Cumberland County
PENNSYLVANIA DIVORCES
1789–1860

Eugene F. Throop

HERITAGE BOOKS
2013

HERITAGE BOOKS
AN IMPRINT OF HERITAGE BOOKS, INC.

Books, CDs, and more—Worldwide

For our listing of thousands of titles see our website at
www.HeritageBooks.com

Published 2013 by
HERITAGE BOOKS, INC.
Publishing Division
100 Railroad Ave. #104
Westminster, Maryland 21157

Copyright © 1994 Eugene F. Throop

Other Heritage Books by the author:
CD: *Cumberland County, Pennsylvania Divorces, 1789–1860*
CD: *Lancaster County, Pennsylvania Divorces, 1786–1832*
CD: *Pennsylvania Divorces*
CD: *Pennsylvania Divorces: Dauphin County, 1788–1867 and York County, 1790–1860*

Cumberland County, Pennsylvania Divorces, 1789–1860
Forest County, Pennsylvania Cemetery Inscriptions
Lancaster County, Pennsylvania Divorces, 1786–1832
Pennsylvania Divorces: Dauphin County, 1788–1867 and York County, 1790–1860

All rights reserved. No part of this book may be reproduced or transmitted in any form or by any means, electronic or mechanical, including photocopying, recording or by any information storage and retrieval system without written permission from the author, except for the inclusion of brief quotations in a review.

International Standard Book Numbers
Paperbound: 978-1-55613-999-4
Clothbound: 978-0-7884-6923-7

CONTENTS

Foreword...v
Cumberland County Divorces 1
Index 395

FOREWORD

For over twenty-five years I have been involved in genealogical research for others. During that time it became increasing apparent that many researchers were overlooking an important aid to their genealogical investigation, and that was the divorce records. Despite the great personal turmoil involved in a divorce case, these records are at times a gold mine of information for family historians. Usually, when a woman filed for a divorce she did so "by her next friend," who often was a close male relative such as a father or brother. Many of the witnesses who testified were neighbors or relatives of the divorcing couple, and their relationships were duly noted.

Having been through a divorce myself, I can certainly attest to the emotional toll it has on all directly affected. I certainly am not in favor of the modern system of divorcing where people often divorce for trifling differences. But, during the time period my book covers, 1789-1860, divorces came as the unavoidable result of very distressing circumstances such as desertion, extreme cruelty, and/or adultery. I also noted distinct similarities such as vindictive wives trying to take their husbands for all they could, and attorneys who played both ends against the middle to get a huge slice of the "pie".

It was amusing to see the strange spellings. Some of the Justices of the Peace were notorious spellers and some were notorious handwriters. For those stuck on the idea a surname should be spelled one way only, please note how careless clerks and Justices of the Peace were. I see instances where the same surname was spelled three different ways on a document written by the same individual!!

This compilation of Cumberland County, Pennsylvania divorce cases, 1789-1860, is invaluable not only for those interested in the history and genealogies of that area, but many other locations as well. When a husband or wife left their mate, they often went quite a distance. I noted such diverse destinations as California, Canada, Georgia, Illinois, Indiana, Ireland, Kentucky, Louisiana, Maryland, Ohio, Washington, D.C. and Wayne County, Michigan. Here in Pennsylvania I found mentions of Adams County, Bucks County, Butler County, Dauphin County, Franklin County, Lancaster County, Lebanon County, Mifflin County, Perry County, Philadelphia, Westmoreland County, and York County. In all, the histories of over 1,000 individuals are documented in this work.

Despite all the legal "mumbo-jumbo," I found some rather interesting sensational events recorded. In a 1790 case, reference was made to a wife's lover, who, when surprised, went fleeing naked into the woods. In an 1836 case, a man found out that while he was toiling in the fields, the farmer who hired him had been romancing his wife. An 1848 case tells of a man who came home after five years in the state penitentiary to find that his wife had borne a child by another man. A husband in an 1848 case complained that not only did his wife want a divorce, but she did not even know the correct date of their marriage! In an 1850 case, a husband had sex with his wife "by laying her on a trunk!" An 1851 case states that a husband threatened his wife in English, knowing that she didn't understand the language. This same winner of a husband said "Peggy Miller wanted him to go to bed with her but he would not do it, when he could get the old woman (her mother) behind the door for a quarter." In an 1853 case the husband used camp meetings for illicit sex. He asked one woman to go with him into the woods and she replied that the leaves were too wet but she would go with him the next night. Afterwards, he told a friend he was going to leave his wife, but only after he made another child for her. His friend replied that he should be tarred and feathered! In an 1856 case, a husband was confined to bed due to an axe cut on his knee. One day, while peeking through the crack in the door, the husband's caregiver observed the wife having sex with another man on the kitchen table!

If this book proves successful, I have plans for a sequel involving divorce cases in Dauphin, York, and Lancaster Counties. The format will differ somewhat, as I will be abstracting only the salient points, rather than copying everything, as I did with Cumberland County. I also plan to continue doing genealogical research for a fee, for those seeking information regarding Pennsylvania and Maryland families. Hopefully, in the future I will also be publishing a book on abstracts of lunacy cases for Cumberland, Dauphin, Lancaster and York Counties.

March 4, 1993
Eugene F. Throop
920 Baltimore St.
Hanover, Pa. 17331

♦ ♦ ♦

Cumberland County, Pennsylvania Divorces, 1789-1860

June 1, 1789 -petition of Sarah Bossler by her next friend and father John Garber, to the Pennsylvania Supreme Court at Philadelphia, Pa. She married Henry Bossler late of Allen township, Cumberland Co., Pa. in Dec. 1781 and had two children by him. In Dec. 1784 he separated from her, leaving the area. He returned in Sept. 1785 when he visited her father's house about two hours and told her father he would not stay with his wife unless her father paid him a sum of money. He made no provision for his wife and children so they have been maintained by her father since her husband's desertion. During their marriage they lived together as man and wife less than twelve months. Testified before William Attlee. Signed by Sarah Bossler and John Garber. Subpoena awarded by court.

June 3, 1789 -John Snyder, yeoman of West Pennsboro Township, Cumberland Co., Pa. testified he left a copy of the subpoena for Henry Bossler to appear in court at the dwelling house of Archibald McAlister in Paxton Township, Dauphin Co., Pa. the last place of abode for Henry Bossler. Henry Bossler had left the state a considerable time ago and is now residing in Georgia.

July 15, 1789 -Commonwealth of Pennsylvania issued a subpoena to Henry Bossler, late of Allen Township, Cumberland County, Pa. to appear in court at Philadelphia Sept. 24, 1789 to answer his wife's libel for divorce.

July 25, 1789 -Charles Leeper, Sheriff of Cumberland County, Pa. testified he made the required three days of proclamation at the Cumberland County Courthouse for Henry Bossler to appear in court to answer his wife's libel for divorce.

Oct. 7, 1789 -Commonwealth of Pennsylvania issued subpoena for Henry Bossler late of Allen Township, Cumberland Co., Pa. to appear in court in Philadelphia, Pa. Jan. 2, 1790 to answer the libel of his wife for a divorce.

Jan. 2, 1790 -Thomas Buchanan, Esq. Sheriff of Cumberland County, Pa. testified he made the required three days of proclamation for Henry Bossler to appear in court to answer his wife's libel for a divorce.

Jan. 2, 1790 -James Ash, Esq. Sheriff of Philadelphia County, Pa. claimed he made the required three days proclamation for the appearance in court of Henry Bossler to answer his wife's libel for a divorce. He made it at the new courthouse, in the public markets and in two public newspapers.

Jan. 2, 1790 -The Commonwealth Of Pennsylvania appointed John Jordan, Ephraim Steel, John Agnew and William Lyon or any two of them to be Commissioners to take testimony in the case of Sarah Bossler vs. Henry Bossler, libel in divorce.

April 15, 1790 -Commonwealth of Pennsylvania issued a subpoena to Henry Bossler, late of Allen Township, Cumberland County, Pa., to appear in Court in Philadelphia, Pa. July 2, 1790 to answer the libel of his wife Sarah Bossler for a divorce.

April 22, 1790 -Deposition of John Garber of West Pennsborough Township, Cumberland County, Pa. before John Jordan and Ephraim Steel. He said Sarah Bossler was his daughter and he was present at her marriage Dec. 1781 in his house in Paxton Township, Lancaster County, Pa. to Henry Bossler. They lived together as man and wife at his house at intervals for eleven or twelve months during which time his daughter always lived in his house. Henry Bossler left his wife without any provisions for her maintenance in Dec. 1784. He returned to her twice, first in Sept. 1785 for five or six days. After his wife had a son he stayed one day. The second time he returned was in June 1786 when he visited for about two hours and he requested from him one hundred guineas which he was refused. The money seemed to be the only reason for his visit. He also testified "Henry Bossler has for several years past resided in Georgia where it has been reported that he has intermarried with a widow."

April 22, 1790 -Deposition of Mary Garber wife of John Garber. She was present at her daughter's wedding to Henry Bossler in 1781 in Paxton Township, Lancaster Co., Pa. by Rev. McKandel now of Lancaster County, Pa. They had a son and a daughter. He left for three years later and returned only twice but at neither occasion had "connection with the said Libellant as his wife." Her daughter and her two children have been provided for by her husband as Henry Bossler made no provision for them. Henry Bossler wrote his wife a letter in the German language in which he said he would never return to his wife unless her father gave him three hundred or four hundred pounds. She personally saw this letter and read it. Signed by Mary Garber.

Undated decree of divorce for Sarah Bossler and Henry Bossler.

◆ ◆ ◆

June 1, 1789 -Petition of William Boor of East Pennsborough Township, Cumberland County, Pa. before William Attlee. He married Mary Baker April 14, (1779. On April 5, 1789 she left him with a Charles Wingler and has lived with him ever since. They now live in the District of Kentucky Commonwealth of Virginia.

April 15, 1789 -Commonwealth of Pennsylvania subpoena to Mary Boor late of East Pennsborough Township, Cumberland

County, Pa. to appear in Court at Philadelphia, Pa. July 2, 1789 (Note -I can't explain why this subpoena was issued prior to the date of the petition but I copied the dates correctly.)

June 6, 1789 -Mathias Saylor testified he served a copy of the subpoena at the dwelling house of William Boor in East Pennsborough Township, Cumberland Co., Pa. because it was the last place of abode of Mary Boor before leaving the state of Pennsylvania.

July 16, 1789 -Commonwealth of Pennsylvania subpoena to Mary Boor late of East Pennsborough Township, Cumberland Co., Pa. to appear in Court in Philadelphia Sept. 24, 1789 to answer the libel of her husband for a divorce.

July 25, 1789 -Charles Leeper, Sheriff of Cumberland County, Pa. testified he made three days proclamation for Mary Boor to appear in Court Sept. 1789 at Philadelphia, Pa.

Oct. 7, 1789 -Commonwealth of Pennsylvania subpoena to Mary Boor late of East Pennsborough Township, Cumberland County, Pa. to appear in Court in Philadelphia, Pa. Jan. 2, 1790 issued by the Honorable Thomas McKean.

Jan. 2, 1790 -Thomas Buchanan, yeoman Sheriff of Cumberland County, Pa. testified he made public proclamation three successive days in Oct. 1789 for Mary Boor to appear in Court to answer her husband's libel for a divorce.

Jan. 2, 1790 -James Ash, Esq. Sheriff of the City and County of Philadelphia, Pa. testified he made public proclamation three days at the courthouse public market and in Messrs. Dunlap and Claypoole and Messrs. Hall and Sellers public newspapers printed in Philadelphia, Pa.

◆ ◆ ◆

Nov. 20, 1789 -petition of Nicholas Wilt late of Cumberland County, Pa. He married Catharine Hoober and they lived together as man and wife over eight years. She was often guilty of infidelity and deserted him in April 1789 and went to Maryland with Jonathan Durre with whom she still lives in a state of adultery.

April 15, 1790 -Commonwealth of Pennsylvania issued a subpoena to Catharine Wilt wife of Nicholas Wilt of Cumberland County, Pa. to appear in Court in Philadelphia July 2, 1790 to answer his libel for a divorce.

June 20, 1790 -Thomas Buchanan, Sheriff of Cumberland County, Pa. testified he could not find Catharine Wilt in his bailiwick after a diligent search.

Nov. 20, 1790 -deposition of Robert Boyce who had lived on the farm of Nicholas Wilt in Cumberland County, Pa. about two years ago. One evening he witnessed a quarrel between Nicholas Wilt and John (Divire?) a person of notorious bad behavior. Nicholas Wilt shut (Divire?) out of his house and (Divire?) broke down his door and windows. Shortly after this quarrel, he saw (Divire?) holding Catharine Wilt on his arm "in a very loving like manner". At another time he went into Nicholas Wilt's barn and saw (Divire?) and Catharine Wilt together in the cow stable and they were very embarrassed at being discovered together. At another time when (Divire?) was apprehended and conveyed to gaol at Carlisle Catharine followed him and attended to him on the journey. Catharine later left her husband and three small children almost "near two years since."

Nov. 18, 1790 -deposition of Thomas James who had known Catharine Wilt since the spring of 1786. He often saw her intimate with John (Divire?) in the absence of her husband and at her husband's house. He and about twelve others had several warrants to serve upon John (Divire?) and they searched for him and found him and Catharine Wilt in an out spring house near the break of day. There was a bed in the spring house and so it appeared that they had spent the night together as well as previous nights. Upon their approach to the spring house John (Divire?) fled to the mountains without his clothes. About twenty-four hours later he was apprehended and then taken to the gaol of Cumberland County, Pa. at Carlisle, Pa. Catharine Wilt then went on foot from her home on the Susquehanna River and accompanied him on his trip to the gaol and during the journey often weeped over his situation. About eighteen months ago Catharine Wilt deserted her husband and her three children the oldest being about nine years old. She went off with John (Drevire?) to the State of Virginia. Thomas James also added that he lived about two miles from Nicholas Wilt and was often employed to work for him. He said that when John (Divire?) was asked if he had had criminal connection with Catharine Wilt instead of denying it he laughed. He also added that "John (Druire?) is a man of bad fame." He signed the deposition by mark. (P.S. I'm sorry I had trouble reading the handwriting on the surname of Catharine Wilt's lover but it was very difficult to decipher and appeared to be spelled differently even in the same deposition!)

◆ ◆ ◆

March 28, 1792 -petition of Elizabeth Lowrey before William Alexander Justice of the Peace for Cumberland County, Pa. She married John Lowry in Ireland. Three weeks later he deserted her and moved to Cumberland County, Pa. She followed him and lived with him there six days. Then "the said John under pretense of taking her to North Carolina decoyed her into Lancaster County in the state of Pennsylvania when he again deserted her taking with him all the money your petitioner had acquired in his absence and stripping her of all her valuable apparel. That from that period which was in the month of July 1787 your petitioner hath not seen nor heard from her said husband and that he hath willfully deserted and abandoned her from that time until the present day. That your petitioner hath resided near five years in the said county of

Cumberland." She signed her petition by mark.

April 2, 1792 -Commonwealth of Pennsylvania issued a subpoena to John Lowry late of Cumberland County, Pa. to appear in Court at Philadelphia, Pa. Sept. 3, 1792 to answer his wife's libel for a divorce.

Sept. 15, 1792 -Commonwealth of Pennsylvania issued subpoena to John Lowry, yeoman late of Cumberland County, Pa. to appear in Court at Philadelphia, Pa. Jan. 7, 1793 to answer his wife's libel for a divorce.

Jan. 6, 1793 -Commonwealth of Pennsylvania issued a subpoena for John Lowry yeoman late of Cumberland County, Pa. to appear in Court in Philadelphia Pa. April 1, 1793.

April 13, 1793 -Commonwealth of Pennsylvania issued subpoena to John Lowry late of Cumberland County, Pa. to appear in Court in Philadelphia, Pa. Sept. 2, 1793.

(undated -possibly April 13, 1793.) Wallace, Sheriff of Cumberland Co., Pa. testified that at the insistence of Thomas Duncan, Esq. attorney he proclaimed a subpoena for John Lowry the fourth and fifth days of April term 1793. He could not find him in his bailiwick.

Jan. 25, 1794 -Commonwealth of Pennsylvania issued subpoena to John Lowry to appear in Court in Philadelphia, Pa. April 7, 1794 to answer the libel of his wife Elizabeth Lowry for a divorce.

Undated document -The Supreme Court of Pennsylvania appointed George Logue and William Alexander, Esq. to take depositions in the case of Elizabeth Lowry vs. John Lowry -libel in divorce.

♦ ♦ ♦

March 2, 1797 -Petition of James Patterson of North Huntington, Westmoreland County, Pa. He married July 8, 1778 Jane Harris of the township of Fermanaugh in Mifflin County, Pa. then in Cumberland County, Pa. They lived together until 1790 and had three sons all now living. About Dec. 1, 1790 he sold his land in Mifflin County, Pa. to Galbreath Patterson, Esq. intending to move his family. At that time his wife left him saying she would not leave and ever since refused to cohabit with him or even speak to him. About Sept. 1, 1791 he moved to North Huntington township, Westmoreland County, Pa. and purchased 200 acres about 60 of which were cleared. He erected a dwelling 40' by 20' hoping that his wife would change her mind and live with him. He wrote her several times to plead for her to join him and he returned to Mifflin County, Pa. about April 1, 1792, about Feb. 1, 1793 about Jan. 4, 1794, about Feb. 5, 1795 about Feb. 10, 1796 and about Sept. 10, 1796. On all occasions his wife refused to even see him.

March 31, 1798 -Commonwealth of Pennsylvania issued subpoena to Jane Patterson to appear in Court at Philadelphia, Pa. the first Monday of Sept. 1798 -Notation on front indicates that

Andrew Nelson, Sheriff served this subpoena Aug. 26, 1798 charging $12.40 for his three hundred mile trip to serve the subpoena.

◆ ◆ ◆

Sept. 1797 term #1352 -Sept. 22, 1797 -Petition of Jacob Buyers of Middleton township, Cumberland County, Pa. who married Anna Dumb. She since eloped with John Metz of Cumberland County, Pa. and moved to Virginia. Where she is now he did not know. Testified before George Logue.

Sept. 26, 1797 -Commonwealth of Pennsylvania issued subpoena to Anna Buyers to appear in Court at Philadelphia, Pa. the second Monday of December 1797 to answer her husband's libel for a divorce.

Aug. 17, 1797 -The Court of General Quarter Sessions of Cumberland County, Pa. Indictment against Ann Beyers late of Cumberland County, Pa. wife of Jacob Beyers. She committed adultery Oct. 1, 1792 with John Metz. Witnesses were Julia Down, Solomon Dentler and Samuel W. McCaskry. Signed by Jared Ingersoll, Attorney General.

Dec. 11, 1797 -Commonwealth of Pennsylvania issued subpoena on Anna Buyers to appear in Court in Philadelphia, Pa. the 3rd Monday of March 1797.

Dec. 28, 1797 -The Supreme Court of Pennsylvania appointed George Logue, Esq. and William Lewis, Esq. to take testimony in the case of Jacob Buyers vs. Anna Buyers -libel in divorce.

Sept. 26, 1797 -Commonwealth of Pennsylvania issued subpoena on Anna Buyers for her to appear in Court in Philadelphia, Pa. the second Monday of December 1797.

Dec. 4, 1797 -testimony of Jacob Crever, Sheriff before John Montgomery that he had made diligent inquiry but could not find Anna Buyers in his bailiwick.

Jan. 6, 1798 -Deposition of Solomon Dentler. Anne Beyers eloped with a man to Virginia. He followed and found them living with the same person near a place called Moorsfield, Virginia. He told Anne that her husband intended to have the man she eloped with "sent to gaol". She replied "that it was not the fault of the man but that she induced him to carry her off."

Jan. 9, 1798 -Deposition of Juliana Dumb, mother of Anne Buyers. She testified that her daughter told her she eloped with a certain man to Virginia and "that they keep house together." She visited her mother, she had "the venereal disease" and she understands that Anne Buyers is now in the state of Kentucky.

Jan. 28, 1798 -Jacob Crever, High Sheriff of Cumberland County, Pa. testified that Anna Buyers could not be found in his bailiwick. He made three days proclamation Jan. 4, 5, 6th for her appearance in court.

Feb. 13, 1798 -Deposition of Jacob Crever, Esq. that he is well acquainted with Jacob Buyers, who has resided seven years and upwards in Cumberland County, Pa.

3rd Monday of March 1798 -John Penrose, Sheriff testified he made public proclamation at open court Feb. 25, 26, 27, and 28th and March 23, 24, 27 in two newspapers for the appearance of Anna Buyers in Court.

◆ ◆ ◆

April 30, 1798 -Petition of Daniel Piper of Tyrone Township, Cumberland County, Pa. who married Anna Myers. In 1790 she deserted him without any just cause and never returned. He testified before James McCormick.

◆ ◆ ◆

Jan. 6, 1800 -Petition of Christian Weaver before John Creigh, Judge of the Court of Common Pleas of Cumberland County, Pa. He married Lydia Long who later committed adultery with a certain Albert and deserted him over five years ago. He signed his name in German script.

March 17, 1800 -Commonwealth of Pennsylvania to Lydia Weaver, late of Cumberland County, Pa. to appear in Court at Philadelphia, Pa. the first Monday of Sept. 1800. -served 24 miles by John Carothers, Sheriff of Cumberland County, Pa.

Dec. 28, 1800 -Commonwealth of Pennsylvania issued subpoena to Lydia Weaver late of Cumberland County, Pa. to appear in Court at Philadelphia, Pa. the third Monday of April 1801. It was served by John Carothers, Sheriff of Cumberland County, Pa.

◆ ◆ ◆

Jan. 14, 1802 -Petition of Mary Black by her next friend Henry Lechler, Jr. before Jacob Crever, Justice of the Peace. She married Anthony Black Feb. 16, 1789. He deserted her Dec. 4, 1794 without any just cause.

Jan. 2, 1802 -Commonwealth of Pennsylvania issued subpoena to Anthony Black to appear in Court at Philadelphia, Pa. the third Monday of March 1802.

March 9, 1802 -Robert Grayson, Sheriff testified that he could not find Anthony Black in his bailiwick and left a copy of the subpoena at his last known residence in Carlisle, Pa.

March 15, 1802 -Commonwealth of Pennsylvania issued a subpoena to Anthony Black to appear in Court at Philadelphia, Pa. the first Monday of Sept. 1802.

March 15, 1802 -Supreme Court of Pennsylvania appointed George Logue, Esq. and James McCormick, Esq. of Carlisle, Pa. to take testimony in the case of Mary Black, Libellant vs. Anthony Black, Respondent.

Sept. 4, 1802 -Deposition of Abraham Loughridge, merchant of Carlisle, Pa. He was present at the marriage of Anthony Black and Mary Black in York County, Pa. about ten or eleven years ago. They lived together over four years and had three children. Anthony Black left his family in the fall of 1794 and went to Virginia. Where he is now he doesn't know. His wife then went to live with her mother in the borough of Carlisle. Anthony Black visited his wife at her mother's home about fifteen months after he left but he only stayed one or two hours. He abandoned his wife "at night with all the property he could take with him and defrauded his creditors and it is reported he took a woman with him from one Fergerson near Mount (Cook?) about six miles west of Carlisle."

Sept. 6, 1802 -Israel Israel, Esq. High Sheriff of the City and County of Philadelphia testified he made public proclamation at the old Courthouse as well as in the market place three successive days for the appearance of Anthony Black in Court to answer his wife's libel for a divorce.

♦ ♦ ♦

August Term 1808 -Cumberland County, Pa. Court of Common Pleas -Subpoena in divorce served by leaving a copy at the late residence of Jane Allen in Derickson Township, Cumberland County, Pa. for the first Monday of Jan. 1811. Exit Subpoena returned made for first Monday of April 1811. Served. Court ordered proclamation to be made by Cumberland County, Pa. Sheriff for three days in April term 1811 on Tuesday, Wednesday and Thursday for Jane Allen to appear.

Aug. 9, 1811 -Court directed notice to be placed in *The Political Register* in Philadelphia, Pa. for four successive weeks prior to the next return day of November session. Exit subpoena served by copy for Jan. 1812 term. Jan. 1812 term ordered an exit subpoena for first day of April 1812 term and if Jane Allen is still not found proclamation is to be made by the Sheriff for three days at the Courthouse plus notice, in some of the public newspapers of Philadelphia for four successive weeks. Depositions to be taken. April 7, 1812 Sheriff reports that the subpoena returned served and the proclamations made. August term 1812 Court heard the depositions and granted the divorce.

♦ ♦ ♦

April term 1809 #151 Cumberland County, Pa. Court of Common Pleas -April 7, 1809 petition of Elizabeth Carothers who married in 1784 Armstrong Carothers. He abused her and endangered her life causing her to leave him Aug. 7, 1808. Elizabeth Carothers petitioned for a divorce and alimony. Subpoena issued April 7, 1809 for Armstrong Carothers to appear in court and answer his wife's libel for a divorce. (Note -Of possible interest -Jan. 1810 #26 Summons in Ejectment involved James Grayson and wife Mary, Isabelle Noble, Samuel Workman and wife Margery, Erasmus Holtsaple and wife Elizabeth and Rebecca Carothers vs. Armstrong Carothers and John

Black. This particular court case dragged on until it was finally settled Feb. 7, 1820.)

♦ ♦ ♦

Aug. 1810 #129 -Aug. 8, 1810 -petition of Margaret Martin by her next friend James Woodburn. She married Jonathan Martin Feb. 1801. He abused her between Jan. 1, 1807 and July 3, 1810 during which "the said Jonathan frequently and without any cause or provocation in a most barbarous and inhuman manner within that period hath abused her person by beating her not only with his hand but with a cow (horn?) and dragged her by the hair and kicking her and within that period hath after menaced her with Declaration of his (illegible word) to destroy her life". Margaret signed "by mark".

Aug. 11, 1810 -subpoena issued to Jonathan Martin for first Monday of Nov. 1810. Served by Luther Crownell Deputy Sheriff Oct. 24, 1810.

Nov. 11, 1810 -alias subpoena issued to Jonathan Martin for first Monday of Jan. 1811. Served Dec. 9, 1810 by Andrew Baden Deputy for Cumberland Co., Pa. Sheriff John Baden.

Jan 9, 1811 -Alias subpoena had been issued to Jonathan Martin issued for first Monday of Jan. 1811. Sheriff John Baden reported that he could not find him in Cumberland Co., Pa. but left the subpoena at his last place of abode in Cumberland Co., Pa. Dec. 13, 1810.

Jan. 9, 1811 -alias subpoena issued for Jonathan Martin for first Monday of April 1811. Served by Sheriff John Boden March 14, 1811.

Aug. 10, 1811 -alias subpoena issued for Jonathan Martin for first Monday of Nov. 1811. Served Oct. 4, 1811 by Andrew Boden, Deputy Sheriff.

♦ ♦ ♦

Apr. 1811 #79 -April 2, 1811 -petition of Elizabeth Weaver by her next friend Henry Shell. She married on or about the last day of Nov. 1808 Jacob Weaver. He abused her and deserted her.

April 21,1811 -subpoena issued for Jacob Weaver.

Aug. 10, 1811 -alias subpoena issued for Jacob Weaver for first Monday of Nov. 1811 left at his home by Cumberland Co., Pa. Sheriff Andrew Boden.

Nov. 9, 1811 -alias subpoena issued for Jacob Weaver for first Monday of Jan. 1812. Sheriff John Boden reported Jan. 9, 1812 that Jacob Weaver could not be found in his bailiwick.

♦ ♦ ♦

Aug. 1813 #138 Aug. 2, 1813 -petition of Elizabeth O'Brien. She married Richard O'Brien March 25, 1799. He abused her, endangered her life and "turned your petitioner out of doors".

Aug. 27, 1813 -subpoena issued for Richard O'Brien for first Monday of Nov. 1813.

Nov. 1, 1813 -Richard O'Brien filed a paper testifying that he was a kind and loving husband and denied "turning her out of doors".

♦ ♦ ♦

Aug. 1815 #154 -Mary Blaine by her next friend James Sharp vs. Thomas Blaine.

Aug. 12, 1815 -subpoena issued for Thomas Blaine for first Monday of 1815. William Glenn substitute sheriff of Cumberland Co., Pa. returned that he could not locate Thomas Blaine.

Jan. 1, 1816 -Court order publication of divorce proclamations in Kline's *Carlisle Gazette* for four successive weeks.

April 1, 1816 -Proof made in Court that the divorce proclamations were printed. Court ordered that depositions be made before John Heap, Esq. of Newton township, Cumberland Co., Pa.

Jan. 13, 1816 -deposition of John Sharp before John Heap, Esq. in Newton township. His daughter Mary Blaine was born April 14, 1775 and has lived at his home since Aug. 7, 1814 and before that at the home of her sister Mrs. Andrew Brackenridge at Culbertson's Row, Franklin Co., Pa. Mary married Thomas Blaine April 13, 1813. About six months after they separated, Thomas Blaine confessed to him that "he had carnal knowledge of Elizabeth Walters but not often."

June 19, 1816 -deposition of Rev. Joshua Williams. He testified that he married Mary Sharp to Thomas Blaine at the house of her father John Sharp in Frankford township, Cumberland Co., Pa. April 14, 1813 by the rules and practices of the Presbyterian Church.

June 24, 1816 -deposition of Frederick Walters before John Heap, Esq. He testified that he heard his daughter Elizabeth Walters say that Thomas Blaine was the father of her child born in Oct. 1815. Testified that the "act of adultery was committed about the later end of January, A.D. 1815 and was in the weaver's shop of this deponent in Frankford Township County aforesaid." Thomas Blaine left property in the amount of ninety-five dollars in his hands "for raising the child aforementioned."

Oct. 12, 1816 -deposition of Eve Walters in Newton township, Cumberland Co., Pa. before John Heap, Esq. Testified she was a sister of Elizabeth Walters and had heard Thomas Blaine confess to his father-in-law John Sharp that he was the father of Elizabeth Walters' male child.

Nov. 4, 1816 -deposition of James Sharp of Frankford Township -"And now to wit November 4th 1816 James Sharp of Frankford Township in the Court of Cumberland, being duly sworn in open court, doth depose and say that he is a brother of Mary Blaine, the within named complainant. That Thomas Blaine the within named libellant, with whom deponent is well acquainted left the County of Cumberland aforesaid about a year ago. That this deponent saw said Blaine last spring in Frankfort Township, where he remained one or two days. The deponent never saw said Blaine but one time from the time he left the county aforesaid. This deponent verily believes the said Blaine is not now in the county of aforesaid. That when deponent saw him last spring, said Blaine told him he then lived in the State of Ohio that he had come from that and would return there."

Nov. 11, 1816 -deposition of Elizabeth Walters at Newville, Newton Township, Cumberland Co., Pa. before John Heap, Esq. Testified that Thomas Blaine committed adultery with her at her father's house about twenty -one months ago and that he is the real father of her male child. She signed "by mark."

Nov. Term 1816 -(no date given) Court granted Mary Blaine a divorce with stipulation "that the said Thomas shall not during the life of the said Mary marry the said Elizabeth Walters."

♦ ♦ ♦

Apr. 1816 Term #144 -Nancy Brady vs. Joseph Brady.

April 2, 1816 -petition of Nancy Brady by her father and next friend Philip Swisher. She married Joseph Brady Dec. 18, 1806 and he deserted her without any just cause more than two years ago.

April 10, 1816 -subpoena issued to Joseph Brady for first Monday Aug. 1816.

Aug. 8, 1816 -William Glenn, deputy Sheriff of Cumberland County, Pa. reported that in June 1816 he made a diligent search and did not find Joseph Brady in Cumberland Co., Pa. so he left the subpoena at his last residence in Cumberland Co., Pa. the house of Philip Swisher.

Nov. 9, 1816 -Alias subpoena issued for Joseph Brady for last Monday of Jan. 1817.

Nov. 20, 1816 -Sheriff Andrew Mitchell testified he could not find Joseph Brady in Cumberland Co., Pa. so he left a copy of the subpoena at the residence of Philip Swisher.

April 8, 1817 -Proof of publication of divorce proclamation in *The American Volunteer* published in Carlisle, Pa. for four successive weeks and depositions to be taken before Levi Owens, Esq. and Alexander Rodgers, Esq. in Rye Township, Cumberland County, Pa.

July 19, 1817 -deposition of Robert Clark before Alexander Rodgers, Esq. Justice of the Peace. Nancy Brady had resided in Petersburgh within one mile of his residence for over fifteen years. She married Joseph Brady and they lived together in Petersburgh two or three years and then he deserted her six or seven years ago. Nancy has lived within one mile of Clark's Ferry ever since she married. He had not seen Joseph Brady for four or five years.

July 19, 1817 -deposition of Mary VanForin. She had known Nancy Brady over fifteen years and resides near her residence in Petersburgh. She was aware that Nancy's husband deserted her in 1809 apparently without just cause.

July 19, 1817 -deposition of Kesiah Martin before Alexander

Rodgers, Esq. She had known Nancy Brady over twenty years. She was born about a mile from Clark's Ferry. She knew she married Joseph Brady and "has been frequently in their house while they lived together and Deponent had seen the said Nancy using Industry to support the family."

Oct. 18, 1817 -deposition of Robert Clark, Esq. before Alexander Rodgers, Esq. He had known Nancy Brady over fifteen years since she was a small girl and resided with her father Philip Swisher in Rye township, Cumberland Co., Pa. where she resided ever since. She married Joseph Brady and two or three years later returned to her father's home in Petersburgh where she has lived ever since. He had known Joseph Brady since 1806 when he resided in the town of Petersburgh, Rye Township where he lived until 1809. He was present in Dec. 1806 when Nancy Brady was married to Joseph Brady at her father's house in Petersburgh. He knew that Joseph Brady left his wife sometime in 1809.

Oct. 18, 1817 -deposition of Eliza Martin before Alexander Rodgers, Esq. She had known Nancy Brady since "she was a suckling child." She lived with her father Philip Swisher until she married after which she lived with her husband in a house in Petersburgh. She knew Joseph Brady from 1806 until he left in 1809 and she knew of no just cause for Joseph Brady to desert his family.

Oct. 18, 1817 -deposition of Philip Swisher before Alexander Rodgers, Esq. He testified that his daughter Nancy was born in Rye township, Cumberland Co., Pa. in March of 1789. He knew Joseph Brady since 1806 and he resided in Rye township until he left in 1809. He was present at the marriage of his daughter Nancy to Joseph Brady at his residence in Petersburgh Dec. 18, 1806. Joseph Brady deserted his wife in Sept. of 1809 leaving her with two small children one only about six months old. He knew of no just cause for desertion.

Oct. 25, 1817 -deposition of Alexander Rodgers, Esq. before John Owens, Esq. a replacement for Levi Owens, Esq. who resigned. He had known Nancy Brady over fifteen years since she was a small girl living with her father, Philip Swisher. He knew Joseph Brady since 1806 until he deserted his family in 1809 and was present at the marriage of Joseph Brady and Nancy Swisher in Dec. 1806 at her father's house in Petersburgh, Pa.

Nov. 2, 1817 -Court granted Nancy Brady a divorce from Joseph Brady.

◆ ◆ ◆

Aug. 1816, #162 Aug. 4, 1816 -petition of Jacob Weaver of Shippensburgh (sic) township, Cumberland Co., Pa. He married Elizabeth Shell Nov. 6, 1807. She deserted him without cause April 1811.

Aug. 10, 1816 -subpoena issued to Elizabeth Weaver for first Monday of 1816.

Aug. 27, 1816 -Deputy Sheriff William Glenn reported that he left the subpoena for Elizabeth Weaver at the house of her father Henry Shell in the Borough of Carlisle, Pa.

Nov. 2, 1816 -Elizabeth Weaver testifies he left her, not her him!

♦ ♦ ♦

Aug. 1816 #164 Aug. 5, 1816 -petition of Catharine Shepley by her next friend Conrad Geese. She testified she had lived in Pennsylvania over a year. She married Aug. 17, 1806 Peter Shepley who deserted her in the first part of Feb. 1813 without just cause.

Aug. 10, 1816 -subpoena issued to Peter Shepley for first Monday of Nov. 1816. Deputy Sheriff William Glenn reported he left subpoena at the home of Mrs. Mull his last place of residence in Cumberland Co., Pa.

♦ ♦ ♦

Aug. 1816 #224 Aug. 26, 1816 -petition of Sarah Rothrock (signed Sally Rodrock) for divorce by her next friend Jacob Swanger (who signed by mark). She married Jacob Rothrock in Jan. 1813 and he deserted her Nov. 10, 1813.

Aug. 10, 1816 -subpoena issued Jacob Rothrock for first Monday of Nov. 1816. William Glenn substitute sheriff of Cumberland Co., Pa. said Jacob could not be found so he left subpoena at his last residence there, that of Henry Bierbrewer in the Borough of Carlisle, Pa. Aug. 26, 1816.

Nov. 9, 1816 -alias subpoena issued to Jacob Rothrock for first Monday of Jan. 1817. Sheriff Andrew Mitchell said he could not find Jacob Rothrock in Cumberland Co., Pa. so left the subpoena at his last residence there.

April 7, 1817 -proof given of publication of divorce proclamation for four successive weeks in *The American Volunteer*. Court appointed George Patterson, Esq. and Isaac Todd, Esq. both of Carlisle, Pa. to take depositions in the case.

June 13, 1817 -deposition of Jacob Swenze before Isaac Todd, Esq. His daughter Sarah was born in (Sweddellen?) township, Cumberland Co., Pa. and lived there until her marriage in Jan. 1813 which was performed by a Rev. P. (Semm?). They lived eight or nine months in Bucks Co., Pa. then in 1813 returned to Cumberland Co., Pa. where her husband deserted her two months later which was over three years ago. He left her in Nov. 1813 when they were living at the house of Henry Bierbrower in the Borough of Carlisle, Pa. He signed "by mark".

June 13, 1817 -deposition of Ann Beirbrewer. She knew Jacob and Sarah Rothrock as they lived in her house in 1813 and she knew he deserted her then. She was present when Doctor Albright was in conversation with Sarah Rothrock. She signed "by mark".

June 13, 1817 -deposition of Samuel (Siverr?). He knew both Sarah and Jacob Rothrock. He knew Jacob Rothrock deserted his wife in Nov. of 1813 but knew of no cause for this. Signed name in German script.

June 13, 1817 -deposition of Doctor Frederick Albright before Isaac Todd, Esq. He testified "that Jacob Rothrock called on Deponent as a physician and deponent inquired what was the matter with his wife and was informed that the said Sarah was two months from home and he believed his wife was with child which child was not his and that she was laboring under a venereal disease in the highest degree. That he the said Jacob was at home on the night before and was solicited by his wife to cohabit and that he was afraid to have anything to do with her and caused deponent to come and examine her. Deponent made several curses saying it was a delicate case and he did not like to go. This was in the forenoon said Jacob went away and returned in the afternoon with his brother-in-law John Traugh and both of them insisted (illegible word) that Deponent would go and Depart. Should have five (Dollars?) for his trouble. Deponent went to the house of Henry Beirbrower and said Jacob stopped in the house of Traugh and answered Deponent after he had examined her his wife to inform him. Deponent stated to Mr. S. Serrert his errand at the request of her husband in the presence of Mrs. Beirbrower. Sarah began to cry bitterly, saying that the cause was to think that such a scandeles (sic) report was brought on her. Deponent conversed with her and then was examined by him and found that no such curse was troubling her and she was perfectly sound. Deponent returned to the house of Traugh and informed her husband that his wife was sound and that nothing of the kind was the matter with her. And the same day ran off from these parts and further saith not."

July 30, 1817 -deposition of Jacob Swenger. Sarah Rothrock is his daughter born in 1795. Jacob Rothrock came from Bucks County and was a stranger to him and his family. His friends said he came from a well-to-do family and he dressed very well. He married his daughter. Jacob Rothrock told him that his father had given him 150 acres back in Bucks County. They lived about five weeks after their marriage in his house then moved to Bucks Co., Pa. where they lived seven or eight months. At that time he and his wife went to visit their daughter in Bucks County. At that time their daughter, Sarah Rothrock, told them how her husband abused her and pleaded to go home with them stating "that she would be a dead woman from the abuse her husband gave her." He tried to persuade her to stay with her husband but gave in to her pleading. Her husband had no business occupation but engaged in gambling. His daughter said "that when he the said respondent came home in the evening he would not show his face to Deponent and that Deponent could have no communication with him." His daughter also stated that all her husband had to his name was one shirt and one hat and that he had in the past borrowed a watch and fancy clothes to impress her and her family that he was well-to-do and of a good family. About two weeks after he had taken his daughter back to Carlisle her husband followed her there. He last saw Jacob Rothrock in the Borough of Carlisle in the fall of 1813. He has not seen him since and he believes his daughter has had no communication with him. Jacob Swenger signed his deposition "by mark".

Aug. 6, 1817 -deposition of Jacob Swager (sic). He knew his son-in-law Jacob Rothrock had rented a room in Beirbrewer's house. He was told it was rented for a three month period and he slept there. However, he lived with his wife there for two of the three months and then left.

Aug. 6, 1817 -deposition of Doctor Frederick Albright who testified that he called at the house of habitation of Jacob Rothrock in Carlisle "in the months of Nov. 1813 being the same day on which he the said Jacob Rothrock ran away."

Aug. term 1817 (no date given) -Divorce granted Sarah Rothrock.

♦ ♦ ♦

Nov. 1818 #256 -Oct. 2, 1818 -petition of Henry Sweigart of North Middleton Township, Cumberland Co., Pa., Schoolmaster. (Signed his petition "Henry Swiger.") He married Wilhelmina otherwise known as Elizabeth Oct. 29, 1807 "daughter of George M. Dininger, late of the Borough of Carlisle, butcher." She deserted him Aug. 25, 1816.

Nov. 2, 1818 -deposition of Conrad Kuntz. Henry Sweigart was born in Martick township, Lancaster Co., Pa. Henry Sweigart "had his home at my house for one year and more before the year 1818." He married in 1807 and they lived together as man and wife about nine years. Wilhelmina deserted him when he lived in the house of John Lane in North Middleton township in the year 1816.

Nov. 7, 1818 -subpoena issued to Wilhelmina Swiger otherwise known as Elizabeth Swiger for first Monday of Jan. 1819. Peter Ritner, substitute Sheriff of Cumberland Co., Pa. left the subpoena with her Dec. 22, 1818 at the house of Samuel Brown of North Middleton Township and he read the subpoena to her.

Jan. 9, 1819 -alias subpoena issued for Wilhelmina Sweiger otherwise known as Elizabeth Sweiger for first Monday of Apr. 1819. Daniel Fisher, substitute Sheriff of Cumberland Co., Pa. reported he served the subpoena on her Feb. 15, 1918 at the house of John Brown in North Middleton township, Cumberland Co., Pa.

March 8, 1820 -deposition of Benjamin Crane. He knew both parties and could testify that Henry Sweigart had lived in North Middleton township for the year previous to 1818. He knew she left him in August 1816 but knew of no reason why she did so.

March 8, 1820 -deposition of John Lane. He knew both parties six or eight years. He knew they lived together as man and wife four or five years before she left him in August of 1816.

March 8, 1820 -deposition of Simon Wonderlich. He knew they lived together as man and wife five or six years before she left him in the fall of 1816. He knew nothing "of the cause or circumstances" of her leaving.

March 20, 1820 -deposition of John P. Helfenstein before Isaac Todd, Justice of the Peace and Elisha Doyle, Justice of the Peace. He had known both parties fourteen years. They were married by Rev. Jonathan Helfenstein. He was present at that marriage and was at that time twelve or thirteen years old.

April 3, 1820 -the court granted Henry Sweigart a divorce.

♦ ♦ ♦

April 1819 #276 May 17, 1819 -petition of Elizabeth Eichelberger now Elizabeth Wolf by her next friend Werner Weitzel. She married Jacob Wolf in 1801 who abused her and deserted her over two years ago. She stated she was a native of Pennsylvania and had always lived here. She signed "by mark".

May 29, 1819 -The Prothonotary James Armstrong issued a subpoena for Jacob Wolf.

April 10, 1819 -Court issued subpoena for Jacob Wolf for first Monday of Aug. 1819.

Aug. 2, 1819 -Daniel Fisher swore he left subpoena at Jacob Wolf's last place of residence in Cumberland Co., Pa. a Mr. Bowman since he could not be found in Cumberland Co., Pa. Jonas Grubb swore that he saw Jacob Wolf in June 1819 at which time he had a copy of the subpoena and Jacob Wolf "stated to deponent the contents of said copy."

Aug. 2, 1819 -deposition of Adam Eichelberger "Adam Eichelberger being duly sworn before me in pursuance of the annexed appointments of Court says that the Elizabeth Wolf in the annexed subpoena mentioned was married to the Jacob Wolf therein named more than twenty years ago. That until eight years ago they lived in Stumpstown and Jonestown in Dauphin County. That for ten years and upwards before he left her in April 1811 he conducted his affairs badly -drank to intemperance and gambled and treated his wife ill. That he still wanted to get into his hands more of the estate coming to said Elizabeth from her father which the said Elizabeth resisted. And that said Jacob Wolf in April 1811 absented himself from the habitation of the said Elizabeth and deserted her because as Deponent believes he could get no more of her father's estate. That he has been absent from the habitation and continued his neglect of the said Elizabeth ever since April 1811. That a few days before said absence the household furniture of the said Jacob Wolf was levied upon and taken away by the constable. That said Elizabeth as deponent believes was always and is a good careful industrious and saving woman and that the said desertion and absence of said Jacob was not as deponent firmly believes owing to any fault of said Elizabeth. That the said Jacob since April 1811 has contributed nothing to the support and maintenance of said Elizabeth." Adam Eichelberger signed "by mark".

Aug. 2, 1819 -Court granted Elizabeth Wolf a divorce.

Aug. 21, 1819 -before Elisha Doyle "And the said Adam Eichelberger before me says that the said Elizabeth Wolf now resides and for eight years past has resided in the county of Cumberland, Pennsylvania." Signed "by mark".

♦ ♦ ♦

Nov. 1821 #21 -Aug. 7, 1821 -petition of Susannah Oliver late Susannah Shelden by her next friend George D. Foulk, doctor of medicine. She was married Jan. 19, 1815 to John Oliver who abused her causing her to leave him June 16, 1821.

Aug. 11, 1821 -subpoena issued to John Oliver of Cumberland Co., Pa. for first Monday of Nov. 1821.

Nov. 8, 1821 -Samuel Scott substitute sheriff of Cumberland Co., Pa. reported that on Oct. 11, 1821 he handed this subpoena to John Oliver who read it in his presence.

Jan. 9, 1822 -John Oliver, late of Cumberland Co., Pa. schoolmaster denys (sic) facts set forth in his wife's petition. Willis Foulk and John Oliver got in an argument over his wife's charges Nov. 8, 1821. As a consequence, John Oliver sued Willis Foulk for $5.00 which he refused to pay and then he raised the amount to $10.00.

♦ ♦ ♦

Aug. 1822 #64 -March 23, 1822 -petition of Jane Wilson by her brother-in-law and next friend Charles Taylor. She married James Wilson in August of 1806 and he deserted her over two years ago.

April 5, 1822 -subpoena issued to James Wilson for first Monday of August 1822.

Nov. 6, 1822 -Peter Ritner, Sheriff of Cumberland Co., Pa. reported that he couldn't find James Wilson.

Nov. 9, 1822 -alias subpoena issued to James Wilson for first Monday of Jan. 1823.

♦ ♦ ♦

Aug. 1822 #109 -May 23, 1822 -petition of Susanna Davis by her next friend Henry Kohlstock. She married William Davis March 15, 1816 and he separated from her May 19, 1820. Susanna signed "by mark."

Nov. 9, 1822 -subpoena to William Davis for first Monday of Jan. 1823.

Jan. 6, 1823 James Neal, Sheriff of Cumberland Co., Pa. reported that William Davis could not be found in Cumberland Co., Pa.

Jan. 6, 1823 -Court ordered Sheriff to make proclamation of divorce once a week for four successive weeks in *The American Volunteer* a Carlisle, Pa. newspaper.

April 3, 1823 -deposition of John Etter before A. Wills, Justice of the Peace. He testified that William Davis left his wife about three years ago.

April 5, 1822 -subpoena to William Davis for first Monday of Aug. 1822. Peter Ritner, Cumberland Co. Sheriff reported that William Davis was "not found in his bailiwick".

April 9, 1823 -deposition of Isiah Leach before A. Wills, Justice of the Peace. He knew that Susannah Davis had lived in Cumberland Co., Pa. for over a year and that her husband left her almost three years ago.

April 11, 1823 -deposition of John Black before A. Wills, Justice of the Peace. He testified that William Davis married Susannah Couser March of 1816 by Alexander Wills, Justice of the Peace." That before his marriage, the said Davis was much embarrassed in his circumstances -That the said Susannah had some property before her marriage which has since been seized by the creditors of said Davis. -That executions were taken out against Davis and that he went away for the purpose of avoiding them and for no other cause according to Deponent's belief. That said Davis left his wife without any means of support and that since his departure the said Susannah has supported herself entirely by her own industry and without receiving any support from her said husband since his departure. Said Deponent further states that said Davis went away more than two years ago and settled in the village of Harmony in the western part of this state and Deponent was informed by a gentleman who was from the west that said Davis there passed himself for a single and unmarried man and endeavored to get married and was about becoming so, but for some cause which he did not recollect was Disappointed. That said Davis was somewhat intemperate before his marriage but became much more so after his marriage, and Deponent verily believes that said Davis never intends to return to his wife and that he the Deponent was informed that said Davis has left Harmony and has gone farther to the west, and that he has never been in this neighborhood since he deserted his wife. Deponent further states that Davis and his wife lived in York County about three fourths of a mile from Haldeman's Forge after their marriage and remained in that neighborhood until he absconded and that Deponent has lived in this neighborhood ever since the above marriage. Deponent states in reply that said Davis taught school a part of his time, and at other times worked as a day laborer."

April 12, 1823 -Court granted Susanna Davis a divorce.

◆ ◆ ◆

Aug. 1822 #252 -Aug. 24, 1822 -petition of Elizabeth Rose by her next friend Lewis Zearing, Esq. She married Josephus Rose July 12, 1818 and he abused her and deserted her about two years later.

Aug. 10, 1822 -subpoena issued to Josephus Rose for first Monday in Nov. 1822. Nov. 5, 1822 Peter Ritner, Cumberland Co., Pa. Sheriff reports that Josephus Rose could not be found in his bailiwick and he left subpoena at his last residence here in East Pennsboro Township.

Nov. 9, 1823 -alias subpoena issued to Josephus Rose for first Monday of Jan. 1823.

Jan. 3, 1823 -Joseph Shields, substitute Sheriff of Cumberland Co., Pa. reports that Josephus Rose could not be found in Cumberland Co., Pa. so he left subpoena at his last residence in East Pennsboro Township.

Jan. 6, 1833 -Court ordered four successive weeks of publication of divorce in *The American Volunteer* Carlisle, Pa. newspaper.

March 9, 1823 deposition of George Bowermaster of Dickinson Township, Cumberland Co., Pa. before Elisha Doyle, Justice of the Peace. From the fall of 1819 to March 1820 Josephus Rose and his wife Elizabeth lived in his house. In March 1820 Josephus deserted her. He heard later he "was about Chambersburg, and afterward he had went to the State of Ohio." He has heard no more of his whereabouts. He left no provision "nor left any means of supporting or maintaining his family consisting of his said wife -one child born before he absconded and another born shortly after he left her."

April 9, 1823 -deposition of John Strayer before Elisha Doyle, Justice of the Peace. "Also personally appears before me, John Strayer, who upon oath duly administered doth depose and say that the above named Josephus Rose has been absent from the habitation of his wife Elizabeth, three years ending in March last and has continued absent. That there was no reasonable cause for which the said Josephus should have deserted her and further believes the desertion to be willful and supposes he has no intention of returning to her again."

April 11, 1823 -Court grants divorce to Elizabeth Rose.

♦ ♦ ♦

August Term 1822 #275 Oct. 2, 1822 -"Came into court Elizabeth Haak by Abraham Hickernell her father and next friend, and preferred a petition to the court therein setting forth that the petitioner is a citizen of the commonwealth of Pennsylvania, and has resided for one whole year and upwards immediately preceding the filing of this her petition or libel, that on or about the twenty fourth day of March one thousand eight hundred and fourteen she was legally joined in the bonds of matrimony with William Haak. That although the libellant at all times since her intermarriage hath behaved and demeaned herself towards the said husband as a dutiful and obedient wife ought to do, yet the said William Haak regardless of matrimonial vows and engagements for a long time to wit, for the space of two years next after his marriage with the libellant offered such indignities to her person as to render her condition intolerable and her life burthensome. And that the said William Haak at the expiration of two years or thereabouts after his marriage with the libellant did willfully and maliciously desert and absent himself from the habitation of the libellant and has continued such desertion or absence up to the time of the filing of this her petition or libel which comprehends a time of two years and upwards. Your petitioner or libellant therefore prayed your honours to award a subpoena directed to the said William Hannk commanding him to appear at the next term of the Court of Common Pleas in and for the said County of Cumberland to answer the matters and things contained in this her petition or libel and to shew cause if any he has, why the libellant should not be divorced from the bonds of matrimony agreeable to the acts of Assembly in such case made and provided. And petition being presented to the Honorable James Armstrong Esquire one of the Judges of the Court of Common Pleas the second day of October A.D. 1822. Whereupon the said Judge awarded a subpoena to issue on due form of law. Returnable to the next term."

Oct. 10, 1822 -"Exit subpoena Returnable to November Term 1822 -Cumberland County S.ct. -The Commonwealth of Pennsylvania to William Haak Greeting -Whereas Elizabeth Haak by her next friend Abraham Hick (sic) her father, did on the second day of October one thousand eight hundred and twenty two last past, preferred her petition to one of our Judges of the Court of Common Pleas for the County of Cumberland prayed that for the causes therein set forth she might be divorced from the bonds of matrimony entered into with the said William Haak, that setting aside all other business and excuses whatsoever, you be and appear in your proper person before our Judges at Carlisle, at a Court of Common Pleas there to be held for the said County on the first Monday of November next to answer the petition or libel of the said Elizabeth, and to shew cause if any you have, why the said Elizabeth your wife should not be divorced from the bonds of matrimony agreeable to the act of General Assembly in such case made and provided. And hereof you are not to fail. Witness John Reed Esquire at Carlisle the tenth day of August (sic) in the year of our Lord one thousand eight hundred and twenty two."

Nov. 5, 1822 -"Cumberland County s.s. -Peter Ritner Esquire high Sheriff of Cumberland County, being duly sworn doth say that William Haak the person named in the within subpoena could not be found in the said county and that he had diligently enquired for the said William Haak at the last place of abode of the said William Haak in the Township of Frankford, with(in) the said County, more than fifteen days before the return day of the within subpoena inclusive. Sworn and subscribed the 5th day of November 1822 in open court." (signed Peter Ritner, Sheriff and Test. B. Aughinbaugh, Prothy.)

"Exit Alias Subpoena Returnable to January Term 1823."

Jan.2,1823 -"Cumberland County, s.s. -James Neal, Esq. High Sheriff of Cumberland County being duly sworn doth say that William Haak the person named in the within subpoena could not be found in the said county, and that a copy of the said subpoena was left by him at the usual and last place of residence and place of abode of the said William Haak in the Township of Frankford within the said county. Sworn and subscribed in open court the 2nd day of January 1823." (signed James Neal and Test. B. Aughinbaugh, Prothy.)

Jan. 6, 1823 -"And now to wit 6th January 1823 proof is duly made to the court that subpoena for the said William Haak to answer to the complaint libel and petition of the said Elizabeth Haak why she should not be divorced from the bonds of matrimony as commanded by the said subpoena issued in the cause were executed as directed by law. Whereupon the court further order that the Sheriff of the County of Cumberland shall cause notice to be published in one of the newspapers printed within the said county, to wit, the paper called *The American Volunteer* published in the Borough of Carlisle for four weeks successively prior to the first day of the next April term of the Court of Common Pleas of said county requiring the said William Haak to appear on the said day to answer to the complaint of the said Elizabeth Haak why she should not be divorced from the bonds of matrimony." (signed John Reed).

April 11, 1823 -"April 11th 1823 on full proof as will appear by affidavit filed the court on ex parte hearing adjudge that the said William Haak has committed willful and malicious desertion and absence from the habitation of the said Elizabeth Haak without a reasonable cause for and during the term and space of two years and upwards and so sentence and decree a divorce and separation of the said William Haak and Elizabeth Haak from the nuptial ties and bonds of matrimony contracted by and between them. By the Court."

◆ ◆ ◆

Nov. 1823 #139 -Nov. 6, 1823 -petition of Hannah Sanno by her next friend John Traugh. She married about 1800 Frederick Sanno. He abused her and left her after thirteen years or thereabouts of marriage.

Nov. 8, 1823 -subpoena issued to Frederick Sanno for first Monday of Jan. 1824. James Neal, Sheriff of Cumberland Co., Pa. reported he was not to be found in Cumberland Co., Pa. so he left the subpoena at his last place of abode in Cumberland Co., Pa. the house of G. D. Foulk Dec. 12, 1823.

Jan. 10, 1824 -alias subpoena issued to Frederick Sanno for first Monday of April 1824. James Neal, Sheriff reported he was not found so the subpoena was left at his last place of abode in Cumberland Co., Pa. at the residence of D. Folk Feb. 20, 1824.

Aug. 10, 1824 -Court ordered Sheriff to publish divorce proclamation for four weeks order in *The Farmer's (Museum?)* a Carlisle, Pa. newspaper. Also ordered Elisha Doyle, Justice of the Peace to take deposition in the divorce case of Hannah Sanno vs. Frederick Sanno.

Aug. 12, 1824 -deposition of John Traugh of the Borough of Carlisle, Pa. before Elisha Doyle, Justice of the Peace. He was present at the marriage of Frederick and Hannah Sanno in Bucks Co., Pa. over twenty years ago. About two years after their marriage they came to Carlisle to live. They lived together there about ten years and he deserted her about ten years ago.

Aug. 12, 1824 -deposition of David Smith of the Borough of Carlisle, Pa. He testified he knew both parties about seventeen years or more. He also knew that Frederick Sanno deserted Hannah Sanno without any just or reasonable cause.

Aug. 12, 1824 -Court granted Hannah Sanno a divorce.

♦ ♦ ♦

Nov. 1823 #140 -Nov. 13, 1823 -petition of Jacob Hyser who married Mary Rodibaugh Aug. 5, 1823. On Aug. 25, 1823 Mary had a female child which during the time of Delivery and several times thereafter she said he was not the father to "Although the said Mary had sworn before a Justice of the Peace that he was the father of said child. The said child lived about eight days after its birth, and about six or seven days after the death of the child the said Mary left the habitation of your petitioner." "He also wishes here to state that he could not live in harmony and peace with his wife after knowing she had willfully and corruptably sworn a child to him to induce him to marry her, which she at the time of so doing must have known was false and which she has since acknowledged was false." Jacob Hyser signed petition "by mark".

Nov. 14, 1823 -subpoena issued to Mary Hyser for first Monday of Jan. 1824. James Neal, Sheriff reported she was not found so he left the subpoena at her last place of residence in the Borough of Carlisle.

Jan. 10, 1824 -alias subpoena issued to Mary Hyser for the first Monday of April 1824. James Neal, Sheriff reports Mary Hyser was not found so he left the subpoena at her last place of abode in the Borough of Carlisle Feb. 19, 1824.

♦ ♦ ♦

Nov. 1823 #174 -Dec. 9, 1823 -petition of Catharine Walt by her next friend Abraham Henwood (both signed "by mark"). She married May 12, 1819 John Walt who deserted her April 5, 1820.

Dec. 9, 1823 -subpoena issued to John Walt for first Monday of Jan. 1824.

Jan. 7, 1824 Joseph Shields, Esq. Deputy Sheriff of Cumberland Co., Pa. reports John Walt could not be found in the county.

Jan. 10, 1824 -alias subpoena issued to John Walt for first

Monday of April 1824.
April 8, 1824 -James Neal, Sheriff says John Walt is not be found in Cumberland Co., Pa.
April 8, 1824 -Court orders the Sheriff to put four weeks notice of this divorce in a Carlisle, Pa. newspaper.

♦ ♦ ♦

Nov. 1823 #175 -Oct. 11, 1823 -petition of Michael Saxton of East Pennsboro Township, Cumberland Co., Pa. He married in 1810 Sarah (Weaver?) and he accused her of adultery.
Nov. 8, 1823 -subpoena to Sarah Saxton for the first Monday of Jan. 1824.
Jan. 10, 1824 Joseph Shields, Sheriff of Cumberland Co., Pa. reported that he served the subpoena on Sarah Saxton.
Jan. 10, 1824 -subpoena issued to Sarah Saxton for the first Monday of April 1824.

♦ ♦ ♦

Apr. 1824 #800 -July 31, 1824 -petition of Jean Cauffman by her next friend George Sponsler. She married in 1812 Joseph Cauffman and about six years later he deserted her. She signed it "Jane A. Kaufman".
Aug. 19, 1824 -subpoena issued to Joseph Cauffman for first Monday of Nov. 1824.
Nov. 15, 1824 -James Neal, Sheriff reports Joseph Cauffman was not found so he left subpoena at his last place of abode in Carlisle, Pa.
Nov. 16, 1824 -subpoena issued to Joseph Cauffman for first Monday in Jan. 1825.
Jan. 8, 1824 -Joseph Shields, Deputy Sheriff of Cumberland Co., Pa. reports Joseph Cauffman not found in Cumberland Co., Pa. so he left subpoena at his last place of abode in Carlisle, Pa.
Jan. 21, 1825 -alias subpoena issued to Joseph Cauffman for second Monday of April 1825.
April 21, 1825 -Joseph Shields, Deputy Sheriff of Cumberland Co., Pa. reports Joseph Cauffman not to be found in Cumberland Co., Pa. so he left subpoena at his last place of abode in Carlisle.
Aug. 10, 1825 -Court orders Sheriff to publish divorce proclamations in *The American Volunteer* and appoints Elisha Doyle, Justice of the Peace to take depositions.
Aug. 10, 1825 -deposition of George Sponsler of North Middleton Township Cumberland Co., Pa. before Elisha Doyle, Justice of the Peace. Jane Cauffman was married to Joseph Cauffman "at the house of her father Jacob Matter in the said Township of North Middleton about the year 1812 about the fall of the year. Deponent was present at the said marriage." He deserted her six years ago. While they lived together about four or five years they lived in the Borough of Carlisle "except some part of said time that he was absent."

Aug. 10, 1825 -deposition of Edward Armor before Elisha Doyle, Justice of the Peace. Jane Matter married Joseph Cauffman Oct. 1812 at the house of her father Jacob Matter in North Middleton Township. They immediately moved to Carlisle and "resided there several years except some time that the said Joseph would be away for several months together." He deserted her six or seven years ago.

Aug. 12, 1825 -Court grants Jean Cauffman a divorce from Joseph Cauffman, for willful and malicious desertion.

♦ ♦ ♦

April 1824 #826 -Jan. 7, 1825 -petition of David James of the Borough of Carlisle. He married his wife Margaret June 10, 1824. He accused her of adultery. She deserted him Sept. 29, 1824.

Jan. 21, 1825 -subpoena issued to Margaret James for second Monday of April 1825.

April 13, 1825 -Joseph Shields, Deputy Sheriff of Cumberland Co., Pa. reports he could not find Margaret James in Cumberland Co., Pa.

April 22, 1825 -alias subpoena issued to Margaret James for second Monday of Aug. 1825.

Nov. 25, 1825 -James Neal, Sheriff of Cumberland Co., Pa. reports Margaret James can not be found in Cumberland Co., Pa.

Nov. 25, 1825 Court orders Sheriff to put four weeks of successive notice of divorce proclamation in County newspaper.

♦ ♦ ♦

Apr 1824 #839 -Jan. 24, 1825 -petition of Mary Bere by next friend Jacob Mussellman. She married Samuel Bere Mar 15, 1821. She accused him of beating her and deserting her Jan. 24, 1823.

Jan. 24, 1825 -subpoena to Samuel Bere for second Monday of April 1825. April 11, 1825 Joseph Shields, Deputy Sheriff for Cumberland Co., Pa. reports he served this subpoena on Samuel Bere March 8, 1825.

March 13, 1825 -deposition of John Black before Elisha Doyle, Justice of the Peace. He was present at the marriage of Samuel Beare and Mary Musselman some time in March four years ago. "He the said Samuel Beare separated from her the said Mary some time in the winter two years ago. He has lived separate from her ever since. He has not kept house ever since that time. She has lived with her grandfather Jacob Musselman ever since or made her home there."

March 13, 1825 -deposition of John Koch before Elisha Doyle, Justice of the Peace. "Also in pursuance of the same order of court personally came before me John Koch who on his oath duly administered doth suppose and say that Samuel Beare and Mary Musselman were married about the middle of March four years ago. Deponent was present at the marriage. About the middle of January two years ago they were separated as deponent understood in consequence of the bad treatment he had given here. He the said Samuel has lived separate from her the said Mary ever since. He the said Samuel told deponent that he would have nothing to do with her the said Mary and that he never would live with her again. This he told me about two or three weeks after he separated from her his said wife. He has not supported her since they separated but has continued working about through the county and driving team and has not kept house since. She the said Mary has lived with her grandfather Mr. Musselman and has been supported by him."

April 13, 1825 -deposition of Rosanna Couffer -"Before the subscriber, one of the Justices of the Peace in and for the County personally came Rosanna Couffer who on her oath duly administered according to law doth depose and say that last winter was two years, she this deponent lived with Mary Bere and Samuel Bere her husband who then lived together. They separated in that winter they have not lived together since. Some short time before they separated one morning before breakfast Samuel Bere took Mary Bere where she was sitting by the throat with his hand and choked her until she was black in the face. He let her go and then choked her again. He struck her twice and knocked her down on the floor. He did not abuse her with his tongue any at that time but did so several times afterwards and before also. Deponent did not hear the said Mary Bear abuse him the said Samuel at any time. The said Samuel Bear has not kept house since they separated. The evening before they separated deponent and Mary Bere were sitting in the room after dark and heard a noise in the kitchen went into the kitchen and saw that a chair had been thrown in at the window that had been hoisted. Deponent and Mary Bere began to cry and Samuel Bere then came in and told deponent that he had thrown in the chair. Deponent was afraid from the conduct of Samuel Bear that night that he would kill his wife the said Mary Bear and the deponent went over to a neighbor's house and staid (sic) there." Rosanna Couffer signed the deposition "by mark".

◆ ◆ ◆

Jan. 1825 (no number given) -May 25, 1824 -petition of Jacob Ewig of Allen township, Cumberland Co., Pa. He married his wife Magdalina June 27, 1811 and was a kind and loving husband. He accused her of adultery and petitioned for a divorce.

◆ ◆ ◆

April 1825 #307 -March 3, 1825 -petition of Lydia Wallace by her next friend Moses Ely stating that she married David Wallace Nov. 4, 1822. She adds "yet so it is that the said Wallace from the first day of November 1823 till the said November 1824 had by cruel and barbarous treatment endangered his wife's (the said libellant's) life and offered such indignities to her person as to render her condition intolerable and life burdensome and thereby forced her to withdraw from his house and family. Wherefore your libellant further showing that she is now and always has been a citizen and resident of this state prays your honors that a subpoena may issue forth to summon him the said David Wallace to appear in the said Honorable Court of April Term next to answer the complaint aforesaid. And also that a decree of the said Honorable Court may be given for the divorcing and separating him the said David Wallace from the said libellant's society fellowship and company in all time to come and her the said libellant from the marriage bond aforesaid as if she had never been married or as if the said David Wallace were naturally dead."

April 22, 1825 -subpoena issued to David Wallace for second Monday of Aug. 1825.

Aug. 11, 1825 -Joseph Shields, Deputy Sheriff of Cumberland Co., Pa. reported that David Wallace could not be found in his bailiwick.

Aug. 20, 1825 -subpoena issued to David Wallace for the second Monday of Nov. 1825.

Nov. 18, 1825 -John Cleppinger, Sheriff of Cumberland Co., Pa. testified that he could not find David Wallace in his bailiwick. The court therefore ordered the Sheriff to publish notice in the *Carlisle Gazette* a Carlisle, Pa. newspaper "once a week for four weeks successively prior to the first day of the next Term of this Court requiring the defendant to appear on the said day to answer the complaint of the libellant as is provided by the aforesaid writ."

Jan. 9, 1826 -Proof was made that the notices were printed in the *Carlisle Gazette* and David Wallace did not appear. The Court appoint Henry D. Overhaltzer, Esq. to take depositions on the case at his office in Leacock Township, Lancaster County on "Saturday the fourteenth instant between the hours of five o'clock in the morning and five o'clock in the afternoon of said day."

Jan. 18, 1826 -deposition of William Line that he knew both Lydia and David Wallace and they lived together as man and wife. To the best of his knowledge Lydia Wallace was born in Penna. and had always lived there. Lydia Wallace withdrew from the house and family of her husband in consequence of his cruel treatment of her.

Jan. 14, 1826 -deposition of Michael Weidknecht who "being duly affirmed according to law deposes and says that sometime in May 1824 I heard David Wallace swear that he would be d____d if he would not kick his wife's guts out, several times Lydia Wallace and Rebecca Line called me in to stay with them that night as they were afraid of Wallace because he was intoxicated, and another night I was called out of bed to go down to Wallace's to stay with them. In the night of the 23rd of July 1824 I was called out of bed to go to Wallace's again telling me that Wallace was beating his wife. I went down seeing him stand at the door with his coat jacket and hat off ready for battle he appeared bloody but I can't say whether from his own or from Lydia. Wallace then called me into the room and asked who all was at his house. I told him who was out, Isaac Rudy Geo. Richardson and others. Wallace then asked me to join him that he wanted to rip all their guts out. He asked where Lydia was that he would like to see her. I observed the fire tongs under the bed and asked him for what the tongs were. Then he replied that he did not know for what, perhaps some of the others brought them in. Wallace still taring (sic) and swearing and inquiring of his wife, then stated that he wanted to play a trick on her. Wallace then took Lydia's clothing. I advised not but he insisted on having them, searched all the drawers and found some money which he put in his pocket. He then said that he did not care a damn about her as he had what would do him a while. He packed up all Lydia's clothes and attempted to go away but the load appeared too heavy and then returned and went to bed." Sworn before H.D. Overholzer at his office in Leacock Township, Lancaster Co., Pa.

Jan. 14, 1826 -deposition of Christina Heller "Christina Heller, being duly affirmed according to law deposes and says that sometime in November in the year 1824 David Wallace came home intoxicated. The first words he said he began to curse and swear at his wife. She flattered him but nothing would do. She then left the house in order to make her escape but could not. He still followed her, that she could not get out of his way. She then again returned to the house and he also. Then he caught her and struck and choked her very much. I heard it and asked what was the matter. She answered but I could not understand what she said, it appeared that she was so much out of breath that she could not speak. When he began to beat her she said David if you don't quit I will call Daddy. Only call him said he God damn him to hell if I only get him in my claws. Then he locked the door and shut the window, and took the fire tong and began to strike on the stove and bench frightful to hear. She made him a good supper but he would not eat and said that he would shit in her supper. She still flattered him and nothing would do. He blew the candle and compelled her to go with him to bed. I then became alarmed and watched the whole night being uneasy that he would kill her. Question, did you ever hear Lydia Wallace give her husband David Wallace any ill language at any time whatsoever? Answer: No, I never did, they lived better than a year in a house in our yard close to our house and I never heard her give him a rash word, and at the time he beat her so severely she said nothing but 'O, David don't!'"

Jan. 14, 1826 -deposition of Rebecca Rayer formerly Rebecca Line -"Affirmed, according to law deposes and says that on the 25th day of May A.D. 1824 David Wallace came home Intoxicated and asked me where Lydia was. I did not like to tell him. He insisted on me telling him where she was. I then told him that she was in John

Bender's corn field planting beans. Wallace seemed to be in a (illegible word) and directly went down to the field. I followed him, being uneasy that he would abuse her. When he went into the field to Lydia he began to scold her and insisted on her coming home. On the way home he swore that he would knock her brains out. They then both went into the house and I do not recollect what then passed. Shortly after Wallace came home again intoxicated and began to abuse and swear at his wife. I and Lydia were afraid of him. We went to Isaac Rudy's and asked Michael Weidknecht and Polly Rudy to come and stay with them that night. They came. When Wallace saw them coming he then appeared to become quiet and behaved himself pretty well that night. Sometime after Wallace came home at midknight (sic) and called Lydia, she got up and opened the door. As soon as he was in the house he began to scold and abuse her. She became alarmed and called me and asked me to let her in my room, which I did. Wallace then came to my room door and requested me to open the door, but I did not. He then went downstairs and directly came up again to my room door, and asked for admittance. I then said if he did not go away from my door that I would call Isaac Rudy. Wallace then began to swear that he did not care whether I would or not. He then went down and walked about the house and sweared dreadfully at his wife. He called the third time at my door and I became alarmed, opened the door and made my escape. Lydia also went out of my room and went into another room, which Wallace heard. He followed her and laid hold upon her but Lydia got loose and got out on the Turnpike towards Isaac Rudy's. Wallace followed her and caught and attempted to beat her. Lydia called me for assistance but I was afraid of him. He got her in the kitchen and then he did cruelly beat her. Lydia again called me to help her. I then went to assist her for she said if I did not that he would kill her. As I came near them Wallace swore very bad that if I did not go away he would do the same to me. I ran to Isaac Rudy's and called murder. George Richardson and William Gilbert came immediately and took him from her. Wallace had Lydia by the neck and choked and scratched her dreadfully. Wallace then shut the door and would not permit any person to come in the house. I was very uneasy because I was afraid he would set my house and barn afire. At last Wallace opened the door after he had taken all linen, clothing and quilts into a bedcase and attempted to take them to Jeremiah Fox. Question: How long did Wallace and Lydia live with you in your house? Answer: About eight months. Question: During the time Wallace and Lydia lived with you did you ever hear Lydia give Wallace any ill language? Answer: I never did hear her give him a bad word but very often heard her flatter him and anything that she thought would please him was done." Rebecca Rayer signed her deposition "by mark".

Jan. 14, 1826 -deposition of Polly Rudy -"Polly Rudy affirmed according to law deposed and says that in the night that Rebecca Line and Lydia Wallace came to our house we were all in bed. They called us up and out of bed, and asked us to come down to their house. I did not like at first to go my brother Isaac then said if they were afraid myself and Michael Weidknecht should go along and stay with them. We went and as we came down Wallace appeared quiet and further he said nothing." Polly Rudy signed her deposition "by mark".

Jan. 14, 1826 -deposition of Samuel Cowan -"Samuel Cowan being duly sworn according to law deposes and says as follows viz. That I and William Gilbert on the evening of the 23rd of July 1824 went to Isaac Rudy's. While we were there we heard some person crying Murder, Murder. We instantly went out and heard Rebecca Line call that Wallace was killing his wife. I did not directly go down. George Richardson and several others went down. Immediately we heard the shout of Murder again. Isaac Rudy begged for God's sake I should go along. As we came down the others had taken Wallace off from her. Lydia came to me crying and saying that she did not know what to do. If it only was daylight for as soon as day she would leave Wallace for it was impossible for her to live with him any longer. At that time a number of people had gathered and Wallace slipped into the house and fastened the door. Rebecca Line seemed very uneasy and did not know where to go or what to do as she stated to me that she was afraid that Wallace would set her house and barn afire."

Jan. 14, 1826 -deposition of John Gillmore -"John Gillmore being duly sworn according to law deposed and says as follows viz. that I lived in the next house to David Wallace. I had not much acquaintance with Wallace as we both only moved to that place in the spring. In the night of the 23rd day of July 1824 I was in bed asleep. My wife wakened me and asked what noise is that. Listened a little and heard some person crying Murder. I got out of bed and went to the door and again heard some person crying Murder. I heard Wallace beat his wife. I then seen George Richardson, Jonathan Simmons and William Gilbert run past my door. I put on my overhawls (sic) and went down as soon as possible. As I came to Wallace's door I met his wife coming out of the door crying and her hair all hanging down very much disordered. I went into the house and Wallace appeared very much outrageous. From that time until Lydia left Wallace she frequently came to my house and stayed all night being afraid that Wallace would kill her and requested that if Wallace would come asking for her that I should say that she was not there. Question: How far did you and Wallace live apart? Answer: About ten or twelve perches. Question: Did you ever see any misconduct of Lydia Wallace towards her husband David Wallace? Answer: I never did, but she always seemed to be friendly and kind toward him, always up early in the morning and appeared to be a very quiet industrious woman."

Jan. 14, 1826 -deposition of Jonas Eby -"Jonas Eby being duly affirmed according to law doth depose and say that at the time I took David Wallace on a State Warrant for assaulting and beating wife Lydia I was compelled to take him to jail. Wallace asked several of his friends to go his security for his appearance but all in vain. I heard Wallace swear that he would have satisfaction of his wife, said that he would be d____d if he would not take me off the horse and kick my guts out. Wallace made many threats on the way to jail but I do not recollect what they were."

Jan. 14, 1826 -deposition of Isaac Rudy -"Isaac Rudy being duly affirmed according to law deposes and says that same in the summer of 1824 Rebecca Line came and called me out of bed and said that David Wallace was so outrageous, they were afraid of him. I then sent my sister and Michael Weidknecht down to stay with them that night. Shortly after one night I heard a noise and immediately went and heard Rebecca Line call for help stating that Wallace was killing his wife. I then called the Boys and told them to run down to Wallace's, that he was beating his wife. Geo. Richardson, Wm. Gilbert and Jonathan Simmons went down. I again went in the house and directly heard Rebecca call me again. I went down with Samuel Cowen and as we came down Lydia Wallace first came out the door crying and very much alarmed. Wallace still taring (sic) and swearing I and my sister went home and shortly Lydia Wallace came too. I asked her what she intended to do. She then said that she wished to stay with me that night. I replied that she would be welcome to stay if it were not for Wallace as I was afraid if she would stay that Wallace perhaps would do me some damage. She should go home this night and I would direct Michael Weidknecht and others to stay with them. I did not like to interfere much, as I was allways (sic) afraid of Wallace that he perhaps would do me some damage."

Jan. 14, 1826 -Court granted Lydia Wallace a divorce.

♦　　　　♦　　　　♦

April 1825 #416 -Nov. 16, 1825 -petition of Mary Keth by her next friend David Croll. Mary Keth testified that she was born in Cumberland Co., Pa. and has always lived there. She married Oct. 17, 1820 Hyram Keth who deserted her Oct. 4, 1821. Her petition was not presented to the court until Jan. 13, 1826.

Jan. 13, 1826 -subpoena issued to Hyram Keth for the second Monday of April 1826.

April 12, 1826 -John Clippinger, Sheriff of Cumberland Co., Pa. states he could not find Hyram Keth in his bailiwick.

April 22, 1826 -alias subpoena issued to Hyram Keth for the second Monday of Aug. 1826.

Aug. 25, 1826 -John Clippinger, Sheriff of Cumberland Co., Pa. stated that he could not find Hyram Keth in his bailiwick.

Aug. 25, 1826 -Ct. ordered publication of divorce proclamation for three weeks in the *Carlisle Herald* and appointed Andrew Matier, Esq. to take depositions.

♦ ♦ ♦

Jan. 1826 #113 -Jan. 9, 1826 -petition of Mary Heiser by her next friend Jacob Rodebaugh for a divorce from Jacob Heiser. She married him July 13, 1822 and he deserted her Dec. 30, 1822 or thereabouts. Signed by mark by both Mary Heiser and Jacob Roudebaugh. Subpoena issued Jan. 9, 1826.

Jan. 21, 1826 -subpoena issued to Jacob Heiser for second Monday of April 1826. Served by John Bowermaster, Deputy Sheriff and John Clippinger, Sheriff.

♦ ♦ ♦

Jan. 1826 #114 -Dec. 15, 1825 -petition of Margaret Markle before John D. Havenstick, Justice of the Peace by her father and her next friend Henry Meyers. She married Dec. 22, 1821 at Allen (now Monroe) township, Cumberland Co., Pa. Henry Markle. He deserted her Nov. 29, 1823. She signed her petition by mark and her father signed his signature in German script. Subpoena issued Jan. 10, 1826.

Jan. 21, 1826 -subpoena issued to Henry Markle for the second Monday of April 1826.

April 10, 1826 -John Clippinger, Sheriff testified in regards to the Jan. 21, 1826 subpoena "Left a copy of the within subpoena at the last place of abode of Henry Markle, the within libellant to wit in the township of Silverspring and that the said Henry had removed from said township to Lancaster county as I was informed."

April 10, 1826 -alias subpoena issued to Henry Markle for second Monday of August 1826.

Aug. 14, 1826 -John Bowermaster, Deputy Sheriff testified "John Bowermaster, substitute sheriff of said county on his affirmation, administered in due form, doth say that he served the within subpoena, on Henry Markle, by leaving a copy thereof, with at the residence and place of abode of the said Henry, on the sixteenth day of June 1826."

Aug. 14, 1826 -answer of Henry Markle to the libel of his wife Margaret Markle. He denied that he deserted his wife and he added "And the said defendant in truth and in fact saith that the said Margaret refused to live with his defendant that he now is and always has been willing to live with her and maintain her and her children and use her as a good husband ought to do."

Nov. 9, 1835 -divorce granted (husband mistakenly referred to as Joseph Markle!)

♦ ♦ ♦

Nov. 1826 #38 -Aug. 15, 1826 -petition before Archibald Ramsey Justice of the Peace, of Susanna Bricker by her next friend Samuel

Smith. She married March 5, 1818 John Bricker. "And from that time until the twentieth day of May in the year of our Lord one thousand eight hundred and twenty lived and cohabitted with the said John Bricker as his wife when she was forced to leave his house and family by cruel and barbarous treatment on his part." Susanna Bricker signed "by mark".

Nov. 25, 1826 -Subpoena issued to John Bricker for second Monday of January 1827. May 22, 1827 John Bowermaster, Deputy Sheriff of Cumberland Co., Pa. testified that he served this subpoena on John Bricker Dec. 16, 1826.

April 16, 1827 -Subpoena issued to Elizabeth Brewster and William Smith to appear before William Richey, Esq. at the office of William Richey, Justice of the Peace in Newville, Pa. Aug. 1, 1827 at 10 o'clcock A.M. concerning the divorce action of Susanna Bricker.

June 5, 1827 -Subpoena issued to John Bricker to appear before William Richey, Justice of the Peace at his office in the borough of Newville, Pa. August 1, 1827 between the hours of 10 o'clock and 2 o'clock.

Aug. 25, 1827 -Subpoena issued to Sarah Hull, Peter Buck, Molly Buck, Samuel Smith, Elizabeth Brewster and Adam Reifsnyder to appear before William Richey, Justice of the Peace Sept. 4, 1827 at his office in the Borough of Newville, Pa. concerning the divorce action of Susanna Bricker.

Sept. 4, 1827 -deposition before William Richey "Personally appeared before the subscriber the Commissioner named in the annexed Commission in pursuance of the same Commission Elizabeth Brewster, who on her oath lawfully administered do then say that she is acquainted with John Bricker and Susanna Bricker named in the said Commission, that she was present at their marriage about nine years ago, and the same marriage was then celebrated in the house of deponent's father John Bisban in the Borough of Carlisle by the Reverend Mr. Helpenstein who at that time officiated as pastor of the German Presbyterian or Reformed Congregation of the Borough of Carlisle."

Sept. 4, 1827 -deposition before William Richey "Personally appeared before the subscriber the Commissioner named in the annexed Commission in pursuance of the same Commission, Sarah Hull who her oath lawfully administered, doth say. That she is acquainted with John Bricker and Susanna Bricker the parties named in the said Commission, that in the later end of the month of March or in the beginning of the month of April in the year of our Lord 1820 she went to live with the said John and the said Susanna who at that time lived together as husband and wife and that from then she continued to live in their family with them till some time in the month of May then next following having been hired and receiving wages for her work. That during the said time that she lived with the said John and the said Susanna he the said John was very seldom sober or out of a state of intoxication. That when he was in a state of intoxication or drunkenness his treatment of his said wife Susanna and the indignities he offered to her person were so bad and barbarous that no woman could live with him and his said wife in consequence such barbarous treatment and indigities was forced to leave him and his family. That on one occassion he caught her hair around his arm and attempted to strike her with his other hand, but was held and prevented from doing so by his mother and deponent. That after he was disengaged from such hold of her his said wife went to his house and for her safety (illegible word) herself in closing the door, which he took a mattock to break open. That deponent then assisted the said Susanna to get out of the house at a window to flee for her safety -and that on this occassion the conduct of the said John was so violent that deponent felt alarmed lest he should kill his said wife. That the said Susanna was forced to leave her said husband and his family sometime in the month of May 1825 on account of his before mentioned barbarous treatment and indignities toward her and has never to the best of deponent's knowledge since cohabitted with him -deponent was living with the said John and Susanna at the time said Susanna left him as above stated." Sarah Hull signed "by mark".

Sept. 4, 1827 -deposition before William Richey "Personally appeared before the subscriber the Commissioner named in the annexed Commission in pursuance of the same Commission James Reed who on his oath lawfully administered doth say that he saw the same Susanna Bricker named in the annexed Commission living at her father's in the said County of Cumberland and believes she resides in the same County with her said father."

Sept. 12, 1827 -Court granted divorce.

◆ ◆ ◆

Nov. 1826 #151 -Nov. 15, 1826 -petition of Esther Call before Edward B. Leonard, Justice of the Peace by her father and next friend Jacob Shelly. Esther Call was married in August of 1816 to Nicholas Call. He deserted her in January of 1823 without a reasonable cause.

Nov. 25, 1826 -Subpoena issued to Nicholas Call for the second Monday of January 1827.

Jan. 17, 1827 -John Bowermaster, Deputy Sheriff of Cumberland Co., Pa. testified that he could not find Nicholas Call in his bailiwick. (Note -original paper says Nicholas Crall which is apparently an error.)

◆ ◆ ◆

Jan. 1827 #77 -Jan. 10, 1827 -petition of Catharine Milizen before Archibald Ramsey by her next friend John Myers. She married Apr. 11, 1822 William Milizen. He deserted her Dec. 18, 1824 when he left their home in Allen township, Cumberland Co., Pa.

Jan. 18, 1827 -Subpoena issued to William Milizen for the second Monday of April 1827 at ten o'clock.

April 16, 1827 -John Bowermaster, Substitute Sheriff testified that he could not find William Millizen when he tried to serve this subpoena.

April 16, 1827 -Subpoena issued to William Millizen for the second Monday in August 1827 at ten o'clock.

Aug. 17, 1827 -John Bowermaster, Deputy Sheriff reported William Millizen could not be found in his bailiwick. "And now August the 17th 1827 upon proof made on the alias subpoena issued in this case the Deft could not be found in the County of Cumberland in the manner pointed out by the act of assembly in such case made and provided and on proclamation made calling on the Deft to appear to answer the complaint of the libelant and in default thereof the court do order and decree that the Sheriff of the County aforesaid shall cause notice to be published in the *American Volunteer* a paper printed in the borough of Carlisle once a week for four weeks successively prior to the first day of the next term of this Court requiring the Deft to appear on said day to answer the complaint of the libelant as is provided by the aforesaid act."

Nov. 12, 1827 -"And now to wit the twelveth day of November A.D. 1827 proof being duly made to the court that notice for the said William Milizen to appear and answer to the complaint libel and petition of the said Catharine Milizen why she should not be divorced from the bonds of matrimony as commanded by the Subpoena issued in this cause, has been given by a publication of the same in the *American Volunteer* a paper printed in the Borough of Carlisle in the County of Cumberland for four weeks successively prior to the first day of this term -and no person appearing to answer the said complaint, libel and petition, the Court orders the examination of witnesses before William Irwin, Esq. of the Borough of Carlisle, County aforesaid at his office between the hours of 11 o'clock A.M. and three o'clock P.M. of this day and that said William Irwin be a Commissioner for the purposes aforesaid."

"In pursuance of the within order personally appeared before me the within named William Irwin at the time and place mentioned in said order, James Anderson, who being duly sworn according to law deposeth and saith that he knew the within named William Milizen and Catharine Milizen to live together as man and wife from some time in the spring of 1824 until sometime about Christmas of said year and that the said William from the time last aforesaid deserted and absented himself from the habitation of her the said Catharine in Allen Township County of Cumberland and still continues to desert and absent himself from the habitation aforesaid of her the said Catharine until the present time without any reasonable cause known to deponent and that said Catharine has lived in the State of Pennsylvania for the last three years."

Nov. 12, 1827 -deposition "At the time aforesaid appeared before me the said William Irvine John Myers who being duly sworn according to law deposeth and saith that he was present at the marriage of the aforesaid William Milizen and Catharine Milizen which took place some time in the spring of 1822 and that they lived together as husband and wife from that time in until some time in the fall of 1824 when the said William deserted and absented himself from the habitation of her the said Catharine in Allen township aforesaid and that he the said William still continues from that time until the present to desert and absent himself from the habitation aforesaid of her the said Catharine without any just or reasonable cause known to said deponent and that said Catharine has lived for the last four years in the state of Pennsylvania."

Nov. 12, 1827 -deposition "Joshua Myers being duly sworn according to law deposeth and saith that the within named Catharine Milizen is his daughter and that she was married to William Milizen within named in the spring of 1822 and that he was present at said marriage and that they the said William and Catharine lived together as man and wife from that time until about the last of December 1824 when he the said William maliciously deserted the said Catharine and left her habitation, and that he the said William has never since lived with said Catharine said deponent further saith that said William and Catharine lived in the same house with him in Allen Township for about nine months previous to said William deserting said Catharine as aforesaid during said time that he said deponent knew said William frequently to get drunk and to threaten said Catharine, that is to say that he would beat her, and he often made use of the most abusive language towards said Catharine, and said deponent and further saith that said William took with him at the time of his desertion -aforesaid all the property which the said Catharine received from deponent her father and that he left her nothing at all to live upon. Said deponent further saith that said William since the time of the desertion aforesaid has lived in the County of Dauphin as deponent believes."

Nov. 13, 1827 -Court granted divorce and added "that nothing contained in their sentence and divorce shall be construed to intend to effect or render illigitimate any children born of the body of the said Catharine."

♦ ♦ ♦

Jan. 1827 #78 -Jan. 15, 1827 petition of Catharine Kentz by her next friend Rudolph Miller. She married Frederick Kentz July 1824. He deserted her in the borough of Newville, Cumberland Co., Pa. sometime in the month of November 1824.

Jan. 18, 1827 -subpoena issued to Frederick Kentz for the second Monday of April 1827 at 10 o'clock in the forenoon.

April 16, 1827 -John Bowermaster, Deputy Sheriff testified that he served the subpoena on Frederick Kentz, Feb. 2, 1827. Court therefore appointed William Ritchy, Esq. of the Borough of Newville to take depositions on the case May 14, 1827 at his office between 10 o'clock A.M. and 6 o'clock P.M.

May 14, 1827 -before William Richey "Personally appeared before me one of the Justices of the Peace in and for said County, the Rev. David Hessinger who being duly sworn as the law directs deposeth and saith that Frederick Kentz was contracted in matrimony and married to Catharine Kentz named in the written order of Court, by him the said David sometime in the month of August in the year 1824 and further this deponent deposeth not."

May 14, 1827 -deposition before William Richey "Personally appeared before me one of the Justices of the Peace in and for the said County Catharine Rutchers who being duly sworn as the law directs deposeth and saith that Frederick Kentz was contracted in matrimony and married to Catharine Kentz named in the within order of Court, by the Rev. David Hessinger sometime in the month of August in the year 1824. That she was present at the marriage and saw them the said Frederick and Catharine married and united together in the bonds of matrimony. Said Deponent further deposeth that she knew the said Frederick and Catharine to live together as husband and wife from the time of said marriage until sometime in the month of November in the year aforesaid -when the said Frederick deserted and absented himself from the habitation of her the said Catharine without any reasonable cause known to deponent and that he the said Frederick still continues to desert and absent himself from the habitation of her the said Catharine without reasonable cause known to said deponent and said deponent further deposeth and saith that said Catharine has lived and resided in the Borough of Newville County aforesaid for the last fifteen or sixteen years."

May 14, 1827 -deposition before William Richey "Personally appeared before me one of the Justices of the Peace in and for said County John Givler who being duly sworn as the law directs deposeth and saith that he knew Frederick Kentz and Catharine Kentz to live together as husband and wife from sometime in the month of August in the year 1824 until sometime in the month of November in said year when said Frederick deserted himself from the habitation of her the said Catharine in the Borough of Newville County aforesaid without any just or reasonable cause known to the deponent and that said Frederick has continued and still doth continue to desert and absent himself from the habitation of her the said Catharine without any just or reasonable cause known to said deponent -and said deponent further deposeth and saith that said Catharine has lived and resided in the Borough aforesaid for the last three years and further this deponent saith not."

May 14, 1827 -deposition before William Richey "Personally appeared before me one of the Justices of the Peace in and for said County Jacob Ketring who being duly sworn as the law directs deposeth and saith that he knew Frederick Kentz and Catharine Kentz to live together as husband and wife from some time in the summer in the Year 1824 until sometime before Christmas in said year when said Frederick deserted and absented himself from the habitation of her the said Catherine in the borough of Newville County aforesaid without any just or reasonable cause known to said deponent and deponent further saith that said Catharine has lived and resided in the Borough aforesaid for the last fourteen or fifteen years. And further this deponent saith not."

May 14, 1827 -deposition before William Richey "Personally appeared before me one of the Justices of the Peace in and for said County Alexander Cox who being duly sworn as the law directs deposeth and saith that he knew Frederick and Catharine Kentz to live together as husband and wife from sometime in the Summer of the year 1824 until sometime before Christmas in said year when said Frederick deserted and absented himself from the habitation of her the said Catharine in the Borough of Newville County aforesaid without any just or reasonable cause known to deponent and the said Frederick has continued from that time and still does continue to desert and absent himself from the habitation of her the said Catharine without any just or reasonable cause known to said deponent. And Deponent further saith that said Catharine has lived and resided in the Borough aforesaid for the last years and further this deponent saith not."

May 21, 1827 -Court granted Catharine Kentz a divorce.

♦ ♦ ♦

Jan. 1827 #98 -Feb. 10, 1827 -petition of Catharine Ketring before Archibald Ramsey, Justice of the Peace by her next friend Rudolph Miller. She married sometime in the month of April 1824 Valentine Ketring. He deserted her willfully and maliciously in August 1824 while they were living in Newton township, Cumberland Co., Pa.

Feb. 20, 1827 -subpoena issued for Valentine Ketring to appear in court the second Monday of April 1827 to answer the libel of his wife.

March 3, 1827 -John Bowermaster, deputy Sheriff of Cumberland Co., Pa. served the Feb. 20, 1827 subpoena on Valentine Ketring.

April 16, 1827 -Court appointed William Ritchey, Esq. to take depositions of witnesses at his office in the Borough of Newville, Pa. May 14, 1827 between 10 o'clock A.M. and 6 o'clock P.M. because Valentine Ketring failed to appear in court.

May 14, 1827 -deposition "Personally appeared before me one of the Justices of the Peace in and for said County Margaret Ann Ketring, who being duly sworn as the law directs deposeth and seyth (sic) that she was present at the marriage of Valentine Ketring and Catharine Ketring and saw them the said parties married and united in the bonds of matrimony by the Rev. Geo. Hiling sometime in the spring of the year 1824 and further this deponent deposeth not."

May 14, 1827 -deposition "Personally appeared before me one of the Justices of the Peace in and for said County Eliza House who being duly sworn as the law directs deposeth and saith that Valentine Ketring was contracted in matrimony and married to Catharine Ketring named in the within Order of Courty, by the Rev. Geo. Hiling sometime in the month of April in the year 1824 -That the said deponent was present at the marriage and saw them the said Valentine and Catharine married and united together in the bonds of matrimony -and said Deponent further deposeth and saith that she has known the said Catharine to live and reside in the County aforesaid for the last four or five years -and further this deponent saith not."

May 14, 1827 -deposition "Personally appeared before me one of the Justices of the Peace in and for said County John Givler who being duly sworn as the law directs deposeth and saith that he knew Valentine Ketring and Catharine Ketring to live together as husband and wife from sometime in the month of April 1824 until sometime in the month of August in said year when said Valentine deserted and absented himself from the habitation of her the said Catharine in the Borough of Newville County aforesaid without any just or reasonable cause known unto deponent and that he the said Valentine hath continued and still doth continue to desert and absent himself from the habitation of her the said Catharine without any just or reasonable cause known to said deponent. Said Deponent further saith that said Catharine has lived and resided in the County aforesaid for the last three years and further he saith not." (signed Johannes Givler).

May 14, 1827 -deposition "Personally appeared before me one of the Justices of the Peace in and for said County Jonas Miller who being duly sworn as the law directs deposeth and saith that he knew Valentine Ketring and Catharine Ketring to live together as husband and wife from sometime in the month of April in the year 1824 until sometime in the month of August in said year when said Valentine deserted and absented himself from the habitation of her the said Catharine in the Borough of Newville County aforesaid without any just or reasonable cause known to deponent and that said Valentine hath continued from that time to desert and absent himself and still doth continue to desert and absent himself from the habitation of her the said Catharine without any just or reasonable cause known to deponent. Deponent further saith that said Catharine has lived and resided in the State of Pennsylvania all her lifetime and further this deponent saith not".

May 14, 1827 -deposition "Personally appeared before me one of the Justices of the Peace in and for said County Nathan Reed who being duly sworn as the law directs deposeth and saith that he knew Valentine Ketring and Catharine Ketring to live together as husband and wife from sometime in the month of April in the year 1824 until sometime in the month of August in said year where said Valentine deserted and absented himself from the habitation of her the said Catharine in the Borough of Newville County aforesaid without any just or reasonable cause known to deponent and that said Valentine hath continued from that time to desert and absent himself and still doth continue to desert and absent himself from the habitation of her the said Catharine without any just or reasonable cause known to deponent. Deponent further saith that he has known said Catharine to have lived and resided in the County aforesaid for the last ten years and further this deponent saith not."

May 14, 1827 -deposition "Personally appeared before me one of the Justices of the Peace in and for said County Catharine Rutchers who being duly sworn according to law deposeth and saith that she knew Valentine Ketring and Catharine Ketring to live together as husband and wife from sometime in the month of April in the year 1824 until sometime in the month of August in said year when said Valentine deserted and absented himself from the habitation of her the said Catharine in the Borough of Neville County aforesaid without any just or reasonable cause known to deponent and then said Valentine hath continued from that time to desert and absent himself and still doth continue to desert and absent himself from the habitation of her the said Catharine without any just or reasonable cause known to deponent and further this deponent saith not."

"May 21 AD 1827 -the depositions of Margaret Ann Ketring, Eliza House, John Givler, Jonas Miller, Nathan Reed and Catharine Rutchers being read, and the facts therein stated being adjudged by the Court to be sufficient cause of divorce, and on full consideration had of the premises on motion of (Mr) Gaullagher the Court do sentence and decree a divorce and separation from the nupitial tie and bonds of matrimony entered unto and hereto existing between the said Catharine Ketring and the said Valentine Ketring, and decree the said marriage to be null and void and of no further effect, and that all and every duties, rights and claims answering to either of said parties at anytime heretofore in pursuance of the said marriage shall cease and determine and that the said parties shall severally be at liberty to marry again in like manner as if they had never been married. --Proclamation made by the court."

♦   ♦   ♦

Aug. 1827 #154 -Sept. 16, 1827 -petition of Sarah Smith by her father and next friend John McCoy. She married in January of 1816 Simon Smith who "on or about the first day of July in the year of our Lord One Thousand Eight Hundred and Twenty Seven at the Borough of Carlisle in the county aforesaid, did violently, cruelly and barbarously whip, beat and kick and wound her the said Sarah." He had done this previously on other occasions and feeling her life endangered Sarah was forced to leave her husband. The petition was signed "Sally Smith". Court awarded subpoena to Nov. Term 1827.

◆ ◆ ◆

Nov. 1827 #112 -Nov. 13, 1827 (before Elisha Doyle) petition of Elizabeth Longnecker by her next friend Christian Erb for a divorce from Joseph Longnecker. They were married April 23, 1800 and he deserted her March 13, 1825. Elizabeth signed "by mark".

Nov. 24, 1827 -subpoena issued to Joseph Longnecker to appear before the Cumberland County Court of Common Pleas at ten o'clock in the forenoon of the second Monday of January 1828.

Jan. 14, 1828 -John Bowermaster, Cumberland County deputy Sheriff reported that he tried to serve the Nov. 24, 1827 subpoena on Joseph Longnecker but he could not be found anywhere in Cumberland Co., Pa.

Jan. 26, 1828 -subpoena issued to Joseph Longnecker to appear in the Court of Common Pleas for Cumberland Co., Pa. on the second Monday in April 1828 at ten o'clock in the forenoon.

April 16, 1828 -John Bowermaster, Deputy Sheriff of Cumberland Co., Pa. reported that Joseph Longnecker could not be found in Cumberland Co., Pa.

April 10, 1828 -Court ordered the Sheriff to publish notice in *The Carlisle Gazette* newspaper for four weeks successively prior to the first day of the next Term of the Common Pleas court requiring Joseph Longnecker to appear in court to answer the complaint of his wife Elizabeth Longnecker.

Aug. 11, 1828 -"To the Honorable Judges of the Court of Common Pleas of the County of Cumberland. The Answer of Joseph Longnecker to the Libel of Elizabeth Longnecker. This respondent saving to himself all manner of benefit and advantage of exceptions to the manifold untruths, uncertainties and imperfections in the said libel contained, for answer thereto, or to so much then of as this respondent is advised, it is in any way material for him to make answer to -answers and says -That true it is, that the said Elizabeth on the 23rd of April A.D. 1801 was lawfully joined in marriage with this respondent. Yet this respondent doth expressly deny the charge of having maliciously and willfully deserted and absented himself from her the said Elizabeth as is stated in the libel of the said Elizabeth. All which matters and things this respondent is ready to verify, to maintain, and prove, as this Honorable Court shall award, and humbly prayeth the same in bar to the libel of the said Elizabeth. This respondent further avers that he did not absent himself two years from the said Elizabeth at any time before the date of her petition or libel to which this is an answer. Joseph Longnecker being duly sworn doth say that the facts set forth in the above answer are just and true to the best of his knowledge and belief. Affirmed subscribed on the 11th Aug. 1828 before me Archibald Ramsey. Signed -Joseph Longnecker."

March 25, 1831 -Bill of "Jacob Clark a witness for Plaintiff (in divorce case of Elizabeth Longnecker vs. Joseph Longnecker)

1 day at January term 1829	.62¢
28 miles circular	.84¢
1 day at Nov. Term 1829	.62¢
28 miles circular	.84¢
4 days at March Court 1831	$2.50
28 miles circular	.84¢
paid for taxing bill	.18 3/4¢
	$6.46

The above bill of costs taxed and sworn to by the above named witness the 25th March 1831 before John Main for John Harper Prothonotary".

March 25, 1831 -Court granted Elizabeth Longnecker a divorce from Joseph Longnecker.

Nov. 15, 1832 -Bill of "Jacob Longnecker a witness for the Plaintiff (in the case of Elizabeth Longnecker vs. Joseph Longnecker)

1 day at Nov. 1829	.62 1/2¢
40 miles circular	$1.20
1 day at August Term 1830	.62 1/2¢
40 miles circular	$1.20
1 day at January Term 1831	.62 1/2¢
40 miles circular	$1.20
2 days at March Court 1831	$1.25
40 miles circular	$1.20
paid for taxing bill	.18 3/4¢
	$8.11 1/4

The above bill of costs taxed and affirmed to by Jacob Longnecker the 15th Nov. 1832 before John Main for John Harper Prothonotary."

March 25, 1831 -Trial by jury found for Libellant. Ct. granted Elizabeth Longnecker a divorce from Joseph Longnecker. Verdict paid by Plaintiff $4.00. Jurors were William Craighead, Jacob Goodyear, Charles Fleeger, George Crockett senr., Fergus R. Kernan, Jacob Hershey, Robert Mclaughlin, Abraham L. McKinney, Samuel Sturgeon, George Keller, Jacob B. Greeger and Samuel Marquart.

◆ ◆ ◆

April 1828 #206 -Aug. 12, 1828 petition of Sarah Smith by her father and next friend John McCoy for a divorce from Simon Smith. They were married Jan. 2, 1816. He abused her and endangered her life forcing her to take protection in the "house and family of her father, the said John McCoy." Subpoena issued Aug. 12, 1828. Petition was signed "Sally Smith".

◆ ◆ ◆

April 1828 #207 -Aug. 11, 1828 -petition of Sarah Saxton by her brother-in-law and next friend Armstrong Irwin before Archibald Ramsey, Justice of the Peace for a divorce from Michael Saxton. They were married in the month of Dec. 1809. He maliciously deserted her over two years ago. Sarah signed "by mark".

Aug. 11, 1828 -Subpoena issued to Michael Saxton for Nov. 1828 term.

March 28, 1829 -Subpoena issued to Michael Saxton to appear in Court on the second Monday of April 1829 at ten o'clock in the forenoon. (Note -this subpoena calls Armstrong Irvine Sarah's *father*-in-law, rather than her brother-in-law, as stated in the Aug. 11, 1828 petition.)

April 20, 1829 -subpoena issued to Michael Saxton to appear in court the second Monday of August 1829 at ten o'clock in the forenoon. (Note -this subpoena also calls Armstrong Irvine the *father*-in-law of Sarah Saxton).

Apr. 13, 1830 -John Irwin, deputy Sheriff reported that he served the April 20, 1829 subpoena personally on Michael Saxton June 29, 1829. On this same date the Sheriff of Cumberland Co., Pa. Martin Dunlap, Esq. reported that the April 20, 1829 subpoena on Michael Saxton was served but he failed to appear in court on the second Monday of August 1829 as he was supposed to do. The Court therefore appointed William Irvin as a commissioner to take testimony to be heard in the case.

April 14, 1830 -"In pursuance of the annexed Commission from the Court of Common Pleas of Cumberland County personally appeared Henry Hough a witness on the part of Sarah Saxton the Complainant. And being duly sworn according to law doth say that he was personally present at the time of the marriage of Michael Saxton and his sister now Sarah Saxton and that they were marryed (sic) by the Reverend Mr. Helfenstine(?) about twenty years ago or thereabouts. That the said Sarah and Michael Saxton lived together about sixteen years perhaps less and that she the said Sarah was turned out of house and home about three years ago and since that time they have lived separate and apart from each other she supporting herself and the family of five children. Said deponent doth further say that said Michael sayed (sic) that he would not do nothing for her and deponent doth say that he has frequently heard said Michael speak very disrespectfully of his wife, and that as far as he knows or believes that said Sarah always conducted herself well towards said Michael and was an industrious and faithful wife to him, and knows of no reasonable cause for his separation from her. Said deponent doth say that he has frequently heard said Michael cursing his wife and abusing her so as to tender her life burdensome. Sworn and subscribed before me April 14, 1830." Signed by William Irvine and Henry Hoch.

May 8, 1830 -deposition "In pursuance of the annexed Commission personally came before me the Commissioner therein named being a Justice of the Peace in and for said County, Rebecca Smith who being sworn according to law doth depose that she is the daughter of Sarah Saxton the within named applicant by her first husband John Weaver, now deceased. Deponent resided with her mother the said Sarah Saxton from the time of her marriage with Michael Saxton her present husband till the time of deponent's marriage with her husband Charles Smith in the month of December 1828 since which time deponent's said mother has resided with deponent and her husband. In the month of February 1826 the said Michael Saxton left the house in which he and his said wife had before that time resided. At the time of his departure he told his wife and said in the presence of deponent that he would go and never return, and that his said wife might go to Hell and be dammed and go for her self (sic), he then went away and since that time has never returned to reside with his said wife. For several years before he left his said wife as aforesaid he treated her with great cruelty by scolding and calling her approbrious names and frequently threatening to hurt her, thereby rendering her life burdensome as deponent believes that the said Sarah was a dutiful affectionate and good wife to the said Michael as deponent verily believes and that his rash will and barbarous conduct to her and his family absenting himself (illegible word), was and is without any just cause as deponent believes. Sworn and subscribed before me May 8th 1830" Signed by Rebecca Smith and William Irvine.

May 8, 1830 -deposition "Also personally came Sarah Ann Saxton who being sworn according to law doth depose that she is a daughter of Michael and Sarah Saxton within named. That deponent was present when her said father left his said wife, and his family upwards of four years since. He said he would go and never return, and that his wife the said Sarah might go to hell and be damned, that he would do for himself and she might do for herself. He then went away and has not since returned to his said wife and family. Deponent has since resided with her said mother ever since and she has not since seen her said father. Before her said father left home as aforesaid for several years he treated his said wife very cruelly by calling her approbrious names and threatening to beat her, and a short time before he went away deponent heard him threaten to burn the house over the heads of his wife and family, if they would not move out of it. That the said Sarah wife of the said Michael, always behaved and conducted herself towards her said husband as a dutiful wife, as deponent believes and his withdrawing from his said wife and family as aforesaid was without any just cause as deponent verily believes. Sworn and subscribed before me May 8th 1830." Signed by Sarah Ann Saxton and William Irvine.

May 11, 1830 -Court granted a divorce for Sarah Saxton.

♦ ♦ ♦

Jan. 1829 #160 -Jan. 10, 1829 petition of Mary Douglas by her next friend Michael Sanno for a divorce from Lewis Douglas. They were married about April 5, 1807. He "did beat and ill treat your petitioner or libelant in a shameful manner" and finally deserted her without any just cause about nine years ago. Mary Douglas signed "by mark." Subpoena issued for Lewis Douglas Jan. 12, 1829.

♦ ♦ ♦

April 1829 #242 -April 15, 1829 petition before John D. Haverstock of Elizabeth Rinard by her next friend John Waggoner for a divorce from John Rinard. They were married Oct. 22, 1821 and he abused her and rendered her life burdensome and her condition intolerable forcing her to leave him Jan. 12, 1829. She also requested alimony. Signed "Elizabeth Rynard". Subpoena issued same day.

Aug. 26, 1829 -Martin Dunlap, Cumberland County Sheriff reported that he personally served a subpoena on John Rinard to appear in court the second Monday of August 1829. Since he failed to appear, the court appointed William Irvine, Esq. to take depositions in the case on ten days notice.

Dec. 11, 1829 -Court issued notice to John Rinard that depositions were to be taken at the office of William Irvin, Esq. in the borough of Carlisle Dec. 29, 1829 between ten o'clock in the forenoon and four in the afternoon regarding his wife's libel for divorce.

Dec. 29, 1829 -Court issued notice to John Rinard that depositions were to be taken at the office of William Irvin, Esq. in the borough of Carlisle on Saturday Jan. 16, 1830 between ten o'clock in the forenoon and four o'clock in the afternoon regarding his wife's libel for a divorce.

Dec. 29, 1829 -Deposition before William Irvine "In pursuance of a commission issued from the Court of Common Pleas of Cumberland County to examine witnesses which is hereto annexed, and due notice having been given, personally appear the following persons to wit: George Christlieb -I am well acquainted with Elizabeth Rinard and John Rinard I live within sight of them. I never saw them fighting. On last March a year towards evening I heard somebody making a dreadful noise, screaming. I stopped my work, as I thought it was one of my children. I heard the same noise it was coming from Rinard's house, the noise continued, and I went over to Rinard's house. When I came there, there was several men there before me, John Rinard was before the house and Mrs. Rinard was in the door. When I came, John Rinard swore an oath, and said there is the constable coming. He rolled up his sleeves, and came towards me as if to fight me. His nose was bleeding at that time, Mrs. Rinard's hair was all pulled down, her arm was bloody and her face also. I didn't know at that time whether it was from John's nose or a cut. The day after this Christmas, a year, I was at my own house and Mrs. Rinard came to my house, on my (illegible word) she looked very badly. She had a black eye, and was cut in several places in the face, and had her head tied up with a handkerchief -Question by the petitioner. How did she look, as if she had been beaten up or otherwise? Objected to by John Williamson, Esq. on the part of the defendant, she looked as if she had been beaten and abused very much. Question by petitioner. At the first time you mentioned, in March, what did Mrs. Rinard state to you in the presence of her husband regarding her appearance and condition. Answer: She said Rinard was endeavouring to get her between the door and the crack of the door, so as he could get a fair opportunity of beating her. Rinard was near her when she said so, and could have heard it, she complained very much at that time of her arm hurting her. At the time she came home on my (illegible word) as mentioned above, she had the clothes of my wife on her, which she left at my house, and went home in her own clothes similarly dressed. Question by petitioner -At this time were you the constable of Mifflin township? Answer: yes. Objected to by Defendant. Question by petitioner. Did Mrs. Rinard at that time, she came to your house bring a warrant from Squire Lusk's for you to Rinard? Answer: She did. Objected to by defendant account of warrant not being produced. Question by petitioner. Did you take him and where did you take him on that warrant? Answer: I took him to Lusk's where he gave bail for his appearance -objected to by defendant. Question: Do you know of any other quarrels between them? Answer: No not to my own knowledge. Question: From what you know of these parties was not the treatment of Rinard towards his wife nearly at all times cruel and barbarous? The question objected to by defendant. Answer: I cannot answer that question. Question by defendant: Did you ever see John speak in presence of his wife respecting her bad treatment towards him? Answer: No. Question by defendant. Where has the petitioner lived since January 1829? Answer: In Perry county with her father, she has lived there ever since as far as I know."

Dec. 29, 1829 -"Also at the same time and place Thomas Torbet who testified as follows -I live near to John Rinards about half a quarter of a mile. I was working in a field near Rinards about the last of March 1828, I heard Mrs. Rinard hollering murder. I knew her voice, she called the second time in the same way. The third time

she called I left my work and went up to Rinard's house. As I was going up, I met Mrs. Rinard coming towards us, she was holding her arm. I went on to the house, and Mrs. Rinard and my son Joseph went along. When we came to the house, Rinard asked us what we wanted. We told him we did not want anything with him, but thought there was murder committing from the noise. Mrs. Rinard then went into the house and stood, and told in the presence of her husband John Rinard, that he viz her husband, had got her down behind the door, and was beating her and that in attempting to get from him and escape from the house she got her arm between the door and the crack of the door, and got her arm almost broken. Question by defendant. Did Rinard say anything at that time in the presence of his wife? Answer: He said nothing excepting that he was going to get a whiskey -at the time I am speaking of Rinard was a good deal in liquor. He is a drinking man, I have seen him frequently in liquor. -this last from the month objected to by defendant. On last Christmas a year when I came home, after being at Major Harper's, I went up to Rinard's, when I got there, the children of Rinard were playing before the door. The oldest daughter went into house and brought the baby of Mrs. Rinard out to me, which I carried in my arms, and took the other three with me to Mrs. Christlieb where I found Mrs. Rinard. I gave her her child and left the other three there. Mrs. Rinard was very much swelled about one of her eyes and was dressed in a flannel frock. At the time Mrs. Rinard had her last child, I went up to Mrs. Rinard's, from there I went to Mrs. Baker's who was away from home. I returned to Mrs. Rinard's and found Mrs. Baker there. I do know anything that happened after that by my own knowledge. Question by defendant. Where has Mrs. Rinard resided away since the January count 1829? Answer: I believe in Perry County. Question by defendant. Did you never hear John Rinard say in the presence of his wife that she struck him? Answer. No, but I have heard John Rinard say that she was a good woman."
---"Thomas Torbett further testifies -that the next day after the quarrel had taken place March 1828, I was going out to my work and John Rinard met me. After talking a little bit, I asked him what he had been doing? He said Och I don't know. I asked him then if he were not ashamed of himself. He turned about and did not make me any answer for a little time. He then said the liquor was the fault of it! This he considered as part of the above by explanation."

Dec. 29, 1829 -"Also George Weise -I live about a mile from Rinards. I never saw them quarreling, but I saw Mrs. Rinard between Christmas a New Year in 1828. She had a black eye. I can state nothing further from my own knowledge. Question by defendant. Where has Mrs. Rinard lived since January 1829. Answer: In Perry County.

Dec. 29, 1829 -deposition "Also John Hefflefinger -I lived near

Mrs. Rinard. I think about three years ago, sometime in the fall of that year, John Rinard was at our house. He then went home, and shortly afterwards Mrs. Rinard came running to our house. She was not abused any. My brother and I went up to Rinard's, we found Rinard setting by the cupboard, when he saw us he told us to keep our distance. I then told him he must come down and make up with his woman. He came down with us. While we were in our kitchen she started home again, Rinard looked for her, and did not see her. He then went home, afterwards in a little time Mrs. Rinard came with the child in her arms and staid (sic) a night at our house. Question by petitioner. Is John Rinard a drinking man? Objected to a leading question by defendant. Answer. I have seen him frequently drunk, he is a drinking man. Question by defendant. Did John Rinard show any unfriendly feelings to his wife? Answer. He appeared to be very cross, and came down, after I coaxed him sometime. I had to offer him some liquor before he would go." John Hefflefinger singed his deposition "by mark".

Dec. 29, 1829 -deposition "Also John Sensebaugh -I live within a half a mile of the place where Rinard lived in 1826. I saw Mrs. Rinnard (sic) several times abused when she lived near me. I never saw Rinard strike her or abuse her. I did not take particular notice how she was abused, until the last time in January. She had a black eye at that time, and looked black in the face. I never hear Mrs. Rinard say in the presence of Rinard how she got the bruise on her face. I never hear Rinard say that he had beeten (sic) his wife. I know nothing more of my own knowledge. Question by petitioner. Is Rinard a drinking man or not? Objected to by defendant as a leading question. Answer. I have seen him several times. The time I refer to when she had a blackened eye was the same time as mentioned by Mr. Christlieb.

Dec. 29, 1829 -deposition "Also Christian Saunders -I live about two miles from Rinard's. I know nothing about Rinard beeten(sic) his wife. I saw Mrs. Rinard sometime in January 1827 with her eye black. This time I saw her eye black I think is the same referred to by Mr. Christlieb. I know nothing more about the matter of my own knowledge."

Dec. 29, 1829 -deposition "Also Jacob Waggoner -I am the brother of the petitioner. I live about three miles from Mr. Rinards. Last summertime a year in 1828, one of the neighbors came down to my house. I could not go up to Rinards last evening, I went up the next morning. As I got near the house I saw Mr. Rinard before the door. He then went into the house, after he has been there a short time, Mrs. Rinard came out, and saw me coming towards the house. She came to meet me we talked a little together, Rinard also came out, and came down towards us. When we noticed him, we then went away from him along the road. I saw he was coming after us, we stopped until he came up. We had some little discourse together, he asked me if it would be a day for hay. I said I thought it would be after some time. He appeared to be fine. I asked John I was informed that Betsey, meaning Mrs. Rinard, was very poorly yesterday afternoon. I asked him whether he was the occasion of her being so unwell. He then made answer, I was whipped by a woman. Mrs. Rinnard then said Oh no John, it was you that abused me. We talked a good while together. He was in liquor then. Mrs. Rinnard and I several times made attempts to go and have a discourse together, but he always followed. Then I told him, John, I would wish to have some discourse with my sister in private, and he said, is it anything in particular. I answered, I would wish to have some private talk with her. He said he would like to hear it, he then swore that he did not like us to talk without him heering (sic) it. She at that time complained that he had pulled her hair and that her head was sore from the pulling of her hair, and the side of her face was swelled, at least in recollecting I think so. John Rinard was present at this time, he still denied that he had abused her, he was a good deal in liquor at this time. I then rode homeward, and they went to their house. Last Christmas was a year in 1828 (I was called upon by two of Christlieb's sons to go with them to their house). This last objected to between brackets by defendant. I did not go up at that time. I went up in the morning to Christlieb's, Mrs. Rinard and her four children were there, she was bruised in the face, had a black eye and some cuts there. She borrowed clothes from Mrs. Christlieb, a cloak and sun bonnet and alone we started with the intention of going to Squire Dalhouser, we did not go there, we then went to Squire Lusk's. From that I went home and she went home. Also a short time after I went over to Perry (County) to see my father, to tell him about what had taken place. I then returned. The next day or so after, I went to Rinard's and went into the house. She was getting breakfast. I then set down, John Rinard was there. He went out to the kitchen, and I talked to her about it. After breakfast was ready, Mrs. John Rinard and children set down to breakfast. I then asked whether they were going to court about it. John said, we will try and court it at home. He was then sober. I said maybe it would be best, I then said, John you have undoubtedly behaved very bad. He answered, I have and must acknowledge it is my fault. I then started out to the kitchen to come away, Mrs. Rinard followed me, and he came out too. I went outside the house, she followed and wanted to talk with me in private. I saw I could not do so. I asked him then, John, did you not strike her or abuse her? He answered he did, and could not deny it. Question by petitioner. Did he say he was sorry for it? Answer. To the best of my recollection he did say so. I then started to go, Mrs. Rinard followed me, and he remained. We talked together, Mrs. Rinard told me of the times mentioned in his presence, that he had abused her. She has resided in Perry County ever since January Session 1829."

Jan. 16, 1830 -deposition before William Irvine "Agreeably to notice the following persons met and testified as follows -Cumberland County I am well acquainted with John Rinard and his wife Elizabeth. I do not know exactly where they lived -on the twenty seventh day of December One thousand eight hundred and twenty eight, Mrs. Rinard came to my house. When she came she had a very black eye, she made a complaint against her husband in pursuance I issued a warrant for him. He was brought before me then on the twenty seventh. I then made out a commitment for him. He returned the next day and entered bail for his appearance at court, on the tenth day of January. Mr. and Mrs. Rinard came to my house together. He made acknowledgement before me, and said before me that he had beaten her, at the time she complained; when she first came to me, she had a large bunch of hair in her hand, and I saw by her head that her hair had been pulled out. The parties settled as per statement now offered, which is a regular and correct transcript from my Docket. I am a Justice of the Peace in Mifflin township. The whole of the above deposition objected to by John Rinard, by J. Williams his counsel." signed R. Lusk.

Jan. 16, 1830 -deposition of Alexander Lindsey before William Irvine, Esq. "I lived a near neighbor to Mr. and Mrs. Rinard. I was at Rinards house about three years ago last summer and saw Mr. and Mrs. Rinard there, she complained to me before him that Rinard had beaten her with the waggon whip. Mr. Rinard said to his wife, mother, you should not tell all things that happens. She said, the abuse is so bad, I cannot help telling it. Mr. Rinard then said, I did strike her twice with the waggon whip, I do not deny it. (When I was leaving the house I then told him I would return him to a Justice of the Peace if he did not behave better.) He then said, it has happened this time but maybe it will not happen again. All enclosed between bracket above objected to by Defendant. A year ago last Summer, Mrs. Rinard came to my house with her hair down, and she was scratched on the cheek and chin and was bleeding at both places. The skin was broken in both places, and her hair appeared as if it had been pulled. She got into the house, and I ran after her. I caught her and held her, and she fainted away on the floor. We got her to the bed, and she remained at my house an hour or more. After she got up she combed her hair, and combed out two bunches of hair, one of which was as large as my little finger. The head was not bleeding but was swelled up in lumps. She then asked me to go home with her. I took a stick in my hand and went. When we got there we found the children there, the oldest one nursing the youngest. I looked about for Mr. Rinard and could not find him. I wasted about an hour, and could not see him. I then went home and was there some time. Mrs. Rinard again came running to my house with her hair down again. She again combed out a great deal of hair. It appeared as if she had received abuse. I then returned again with her, and another man went with me. When we got to the house Mr. Rinard was setting on the steps. I asked him what was the reason he was continually abusing his wife (he was very full of liquor). He said there are too many complaints against me. I don't know how he would bear them. He hardly knew what he was saying. We then went to Mr. Larkin, and took Mr. Rinard with us. Mr. Rinard told me afterwards that he denied striking her but that he did pull her hair. The same harvest I was there, Mrs. Rinard had come to my house and begged me to come up and cut the grain as it would fall. I was working in the field. Thom. Plicht came into the field and Rinard and he commenced drinking. Mrs. Rinard called from the house not to let that man come there, as he had abused her house very much. Mr. Rinard then got a piece of a limb of a tree and went towards the house. I followed him with another and prevented him from striking her." Alexander Lindsay signed by mark.

undated document -"In the case of the petition or libel of Elizabeth Rinard by her next friend John Waggoner. The said John Rinard saith that the said libel of the libellant the matters therein contained and the matters therein contained, in manner and form as they are stated are not sufficient in law for the said Elizabeth Rinard to have or maintain her aforesaid action of divorce against the said John Rinard and that the said John Rinard is not bound by law to answer unto the same and this he is ready to verify.

That the said Elizabeth Rinard did not reside in the said County of Cumberland at the time of presenting the said libel nor is the same alleged, or attempted to be alleged in the same libel and therefore for want of sufficient libel and in this behalf the said John Rinard pray judgment and that the said libellant may be barred from having or maintaining her aforesaid action of divorce against him. And further the said libellant and the said petitioner replies that she was a resident of Cumberland County at the time of presenting her said petition."

Aug. 6, 1830 -"In the Court of Common Pleas of Cumberland County Application for a divorce. To John Rinnard Sir, Take notice that depositions to be read in this case will be taken at the office of William Irvin Esq. in the borough of Carlisle on Thursday the 19th day of August at 10 o'clock in the forenoon of said day -Samuel A. McCorksay atty for Elizabeth Rinnard."

Aug. 19, 1830 "Before me the subscriber one of the Justices of the Peace in and for Cumberland County, appeared Jacob Waggoner who being duly sworn according to law deposes and says that he served the within notice by leaving a copy at the residence of John Rinnard on the 7th day of August 1820. Sworn and subscribed before me August 19th 1830 William Irvine."

Aug. 6, 1830 -Martin Dunlap, Esq. High Sheriff of Cumberland County, Pa. testified he had served notice on John Rinard to appear in court that day regarding the libel served against him by his wife. Since he did not appear, the court ordered that there be an examination of witnesses on ten days notice before William Irvine, Esq. on this divorce case.

Aug. 19, 1830 -deposition of John C. Mitchell before William Irvine" I am the son of John Mitchell, Esq. of Mifflin township, Cumberland County. He was for many years a Justice of the Peace in that township. He was a Justice there in 1821 -this is a leaf from the Docket of my father (here the witness produced the leaf) it is in the handwriting of my father and the following entry is in the handwriting "1821 October the 23rd married John Rayner and Elizabeth Brant now Raynor". This is the same person who is the daughter of John Waggoner, and also the same John Raynard who is a party to this transaction. John Rinnard has told me that my father married him and Elizabeth Brant now Elizabeth Rinnard and that they were lawfully married and further saith not."

Aug. 31, 1830 -Court decreed Elizabeth Rinnard divorced from her husband John Rinnard and the Prothonotary of Cumberland County, Pa. John Hooper certified he had made a true conscript of the record of the decree.

◆ ◆ ◆

April 1829 #243 -April 15, 1829 -petition of David Groman who married Catharine Tranger May 4, 1815, "and from that time until the fourth day of October One Thousand eight hundred and twenty eight lived and cohabited with the said Catharine as his wife." She deserted him Nov. 22, 1828 "without any just or reasonable cause."

April 20, 1829 -Court issued a subpoena for Catharine Groman to appear in court on the second Monday of August 1829 at ten o'clock in the forenoon. Signed by W. Foulk, Prothonotary.

August 22, 1829 -Court issued an alias subpoena for Catharine Tranger now Catharine Groman to appear in court on the second Monday of November 1829 at ten o'clock in the forenoon to show cause why her husband David Groman should not be divorced from her.

◆ ◆ ◆

April 1829 #261 -April 16, 1829 -petition of Elizabeth Holsapple by her next friend William Ewing. She testified she married Erasmus Holsapple March 15, 1807 "and from that time until November one thousand eight hundred and twenty eight lived and cohabited with him as his wife." He deserted her at that time without just or reasonable cause. She requested a divorce and alimony.

April 20, 1829 -Court issue subpoena to Erasmus Holsapple for the second Monday of August at ten o'clock in the forenoon.

August 17, 1829 -Martin Dunlap, Esq. Sheriff of Cumberland Co., Pa. testified he had served the subpoena on Erasmus Holsapple to appear in court that day. Since he did not appear the court ordered that witnesses were to be examined on this case Sept. 4, 1829 at the office of William Irvine, Esq. between ten o'clock and four o'clock.

Sept. 4, 1829 -Deposition of William Ewing before William Irvine in the presence of Erasmus Holshopple "In pursuance of the annexed Commission from the Court of Common Pleas of Cumberland County and before the subscriber one of the Justices of the Peace in said County notice thereon personally appeared William Ewing a witness on part of the Plaintiff who being duly sworn according to law doth say that he is a son of Elisabeth Holshopple the plaintiff and that he resided in the family of his mother until sometime in April last, and that Erasmus Holshopple left his house sometime in November preceding. Before that time the parties lived together as man and wife on a farm of Erasmus Holshopple held in right of his wife. And prior to Erasmus Holshopple leaving his dwelling there was frequent disturbances and quarrels in the family. So much so as to render her life uncomfortable from the time of Erasmus Holshopple's leaving his house and family he Erasmus Holshopple has worked the farm and has received the entire proceedings of the farm since that time. This deponent further states that he hired out and appropriated part of his wages in support of his mother Elizabeth Holshopple and that the Elizabeth Holshopple was sometime in May last taken forcibly away from the premises on an alleged breach of the peace and thrown into the jail of Cumberland County. And sometime in August last has been on the township of West Pensborough as a pauper and still remains there she being sick and unable to gain her own livelyhood and that she is about sixty years of age." Interrogation on part of defendant Erasmus Holshopple -"Did I not lend to Elisabeth Holshapple at several times both wheat and coffey?" Answer "I do not know nor recollect of any."

Sept. 4, 1829 -Deposition of John Holshopple before William Irvine in the presence of Erasmus Holshople "Also appeared John Holshopple witness on the part of the Plaintiff who being duly sworn according to law Doth say that he is a son of Erasmus and Elisabeth Holshopple. That he resided in the family all his life up to November last on the farm of Erasmus Holshopple held in right of his wife in West Pennsborough township. Deponent on account of disturbances in the family left the family in the month of November last and hired out at Sheriff Neal's, at which time Erasmus Holshopple left the premise. Deponent entreated Erasmus Holshopple to remain and take care of his mother, since which time Erasmus Holshopple has worked the farm and received the entire proceeds of the farm. From last November William Ewing, James Holshopple and said deponent supported Elisabeth Holshopple out of their earnings. That some time in the month of May last Elisabeth Holshopple was forcibly taken away from the premises and lodged in jail and since her discharge has been on the township of West Pennsborough as a pauper and still remains a charge to said township. And from November last up to the present time the parties have not resided together." Interrogatory by Defendant "Did I at any time since November last send her wheat or coffey?" Answer "There was Coffey come once but I did not know who sent it but I allowed that you sent it. But I do not know of any wheat by sent at any time."

Sept. 4, 1829 -deposition of James Holshople before William Irvine" Also appeared James Holshople witness on part of the Plaintiff who being duly sworn according to law doth say, that he is a son of Erasmus Holshopple and Elizabeth Holshopple and that he resided in the family up to April last on the farm of Erasmus Holshopple in West Pennsborough township held in right of his wife. That Erasmus Holshopple left the premises in November last and has not since that time resided with deponent's mother. Since November Erasmus Holshopple has farmed the land and received the entire proceeds of the farm. His mother lived in a house of said farm up to May last at which time she was forcibly taken to jail on an alleged breach of the peace. During her residence on the farm after Erasmus Holsopple had left her, William Ewing, John Holshopple and deponent supported her generally and since the time of her discharge from prison she has been a pauper on the township of West Pennsborough and still remains on said township as such. Interrogatory on part of Erasmus Holshopple Do you not know of my having sent grain and coffey at different times to Elizabeth Holshopple since November last? Answer I do know that Erasmus Holshopple sent at one time three bushels of wheat and the flower (sic) of three bushels of wheat at an other time and two or three pounds of Coffey at one time."

Sept. 8, 1829 -The defendant appears in court and does not object to a divorce from bed and board or to the payment of 50 dollars a year alimony for the said petitioner. The court therefore and upon the testimony decrees a divorce from the bed and board and the said Erasmus Holshopple pay the sum of fifty dollars per annum of alimony for the said Elizabeth to be paid monthly.

◆ ◆ ◆

April 1829 Term #323 -Aug. 7, 1829 -petition of Sarah Wilson by her next friend James McElwain --"To the Honorable Judge of the Court of Common Pleas of Cumberland County now holding said court at Carlisle August 10, 1829 -The libel of Sarah Wilson by her next friend Respectfully Showeth -That your libellant on the sixteenth day of January in the year of our Lord one thousand eight hundred and twenty five was contracted and married to a certain Andrew Wilson and from that time until the second day of August in the year of our Lord one thousand eight hundred and twenty eight, lived and cohabited with the said Andrew Wilson as his wife and as such was owned and acknowledged by him, and so deemed and reputed by her neighbors and acquaintances. And although by the laws of God, as well as by their mutual vows and faith plighted to each other, they were bound to that uniform constancy and regard which ought to be inseparatable (sic) from the marriage state, yet so it is that the said Andrew Wilson from the second day of August in the year of our Lord one thousand eight hundred and twenty eight, hath wilfully and maliciously deserted and absented himself from the habitation of this libellant without any just or reasonable cause. And said desertation (sic) hath persisted for the term of one year, and yet doth continue to absent himself from the said libellant. Wherefore your libellant prays your Honor that a subpoena may issue forth to summon the said Andrew Wilson to appear in this Honorable court at November term next to answer the complaint as aforesaid and also that a decree of this Honorable Court may be made for the divorcing of him the said Andrew Wilson from the society, fellowship and company of this libellant in all time to come and her this libellant from the marriage bond aforesaid, as if she had never been married, or as if the said Andrew Wilson were naturally dead." ---" The above named Sarah Wilson being duly sworn according to Law, says the facts contained in the above libel are true to the best her knowledge, belief and that the said complaint is not made out of levity or collusion between the said Andrew Wilson and the said Sarah Wilson, and for the mere purpose of being freed and separated from each other, but in sincerity and truth, for the causes mentioned in the said libel."

♦ ♦ ♦

Jan. 1830 term #182 -Feb. 7, 1830 -petition of Andrew Wilson before Archibald Ramsey --"To the Honourable Judges of the Court of Common Pleas of the County of Cumberland -The Petition of Andrew Wilson Respectfully showeth That your petitioner, on the sixteenth day of January A.D. One thousand Eight Hundred and twenty four was lawfully joined in marriage with Sarah McElwine his present wife and from that time hath lived and in all respects demeaned himself as a kind and loving husband. And although by the laws of God, as well as by the natural vows plighted to each other, they were bound to that chastity which ought to be inseparable from the marriage state, yet the said Sarah in violation of her marriage vow, hath for a considerable time past given herself up to adulterous practices, and been guilty of adultery with a certain Alexander Smith, and diverse other persons to your petitioner unknown. Wherefore your Libellant further showeth that he is a Citizen of the State of Pennsylvania, and has resided therein for upwards of one whole year previous to the filing of this his libel and prays your Honors that a subpoena may issue forth to summon the said Sarah McElwine now Sarah Wilson, to appear in this Honourable Court at August Term next, to answer the complaint aforesaid. And also that a decree of this Honourable Court may be made for the divorcing of her the said Sarah McElwine now Sarah Wilson from the society, fellowship and company of this Libellant in all time to come, and him this Libellant from the marriage bond aforesaid as if he had never been married or as if the said Sarah McElwine now Sarah Wilson were naturally dead. And this Libellant will pray be." signed And. Wilson "The above named Andrew Wilson being duly sworn, says that the facts contained in the above libel are true to the best of his knowledge and belief, and that the said Complaint is not made out of levity and by collusion between him and the said Sarah McElwain now Sarah Wilson and for the mere purpose of being freed and separated from each other but in sincerity and truth for the causes mentioned in the said libel." signed And. Wilson "Sworn before me this eleventh day of February A.D. 1830" signed Archibald Ramsey.

April 13, 1830 -subpoena issued for Sarah McElwaine now Sarah Wilson to appear in court on the second Monday of August 1830 at ten o'clock in the forenoon to answer the libel of Andrew Wilson.

♦   ♦   ♦

Jan. 1831 Term #93 -Jan. 10, 1831 -"To the Honourable John Reed Esquire president and his associates Judges of the Court of Common Pleas of the County of Cumberland. The Petition of Elizabeth Sayler by her next friend Baltzer Kunkle Humbly Sheweth That your libellant on the first day of February One Thousand Eight Hundred and Twenty Seven was contracted in Matrimony and married to a certain Jacob Sayler, and from that time until the first of August following lived and cohabited with him the said Jacob as his wife; and as such was owned and acknowledged as such by him, and so deemed and reported by all her neighbours and acquaintances, and altho by the laws of God, as well as their mutual vows and faith plighted to each other, they were reciprocally bound to that constancy and uniform regard which ought to be inseparable from the marriage state -yet so it is that the said Jacob from the first day of August One Thousand Eight Hundred and Twenty Seven hath wilfully and maliciously deserted and absented himself from her the said Elizabeth and such desertion and absence hath persisted in for the term of two years and more without any just or reasonable cause and yet doth continue to absent himself from her the said Elizabeth. Wherefore your libellant further sheweth that she was born in the state of Pennsylvania and resided in the county of Cumberland since her marriage with the said Jacob; and prays your Honours that a subpoena may issue forth to summon him the said Jacob appear in the said Honourable Court at the next term, to answer the complaint aforesaid; and also that a Decree of the said Honourable Court may be given for divorcing and separating him the said Jacob from the said libellant's Society fellowship and company in all time to come, and her the said libellant from the marriage bond aforesaid as if she had never been married or as if he the said Jacob were naturally dead. And the said libellant as in duty bound will ever pray. Elizabeth Saylor by her next friend." (signed in German script by Baltzer Kunkle.)

"Cumberland County Pa. Before me the subscriber one of the justices of the peace in and for said County personally appeared Elizabeth Saylor who upon her solemn oath lawfully administered doth declare and say that the facts contained in the within petition or libel are true to the best of her knowledge and belief, and that the said complaint is not made out of levity or by collusion between her and her said husband and not for the mere purpose of being freed and separated from each other but in sincerity and truth for the causes mentioned in the said petition or libel. Sworn and subscribed the 10th day January Anno domini 1831 Before me." (signed Andrew Mateer and Elizabeth Sayler who signed by mark)

Jan. 1831 Term #393 -Jan. 22, 1831 -"Cumberland County s.s. -The Commonwealth of Pennsylvania to Jacob Saylor Greeting -Whereas Elizabeth Saylor by her next friend Baltzer Kunkle did on the Eleventh day of January A.D. 1831 prefer a petition to and of the Court of Common Pleas of the County of Cumberland at a Court held at Carlisle for said County praying that for the causes therein set forth she might be divorced from the bonds of matrimony entered into with you the said Jacob Sailor -We do therefore command you the said Jacob Saylor that setting aside all business and excuses whatsoever you be and appear in your proper person before our Judges at Carlisle at a Court of Common Pleas there to be held for the said County on the second Monday of April next to answer the petition or libel of the said Elizabeth and shew cause why the said Elizabeth your wife should not be divorced from the bonds of matrimony agreeable to the act of General Assembly in such case made and provided and hereof you are not to fail. Witness John Reed Esquire at Carlisle the twenty second day of January in the year of our Lord one thousand eight hundred and thirty one. for John Harper, Prothy." (signed John Main.) Notation on the front -"Non Est Inventes 25 March 1831 so answers Martin Dunlap Shrff. Shrff.'s fee $0.98"

◆ ◆ ◆

Nov. 1832 Term #158 -"To the Honorable Judge of the Court of Common Pleas of the County of Cumberland holding said court at Carlisle the 20th Nov. 1832. The libel of Charlott Thompson by her next friend Nathan Harrison Respectfully Represents that your libellant in April in the year one thousand eight hundred and ten was contracted in matrimony and married to a certain Henry Thompson, and from that time until the year one thousand eight hundred and eighteen lived and cohabited with the said Henry Thompson as his wife and as such was owned and acknowledged by him and so deemed and reputed by her neighbours and acquaintances. And although by the laws of God as well as by their mutual vows and faith plighted to each other they were bound to that uniform constancy and regard which ought to be inseparable from the marriage state yet so it is that the said Henry Thompson from the said year 1818 hath willfully and maliciously deserted and absented himself from the habitation of this libellant, without any just or reasonable cause, and such desertion hath persisted in for the term of two years and upwards, and yet doth continue to absent himself from the said libellant. Wherefore your libellant further showing that she is a citizen of the State of Pennsylvania and has resided therein for upwards of one whole year previous to filing of the libel prays your honors that a subpoena may issue forth to summon the said Henry Thompson to appear in this honourable court, at the January Term next to answer the complaint aforesaid. And also that a decree of this honorable Court may be made for the divorcing of him the said Henry Thompson from her society fellowship and company of this libellant in all time to come, and her this libellant from the marriage bond aforesaid as if she had never be married or as if the said Henry Thompson were naturally dead. And she will pray." (signed by mark Charlott Thompson) by her next friend (signed by mark Nathan Harrison)." The above named Charlott Thompson being duly sworn says that the facts contained in the above libel are true to the best of her knowledge and belief and that the said complaint is not made out of levity and collusion between her and her said husband, and for the mere purpose of being freed and separated from each other but in sincerity and truth for the causes mentioned in the said libel. Sworn and subscribed before me this 20th day of November A.D. 1832." (Signed by Jacob Lynn? and Charlott Thompson who signed by mark).

Nov. 23, 1832 -Court issued subpoena for Henry Thompson to appear in court the second Monday of January 1833 at ten o'clock in the forenoon to answer his wife's libel. George Beetem, Sheriff reported "The above stated Henry Thompson not to be found in my bailiwick."

Aug. 21, 1833 -subpoena issued to Henry Thompson to appear in court to answer his wife's libel of divorce on the second Monday of November 1833 at ten o'clock in the forenoon. Sheriff George Beetom reported "Henry Thompson not to be found in my bailiwick."

◆ ◆ ◆

Jan. 1833 #149 -Dec. 24, 1832 -"To the Honorable Judges of the County of Cumberlin (sic) and for the County of Cumberland. The libel of Agnes Weist by her next friend Sarah Barnet, respectfully sheweth, That your libellant on the twentieth day of March in the year of our Lord one thousand eight hundred and twenty seven was contracted in matrimony and married to a certain Adam Weist and from that time till the fifteenth day of November in the year of our Lord one thousand eight hundred and twenty eight lived and cohabited with the said Adam Weist and as such was owned and acknowledged by him and was so deemed and reputed by her neighbors and her acquaintances. And though by the laws of God as well as by their mutual vows and faith plighted to each other, they were bound to that uniform constancy and regard which ought to be inseparable from the marriage state; yet so it is, that the said Adam Weist from the said fifteenth day of November in the year of our Lord one thousand eight hundred and twenty eight, hath wilfully and maliciously deserted and absented himself from the habitation of this libellant without any just or reasonable cause. And such desertion he hath persisted in from the said fifteenth day of November in year of our Lord 1828 till the present time and still persists therein and continuing to absent himself from the said Libellant. Wherefore this libellant further shewing that she is a citizen of the State of Pennsylvania and hath resided therein and in the said County of Cumberland one whole year previous to the filing of this libel, prays your Honours that a subpoena may issue forth to summon the said Adam Weist to appear in this Honourable Court at the next term to answer this complaint aforesaid. And also that a decree of this Honourable Court may be made for the divorcing of him the said Adam Weist from the society fellowship and company of this libellant and from all time to come and she this libellant from the marriage bond aforesaid as if she had never been married, or as if the said Adam Weist were naturally dead. And this libellant will pray." (signed Agnes Weist) by her next friend (signed by mark by Sarah Barnet). "Cumberland County, Pa. Personally appeared before the subscriber one of the justices in and for the said County of Cumberland the within named Agnes Weist who on her oath lawfully administered doth say, that the facts contained in the above libel and within libel are true to the best of her knowledge and belief and that the within complaint is not made out of levity and collusion between her and the said Adam Weist and for the mere purpose of being freed and separated from each other, but in sincerity and truth for the causes mentioned in the said libel. Sworn and subscribed before me this 24th December 1832" (signed by G. Carver and Agnes Weist).

Jan. 26, 1833 -subpoena issued to Adam Weist to appear in court to ans. his wife's libel for divorce on the second Monday of April 1833. "May 2nd 1833 on proof made by Geo. Beetem, Esq. Shff that the said Adam Weist is not to be found in this County of Cumberland, an alias subpoena is awarded."

April 20, 1833 -subpoena issued to Adam Weist to appear in

court to answer his wife's libel for divorce on the second Monday of August 1833. George Beetem, Sheriff reported "The defendant could not be found in said County."

Aug. 23, 1833 -"23 August 1833 due proof having been made, on the return of the alias supbeona in this, that the said defendant Adam Weist could not be found in the said County, the court orders that the Sheriff of the same County shall cause notice to be published in one newspaper published within the said County for four weeks successively prior to the first day of the next term of the said Court requiring the said defendant to appear on the said day to answer to the said complaint of the said plaintiff."

Nov. 12, 1833 -"In the Court of Common Pleas of Cumberland County No. 149 January Term 1833 In the case of the application of Agnes Weist for divorce from Adam Weist her husband. And now to wit 12th November 1833 It appearing to the Court that due notice to the said Adam Weist was published according to law -William D. Ramsey Esq. is appointed a commissioner to take depositions to be read on the hearing of this case, and the same is continued to the Orphan's Court on the 3rd Dec. 1833.

Dec. 24, 1833 -"Cumberland County, Pa. I certify that the above is a true extract taken from the records of the Court of Common Pleas of said County -In testimony whereof I have hereunto set my hand and the seal the said court at Carlisle this 24th day of December A.D. 1833 For John Harper Prothy. John Main."

Jan. 18, 1834 -"Cumberland County, Pa. In pursuance of the above commission personally appeared before me, the above named commissioned Samuel Barnet who being duly sworn according to law deposes and says that Adam Weist, the husband of the above named Agnes Weist, on or about the fifteenth day of November One thousand eight hundred and twenty eight, deserted his said wife, Agnes and has ever since that time, been absent from her habitation. Deponent further says that he is intimately acquainted with the said parties, and never heard of any reasonable cause for the said desertion and absence of the said Adam and from his wife Agnes; and is sure there was no cause other than his own willfulness. Deponent heard the said Adam Weist say, that he would go away to the canal and would not stay with his wife. The said Adam Weist was subject to intemperate habits, and would always endeavor to be where he could get liquor. Deponent further says than on account of the absence of the said Adam from his said wife, Sarah Barnet, her mother, has been under the necessity of taking her, the said Agnes, and her child, from the place where she and her said husband were living previous to his desertion, to her own house, and has kept and supported them ever since. Deponent heard the said Adam Weist and Agnes both that they were married by the Rev. Mr. Keller in Carlisle sometime in the month of March 1827; That deponent has not heard of the said Ada Weist since in the spring of 1829 -he then heard of his living at his father's in Westmoreland County in Pennsylvania. (signed by Samuel Barnet) Sworn and subscribed the 18th day of January 1834 before me half an hour after 12 o'clock of said day. W.D. Ramsey"

Jan. 20, 1834 -"Cumberland County, Pa. Before me the subscriber the Commissioner within named personally came, Henry Knettle who upon his solemn oath deposes and says that he has heard and believes it to be true, that Adam Weist husband of the within Agnes Weist has left his said wife, and has been absent from her about three or four years as deponent thinks. It may be more or it may be less. Deponent further says that he knows Samuel Barnet, the above deponent, and from what he knows of him he believes him to be a person of good moral character, and has never heard his character for truth or otherwise doubted." (Signed Henry Knettle) "Sworn and subscribed before me the 20th day Jany. 1834 W.D. Ramsey"

Jan. 20, 1834 -"Cumberland County, Pa. Before me the within named commissioner personally came John H. Weaver who being duly sworn according to law deposes and says that he kept store in Newville before Adam Weist and Agnes, were married; that he was well acquainted with both the parties; that they lived together as man and wife till the fall of the year 1828, as deponent thinks, that since that time deponent has never heard of the said Adam Weist being in that part of the country and believes that he has been absent from his said wife ever since. Deponent further says that he often heard of the said Adam Weist doing badly, being addicted both to intemperance and gambling previously to his leaving his said wife. Deponent is well acquainted with Samuel Barnet the first named deponent, and knows him to be a young man of very good character with regard to truth, and in every other respect; that the deponent considering that the said Samuel Barnet is a young man rather remarkable for his good conduct. Deponent further says that he is well aquainted with Sarah Barnet, the mother of the said Agnes, and also with the said Agnes, and knows them to be women of very good character. Deponent further says that he left Newville last spring, and had been living there from the 22nd day of March 1825 till that time; and that the said Sarah Barnet and her family lived about two and one half miles from Newville during all that time. Sworn and subscribed the 20th day of Jany. 1834 before me." (signed by John H. Weaver).

Jan. 20, 1834 -"And now the 20th day of January 1834 the commissioner William D. Ramsey Esquire having returned to the court the deposition of the witnesses taken before him on the part of the Libellant and the same being heard and read by the court, and the court on consideration then of, being satisfied then with and proclamation being duly made of the Respondent to come forth and he not appearing, the court do order adjudge and decree that the said Agnes Weist the Libellant be divorced and separated from the nuptial tie and bond of matrimony contracted with the said Respondent A. Weist and that all and every the duties, rights and claims occuring to either of the said parties by reason of the said marriage shall henceforth cease and determine, and the said parties be severally at liberty to marry again in like manner as if they never had been married. By the Court." (signed John Reed)

♦ ♦ ♦

April 1833 Term #240 -April 30, 1833 -"To the Honorable John Reed, President Judge and his associate Judges of the Court of Common Pleas of Cumberland County. The petition of Sarah Galbraith, by her next friend, Alexander Spence respectfully sheweth -That your libellant, the said Sarah, in the latter part of December in the year of our Lord 1807 was contracted in matrimony and married to a certain John Galbraith, from that time until in the month of January Anno Domini eighteen hundred and twenty five lived and cohabited with him the said John Galbraith as his wife, and as such was owned and acknowledged by him so deemed and reported by all her neighbors and acquaintances; and altho by the laws of God, as well as by their mutual vows and faith plighted to each other, they were reciprocally bound to that constancy and uniform regard which ought to be inseparable from the marriage state. Yet so it is that the said John Galbraith from the said month of January 1825 up to the present time, viz April the thirteenth A.D. 1833, hath wilfully and maliciously deserted and absented himself from her the said Sarah, and from her habitation, without any just or reasonable cause and yet doth continue to absent himself from her the said Sarah. Wherefore your libellant further shewing that she has resided for one year and more within this state and in said County of Cumberland, prays your Honour, that a subpoena may issue furth to summon him the said John Galbraith to appear in the said Court of Common Pleas at August Term next to answer the complaint aforesaid. And also that a decree of the said Honorable Court may be given for the divorcing and separating him the said John Galbraith from the said libellant's society, fellowship and company in all time to come and her the said libellant from the bond of matrimony aforesaid as if she had never been married or as if the said John Galbraith were naturally dead. And the said libellant in duty bound will ever pray. (signed by mark Sarah Galbraith). The said Sarah on her oath doth declare that the facts contained in the above petition or libel are true, to the best of her knowledge and belief, and that the said complaint is not made out of levity, or by collusion between her and her husband, and for the mere purpose of being freed and separated from each other, but in sincerity and truth for the causes mentioned in said libel (signed by mark Sarah Galbreath). Sworn and subscribed April 30th 1833 before me Archibald Ramsey."

April 20, 1833 -"Cumberland County Pa. The Commonwealth of Pennsylvania to the sheriff of Cumberland County Greeting: Whereas Sarah Galbraith by her next friend Alexander Spence did on the first day of May A.D. 1833 prefer a petition to the Judges of the Court of Common Pleas of the County of Cumberland at a court held at Carlisle in and for said county praying that for the causes therein set forth she might be divorced from the bonds of matrimony entered into with John Galbraith. We do therefore command you the said John Galbraith that setting aside all other business and excuses whatsoever you be and appear in your proper person before our-Judges at Carlisle at our Court of Common Pleas there to be held for the said County of Cumberland the second Monday of August next to answer the petition or libel of the said Sarah Galbraith and to shew cause if any you have why the said Sarah your wife should not be divorced from the bonds of matrimony agreeable to the act of General Assembly in such case made and provided and hereof you are not to fail. Witness John Reed Esquire at Carlisle the twentieth day of April in the year of our Lord one thousand eight hundred and thirty three. For John Harper Prothy. John Main." (Note -I have no explanation why the petition was dated ten days prior to the issuing of the subpoena but I just copied the dates as they were written -E.T.)

"I do hereby certify that John Galbrath and Sarah Davenport, the bearer of this, as I suppose, were lawfully joined together by the subscriber, on the twenty second day of December, eighteen hundred and seven -given at Shippensburg August 8th 1833 by John Moodry. "

Aug. 13, 1833 -"In the Court of Common Pleas of Cumberland County No. 240 April term 1833. Now to wit 13th August 1833, George Beetem Esquire high Sheriff of said County made return to the Judges of said Court at Carlisle, that he had served, the subpoena issued out of the same court to him direct, commanding John Galbraith to appear before said Judges on the second Monday of April last past to answer the petition of libel of Sarah Galbraith and to Shew cause why she should not be divorced from the Bonds of matrimony and he not appearing nor any person for him to answer the complaint, libel and petition of said Sarah -The court orders the examination of witnesses this evening at 7 o'clock before William Ramsey Esquire the commissioner appointed for that purpose. By the Court. Cumberland County, Pa. I certify that the above is a true extract taken from the records of the Court of Common Pleas of said County. In testimony whereof I have hereunto set my hand and the seal of said Court at Carlisle this 13th August 1833." (signed John Harper Prothonotary)

Aug. 13, 1833 -"In pursuance of the order of the Court of Common Pleas of Cumberland County, appointing me Commissioner to take depositions in the case of the application of Sarah Galbreath to be divorced from bonds of matrimony from her husband John Galbreath the following depositions were taken before me (to wit). Margaret Donnelly upon oath doth depose and say that she has known Sarah Galbreath, the libellant for upwards of ten years, and that at that time she and her husband John Galbreath lived for one year in the same house, upstairs, in which this deponent lived; that after a year's interval they again lived in the same house with deponents in Carlisle for a period of six months. During the time this deponent was acquainted with Mrs. Galbreath she was a very industrious hard working woman, making a penny in every honest way in her power. That her said husband was very much addicted to hard drinking, and when drunk, very often abused and beat his wife, and neglected to provide necessary provision for his family; that this deponent though a poor woman herself, has frequently out of compassion for the condition of the family given them victuals to eat, and wood to make fire to keep them from perishing; that so far as this deponent knows she (Mrs. Galbreath) never gave her husband any provocation to justify his bad treatment. It is seven years ago last spring that the said John Galbreath deserted his wife and family, since which time he has not been in this part of the country with his family except one night to deponent's knowledge. Deponent knows no just cause given by the said Sarah Galbreath for her husband's so deserting and abandoning her. Deponent says that she has always understood that the maiden name of said Sarah Galbreath was Sarah Davenport. Deponent further states that she believes the desertion of said Galbreath from his wife and family was wilful and malicious, and deponent further states that the said John Galbreath still continues to absent himself from his wife and family. Sworn and subscribed before me the 13th day of August A.D. 1833. W. D. Ramsey. " (signed by mark by Margaret Donnelly.)

Aug. 13, 1833 -"William (Hause? Humes?) sworn says that he has known John Galbreath and his wife Sarah for upwards of twelve years, and that during that time the said Sarah has always been a hardworking industrious and sober woman; but that the said John Galbreath since this deponent has known him, has been very much addicted to hard drinking, that when drunk he was in the habit, as this deponent understood from report of beating and abusing his said wife; that on one occasion deponent saw marks on said Sarah's shoulders of blows, which she said were inflicted with a stick by her said husband, she was then living in the country about two miles from Carlisle. Deponent further states that it is something like seven years last spring since the said John Galbreath deserted his wife Sarah, without any just cause or provocation given by the said

Sarah his wife for desertion, so far as deponent knows and believes, and that said Galbreath still continues to absent himself from his wife and family and neglects to provide necessaries for them. Deponent states further that said Sarah is now living in Shippensburg and makes a living for herself and family by taking in sewing. Two of said Sarah's children are under age and reside with her and are supported by her. Deponent is a shoemaker by trade and is married to Mary Jane Galbraeth one of said John and Sarah's daughters. Sworn and subscribed before me the 13th day of August 1833. W. D. Ramsey." (signed William Humes? Hause?)

Aug. 13, 1833 -"Elizabeth Egulf sworn says that she has known John Galbreath and his wife Sarah for fourteen or fifteen years and that during part of said time she lived neighbor to them. So long as this deponent has known the said Sarah she has considered her a hardworking industrious woman; but that the said John was very intemperate in his habits, and had the name of being a bad provider for his family; that frequently this deponent furnished the said Sarah and family with flour and wood; that it is seven years past since the said John Galbreath deserted his wife and family; Deponent further says that about a year after he (the said John) left his wife and family that his wife had no house to live in; that the few goods she had, were thrown out of doors, by the tenant who succeeded her; that at that time she had three small children to take care of without any means of supporting them, that deponent procured her the said Sarah and her youngest child a situation at three dollars a month under the Overseers of the Poor to take care of the poor of the borough of Carlisle. Dr. Foulk and Frederick Sharretts were the overseers of the poor at that time. Sworn and subscribed the 13th day of August A. D. 1833 before me. W. D. Ramsey." (signed by mark by Elizabeth Egulf.)

Aug. 13, 1833 -"Dr. George D. Foulk affirmed says that he has known John and Sarah Galbreath for twenty years; that the said John was a tenant of his at that time and lived on his farm for one year. Deponent further states that the said John Galbreath was a drinking, troublesome quarrelsome and bad-doing man in every sense of the word. He neglected his duty as a parent and a husband, and did not provide for his family in a proper manner; that he was, when under the influence of liquor in the habit of beating and abusing his wife. Deponent states further that the said John deserted his wife and family about seven years ago; and that about a year after his desertion, to wit, in 1828, she the said Sarah was in a very destitute condition, and that as Overseers of the Poor Frederick Sharretts and this deponent employed said Sarah at three dollars a month to keep and manage the poor house of the borough of Carlisle. Deponent further says that said Sarah's conduct was unexceptionable, whilst in the employment of the overseers, was a good housekeeper and kept the house in excellent order. Deponent further says that the desertion of the said John from the said Sarah, was as far as he is acquainted without any just cause or provocation on the part of the said Sarah. Deponent has known nothing immoral or improper in the conduct of the said Sarah during the twenty years he has known her, and that during the greater part of said time the said Sarah has resided in the borough of Carlisle and its vicinity. Affirmed and subscribed the 13th day of August A. D. 1833 before me. W. D. Ramsey." (signed by Dr. George D. Foulk.)

"In the case of the application of Sarah Galbraith to be divorced from her husband, John Galbraith. And now to wit 23d August A. D. 1833 The Commissioner William D. Ramsay having returned to the Court the Depositions of witnesses taken before him on the part of the libellant and the same being read and heard by the Court, after mature and solemn deliberation being satisfied therewith the Court do order, adjudge and decree that the said Sarah Galbraith the libellant be divorced and separated from the bonds of matrimony contracted with the said John Galbraith, and that all and every the duties, rights and claims accruing to either of the parties by reason of the said Marriage shall henceforth cease and determine and the said parties shall severally be at liberty to marry again in like manner as if they never had been married. By the Court." (signed John Reed.)

◆ ◆ ◆

August 1833 Term #219 -Aug. 22, 1833 -"To the Honorable John Reed, President, and his associates, Judges of the Court of Common Pleas of the County of Cumberland. The petition of George Gensler, of North Middleton Township in said County, Miller, humbly sheweth, That your petitioner on the eleventh day of May in the year of our Lord eighteen hundred and thirty was lawfully joined in marriage with Catherine his present wife. And although by the laws of God, as well, as by the mutual vows plighted to each other, they were bound to that chastity which ought to be inseparable from the marriage state, yet the said Catherine, in violation of her marriage vow, hath for a considerable time past given herself up to adulterous practices, and been guilty of adultery. Your petitioner therefore prays that your Honors will please to order and direct that a subpoena do issue, in due form of law, directed to the said Catherine commanding her to appear at the next Court of Common Pleas to be held in said County, to answer the petitioner's libel, and to show cause, if any she hath, why the petitioner should not be divorced from the bond of matrimony. And he will pray etc. The said George Gensler on his oath doth declare that the facts contained in the above petition or libel are true to the best of his knowledge and belief, and that the said complaint is not made out of levity, or by collusion between him and his wife, and for the mere purpose of being freed and separated from each other, but in sincerity and truth, for the causes mentioned in the said petition or libel. Sworn and subscribed before me the 22nd day of August A.D. 1833. W.D. Ramsey." (signed George Gensler.)

Aug. 24, 1833 -"Cumberland County, Pa. The Commonwealth of Pennsylvania to Catherine Gensler, Greeting: Whereas George Gensler did on the 23rd August 1833 prefer a petition to our Judges of the Court of Common Pleas of the County of Cumberland at a court held at Carlisle in and for said county praying that for the causes therein set forth he might be divorced from the bonds of matrimony entered into with you the said Catharine -We do therefore command you the said Catharine that setting aside all other business and excuses whatsoever, you be and appear in your proper person before our Judges at Carlisle at our County Court of Common Pleas there to be held for the County of Cumberland on the second Monday of November next to answer the Petition or libel of the said George and to shew cause if any you have why the said George your Husband should not be divorced from the bonds of matrimony agreeably to the act of General assembly in such case made and provided and hereof fail not. Witness John Reed Esquire at Carlisle the twenty fourth day of August in the Year of our Lord one thousand eight hundred and thirty three. For John Harper, Prothy." (signed John Main).

"Nov. 18, 1833 -Michael Holcomb being duly sworn according to law doth say that he served the within subpoena personally, on 4th Oct. 1833, on Catherine Gensler. Sworn and subscribed in open court Nov. 18th 1833 before John Harper, Prothy." (signed M. Holcomb.)

"18th Nov. 1833 -William D. Ramsey Esqr. appointed a commissioner to take depositions at such times as he may think proper to be read hearing at next January term to wit. 13th Jany. 1834. By the Court."

Dec. 23, 1833 -"In the case of George Gensler for a Divorce No. 219 August term 1833 in the court of Common Pleas of Cumberland County. And now, to wit, 18th November 1833 William D. Ramsey Esquire appointed a Commissioner to take depositions at such time and place as he may think proper to be read on hearing at next January term, to wit, 13th January 1834. --Cumberland County, Pa. I certify that the above is a true extract taken from the records of the Court of Common Pleas of said County. In testimony whereof I have hereunto set my hand and the seal of said Court at Carlisle the 23d December 1833." (signed John Harper, Prothy.)

Jan. 13, 1834 -"And now to wit Jany. 13th 1834 -The commissioner William D. Ramsay, having returned to the Court, the Depositions of witnesses taken before him on the part of the libellant, and the same being read and heard by the Court, after mature and solemn deliberation, being satisfied therewith, the Court do order, adjudge and decree that the said George Gennsler, the libellant, be divorced and separated from the bonds of matrimony contracted with the said Catherine Gennsler, and that all and every the duties, rights and claims accruing to either of the parties, by reason of the said marriage shall henceforth cease and determine, and the said parties shall severally be at liberty to marry again in like manner as if they never had been married. By the Court."

Commissioner fees	$1.30 1/2
Isaac Augney serving subpoena on 5 witnesses	.62
Witnesses	
John Gould	.25
James Allen	.25
Joseph Miller	.25
Susan Jones	.25
	$2.92 1/2

◆ ◆ ◆

August 1833 Term #235 -Nov. 22, 1833 -"To the Judges of the Court of Common Pleas of Cumberland County. The Petition of Peter Hartzel the father and next friend of Catherine McCurdy Respectfully represents that sometime in the year 1824 the said Catherine was married to James McCurdy in Shippensburg Cumberland County; that the said James McCurdy and his wife the said Catherine continued to live together as man and wife for the space of about three years, during which time the conduct of the said James McCurdy was such that it was indignant and insulting to the person of his said wife and rendered her condition intolerable and her life burthensome, whereby she was forced to withdraw from his house and family. The said James McCurdy was so intemperate in his habits as to render the person and situation of his said wife unsafe and uncomfortable. Sometime in the year 1827 the said James McCurdy left this state and went to the west leaving his said wife in Shippensburg since which time he has never returned to his said wife but continues to absent himself. Your petitioner therefore prays your Honors to award a subpoena to the said James McCurdy to appear at the next Court of Common Pleas to shew cause why she the said Catherine should not be disolved from the bands (sic) of matrimony which the said Catherine will pray your Honors to decree." (signed Peter Hartzel.)

Nov. 22, 1833 -"Cumberland County Personally appeared before me a Justice of the Peace in and for said County Catherine McCurdy who being duly sworn doth depose and say that the facts set forth in the foregoing petition are true to the best of her knowledge and belief: and that the said complaint is not made out of levity or by collusion between her and the said James McCurdy and for the mere purpose of being freed and separated from each other, but in sincerity and truth for the causes mentioned in the said petition." (signed Catharine McCurdy.) "Sworn and subscribed the 22d day of November A.D. 1833 Before me Geo. W. Ginney."

Nov. 21, 1833 -"Cumberland County The Commonwealth of Pennsylvania to James McCurdy Greeting. Whereas Catharine McCurdy late Catharine Hartzel did on the third day of December 1833 prefer her petition to our Judges of the Court of Common Pleas of the County of Cumberland a court held at Carlisle in and for said county praying that for the causes therein set forth she might be divorced from the bonds of matrimony entered into with you the said James McCurdy we do therefore command you the said James McCurdy that setting aside all other business and excuses whatsoever, you be and appear in your proper person before our Judges at Carlisle at a court of Common Pleas there to be held for said county on the second Monday of January next to answer the petition or libel of the said Catharine and to show cause if any you have why the said Catharine your wife should not be divorced from the bonds of matrimony provided. And hereof you are not to fail. Witness John Reed Esquire at Carlisle the twenty first day of November in the year of our Lord one thousand eight hundred and thirty three. For John Harper, Prothy. John Main."

"James McCurdy not to be found in my Bailiwick. So answers Geo. Beetem, Sheriff. B. $1.78."

◆   ◆   ◆

August Term 1833 #337: Nov. 12, 1833 -"To the Honorable Judges of the Court of Common Pleas of Cumberland County -The petition of John Friese Respectfully therewith that your libellant on the eighth day of December in the year one thousand eight hundred and twenty nine was contracted in matrimony and married to a certain Sarah Miller and from that time until the 24th day of March in the year of our Lord one thousand eight hundred and thirty one lived and cohabited with her as her husband and as such was owned and acknowledged by her and so deemed and reputed by all his neighbours and acquaintances and although by her vows of God as well as their mutual vow and faith plighted to each other they were reciprocally bound to that kindness and uniform regard which ought to be inseparable from the marriage state yet so it is that the said Sarah from the said 24th day of March in the year of our Lord one thousand eight hundred and thirty one has wilfully and maliciously absented herself from the habitation of this libellant without past or reasonable cause and such desertion has persisted via for the term of two years and upwards and yet doth continue to absent herself from the said libellant. Wherefore your libellant further showing that he is a citizen of this state and hath resided therein for one whole year and more previous to the filing of this petition prays your honors that a subpoena may issue from the said Court directed to the said Sarah Freis commanding her to appear at the next January Term of the said Court to answer this petition and also that a decree of the said Court may be given granting this libellant a divorce from the marriage bond aforesaid as if he had never been married or as if the said Sarah were naturally dead. And this libellant will pray be." (signed John Friese.) "Cumberland County, Pa. The above named John Friese being duly affirmed according to law affirmeth and saith that the facts contained in the above libel are true to the best of his knowledge and belief and that the said complaint is not made out of levity and by collusion between the said Sarah and this affirmant and for the mere purpose of being free and separated from each other but in sincerity and truth for the causes mentioned in the said libel." (signed John Friese.) "Affirmed and subscribed this 12th Nov. 1833 before And. Baden."

Nov. 21, 1833 -Cumberland County, Pa. The Commonwealth of Pennsylvania to Sarah Friese Greeting -Whereas John Friese did on the eleventh day of November A.D. 1833 preferred a Petition to the Judges of the Court of Common Pleas of Cumberland County at a court held at Carlisle in and for said County praying that for the causes therein set forth he might be divorced from the bonds of matrimony entered into with you the said Sarah Friese late Sarah Miller. We do therefore command you the said Sarah Friese that setting aside all other business and excuses whatsoever you be and appear at our county Court of Common Pleas there to be held for the county of Cumberland on the second Monday of January next to answer the petition of libel of the said John Friese and to shew cause if any you have why the said John Friese your Husband should not be divorced from the bonds of matrimony agreeably to the act of assembly in such case made and provided. And hereof you are not to fail. Witness John Reed Esquire at Carlisle the twenty first day of November in the year of our Lord one thousand eight hundred and thirty three. For John Harper Prothy. John Main." "Served 4th December 1833 on Sarah Friese. So answers, George Beetem, Sheriff B. $0.98."

Jan. 13, 1834 "The subpoena which was issued in pursuance of the prayer contained in the within petition was duly served upon Sarah Fries. And now 13 Jan. 1834 I appear for the said Sarah Fries and deny the allegations the said John Fries in his petition contained and desire the Court to direct an issue to be joined between the parties that the same may be tried by a Jury." (signed Fred. Watts atty. for the Respondent.)

◆ ◆ ◆

April Term 1834 #339 -Aug 13, 1834 "To the Honourable the Judges of the Court of Common Pleas of Cumberland County -The petition of Ephraim A. Fahnestock of said county Humbly sheweth, That your petitioner, on the twenty second day of November in the year of our Lord one thousand eight Hundred and thirty two, was lawfully joined in marriage with Amelia W. Lewis his present wife, and from that time until some time in the month of July one thousand eight hundred and thirty three he lived and cohabited with her at their residence in the town of New Cumberland in said county of Cumberland, and in all reports demeaned himself as a kind and loving husband: And although by the laws of God as well as by their mutual vow plighted to each other, they were bound to that chastity which ought to inseparable from the marriage state, yet the said Amelia, in violation of her marriage vows, did for a long time after her said marriage and before the said month of July one thousand eight hundred and thirty three, and hath ever since, given herself up to adulterous practices, and been guilty of adultery -Your petitioner therefore prays your Honors to order and direct that a subpoena do issue in due form of court, directed to the said Amelia, commanding her to appear at the next term of your Honourable court to answer your petitioner's libel, and to show cause, if any she hath, why your petitioner should not be divorced from the bond of matrimony. And he will pray." (signed E.A. Fahnestock) "Cumberland County, Pa. Ephriam A. Fahnestock the above named petitioner appeared in open court and being duly affirmed according to law doth say, that the facts contained in the above petition or libel are true, to the best of his knowledge and belief, and that the said complaint is not made out of levity, or by collusion between him and his wife, and for the mere purpose of being freed and separated from each other, but in sincerity and truth for the causes mentioned in said petition or libel." (signed E.A. Fahnestock.) "Affirmed and subscribed in open court the 13th Augt. 1834 -J.W. Harper, Prothy."

Aug. 14, 1834 -"Cumberland County, Pa. The Commonwealth of Pennsylvania to Amelia W. Fahnestock late Amelia W. Lewis. Greeting Whereas Ephraim A. Fahnestock of the town of New Cumberland in said county did on the 14th day of August A.D. 1834 prefer his petition to the Judges of the Court of Common Pleas of the county of Cumberland at a court held at Carlisle in and for said county, praying that for the causes therein set forth he might be divorced from the Bonds of Matrimony entered into with you the said Amelia W. Fahnestock late Amelia W. Lewis. We do therefore command you the said Amelia that setting aside all other business and excuses whatsoever, you be and appear in your proper person before our Judges at Carlisle at our county Court of Common Pleas there to be held for the said County of Cumberland on the second Monday of November next to answer the petition or libel of the said Ephraim A. Fahnestock and shew cause if any you have why the said Ephraim your husband should not be divorced from the bonds of matrimony agreeably to the act of assembly in such case made and provided and hereof you are not to fail. Witness John Reed Esquire at Carlisle the 14th day of August in the year of our Lord one thousand and eight hundred and thirty four. For John Harper Prothy. John Main."

Nov. 12, 1834 -"Cumberland County, Pa. Before me the subscriber a Justice of the Peace of said county personally came And. Young and being sworn according to Law doth depose that he served this within subpoena upon the within named Amelia W. Fahnestock on the 16th day of August 1834 by reading the same to her and serving her a copy thereof. Sworn and subscribed before me this 12th Novr. 1834." (signed John Black, A. Young.)

Aug. 14, 1834 -"14 Aug. 1834 I do hereby authorize and depute Andrew Young to execute the within writ agreeably to law." (signed George Beetem.)

Nov. 13, 1834 -"In the Court of Common Pleas of Cumberland County No. 339 Apr. Term 1834 Libel sur Divorce -Now 13th November 1834 The court having received due proof of the service of the subpoena upon the above named Amelia W. Fahnestock, and she not appearing to answer the matters charged in the Libel of the said Ephraim A. Fahnestock, the Court upon motion appoints Joseph Irwin Esquire of New Cumberland in Cumberland County to take the testimony of witnesses exparte, to be read in evidence on the further hearing of the case, on Wednesday the 3rd day of Decr. next, to which day, the case is now adjourned -notice of the time and place of taking the Testimony, to be served on the said Amelia -or if absent, to be left at her present, or late place of residence. By the Court. Cumberland County, Pa. I John Harper Prothonotary of the Court of Common Pleas of said County, do certify, the above to be a true copy of the appointment of a commission to take Testimony, in the above case. In testimony whereof I have hereunto subscribed my name and affixed the seal of the said Court, at Carlisle the 13th day of November A.D. 1834 Jno. Harper, Prothy."

Nov. 21, 1834 -"In the Court of Common Pleas of Cumberland County No. 339 April Term 1834 Libel for divorce -On motion the Court appointed Joseph Irvin Esq. of New Cumberland in Cumberland County to take testimony of witnesses. -Cumberland County, Pa. The Commonwealth of Pennsylvania to Dr. Lewis Lemer, Robert R. Church, George Christ, Revd. Daniel Zacharias, Emanuel Erb, James Miller and Mary Bare. Commanding that laying aside all business and excuses whatsoever you and each of you be and appear in your proper persons before Joseph Irwin Esq. the aforesaid Commissioner appointed as aforesaid at the House of Jacob Baxter Innkeeper in said town of New Cumberland and said county on the first day of December A.D. 1834 at 10 o'clock in forenoon of same day to testify the truth and give evidence on behalf of the Plaintiff above stated in the action above stated. Herein fail not on pain of such penalty as the law imposes in such cases. Witness the hand and seal of the said Commissioner and Justice of the Peace

Novr. 21st 1834." (signed J. Irwin.) "Served personally Nov. 21, 1834 on Dr. Lewis Lemer, Same day on George Crist, Served personally Nov. 22. 18 on the Revd. Danl. Zacharias. Served personally on Emanuel Erb Nov. 22 1834. Served personally on R.R. Church and Mary Bare Nov. 27, 1834." (signed A. Young.)

Nov. 26, 1834 -"Ephrahim A. Fahnestock Libellant vs. Amelia W. Fahnestock Libel sur divorce in the common pleas of Cumberland County -Madam -Take notice that depositions of witnesses to be read on the further hearing of this case, will be taken at the house of Jacob Baxter in the Borough of New Cumberland, in the County of Cumberland on Monday the first day of December next between the hours of 10 o'clock A.M. and 4 o'clock P.M. before Joseph Irvin the Commissioner appointed for that purpose, when and where you may attend to cross examine, if you think proper." (signed E.A. Fahnestock) "Ephraim A. Fahnestock Libellant vs. Amelia W. Fahnestock late Amelia W. Lewis -Case of Divorce in the Common Pleas of Cumberland County -I the above named Amelia W. Fahnestock -do hereby constitute and appoint Washington Hammersley, as my next friend for me, and in my name behalf and stead -to attend at the house of Jacob Baxter in the county of Cumberland on Monday the first day of December next -and then and there to do all matters and things which, I, in the premises could or might legally do were I personally present -and generally to act for me in said case -Witness my hand and seal this twenty sixth day of November A.D. 1834. Attest Jacob Kirk." (signed Amelia W. Fahnestock.)

Dec. 1, 1834 -"Served personally on Amelia W. Fahnestock by read the within and giving her a copy of the same Nov. 22, 1834." (signed A. Young.) "Cumberland County, Pa. Before me the subscriber a Justice of the Peace personally appeared A. Young and being duly sworn according to law saith on his oath that he served the within notice on Amelia W. Fahnestock at the time and in the manner as above recorded. (signed A. Young) Sworn and subscribed before me December 1st 1834 (signed Jas. surname illegible.) "York County, Pa. On the day and year within mentioned -to wit -the 26th of November A.D. 1834 -the within named Amelia W. Fahnestock appeared before me and acknowledged the within instrument of writing to be her act and deed -consenting that the same might be recorded of necessity. Witness my hand." (signed Jacob Kirk Jr. a Justice of the Peace in and for said county.)

Dec. 1, 1834 -"In obedience to the above Commission also appeared Mary Bear also appeared as a witness on behalf of the libellant and being duly sworn as aforesaid doth depose and says as follows viz I am acquainted with Mrs. A.W. Fahnestock wife of E.A. Fahnestock. I was acquainted with a man named Jones from the State of New York who boarded at Mrs. Lewis her mother's house for sometime while Mrs. Fahnestock boarded there. On Mr. Fahnestock's return from York she said she was unwell and Mr. Fahnestock must go to Harrisburg for her. Mr. Fahnestock did so and asked me to take care of her until his return. I went up to the room with her but had not been long there when she told me go to down and send Jones up to her. I went down for a drink of water for her when I went up Jones was sitting on the edge of her bed. I went down, and went up a second time Jones was there laying behind her in the bed. Mrs. Fahnestock got angry at me for coming up and told me to go down. When I went up again soon after, the door was locked. Jones and she in the room, they coming down stairs in the evening different ways. She first got sick and went to bed a little after dinner. Two or three weeks after this I heard her say she would leave her husband and go with Jones and wanted me to go with them. She said she did not think much of Fahnestock and did not like him at all. Cross examined. She said she married Fahnestock because he coaxed her to it. She was young and foolish. I heard them talk in the room while they were locked in. She complained no more when she came down stairs." (signed by mark "being very sick" Mary Bare.) "Sworn and subscribed before me this 1st day of Dec. 1834 between the hours of 10 o'clock A.M. and 4 P.M. at the house of Jacob Baxtser in the town of New Cumberland affd. County Washington Hammersly appearing and cross examining the witnesses on behalf of the deffendant." (signed J. Irvin.)

Dec. 1, 1834 -"Cumberland County, Pa. -In obedience to the above and hereto attached rule and Commission to me directed by the Court of Cumberland County, Daniel Zacharias was produced as a witness on behalf of Ephraim A. Fahnestock the above libellant who being duly sworn does depose and say as follows viz. -I married Amelia W. Fahnestock, then Lewis, to Ephraim A. Fahnestock on the 22d day of November A.D. 1832. I performed the ceremony as clergyman of the Synod of the German Reformed Church, her mother attending at the wedding which was held at her own house in New Cumberland in the affd. County." (signed Daniel Zacharias) "Sworn and subscribed before me, the 1st day of Dec. 1834 between the hours of 10 o'clcock A.M. and 4 o'clock P.M. at the house of Jacob Baxtesser in the town of New Cumberland affd. County, Washington Hammersly appearing and cross examining on behalf of defendant." (signed J. Irvin Commissioner).

Dec. 1, 1834 "In pursuance of the above rule and Commission also appeared as a witness on behalf as aforesaid Emanuel Erb who being duly sworn according to law doth depose and say as follows viz. I am acquainted with Amelia W. Fahnestock wife of Ephraim A. Fahnestock since her marriage, while she boarded in York, Pennsylvania. She frequently sent to his lodging at White Hall after McCormick a stage driver and several times called to see him herself. When she appeared to be too familiar with him for a married woman. She at one time addressed a note to McCormick requesting to come to see her immediately or if he would she would go with Jones. I once saw him go into her boarding house about the middle of the day and he did not return home untill after midnight. I asked him next morning if he had been with Mrs. Fahnestock that night. He said he had and had to do with her three times that night and hard work to get away from her then. I also saw her walk the streets at different times with other young men whose characters were noted for libertinism. McCormick was a libidinous character, who had to discharge him for an attempt upon a female passenger in the state he drove." (signed Emml. Erb.) "Sworn and subscribed before me this 1st day of December 1834 between the hours ten o'clock A.M. and four o'clock P.M. at the place in the said rule named at the house of Jacob Baxtesser in the Town of New Cumberland affd. County, Washington Hammersly appearing and cross examining the witnesses on behalf of the defendant." (signed J. Irvin Commissioner.)

Dec. 1, 1834 "Dr. Lerue Lemor also appeared as a witness on behalf of the libellant and being duly sworn afforesaid doth depose and say as follows viz. -I was acquainted with Mrs. A.W. Fahnestock before and after marriage, a short time after their return from York, being then the wife of Ephraim A. Fahnestock. She complained to me of being unwell, having a sore on her private parts. I told her I believed it was the veneral disease. She denied it, but after considerable talking I gave her medicine and told her expressly it was for that complaint. She took with her, in further inquiry I asked her of whom she contracted the disease. She said she had connection with no one but a man from up the river by the name of Jones. All this took place after marriage as before stated." (signed Lerue Lemor) "Sworn and subscribed before me this 1st day of Decr. 1834 between the hours of 10 A.M. and 4 P.M. at the house of Jacob Batesser in the Town of New Cumberland affd. County. Washington Hammersly appeared and cross examining the witnesses on behalf of the defendant." (signed J. Irvin Commissioner.)

Dec. 3, 1834 -"Ep. A. Fahnestock Libellant vs. Amelia W. Fahnestock: Libel for divorce. Nov viz 3rd Dec. 1834, the further hearing of this case continued by court appointing till the first day of next Jan. term 1835, at which time it is agreed that the court shall finally continue the same upon deposition. The depositions accordingly taken and now filed to be read and upon other depositions are to be taken upon ten days notice to either of the parties. All the depositions judged to be legal objection to the matters contained within." (signed Jno. Williamson Atty. for A.W. Fahnestock.)

Jan. 7, 1835 "E. Fahnestock Libellant vs. Amelia W. Fahnestock -In the Common Pleas of Cumberland County No. 339 April Term 1834 -Rule to take Depositions on the 9th and 10th Jany. 1835 -Cumberland County, Pa. -The Commonwealth of Pennsylvania to

R.R. Church, Larue Lemer, Mary Barr, Geo. Christ, Wm. Boggs, James Miller, John Miller Jr. and each of you hereby subpoenaed to attend at the house of William Boggs in New Cumberland, Cumberland County, Penna. on the 9th and 10th of Jany. Instant to give testimony before a Justice of the Peace for said County between the hours of 10 o'clock A.M. and 3 o'clock P.M. of said days, in the above case. Hereof fail not." (signed J. Irvin Jany. 7th 1835) "Served personally Jany. 7th 1835 on Wm. Boggs, same day on R.R. Church, Dr. Lerue Lemer, Mary Bare, John Miller, Jr. Served personally Jany. 8th 1835 on James Miller and on same day on George Crist." (signed E.A. Fahnestock.)

Jan. 9, 1835 "Ephraim A. Fahnestock Libellant vs. Amelia W. Fahnestock -In the Court of Common Pleas of Cumberland County No. 339 April term 1834 -In pursuance of the agreement of the parties in the above stated action to take depositions to be read on the trial thereof John Miller personally appeared before the subscriber, a Justice of the Peace for said county who being duly sworn according to law deposeth and saith under his said oath that he is acquainted with the parties in the above stated suit and that after the marriage of the plaintiff with the defendant therein he has known the said Amelia W. Fahnestock to have been in the habit of having interviews with a stage driver by the name of McCormick frequently; particularly at one time in July or August 1833, when one night he after all in the house were gone to bed, except the said Amelia W. Fahnestock who made a practice, when McCormick drove up, to stay downstairs until he returned from Harrisburg, which was generally about one or two o'clock in the morning, got up when downstairs and was met by a fellow boarder at the gates of the backyard, and on being asked why I was up so late replied that I have got up to see some fun. We then stood at the gate untill the stage drove up to the door, which was unlocked. McCormick then entered and after he had been in about ten or twelve minutes we walked forward to the bar-room door, and same McCormick came out of the parlor and went towards us, and on seeing us inquired if there was any person up, that he wanted a drink. I replied that there was none that I knew of. He then drove off, we then went into the parlor, and found her lying on a Settee and when we called to her she made no answer as though she was asleep. We then awakened her with good deal of pulling and noise. She asked whether the stage had gone down, and on being answered in the affirmative got up and started upstairs. In the fall of the same year she wanted to go down in the stage one night, and on being refused by her mother, she started when she heard the stage approaching and went off down the road until the stage came up to her. She then got in, McCormick at the time was driving. I also in the spring of 1833 saw her and a Mr. James Jones, (a waterman) from Steuben County in the State of

New York who at the time was a boarder in the house very intimate, and one day she pretended and said she was sick. A girl in the house came downstairs and told me that her and Jones were upstairs in one bed, and she also told me that she would tell her mother. I said that she had better not, as she would only make a useless noise, but went myself upstairs and saw Mr Jones and her lying on the bed, and on my coming down found that the girl had told her mother and that she was very angry and did not believe it. Jones and her were in the same room with the door locked untill they were called to supper, which was at least one hour after I saw them. At the time he went away he gave her a ring, and promised to write a letter to him, which she afterward asked me to do. I do not however recollect of having done it, or whether it was done for her by any other person. I have frequently heard her say since that she would not live with her husband for any consideration, and she would rather suffer death. I have known her since to have been intimate with several other men, Mr. Carothers another stage driver who I knew her to have given her pocketbook with a small sum of money in, and he took with him, and a Mr. Lewis Disbrow, a waterman in the spring of 1834. I have been in bed for hours after all the rest of the family and boarders were bed and on getting up found her and him sitting up still. I have also known her to be in the company of other men. The girl that told me that Mr. Jones and Mrs. Fahnestock were in bed together was a Miss Catharine Linesweaver, who at the time lived in the house of Mrs. Lewis with Mary Bare. All the above transpired after her marriage with Ephraim A. Fahnestock. I believe her to be of sound and rational mind. (signed John Miller.) "Sworn to and subscribed before me a Justice of the Peace in and for Cumberland County a little before 3 o'clock P.M. 9th Jany. 1835 at the house of William Boggs, no one appearing to cross examine." (signed J. Irvin.)

Jan. 9, 1835 -"In pursuance of the said agreement, as mentioned in the foregoing deposition of John Miller also personally appeared before in the said Justice of the Peace in the aforesaid County George Crist who being duly sworn as aforesaid deposeth and saith as follows. I am acquainted with Amelia W. Fahnestock named in the above stated action, and that her general character for chastity and fidelity towards her husband was very bad especially after her return from York in the summer of 1833, it being the general opinion that she was improperly familiar with other men and that I have seen her too familiar with other men for a married woman in the barroom of her mother's house. I believe her to be of sound mind, sufficient to conduct herself prudently." (signed George Crist.) "Sworn to and subscribed before me a Justice of the Peace in and for Cumberland County a little before 3 o'clock P.M. Jany. 9th 1835 at the house of William Boggs, no one appearing to cross examine." (signed J. Irvin.)

Jan. 9, 1835 -"In pursuance of the said agreement as mentioned in the foregoing deposition of John Miller also appeared before me the said Justice of the Peace in the aforesaid County James Miller who being duly sworn as aforesaid deposeth and saith as follows viz, that in the year 1833 in the summer I saw Amelia W. Fahnestock named in the above action laying on the Settee with McCormack a stage driver he laying on top of her loving one another. This I saw on passing through the room in the dusk of the evening in the house then occupied by her mother (now by Mr. Boggs) in New Cumberland. She uniformly sat up the night McCormack's stage came and ran to the door to meet him and took him in through the entry (signed by mark by James Miller.) "Sworn to and subscribed before me a Justice of the Peace in and for Cumberland County a little before 3 o'clock 9th Jany. 1835 in the afternoon (no one appearing this day to cross examine), at the house of William Boggs in New Cumberland." (signed J. Irvin.)

Jan. 9, 1835 -"In pursuance of the above said agreement as mentioned in the foregoing deposition of John Miller also personally appeared before me the said Justice of the Peace in the aforesaid County Mary Miller who being duly sworn as aforesaid doth depose and say as follows viz -that in addition to the facts stated in her former deposition she saw Mrs. Amelia Fahnestock in August 1833 put her arms round the neck of McCormack the stagedriver as he came off the stage which he then drove from Harrisburg and kiss him on his mouth, and he did the same to her. She first caught him around the neck. I also saw her walk to the Camp meeting at night with a man named Fisher he having his arm round her waste (sic) and she round his. I also saw her at another time, at 11 or 12 o'clock at night walk in the same familiar way around the town with a peddlar. These facts took place all near about the same time and were omitted in my former deposition being then on a sick bed I did not recollect them." (signed Mary Bere.) "Sworn to and subscribed before me a Justice of the Peace in for Cumberland Co. a little before 3 o'clock P.M. 9th Jany. 1835 at the house of William Boggs in New Cumberland, no one appearing to cross examine." (signed J. Irvin.)

Jan. 10, 1835 -"I do hereby certify that the witnesses in the foregoing depositions were all again produced before me the said Justice of the Peace named therein for the purpose of being cross examined by the defendant in the agreement therein mentioned but that no one appeared for said purpose on the part of said defendant between the hours of 10 o'clock A.M. and 3 o'clock P.M. of said day." (signed J. Irvin January 10th 1835.)

Jan. 12, 1835 "Ephraim A. Fahnestock Libellant vs. Amelia W. Fahnestock. Libel for divorce in the Common Pleas of Cumberland County -and now, viz 12th Jany. 1835, the court having heard and duly considered the evidence the part of the libellant, the Deft. not having produced any, do adjudge that the complaint of the said Libellant, made and stated in his libel has been fully sustained and provided, and do sentence and decree that the said Ephraim A. Fahnestock, the libellant is hereby divorced and separated from the nuptial ties and bonds of matrimony with the said Amelia W. Fahnestock, the Deft. and that the costs be paid by the defendant. By the court."

Jan. 13, 1835 -"Ephraim A. Fahnestock vs. Amelia W. Fahnestock No. 339 April term 1834 Case of Divorce -Plaintiffs bill of expenses in taking testimony before Joseph Irvin Esquire the commissioner appointed by court to take the same.

Cash paid for first subpoena for 7 witnesses	$0.21
Cash paid Constable Young for serving the same	3.12
Cash paid for 2d subpoena for 7 witnesses	0.21
Serving the same and mileage	1.00
Cash paid Constable Young for serving notice on Deft. of the time and place of taking testimony	2.63 1/2
Cash paid Commissioner for taking testimony	2.50
	$9.67 1/2

Cash paid by Plaintiff to the following named witnesses for appearing and giving testimony
To wit

Dr. Lerew Lemer 1 day		.50
Rev. Daniel Zacharias 1 day	.62 1/2	
6 miles circular	.18	.80 1/2
Emanuel Erb 1 day	.62 1/2	
44 miles circular	1.34	1.96 1/2
Mary Bare 3 several days		1.50
George Crist 2 several days		1.00
James Miller 2 several days	1.25	
2 miles circular	.06	1.31
John Miller 2 several days	1.25	
2 miles circular	.06	1.31
		$18.06
Docket costs Shff. B.	$3.00	
Clk. Harper	2.75	5.75
		$23.81
Copy and Certificate		1.25
		$25.06
taxing Bill		.18 3/4
		$25.24 3/4

Filed 13th January 1835"

♦ ♦ ♦

January 1835 Term #137 -Feb. 27, 1835 -"To the honorable the Judges of the Court of Common Pleas of Cumberland County -The petition of Sarah Black by her next friend Miles Crowley -Respectfully Sheweth that your libellant on the 22d day of Feb. in the year of our Lord One Thousand Eight hundred and thirty one was contracted in matrimony and married to a certain Anthony Black, and from that time untill the seventeenth day of Jan. in the year of our Lord One thousand and eight hundred and thirty five lived and cohabited with him as his wife and as such was owned and acknowledged by him and so deemed and reputed by all her neighbors and acquaintances; and altho, by the laws of God as well as by their mutual vows and faith plighted to each other they were reciprocally bound to that kindness and uniform regard which ought to be inseparable to the marriage state; yet so it is that the said Anthony Black did prior to the said 17th day of January offer such indignities to her person as to render her condition intolerable and life burdensome and thereby force her to withdraw from his house and family. Wherefore your libellant further shewing that she is a citizen of this state and hath resided therein for one whole year and more previous to the filing of this petition and prays your honors that a subpoena shall issue from the said Court directed to the said Anthony Black commanding him to appear at the next April term of the said Court to answer this petition and also that a decree of the said Court may be given granting this libellant a divorce from bed and board and also allowing such alimony as the said Anthony Black's circumstances will admit of so as the same do not exceed the third part of profit or income of his estate or of his occupation and labour. And as in duty found this libellant will ever pray etc." (signed by mark Sarah Black by her next friend Miles Crowley.) "The above named Sarah Black being duly sworn according to law doth depose and say that the facts contained in the above petition or libel are true to the best of her knowledge and belief and that the said complaint is not made out of levity or by collusion between her and the said Anthony Black, and for the mere purpose of being freed and separated from each other but in sincerity and truth for the causes mentioned in said petition or libel." (signed by mark Sarah Black.) "Sworn and subscribed before me a Justice of the Peace in and for Cumberland County Feb. 27, 1835." (signed Robert Snodgrass) 28 Feb. 1835 subpoena awarded.

March 2, 1835 -"Cumberland County, Pa. -The Commonwealth of Pennsylvania to Anthony Black Greeting: Whereas Sarah Black by her next friend Miles Crowley did on the 28th day of February 1835 prefer her petition to the Judges of the Court of Common Pleas of the County of Cumberland, praying that for the causes therein set forth she might be divorced from the bed and board of the said Anthony Black and also that she be allowed such alimony as the said Anthony Black's circumstances will admit of etc. We do therefore command you the said Anthony Black that setting aside all other business and excuses whatsoever you be and appear in your proper person before our Judges at Carlisle at our County Court of

Common Pleas there to be held for the said County of Cumberland on the second Monday of April next to answer the Petition or libel of the said Sarah, and to show cause if any you have why the said Sarah your wife should not be divorced from your bed and board, and allowed such alimony as your circumstances will admit of so as the same does not exceed the third part of the profits or income of your estate or occupation and labour agreeably to the act of assembly in such case made and provided. And hereof you are not to fail. -Witness John Reed Esquire at Carlisle the second day of March in the year of our Lord one thousand eight hundred and thirty five. For John Harper, Prothy." (signed John Main.)

March 16, 1835 -"To the Honourable the Judge of the Court of Common Pleas of the County of Cumberland -The petition of Anthony Black of Dickinson Township in said county -Humbly sheweth, That your petitioner on the 22d day of Feby. 1831, was lawfully joined in marriage with Sarah his present wife, and from that time until the 17th Jany. 1835, has lived and cohabited with her, and he hath in all respects demeaned himself as a kind and loving husband: and although by the laws of God as well as by the mutual vows plighted to each other, they were bound to that chastity which ought to be inseparable from the marriage state yet the said Sarah in violation of her marriage vows hath for a considerable time past given herself up to adulterous practices, and been guilty of adultery -And that on or about the 15th day of Jany. 18 your petitioner being then confined to his bed by sickness under which he had laboured for several weeks previous (illegible word), then the said Sarah made an attempt with a butcher knife upon the person of your petitioner and with profane oaths and improvacations threatened to destroy his life, which she was then prevented from doing by the kind intercession of other persons who were providentially present -and the said Sarah continued her cruel and barbarous treatment as aforesaid untill the 17th day of Jany 1835, on which last mentioned day, she left the habitation of your petitioner -And that the said Sarah by her cruel and barbarous treatment of your petitioner as aforesaid, has rendered his life burthersome, and from the violent threats uttered by the said Sarah as aforesaid he believes his life is in danger. Your petitioner therefore prays your Honors to award a subpoena in due form of law directed to said Sarah commanding her to appear at the next time of your honorable Court, to answer your petitioner's libel, and to show cause, if any she hath, why your petitioner should not be divorced from the bonds of matrimony -and he will pray etc." (signed Anthony Black.) "Cumberland county, Pa. Before me the subscriber a Justice of the Peace in and for said county personally came Anthony Black the above named petitioner and being sworn according to law doth depose and say that the facts stated in his said petition or libel are true as he firmly believes, and that the said complaint is not made out of levity, or by collusion between deponent and his said wife, and for the mere purpose of being freed and separated from each other, but in sincerity and truth for the causes mentioned in his said petition or libel." (signed Anthony Black) "Sworn and subscribed the 16th March 1835 before" (signed Robert Snodgrass.) Notation on front -"May 8th 1835 Subpa. sux Divorce awarded by the court."

April 13, 1835 -"Anthony Black the respondent in the within libel of Sarah Black now comes and defends the complaint of the said libellant in the first libel stated and says that although true it is that said libellant and this respondent were lawfully joined in the bonds of matrimony on the 22 Feby. 1831 and lived and cohabited together as man and wife from that time until the 17 Jany. 1835; it is not true as the said libellant has in her said libel falsely alleged that the said respondent did prior to the said 17 Jany. 1835 offer such indignities to the person of her the said Libellant as to render her condition intolerable and life burthensome, and thereby force her to withdraw from the house and family of this respondent -and the said respondent further in fact doth respond ever and say that the said Libellant from the said 22d Feby. 1831 until the said 17 Jany. 1835 did not demean and behave kindly towards this respondent as a loving and dutiful wife ought to do, but on the contrary she the said Libellant altogether gave herself up to adulterous practices, and did between the days and years last aforesaid at the county of Cumberland commit the crime of adultery; and also that she the said Libellant during the time aforesaid did conduct and behave herself towards this respondent so unruly, indecently, maliciously mistreating him, and in such violence as to destroy all the comfort of this respondent, and endanger his life and render it burthensome; and further that she the said Libellant on the said 17 Jany. 1835, did voluntarily withdraw herself and abandon this respondent and his habitation and family, of her own free will and accord, without the consent or knowledge of this respondent, and without any just cause -all which previous the respondent is ready to verify etc." (signed A. Carothers for Respondent) Notation -Respondents plea read and filed 13th Apl. 1835.

April 14, 1835 -"Sarah Black vs. Anthony Black -In the Com. Pleas of Cumberland Co. Jany. term 1835 No. 137 -Sarah Black the Libellant in the within libel by Chas. McClure her attorney comes and says that protesting all and singular the matters and things in the Respondent's plea alleged in bar of her libel and prayer, are not true -she is ready to verify the said matters and things by her in her said libel and prayer set forth and prays that a Jury may be called to inquire thereof according to the several acts of Assembly in this behalf made and provided. Apl. 14th 1835" (signed Chas. McClure for Libellant)

♦ ♦ ♦

Nov. 1835 Term #87 -Nov. 20, 1835 -"To the Honorable the Judges of the Court of Common Pleas of Cumberland County -The Petition of Rudolph Kindig humbly showeth that your petitioner on the tenth day of January A.D. 1819 was lawfully joined in marriage with Elizabeth his present wife -And although by the laws of God as well as by their mutual vows plighted to each other they were bound to live together -yet the said Elizabeth in violation of her marriage vows in the month of August A.D. 1831, wilfully and maliciously did desert and absent herself from the habitation of your petitioner without a reasonable cause and hath remained absent from that date to the present time, a period of upwards of four years. Your Petitioner therefore prays that your Honors will please to direct and order that a subpoena do issue in due form of law directed to the said Elizabeth commanding her to appear at the next Court of Common Pleas to be held in said County to answer the Petitioner's libel and to show cause if any she hath why the Petitioner should not be divorced from the bonds of matrimony and he will pray etc." (signed Rudolph Kindig) "Cumberland County, Pa. The said Rudolph Kindig on his solemn affirmation doth declare and say that the facts contained in the above Petition or libel are true to the best of his knowledge and belief, and that the said complaint is not made out of levity, or by collusion between him and his wife, and for the mere purpose of being freed and separated from each other but in sincere- ity and truth for the causes mentioned in the said petition or libel." (signed Rudolph Kindig.) "Affirmed and subscribed before me the 20th Novr. A.D. 1835" (signed John Creigh.) "20th November 1835 Petition presented and Subpoena awarded the Court."

♦ ♦ ♦

January 1836 Term #69 Jan. 16, 1836 -"To the Honourable the Judges of the Court of Common Pleas of Cumberland County -The petition of Sarah Smith by John McCay her father and next friend -Humbly sheweth, That your petitioner or libellant, was intermarried with her present husband Simon Smith about twenty years since, and hath during all that time demeaned herself towards her said husband as a dutiful wife ought to do -yet her husband, the said Simon Smith, in violation of his marriage vows and of his duties as a Husband, at sundry times within the last two years, by his cruel and barbarous treatment, has endangered her life, and offered such indignities to her person as to render her condition intolerable and her life burthensome, and has thereby forced her to withdraw one month last past, finally to withdraw from his house and family -That your petitioner is a citizen of the Commonwealth of Penna., and has resided therein for one year and upwards previous to the filing of this her complaint or libel. Your petitioner therefore prays your Honours to award a subpoena directed to the said Simon Smith to appear, at the next term of this Honorable court or at some other time as your Honours may appoint, and there show cause if any he has why your petitioner or libellant should not be divorced from the bed and board of her said Husband, and allowed such alimony as his circumstances will admit of, so as the same do not exceed the third part of the annexed profits or income of his estate, or of his occupation and labour, agreeably to the act of assembly in such case made and provided -and your petioner will pray etc." (signed by mark by John McCay and witness Andrew Carothers.) "Cumberland County, Pa. Before me the subscriber a Justice of the Peace in and for said county personally came Sarah Smith the petitioner or libellant within named and being sworn according to law did depose and say that the facts stated in the within petition or libel are just and true and that the said complaint and application was not made by collusion between her and her said Husband, but in sincerity and truth for the causes therein stated." (signed Sally Smith.) "Sworn and subscribed the 16th Jany. 1836 before" (signed Archibald Ramsey.)

Jan. 18, 1836 -"Cumberland 1836 -"Cumberland 1836 -"Cumberland County, Pa. The Commonwealth of Pennsylvania to Simon Smith Blacksmith of the Borough of Carlisle Greeting -Whereas Sarah Smith by John McCoy her Father and next friend did on the 18th day of January 1836 prefer her petition to our Judges of the court of Common Pleas of the county of Cumberland at a court held at Carlisle in and for said county praying that for the causes therein set forth she might be divorced from your Bed and Board, and allowed such alimony as your circumstances will admit of etc. We do therefore command you the said Simon Smith that setting aside all business and excuses whatsoever you be and in appear your proper person before our Judges at Carlisle at a Court of Common Pleas there to be held for the said county on the second Monday of April next to answer the petition or libel of the said Sarah Smith and to shew cause if any you have why the said Sarah your wife should not be divorced from your bed and board and allowed such alimony as your circumstances will admit of so as the same do not exceed the third part of the annual profits or income of your Estate or of your occupation and labour and agreeably to the act of assembly in such case made and provided. And hereof you are not to fail. Witness John Reed Esquire at Carlisle the 18th day of January in the year of our Lord one thousand eight hundred and thirty six." (signed George Fleming, Prothy.) "Served personally 27th February, 1836, So answers M. Holcomb, Sheff. Sheriff bill $0.83." (signed Carothers.)

◆ ◆ ◆

January 1836 Term #97 -Feb. 10, 1836 -"To the Honorable the Judges of Court of Common Pleas of the County of Cumberland -The Petition of Susannah Maxwell by her next friend Isaac Christlieb

-Respectfully sheweth That your petitioner on the 24th day of October A.D. 1832 was lawfully joined in marriage with James Maxwell and from that time untill the first day of April A.D. 1834 lived and cohabited with the said James Maxwell as his wife and was owned and acknowledged by him and so deemed or reputed by all her neighbors and acquaintances, and although by the laws of God, as well as by their mutual vows, they were reciprocally bound to that uniform regard which ought to be inseparable from the marriage state, yet so it is that the said James Maxwell has offered such indignities to the person of your petitioner as to render her condition intolerable, and her life burthensome, and thereby force her to withdraw from his house and company. Wherefore your libellant further showing that she is a citizen of the State of Pennsylvania and has resided therein for upwards of one whole year previous to the filing of this her libel prays your honors that a subpoena may issue forth to summon the said James Maxwell to appear in this Honorable Court at the April Term next to answer the complaint aforesaid. And also that a decree of this Honorable Court may be made for the divorcing of him the said James Maxwell from the society, fellowship and company of this Libellant in all time to come, and Susannah Maxwell the Libellant from the Marriage bond aforesaid as if she had never been married or as if the said James Maxwell were naturally dead. And this Libellant will ever pray etc." (signed Susannah Maxwell by her next friend Isaac Christleib.) "Cumberland County, Pa. The within and before named Susannah Maxwell being duly sworn says that the facts contained in the within Libel are true to the best of her knowledge and belief and that the said complaint is not made out of Levity and Collusion between James Maxwell and her the said Susannah Maxwell and for the mere purpose of being freed and separated from each other but in sincerity and truth for the causes mentioned in the said libel." (signed Susannah Maxwell) "Sworn and subscribed before me at Carlisle the 10th day of February A.D. 1836" (signed Robert Snodgrass.)

10 Feby. 1836 -subpoena awarded.

April 11, 1836 -"Susannah Maxwell by her next friend Isaac Christleib vs. James Maxwell -In the Court of Common Pleas of Cumberland County No. 97 Jan. Term 1836 -Now, to wit 11th April 1836 -Due proof having been made of the service of the subpoena awarded, and the same James Maxwell not appearing, the Court do hereby appoint Robert Lusk Esquire as a commissioner to take testimony on the subject and do fix Tuesday the 10th of May next for the final hearing of the case. By the court."

April 13, 1836 -"Cumberland County, Pa. I George Fleming, Prothonotary the Court of Common Pleas of Cumberland County, do certify the above to be a true copy of the appointment of a commissioner to take testimony in the above case. In testimony whereof I have hereunto subscribed my name, and affixed the seal of said court at Carlisle, the 13th day of April, A.D. 1836." (signed George Fleming, Prothy.)

April 14, 1836 -"Susannah Maxwell by her next friend Isaac Christlieb vs. James Maxwell In the Common Pleas of Cumberland County Libel for Divorce -To Mr. James Maxwell -Sir You will please to take notice that the depositions of witnesses to be read in evidence on the hearing of the above case will be taken at the office of Robert Lusk Esquire in Mifflin township Cumberland County on Saturday the thirtieth day of April 1836 between the Hours of ten o'clock in the forenoon and five o'clock the afternoon of that day -at which time and place you may attend if you think proper. -Carlisle April 14th 1836" (signed Saml. Hepburn attorney for Susannah Maxwell).

April 30, 1836 "Cumberland Co., Pa. Personally before me the subscriber one of the Justices of the Peace etc. came George Hoon who after being sworn according to law, sayeth that he served the within notice on James Maxwell personally on Monday the 18th April A.D. 1836." (signed Geo. Hoon.) "Sworn and subscribed the 30th April 1836" (signed R. Lusk.)

Jan. 23, 1836 -"Cumberland County, Pa. The Commonwealth of Pennsylvania to James Maxwell Greeting -Whereas Susannah Maxwell by her next friend Isaac Christlieb, did on the 10th day of February A.D. 1836 prefer her petition to our Judges of the Court of Common Pleas of said county at court held at Carlisle praying there for the causes therein set forth, she might be divorced from the society, fellowship and company of the said James Maxwell etc. Therefore we command you the said James Maxwell that setting aside all business and excuses whatsoever you be and appear before our Judges at Carlisle at a Court of Common Pleas there to be held for the said county on the second Monday of April next to answer the petition or Libel by the said Susannah, and to show cause if any you have why the said Susannah Maxwell your wife should not be divorced from the bonds of Matrimony agreeably to the acts of General assembly in such case made and provided and hereof you are not to fail. Witness John Reed Esquire at Carlisle the twenty third day of January in the year our Lord one thousand eight hundred and thirty six." (signed George Fleming Prothonotary.) (Note -Susannah Maxwell's original petition was dated Feb. 10, 1836 yet this subpoena was dated Jan. 23, 1836. I have no explanation but I did double-check that these were the dates recorded.) On the back of this subpoena "I do hereby authorize and deputise John Elliott to execute the within writ agreeably to Law -Witness my hand and seal the 14th March 1836." (signed M. Holcomb, Sheriff.) "Cumberland County -John Elliott being duly sworn doth depose and say that he served this subpoena personally on James Maxwell on the 15th March, 1836." (signed John Elliott.) "Sworn and subscribed in open court 11th April, 1836." (signed George Fleming, Prothy.) Sheriff's bill $2.84.

April 30, 1836 -"Agreeably to the within order or appointment of the Court, the following depositions were taken by the within named Commissioner in the presence of James Maxwell on Saturday the thirtyeth (sic) April 1836. Sarah Christlieb the elder, sworn sayeth that when Susannah Maxwell was lying ill with a swelled throat, that her husband James Maxwell instead of trying to comfort and solace her and make her case more easy by administering necessary help he went away and left her without any one to so much as give her a drink of water and also without fire and that she the deponent went and staid (sic) with her about four days and that his conduct for that time was intolerable that he did not once go to see her nor ask how she was, during that time, this took place while he lived on the plantation of Ludwick Miller about five months after they were married he then moved to a tenant house on the farm of John Graham and she was still unwell. He did not so much as see her into her new house but just unloaded went away and did not come back untill the next evening. About two weeks after he commenced abusing her at night (not being much in the house through the day) and continued abusing her four nights in succession almost from dark to day (this abuse was with the tongue) and was to such an extent that he repeatedly said she would mix with blacks if she had any convenient, that his conduct was most intolerable about the time she had her child. That the morning before she was delivered, she plead with and that with tears, catching him by the arm and telling him not to go away and leave her. But he went away in the morning and left her and that entirely alone, and seen her not, excepting a sight through the door of deponent, where she had fled for refuge untill after she had been delivered. That about one month before he caught her and gave her a drive from him in anger by which she would have fell, after plunging about ten feet had she not came against Deponent, that he once lifted a chair and drew over her and swore that he made her tremble, that he would not suffer others, nor carry water or cut wood for her himself, lest it would be doing it for his wife and that his conduct towards his wife throughout was intolerable she being in continual fear, not having as he himself said he would give her the life of a dog." (signed by mark Sarah Christlieb senr.) "Sworn and subscribed the 30th April 1836." (signed R. Lusk.)

April 30, 1836 -"Seawright Christlieb sworn -sayeth that he observed on the day he, James Maxwell was married that he treated his wife Susan Maxwell with wanton contempt, when he moved to his dwelling. I was there frequently and do not recollect that he once spoke to her unless it was to ridicule her, sometime after they lived there she took sick, and he came by our house on his way to a two day meeting which he said was to be held in Germantown Perry County and with eloquent solicitations requested me to accompany him. I did and we were away about two days. He was playing the fool all the time and his wife at home sick, without any person to care of her, he had no errand and had no religious desire. I boarded there one week, his treatment and conduct towards her was intolerable, or to my notion not good. During that time he was scolding her about using so much firewood and she generally had breakfast at dawn of day but he would lie till sunrise, although requested to rise to breakfast. I have frequently seen him going to work at 10 o'clock in the day he is of such indolent habits." Question by James Maxwell "Who told you that she was sick?" Answer "You told me that she was sick." (signed Searight Christlieb.) "Sworn and subscribed the 30th April 1836." (signed R. Lusk.)

April 30, 1836 -"Catharine Miller the younger, sworn Sayeth, that one evening he came home from a vendue (and I was living there) he began to scold his wife about the money which was coming to her and said he would not trust her anything and he would take the child from her, and when she went to bed she trembled like a leaf, she was so afraid of him. I slept, or lay with her that night. She was as fearful of him as death that night he scolded so much. I lived there three months and almost every time he came in he scolded about something. His conduct was most intolerable towards his wife all the time I was there he was always scolding about firewood and would not let us have enough. I cut some of the wood we used and his wife cut some, that he went through the house shaking his fist and told his wife she ought to be wagon-whipt every day." (signed by mark by Catharine Miller.) "Sworn and subscribed the 30th April 1836." (signed R. Lusk.)

April 30, 1836 -"Sarah Christlieb the younger sworn sayeth that the winter after they were married Susannah Maxwell wife of James Maxwell was sick. That when she went to the house the doors were open and no fire in the room where his wife was lying in bed, that they moved to a house on the farm of John Graham, that he unloaded and went away and was not back untill the next evening. Sometime afterwards I was there at the house of James Maxwell and when at breakfast with his wife he got offended because his wife did not fill his cup without him handing it as usual and he got up and drew the chair in a position to strike swearing at the the time he set it down, and then lifted and drew it again. He then laid it down and went round to where his wife was and shaked (sic) his fist at her and swore he would strike her if it was not for the civil law and did not know but what he would do it anyhow. One evening after he began to scold her and said that she was in the way now that she would be likely soon to go off, my mother then said she supposed he would be glad. He said yes he would be glad to get rid of the damned breed. The same evening he cast up to her that she would meddle with black and white. That she left the house of James Maxwell the morning before his wife was delivered of a child that James Maxwell was at home when she went away that there was no other person at the house that before She got home which was between two and three miles she saw James Maxwell on horseback about a mile from his house. That after she went home about one hour Mrs. Maxwell came likewise to our house and that night was delivered of a child all the time and every time I was there his conduct towards his wife was very intolerable." (signed Sarah Christlieb Jr.) "Sworn and subscribed the thirtieth day of April A.D. 1836 Before" (signed R. Lusk.)

May 10, 1836 -"Susannah Maxwell by her next friend Isaac Christlieb vs. James Maxwell -In the Court of Common Pleas of Cumberland County No. (left blank) Term 1836 -And now the 10th day of May A.D. 1836 -the Commissioner Robert Lusk Esquire have returned to the Court here the depositions of witnesses taken before him on the part of the Libellant and in the presence of the said James Maxwell -and the same being read and heard by the court, and the Court after mature and solemn deliberation being satisfied therewith -and this being the day appointed by the said Court for the final hearing and determining the said matter -and the said James Maxwell not appearing -the Court do order adjudge and decree that the said Susannah Maxwell the libellant be divorced and separated from the bond of matrimony contracted with the said James Maxwell and that all and every the duties rights and claims accruing to either of the said parties at any time by reason of the said marriage shall cease and determine and the said parties be severally at liberty to marry again in like manner as if they had never been married -and that the said James Maxwell pay the costs of this application. By the Court."

◆ ◆ ◆

April Term 1836 #35 March 1, 1836 -To the Honorable John Reed President Judge of the Court of Common Pleas of Cumberland County, Pa. -The petition of Jacob Herman of Silverspring Township, Cumberland County represents that he was lawfully married to Jane Young on the twenty sixth day of March one thousand eight hundred and twenty two and did live and cohabit with her as his lawful wife for about eleven years and during that time had by her five children. That on the 26 Feb. 1834 she the said Jane Herman the wife of your petitioner, did wilfully and maliciously desert and absent herself from the habitation of your petitioner without a reasonable cause and hath been absent for the space of two years and more before the presentation of this petition. Your petitioner therefore prays your Honor to award a subpoena directed to the said Jane Herman commanding her to appear at the next Court of Common Pleas of

Cumberland County to answer this petition, and shew cause why the said Jacob Herman should not obtain from the said Court a divorce from the bonds of matrimony. And he will pray etc." (signed Jacob Herman.) "Cumberland County, Pa. personally appeared before me a Justice of the Peace in and for said County Jacob Herman who being duly sworn doth depose and say that the facts mentioned in the foregoing petition are true to the best of his knowledge and belief and that the said complaint is not made out of levity or by collusion between him and his wife and for the mere purpose of being freed and separated from each other, but in sincerity and truth for the causes mentioned in the said petition or libel." (signed Jacob Herman. "Sworn and subscribed the 1 March 1836 Before me" (signed William Irvine.)

March 2, 1836 -"The Commonwealth of Pennsylvania To Jane Herman. Greeting -Whereas Jacob Herman of Silverspring Township, Cumberland County has presented his petition to the Hon. John Reed President Judge of the Court of Common Pleas of Cumberland County which represents That he was lawfully married to Jane Young on the 26 March 1822 and did live and cohabit with her as his lawful wife for about eleven years and during that time had by her five children: that on the 26 February 1834 she the said Jane Herman the wife of the petitioner did wilfully and maliciously desert and absent herself from the habitation of the petitioner without a reasonable cause and hath been absent for the space of two years and more before the presentation of his petition: and praying the Hon. John Reed President Judge to award a subpoena directed to the said Jane Herman commanding her to appear and answer his petition and show cause why the said Jacob Herman should not obtain a divorce from the bonds of matrimony. We therefore command you the said Jane Herman that you be and appear at the next Court of Common Pleas of Cumberland County to be held at Carlisle on Monday the 11 April 1836 to answer the said petition of the said Jacob Herman. Witness the Hon. John Reed President Judge at Carlisle the 2nd day of March 1836. Allowed by John Reed Pres. Judge Seal of the Court of Common Pleas of Cumberland County. Attest" (signed George Fleming Prothy.)

April 11, 1836 -"Cumberland County Joseph Lobach Deputy Sheriff being duly sworn doth depose and say that he served this subpoena personally on Jane Herman on the 25 of March 1836." (signed J. Lobach.) "Sworn and Subscribed in open court 11 April 1836" (signed George Fleming Prothy.)

May 30, 1836 -"To Jane Herman In the case of the application of Jacob Herman for a divorce. Depositions to prove the facts relating thereof will be taken at the office of John Clendenin Esq. in Hogestown Saturday the Fourth day of June A.D. 1836 where you may attend if you think proper between 10:00 A.M. and 4:00 P.M."

(signed Fred. Watts Atty. for petitioner 10 May 1836) on back of this paper "Cumberland County, Pa. Adam Longsdorf being duly sworn before the subscriber a Justice of the Peace in and for said county deposeth and saith that he served the within notice on Jane Herman by leaving a copy thereof with old Mr. Young with whom the said Jane resides the fourteenth day of May instant." (signed Adam Longsdorf.) "Sworn and Subscribed May 30th 1836 before Jno. Clendenin."

June 4, 1836 -"Cumberland County, Pa. Personally appeared before the subscriber one of the Justices of the Peace in and for said county William Fisher who being sworn doth say that he lived with Jacob Herman and his wife almost two years during the time they kept house together; they always had plenty to eat, and to ware (sic); Deponent further saith that he never knew Herman to use his wife ill; further saith not." (signed William Fisher.) "Sworn and Subscribed June 4th A.D. 1836 Before Jno. Clendenin."

June 4, 1836 -"Jacob Harman vs. Jane Harman: In the Court of Common Pleas of Cumberland County No. 35 April Term, 1836. Now, to wit, 11th Apr 1836 due proof having been made of the service of the subpoena awarded, and the said Jane Harman not attending the Court do hereby appoint John Clendenin Esquire as a Commissioner to take testimony on the subject and do fix the second Monday of August next for the final hearing of the case. By the Court. Cumberland County Pa. I, George Fleming, Prothonotary of the Court of Common Pleas of Cumberland County Do certify the abov to be a true copy of appointment of a Commissioner to take testimony in the above case. In testimony whereof I have hereunto subscribed my name and affixed the seal of said court, the tenth day of May, A.D. 1836." (signed George Fleming, Prothy.)

June 4, 1836 -"Cumberland County, Pa. In pursuance of the above Commission authorizing the taking of testimony to be read in evidence on the final trial of the above cause, Personally came before me the subscriber, one of the Justices of the Peace, in and for said county of Cumberland, at my office, in and for said county of Cumberland, at my office in Hogestown, Martin Diller, who being duly affirmed, doth depose and say; that he is well aquainted with Jacob Harman and Jane his wife; that he was present at the house of Peter Young (the father-in-law of said Jacob) on the day that said Jacob removed with his family from the premises of said Young, after the wagon was loaded and ready to go said Jacob asked Jane his wife if she was not going with him. She said she would not, Jacob then said to her if you will not go for my sake; go for sake of the children. She again said she would not go, this was sometime in the month of February one thousand eight hundred and thirty four; deponent further saith that said Jane has been living with her father Peter Young from that time, to this day; and further affirmant saith that said Jane had declared to him that her husband had never used her ill, or scolded her. I never heard that Harman used his wife ill, I always heard him well spoken of -further said not." (signed Martin Diller in what appears to be a very shaky signature.) "Affirmed and subscribed June 4th A.D. 1836 at 4 o'clock P.M. no person appeared to cross examine before Jno. Clendenin."

June 4, 1836 -"Also, Personally appeared before the subscriber at the same time and place John Goodyear who being sworn according to law doth depose and say; Jacob Harman invited him to come and help to load his goods, on the day he removed from Peter Young's which was two years ago the last of February last past; he went accordingly, before they began to load said Jacob told his wife Jane to make ready to go along. She said she would not go. After the waggons were loaded, in presence of deponent, and in presence of Peter Young and wife and several neighbors Jacob Harman again asked his wife to go along with him. She said she would not. He then said to her if you will not go on my account, go on account of the children. She again said she would no go (sic). Deponent further saith that he lives about a fourth of a mile from said Young's dwelling house; in passing said house he has often seen said Jane Harman and believes she has been living with her father, the said Peter Young from the time Jacob left there to the present time. I never heard of any quarrel or dispute between said Harman and his wife -further saith not." (signed Johannes Goodyear in German script.) "Sworn and subscribed June 4th 1836 at 4 o'clock (taken exparte) before Jno. Clendenin."

June 4, 1836 -"Michael G. Belshoover appeared and being affirmed doth declare and affirm that Jacob Harman asked him to come and help him to move from the premises of his father-in-law Peter Young, to his own farm with the deposition of Michael G. Belshoover: in Silver Spring township, and to bring his Barouch to haul his wife and family. Deponent went with his Barouch after the waggons were loaded and all ready to start, Jacob went into the house and asked his wife to go with him. She said she would not go. Said Jacob then went down on his knees before her and begged of her to go, and if she would not go for his sake to go for the sake of the children. She said she would not go along. Deponent then told her he had his Barouch there and he would haul her over and if she did not like to stay he would haul her back again. She told him she would not go. Deponent further saith that said Jane has been living with her father from that time to this. I never heard of any quarrel between said Harman and his wife." (signed Michael G. Beltzhoover.) "Affirmed and Subscribed June 4th 1836 at 4 o'clock P.M. (in presence of complainant only) before Jno. Clendenin."

June 4, 1836 -"Personally appeared Catharine Orris who being duly sworn doth say that she has been living with Jacob Harmand (sic) of Silvers Spring township from the seventh day of March one thousand eight hundred and thirty four to the present time; in the capacity of house-keeper and during all this time she has not seen Jane, the wife of said Jacob at his dwelling house or elsware (sic); to her knowledge -further saith not." (signed by mark Catharine Orris.) "Sworn and subscribed June 4th 1836 at 4 o'clock P.M. at my office in Hogestown -before Jno. Clendenin."

June 4, 1836 -"Cumberland County, Pa. In pursuance of the foregoing commission personally appeared before the subscriber a Justice of the Peace for said county, William Keller who being duly sworn doth depose and say that Jacob Harman called on him a few days after he removed from Peter Young's to his farm in Silver Spring township, to go with him (the said Jacob) to the house of his father-in-law, Peter Young, for the purpose of being a witness to the service of a notice on said Peter that he would not be accountable or liable to him for the support of his wife who had (as deponent understood) remained behind with her father and also notifying him the said Peter not to harbour his wife and children. Deponent went with Harman to Mr. Young's. Mr. Harman told Mr. Young he had come to notify him that he would not be responsible to him for the keeping of his wife and that he had with him a notice to that effect. At the request of Harman deponent read the notice and handed a copy of it to Young. Young said to Harman, do yo think I would charge you, with keeping my child? I can keep her, as I have done, I have bread and meat enough. Jacob's wife was present; Mr. Harman asked his wife where the children was. She asked what he wanted with them. He said if he had the children at home he thought she would come too. She said he might do as he pleases he should never have Mary Ann; if he should split open in the back; deponent heard Jane say during the talk that she would not go with him (Jacob) -further saith not." (signed William Keller.) "Sworn and subscribed June 4th 1836 at 4 OC. P.M. Before Jno. Clendenin."

June 4, 1836 -"Isaac Slonaker being sworn deposeth and saith that sometime in March one thousand eight hundred and thirty four he went with Jacob Harman to the house of Peter Young for some hogs Harman had left when he removed from them. As they approached the house, deponent seen some person looking out of the window which he believed to be the wife of Jacob Harman. When they went to the house Mr. Harman attempted to go in but could not. Every door appeared to be fastened. After Harman had called sometime, Mr. Young came out, when the door was instantly fastened behind him. After being there sometime Mr. Harman invited deponent to go with him into the house stating that he would like to the children if he would get them he would take them along with him. They went to the house and found all the doors fastened further saith not." (signed Isaac Slonaker.) "Sworn and subscribed June

4th 1836 before Jno. Clendenin."

April Term 1836 #35 June 4, 1836 -"David Nay appeared and being sworn doth depose and say that he has lived with Jacob Harman from the time he removed in February 1834 from Peter Young's to his own farm in Silver Spring township. All during at that time he has not seen Jane the wife of said Jacob at the house or on the premises of her husband. Deponent further saith that he lived with Harman for some months before him and his wife parted, and that the family appeared to have plenty both to eat and to ware (sic) -further saith not." (signed David Nay.) "Sworn and Subscribed June 4th 1836 Before Jno. Clendenin."

Aug. 6, 1836 -"Cumberland County, Pa. Before me the subscriber a Justice in and for said county personally came David Wolf who being duly sworn according to law doth depose and say that sometime in the latter end of May one thousand eight hundred and thirty four Jacob Harman called on him with a request that he would go with him to the house of his father-in-law Peter Young stating that he wanted to get his children that were living there with their mother. Deponent went with said Harman to Mr. Young's. After some conversation between Harman and his wife (who was then living at her father's) one of the children came to Harman. He asked it, if it would go along with him. It said it would. He then asked for the child's shoes. Harman's wife then came up to him whilst he held the child in his arms and said Jake, you are not going to take the child away and began to strike at him with both her hands. Old Mrs. Young then came and seized the child and pulled it from its father, the mother was striking all the time and continued to strike at, and followed her husband across the house until she put him out. Harman and deponent then went away without any of the children." (signed David Wolf.) "Sworn to and subscribed Augt. 6th A.D. 1836 Jno. Clendenin."

August 8, 1836 -"In the case of the Petition or libel of Jacob Harman to be divorced from the bonds of matrimony entered into with Jane his wife. Now to wit, 8 August 1836 upon due consideration of the premises and due proof having been made of the facts contained in the petition or libel of the said Jacob Herman the Court do hereby sentence and decree that the said Jacob Herman and the said Jane Herman be divorced and separated from the nuptial ties or bonds of matrimony and that the said marriage be and is null and void and that all and any duties rights and claims accruing to either of the said parties at any time heretofore in pursuance of the said marriage shall cease and determine and the said parties shall severally be at liberty to marry again in the like manner as if they had never been married. By the court." (signed John Reed.)

April 11, 1836 -"In the case of the Petition of Jacob Herman for a divorce from his wife Jane Herman. Now, to wit, 11 April 1836 due proof having been made of the service of the subpoena awarded and the said Jane Herman not attending the Court do hereby appoint John Clendenin, Esq. as a commissioner to take testimony on the subject and do fix the second Monday of August next for the final hearing of the case. By the Court."

♦ ♦ ♦

August Term 1836 #38 -May 10, 1836 -"To the Hon. John Reed President Judge of the Court of Common Pleas of the County of Cumberland The petition of Nancy M. Logue by her next friend -Respectfully represents: That she was lawfully joined in wedlock with George Logue on the 4 day of October A.D. 1827 and for the last three years and more the said George Logue has been an habitual drunkard and by his cruel and barbarous treatment and indignities offered to the person of your petitioner has rendered her condition so intolerable and her life so burthensome as to force her to withdraw from his house and family; and your petitioner also represents that the said George Logue has since his intermarriage with your petitioner been guilty of adultery. She therefore prays your Honor to award a subpoena directed to the said George Logue to appear at the next Court of Common Pleas to shew cause why your petitioner should not obtain a divorce from the bond of matrimony." (signed Nancy M. Logue by her next friend Thos. Carothers.) "Cumberland County, Pa. Personally appeared before me a Justice of the Peace in and for said County Nancy M. Logue the above named petitioner who being duly sworn doth depose say that the facts set forth in the foregoing petition are true to the best of her knowledge and belief; and that the said complaint is not made out of levity or by collusion between her and her said husband and for the mere purpose of being freed and separated from each other, but in sincerity and truth for the causes mentioned in her said petition. (signed Nancy M. Logue.) "Sworn and Subscribed the 10th day of May A.D. 1836 Before me." (signed Thos. Trimble.)

June 8, 1836 -"The Commonwealth of Pennsylvania, To George Logue, Greeting: Whereas Nancy M. Logue by her next friend Thos. Carothers has presented her petition to the Hon. John Reed, President Judge of the Court of Common Pleas of Cumberland County which represented that she was lawfully married to George Logue on the 4th day of October A.D. 1827, and for the last three years and more, the said George Logue had been an habitual drunkard, and by his cruel, and barbarous treatment and indignities offered to the person of said petitioner, has rendered her condition so intolerable and her life so burthensome, as to force her to withdraw from his house and family. That the said George Logue has since his intermarriage with petitioner been guilty of adultery; and praying the said Hon. John Reed, President Judge, to award a Subpoena directed to the said George Logue commanding him to appear and answer her petition and shew cause why the said Nancy M. Logue should not obtain a divorce from the bonds of Matrimony. We, therefore, command you the said George Logue, that you be and appear at the next Court of Common Pleas of Cumberland County, to be held at Carlisle on Monday the 8th day of August next, to answer the said petition of the said Nancy Logue. Witness the Hon. John Reed Esq. President Judge, at Carlisle, the 8th day of June in the year of our Lord, one thousand eight Hundred and thirty-six." (signed George Fleming Prothy.) Notation on front of this subpoena "Not to be found in my Bailiwick. So answers, M. Holcomb, Sheff. Sheriff bill $0.18 3/4"

♦ ♦ ♦

August Term 1836 #39 May 24, 1836 -"To the Hon. John Reed President of the Court of Common Pleas of Cumberland County. The petition of Barbara Yohe by her next friend Jacob Gross Respectfully represents that she was lawfully married to Jacob Yohe on the 10th of August 1834 and continued to live with him for two months and that since that time they have been separate and apart from each other. That the said Jacob Yohe hath been guilty of adultery since his intermarriage with the said Barbara. She therefore prays your Honor to award a subpoena to the said Jacob Yohe to appear at the next Court of Common Pleas of said County to be held on the second Monday of August next to answer this petition." (signed Barbara Yohe by her next friend Jacob Gross.) "Cumberland County, Pa. Personally appeared before me a Justice of the Peace in and for said County Barbara Yohe who being duly sworn doth depose and say that the facts set forth in the foregoing petition are true to the best of her knowledge and belief and that the said complaint is not made out of levity or by collusion between her and her said husband and for the mere purpose of being freed and separated from each other, but in sincerity and truth for the causes mentioned in her said petition." (signed by mark Barbara Yohe.) "Sworn and Subscribed the 24 May 1836 Before me" (signed William Irvine.)

June 8, 1836 -"The Commonwealth of Pennsylvania To Jacob Yohe: Greeting: Whereas Barbara Yohe by her next friend Jacob Gross had presented her petition to the Hon. John Reed, Esq. President Judge of the Court of Common Pleas of Cumberland County, which represents that she was lawfully married to Jacob Yohe on the 10th of August 1834, and continued to live with him for two months, and that since that time they have been separate and apart from each other. That the said Jacob Yohe hath been guilty of adultery since his intermarriage with the said Barbara: and praying the said Hon. John Reed, Esq. President Judge to award a subpoena directed to the said Jacob Yohe commanding him to appear and answer her petition and shew cause why the said Barbara Yohe should not obtain a divorce from the bonds of matrimony. We, therefore command you, the said Jacob Yohe, that you be and appear at the next Court of Common Pleas of Cumberland County be to held at Carlisle, on Monday the 8th day of August next, to answer the said petition of the said Barbara Yohe. Witness the Hon. John Reed, Esq. President Judge, at Carlisle, the 8th day of June in the year of our Lord, one thousand eight hundred and thirty six." (signed George Fleming, Prothy.)

Sept. 14, 1836 -"Cumberland County -Jos. Lobaugh, Dep. Sheff. being duly sworn doth depose and say that he served a true copy of the within subpoena on the 15 July 1836 by leaving it with a member of Jacob Yohe at his house." (signed Jos. Lobach.) "Affirmed and Subscribed the 14 Sep. 1836." (signed George Fleming Prothy.)

Sept. 14, 1836 -"Barbara Yohe vs. Jacob Yohe: No. 39 August Term 1836 In the Court of Common Pleas of Cumberland County: Subpoena sur divorce served by copy 15th July, 1836. And now to wit: 14th Sept. 1836 The Court having received due proof of the service of the Subpoena on Jacob Yohe, and he not appearing, the Court appoints John Clendenin, Esquire, a Commissioner to take testimony in support of the facts alleged in the petition, and appoint the second Monday of November next for the final hearing of the case. By the Court."

Sept. 27, 1836 -"Cumberland County, Pa. I George Fleming Prothonotary, the Court of Common Pleas of Cumberland County Do certify the above to be a true copy of the Docket entry of the above case. In testimony whereof I have hereunto subscribed my name and affixed the seal of said Court at Carlisle, the twenty-seventh day of September, A.D. 1836." (signed Geo. Fleming Prothy.)

Nov. 4, 1836 -"Cumberland Co., Pa. Barbara Yohe vs. Jacob Yohe: In the Court of Common Pleas of Cumberland County No. 39 Augt Term 1836: In pursuance of the within commission to take depositions to be used in evidence on the trial of the above cause Personally came before me the subscriber a Justice of the Peace in and for said County Peter Emmerick who being duly sworn doth depose and say that he is well aquainted with Jacob Yohe above named. That said Yohe was married (as deponent was informed by said Yohe) to Barbara Shelly sometime in the summer of one thousand eight hundred and thirty four, that Yohe lived on with his family as before from the time of his marriage until the spring following. During that time he had a certain Polly Walters to keep house for him. Sometime in the winter said Polly had a child born of her body. Yohe told deponent that he was the father of said child. About the last of March or first of April 1835, said Yohe removed with his children and goods to Barbara Shelly's or Yohe's. Some few weeks after (Perhaps the last of May) he rented a house in Hogestown and removed there with his family, from the said Barbara. He came to the house of deponent where said Polly Walters was then living and took to live with him again. They lived together from that time, as deponent has reason to believe like man and wife until they removed from this to the state of Ohio in August last -further saith not." (signed Peter Emmerick.) "Sworn and Subscribed November 4th A.D. 1836" (signed Jno. Clendenin.)

Nov. 17, 1836 -"17th Nov. 1836 -Commission remanded back to Commissioner that fuller evidence be taken by him. By the Court." (signed G. Fleming, Prothy.)

Jan. 7, 1837 -"Cumberland County, Pa. Personally appeared before the subscriber a Justice of the Peace in and for said county David Capp who being sworn doth say that he was well acquainted with Jacob Yohe and Polly Walters his housekeeper. That said Polly lived in deponent's house for sometime, that Yohe visited her after his marriage with Barbara Shelly: and further that he believes they were in the habit of sleeping together during the time they lived together after the said Jacob left his wife. Deponent also further saith that the said Yohe removed to the west last Augt. and took the said Polly Walters with him." (signed David Capp.) "Sworn and Subscribed Jany. 7th A.D. 1837." (signed Before Jno. Clendenin.)

Jan. 7, 1837 -"Cumberland County, Pa. Abraham Bosler appeared before the subscriber and being duly sworn doth depose and say that Jacob Yohe lived sometime in the same house with him that a certain Polly Walters kept house for Yohe, that he believes they were in the habit of sleeping together. There was nothing but a board partition between deponent's room and theirs. They removed to the west together. The time Yohe lived in the house with deponent was after he left his wife." (signed Abm. Bosler.) "Sworn and Subscribed Jany. 7th 1837 Before" (signed Jno. Clendenin.)

Jan. 7, 1837 -"William Bell appeared before the subscriber and being sworn doth depose and that Jacob Yohe lived in the same house with him in Hogestown after he left his wife. That a certain Polly Walter kept house for said Yohe that during the time Yohe lived in said house. He (deponent) believes that the said Jacob and Polly were in the constant habit of sleeping together. He could and did often hear them talking together in their sleeping room adjoining deponent's room." (signed William Bell.) "Sworn and subscribed Jany. 9th 1837 Before" (signed Jno. Clendenin.)

Jan. 12, 1837 -"Now, to wit, 12 Jany. 1837 The Court upon due consideration of the premises and upon the evidence they deem the same sufficient in law to entitle the said Barbara Yohe to be divorced from the bonds of matrimony and the said Court do hereby order and decree that the said Barbara Yohe be and is hereby divorced from the bonds of matrimony existing between her and the said Jacob Yohe and that she the said Barbara be now at liberty to marry again as if she had never been married. By the Court."

◆   ◆   ◆

November Term 1836 #2 -Aug. 8, 1836 -"To the Honourable the Judges of the Court of Common Pleas of Cumberland County. The petition of Jacob Berch respectfully showeth that your Libellant, in the month of March in the year of our Lord one thousand eight hundred and twenty nine was contracted in matrimony and married to a certain Jane Small and from that time untill about three months thereafter, lived and cohabited with her, as her husband, and as such was owned and acknowledged by her, and so deemed and reputed by all his neighbors and acquaintances; and although by the laws of God, as well as by their mutual vows and faith plighted to each other, they were reciprocally bound to that kindness and uniform regard which ought to be inseparable from the marriage state; yet so is, that the said Jane from the month of June in the year of our Lord one thousand eight hundred and twenty nine, hath wilfully and maliciously absented herself from the habitation of this libellant without just or reasonable cause, and such desertion has persisted in for the term of two years and upwards and yet doth continue to absent herself from the said Libellant. Wherefore your Libellant further showing that he is a citizen of this State, and hath resided therein for one whole year and more previous to the filing of this petition prays your Honours that a subpoena shall issue from the said Court directed to the said Jane his wife commanding her to appear at the next Term of the said Court to answer this petition and also that a divorce of the said Court may be given granting this Libellant a divorce from the society, fellowship and company of the said Jane his wife in all time to come and this Libellant from the marriage bond aforesaid, as if he had never been married or as if the said Jane his wife were naturally dead. And this Libellant as in duty bound will pray etc." (signed Jacob Berch in German script.) "Cumberland County, Pa. Personally before the subscriber a Justice of the Peace in and for said county came the within named Jacob Berch, who being sworn according to law doth say, that the facts contained in the within libel are true to the best of his knowledge and belief, and that the same is not made out of levity and by collusion between him and his said wife, and for the mere purpose of being freed and separated from each other, but in sincerity and truth for the causes mentioned in the said libel." (signed in German script by Jacob Berch) "Affirm and subscribed this 8th day of Augt. A.D. 1836 Before me" (signed Robert Snodgrass.)

Aug. 12, 1836 -"Cumberland County, Pa. To Jane Berch Greeting: Whereas Jacob Berch of Cumberland County has presented his petition to the Court of Common Pleas of Cumberland County, which he represented that in the month of March in the year of our Lord one thousand eight hundred and twenty nine he was lawfully married to a certain Jane Small and from that time untill about three months thereafter, lived and co-habited with her, as her husband,

and as such was owned and acknowledged by her and so deemed and reputed by all his neighbours and acquaintances and that the said Jane from the month of June in the year of our Lord one thousand eight hundred and twenty nine hath wilfully and maliciously absented herself from the habitation of the petitioner without just or reasonable cause, and such desertion has persisted on for the term of two years and upwards and yet doth continue to absent herself from the said Petitioner and praying the said Court that a Subpoena be issued from the said Court directed to the said Jane Berch commanding her to appear at the next Term of said Court to answer his petition, and shew cause why the said Jacob Berch should not obtain obtain a divorce from the bonds of matrimony. We therefore command you the said Jane Berch that you be and appear at the next Court of Common Pleas of Cumberland County to be held at Carlisle on Monday the 14th November 1836 to answer the said petition of the said Jacob Berch. Witness the Hon. John Reed President Judge at Carlisle the 12th August 1836." (signed George Fleming, Prothy.)

Nov. 14, 1836 -"Cumberland County S.S. Andrew Young being duly sworn according to law deposeth and says that he served the within subpoena personally on the within named Jane Berch on the 27th day of Septm. A.D. 1836." (signed A. Young.) "Sworn and subscribed 14th Nov. 1836 Before" (signed G. Fleming Prothy.)

Nov. 14, 1836 -"November Term 1836 At a Court of Common Pleas began on Monday the fourteenth day of November Anno Domini one thousand eight hundred and thirty six and held at Carlisle for the County of Cumberland before the Honourable John Reed Esquire President and John Stuart and John Lefever Esquires his associate Judges of the same court and ca inter alia it is thus contained."

Dec. 15, 1836 -Bradeberry -Jacob Berch vs. Biddle -Jane Berch entered 9th August 1836 Subpoena sur Divorce -Returned on oath by Andw. Young Constable served personally on Jane Berch 27th September 1836. 15th December 1836, Henry Zearing Esquire appointed Commissioner to take depositions in this case to be read in evidence at the February Orphan's Court, at which time this case is to be decided: notice to be given according to law. By the Court."

Dec. 22, 1836 -"Cumberland County Pa. I certify that the above is a true copy taken from the records of the Court of Common Pleas of said county. In testimony whereof I have hereunto set my hand and affixed the seal of same Court at Carlisle the twenty second day of December A.D. 1836." (signed G. Fleming, Prothy.)

Dec. 22, 1836 -"Jacob Berch vs. Jane Berch: No. 2 November Term 1836 Sub. sax Divorce. In the case of the Petition of Jacob Berch for a divorce in the Court of Common Pleas of Cumberland County. You will take notice that depositions to be read at the hearing of the above cause, at the Orphan's Court of Cumberland County in February next, will be taken in Shiremanstown, on Saturday the seventh day of January next between the hours of 10 o'clock A.M. and 4 o'clock P.M. of said day, before Henry Zearing Esq. the Commissioner appointed by the court, for that purpose when and where you may attend if you think proper. To Jane Berch Respondent." (signed L.G. Brandebury Attorney for Libellant Decr. 22d 1836.)

Dec. 31, 1836 -"Cumberland County S.S. Personally before the subscriber one of the Justices in and for said County came Andrew Lewis who being duly affirmed according to law doth say that he served a copy of the within notice on the within named Jane Berch on the 28th day of Decr. A.D. 1836." (signed Andrew Lewis.) "Affirmed and subscribed this 31st day of Decr. A.D. 1836 Before me" (signed Henry Zearing.)

Jan. 7, 1837 -"In the pursuance of the above commission to me directed by the Court of Common Pleas of Cumberland County Personally appeared John Megary who deposeth and saith, I reside in Shiremanstown. I lived here about ten or eleven years. I am acquainted with Jacob Berch and Jane Berch the parties in this case. I was present when they were married. As near as I can recollect they were married in March 1829 by the Reverend Simon Drisbauch. They commenced house keeping in this place about the first of April. He paid to me her boarding a weak (sic) or two before they commenced house keeping. They lived together untill about the last of June 1829. A night or two before this she came to my house and told me that she would not stay with him. The question was put to her why she would not stay with him any longer, and she said because he would not let my mother stay, she would not stay either, she left his dwelling soon after this, and went to Harrisburg. She never returned to his house that I know of. Mr. Berch kept her and her mother and her two sisters up untill the time she left him. I saw her soon after he commenced suit for a divorce in Harrisburg. I had a conversation with her. She said she never would go back. She said she would not give him clear for less than five hundred dollars. She said she had not seen him since she left him only once at a camp meeting then she hid herself so he would not get to see her. Jacob Berch owns the property he lives on, he is a day laborer, pretty far advanced in life. He is nearly blind. Jacob is an honest upright man, and further deponent saith not." (signed John Megery.) "Affirmed and Subscribed Jany. 7, 1837 Before me." (signed Henry Zearing Commissioner.)

Jan. 7, 1837 -"At the same time and place also George Berch appeared who deposeth and saith. I live in Shiremanstown. I lived here about fourteen years. I am acquainted with Jane Berch and Jacob Berch the parties to this. Jacob Berch is my brother. They were reputed to be man and wife. I was not present at the wedding but they were married in the Spring of 1829. Her name was Jane Small before she was married. They commenced house keeping in Jacob's own house as soon as John Megary moved out. It was about the first April 1829. Her mother lived with them and sometimes three or four of her sisters were boarding with them. About the beginning of June 1829 I ate my breakfast at home. I went there to work one day when Jacob and I sat down to dinner she said she never would set down to dinner with a half blind man alluding to Jacob her husband. When we were eating supper she said (swearing an oath) that she would stay about two months with him, she would leave him and he would have to pay her boarding for all. She got into a dreadful passion and threw her tea pot against the door. I don't know what she got angry about, unless it was about the meat. He brought ten or twelve lbs. of meat from the butchers, and she threw it on his back because he did not bring salt along. He went then and got salt. Her mother was there and two of her sisters at the same time. Jane left her husband's house sometime in June 1829, her mother and sisters left then too. Jacob was out doing days work when she went away. She went to Harrisburg when she left him. She took about forty dollars worth of his things when she went away. When we were eating supper that time she said she only married a half blind man (meaning Jacob) for his fortune. She said she would as soon live with the devil as with a half blind man. For all I know she was in Harrisburg ever since. I saw her this forenoon. Jacob owns some property in town it's worth about fifteen hundred dollars. Jacob was sued for debts of her contracting in Harrisburg, after she left him. The day after I went to Harrisburg to advertise her for my brother. When I went there Mr. Snavely (a store keeper) told me she had bot (sic) goods of him on her husband's account to the amount of between twenty and thirty dollars. Jacob was sued for it afterwards. I saw the constable serve a summons on Jacob. I was in the Justice's office and saw him pay the Justice. I was frequently in my brother's house and I never saw her there since. And further deponent saith not." (signed in German script by George Berch.) "Affirmed and Subscribed Jany. 7 1837 Before me" (signed Henry Zearing Commissioner.)

Jan. 7, 1837 -"At the same time and place Also appeared Margaret Boyer who deposeth and saith I live in Shiremanstown. I was acquainted with Jacob Berch and Jane Berch his wife. I and my husband and family moved into his house on the first April 1829. We lived upstairs and they lived below. Mrs. Berch's mother and sister lived with Jacob and sometimes one or two others lived with them. I think Jacob and his wife lived together about three months after we moved into the house. She left his home about the last of June for what I know she went to Harrisburg. We lived three weeks in the house with them. As long as we lived there he provided for his house as a man ought have done. The day she left him she was in her garden and I was in ours. She spoke to me across the fence and said I have a mind to leave him, and I said why? She said she knowed, then she said she had no more regard for him than for a negro in the street. She left him that afternoon. I went for water and saw the house empty. I have been in Shiremanstown ever since, I have never seen her here since she left him, and further the deponent saith not." (siged by mark by Margaret Boyer.) "Affirmed and Subscribed this 7th day of January 1837 Before me" (signed Henry Zearing Commissioner.)

Jan. 7, 1837 -"At the same time and place Also appeared Mrs. Frances Whisler who deposeth and saith. I reside in Shiremanstown. I knew Jacob Berch and Jane Berch his wife. They were reputed to be man and wife. I was not at the wedding. I knew they lived together about three months as near as I can recollect. It was in spring of the year. I was over there one afternoon, Jacob was out in the country chopping wood, I saw Mrs. Berch her mother and two sisters. They had a good supper. Short time afterwards I called again, Jacob came in about that time. He then asked for his supper. His wife told him to go to the drawer or cupboard and get it himself. He said he worked hard and wanted a warm supper. She swore he might get it himself. He then said you must have had a good supper this afternoon. His wife said it was none of his business. I thought the treatment he received was bad. I went away. All I seen he provided well. I knew her and her sister Nancy to make very hard expressions about Jacob. Her sister once rolled up her sleeves in presence of Mrs. Berch and swore would take a fight with him. His wife seemed to be delighted with it. Jacob was not present. I and my mother went to Harrisburg sometime after she left her husband. I wanted to see her about some things of mine that she took away. I saw her and her mother at Mr. Peters' and she shewed me two silk dresses and some other things she bought of my brother (John Shardy.) She said she bought the on her husband's account. She seemed glad that she could throw him into debt. She has never lived with him since that I know of and further deponent saith not." (signed Frances Whisler.) "Affirmed and Subscribed Jany. 7th 1837 Before me" (signed Henry Zearing Commissioner.)

Jan. 7, 1837 -"At the same time and place also appeared Sarah Zearing, who deposeth and saith. I live in Shiremanstown. I know Jacob Berch and his wife. I know them reported to be married. I think it was about seven years ago. I was then young. I can't remember it so well. They lived together about three months. Her mother and one of her sisters lived there. I don't recollect the time she left but she has never been here since. I saw her once or twice in Harrisburg since and further deponent saith not." (signed Sarah Zearing.) "Affirmed and Subscribed Jany 7th 1837 Before me"

(signed Henry Zearing, Commissioner.)

Jan. 31, 1837 -"Jacob Berch Libellant vs. Jane Berch: Lib. Sur Divorce No. 2 Nov. Term 1836 In the Court of Common Pleas of Cumberland County -And now to wit: 31st January 1837. The Court having heard and duly considered the evidence on the part of the Libellant, the defendant not having produced any, do adjudge that the complaint of the said Libellant, charged and stated in his said libel, has been fully sustained and proved, and do sentence and decree that the said Jacob Berch the libellant, be, and he is hereby divorced and separated from the nuptial ties or bonds of matrimony with the said Jane Berch the defendant and that the costs be paid by the defendant. By the Court."

♦ ♦ ♦

November Term 1836 #3 July 23, 1836 -"To the Honourable, the Judges of the Court of Common Pleas of Cumberland County. The petition of Mary Susan Robertson by her father and next friend John Clippinger respectfully showeth: That your Libellant on the twenty-sixth day of July in the year of our Lord one thousand eight hundred and thirty one was contracted in matrimony and married to a certain Andrew D. Robertson and from that time untill the seventeenth day of September in the year of our Lord one thousand eight hundred and thirty three lived and cohabited with him as his wife, and as such was owned and acknowledged by him and so deemed and reputed by all her neighbours and acquaintances; and although by the laws of God as well as by their mutual vows and faith plighted to each other they were reciprocally bound to that kindness and uniform regard which ought to be inseparable from the marriage state; yet so it is, that the said Andrew D. Robertson from the seventeenth day of September in the year of our Lord one thousand eight hundred and thirty three hath wilfully and maliciously absented himself from the habitation of this Libellant without a reasonable cause. And such desertion has persisted in for the term of two years and upwards, and yet doth continue to absent himself from the said Libellant. Wherefore your Libellant further showing that she is a Citizen of this State and hath resided therein for one whole year and more previous to the filing of this petition, prays your Honours that a subpoena shall issue from the said Court directed to the said Andrew D. Robertson commanding him to appear at the next Term of the said Court, to answer this petition; and also that a decree of the said Court may be given granting this Libellant a divorce from the society, fellowship and company of the said Andrew D. Robertson in all time to come, and this Libellant from the marriage bond aforesaid as if she had never been married or as if the said Andrew D. Robertson were naturally dead. And this Libellant as in duty bound will ever pray etc." (signed Mary S. Robertson by her father and next friend John Cleppinger.) "Cumberland County S.S.

Personally before the subscriber a Justice of the Peace in and for said County came the within named Mary Susan Robertson, who being duly sworn according to law says that the facts contained in the within libel are true to the best of her knowledge and belief, and that the said complaint is not made out of levity and by collusion between her and her said husband, and for the mere purpose of being freed and separated from each other, but in sincerity and truth for the causes mentioned in the said Libel." (signed Mary S. Robertson.) "Sworn and subscribed this 23d day of July A.D. 1836 Before me" (signed Samuel Davis.)

Aug. 12, 1836 -"Cumberland County, Pa. To Andrew D. Robertson, Greeting: Whereas Mary Susan Robertson has presented her petition to the Court of Common Pleas of Cumberland County, which represents that she was lawfully married to Andrew D. Robertson on the 26th day of July 1831, and from that time until the 17th day of September, 1833, lived and co-habited with him as his wife, that the said Andrew D. Robertson from the said 17th day of Sept. in the year of our Lord 1833, hath wilfully and maliciously absented himself from the habitation of the petitioner without just or reasonable cause, and such desertion has persisted in for the term of two years and upward and yet doth continue to desert himself from the said petitioner; and praying the said Court to award a Subpoena, directed to the said Andrew D. Robertson, commanding him to appear at the next term of said Court to answer this petition etc. We therefore command you, the said Andrew D. Robertson that you be and appear at the next Court of Common Pleas of Cumberland County, to be held at Carlisle, on Monday the fourteenth day of November next, to answer the said petition of the said Mary Susan Robertson. Witness the Honorable John Reed, President of the said Court, at Carlisle the twelfth day of August, A.D. 1836." (signed George Fleming, Prothy.) On front of this subpoena -"Defendant not to be found in my bailiwick. So answers M. Holcomb, Shrff. Return sworn to in open court. Shrff. bill $1.48 3/4."

Nov. 28, 1836 -"Cumberland County S.S. To Andrew D. Robertson Greeting: Whereas Mary Susan Robertson has presented her petition to the Court of Common Pleas of Cumberland County, which represents that she was lawfully married to Andrew D. Robertson, on the 26th day of July 1831, and from that time until the 17th day of September, 1833 lived and co-habited with him as his wife: That the said Andrew D. Robertson from the said 17th day of September, A.D. 1833, hath wilfully and maliciously absented himself from the habitation of the petitioner, without just or reasonable cause, and such desertion has persisted in for the term of two years and upwards and yet doth continue to absent himself from the said petitioner; and praying the said Court to award a Subpoena directed to the said Andrew D. Robertson commanding him to appear at the next term of said Court to answer this petitioner, etc. We therefore command you, the said Andrew D. Robertson, as you were heretofore commanded, that you be and appear at the next Court of Common Pleas of Cumberland County, to be held at Carlisle, on the Second Monday of January next to answer the said petition of the said Mary Susan Robertson. Witness the Hon. John Reed, President of the said Court, at Carlisle, the 28th day of November, A.D. 1836." (signed G. Fleming, Prothy.) On front of this subpoena "Defendant not to be found in my Bailiwick. So answers. M. Holcomb, Shrff. Shrff. bill $1.00."

Jan. 16, 1837 -"The following Interrogations are filed in pursuance of the above rule to be propounded to the witnesses appearing before the above named Commissioners on part of the Libellant viz: First What is your name -your place of residence and how long have you resided there? Second Were you acquainted with Andrew D. Robertson and Mary Susan Robertson (late Mary Susan Clippinger) the above named parties? If yes, do you know if they were married or reputed to be man and wife by their neighbors? Third -Do you know when they were married -where they resided and how long they lived together? Fourth -Do you know if the said Andrew D. Robertson deserted from the said Mary Susan Robertson his wife? If yes, when did he leave her? Fifth -Do you know for what causes or reasons, if any, the said Andrew D. Robertson deserted the said Mary Susan Robertson his wife? If yes, state them at length. Sixth -If the said Andrew D. Robertson deserted his said wife Mary D. Robertson, do you know how long she resided where he left her, and where she resides now? Seventh -Do you know where the said Andrew D. Robertson has been living since? Eight -If the parties were married Do you know if the said Mary Susan Robertson had issue any children to the said Andrew D. Robertson. Ninth -If the said Andrew D. Robertson deserted his said wife Mary Susan Robertson, do you know what her age and condition was at that time? Tenth -Do you know if the said Andrew D. Robertson has provided any maintenance for his said wife Mary Susan Robertson since he deserted her? Eleventh -Do you know of any other facts which would be of advantage to these parties or either of them? If yea, state them at length." (signed January 16th 1837 Lemuel G. Brandebury Attorney for Libellant.)

Feb. 6, 1837 -"State of Pennsylvania Cumberland County -The Commonwealth of Pennsylvania to Jesse Miller, Esquire Washington City Greeting: Mary Susan Robertson by her father and next friend John Clippinger vs. Andrew D. Robertson: No. 3 November Term 1836 in the Court of Common Pleas of Cumberland County Sub. sur Divorce On motion of L. G. Brandebury Esq. the Court grants a rule to take depositions to be read on the hearing of this case at the April Term 1837, and the said Court appoints Jesse Miller Esquire

Washington City, D.C. and any Justices of the Peace of the State of Indiana to be named by Plaintiff commissioners to take depositions their respective residences upon interrogatories to be filed. Know ye that in confidence of your prudence and fidelity we have appointed you and by these presents do give unto you full power and authority in pursuance of a rule entered in the Court of Common Pleas of said County of Cumberland in a certain action of divorce there pending as above stated wherein Mary Susan Robertson by her father and next friend John Clippinger is complainant or Libellant and Andrew D. Robertson is defendant at a certain day and place by you to be appointed, diligently to examine all witnesses upon certain Interrogatories hereto attached, and when you shall have so examined said witness or witnesses, touching the premises and reduced their testimony to writing you are to send the same before us, in our County Court of Common Pleas aforesaid together with the Interrogatories aforesaid and this writ certified under your hand and seal. Witness the Honorable John Reed Esquire President of our said Court at Carlisle, the sixth day of February in the year of our Lord one thousand eight hundred and thirty seven." (signed Geo. Fleming, Prothy.)

Feb. 6, 1837 -"State of Pennsylvania Cumberland County S.S. I George Fleming Prothonotary of the Court of Common Pleas of said County of Cumberland Do certify that the above and foregoing is a true copy of the original Interrogatories filed on part of the Libellant in the case abovementioned and of record in said Court. In testimony whereof I have herunto set my hand and affixed the seal of said court at Carlisle the sixth day of February Anno Domini one thousand eight hundred and thirty seven." (signed Geo. Fleming, Prothy.)

Feb. 22, 1837 -"The execution of this commission appears in certain schedule hereunto annexed paged or numbered from one to five inclusive. Witness my hand at the City of Washington in the District of Columbia this 22d day of Feby A.D. 1837." (signed J. Miller, Commissioner.)

Feb. 6, 1837 -identical document as that directed to Jesse Miller, Esquire was directed to Milner E. Nash, Esquire of Carlisle, Sullivan County, and State of Indiana.

March 6, 1837 -"State of Indiana Sullivan County: The execution of this commission appears in a certain schedule hereunto annexed given under my hand and seal this 6th day of March in the year Eighteen hundred and thirty seven." (signed Milner E. Nash Justice of the Peace.)

Feb. 22, 1837 -"District of Columbia -Deposition of Witness produced sworn and examined on the twenty second day of February in the of our Lord one thousand eight hundred and thirty seven at the office of Milner E. Nash, Esq. in the town of Carlisle, County of Sullivan, and State of Indiana, by virtue of a commission issuing from the Court of Common Pleas of Cumberland County, State of Pennsylvania to Milner E. Nash of Carlisle, Sullivan County, State of Indiana, directed for the examination of witnesses in a certain cause depending in said Court wherein Mary Susan Robertson by her father and next friend John Clippinger is Plaintiff or Libellant and Andrew D. Robertson is platf. -Joseph W. Briggs of the town of Carlisle, Sullivan County and State of Indiana being produced, sworn and examined on behalf of the Plaintiff or Libellant, he deposeth as follows -1st To the first interrogatory on the part of the Plaintiff or Libellant, he deposeth as follows. His name is Joseph W. Briggs; his residence Carlisle, Sullivan County, Ind. and has resided there for near six years. 2nd To the second interrogatory on the part of the plaintiff etc., he deposeth as follows -I have been acquainted with Andrew D. Robertson and Mary Susan Robertson late Mary Susan Clippinger since the year 1829 part of which time they lived in my family as man and wife. 3rd To the third interrogatory on the part of the plaintiff etc. he deposeth as follows -They were married sometime in the month of July 1831 -a few weeks after they were married Robertson came to Carlisle, Ind. and in the spring of 1832 Mrs. Robertson came out also. During the summer and fall they resided part of the time with the family of Dr. Davis and part in the family of Philip Hoover. In November 1832, he moved to my house and resided there untill sometime in September 1833. They lived together from the time they were married in 1831 to Septebr. 1833 except for the short time before mentioned in 1831 and 1832 and their not being together then was occassioned by Robertson's being in the west seeking a place of residence. 4th To the fourth interrogatory on the part of the pltff. he deposeth as follows -Andrew D. Robertson deserted his wife, or rather was compelled to leave her in the month of September 1833. 5th To the fifth Interrogatory on the part of the pltff. he deposeth as follows -On the evening of the 4th of July 1833 one hundred and sixty dollars was stolen from my house, while the family was absent -Robertson appeared very anxious to discover the thief and directed attention to two or three individuals residing in the neighborhood of suspicious characters. His anxiety to fasten guilt upon them, together with some other circumstances, directed suspicion towards him. He was watched closely and it was discovered that he was remitting money of the kind stolen to a gentleman by the name of Zooker in Orange County, N. York. As soon as this was discovered I charged him with having stolen the money -which after some considerable hesitation he confessed -and gave as an excuse for his so doing that he was afraid Zooker would put into execution a threat he had made sometime before of exposing Robertson's conduct while living in the state of New York to his wife's friends, unless he would send him a certain amount of money -and that he could not get the money in any other way than by stealing it, in time to prevent the disclosure. A State's Warrant was issued upon the affidavit of John Gauman one of those suspected, for his apprehension, but he made his escape before it could be served by the office in whose hands it was placed. This was the only reason of his leaving his wife. 6th To the Sixth Interrogatory on the part of the plaintiff he deposeth as follows -after he left his wife, she resided with me untill the spring of 1835 when she returned to her father's family in Cumberland County Pennsylvania, where she has since resided. 7th To the 7th Interogatory on the part of the plaintiff he deposeth as follows -that said Robertson has resided somewhere in the northern part of Illinois -the precise place I can not exactly tell. 8th To the 8th Interrogatory on the part of the plaintiff he deposeth as follows -Mrs. Robertson had no issue by her husband. 9th To the 9th Interrogatory on the part of the plaintiff he deposeth as follows -When he left her, she was between eighteen and nineteen years of age. 10th To the 10th Interrogatory on the part of the plaintiff he deposeth as follows. At the time Robertson left his wife, she was entirely dependent for support upon her friends and I believe still remains. I do not know and have not heard of his providing any maintenance for her since he left her. 11th To the eleventh Interrogatory on the part of the plaintiff he deposeth as follows -after the statute of Limitations had barred a prosecution for the offence -which was in the fall of 1835 -Robertson returned to the place and remained there for a few hours. I saw him and conversed with him respecting his wife. He told me that he had treated her so badly that he never expected to live with her again, that if she should get a divorce he would be perfectly satisfied with it. He came here then for the purpose of seeing her, but as she had then returned to her father's in Pennsylvania, he would not look after her any more. I asked him if he would provide in any way for her support, he said he would have no objections to doing so if he ever expected to live with her again -but that as he never would see her, he should not. Since his leaving then I have not heard anything of him." (signed Joseph W. Briggs.) "State of Indiana -Sullivan County: Personally appeared before the subscriber a Justice of the Peace within and for said County Joseph W. Briggs. Reasonable notice having been given him and after having taken an oath to make true answers to all such questions as shall be asked upon the interrogations annexed to the Commission without favour or affection to either party and therein to speak the truth the whole truth and nothing but the truth subscribed his name to the above answers this 6th day of March 1837 Before me." (signed Milner E. Nash, J.P.)

March 6, 1837 -"John H. Eaton of the town of Carlisle in Sullivan County State of Indiana being produced sworn and examined on behalf of the Plaintiff or libellant. He deposeth as follows. 1st To the first interrogatory on the part of the Plaintiff or Libellant he deposeth as follows. My name is John H. Eaton my place of residence is in the town of Carlisle in Sullivan County State of Indiana in which place I have resided some little more than five years. 2nd To the second interrogatory on the part of the Plaintiff or Libellant he deposeth as follows -I was acquainted with a man called A.D. Robertson and also with a woman by the name of Susan Robertson who passed for his wife. I know nothing in relation to their being married only from information. But I know they were reputed man and wife by their neighbors. 3rd To the third interrogatory on the part of the Plaintiff or Libellant he deposeth as follows -I do not know when they were married nor where they resided at that time but they resided together in Carlisle Indiana upwards of one year. 4th To the fourth interrogatory on the part of the Plaintiff or Libellant he deposeth as follows -On the 17th day on night of September 1833 the said A.D. Robertson deserted or rather was compelled to leave his wife to prevent being apprehended by virtue of a State's Warrant which was then in the hands of an officer charging him with Larceny. 5th to the fifth interrogatory on the part of the Plaintiff or Libellant he deposeth as follows -I know of no other reasons for his deserting his wife Susan Robertson than the reason stated in the previous answer. 6th To the sixth interrogatory on the part of the Plaintiff or Libellant he deposeth as follows -the said Mary Susan Robertson resided in Carlisle, Indiana from the time the said A.D. Robertson (her husband) left her in September 1833 till in the spring or summer following. Her place of residence since from information is in Pennsylvania. 7th To the seventh interrogatory on the part of the Plaintiff or Libellant he deposeth as follows -I do not know where he has resided. 8th To the eighth interrogatory on the part of the Plaintiff or Libellant he deposeth as follows -From information they were married but the said Mary Susan Robertson had no issue to the said A.D. Robertson or any other person to my knowledge. 9th To the ninth interrogatory on the part of the Plaintiff or Libellant he deposeth as follows -I know not what her age and condition was at the time her husband A.D. Robertson deserted her. 10th To the tenth interrogatory on the part of the Plaintiff or Libellant he deposeth as follows -The said A.D. Robertson has made no provision for the maintenance of his wife Mary Susan Robertson since he deserted her that I know of. 11th To the eleventh interrogatory on the part of the Plaintiff or Libellant he deposeth -I known of no other facts that would be of any advantage to either or both parties." (signed John H. Eaton.) "State of Indiana Sullivan County: Personally appeared before the subscriber a Justice of the Peace within and for said County John H. Eaton (reasonable notice having been given him) and after taking an oath to make true answers to all such questions as shall be asked upon the interrogatories annexed to the Commission hereto attached without favour or affection to either party and therein to speak the truth the whole truth and nothing but truth subscribed his name to the above answers this 6th day of March A.D. 1837 Before me" (signed Milner E. Nash, J.P.)

March 6, 1837 -"Philip Hoover of the town of Carlisle in Sullivan County and State of Indiana being produced sworn and examined on behalf of the Plaintiff or Libellant. He deposeth as follows, to wit: 1st To the first interrogatory on the part of the Plaintiff or Libellant He deposeth as follows My name is Philip Hoover. I reside in Carlisle in the State of Indiana in which place I have resided ever since the fall of 1819 (the time of being absent on business excepted.) 2nd To the second interrogatory on the part of the plaintiff or Libellant -He deposeth as follows -I was acquainted with Andrew D. Robertson and Mary Susan Robertson while they lived in Carlisle Indiana also with the said Mary Susan wife of the said Andrew D. Robertson when she resided as a child with her father in Pennsylvania. As to the facts of Andrew D. Robertson and the said Mary Susan Robertson (late Mary Susan Clipinger) being married I know nothing only from information but I know they we reputed man and wife by their neighbors. 3rd To the third interrogatory on the part of the Plaintiff or Libellant He deposeth as follows -If they were married, where they resided at that time and how long they lived together I know not. 4th To the fourth interrogatory on the part of the Plaintiff or Libellant He deposeth as follows -I know the said Andrew D. Robertson deserted from the said Mary Susan Robertson his wife in the fall of 1833. 5th To the fifth interrogatory on the part of the plaintiff or Libellant He deposeth as follows -I know of no causes of the said Andrew D. Robertson, deserting his wife Mary Susan Robertson only from information. 6th To the sixth interrogatory on the part of the Plaintiff or libellant He deposeth as follows -The said Mary Susan Robertson resided in Carlisle, Indiana when her husband Andrew D. Robertson deserted her and when she left that place and for some time before I was absent from home. Consequently I cannot tell how long she remained there. I understood she has resided since at her father's in Pennsylvania. 7th To the seventh interrogatory on the part of the Plaintiff or Libellant He deposeth as follows -I understand the said Andrew D. Robertson has been living since he deserted his wife at Galena in the State of Illinois. 8th To the eighth interrogatory on the part of the Plaintiff or Libellant He deposeth as follows -If the parties were married I know of no issue any children of the said Mary Susan Robertson to the said Andrew D. Robertson. 9th To the ninth interrogatory on the part of the Plaintiff or Libellant He deposeth as follows -Where the said Andrew D. Robertson deserted his wife Mary Susan Robertson I know nothing in regard to her age and condition. 10th To the tenth interrogatory on the part of the Plaintiff or Libellant He deposeth as follows -I know of no provision made by the said

Andrew D. Robertson for his wife's maintenance since he left her except a few school accounts he left her and they were small. 11th To the eleventh interrogatory on the part of the Plaintiff or Libellant He deposeth as follows -I know of no other facts which would be of advantage to the parties or either of them." (signed Philip Hoover.) "State of Indiana Sullivan County Sct: Personally appeared before the subscriber a Justice of the Peace within and for said County Philip Hoover (reasonable notice having been given him) and after taking an oath to make a true answer to all such questions as shall be asked upon the interrogatories annexed to the Commission hereto attached without favour or affection to either party and therein to speak the truth the whole truth and nothing but the truth subscribed his name to the above answers this 6th day of March A.D. 1837 before me" (signed Milner E. Nash J.P.S.C.)

Feb. 22, 1837 -"District of Columbia -Deposition of Witnesses produced sworn and examined on the twenty second day of February in the year of our Lord one thousand eight hundred and thirty seven at the house of Joseph Harbaugh in the city of Washington and District of Columbia by virtue of a Commission issuing from the Court of Common Pleas of Cumberland County in the state of Pennsylvania to Jesse Miller, Esquire, directed, for the examination of witnesses in a certain cause depending in said Court wherein Mary Susan Robertson by her father and next friend John Clippinger is Plaintiff or Libellant and Andrew D. Robertson is defendant as follows to wit: John W. Davis being produced sworn and examined on behalf of the Plaintiff or Libellant deposeth as follows: 1st To the first interrogatory on the part of the Plaintiff he deposeth as follows -My name is John W. Davis. My place of residence is Carlisle, Sullivan County State of Indiana at which place I have lived nearly fourteen years with the exception of a few months in the year one thousand eight hundred and twenty six. 2nd To the second interrogatory on the part of the Plaintiff or Libellant he deposeth as follows -I have been acquainted with Andrew D. Robertson and Mary Susan Robertson late Mary Susan Clippinger. The former about five or six years, the latter for about sixteen or eighteen years. I was not present at their marriage, but have no doubt they were married. They lived together as man and wife for a period of between one and two years to my knowledge and they were reputed to be man and wife by their neighbors. 3rd To the third interrogatory on the part of the Plaintiff or Libellant he deposeth as follows: I do not know positively when they were married but believe it was in the year one thousand eight hundred and thirty one. Andrew D. Robertson moved to Carlisle, Indiana some few months after their marriage. To the best of my recollections in the summer of the year one thousand eight hundred and thirty two Mrs. Mary Susan Robertson his wife came also to reside at Carlisle aforesaid and they lived at that place together until about the month of September one thousand eight hundred and thirty three. 4th To the fourth interrogatory on the part of the plaintiff or Libellant he deposeth as follows -Andrew D. Robertson abandoned his wife Mary S. Robertson and his residence at Carlisle, Indiana in a clandestine manner about the month of September in the year one thousand eight hundred and thirty three. 5th To the fifth interrogatory on the part of the Plaintiff or Libellant he deposeth as follows -About the month of July one thousand eight hundred and thirty three Andrew D. Robertson was suspected of having stolen some money from Briggs and Clippinger his brothers-in-law (merchants) of Carlisle aforesaid. The amount of money so stolen I understand was about one hundred and sixty dollars and had been taken about the month of April or May one thousand eight hundred and thirty three. The suspicions against Andrew D. Robertson were confirmed by his remitting money of the description of that which had been stolen through the Post Office at Carlisle aforesaid at which place I was then Post Master. After Mr. Briggs, myself and one or two others had satisfied ourselves that a certain letter put into my hands as Post Master by the said Andrew D. Robertson to be mailed about the month of July one thousand eight hundred and thirty three contained a part of the money that had been stolen. Mr. Briggs as I understood informed the said Andrew D. Robertson of the fact and that there was no doubt in the minds of those who examined the letter but that he Robertson had stolen the money and that the only means left him to convince us of his innocence was to open the letter and exhibit the contents to shew that they did not correspond with any part of the stolen money. The said Andrew D. Robertson as I was informed and believe then confessed that he had stolen the money and gave Mr. Briggs an order to me as Post Master to deliver to him (Briggs) the aforesaid letter, which order was delivered to me and the letter was given to Briggs. In a few weeks after this discovery a warrant was issued at the insistence of one John Gannan to arrest the said Andrew D. Robertson on a charge of Larceny for stealing the said money but before the execution of the warrant Robertson run away leaving his wife Mary Susan Robertson with Mr. Briggs her brother-in-law. 6th To the sixth interrogatory on the part of the Plaintiff or Libellant he deposeth as follows -Mrs. Mary Susan Robertson remained at Carlisle aforesaid to the best of my recollection between one and two years after her husband left her. She now resides with her father John Clippinger near Shippensburg in Penna. 7th To the seventh interrogatory on the part of the Plaintiff or Libellant he deposeth as follows -I do not know where the said Andrew D. Robertson has been living since he run away from Carlisle in Indiana but have heard within the last year that a man answering to his description was living at Galena in Illinois. 8th To the Eighth interrogatory on the part of the Plaintiff or Libellant he deposeth as follows -Mrs. Mary Susan Robertson aforesaid has never had any child or children to my knowledge. 9th To the Ninth interrogatory on the part of the Plaintiff or Libellant he deposeth as follows -At the time the said Andrew D. Robertson abandoned his wife Mary Susan Robertson her age was about eighteen or nineteen years. Her condition so far as I know a dependent one on her friends though enjoying good health. 10th To the tenth interrogatory on the part of the plaintiff or Libellant he deposeth I know of no maintenance provided by the said Andrew D. Robertson for said wife Mary Susan Robertson since he left her. 11th To the Eleventh interrogatory on the part of the Plaintiff or Libellant he deposeth as follows -I know of no other facts than those above stated which I believe material to the rightful decision of the case or that would be of advantage to either of the said parties. I may not be strictly correct as to dates in the foregoing answer having no memorandums with me to refresh my recollections or memory." (signed Jno. W. Davis.) Test. (J. Miller Commr.)

March 18, 1837 -"Carlisle, Indiana 18th March 1837 Mr. George Fleming, Sir enclosed you will find the Commission directed to me authorizing me to take depositions to be read in evidence in a certain case now pending in your Court wherein Mary Susan Robertson by her father and next friend John Clipinger is plaintiff or Libellant and Andrew D. Robertson is defendant. The depositions required are attached to the Commission all of which I would have mailed at an earlier period but was delayed in consequence of bring forward some of the deponents they being absent. Yours Respectfully" (signed M.E. Nash, J.P.S.C.) Addressed to George Fleming Prothonotory Carlisle Cumberland County, Pennsylvania.

April 10, 1837 -"Mary Susan Robertson by her father and next friend John Clippinger vs. Andrew D. Robertson: No. 3 November Term 1836 Sub. sur Divorce in the Court of Common Pleas of Cumberland County -And now to wit this tenth day of April in the year one thousand eight hundred and thirty seven, the Court having heard and duly considered the evidence, on the part of the Libellant, the defendant not having produced any nor appeared to answer the complaint, and it being made to appear to the Court that a subpoena and an alias subpoena were issued and returned, and notice to the defendant published according to the Act of Assembly in such cases made and provided, do adjudge that the complaint of the said Libellant charged and stated in her said Libel, has been fully sustained and proved, and do sentence and decree that the said Mary Susan Robertson the Libellant be, and she is hereby divorced and separated from the nuptial ties or bonds of matrimony with the said Andrew D. Robertson the defendant; and that the costs be paid by the defendant. By the Court." (signed John Reed.)

◆   ◆   ◆

November Term 1836 # 4 -August 4, 1836 -"To the Honorable the

Judges of the Court of Common Pleas of Cumberland County -The libel of Elizabeth Hostler by her next friend Robert Moore -Respectfully sheweth -That your libellant on the second day of October 1821 was contracted in matrimony and married to a certain John Hostler and from that time until __ day of November 1833 -lived and cohabited with the said Elizabeth as wife and as such was owned and acknowledged by him and so deemed and reputed by her acquaintances and neighbors. And although by the laws of God as well as by their mutual vows and faith plighted to each other they were bound to that uniform constancy and regard which ought to be inseparable from the marriage state, yet so it is that the said John Hostler from the __ day of November in the year 1833 hath wilfully and maliciously deserted and absented himself from the habitation of this Libellant without any just and reasonable cause and such desertion hath persisted in for two years and upwards and yet doth continue to absent himself from said Libellant. Wherefore your Libellent further shewing that she is a citizen of the state of Penna. and hath resided therein for upwards of one whole year previous to filing this her Libel prays your honors that a subpoena may issue forth to summon the said John Hostler to appear in this Honl. Court at November term next to answer the complaint aforesaid. And also that a decree of this honl. court may be made for the divorcing of him the said John Hostler from the society fellowship and company of this libellant in all time to come and her this Libellant from the marriage bond aforesaid as if she had never been married or as if the said John Hostler were naturally dead. And this Libellant will pray." (signed by mark Elizabeth Hostler.) By her next friend (signed R. Moore senr.) "The above named Elizabeth Hostler being duly sworn says the facts contained in the above Libel are true to the best of her knowledge and belief and that the said complaint is not made out of levity and collusion between her and her said husband and for the mere purpose of being freed and separated from each other but in sincerity and truth for the causes mentioned in said libel. Sworn before me this 4th day of August 1836." (signed Jacob? Lynn?) (Note -signature is difficult to read.)

August 12, 1836 -"Cumberland County, Pa. To John Hostler Greeting -Whereas Elizabeth Hostler has presented to the Court of Common Pleas of Cumberland County her petition, which represented, That on the second day of October 1821 was was married to a certain John Hostler, and from that time until the __ day of November, 1833, she lived and cohabited with him as his wife, and as such was owned and acknowledged by him: That the said John Hostler from the __ day of November in the year 1833, hath wilfully and maliciously deserted and absented himself from the habitation of the petitioner without any just and reasonable cause, and such desertion hath persisted in for two years and upwards, and yet doth continue to absent himself from said petitioner, and praying the Court to award a subpoena directed to the said John Hostler, commanding him to appear at the next term of said court, to answer the complaint aforesaid. We therefore command you the said John Hostler that you be and appear at the next Court of Common Pleas of Cumberland County, to be held at Carlisle, on Monday the fourteenth day of November next, to answer the petition of the said Elizabeth Hostler. Witness the Honorable John Reed president of the said Court, at Carlisle, the twelfth day of August, A.D. 1836." (signed George Fleming, Prothy.)

Nov. 15, 1836 -"Not to be found in my Bailiwick, so answers M. Holcomb, Sheff. Sheff's fee $1.108 affidavit of return made in open court. Alias subpoena awarded by the court 15th Nov. 1836."

Nov. 28, 1836 -"Cumberland County, Pa. -To John Hostler Greeting -Whereas Elizabeth Hostler, has presented to the Court of Common Pleas of Cumberland County, her petition, which represents that on the second day of October, 1821, she was married to a certain John Hostler, and from that time until the ___ day of November, 1833, she lived and cohabited with him as his wife, and as such was owned and acknowledged by him: That the said John Hostler from the ___ day of November, in the year 1833, hath wilfully and maliciously deserted and absented himself from the habitation of the petitioner without any just and reasonable cause, and such desertion hath persisted in for two years and upwards, and yet doth continue to absent himself from said Petitioner, and praying the Court to award a subpoena directed to the said John Hostler, commanding him to appear at the next term of said Court, to answer the complaint aforesaid. We therefore command you the said John Hostler, as we have heretofore commanded you, that you be and appear at the next Court of Common Pleas of Cumberland County, to be held at Carlisle on the second Monday of January next, to answer the petition of the said Elizabeth Hostler, Witness the Hon. John Reed, president of the said Court at Carlisle, the 28th day of November, A.D. 1836." (signed G. Fleming, Prothy.)

Jan. 31, 1837 -"Defendant not to be found in my Bailiwick. So answers M. Holcomb, Shrff. Shrff.'s fee $1.00. Return sworn to in open court 31st Jany. 1837. Attest G. Fleming, Prothy."

April 10, 1837 -"Cumberland County, Pa. Personally appeared before me the subscriber a Justice of the Peace in and for said County Jacob Faust who being duly sworn according to law deposeth and saith that he was personally acquainted with John Hostler the husband of Elizabeth Hostler and that he knows that the said John Hostler has absented himself from the said Elizabeth for upwards of three years last past and that he has totally neglected and deserted her said Elizabeth for and during that time -and left her to provide for herself. Deponent knows no just cause for said Hostler's desertion of his wife but believes he was not a very well doing man. Deponent further states that he knew said Hostler to have left two of his children with the said Elizabeth who has been obliged to support them without any assistance from him. Sworn and subscribed to this 10th day of April 1837." (signed J.S. Faust.) "Sworn to and subscribed the 10th day of April A.D. 1837 Before" (signed Robert Snodgrass.)

April 10, 1837 -"Cumberland County, Pa. Personally appeared before me the subscriber a Justice of the Peace in and for said County Jacob Wetzel who being duly sworn according to law deposeth and saith that he was personally acquainted with John Hostler husband of Elizabeth Hostler that he was not a well doing man and that more than three years ago he left his home and the said Elizabeth and has never returned to the same nor held any communciation with her since his going away. Said Hostler left two children for his wife Elizabeth to support and some debts which she has since paid. He had no just cause for deserting his wife having always been treated kindly by her so far as deponent had opportunity to observe. Deponent was frequently at the house of said Hostler. Sworn and subscribed this 10th day of April 1837." (signed Jacob Wetzel.) "Sworn to and subscribed the 10th day of April A.D. 1837, Before" (signed Robert Snodgrass.)

April 10, 1837 -"Elizabeth Hostler by her next friend R. Moore vs. John Hostler: In the Court of Common Pleas of Cumberland County -And now the tenth day of April A.D. 1837 the Examiner Robert Snodgrass, Esqr. having returned to the Court hear the depositions of witnesses taken before him on the part of the Libellant and the same being read and heard by the Court and the Court after mature and solemn deliberation being satisfied therewith and proclamation being duly made for the Respondent to come forth and he not appearing, the Court do order adjudge and decree that the said Elizabeth Hostler the libellant be divorced and separated from the bond of matrimony contracted with the said John Hostler the Respondent and that all and every the duties rights and claims accruing to either of the parties by reason of said marriage shall henceforth cease and determine and the said parties be severally at liberty to marry again in like manner as if they never had been married. By the Court. Attest." (signed John Reed.)

♦ ♦ ♦

November Term #30 1836 -Sept. 8, 1836 -"To the Hon. John Reed President of the Court of Common Pleas of Cumberland County -The petition of Ann Bowers by her next friend Jonas Rupp Respectfully Represents that she was lawfully married to Gabriel Bower on the 20 Novr. 1813 and continued to live and cohabit with him as his wife for several years until the year 1828 in the month of October when the said Gabriel Bower did wilfully and maliciously desert your said petitioner the said Ann Bower and absent himself from her habitation without any reasonable cause and has ever since continued to be absent from her habitation without any reasonable cause. She therefore prays your Honors to award a subpoena directed to the said Gabriel Bower to appear at the next Court of Common Pleas to answer this petition and shew cause if any he hath why the said Ann Bower should not be divorced from the bonds of matrimony." (signed Ann Bower by her next friend Jonas Rupp.) "Cumberland County, Pa. -Personally appeared before me a Justice of the Peace in and for said County Ann Bower who being duly affirmed and Jonas Rupp who being duly affirmed do depose and say that the facts set forth in the above petition are true to the best of their knowledge and belief and that the said complaint is not made out of levity or by collusion between the said Ann and her said husband and for the mere purpose of being freed and separated from each other, but in sincerity and truth for the causes mentioned in the said petition." (signed Ann Bower and Jonas Rupp.) "Affirmed and subscribed the 8th Sep 1836 Before me." (signed William Irvine.)

Sept. 26, 1836 -"Cumberland County -The Commonwealth of Pennsylvania to Gabriel Bower Greeting -Whereas Ann Bower by her next friend Jonas Rupp has presented her petition to the Honorable John Reed Esquire President Judge of the Court of Common Pleas of Cumberland County which represents that she was lawfully married to Gabriel Bower on the 20th November 1813 and continued to live and cohabit with him as his wife for several years untill the year 1828 in the month of October when the said Gabriel Bower did wilfully and maliciously desert the said petitioner the said Ann Bower and absent himself from the habitation without any reasonable cause. And praying the said Honorable John Reed Esq. President Judge to award a Subpoena directed to the said Daniel (sic) Bower commanding him to appear and answer her petition at the next Court of Common Pleas and shew cause if any he hath why the said Ann Bower should not be divorced from the bonds of matrimony. We therefore command you the said Daniel (sic) Bower that you be and appear at the next Court of Common Pleas of Cumberland County to be held at Carlisle on Monday the fourteenth day of November next, to answer the Petition of the said Ann Bower. Witness the Honorable John Reed, Esq. President Judge at Carlisle the twenty sixth day of September in the year of our Lord one thousand eight hundred and thirty six." (signed G. Fleming, Prothy.) Written on the front "Gabriel Bower not to be found in my Bailiwick. So answers, M. Holcomb, Shff. Shff's fee $0.18 3/4."

June 26, 1837 -"Cumberland County -The Commonwealth of Pennsylvania to Gabriel Bower Greeting -Whereas Ann Bower by her next friend Jonas Rupp presented her petition to the Honorable John Reed Esq. President Judge of the Court of Common Pleas of the said County of Cumberland at November Term 1836 -representing that she was lawfully married to Gabriel Bower on the twentieth day of November A.D. one thousand eight hundred and thirteen, and continued to live and cohabit with him as his wife for several years until the year 1828, in the month of October, when the said Gabriel Bower did wilfully and maliciously desert the said petitioner Ann Bower, and absent himself from her habitation without any reasonable cause. And praying the Honorable John Reed Esquire President Judge as aforesaid to award a Subpoena directed to the said Daniel (sic) Bower commanding him to appear and answer her petition at the next Court of Common Pleas, and shew cause if any he hath why the said Ann Bower should not be divorced from the bonds of matrimony. We therefore command you, as you were heretofore commanded, that you the said Daniel (sic) Bower be and appear at the next Court of Common Pleas of the said County of Cumberland to be held at Carlisle on Monday the fourteenth day of August next to answer the said Petition of Ann Bower. Witness the Honorable John Reed Esquire at Carlisle the twenty sixth day of June Anno Domini one thousand Eight hundred and thirty seven." (signed Geo. Fleming Prothy.) On front of this page -"Not to be found in my Bailiwick. So answers M. Holcomb Shff. Shff. fee $1.00"

Nov. 28, 1837 -"Ann Bower vs. Gabriel Bower: In the Court of Common Pleas of Cumberland County No. 30 Nov. Term 1836 -Now to wit 28th Novr. 1837 A subpoena and alias Subpoena having issued in this case which were returned "not to be found in my bailiwick" and due publication made according to law, the Court do hereby appoint Henry Zearing Esq. to take the testimony of witnesses to be read upon the final hearing of this case on the second Monday of January next, By the Court."

Nov. 29, 1837 -"Cumberland County, s.s. -I George Fleming Prothonotary of the Court of Common Pleas of Cumberland County Do certify that the above is a true copy of a Decree of the Court of Common Pleas in the above mentioned case. In testimony whereof I have hereunto subscribed my name, and affixed the seal of said Court at Carlisle, this twenty-ninth day of November A.D. 1837." (signed Geo. Fleming Prothy.)

Dec. 15, 1837 -"Cumberland County, S.S. -In pursuance of the above rule personally appeared before me one of the Justices of the Peace in and for the said County Daniel Sherban Senr. who being duly affirmed according to Law doth depose and say -That I have known Mrs. Ann Bower the libellant in this case, about thirty years. She is the daughter of Jonas Rupp decd. She is married to Gabriel Bower about fourteen years. Mr. Bower got with her a fortune of about five thousand dollars, he has since spent the whole of it, and afterwards about nine years since he abandoned her, leaving her with two small children. I was sent for one time soon after he left her. Her smallest child was sick, and then died, about that time her effects were seized by a constable and sold. She appeared to be in great want, and shortly afterwards removed to her mother where she remained till last April ever since. He, Mr. Bower, never contributed to her support ever since to the best of my knowledge. He took to drinking soon after his marriage and was an habitual drunkard ever since to the last account I have of him which is about four years and further saith not." (signed Daniel Sherban.) "Affirmed and subscribed Before me Dec. 15, 1837" (signed Henry Zearing.)

Dec. 15, 1837 -"In pursuance of the above rule etc. also appeared before me one of the Justices of the Peace in and for the said County Abraham Warner who being duly affirmed according to Law, doth depose and say, That I know Mrs. Ann Bower. I was present at the wedding when she was married to Mr. Gabriel Bower. She got married about fourteen years ago. He has deserted and abandoned her about nine years since. Soon after her effects were seized and sold to the best of my knowledge, she then removed to her Mother where she lived ever since, until last spring. Mr. Bower has never since contributed any to her support to the best of my knowledge, and further saith not." (signed in German script by Abraham Warner.) "Affirmed and subscribed December 15, 1837 Before me" (signed by Henry Zearing.)

Dec. 15, 1837 -"In pursuance of the above rule etc. also appeared before me Jacob Rupp Esquire, who being duly affirmed according to Law deposeth and saith, That I know Mrs. Anne Bower. I was present when she was intermarried to Gabriel Bower. She was married about fourteen years. Bower has abandoned her about eight or nine years since, soon after he left her her effects were sold. To the best of my knowledge, she then removed to her Mother, where she lived ever since untill the death of her Mother and sometime afterwards in her Mother's house until last March. She has been dealing in my store for about four years in her own name. I know her to take in work to sustain her, a support. To the best of my knowledge she never received any support from G. Bower for her or her child, since he left her. I know that G. Bower got to drinking to excess shortly after he was married, and remained a drunkard ever since to the last knowledge I had of him, and further saith not." (signed Jacob Rupp.) "Affirmed and Subscribed Decr. 15, 1837 Before me." (signed Henry Zearing.) "I do certify that the above depositions were this day taken at my office, in Shiremanstown, the fifteenth day of December, Anno Domini 1837." (signed Henry Zearing.)

Jan. 8, 1838 -"Ann Bower vs. Gab. Bower: Now to wit, 8th Jany. 1838 -The Court having heard the proof taken in this case by Henry Zearing the commissioner appointed for the purpose and satisfied that it is sufficient in law to entitle the said Ann Bower to be divorced from her said Husband and they do hereby decree that the said Ann Bower be and she is hereby divorced from the bonds of matrimony entered into with Gabriel Bower and that she be at full liberty to marry again as though she had never been married and in all particulars that she be free and clear from all matrimonial obligations to the said Gabriel Bower. By the Court."

♦ ♦ ♦

January Term 1836 #5 -Sept. 24, 1836 -"To the Honorable the Judges of the Court of Common Pleas of Cumberland County -The Libel of Catharine Hippel of the Township of North Middleton in the county aforesaid by George Simon her father and next friend -Respectfully sheweth -That your Libellant on the nineteenth day of September in the year of our Lord one thousand eight hundred and thirty four was contracted in matrimony and married to a certain Henry Hippel, who the day following the said marriage deserted and left her after having remained and cohabited with her but one night. And although by the laws of God as well as by their mutual vows and faith plighted to each other they were bound to that uniform constancy and regard which ought to be inseparable from the marriage state; yet so it is that the said Henry Hippel from the day aforesaid to wit the twentieth day of September in the year aforesaid hath wilfully and maliciously deserted and absented himself from the habitation of this Libellant without any just or reasonable cause. And such desertion hath persisted in for the term of two years and upwards, and yet doth continue to absent himself from the said Libellant. Wherefore your Libellant further sheweth that she is a citizen of Pennsylvania and has resided therein for upwards of one whole year previous to the filing of this her Libel. Your Libellant therefore prays your Honors that a subpoena may issue forth to summon the said Henry Hippel to appear in this Honorable court at January Term next to answer the complaint aforesaid and also that a divorce of this Honorable court may be made for the divorcing of him the said Henry from the society, fellowship and company of this Libellant in all time to come, and of her this Libellant from the marriage bond aforesaid as if she had never been married or as if the said Henry were naturally dead. And this Libellant etc. Catherine Hippel by her father and next friend." (signed in German script by George Simon.) "The above named Catharine Hippel being duly affirmed as the law directs doth say that the facts contained in the above libel are true the best of her knowledge and belief and that the said complaint is not made out of levity and collusion between her and the said Henry Hippel and for the mere purpose of being freed and separated from each other, but in sincerity and truth, for the causes mentioned in the said Libel. Affirmed and subscribed before me one of the Justices of the Peace in and for the Borough of Carlisle on this 24th day of Sept. A.D. 1836." (signed Isaac Good and by mark Catherine Hippel.)

Nov. 28, 1836 -"Cumberland County -To Henry Hippel, Greeting Whereas Catharine Hippel, by her father and next friend Geo. Simon, has presented her petition to the Court of Common Pleas of Cumberland County which represents that on the nineteenth day of September in the year of our Lord 1834, was contracted in matrimony to a certain Henry Hippel, who the day following the said marriage deserted and left her after having remained and co-habited with her but one night. That the said Henry Hippel from the day aforesaid, hath wilfully and maliciously deserted and absented himself from the habitation of the petitioner, without just or reasonable cause, and such desertion has persisted in for the term of two years and upwards, and yet doth continue to absent himself from the said Petitioner; and praying the said Court to award a subpoena directed to the said Henry Hippel commanding him to appear at the next term of the said Court to answer this petitioner etc. We therefore command you, the said Henry Hippel that you be and appear at the next Court of Common Pleas of Cumberland County, to be held at Carlisle on the second Monday of January next to answer the said Petition of the said Catharine Hippel. Witness the Hon. John Reed President of the said Court at Carlisle, the 28th day of November A.D. 1836." (signed G. Fleming, Prothy.)

Jan. 10, 1837 -"Defendant not to be found in my Bailiwick. So answers M. Holcomb, Shff. Alias subpoena awarded 10th Jany. 1837 By the Court. Shrff. fee $1.00 Gaullagher."

Jan. 16, 1837 -"Cumberland County, Pa. To Henry Hipple Greeting: Whereas Catharine Hippel, by her father and next friend George Simon has presented her petition to the Court of Common Pleas of Cumberland County, which represents that on the nineteenth day of September in the year of our Lord A.D. 1834, was contracted in matrimony to a certain Henry Hippel, who the day following the said marriage deserted and left her after having remained and co-habited with her but one night. That the said Henry Hippel from the day aforesaid, hath wilfully and maliciously deserted and absented himself from the habitation of the petitioner, without just or reasonable cause, and such desertion has persisted in, for the term of two years and upwards, and yet doth continue to absent himself from the said petitioner; and praying the said Court to award a subpoena directed to the said Henry Hippel commanding him to appear at the next term of the said Court to answer this petition, etc. We therefore command you, the said Henry Hippel, as heretofore you have been commanded that you be and appear at the next Court of Common Pleas of Cumberland County to be held at Carlisle on the second Monday of April next to answer the said petition of the said Catharine Hippel. Witness the Hon. John Reed, President of the said Court at Carlisle the sixteenth day of January, A.D. 1837." (signed George

Fleming, Prothy.)

April 14, 1837 -"Michael Holcomb being duly sworn as the law directs doth say that the within named defendant Henry Hipple is not to be found in his bailiwick. Sworn and subscribed in open court 14 April 1837. Test. Geo. Fleming, Prothy." (signed M. Holcomb, Shrff.) "Now to wit the 14 April 1837 the court upon motion directs the Sheriff to cause notice to be published in one newspaper printed in the Borough of Carlisle for four weeks successively prior to the first day of the next August term requiring the said Henry Hipple to appear on the said first day of said term to answer to the said complaint of the said Catharine Hipple. By the Court." "Shrff fee $1.00 Gaullaugher."

Aug. 15, 1837 -"Catharine Hipple by her father and next friend George Simon vs. Henry Hipple: In the Court of Common Pleas of Cumberland County Subpoena Sur Divorce. No. 5 January Term 1837 -Now to wit: 15th Augt. 1837 It appearing to the court that the said Henry Hipple does not appear in Court as required by the publication of their order and decree, they do further order and direct that Robert Snodgrass Esquire be a Commissioner before whom depositions shall be taken to be read in evidence on the trial and hearing of this case at the coming September Orphan's Court. the Court.

Aug. 17, 1837 -"Cumberland County, Pa. -I George Fleming, Prothonotary of Court of Common Pleas of Cumberland County, do hereby certify, that the above is a true copy of an order and decree of said court in the case stated. In testimony whereof I have hereunto subscribed my name and affixed the seal of said court at Carlisle, this 17th day of August, A.D. 1837." (signed Geo. Fleming, Prothy.)

Sept. 9, 1837 -"Personally appeared before me at my office in Carlisle, George Simon Junior who being duly affirmed as the law directs doth say that Catharine Hipple and Henry Hipple the persons mentioned in the foregoing order of Court were married on the nineteenth day of September eighteen hundred and thirty four at the house of George Simon Senior the father of said Catharine by Abraham Lamberton Esqr -that he the said deponent was present at said marriage -and he the said deponent doth further say that the said Henry Hipple the day after said marriage wilfully and maliciously deserted and absented himself from the habitation of the said Catharine and has continued to do so from that time, and still doth continue to do so, without any reasonable cause. Affirmed and subscribed before me this 9th day of Sept. 1837." (signed Robert Snodgrass and George Simon Junr. by his mark.)

Sept. 9, 1837 -"Also at same time and place appeared Joseph Cockly who being duly affirmed as the law directs doth say that he was present at the marriage of the aforesaid Catharine Hipple and Henry Hipple -that they were married by Abraham Lamberton Esqr.

on the nineteenth day of September eighteen hundred and thirty four -and he doth further say that the said Henry the day after the said marriage wilfully and maliciously deserted and absented himself from the habitation of the said Catharine, and has continued to do so from that time, and still doth continue to do so without any reasonable cause. Affirmed and subscribed before me this 9th day of Sept. A.D. 1837." (signed Robert Snodgrass also Joseph Cockley.)

Sept. 9, 1837 -"Also at same time and place appeared George Simon Senior who being duly affirmed doth say that he is the father of the aforesaid Catharine Hipple -that she was married to the said Henry Hipple at his house in North Middleton Township by Abraham Lamberton Esqr. on the nineteenth day of September eighteen hundred and thirty four -and he doth further say that the said Henry the day after said marriage wilfully and maliciously deserted and absented himself from the habitation of the said Catharine, and has continued to do so from that time, and still doth continue to do so, without any reasonable cause. Affirmed and subscribed before me this 9th day of Sept. 1837." (signed Robert Snodgrass and George Simon who signed in German script.)

Sept. 9, 1837 -"Also at same time and place appeared Abraham Lamberton Esqr. who being duly sworn according to law doth say that he married the aforesaid Catharine Hipple and Henry Hipple at the house of her father on the nineteenth day of September eighteen hundred and thirty four -and that he believes that the said Henry the day after said marriage wilfully and maliciously deserted and absented himself from the habitation of the said Catharine and has continued do so from that time and still doth continue to do so without any reasonable cause. Sworn and subscribed before me this 9th day of Sept. 1837." (signed Robert Snodgrass and Abraham Lamberton.)

Sept. 13, 1837 -"Catharine Hipple by her father and next friend vs. Henry Hipple: Action of Divorce in the Common Pleas of Cumberland County: And now to wit the 13th day of September A.D. 1837 the court after hearing the depositions taken by and before Robert Snodgrass Esqr. on the part of the aforesaid Libellant, and being satisfied with the same, do order, adjudge, and decree that the said Catharine Hipple the said Libellant be divorced and separated from the bond of matrimony contracted with the said Henry Hipple, and that all and every the duties rights and claims, accruing to either of the said parties by reason of the said marriage shall henceforth cease and determine and the said parties be severally at liberty to marry again in like manner as if they never had been married and that the defendant pay the costs in this case to the said Catharine Hipple. By the Court."

Oct. 14, 1837 -"Catharine Hipple vs. Henry Hipple: Divorce in the Common Pleas of Cumberland County to Geo. Fleming Prothy. Sir,

Please let George Simon Senior have my costs paid in this case 14 Oct. 1837." (signed Abram. Lamberton.)

Oct. 14, 1837 -"Rec'd from Clk. Fleming 62 1/2 cents the costs due the above witness." (signed George Simon -above witness was Abraham Lamberton.)

Feb. 28, 1838 -"Rec'd from Geo. Fleming 62 1/2 cents my costs as a witness in this case 28 Feby. 1838." (signed Joseph Cockley.)

◆ ◆ ◆

January Term 1837 #6 Nov. 25, 1836 -"To the Honorable the Judges of the Court of Common Pleas of Cumberland County: The Petition of Anna Maria Williams by her next friend Elizabeth Thomas Respectfully represents that your Libellant on the ninth day of April A.D. 1832 was contracted in matrimony and married to a certain Joseph Williams and from that time until the beginning of September A.D. 1833 lived and cohabited with her as his wife and as such was owned and acknowledged by him and so deemed and reputed by all her neighbors and acquaintances; and although by the laws of God as well as by their mutual vows and faith plighted to each other, they were reciprocally bound to that uniform kindness and regard which ought to be inseparable from the marriage state; yet so it is that the said Joseph Williams from the said month of September A.D. 1833, hath wilfully and maliciously absented himself from the habitation of this Libellant without just or reasonable cause, and such desertion hath persisted in for the term of two years and upwards and yet doth continue to absent himself from your Libellant -Wherefore your Libellant further showing that she hath resided within this state for two years and upwards previous to the filing of this petition prays your Honors that a subpoena shall issue from the said Court directed to the said Joseph Williams, commanding him to appear at the next term of the said Court to answer this petition, and also that a decree of said court may be made granting this Libellant a divorce from the society, fellowship, and company of the said Joseph Williams, in all time to come, and this Libellant from the marriage bond aforesaid, as if she had never been married, or as if the said Joseph Williams were naturally dead and she will Pray etc." (signed Ann Williams.) By her next Friend (signed by mark by Elizabeth Thomas.) "Witness" (signed M. Graham.) "Cumberland County, Pa. Before me a Justice of the Peace in and for said County personally came the within named Ann Maria Williams who being duly sworn according to Law says that the facts contained in the within Libel are true to the best of her knowledge and belief -and that the said complaint is not made out of levity or by collusion between her and her said husband and for the mere purpose of being freed and separated from each other, but in sincerity and truth for the causes mentioned in the within petition or libel. Sworn and subscribed the 25 Novr. 1836 Before" (signed John Creigh also Ann Williams.)

Nov. 29, 1836 -"Cumberland County, Pa. -To Joseph Williams Greeting: Whereas Ann Maria Williams by her next friend Elizabeth Thomas has presented her petition to the Court of Common Pleas of Cumberland County, which represents that on the ninth day of April, A.D. 1832 she was contracted in matrimony and marriage to a certain Joseph Williams and from that time until the beginning of September A.D. 1833, lived and cohabited with him as his wife and as such was owned and acknowledged by him; That from the said month of September, A.D. 1833 the said Joseph Williams hath wilfully and maliciously absented himself from the habitation of the petitioner, without just or reasonable cause, and such desertion hath persisted in for the term of two years, and upwards, and yet doth continue to absent himself from the said petitioner, and praying the said court to award a subpoena directed to the said Joseph Williams, commanding him to appear at the next term of said court to answer this petition etc. We therefore command you the said Joseph Williams that you be and appear at the next court of Common Pleas of Cumberland County, to be held at Carlisle, on the second Monday of January next, to answer the said petition of the said Ann Maria Williams. Witness the Hon. John Reed, President of the said Court, at Carlisle, the 29th day of November, A.D. 1836." (signed G. Fleming, Prothy.) Note on front -"Not to be found in my Bailiwick. So answers, M. Holcomb Shrff. Shrff's fee $0.18 3/4 Graham."

Feb. 8, 1837 -"Cumberland County, Pa. -To Joseph Williams Greeting: Whereas, Ann Maria Williams by her next friend, Elizabeth Thomas, has presented her petition to the Court of Common Pleas of Cumberland County, which represents, That on the ninth day of April, A. D. 1832, she was contracted in matrimony and marriage to a certain Joseph Williams, and from that time until the beginning of September, A.D. 1833, lived and cohabited with him as his wife, and as such was owned and acknowledged by him: that from the said month of September, A.D. 1833, the said Joseph Williams hath wilfully and maliciously absented himself from the habitation of the said petitioner, without just or reasonable cause, and such desertion hath persisted in for the term of two years and upwards, and yet doth continue to absent himself from the said petitioner -and praying the said court, to award a subpoena directed to the said Joseph Williams commanding him to appear at the next term of said court to answer this petition etc. We therefore command you the said Joseph Williams as heretofore we have commanded you, that you be and appear at the next court of Common Pleas of Cumberland County to be held at Carlisle on the second Monday of April next, to answer the said petition of the said Ann Maria Williams. Witness the Hon. John Reed President of the said Court, at Carlisle, the eighth day of February, A.D. 1837." (signed Geo.

Fleming, Prothy.) Notation on front -"Alias Subpoena sur Divorce -Defendant not to be found in my Bailiwick. So answers M. Holcomb Sheriff. Shrff. fees $1.00 Graham."
undated -"A.M. Williams by her next friend vs. Joseph Williams: Alias Sub. sur divorce -On motion of J.H. Graham the Shrff. authorised to publish notice in this case agreeably to the act of assembly in such case provided. By the Court. Mr. Fleming will enter this in his rough docket."

Aug. 14, 1837 -"Ann Maria Williams by her next friend Elizabeth Thomas vs. Joseph Williams: No. 6 January Term 1837 -In the Common Pleas of Cumberland County Subpoena Sur Divorce -14th August 1837 -On proof of the publication of notice agreeably to the Order of Court Defendant being called and not appearing the court appoint R. Snodgrass Esquire a Commissioner to take depositions to be read in evidence in this case. By the Court."

Aug. 17, 1837 -"Cumberland County, Pa. -I George Fleming, Prothonotary of the Court of Common Pleas of Cumberland County do certify that the above is a true copy of an order of said Court in the case stated. In testimony whereof I have hereunto subscribed my name and affixed the seal of said Court at Carlisle this 17th day of August A.D. 1837." (signed Geo. Fleming, Prothy.)

Sept. 16, 1837 -"Cumberland County, Pa. -Personally appeared before me the subscriber a Justice of the Peace in and for said County John Thomas who being duly sworn according to law doth depose and say that Anna Maria Williams and Joseph Williams, the persons mentioned in the foregoing order of court were married in the month of April A.D. 1832, that deponent was present and saw them married. That the said Joseph Williams lived and cohabited with his said wife from the time of their marriage until the month of September A.D. eighteen hundred and thirty three, during which time the said Anna Maria had issue one child. That in the month of September A.D. 1833 the said Joseph Williams did wilfully and maliciously desert and absent himself from the habitation of his said wife Anna Maria without any reasonable cause and hath continued to do so from that time and still continues to do so. From information which deponent had from the post master at Covington Kentucky deponent believes said Joseph Williams is, or recent was confined in the State Penitentiary of Louisiana. Sworn and subscribed before me at my office the 16 Sept. 1837." (signed Robert Snodgrass also John Thomas.)

Sept. 16, 1837 -"Also at the same time and place personally appeared Francis Thomas who being duly sworn according to law says that he waw present at the marriage of the aforesaid Joseph Williams and Anna Maria Williams and that they were lawfully married in the month of April A.D. one thousand eight hundred and thirty two and that in the month of September Anno Domini eighteen hundred and thirty three the said Joseph Williams did wilfully and maliciously desert the habitation of his said wife, near Waynesburg in the County of Franklin and State of Penna. and absented himself from his said wife and continued so to do from that time and still doth continue to do so without any reasonable cause. Sworn and subscribed the 16 Sept. A.D. 1837 before me at my office in the Borough of Carlisle." (signed Robert Snodgrass also signed by mark by Francis Thomas.)

Nov. 13, 1837 -"Anna Maria Williams by her next friend Elizabeth Thomas vs. Joseph Williams: Action of Divorce in the Court of Common Pleas of Cumberland County -And now to wit, 13th Novr. A.D. 1837 the court after hearing the depositions taken before Robert Snodgrass Esq., a commissioner appointed by the Court for that purpose, on the part of aforesaid Libellant, and being satisfied with the same; do order, adjudge and decree that the said Anna Maria Williams the aforesaid Libellant, be divorced and separated from the nuptial ties, or bonds of matrimony contracted with the said Joseph Williams and that all and every the duties, rights and claims accruing to either of the said parties by reason of the said marriage, shall henceforth cease and determine, and, the said parties be severally at liberty to marry again in like manner as if they never had been married. By the Court." (signed Jno. Reed.)

◆ ◆ ◆

April Term 1837 #22 -Jan. 26, 1837 -"To the Honorable the Judges of the Court of Common Pleas of Cumberland County -The petition of Mary Ann Weigandt by her next friend Samuel F. Gaenslen -Respectfully Sheweth -That your Libellant on the second day of August A.D. One thousand Eight hundred and thirty two was contracted in matrimony and married to a certain Barnet Christian Weigandt, and from that time to the 30th day of May A.D. One thousand Eight hundred and thirty four lived and cohabited with him as his wife, and as such was owned and acknowledged by him, so deemed and reputed by all her neighbors and acquaintances, and although by the laws of God as well as by their mutual vows and faith plighted to each other, they were reciprocally bound to that kindness and uniform regard which ought to be inseparable from the marriage state: yet so it is that the said Barnet Christian Weigandt from the said 30th of May A.D. 1834 hath wilfully and maliciously absented himself from the habitation of this libellant without just or reasonaable cause. And such desertion has persisted in for the term of two year and upwards, and yet doth continue to absent himself from the said Libellant. Wherefore your Libellant further showing that she is a citizen of this state and hath resided therein for one whole year and more previous to the filing of this petition prays your Honors that a subpoena shall issue from the said court directed to the said Barnet Christian Weigandt, commanding him to appear at the next April term of the said court to answer this petition, and also that a decree of said court may be made for the divorcing of him the said Barnet Christian Weigandt from the society, fellowship and company of this Libellant in all time to come, and her this Libellant from the marriage bond aforesaid as if she had never been married or as if the said Barnet were naturally dead and this Libellant will pray etc." (signed Mary Ann Weigandt by her next friend Samuel F. Gaenslen.) "Cumberland County -The within named Mary Ann Weigandt being duly sworn says the facts contained in the foregoing libel are true to the best of her knowledge and belief and that the said complaint is not made out of levity or collusion between her and the said Barnet Christian Weigandt, and for the mere purpose of being freed and separated from each other, but in sincerity and truth for the causes mentioned in the said libel. Sworn and subscribed before me this 26th January A.D. 1837." (signed Robert Snodgrass and Mary Weigandt.)

March 6, 1837 -"Cumberland County ss -To Barnet Christian Weigandt Greeting - Whereas Mary Ann Weigandt by her next friend Samuel F. Gaenslen has presented her petition to the Court of Common Pleas of Cumberland County which represents that she the said Mary Ann Weigandt on the second day of August A.D. one thousand eight hundred and thirty two, was contracted in matrimony and married to a certain Barnet Christian Weigandt, and from that time to the 30th day of May A.D. one thousand eight hundred and thirty four, lived and cohabited with him as his wife, and as such was owned and acknowledged by him and so deemed and reputed by all her neighbors and acquaintances, and although by the laws of God as well as by their mutual vows and faith plighted to each other, they were reciprocally bound to that kindness and uniform regard which ought to be inseparable from the marriage state. Yet so it is that the said Barnet Christian Weigandt from the said 30th of May A.D. 1834, hath wilfully and maliciously absented himself from the habitation of this libellant, without just or reasonable cause, and such desertion has persisted in for the term of two years and upwards, and yet doth continue to absent himself from the said Libellant. Whereupon the libellant further shewing that she is a citizen of this State, and hath resided therein for one whole year and more previous to the filing of her petition, prayed the Court that a subpoena should issue from the said Court directed to the said Barnet Christian Weigandt commanding him to appear at the next April Term of the said Court, to answer the said petition, and also that a decree of said Court may be made for divorcing of him the said Barnet Christian Weigandt from the society, fellowship and company of this libellant, in all time to come, and her the said libellant from the marriage bond aforesaid as if she had never been married or as if the said Barnet Christian Weigandt were naturally dead. We therefore command you the said Barnet Christian Weigandt that you be and appear at the next Court of Common Pleas of the County of Cumberland to be held at Carlisle in and for said County on the tenth day of April next, to answer the petition of the said Mary Ann Weigandt. Witness the Honorable John Reed, President of the said Court at Carlisle the sixth day of March Anno Domini one thousand eight hundred and thirty seven." (siqned G. Fleming, Prothy.) Note on front -"Not to be found in my Bailiwick. So answers M. Holcomb, Shff. Shff's fee $1.00 Biddle."

♦   ♦   ♦

August Term 1837 #37 -April 25, 1837 -"To the Judges of the Court of Common Pleas of Cumberland County -The petition of Sarah Gross by her next friend George Brindle respectfuliy represents -That she was lawfully married to Henry Gross on or about the first of September 1833 and continued to live and co-habit with him until about the 1 May 1835 during which time the said Henry Gross did so cruelly and barbarously treat his said wife as to endanger her life in consequence of which she separated herself from him and remained separate for about two weeks, when she was induced by her said husband to return to his house upon his promise made in writing that his conduct towards his wife and her children should not be cruel. She the said Sarah then continued to reside with the said husband until the 12 March last during which latter period, the said Henry Gross did so cruelly and barbarously beat his said wife as to endanger her life and offered such indignities to her person as to render her condition intolerable and life burthensome and has thereby forced her to withdraw from his house and family. She therefore prays your Honors to award a subpoena directed to the said Henry Gross to appear on the second Monday in August next to answer this the petition of the said Sarah Gross and shew cause why she should not be divorced from the bonds of matrimony entered into with her said husband." (signed George Brindle.) "Cumberland County sct -Personally appeared before me a Justice of the Peace in and for said County Sarah Gross who being duly sworn doth depose and say that the facts set forth in the foregoing petition are true to the best of her knowledge and belief and that the said complaint is not made out of levity or by collusion between the said husband and wife and for the mere purpose of being freed and separated from each other, but in sincerity and truth for the causes mentioned in the said petition or libel. Sworn and subscribed the 25th April 1837 Before me." (signed Robert Snodgrass and by mark by Sarah Gross.) "25 April T. 1837 Subpoena award by the Court. Watts"

May 9, 1837 -"Cumberland County ss -The Commonwealth of Pennsylvania Henry Gross -Greeting Whereas Sarah Gross, by her next friend George Brindle, has presented to the Court of Common

Pleas of Cumberland County, her petition, which represents That she was lawfully married to Henry Gross on or about the first of September 1833 and continued to live and cohabit with him until about the first of May 1835, during which time the said Henry Gross did so cruelly and barbarously treat her his said wife as to endanger her life, in consequence of which, she separated herself from him and remained separate for about two weeks when she was induced by her said husband to return to his house upon his promise made in writing that his conduct towards his wife and her children should not be cruel. That she the said Sarah then continued to reside with her said husband until the 12th March last, during which latter period the said Henry Gross did so cruelly and barbarously treat his said wife as to endanger her life and offered such indigities to her person as to render her condition intolerable and life burthensome and has thereby forced her to withdraw from his house and family, and praying the court to award a subpoena directed to the said Henry Gross and shew cause why she should not be divorced from the bonds of matrimony entered into with her said husband. We therefore command you the said Henry Gross that you be and appear before our Judges at our next court of Common Pleas of Cumberland County to be held at Carlisle on Monday the fourteenth day of August next to answer the petition of the said Sarah Gross. Witness the Honorable John Reed Esquire President of the said Court at Carlisle the ninth day of May Anno Domini one thousand eight hundred and thirty seven." (signed Geo. Fleming Prothy.)

July 31, 1837 -"I do hereby authorise and deputise Joseph Lobach to execute the summons of divorce according to law. Witness my hand and seal this 31st day of July 1837." (signed M. Holcomb.) "Cumberland County sct -Joseph Lobach by being duly affirmed doth depose and say that he served the within subpoena personally on Henry Gross on the July 1837. Affirmed and subscribed the 15th Aug. 1837." (signed by Jos. Lobach and Geo. Fleming Prothy.)

Aug. 16, 1837 -"Sarah Gross vs. Henry Gross: No. 13 Aug. Term 1837 -Now to wit 16 Aug. 1837 the Court having received due proof of the service of the subpoena in this cause do order and decree that Michl. Hoover, Esq. of Mechanicsburg be a commissioner to take the testimony of witnesses to be read in evidence to the Court upon the final hearing of the cause -By the Court."

Aug. 17, 1837 -"Cumberland County s.s. -I George Fleming Prothonotary of the Court of Common Pleas of Cumberland County do certify that the above is a true copy of a decree of the Court of Common Pleas in the above mentioned case. In testimony whereof I have hereunto subscribed my name and affixed the seal of said Court at Carlisle, this 17th day of August A.D. 1837." (signed Geo. Fleming Prothy.)

Nov. 27, 1837 -"In the case of the petition or libel of Sarah Gross to be divorced from the bonds of matrimony entered into with Henry Gross her husband -Now to wit: 27th November, 1837 Upon due consideration of the premises and due proof having been made of the facts contained in the petition or libel of the said Sarah Gross the Court do hereby sentence and decree that the said Sarah Gross and the said Henry Gross be divorced and separated from the nuptial ties or bonds of matrimony and the said marriage be and is null and void; and that all and every the duties, rights and claims accruing to either of the said parties at any time heretofore in pursuance of the said marriage shall cease and determine and the said parties shall severally be at liberty to marry again in like manner as if they had never been married. By the Court."

♦ ♦ ♦

November Term 1837 #8 -Aug. 24, 1837 -"To the Honorable the Judges of the Court of Common Pleas of Cumberland County -The petition of Catherine Kutz by her next friend Jacob Beltzhoover -Respectfully sheweth -That your libellant on the 24th day of March A.D. One thousand Eight hundred and thirty six was contracted in matrimony and married to a certain Samuel Kutz and from that time until the twenty first of August A.D. 1837 lived and cohabited with him as his wife and as such was owned and acknowledged by him and so deemed and reputed by all her neighbors and acquaintances; and although by the laws of God as well as by their mutual vows plighted to each other, they were reciprocally bound to that kindness and uniform regard which ought to be inseparable from the marriage state: yet so it is that the said Samuel Kutz did prior to the said twenty first day of August offer such indignities to her person as to render her condition intolerable and life burdensome and thereby and by compulsion did force her to withdraw from his house and family. Wherefore your libellant further showing that she is a citizen of this state and hath resided therein for one whole year and more previous to the filing of this petition prays your Honors that a subpoena shall issue from the said Court directed to the said Samuel Kutz commanding him to appear at the next November term of the said Court to answer this petition and also that a decree of the said court may be given granting this libellant a divorce from bed and board, and also allowing such alimony as the said Samuel Kutz's circumstances will admit of according to the laws in such case made and provided -and the said libellant will ever pray etc." (signed Catherine Kutz by her next friend Jacob Beltzhoover.)

Aug. 29, 1837 -"Cumberland County s.s. -To Samuel Kutz, Greeting: Whereas Catharine Kutz, by her next friend Jacob Beltzhoover, has presented her petition to the Court of Common Pleas of Cumberland County, which represents, that on the 26th day of March, A.D. 1836 she was contracted in matrimony and married to a certain Samuel Kutz, and from that time until the 21 of August, 1837, lived and co-habited with him as his wife, that the said Samuel Kutz did, prior to the said 21 day of August offer such indignities to her person as to render her condition intolerable and life burdensome, and thereby, and by compulsion, did force her to withdraw from his house and family, and praying the Court that a subpoena shall issue from the said Court directed to the said Samuel Kutz commanding him to appear at the next November Term of the said Court to answer this petition, and also that a decree of the said Court may be given, granting the said Catharine a divorce from bed and board, and also allowing such alimony as the said Samuel Kutz's circumstances will admit of, according to the laws in such case made and provided etc. We therefore command you, the said Samuel Kutz, that you be and appear at the next Court of Common Pleas of Cumberland County to be held at Carlisle, on the second Monday of November next to answer the said petition of the said Catharine Kutz by her next friend Jacob Beltzhoover. Witness John Reed Esquire President of the said Court, at Carlisle, this twenty-ninth day of August, A.D. 1837." (signed George Fleming, Prothy.)

♦ ♦ ♦

November Term 1838 #2 -Aug. 13, 1838 -"To the Judges of the Court of Common Pleas of the County of Cumberland -The Libel of Mary Black by her brother and next friend Thomas Fraley -Respectfully showeth -That your Libellant on the nineteenth day of July one thousand eight hundred and twenty four was contracted in matrimony and married to a certain John Black and from that time untill about the first day of January one thousand eight hundred and thirty five, lived and cohabited with the said John Black as his wife, and as such was owned and acknowledged by him, and so deemed and reputed by her neighbours and acquaintances. And although by the laws of God, as well as by their mutual vows and faith plighted to each other, they were bound to that uniform constancy and regard which ought to be inseparable from the marriage state; yet so it is, that the said John Black from the said first day of January in the year of our Lord one thousand eight hundred and thirty five, hath wilfully and maliciously deserted and absented himself from the habitation of this Libellant without any just or reasonable cause and such desertion hath persisted in for the term of two years and upwards and yet doth continue to absent himself from the said Libellant. Wherefore your Libellant further shewing that she is a citizen of the state of Pennsylvania and has resided therein for upwards of one whole year previous to the filing of this her libel, prays your Honours that a subpoena may issue forth to summon the said John Black to appear in this Honourable court at its next term to answer this complaint aforesaid. And also that a decree of this Honourable court may be made for the divorcing of him the said John Black from the society, fellowship and company of this Libellant in all time to come, and she this Libellant from the marriage bond aforesaid as if she had never been married, or as if the said John Black were naturally dead -and this Libellant will pray etc." (signed Mary Black by her next friend Thomas Fraley.) "Mary Black the within named Libellant being duly sworn doth depose and say that the facts contained in the within Libel are true to the best of her knowledge and belief; and that the said complaint is not made out of levity and collusion between her and her said husband and for the mere purpose of being freed and separated from each other, but in sincerity and truth for the causes mentioned in the said Libel. Sworn and subscribed this 13th day of Augt. 1838 Before." (signed Isaac Todd and Mary Black by her mark.)

Aug. 17, 1838 -"Cumberland County ss -The Commonwealth of Pennsylvania to John Black -Greeting -Whereas Mary Black by her brother and next friend Thomas Fraley, has presented to the Court of Common Pleas of Cumberland County, her petition which represents that she was lawfully married to John Black on the 19th day of July A.D. 1834 and continued to live and cohabit with him until the first day of January 1835, during which time the said John Black hath wilfully and maliciously deserted and absented himself from the habitation of the Libellant without any just or reasonable cause, and such desertion hath persisted in for the term of two years and upwards and yet doth continue to absent himself from the said Libellant, and praying the Court to award a subpoena directed to the said Jno. Black to appear, on the second Monday of November next, to answer this the petition of the said Mary Black, and shew cause why she should not be divorced from the bonds of matrimony entered into with her said husband. We therefore command you the said John Black that you be and appear before our Judges at our next court of Common Pleas of Cumberland County to be held at Carlisle on Monday the twelfth day of November next, to answer the petition of the said Mary Black. Witness the Honorable John Reed Esquire President of the said court at Carlisle the seventeenth day of August in the year of our Lord one thousand Eight hundred and thirty eight. For George Fleming, Prothy." (signed Wm. M. Beetem.)

Nov. 22, 1838 -"Cumberland County, s.s. -John Myers Esqr. high Sheriff of said county being duly sworn saith that his return made to this summons, "that the defendant was not found in my Bailiwick" is true. Sworn and subscribed in open court this 22nd day of Novr. 1838." (signed Geo. Fleming Prohy. and John Myers.)

◆ ◆ ◆

January Term 1839 # 252 April 8, 1839 -"To the Honorable the Judges of the Court of Common Pleas of Cumberland County -The petition of Elizabeth Fleming by her next friend Martin Diller respectfully represents -That your Libellant in the month of October A.D. 1803 was contracted in matrimony and married to a certain Timothy

Fleming and from that time until the month of October A.D. 1819 lived and cohabited with him as his wife and as such was owned and acknowledged by him and so deemed and reputed by all her neighbors and acquaintances and altho by the laws of God as well as by their mutual vows and faith plighted to each other, they were reciprocally bound to that uniform kindness and regard which ought to be inseparable from the marriage state, yet so it is that the said Timothy Fleming in the month of June 1824 did wilfully and maliciously absent himself from the habitation of this libellant without just or reasonable cause and such desertion hath persisted in for the term of fourteen years and upwards, and yet doth continue to absent himself from your Libellant and during the term of his aforesaid desertion hath lived and cohabited with other women -Wherefore your Libellant further showing that she is a citizen of this state prays your Honors that a subpoena may issue from said Court directed to the said Timothy Fleming commanding him to appear at a Court of Common Pleas to be held in and for said County on the 20th day of April 1839 to answer this petition and also that a decree of said Court may be made granting this Libellant a divorce from the society fellowship and company of the said Timothy Fleming in all time to come and from the marriage bond aforesaid as if she had never been married or as if the said Timothy Fleming were naturally dead. And she will pray etc. Witness" (signed D.H. Graham also signed by her mark Elizabeth Fleming.) "by her next friend" (signed Martin Diller.) -"Cumberland County, s.s. -Before me a Justice of Peace in and for said County personally came the within named Elizabeth Fleming who being duly sworn according to law says that the facts contained in the within Libel are true to the best of her knowledge and belief and that the said complaint is not made out of levity or by collusion between her and her said husband and for the mere purpose of being freed and separated from each other, but in sincerity and truth for the causes mentioned in the within petition or libel. Sworn and subscribed the 8th day of April 1839 Before" (signed Michael Hoover) also signed by mark (Elizabeth Fleming).

April 8, 1839 -"Cumberland County s.s. -The Commonwealth of Pennsylvania to Timothy Fleming -Greeting -Whereas Elizabeth Fleming by her next friend Martin Diller, has presented to the Court of Common Pleas of Cumberland County, her petition which represents that she was Lawfully married to Timothy Fleming in the month of October A.D. 1803 and from that time until the month of October A.D. 1819 lived and cohabited with him as his wife and as such was owned and acknowledged by him and so deemed and reputed by all her neighbors and acquaintances and that the said Timothy Fleming in the month of June 1824 did wilfully and maliciously absent himself from the habitation of this libellant, without any just or reasonable cause and such desertion hath persisted in for the term of fourteen years and upwards and yet doth continue to absent himself from your Libellant and during the term of his aforesaid desertion hath lived and cohabited with other women. Wherefore your Libellant further shewing that she is a citizen of this state prays your Honors that a subpoena may issue from said Court directed to the said Timothy Fleming commanding him to appear at a Court of Common Pleas to be held in and for said County on the 30th day of April A.D. 1839 to answer this petition and also that a decree of said court may be made granting this Libellant a divorce from the society fellowship and company of the said Timothy Fleming in all time to come and from the marriage bond aforesaid, as if she had never been married or as if the said Timothy Fleming were naturally dead. We therefore command you the said Timothy Fleming that you be and appear before our Judges at Carlisle the 30th day of April instant, to answer the petition of the said Elizabeth Fleming. Witness the Honorable Samuel Hepbun Esquire President of the said Court at Carlisle the 8th day of April in the year of our Lord one thousand Eight hundred and thirty nine. To George Sanderson Prothy." (signed Wm. M. Beetem.)

April 9, 1839 -"I do hereby authorize and deputize Snider Rupley Execute the within subpoena according to law. Witness my hand and seal this 9th day of April 1839." (signed John Myers. Shrff. and Test. Jos. Lobach.)

April 15, 1839 -"Cumberland County s.s. -Personally appeared Snider Rupley in open court who deposeth and says he served the within writ personally on Timothy Fleming on the 15th day of April 1839. Sworn and subscribed in open court the 16th day of Apr. 1839." (signed Geo. Sanderson, Prothy.) "Cumberland County s.s. -Snyder Rupley being duly sworn according to Law says that he served the within writ personally on Timothy Fleming the 1 April 1839." (signed Snider Rupley.) Notation on front of document -"served personally by copy 9th April 1839 So answers." (signed John Myers, Shrff.) "Shrff. fee $1.80 Graham."

April 29, 1839 -"Elizabeth Fleming by her next friend Martin Diller vs. Timothy Fleming -In the Court of Common Pleas of Cumberland County -Summons in Divorce etc. -In addition to the facts set forth in the petition of Libellant in this case, the libellant will prove and rely upon the following additional facts and asks this statement to be filed by the Court and considered as a part of the cause of complaint of this Libellant -The said Timothy Fleming the husband of the Libellant prior to the time of his desertion and absence found the habitation of Libellant as set forth in said Libellant's petition, did by cruel and barbarous treatment of the libellant endanger her life and offered such indignities to her person as to render her condition intolerable and life burthensome. Cumberland County, s.s. -Elizabeth Fleming the libellant above named being duly sworn according to Law doth depose and say that the facts set forth in the above statement are true to the best of her knowledge and belief. Sworn and subscribed the 29th April 1839 Before" (signed John Creigh also Elizabeth Fleming signed by her mark.)

♦ ♦ ♦

August Term 1839 #13 April 4, 1839 -"To the Honorable the Judges of the Courts of Common Pleas of Cumberland County -The Petition of Harriet Cairns by her next friend James Davis Respectfully Represents -That your libellant in the month of June A.D. 1808 was contracted in matrimony and married to a certain Joseph Cairns and from that time until the month of October A.D. 1810 lived and cohabited with him as his wife and as such was owned and acknowledged by him, and so deemed and reputed by all her neighbors and acquaintances; and although by the Laws of God, as well as by their mutual vows and faith plighted to each other, they were reciprocally bound to that uniform kindness and regard which ought to be inseparable from the marriage state; yet so it is that the said Joseph Cairns from the said month of October A.D. 1810, hath wilfully and maliciously absented himself from the habitation of this libellant, without just or reasonable cause and such desertion hath persisted in for the term of twenty eight years and upwards, and yet doth continue to absent himself from your Libellant -Wherefore your Libellant further showing that she hath resided in this state for two years and upwards previous to the filing of this petition prays your Honors that a subpoena shall issue from said Court directed to the said Joseph Cairns, commanding him to appear at the next term of the said Court to answer this petition; and also that a decree of said Court may be made granting this Libellant a divorce from the society, fellowship and company of the said Joseph Cairns in all time to come, and from the marriage bond aforesaid, as if she had never been married, or as if the said Joseph Cairns were naturally dead. And she will pray etc. (signed Harriet Cairns.) "By her next friend (signed James Davis.) "Cumberland County s.s. -Before me a Justice of the Peace in and for said County personally came the within named Harriet Cairns, who being duly sworn according to Law says that the facts contained in the within Libel are true to the best of her knowledge and belief -And that the said complaint is not made out of levity or by collusion between her and her said husband and for the mere purpose of being freed and separated from each other, but in sincerity and truth for the causes mentioned in the within petition or Libel. Sworn and subscribed the 4th day of April A.D. 1839 Before (signed Robert Snodgrass, J.P. and Harriet Cairns.)

April 13, 1839 -"Cumberland County, s.s. -The Commonwealth of Pennsylvania to Joseph Cairns -Greeting Whereas Harriet Cairns by her next friend James Davis, has presented to the Court of Common Pleas of Cumberland County her Petition which represents that she was lawfully married to Joseph Cairns in the month of June A.D. 1808 and from that time until the month of October A.D. 1810 lived and cohabited with him as his wife and as such was owned and acknowledged by him and so deemed and reputed by all her neighbors and acquaintances, and although by the laws of God, as well as by their mutual vows and faith plighted to each other, they were reciprocally bound to that uniform kindness and regard which ought to be inseparable from the marriage state; yet so it is that the said Joseph Cairns from the said month of October A.D. 1810 hath wilfully and maliciously absented himself from the habitation of this Libellant, without just or reasonable cause and such desertion hath persisted in for the term of twenty eight years and upwards and yet doth continue to absent himself from your Libellant. Wherefore your Libellant further showing that she hath resided in this state for two years and upwards previous to the filing of this petition, prays your Honors that a subpoena shall issue from said Court directed to the said Joseph Cairns, commanding him to appear at the next term of the said Court to answer this petition; and also that a decree of Court may be made granting this Libellant a divorce from the society, fellowship and company of the said Joseph Cairns in all time to come and from the marriage bond aforesaid, as if she had never been married, or as if the said Joseph Cairns were naturally dead. We therefore Command you the said Joseph Cairns that you be and appear before our Judges at our next Court of Common Pleas of Cumberland County to be held at Carlisle, on Monday the twelfth day of August next, to answer the petition of the said Harriet Cairns. Witness the Honorable Samuel Hepburn, Esquire President of the said Court at Carlisle the thirteenth day of April in the year of our Lord one thousand eight hundred and thirty nine." (signed Geo. Sanderson, Prothy.) Notation on front of this document "Defendant not to be found in my Bailiwick. So answers. (signed John Myers, Shrff.) "Shrff. fee $0.18 3/4 Graham."

♦   ♦   ♦

August Term 1839 #113 August 12, 1839 -"To the Honorable The Judges of the Court of Common Pleas of Cumberland County. The petition of Catharine Roland by her next friend C. Myers respectfully represents -That your libellant on the second day of August 1834 was contracted in matrimony and married to a certain Frederick Roland and from that time for six weeks lived and cohabited with her as his wife, and as such was owned and acknowledged by him and deemed and reputed by all her neighbors and acquaintances and although by the laws of God as well as by their mutual vows and faith plighted to each other, they were reciprocally bound to that uniform kindness and regard which ought to be inseparable from the marriage state, yet the said Frederick Roland in the month of October 1834 did wilfully and maliciously absent himself from the habitation of this libellant without just or reasonable cause and such desertion hath persisted in for the term of four years and upwards, and yet doth continue to absent himself from your libellant. Whereupon your libellant further shewing that she is a citizen of this state prays you honors that a subpoena may issue from said court directed to said Frederick Roland commanding him to appear at a Court of Common Pleas to be held in and for said County on the eleventh day of November 1839 to answer this petition and also that a decree of said Court may be made granting this libellant a divorce from the society, fellowship and company of the said Frederick Roland in all time to come, and from the marriage bond aforesaid, as if she had never been married, or as if the said Frederick Roland were naturally dead and she will pray etc. Witness" (signed William Ramsey and Catharine Roland by her mark.) "by her next friend" (signed C. Myers by his mark.) "Cumberland Co., s.s. -Before me a Justice of the Peace in and for said County personally appeared the within named Catherine Roland who being duly sworn according to law says that the facts contained in the within libel are true to the best of her knowledge and belief and that the said complaint is not made out of levity or by collusion between her and her said husband for the mere purpose of being freed and separated from each other, but in sincerity and truth for the causes mentioned in the within petition or libel. Sworn and Suscribed the 12th day of Aug. 1839 before me." (signed Robert Snodgrass, J.P. and Catherine Roland by her mark.)

Aug. 20, 1839 -"Cumberland County, s.s. -The Commonwealth of Pennsylvania Frederick Roland -Greeting: Whereas Catharine Roland by her next friend C. Myers, has presented to the Court of Common Pleas of Cumberland County, her Petition which represents that she was lawfully married to Frederic Roland on the second day of August 1834, and from that time for six weeks lived and cohabited with her as his wife and as such was owned and acknowledged by him and deemed and reputed by all her neighbors and acquaintances, and that the said Frederick Roland in the month of October 1834 did wilfully and maliciously absent himself from the habitation of this libellant, without just or reasonable cause and such desertion hath persisted in for the term of four years and upwards, and yet doth continue to absent himself from your libellant. Wherefore your Libellant further shewing that she is a citizen of this state prays your honors that a subpoena may issue from said Court directed to said Frederick Roland commanding him to appear at a Court of Common Pleas to be held in and for said County on the eleventh day of November 1839 to answer this Petition and also that a decree of said Court may be made granting this libellant a divorce from the society, fellowship and company of the said Frederick Roland in all time to come and from the marriage bond aforesaid as if she had never been married or as if the said Frederick Roland were naturally dead. We therefore command you the said Frederick Roland that you be and appear before our Judges at Carlisle the eleventh day of November next, to answer the petition of the said Catharine Roland. Witness the Honorable Samuel Hepburn Esquire President of the said Court at Carlisle the 20th day of August in the year of our Lord one thousand eight hundred and thirty nine." (signed Geo. Sanderson, Prothy.)

Nov. 16, 1839 -"John Myers Sheriff being duly sworn according to law doth say that the Deft. named in the within writ is not to be found in the County of Cumberland." (signed John Myers Shrff.) "Sworn and subscribed in open Court 16 Nov. 1839." (signed Geo. Sanderson, Prothy.)

Nov. 18, 1839 -"Cumberland County, s.s. -The Commonwealth of Pennsylvania to Frederick Roland -Greeting: Whereas Catharine Roland by her next friend C. Myers has presented to the Court of Common Pleas of Cumberland County her petition which represents that she was lawfully married to Frederick Roland on the second day of August 1834, and from that time for six weeks lived and cohabited with her as his wife, and as such was owned and acknowledged by him, and deemed and reputed by all her neighbors and acquaintances, and that the said Frederick Roland in the month of October 1834, did wilfully and maliciously absent himself from the habitation of this libellant. Wherefore your Libellant further shewing that she is a citizen of this state, prays your Honors that a subpoena may issue from said Court directed to said Frederick Roland commanding him to appear at a Court of Common Pleas to be held in and for said County on the eleventh day of November 1839, to answer this petition, and also that a decree of said Court may be made granting this libellant a divorce from the society, fellowship and company of the said Frederick Roland in all time to come, and from the marriage bond aforesaid, as if she had never been married, or as if the said Frederick Roland were naturally dead. We therefore command you the said Frederick Roland, as we have heretofore commanded you, that you be and appear before our Judges at Carlisle the second Monday of January next to answer the petition of the said Catharine Roland. Witness the Honorable Samuel Hepburn Esquire President of the said Court at Carlisle the 18th day of November in the year of our Lord One thousand eight hundred and thirty nine." signed Geo. Sanderson Prothy.)

Jan. 15, 1840 -"John Myers Sheriff being sworn in open court doth say that the defendent Frederick Roland is not to be found in his bailiwick. Sworn and subscribed 15 Jany. 1840. (signed John Myers Shrff. and Geo. Sanders Prothy.) "Shrff. bill $0.18 3/4 Ramsey 15 Jany 1840. On motion of Mr. Gallagher Sheriff to give notice according to act of assembly. By the Court."

Filed April 14, 1840 -"In case of the application of Catharine Roland for a divorce it appearing to the Court that the Sheriff gave notice according to law requiring Frederick Roland the husband of the said Catharine to appear on the first day of this term in Court to answer to the complaint of the said Catharine and it also appearing that the said Frederick does not appear or attend. Whereupon the Court do order and direct that depositions be taken exparte by the said Catharine before William Irvine Esqr. to be read in evidence on the hearing of her application or aforesaid at the next Orphan's Court. By the Court. Test." (signed Geo. Sanderson.)

April 14, 1840 -"Catharine Roland by her next friend Myers vs. Frederick Roland: No. 113 August Term 1839 -14th April 1840 On Motion of Mr. Gallagher, Rule that depositions be taken exparte by Catharine Roland Before William Irvine, Esq. to be read in evidence on the hearing of her application, at the next Orphan's Court."

April 24, 1840 -"Cumberland County, s.s. -I George Sanderson Prothonotary of the Court of Common Pleas of said County do certify that the above is a true extract of a rule entered in the above case. In testimony whereof I have hereunto set my hand and affixed the seal of said Court, at Carlisle, the 24th day of April, A.D. 1840. Test. (signed Wm. W. Beetem for Geo. Sanderson Prothy.)

April 24, 1840 -"Cumberland County, s.s. -Personally appeared before the subscriber a Justice of the Peace in and for the county aforesaid in pursuance of the above rule of Court Catharine Myers who being duly sworn according to law doth say that she was present at the marriage of Catharine Roland and Frederick Roland that they were married in August 1834 by Squire Gibson of Perry County -that the said Frederick has wilfully and maliciously deserted and absented himself from the habitat of his said wife Catharine without a reasonable cause for the last five years and doth still continue to absent himself from the habitation of the said Catharine. Sworn and subscribed this 24th day of April 1840. (signed Catharine Myers in a German script also William Irvine.)

April 24, 1840 -"Also at same time appeared Henry Myers who being duly sworn according to law doth say that Frederick Roland has wilfully and maliciously deserted and absented himself from the habitation of his wife Catharine without a reasonable cause for the last five years and upwards and doth still continue to absent himself from her habitation. Sworn and subscribed this 24th day of April 1840. (signed Henry Myers and William Irvine.)

April 24, 1840 -"At same time also appeared John White who being duly affirmed doth say that he is acquainted with Frederick Roland and Catharine his wife and that the said Frederick has wilfully and maliciously deserted and absented himself from the habitation of his said wife Catherine without a reasonable cause for the last five years and upwards and doth still continue to absent himself from her habitation. Affirmed and subscribed this 24th day of April 1840. (signed John White and William Irvine.)

April 24, 1840 -"Also at same time appeared Henry Beader who being duly affirmed according to law doth say that he was present at the marriage of Frederick Roland and Catharine Roland that they were married sometime in the summer of 1834 by Squire Gibson of Perry County and that he believes that the said Frederick has not lived with his said wife for the last five years that he has deserted and absented himself from the habitation of his said wife for at least five years past without any reasonable cause and still doth continue to absent himself from her habitation as affirmant verily believes. Affirmed and subscribed this 24th day of April 1840. (signed Henry Beader and William Irvine.)

April 28, 1840 -"Now to wit the 28th of April 1840 in the case of the application of Catherine Roland for a divorce the Court after hearing the depositions taken exparte in pursuance of an order of said Court and after a full consideration of the testimony do order and decree that the said Catharine Roland the Libellant be divorced and separated from the bonds of matrimony contracted with the said Frederick Roland and that the said marriage be null and void and that all and every the duty, rights and claims accruing to either of the said parties by reason of the said marriage shall hence forth cease and determine, and the said parties be severally at liberty to marry again in like manner as if they never had been married. By the Court April 28, 1840."

◆ ◆ ◆

August Term 1839 #120 Aug. 3, 1839 -"To the Judges of the Court of Common Pleas of Cumberland County -The petition of Archibald Peck of said County Respectfully Represents That he was lawfully married to Caroline Hamilton about the year 1832 and continued to live with her as her husband for (many, which was crossed out and, one, written above); but about (four, which was crossed out and, eight, written above) years ago the said Caroline deserted and left your petitioner and about that time she knowingly entered into a second marriage in violation of her previous vows she had made to your petitioner and that the said Caroline hath since been guilty of adultery and of wilful and malicious desertion and absence from the habitation of your petitioner without a reasonable cause, for and during the term and space of (two, crossed out and eight written above) years. He therefore prays your Honors to grant him a divorce from the bonds of matrimony entered into by him with the said Caroline and he will pray etc. (signed Archd. Peck by his mark.) "Cumberland County, s.ct. -Personally appeared before me a Justice of the Peace in and for said County Archibald Peck the above named petitioner who being duly sworn doth depose and say that the facts set forth in the above petition are true to the best of his knowledge and belief and that the said complaint is not made out of levity or by collusion between the said petitioner and his wife and for the mere purpose of being freed and separated from each other, but in sincerity and truth for the causes mentioned in his petition. Sworn and subscribed the 3 Aug. 1839 Before me. (signed Robert Snodgrass J.P. and Archibald Peck by his mark.) Notation on front of petition "13th August 1839 Subpoena awarded. Watts."

◆ ◆ ◆

August Term 1839 #157 -Sept. 19, 1839 -"To the Honorable John Stuart one of the Judges of the Court of Common Pleas of Cumberland County -The petition of Barbara Ann Krone a resident and citizen of the County aforesaid by her next friend John A. Clark -Respectfully represents that your petitioner or Libellant on the second day of January in the year of our Lord one thousand eight hundred and thirty three was contracted in matrimony and married to a certain George Krone and from that time until the fifteenth day of March in the year of our Lord one thousand eight hundred and thirty five lived and cohabited with the said Barbara Ann as his wife and as such was owned and reputed by her neighbors and acquaintances. And although by the laws of God as well as by their mutual vows and faith plighted to each other, they were bound to that uniform constancy and regard which ought to be inseparable from the marriage state; yet so it is that the said George Krone from the fifteenth day of March in the year last aforesaid hath wilfully and maliciously deserted and absented himself from the habitation of your Libellant without any just or reasonable cause -and such desertion hath persisted in for the term of two years and upwards and yet doth continue to absent himself from the said Libellant. Wherefore your Libellant further showing that she is a citizen of the State of Pennsylvania and has resided therein for upwards of one whole year previous to the filing of this her libel prays your honors that a subpoena may issue forthwith to summon the said George Krone to appear in the next Court of Common Pleas to be held in Nov. next in and for the County aforesaid to answer the complaint aforesaid and also that a decree of the said Court may be made for the divorcing of him from the society, fellowship and company of this your Libellant in all time to come and her this Libellant from the marriage bond aforesaid as if she had never been married or as if the said George Krone was naturally dead. And this Libellant will pray etc." (signed by her mark Barbara Ann Krone.) "by her next friend" (signed John A. Clark.) "Test" (signed H. Gallagher.) "The above named Barbara Ann Krone being duly sworn according to law doth say that the facts contained in the foregoing are true to the best of her knowledge and belief -and that the said complaint is not made out of levity and collusion between her and the said George Krone and for the mere purpose of being freed and separated from each other, but in sincerity and truth and for the causes mentioned in the said libel. Sworn and subscribed before me this 19th day of Sept. 1839. (signed Robert Snodgrass, J.P. and Barbara Ann Krone by her mark.)

Sept. 27, 1839 -"Cumberland County, s.s. -The Commonwealth of Pennsylvania to George Krone Greeting: Whereas Barbara Ann Krone, a citizen of Cumberland County did on the 27th day of September A.D. 1839 prefer her petition to one of the Judges of the Court of Common Pleas of Cumberland County praying that for the causes therein set forth, she might be divorced from the bonds of matrimony entered into with you the said George Krone. We therefore command you the said George Krone, that setting aside all other business and excuses whatsoever, you be and appear in your proper person before our Judges at Carlisle at our County Court of Common Pleas, there to be held the second Monday of November next, to answer the petition or libel of the said Barbara Ann Krone, and show causes if any you have why the said Barbara Ann Krone your wife, should not be divorced from the bonds of matrimony agreeably to the Act of Assembly in such case and provided -and hereof you are not to fail. Witness Samuel Hepburn Esquire, President of our said Court at Carlisle the 27th day of September in the Year of our Lord one thousand eight hundred and thirty nine. (signed Geo. Sanderson, Prothy.)

Nov. 16, 1839 -"John Myers Sheriff being duly sworn according to law doth say that the Deft. named in the within writ is not to be found in the County of Cumberland. Sworn and subscribed in open court 16 Nov. 1839." (signed John Myers, Shrff. and Geo. Sanderson, Prothy.)

Nov. 18, 1839 -"Cumberland County, s.s. -The Commonwealth of Pennsylvania to George Krone Greeting: Whereas Barbara Ann Krone, a citizen of Cumberland County, did on the 27th day of September A.D. 1839, prefer her petition to one of the Judges of the Court of Common Pleas of Cumberland County, praying that for the causes therein set forth, she might be divorced from the bonds of matrimony entered into with you the said George Krone. We, therefore, command you the said George Krone, that setting aside all other business and excuses whatsoever, you be and appear in your proper person before our Judges at Carlisle, at a County Court of Common Pleas, there to be held the second Monday of November next, to answer the Petition or Libel of the said Barbara Ann Krone, and show cause if any you have, why the said Barbara Ann Krone your wife, should not be divorced from the bonds of matrimony agreeably to the acts of Assembly in such case made and provided, and hereof you are not to fail. Witness Samuel Hepburn, Esquire President of our said Court at Carlisle, the 18th day of November in the year of our Lord one thousand eight hundred and thirty nine." (signed Geo Sanderson, Prothy.)

Jan. 15, 1840 -"John Myers Sheriff being sworn in open court doth say that the defendant George Krone is not to be found in his bailiwick. Sworn and subscribed 15 Jany. 1840." (signed John Myers, Shrff. and Geo. Sanderson, Prothy.) "Shrff. fee $0.18 3/4 15th Jany. 1840 On motion of Mr. Gallagher Sheriff to give notice according to act of Assembly. By the Court."

April 16, 1840 -"In the Court of Common Pleas of Cumberland County -In the case of the application of Barbara Ann Krone for a Divorce from the bonds of matrimony entered into with George Krone, on motion of Mr. Gallagher, Rule that depositions be taken ex-parte, by Barbara Ann Krone, before Rudolph Krysher, Esquire, to be read in evidence on the hearing of her application at the next Orphan's Court -By the Court."

April 16, 1840 -"Cumberland County, s.s. -I George Sanderson, Prothonotary of the Court of Common Pleas of Cumberland County do certify that the above is a true extract of a rule entered in the above case. -In testimony whereof I have hereunto set my hand and affixed the seal of said Court, at Carlisle, the 16th day of April, A.D. 1840." (signed Geo. Sanderson, Prothy.)

April 25, 1840 -"Cumberland County, s.s. -Personally appeared before me the subscriber one of the Justices of the Peace in and for said County George Beltzhoover Senior who Doth say that he was present at the marriage of Barbara Krone to George Krone in the year 1834 and saw them married and that the said George Krone has wilfully and maliciously deserted and absented himself from the habitation of the said Barbara for any reasonable cause for upwards of three years from the application of the said Barbara for a divorce and doth still continue to absent himself from her and her habitation. Sworn and subscribed April 25th 1840 before." (signed Rudolph Krysher and George Belshoover.)

April 25, 1840 -"Cumberland County -Personally appeared before me the subscriber one of the Justices of the Peace in and for said County Barbara Hopple who doth say that she was present at the marriage of her daughter Barbara to George Krone that she saw them married on or about the 2nd day of January 1834 and that the said George Krone has wilfully and maliciously deserted and absented himself from the habitation of the said Barbara without any reasonable cause for upward of three years from the application of the said Barbara for a divorce and doth still continue to absent himself from her and her habitation. Sworn and Subscribed April 25th 1840 Before" (signed Rudolph Krysher and Barbara Hopple widow by her mark.)

April 25, 1840 -"I do hereby certify that I married the said Barbara to George Krone on the 2nd day of January A.D. 1834 And I know that he absconded and left her." (signed Rudolph Krysher.)

April 28, 1840 -"Now to wit the 28th of April 1840 in the case of the application of Barbara Ann Krone for a divorce the Court after hearing the depositions taken exparte in pursuance of an order of said Court and after a full consideration of the testimony do order adjudge and decree that the said Barbara Ann Krone the Libellant be divorced and separated from the bonds of matrimony contracted with the said George Krone, and that the said marriage be null and void, and that all and every the duty, rights and claims accruing to either of the said parties by reason of the said marriage shall henceforth cease and determine, and the said parties be severally at liberty to marry again in like manner as if they had never been married. By the Court, April 28, 1840."

♦ ♦ ♦

August Term 1839 #160 Oct. 9, 1839 -"To the Honorable John Stuart one of the Judges of the Court of Common Pleas of Cumberland County -The Libel of Mary Wagner a resident and citizen of the County aforesaid by her next friend Jacob Longnecker -Respectfully showeth that your Libellant on the tenth day of January in the year of our Lord one thousand eight hundred and Twenty one was contracted in matrimony and married to a certain Joseph Wagner and from that time until the last day of May in the year of our Lord one thousand eight hundred and thirty seven lived and cohabited with the said Libellant as his wife and as such was owned and acknowledged by him and so deemed and reputed by her neighbors and acquaintances. And although by the laws of God as well as by their mutual vows and faith plighted to each other they were bound to that uniform constancy and regard which ought to be inseparable from the marriage state; yet so it is that the said Joseph Wagner from the said last day of May in the year of our Lord one thousand eight hundred and thirty seven hath wilfully and maliciously deserted and absented himself from the habitation of this Libellant without any just or reasonable cause -and such desertion hath persisted in for the term of two years and upwards, and yet doth continue to absent himself from the said Libellant. Wherefore your libellant further shewing that she is a citizen of the State of Pennsylvania and has resided therein for upwards of one whole year previous to the filing of this her libel prays your honor that a subpoena may issue forth to summon the said Joseph Wagner to appear in the Court of Common Pleas for the County aforesaid at the next November term to answer the complaint aforesaid. And also that a decree of the said court may be made for the divorcing of him the said Joseph Wagner from the society, fellowship and company of this libellant from the marriage bond aforesaid as if she had never been married or as if the said Joseph Wagner were naturally dead. And this Libellant etc." (signed Mary Wagner by her mark.) "by her next friend" (signed Jacob Longnecker.) "Test" (signed H. Gaullagher.) "The above named Mary Wagner being sworn according to law doth say that the facts contained in the above libel are true to the best of her knowledge and belief, and that the said complaint is not made out of levity and collusion between her and the said Joseph Wagner and for the mere purpose of being freed and separated from each other, but in sincerity and truth and for the causes mentioned in the said libel. Sworn and subscribed this 9th day of Oct. 1839." (signed Robert Snodgrass, J.P. and Mary Wagner by her mark.)

Oct. 10, 1839 -"Cumberland County, s.s. -The Commonwealth of Pennsylvania to Joseph Wagner, Greeting: Whereas Mary Wagner of Cumberland County, did on the 10th day of October A.D. 1839 prefer her petition to John Stuart one of the Judges of the Court of Common Pleas of Cumberland County, praying that for the causes therein set forth, she might be divorced from the bonds of matrimony entered into with you the said Joseph Wagner. We do therefore command you the said Joseph Wagner, that setting aside all other business and excuses whatsoever, you be and appear in your proper person before our Judges at Carlisle, at our County Court of Common Pleas, there to be held for the said County of Cumberland, on the second Monday of November next, to answer the petition or libel of the said Mary Wagner, and shew cause if any you have why the said Mary your wife should not be divorced from the bonds of matrimony agreeably to that Act of Assembly in such case made and provided, and hereof you are not to fail. Witness Samuel Hepburn, Esquire at Carlisle, the 10th day of October in the year of our Lord one thousand eight hundred and thirty nine." (signed Geo. Sanderson, Prothy.)

Nov. 16, 1839 -"John Myers sheriff being duly sworn according to law doth say that the Deft. named in the within writ is not to be found in the County of Cumberland. Sworn and subscribed in open court 16th Nov. 1839." (signed John Myers Shrff. and Geo. Sanderson, Prothy.)

Nov. 18, 1839 -"Cumberland County, s.s. -The Commonwealth of Pennsylvania to Joseph Wagner, Greeting: Whereas Mary Wagner of Cumberland County, did on the 10th day of October A.D. 1839, prefer her petition to John Stuart one of the Judges of the Court of Common Pleas of Cumberland County, praying for the causes therein set forth, she might be divorced from the bonds of matrimony entered into with you the said Joseph Wagner. We do, therefore, command you the said Joseph Wagner, as we have heretofore commanded you, that setting aside all other business and excuses whatsoever, you be and appear in your proper person before our Judges at Carlisle, at our County Court of Common Pleas, there to be held for the said County of Cumberland, on the second Monday of January next, to answer the petition or libel of the said Mary Wagner and shew cause if any you have why the said Mary your wife should not be divorced from the bonds of matrimony agreeably to the acts of

Assembly in such case made and provided, and hereof you are not to fail. Witness, Samuel Hepburn, Esquire at Carlisle, the 18th day of November in the year of our Lord one thousand eight hundred and thirty nine." (signed Geo. Sanderson, Prothy.)

August Term 1839 #160 Jan. 15, 1840 -"John Myers, Sheriff being sworn in open court doth say that the defendant Joseph Wagner is not to be found in his bailiwick. Sworn and subscribed 15 Jany. 1840." (signed John Myers, Shrff. and Geo. Sanderson, Prothy.) "15 Jany. 1840 On motion of Mr. Gallagher Sheriff to give notice according to Act of Assembly. By the Court."

Filed April 14, 1840 -"In case of the application of Mary Wagner for a divorce it appearing to the Court that the Sheriff gave notice according to law requiring Joseph Wagner the husband of the said Mary to appear on the first day of this term to answer to the complaint of the said Mary and it also appearing that the said Joseph did not appear at all and whereupon the Court do order and direct that depostions be taken exparte by the said Mary before Jacob Longnecker to be read in evidence on the hearing of her application as aforesaid at the next Orphan's Court. Test." (signed Geo. Sanderson.) "By the Court."

April 16, 1840 -"In the Court of Common Pleas of Cumberland County -In the case of the application of Mary Wagner for a divorce from the bonds of matrimony entered into with Joseph Wagner, on motion of Mr. Gaullagher, Rule to take depositions ex-parte by the said Mary Wagner before Jacob Longnecker to be read in evidence on the hearing of her application at the next Orphan's Court. By the Court." --"Cumberland County, s.s. -I George Sanderson Prothonotory of the Court of Common Pleas of said County do certify that the above is a true extract of a rule entered in the above case. In testimony whereof I have hereunto set my hand and affixed the seal of said Court at Carlisle, the 16th day of April A.D. 1840." (signed Geo. Sanderson, Prothy.)

April 27, 1840 -"Cumberland County, s.s. -Personally appeared before me the subscriber a Justice of the Peace in and for said County in pursuance of the above rule of Court, Samuel Mumma who being duly affirmed according to law doth say that he is acquainted with Mary Wagner and her husband Joseph Wagner that he was present at the marriage of the said Mary and Joseph that they were married by the Rev. Agustus Lochman, of Harrisburg, on the tenth day of January A.D. 1822. Sworn and subscribed before me this 27th day of April A.D. 1840." (signed Samuel Mumma.)

April 27, 1840 -"Cumberland County, s.s. -Personally appeared before me the subscriber a Justice of the Peace in and for the said County in pursuance of the above rule of Court, Henry Brets and Mary Miller who being duly sworn according to law doth say that they are acquainted with Mary Wagner and her husband Joseph

Wagner and that they know that the said Joseph Wagner hath wilfully and maliciously deserted and absented himself from the habitation of the said Mary Wagner for two years and upwards previous to her application for a divorce and doth still continue to absent himself from her habitation. Sworn and subscribed before me this 27th day of January" (sic) A.D. 1840." (signed J. Longnecker, Henry Brets by his mark and Mary Miller by her mark.)

April 28, 1840 -"Now to wit the 28th of April 1840 in the case of the application of Mary Wagner for a divorce the Court after hearing the depositions taken exparte in pursuance of an order of said Court and after a full consideration of the testimony do order, adjudge and decree that the said Mary Wagner the Libellant be divorced and separated from the bonds of matrimony contracted with the said Joseph Wagner and that the said marriage be null and void, and that all and every the duty, rights, and claims accruing to either of the said parties by reason of the said marriage shall henceforth cease and determine, and the said parties by severally at liberty to marry again in like manner as if they had never been married. By the Court. April 28th, 1840."

◆ ◆ ◆

November Term 1839 #2 July 29, 1839 -"To the Honorable The Judges of the Court of Common Pleas of Cumberland County -The petition of Margaret Woods Respectfully Represents -That your Libellant in the month of June A.D. 1833 was contracted in matrimony and married to a certain Samuel Woods and from that time until the fifth day of June 1835 lived and cohabited with him his wife and as such was owned and acknowledged by him and so deemed an reputed by all her neighbors and acquaintances, and altho by the laws of God as well as by their mutual vows and faith plighted to each other, they were reciprocally bound to that uniform kindness and regard which ought to be inseparable from the marriage state, yet so it is that the said Samuel Woods hath by cruel and barbarous treatment endangered the life of your Libellant and hath offered such indignities to her person as to render her condition intolerable and life burthensome and thereby forced her to withdraw from his house and family. Wherefore your Libellant further showing that she hath resided in this state for two years and upwards previous to the filing of this petition prays your Honors that a subpoena may issue from said Court directed to the said Samuel Woods, commanding him to appear at the next term of said Court to answer this petition and also that a decree of said Court may be made granting this Libellant a divorce from the society fellowship, and company of the said Samuel Woods, in all time to come and from the marriage bond aforesaid as if she had never been married or as if the said Samuel Woods were naturally dead. And she will pray etc. Witness at signing." (signed Margaret Woods, M. Graham and Margaret Woods by her mark.) "By her next friend." --"Cumberland County s.s. -Before the subscriber a Justice of the Peace in and for said County personally came the within named Margaret Woods who being duly affirmed according to law doth on her solemn affirmation say that the facts contained in the within libel are true to the best of her knowledge and belief. And that said complaint is not made out of levity or collusion between her and her said husband and for the mere purpose of being freed and separated from each other, but in sincerity and truth for the causes mentioned in the within petition or libel. Affirmed and subscribed the 29 July 1839 Before" (signed Isaac Todd and Margaret Woods by her mark.)

Aug. 20, 1839 -"Cumberland County, s.s. -The Commonwealth of Pennsylvania to Samuel Woods Greeting: Whereas Margaret Woods, has presented to the Court of Common Pleas of Cumberland County her petition which represents that she was lawfully married to Saml. Woods in the month of June A.D. 1833 and from that time until the fifth day of June 1835 lived and cohabited with him as his wife and as such was owned and acknowledged by him and so deemed and reputed by all her neighbors and acquaintances and that the said Saml. Woods in the month of June A.D. 1835 hath by cruel and barbarous treatment endangered the life of your Libellant and hath offered such indignities her person as to render her condition intolerable and life burthensome and thereby forced her to withdraw from his house and family wherefore your Libellant further showing that she hath resided in this state for two years and upwards previous to the filing of this petition prays your Honors that a subpoena may issue from said Court directed to the said Samuel Woods, commanding him to appear at the next Term of said Court to answer this petition and also that a decree of said Court may be made granting this Libellant a divorce from the society, fellowship and company of the said Samuel Woods in all time and from the marriage bond aforesaid as if she never been married or as if the said Samuel Woods were naturally dead. We therefore command you the said Samuel Woods that you be and appear before our Judges at Carlisle the second Monday of November next to answer the petition of the said Margaret Woods. Witness the Honorable Samuel Hepburn, Esquire President of the said Court at Carlisle the twentieth day of August, in the year of our Lord one thousand eight hundred and thirty nine." (signed Geo. Sanderson, Prothy.) Notation on front of this document -"defendant not to be found my bailiwick so answers" (signed John Myers, Shrff.) "Sheriff's fee $0.18 3/4 Graham."

Nov. 20, 1839 -"Cumberland County, s.s. -The Commonwealth of Pennsylvania to Samuel Woods, Greeting: Whereas Margaret Woods, has presented to the Court of Common Pleas of Cumberland County, her petition, which represents, that she was lawfully married to Samuel Woods in the month of June A.D. 1833, and from that time until the 5th day of June 1835, lived and co-habited with him as his wife, and as such was owned and acknowledged by him and so deemed and reputed by all her neighbours and acquaintances, and that the said Samuel Woods in the month of June A.D. 1835, hath by cruel and barbarous treatment endangered the life of your Libellant, and hath offered such indignities to her person as to render her condition intolerable and life burthensome, and thereby forced her to withdraw from his house and family. Wherefore your Libellant further showing that she hath resided in this state for two years and upwards, previous to the filing of this petition. Prays your honors that a subpoena may issue from said court directed to the said Samuel Woods, commanding him to appear the next term of said court, to answer this petition, and also that a decree of said court may be made, granting this Libellant a divorce from the society, fellowship and company of the said Samuel Woods in all time to come, and from the marriage bond aforesaid, as if she had never been married, or as if the said Samuel Woods were naturally dead. We, therefore, command you the said Samuel Woods, as we hath heretofore commanded you that ye be and appear before our Judges at Carlisle, the second Monday of January next, to answer the petition of the said Margaret Woods. Witness the Honorable Samuel Hepburn, Esquire, President of the said court at Carlisle, the twentieth day of November in the year of our Lord one thousand eight hundred and thirty nine." (signed Geo. Sanderson, Prothy.) Notation on the front of this document -"Defendant not to be found in my Bailiwick. So answers" (signed John Myers, Shrff." "Shrff. fee was $0.18 3/4 Graham."

April 28, 1840 -"Notice not having been published agreeably to the order of Court -Now to wit 28 April 1840 This court grants the order for publications returnable to the next August Court. By the Court."

◆ ◆ ◆

November Term 1839 #15 -Aug. 14, 1839 -"Cumberland County, s.s. -The Commonwealth of Pennsylvania to Joseph Cairns, Greeting: Whereas Harriett Cairns by her next friend James Davis, has presented to the Court of Common Pleas of Cumberland County her petition which represents, that she was lawfully married to Joseph Cairns in the month of June A.D. 1808 and from that time until the month of October A.D. 1810 lived and cohabited with him as his wife and as such was owned and acknowledged by him and so deemed and reputed by all her neighbors and acquaintances, and although by the laws of God as well as by their mutual vows and faith plighted to each other, they were reciprocally bound to that uniform kindness and regard which ought to be inseparable from the marriage state; yet so it is that the said Joseph Cairns from the said month of October A.D. 1810 hath wilfully and maliciously absented himself from the habitation of this Libellant; Wherefore your Libellant further showing that she hath resided in this state for two years and upwards previous to the filing of this petition. Prays your Honors that a subpoena shall issue from said Court directed to the said Joseph Cairns, commanding him to appear at the next term of the said Court, to answer this petition, and also that a decree of Court may be made granting this Libellant a divorce from the society, fellowship and company of the said Joseph Cairns in all time to come and from the marriage bond aforesaid, as if she had never been married, or as if the said Joseph Cairns were naturally dead. We therefore command you the said Joseph Cairns as we have heretofore commanded you, that you be and appear, before our Judges at our next Court of Common Pleas of Cumberland County to be held at Carlisle, on Monday the eleventh day of November next, to answer the petition of the said Harriet Cairns. Witness the Honorable Samuel Hepburn, Esquire, President of the said Court at Carlisle the fourteenth day of August, in the Year of our Lord one thousand eight hundred and thirty nine. For George Sanderson, Prothonotary." (signed Wm. M. Beetem.) Notation on front of this document -"defendant not to be found in my Bailiwick. So answers" (signed John Myers, Shff.) "Shrff.'s fee is $0.18 3/4 Graham."

◆   ◆   ◆

January Term 1840 #53 Dec. 17, 1839 -"To the Judges of the Court of Common Pleas of Cumberland County -The petition of Mary Whiteman formerly Mary Dunfee Respectfully represents That she was lawfully joined in wedlock to William Whiteman more than ten years ago and that the said William Whiteman her husband hath wilfully and maliciously deserted and absented himself from the habitation of his said wife your petitioner without a reasonable cause, and for and during the term and space of two years and upwards. She the said Mary Whiteman by her next friend Jacob Myers presents this her petition to the said Court to grant her a divorce from the bonds of matrimony entered into between her and the said William Whiteman." (signed Mary Wightman.) "by her next friend" (signed Jacob Myers.) "Cumberland County sct. -Personally appeared before me a Justice of the Peace in and for said County Mary Whiteman who being duly sworn doth depose and say that the facts set forth in the above petition are true to the best of her knowledge and belief and that the said complaint is not made out of levity or by collusion between her and her said husband and for the mere purpose of being freed and separated from each other, but in sincerity and truth for the causes mentioned in her said petition, and for no other purpose. Sworn and subscribed the 17th day of December A.D. 1839 Before me." (signed Jas. N. Allen.)

Jan. 28, 1840 -"Cumberland County, s.s. -The Commonwealth of Pennsylvania William Wightman, Greeting: Whereas Mary Wightman, a citizen of Cumberland County, did on the 13th day of January, A.D. 1840, prefer her petition to the Judges of the Court of Common Pleas of Cumberland County praying that for the causes therein set forth, she might be divorced from the bonds of matrimony entered into with you the said William Wightman -We, therefore, command you the said William Wightman that setting aside all other business and excuses whatsoever, you be and appear in your proper person before our Judges at Carlisle, at our County Court of Common Pleas, there to be held the second Monday of April next, to answer the petition or libel of the said Mary Wightman, and shew cause if any you have why the said Mary Wightman your wife, should not be divorced from the bonds of matrimony agreeably to the Act of Assembly in such case made and provided -and hereof you are not to fail. Witness Samuel Hepburn, Esquire, President of our said Court, at Carlisle, this 28th day of January in the year of our Lord one thousand eight hundred and forty." (signed Geo. Sanderson, Prothy.) Notation on front of this document -"Not to be found in my Bailiwick. So answers." (signed John Myers Shrff.) "Watts"

April 16, 1840 -"Cumberland County, s.s. -The Commonwealth of Pennsylvania to William Wightman -Greeting: Whereas, Mary Whiteman, a citizen of Cumberland County, did on the 13th day of January, A.D. 1840, prefer her petition to the Judges of the Court of Common Pleas of Cumberland County, praying that for the causes therein set forth, she might be divorced from the bonds of matrimony entered into with you the said William Whiteman. We, therefore command you as we have heretofore commanded you the said William Whiteman that setting aside all other business and excuses whatsoever, you be and appear in your proper person before our Judges at Carlisle, at our County Court of Common Pleas, there to be held the second Monday of August next, to answer the petition or libel of the said Mary Whiteman and shew cause if any you have why the said Mary Whiteman your wife, should not be divorced from the bonds of matrimony agreeably to the Acts of Assembly in such case made and provided -and hereof you are not to fail -Witness Samuel Hepburn, Esquire, President of our said Court, at Carlisle, this 16th day of April A.D. 1840." (signed Geo. Sanderson, Prothy.)

Aug. 11, 1840 -"Cumberland County, sct. -John Myers being duly sworn doth depose and say that he served a true copy of the within subpoena on William Wightman on the 16 April 1840 by giving the same to him. Sworn and subscribed in open Court 11 Aug. 1840" (signed Geo. Sanderson, Prothy.)

Aug. 11, 1840 -"In the Court of Common Pleas of Cumberland County -Mary Wightman formerly Mary Dunfee vs. William Wightman -No. 53 January Term 1840 -Now to wit; 11th August 1840 The Court having received due proof of the service of the subpoena in this case upon William Wightman on the 16th April 1840 and the said William Wightman not now appearing, the Court do hereby order and appoint James Kennedy, Esq. of Newville as a Commissioner to take the testimony of witnesses to prove the complaint of the said Mary Wightman as set forth in her petition, and do hereby appoint Tuesday the 25 August next for the final hearing of the case -By the Court." --"Cumberland County, s.s. -I George Sanderson, Prothonotary of the Court of Common Pleas of said county, do certify, that the above is a true copy of the order of Court for a Commissioner in the above case -In testimony whereof I have hereunto set my hand and affixed the seal of said Court at Carlisle, the 11th day of August, A.D. 1840." (signed Geo. Sanderson, Prothy.)

August 14, 1840 -"Cumberland County, s.s. -Personally appeared before me a Justice of the Peace in and for said County William Barr who being duly sworn doth depose and say that more than three years ago William Wightman, willfully and maliciously deserted and absconded himself from the habitation of his said wife Mary Wightman without any reasonable cause known to the deponent. That the deponent has known the said Mary Wightman for more than two years and that during that time he verily believes that the said William Wightman has not in any way provided for or aided to maintain his said wife but has wholly abandoned her to make her own living as she can and further deponent sayeth not. Sworn and subscribed this 14th day of August 1840." (signed William Barr and Jas. Kennedy.)

August 14, 1840 -"Cumberland County, s.s. -Personally appeared before me a Justice of the Peace in and for said County Nathan Reed who being duly sworn doth depose and say that more than three years ago William Wightman willfully and maliciously deserted and absconded himself from the habitation of his said wife Mary Wightman without any reasonable cause known to the deponent that the deponent has known the said Mary Wightman for more than two years and that during that time he verily believes that the said William Wightman has not in any way provided for or aided to maintain his said wife but has wholly abandoned her to make her own living as she can further deponent sayeth not. Sworn and subscribed the 14th day of August 1840." (signed Nathan Reed and Jas. Kennedy.)

August 14, 1840 -"Cumberland County, s.s. -Personally appeared before me a Justice of the Peace in and for said County William Laughlin who being duly sworn doth depose and say that more than three years ago William Wightman willfully and maliciously deserted and absconded himself from the habitation of his said wife Mary Wightman without any reasonable cause known to the deponent. That the deponent has known the said Mary Wightman for more than two years and that during that time he verily believes that the said William Wightman has not in any way provided for or aided to maintain his said wife, but has wholly abandoned her to make her own living as she can further deponent sayeth not. Sworn and subscribed this 14th day of August A.D. 1840." (signed Wm. Laughlin and Jas. Kennedy.)

August 25, 1840 -"Mary Wightman formerly Mary Dunfee vs. William Wightman: No. 53 Jan Term 1840 In the Common Pleas of Cumberland County -Now to wit 25 Aug. 1840. The Court having heard the evidence taken in this case upon due consideration of the premises do hereby sentence and decree that the said Mary Wightman formerly Mary Dunfee be divorced and separated from the nuptial ties or bonds of matrimony entered into with the said William Wightman and that the said marriage is null and void, and that all the duties rights and claims accruing to either of the said parties at any time heretofore in pursuance of the said marriage do now cease and determine and the said parties shall severally be at liberty to marry again in like manner as if they never had been married. By the Court."

◆ ◆ ◆

January Term 1840 #214 March 21, 1840 -"To the Honorable the Judges of the Court of Common Pleas of Cumberland County -The Libel of Mary Ann Snavely by her next friend George Moltz Respectfully Showeth -That your Libellant in the nineteenth day of December A.D. One thousand eight hundred and thirty three was contracted in matrimony and married to a certain John Snavely, and from that time until the fourteenth of March A.D. one thousand eight hundred and thirty six lived and cohabited with the said John Snavely as his wife, and as such was owned and acknowledged by him, and so deemed and reputed by her neighbors and acquaintances. And although by the laws of God as well as by their mutual vows and faith plighted to each other, they were bound to that uniform regard and constancy which ought to be inseparable from the marriage state: yet so it is, that the said John Snavely from the said fourteenth of March A.D. One thousand eight hundred and thirty six hath wilfully and maliciously deserted and absented himself from the habitation of this Libellant without any just and reasonable cause and such desertion hath persisted in for the term of two years and upwards, and yet doth continue to absent himself from the said Libellant. Wherefore your Libellant further showing that she is a citizen of the State of Pennsylvania, and has resided therein for upwards of one whole year previous to the filing of this her libel prays your Honors that a subpoena may issue forth to summon the said John Snavely to appear in this Honorable Court at August term next, to answer the complaint aforesaid and also that a decree of this court may be made for the divorcing of him the said John Snavely from the society, fellowship and company of this Libellant in all time to come, and she this Libellant from the marriage bond aforesaid, as if she had never been married or as if the said John Snavely were naturally dead, and this Libellant will pray etc." (signed Mary Ann Snavely by her next friend George Moltz.) "Cumberland County, ss. -The above named Mary Ann Snavely being duly affirmed says the facts contained in the above Libel are true to the best of her knowledge and belief, and that the said complaint is not made out of levity and collusion between her and her said husband and for the mere purpose of being freed and separated from each other but in sincerity and truth for the causes mentioned in said Libel. Affirmed and subscribed before me this 21st day of March A.D. 1840." (signed Henry Zearing and Mary Ann Snavley.)

April 17, 1840 -"Cumberland County, s.s. -The Commonwealth of Pennsylvania to John Snavely, Greeting: Whereas, Mary Ann Snavely, a citizen of Cumberland County, did, on the 13th day of April, A.D. 1840, prefer her petition to the Judges of the Court of Common Pleas of Cumberland County, praying that for the causes therein set forth, she might be divorced from the bonds of matrimony entered into with you the said John Snavely -We therefore command you the said John Snavely that setting aside all other business and excuses whatsoever, you be and appear in your proper person before our Judges at Carlisle, at our County Court of Common Pleas, there to be held the second Monday of August next, to answer the petition or libel of the said Mary Ann Snavely, and shew cause if any you have why the said Mary Ann Snavely your wife, should not be divorced from the bonds of matrimony agreeably to the Act of Assembly in such cases made and provided -and hereof you are not to fail -Witness Samuel Hepburn, Esquire, President of our said court, at Carlisle, the 17th day of April in the Year of our Lord one thousand eight hundred and forty." (signed Geo. Sanderson Prothy.) --Notation on front of this document "defendant not to be found in my Bailiwick. So answers." (signed John Myers, Sheff.) "16th January 1841 Alias subpoena awarded by the Court. Sheriff's fee $0.18 3/4 Biddle."

Jan. 16, 1841 -"Cumberland County, s.s. -The Commonwealth of Pennsylvania to John Snavely, Greeting: Whereas, Mary Ann Snavely a citizen of Cumberland County, did on the 13th day of April, A.D. 1840, prefer her petition to the Judges of the Court of Common Pleas of Cumberland County praying that for the causes therein set forth, she might be divorced from the bonds of matrimony entered into with you the said John Snavely -We therefore command you the said John Snavely as we have heretofore commanded you, that setting aside all other business and excuses whatsoever, you be and appear in your proper person before our Judges at Carlisle, at our County Court of Common Pleas there to be held the 2d Monday of April next, to answer the petition or libel of the said Mary Ann Snavely, and shew cause if any you have why the said Mary Ann Snavely your wife, should not be divorced from the bonds of matrimony agreeably to the act of Assembly in such case made and provided -and hereof you a not to fail -Witness Samuel Hepburn, Esquire, President of our said Court at Carlisle, the 16th day of January, A.D. 1841." (signed Geo. Sanderson, Prothy.) Notation on front of document -"Defendant not to be found in my Bailiwick So answers," (signed Paul Martin, Shrff.) "Shrff. Martin's fee $0.18 3/4 Sheriff Martin sworn to the service. Biddle"

Nov. 8, 1841 -"In the Court of Common Pleas of Cumberland County -In the case of the application of Mary Ann Snavely for a divorce from the bonds of matrimony entered into with John Snavely -And Now to wit, 8th November, 1841 on motion of Mr. Biddle Rule that depositions be taken exparte on the part of said applicant before David Hume Esquire to be read in evidence on the hearing of her case at next argument Court. -Cumberland County, s.s. -I George Sanderson Prothonotary of the Court of Common Pleas of said County do certify that the above rule is entered of Record in said Court. In testimony whereof I have hereunto set my hand and the seal of said Court at Carlisle the 8th November 1841." (signed Geo. Sanderson Prothy.)

Nov. 22, 1841 -"Cumberland County, s.s. -Personally appeared before me the subscriber, a Justice of the Peace, in and for said county, John Sherburn, who doth depose and say, that he was present at the marriage of John Snavely and Mary Ann Snavely, which took place the 19th day of December, in the year one thousand eight hundred and thirty-three, and further deponent saith, that on or about the 14th day of March, eighteen hundred and thirty-six, the said John Snavely wilfully and maliciously deserted the said Mary Ann without any reasonable or just cause, and further deponent saith, that since said desertion, he the said John Snavely, has not been with said Mary Ann, having left the state, and enlisted in the United States Army, and now resides in some of the western states or territories, and has not returned, but where he still resides, and deponent further saith not. Affirmed and subscribed the 22d day of November 1841 Coram me." (signed David Hume and John Sherbahn.)

Nov. 22, 1841 "Cumberland County, s.s. -Personally appeared before me the subscriber, a Justice of the Peace, in and for said county, Michael P. Dill, who doth depose and say, that on the 19th day of December, 1833, John Snavely and Mary Ann Snavely were married, and further deponent saith, that on the 14th of March, 1836, the said John Snavely, wilfully and maliciously deserted the said Mary Ann without any reasonable or just cause, and further deponent saith, that since said desertion, he has not been with said Mary Ann, having left the state, and enlisted in the United States army, and now resides in some of the western states or territories, and has not returned, but where he still resides, and deponent further saith not. Sworn and subscribed this 22d day of November, 1841 Coram me." (signed David Humes and Michael P. Dill.)

Dec. 14, 1841 -"Mary Ann Snavely by her next friend vs. John Snavely: In Common Pleas of Cumberland County No. 214 January 1840 Libel for Divorce: Now to wit 14th December 1841 the Court having heard the evidence taken in this case upon due consideration of the premises do hereby sentence and decree that the said Mary Ann Snavely formerly Mary Ann Moltz be divorced and separated from the nuptial ties or bonds of matrimony entered into with the said John Snavely, and that the said marriage is null and void, and that all and every the duties rights and claims accruing to either of the said parties at any time heretofore in pursuance of the said marriage do now cease and determine and that the said parties shall severally be at liberty to marry again in like manner as if they never had been married. By the Court." Notation on front of this document "14th Decr. 1841 Decree of Court filed."

◆ ◆ ◆

November Term 1840 #88 Nov. 16, 1840 -"To the honorable the Judges of the Court of Common Pleas of Cumberland County -The Libel of Elizabeth Wilson by her brother and next friend James Steen -Respectfully showeth -That your Libellant sometime in the month of May in the year of our Lord one thousand eight hundred and thirty eight was contracted in matrimony and married to a certain George Wilson and from that time until sometime in the month of August in the year aforesaid lived and cohabited with the said George Wilson as his wife and as such was owned and acknowledged by him and so deemed and reputed by her neighbors and acquaintances and although by the laws of God as well as by their mutual vows and faith plighted to each other, they were bound to that uniform constancy and regard which ought to be inseparable from the marriage state; yet so it is that the said George Wilson from the month of August last aforesaid in the year aforesaid hath wilfully and maliciously deserted and absented himself from the habitation of this Libellant without any just or reasonable cause and such desertion hath persisted in for the term of two years and upwards, and yet doth continue to absent himself from the said Libellant Wherefore your Libellant further shewing that she is a citizen of the state of Pennsylvania, and has resided therein for upwards of one whole year previous to the filing of this her Libel, prays your honors that a subpoena may issue forth to summon the said George Wilson to appear in this honorable Court at the next January term to answer the complaint aforesaid and also that a decree of this Court may be made for the divorcing of him the said George Wilson from the society, fellowship and company of this Libellant in all times to come, and her this Libellant from the marriage bond aforesaid as if she had never been married or as if the said George Wilson were naturally dead and this Libellant will pray etc." (signed test. Abam Mayhr and Elizabeth Wilson by her mark.) "by her next friend" (signed James Steen.) -The above named Elizabeth Wilson being sworn according to law says that the facts contained in the above Libel are true to the best of her knowledge and belief and that the said complaint is not made out of levity and collusion between her and the said George Wilson her husband and for the mere purpose of being freed and separated from each other, but in sincerity and truth for the causes mentioned in the said Libel Sworn and subscribed before me this 16th day of Nov. A.D. 1840." (signed William Irwin also by her mark Elizabeth Wilson.)

Nov. 17, 1840 -"Cumberland County, s.s. -The Commonwealth of Pennsylvania, to George Wilson Greeting: Whereas Elizabeth Wilson, a citizen of Cumberland County, did on the 17th day of November, A.D. 1840, prefer her petition to the Judges of the Court of Common Pleas of Cumberland County, praying that for the causes therein set forth, she might be divorced from the bonds of matrimony entered into with you the said George Wilson -We therefore command you the said George Wilson, that setting aside all other business and excuses whatsoever, you be and appear in your proper person before our Judges at Carlisle, at our County Court of Common Pleas there to be held the second Monday of January next, to answer the petition or libel of the said Elizabeth Wilson, and shew cause if any you have why the said Elizabeth Wilson your wife, should not be divorced from the bonds of matrimony agreeably to the act of Assembly in such case made and provided, and hereof you are not to fail. -Witness Samuel Hepburn, Esquire, President of our said Court, at Carlisle, the 17th day of November in the year of our Lord one thousand eight hundred and forty." (signed Geo. Sanderson, Prothy.)

Jan. 26, 1841 -"Cumberland County, s.s. -Paul Martin Sheriff of said County being sworn according to law doth say that his return to this writ that Defendant Geo. Wilson is not to be found in his bailiwick is true and further saith not. Sworn and subscribed the 26th Jany. 1841." (signed Geo. Sanderson, Prothy. and Paul Martin, Shrff.) Notation on front of this document "Shrff. Martin's fee $0.18 3/4 Gaullagher."

Jan. 27, 1841 -"Cumberland County. s.s. -The Commonwealth of Pennsylvania to George Wilson Greeting: Whereas Elizabeth Wilson, a citizen of Cumberland County, did on the 17th day of November A.D. 1840 prefer her petition to the Judges of the Court of Common Pleas of Cumberland County, praying that for the causes therein set forth, she might be divorced from the bonds of matrimony entered into with you the said George Wilson. -We therefore command you the said George Wilson that setting aside all other business and excuses whatsoever, you be and appear in your proper person before our Judges at Carlisle, at our County Court of Common Pleas there to be held the 2d Monday of April next, to answer the petition or libel of the said E. Wilson, and shew cause if any you have why the said E. Wilson your wife should not be divorced from the bonds of matrimony agreeably to the act of Assembly in such case made and provided, and hereof you are not to fail. -Witness Samuel Hepburn, Esquire, President of our said Court, at Carlisle, the 27th day of January, A.D. 1841." (signed Geo. Sanderson, Prothy.)

May 12, 1841 -"Cumberland County, s.s. -Paul Martin Sheriff of said County being sworn according to law doth say that his return to this writ that the Deft. Geo. Wilson is not to be found in his bailiwick is true and further saith not. Sworn and subscribed 12 May 1841." (signed Geo. Sanderson, Prothy. and Paul Martin.)

May 12, 1841 -"Now to wit 12 May 1841 the Court order and direct the said Sheriff to cause notice to be published in one or more newspapers printed and published within the said County of Cumberland for four weeks sucessively prior to the first day of next term requiring said Geo. Wilson to appear on said day to answer to the complaint of the said Libellant By the Court." Notation on the front of this document -"Shrff. Martin's fee $0.18 3/4 Gaullagher."

♦ ♦ ♦

Jan. 1841 #68 May 19, 1842 -"19th May 1842 on hearing of this case, and it appears from the record that issue is joined it is ordered that it be put at the head of the trial list for August term next. By the Court."

Aug. 1842 -"Stewart vs. Stewart: Samuel Sidle a witness for Deft.

2 days at Augt. Term 1842	$1.25
20 miles	.60
	1.85

Stuart vs. Stuart: William Knettle a witness on the part of the Plaintiff

2 days at Augt. Term 1842	$1.25
34 miles circular	1.02
	$2.27

Taxed and sworn to be witnesses the 9th August 1842 Before John Main for Geo. Sanderson Prothy. David Ralston a witness for plff.

2 days at Augt. Term 1842	$1.25
8 miles circular	.24
	$1.49

Taxed and sworn to be witnesses the 9th August 1842 Before John Main for Geo. Sanderson Prothy.

Mrs. Mary Cook a witness for Plff.
2 days at Augst. Term 1842	$1.25	
6 miles circular	.18	1.43
Jane McClelland 2 days	$1.25	
96 miles circular	2.88	4.13
		$11.17

Henry D. Daelhousen a witness for Deft.
2 days	$1.25
36 miles	1.08
	$2.33

Aug. 8, 1842 -"And now to wit 8th August 1842 a Jury of the County being called came to wit Henry Thrush, Samuel Pague, James Weakley, John Ruth, James Kelso, Adam Hauk, Jacob Mumma, George Martin, John K. Longnecker, John Eberly, Henry A. Mackley and Samuel Eberly who being severally balloted for elected, empannelled sworn and affirmed respectfully do say that they find for the plaintiff Forty dollars per year alimony from the time of filing the petition with costs."

Dec. 13, 1842 -"And now to wit 13th December 1842 the Court overrules the motion for a new trial, and do adjudge and decree that the said Mary Stuart be and she is hereby divorced from the bed and board of her husband the said James Stuart. And on motion of the counsel for the said James Stuart the further hearing of the parties upon the subject of alimony is continued until the 14th day of February 1843, at which day the said parties by their counsel appeared in Court and on motion of Defendant's counsel, the further hearing of the cause upon the question of alimony, is continued until the 21st day of February 1843 in order to afford Defendant an opportunity of shewing the circumstances of Defendant's estate and that the amount of the income of Defendant's estate, as sworn to by the witnesses and ascertained by the jury erroneous and that the said Defendant is in debt."

Feb. 21, 1843 -"Mary Stuart by her Aunt and next friend Margaret Bigham vs. James Stuart: In the Court of Common Pleas of Cumberland County No. 68 January Term 1841 Subpoena Sur divorce -And now, to wit, 21st February 1843 the parties by their counsel appear in Court, and defendant's counsel declining to give any further proof or information, on proof given on the subject of alimony, and of the circumstances of defendant's estate do adjudge and decree that the said Plaintiff recover from the Defendant alimony to the amount of forty dollars per year, to be computed from the 11th day of January 1841 being the day when libellant's petition was filed and now amounting to the sum of eighty four dollars and forty four cents to be paid to her by the Defendant yearly and every year during the continuance of said divorce, and the Court do also award costs of suit to be allowed and paid to the Plaintiff by the Defendant to be taxed. By the Court. -Cumberland County s.s. -I Thomas H. Criswell Prothonotary of the Court of Common Pleas of said county do certify that the above is a true copy of the decree of the court made in the case of the application of Mary Stuart for a divorce from her husband James Stuart taken from the records of said court. In testimony whereof I have hereunto set my hand and the seal of said court at Carlisle the 31st July A.D. 1843." (signed Thos. H. Criswell, Prothy.) Notation on the front of this document:

"R. Dt.	$84.44
Int. from 21st Feby. 1843	
Shff. Martin	$1.91
witnesses	11.17
H.D. Daelhousen	2.33
verdict fee	4.00
Atty	3.00
Clk. S.	3.52
Do C	3.96
Cost in Sup. Court	12.50
	$42.39
Shff. Martin for	
serving subpoena	5.95
	$48.34
Sheriff Martin	1.28
Alexander	$49.62

"Money made and paid over so answers." (signed Paul Martin Sherriff.)

May 9, 1843 -"9th May 1843 James Stuart appeals from the decree of the Court in this case. See paper filed."

May 12, 1843 -"12th May 1843 Record delivered to Mr. Brandeberry."

July 29, 1843 -"Stuart vs. Stuart: No. 68 Jany. Term 1841 -Make a copy of the decree for the shff. to collect the money and costs. Samuel Alexander Atty for Libellant 29 July 1843." (signed T.H. Criswell, Esq. Prothy.)

July 31, 1843 -"Exit copy of decree to Sheriff the 31st July 1843."

Apr. 20, 1844 -To the Honourable the Judges of the Court of Common Pleas of Cumberland County -The Petition of James Stewart Respectfully represents: That upon the application of Mary M. Stewart wife of your petitioner, your Honours granted the said Mary M. Stewart a Decree of Divorce from the bed and board of your petitioner and allowed her Alimony. -Your petitioner represents that he is willing to receive and cohabit with the said Mary and to use her as a good husband ought to do, and prays your Honours to suspend the aforesaid sentence or decree or in case of her refusal to return and cohabit under the protection of the Court, with the said James, your petitioner, to discharge and annul the same. And he will pray etc." (signed James Stewart.) Notation on the front of this document -"filed 20th April 1844 and further proceedings stayed until the adjourned court By the Court. Brundebury."

Aug. 20, 1844 -"20th August 1844 Rule to shew cause why the decree of divorce shall not be suspended."

Apr. 29, 1845 -"29th Apl. 1845 Deft. being dead Rule discharged. By the Court."

♦ ♦ ♦

April Term 1841 #36 March 3, 1841 -"To the Honourable Samuel Hepburn, President Judge of the Court of Common Pleas of Cumberland County -The Petition of Martin Brandt respectfully represents -That your petitioner on the twenty first day of August in the year of our Lord one thousand eight hundred and twenty eight was contracted in matrimony and married to a certain Sarah Wymer, and from that time until and during the committing of the grievances hereinafter mentioned, lived and cohabited with her as her husband, and as such was owned and acknowledged by her, and so deemed and reputed by all his neighbours and acquaintances; and although by the laws of God they were bound reciprocally, to that kindness and uniform regard which ought to be inseparable from the marriage state, yet so it is, that the said Sarah, disregarding her marriage vow has been guilty of wilful and malicious desertion and absence from the habitation of your petitioner for and during the term and space of two years and upwards, to wit from the month of April A.D. 1838, without a reasonable cause. Wherefore your petitioner further shewing that he is a citizen of this state, and hath resided therein for one whole year and more, previous to the filing of this his petition, prays your Honour to award the issuing of a subpoena from the said Court, directed to the said Sarah, commanding her to appear at the next term of said Court to answer this petition, and also that a decree of the said Court may be given granting this Libellant a divorce from the bonds of matrimony and he will pray etc." (signed Martin Brandt.) "Cumberland County S.S. -Martin Brandt the within named petitioner being duly affirmed according to law doth say that the facts set forth in the within petition are true to the best of his knowledge and belief, and that the said complaint is not made out of levity or by collusion between the said Sarah and affirmant, for the mere purpose of being freed and separated from each other, but in sincerity and truth for the causes mentioned in the said petition. Affirmed and subscribed Before me March 3d 1841." (signed Saml. Hepburn and Martin Brandt.) "Subpoena awarded Saml. Hepburn March 3d 1841."

March 3, 1841 -"Cumberland County s.s. -The Commonwealth of Pennsylvania to Sarah Brandt, Greeting: Whereas Martin Brandt, a citizen of Cumberland County did on the 3d March 1841 prefer his petition to the Honorable Samuel Hepburn, President Judge of the Court of Common Pleas of Cumberland County, in vacation, praying that for the causes therein set forth, he might be divorced from the bonds of Matrimony entered into with you the said Sarah Brandt, and the said Judge having awarded a subpoena -We therefore command you the said Sarah Brandt, that setting aside all other business and excuses whatsoever, you be and appear in your proper person before our Judges at Carlisle, at our County Court of Common Pleas, there to be held, the second Monday of April next, to answer the petition or libel of the said Martin Brandt, and shew cause if any you have why the said Martin Brandt, your husband should not be divorced from the bonds of matrimony agreeably to the acts of Assembly in such case made and provided -and hereof you are not to fail. Witness Samuel Hepburn Esquire President of our said court at Carlisle this 3d day of March in the year of our Lord one thousand eight hundred and forty one." (signed Geo. Sanderson Prothonotary.)

April 12, 1841 -"Cumberland County S.S. -John Stine being duly affirmed according to law doth say that he served the within subpoena personally on Sarah Brandt and by copy on the fifth day of March A.D. 1841. Affirmed and subscribed this 12th day of April 1841 in open Court." (signed by John Stine and Geo. Sanderson Prothy.)

April 13, 1841 -"In the Court of Common Pleas of Cumberland County Martin Brandt vs. Sarah Brandt No. 36 April Term 1841 -13th April 1841. On motion of Mr. Brandebury, the Court appoints Rudolph Krysher, Esq. Commissioner to take depositions exparte on ten days notice, and the case to be heard at the adjourned Court on the 11th of May." -"Cumberland County s.s. State of Pennsylvania: I George Sanderson, Prothonotary of the Court of Common Pleas of said County, do certify that the above is a true copy of the Rule entered in this case. In testimony whereof I have hereunto set my hand, and affixed the seal of said Court, at Carlisle, the 13th day of April A.D. 1841." (signed Geo. Sanderson, Proth.)

April 15, 1841 -"To Mrs. Sarah Brandt -You will take notice that in pursuance of the above rule, depositions to be read on the hearing of the above case, will be taken before Rudolph Krysher Esquire, at his office in Churchtown on Friday the 30th day of this month between the hours of 10 o'clock A.M. and 2 o'clock P.M. of said day when and where you may attend if you think proper." (signed Martin Brandt April 15, 1841.)

May 11, 1841 -"Cumberland County S.S. -Martin Brandt being duly affirmed according to law doth say that he served a copy of the within rule and notice on Sarah Brandt on Tuesday the twentieth day of April last. Affirmed and subscribed this 11th day of May A.D.

1841 in open Court Coram." (signed Martin Brandt and Geo. Sanderson, Prothy.)

April 30, 1841 -"Cumberland County S.S. -Agreeable to a Rule from Court of Cumberland County appeared before me Rudolph Krysher one of the Justices of the Peace in and for the said County Frederick Hoke and being duly sworn according to law saith I met Sarah one time after she had left Brandt. I said what came over you that you left Brandt, that you parted was the meaning. She said I will not keep house with him no more. I then asked her whether Martin Brandt was cross to her or whether he abused her. She made answer No that he was not. I then asked her Sarah was his children cross to you. She made answer No and smiled they were not. I then said Sarah what made you go away? Because I would not live with him any more further saith not. Sworn and subscribed April 30th 1841 Before me." (signed Fred. Hoke and Rudolph Krysher.)

April 30, 1841 -"Peter Wolford Esquire on his solemn affirmation saith three years last Easter myself and several neighbours had been called to arrange a settlement at David Low's house between Sarah Brandt and her son-in-law David Low and George Byers who was the guardian of Mrs. Brandt's daughter Elizabeth Wiemer. Martin Brandt was not there at the commencement of our business but in a short time came. After Brandt had come he and his wife Sarah went into another apartment, and in a short time returned into the room where we were at business. Then Sarah in substance said that she would never go back to keep house with Brandt again. Then Mr. Brandt questioned her, if ever he abused her or treated her ill. Sarah said No. Then Mr. Brandt questioned further more whether his children abused her or treated her ill. She replyed (sic) No, but I will keep house with you no more. Further saith not. Affirmed and subscribed April 30th 1841 Before" (signed Rudolph Krysher and Peter Wolford.)

April 30, 1841 -"David Brandt on his solemn affirmation saith that on the 27th day of January last past as near as I can recollect Martin Brandt came to my house and requested me to go along with him to Sarah Brandt his wife. He then asked her to come back and live with him. The answer she made was she would not. Mr. Brandt then stated that it would be mutch (sic) better for them both. She then answered again she would not. Further saith not. Affirmed and subscribed April 30th 1841 Before me." (signed Rudolph Krysher and David Brandt.)

April 31, 1841 -"James Livingston on his solemn oath according to law saith he lived with Mr. Martin Brandt three years while Sarah Brandt was there, and that he never seen nor heared (sic.) any quarrell between Brandt and his wife nor with the children neither. She told me she would go when she pleased and come when she pleased. She was her own Master. Further saith that she always had plenty to eat while I was there. Further saith not. Sworn and subscribed April 31st 1841 Before Me." (signed Rudolph Krysher and James Livingston.)

May 3, 1841 -"Cumberland County S.S. -Personally appeared before me the subscriber one of the Justices of the Peace in and for said County Daniel Bollinger and on his solemn affirmation according to law deposeth and saith that Mr. Martin Brandt and Sarah Wiemer were legally joined in wedlock and that he had maried (sic.) them but how long since he doth not recollect. Further saith not. Affirmed and subscribed May 3rd 1841 Before Me." (signed Rudolph Krysher and Daniel Bollinger.)

May 11, 1841 -"Now to wit 11th May A.D. 1841 the Court, upon due proof having been made, by the petitioner that he has complied with all the requisition of the acts of Assembly in the premises, and after hearing the proofs of petitioner, the defendant not appearing nor any person for her, do order and decree that the said Martin Brandt be divorced from the bonds of matrimony with the said Sarah Brandt, so that their said marriage be null and void, and that all and every the duties, rights and claims accruing to either of said parties at any time heretofore in pursuance of said marriage now cease and determine, and the said parties be severally at liberty to marry again in the like manner as if they never had been married. The Court do further order and decree that the costs of the proceedings in this case, be paid by the defendant Mrs. Sarah Brandt. By the Court." Notation on front of document -"Filed 11 May 1841."

◆　　　　◆　　　　◆

January Term 1842 #14 Dec. 1, 1841 -"To the Hon. Samuel Hepburn, President Judge of the Court of Common Pleas of Cumberland Co. -The libel of Jane Sheaner by her next friend David Lamb Respectfully Sheweth -That your libellant on the 22 day of October 1835 was contracted in matrimony and married to a certain Jacob Sheaner who from that time until March 1836 lived and cohabited with the said Jane as his wife and as such she was owned and acknowledged by him and so deemed and reputed by her acquaintances and neighbors. And although by the laws of God as well as by their mutual vows and faith plighted to each other they were bound to that uniform constancy and regard which ought to be inseparable from the marriage state, yet so it is that the said Jacob Sheaner from March 1836 hath wilfully and maliciously deserted and absented himself from the habitation of this libellant without any just and reasonable cause and in such desertion hath persisted for the space of two years and upwards. Wherefore your libellant further shewing that she is a citizen of the state of Pennsylvania and hath resided therein for one whole year previous to filing this her bill, prays your Honor that a subpoena may be awarded to summon the said Jacob to appear in the Court of Common Pleas of Cumberland County at

January Term next to answer the complaint aforesaid. And also that a decree of the said Court be made for the divorcing of him the said Jacob Sheaner from the society, fellowship and company of this libellant in all time to come and her this libellant from the marriage bond aforesaid as if she had never been married or as if the said Jacob Sheaner were naturally dead. And this libellant will pray." (signed by her mark Jane Sheaner.) "by her next friend" (signed David Lamb.) -"Cumberland County s.s. -The above libellant being duly sworn says the facts contained in the above libel are true to the best of her knowledge and belief, and that the said complaint is not made out of levity and collusion between her and her said husband, but in sincerity and truth for the causes mentioned in said libel. Sworn and subscribed before me this 1st Dec. 1841." (signed David Smith and Jane Sheaner by her mark.)

Dec. 1, 1841 -"Cumberland County s.s. -The Commonwealth of Pennsylvania to Jacob Sheaner Greeting -Whereas Jane Sheaner by her next friend David Lamb, on the 1st day of December A.D. 1841, preferred a petition to the Honorable Samuel Hepburn President Judge of the Court of Common Pleas of Cumberland County in vacation praying that for the causes therein set forth, she might be divorced from the bonds of matrimony entered into with you the said Jacob Sheaner and the said Judge having awarded a subpoena -We command you the said Jacob Sheaner that setting aside all other business and excuses, whatsoever, you be and appear in your proper person before our Judges at Carlisle at our County Court of Common Pleas there to be held the second Monday of January next, to answer the petition or libel of the said Jane Sheaner and shew cause if any you have why the said Jane Sheaner, you wife should not be divorced from the bonds of matrimony, agreeably to the acts of Assembly in such case made and provided. And hereof you are not to fail -Witness Samuel Hepburn Esquire President Judge of our said court at Carlisle the 1st day of December A.D. 1841 for George Sanderson Prothonotary." (signed John Main.) "Cumberland County -Michael Holcomb Dep. Shf. being sworn in open court says his return to this writ is true. Sworn and subscribed in open court 10 Jany. 1841." (signed M. Holcomb, D.S. and Geo. Sanderson, Prothy.) Notation on front of this document -"Not to be found in my Bailiwick, So answers" (signed Paul Martin Shrff.) "Shff. Martin's fee 18 3/4 cts. Adair."

Jan. 14, 1842 -"Cumberland County s.s. -The Commonwealth of Pennsylvania to John (sic) Sheaner Greeting -Whereas Jane Sheaner by her next friend Davd Lamb on the 1st day of December A.D. 1841 preferred a petition to the honorable Samuel Hepburn President Judge of the Court of Common Pleas of Cumberland County, in vacation praying that for the causes therein set fourth (sic) she might be divorced from the bonds of matrimony entered into with you the said Jacob Sheaner, and the said Judge having awarded a subpoena, we command you the said John (sic) Sheaner that setting aside all other business and excuses whatsoever you be and appear in your proper person before our judges at Carlisle at our County Court of Common Pleas there to be held the second Monday of January next to answer the libel or petition of the said Jane Sheaner by etc. and shew cause if any you have why the said Jane Sheaner your wife should not be divorced from the bonds of matrimony agreeably to the acts of Assembly in such case made and provided. And hereof you are not to fail -witness Samuel Hepburn Esquire President of our said Court at Carlisle the fourteenth day of January A.D. 1842 for George Sanderson Prothy." -(signed John Main.) Notation on the front of the document -"Not to be found in my Bailiwick, So answers" (signed Paul Martin, Shrff.) "Shff. Martin's fee 18 3/4 cents Adveg. $1.00 Adair."

Aug. 8, 1842 -"Cumberland Co., s.s. -M. Holcomb Depy. Sheriff being duly sworn says that the return to this writ is true and that the proper notice was published for four successive weeks in the *Carlisle Herald and Expositor*. Sworn and subscribed in open court 8 Aug. '42" (signed Geo. Sanderson, Prothy. and M. Holcomb.)

Aug. 8, 1842 -"In the matter of the application by Jane Sheaner for a Divorce: No. 14 January term 1842 -Now to wit August 8th 1842 It being made to appear to the Court that notice of said application has been published in the *Carlisle Herald and Expositor* for four successive weeks in accordance with the terms of the act of Assembly. On motion of Mr. Adair Lewis Zearing is appointed a commissioner to take the depositions of witnesses to be read on the hearing of this application on the part of the libellant. By the Court." -"Cumberland County s.s. -I George Sanderson, Prothonotary of the Court of Common Pleas of said County do certify that the above is a true extract from the records of said court. In testimony whereof I have hereunto set my hand and the seal of said court at Carlisle this 8th day of August A.D. 1842." (signed Geo. Sanderson, Prothy.)

Aug. 24, 1842 -"Cumberland County S.S. -Before me the subscriber, one of the Justices of the Peace in and for the said County, the following depositions were taken before me in pursuance of the above rule of Court, on the part of the said libellant, to wit. Henry Leas personally appeared before me, and after being duly sworn, doth depose and say, that he knew Jacob Shanor (sic) the husband of the above named libellant in the Year A.D. 1835 and 1836 at which time he lived in the borough of Mechanicsburg in said County, said Shanor (sic) and wife both gave deponent to understand that they were married, and that both said Shanor (sic) and wife came to the store of H. & C. Leas (said deponent being one of the firm of H. & C. Leas.) that they purchased some goods of said firm during the above mentioned two years, and that said Shaner (sic) worked for deponent in the winter of 1835-6. That in the month of April 1836 there was a balance of five dollars and fifteen cents owing by him. Said Shaner (sic) left said borough in the said month of April, and it was believed that had left the place not to return again. I then called on Mrs. Shaner (sic) said libellent and told her she might as well give me some of his tools for the balance which said Shaner (sic) owed said firm. Mrs. Shaner (sic) then accordingly gave me two crupping hoes and one axe. I think shortly afterwards said Shaner (sic) returned, and him (said Shaner) or some person for him came to our store, and we fixed a price on said tools, and a balance of sixty five cents was still owing to said firm which was paid at the same time. I think shortly afterwards he went away again, and I do not recollect of ever having seen him afterwards. Further saith not. Sworn and subscribed the 24th day of August A.D. 1842 before me." (signed Lewis Zearing and Henry Leas.)

January Term 1842 #14 Aug. 24, 1842 -"Cumberland County S.S. -Henry Kimmel of the borough of Mechanicsburg personally came as above, who being duly sworn as the law directs doth depose and say, that he knew Jacob Sheaner the husband of the said Jane Shaner (sic) said libellant. I understood from both them that they were married as from common report I recollect the night of the serenading of their marriage. I think this matter took place in the year A.D. 1835 in the fall of that year. I recollect that said Shaner (sic) left said borough in the spring of the year 1836 and soon afterwards returned again, but soon afterwards left his wife and home. I afterwards heard that he was somewhere on the Baltimore and Ohio Rail Road. I know that said Shaner (sic) hath not since come to this part of the country to my knowledge. Further saith not. Sworn and subscribed the 24th day of August A.D. 1842 before me. (signed Lewis Zearing and Henry Kimmel.)

Aug. 24, 1842 -"Robert Wilson of Mechanicsburg, sworn as the law directs, doth depose and say, that I knew Jacob Shaner (sic) and Jane his wife the said libellant. I understand from the peoble (sic) of said town that said Jacob and Jane were married, and lived together like man and wife, I think that said Shaner (sic) left here some time after, and returned again, and soon afterwards left his wife and home and never returned again to the best of my knowledge. I afterwards heard that he was about the Gettysburg Rail Road; and that he got married again, and that I have not heard of him for three or four years past. Further saith not. Sworn and subscribed the 24th day of August A.D. 1842 before me." (signed Lewis Zearing and Robert Wilson.) Notation on front of document -"50 cents paid by Mr. D. Lamb to Lewis Zearing."

Nov. 15, 1842 -"Jane Shaner (sic) by her next friend David Lamb vs. Jacob Shaner (sic): No 14 January Term 1842 -And now to wit, November 15th 1842, Lewis Zearing Esq. the Commissioner appointed by the Court, having returned here the depositions taken before him on the part of the Libellant and the same being read and heard by the Court, and the Court after mature deliberation being satisfied therewith, it is ordered adjudged and decreed, that the said Jane Shaner the Libellant be divorced and separated from the bond of matrimony contracted with the said Jacob Shaner (sic) the Respondent and that all and every the duties rights and claims accruing to either of the said parties by reason of the said marriage shall henceforth cease and determine, and the said parties be severally at liberty to marry again in like manner as if they never had been married." Notation on front of this document -"15th November 1842 Granted by the Court Filed 15 November 1842."

♦ ♦ ♦

April Term 1842 #2 Dec. 15, 1841 -"To the Judges of the Court of Common Pleas of the County of Cumberland -The petition of Mary Ann Davis by her father and next friend John T. Kepler Respectfully Represents -That the said Mary Ann was lawfully joined in marriage with Luther Davis a number of years ago. That the said Luther Davis wilfully and maliciously deserted and absented himself from the habitation of his wife the said Mary Ann Davis without any reasonable cause and has been absent for and during the space of two years and more during which time he has not contributed in any way to the support of his said wife and family. She therefore prays the Court to award a subpoena directed to the said Luther Davis to appear on the second Monday of January next to answer this petition and shew cause why the Court should not decree a divorce in favour of the said petitioner. By her next friend." -"Cumberland County sct -Mary Ann Davis personally appeared before me a Justice of the Peace in and for said County and being duly sworn doth depose and say that the facts contained in the above petition are true to the best of her knowledge and belief; and that the said complaint is not made out of levity or by collusion between her and her said husband, and for the mere purpose of being freed and separated from each other, but in sincerity and truth for the causes mentioned in the petition. Sworn and subscribed the 15th December 1841 Before me." (signed William Irwin and Mary Ann Davis.) Notation on front of this document -"10th January 1842 Petition presented and Subpoena awarded By the Court."

Jan. 11, 1842 -"Cumberland County, s.s. -The Commonwealth of Pennsylvania to Luther Davis Greeting -Whereas Mary Ann Davis by her father and next friend John T. Kepler on the 10th day of January A.D. 1842 preferred a petition to the Judges of the Court of Common Pleas of Cumberland County, praying that for the causes therein set forth she might be divorced from the bonds of matrimony entered into with you the said Luther Davis, and the said Judges, having awarded a subpoena We command you the said Luther Davis that setting aside all other business and excuses whatsoever you be and appear in your proper person before our Judges at Carlisle at our County Court of Common Pleas there to be held the second Monday of April next to answer the petition or libel of the said Mary Ann Davis by etc. and shew cause if any you have why the said Mary Ann Davis your wife should not be divorced from the bonds of matrimony agreeably to the acts of Assembly in such case made and provided -And hereof you are not to fail -Witness Samuel Hepburn Esquire at Carlisle the 11th day of January A.D. 1842." (signed Geo. Sanderson, Prothy.) Notation on front of this document -"Subpoena Sur divorce to Luther Davis Returnable 11th Apl. 1842 Not to be found in my Bailiwick So answers." (signed Paul Martin Shrff.) -"Shrff. Martin's fee $ 0.18 cts Watts."

April 15, 1842 -"Cumberland County, s.s. -The Commonwealth of Pennsylvania to Luther Davis Greeting -Whereas Mary Ann Davis by her father and next friend John T. Kepler on the 10th day of January A.D. 1842 preferred a petition to the Judges of the Court of Common Pleas of Cumberland County, praying that for the causes therein set forth she might be divorced from the bonds of matrimony entered into with you, the said Luther Davis, and the said Judges having awarded an alias subpoena. We command you as we have heretofore commanded you, that setting aside all other business and excuses whatsoever you be and appear in your proper person before our Judges at Carlisle at our County Court of Common Pleas there to be held the second Monday of August next, to answer the petition or libel of the said Mary Ann Davis by etc., and shew cause if any you have why the said Mary Ann Davis your wife shall not be divorced from the bonds of matrimony agreeably to the acts of Assembly in such case made and provided -and hereof you are not to fail. Witness Samuel Hepburn Esquire at Carlisle the fifteenth day of April A.D. 1842." (signed Geo. Sanderson, Prothonotary.) -Notation on the front of this document -"Alias subpoena in Divorce to Luther Davis Returnable 8th August 1842. Not to be found in my Bailiwick. So answers." (signed Paul Martin, Shrff.) -"Shrff. Martin's fee 18 3/4 cts. Watts."

Oct. 10, 1842 -"Cumberland County s.s. -The Commonwealth of Pennsylvania to Luther Davis Greeting -Whereas Mary Ann Davis by her father and next friend John T. Kepler on the 10th day of January A.D. 1842 preferred a petition to the Judges of the Court of Common Pleas of Cumberland County praying that for the causes therein set forth she might be divorced from the bonds of matrimony entered into with you the said Luther Davis and the said Judges having awarded a subpoena, we command you as we have heretofore commanded you, that setting aside all other business and excuses whatsoever and be in your proper person before our Judges at Carlisle at our County Court of Common Pleas there to be held the second Monday of November next to answer the petition or libel of the said Mary Ann Davis by etc. and shew cause if any you have why the said Mary Ann Davis your wife shall not be divorced from the bonds of matrimony agreeably to the acts of Assembly in such case made and provided and hereof you are not to fail. Witness Samuel Hepburn Esquire at Carlisle the tenth day of October A.D. 1842 for Geo. Sanderson Prothy." (signed John Main.) Notation on the front of this document -"Pluries subpoena in Divorce to Luther Davis Returnable 14th Nov. 1842 Advertised as by the within writ directed. So answers," (signed Paul Martin Shrff.) "Shrff. Martin $1.00 Advert. $1.00 total bill $2.00 Watts."

Nov. 14, 1842 -"In the matter of the application of Mary Ann Davis for a decree of divorce from her Husband -Now, to wit, 14 Nov. 1842 The Court having received due proof of the truth of the returns to the several writs of subpoena directed to the Sheriff and that the same has been duly published according to law -Do now appoint Wm. Irvine Esq. as a Commissioner to take the testimony of witnesses to be read in the final hearing and the Court appoint Tuesday the 13 Decr. next for the final hearing. By the Court." "Filed 17 Novr. 1842."

Dec. 15, 1842 -"Cumberland County s.s. -I do certify that the above is a true extract taken from the records of the Court of Common Pleas of said County. In testimony whereof I have hereunto set my hand and the seal of said Court at Carlisle this 15th day of December A.D. 1842 for Thos. H. Criswell Prothonotary." (signed John Main.)

March 2, 1843 -"Cumberland County sct. -In pursuance of the above commission to me directed I caused to come before me John T. Kepler who being duly sworn according to law doth depose and say that he was well acquainted with Luther Davis and was present at his marriage with Mary Ann his present wife who is the above named plaintiff that they were married about twenty years ago or more. Soon after his marriage it was discovered that he the said Luther Davis was addicted to drinking spirted liquors. He continued to live with his wife about three or four years and during that time was in the habit of treating his wife cruelly so much so that deponent believes that her life was endangered. About that time he deserted his wife went to Philadelphia as deponent heard and has never since lived with his said wife or conduced in any manner to her support or that of her children. Deponent has not seen the said Luther Davis for several years but heard that he was in Carlisle about four years ago and that he was then drunk. Sworn and subscribed before me March 2 1843." (signed William Irvine and J.T. Keppler.)

March 2, 1843 -"Also appeared before me at the same time Abel Keeney who being duly affirmed doth depose and say that he is well cquainted with Mrs. Mary Ann Davis the wife of Luther Davis and that he has known her for about eight years ever since she came to Carlisle to live. He saw Luther Davis the husband of the said Mary Ann about four years ago and his knowledge of the parties enables him to say that the said Luther Davis has not lived with his said wife or conduced in any manner to her support or that of her children so far as deponent believes. Affirmed and subscribed Before me March 2nd 1843." (signed William Irvine and Abel Keeney.)

March 2, 1843 -"Also appeared before me at the same time Samuel Keppler who being duly sworn doth depose and say that he was acquainted with Luther Davis and was present at his marriage which was more than twenty years ago. That the said Luther Davis continued to live with his wife Mary Ann for a few years and then left her. That during the time he lived with her he was a man of intemperate habits and treated his wife cruelly so much so that her life was not always safe. Deponent can say that he verily believes the said Luther Davis has not lived with his wife for many years nor contributed in any manner to her support or that of her children. Sworn and subscribed the 2 March 1843 Before me." (signed William Irvin and Saml. Keppler.)

April Term 1842 #2 April 15, 1843 -"Now, to wit, 15 April 1843 the said proceedings having been continued to that time the Court having received and examined the evidence in the foregoing case of divorce and taking the care unto consideration do hereby order and decree that the said Mary Ann Davis be and she is hereby divorced from the bonds of matrimony contracted with the said Luther Davis so that she be now as free therefrom as if she had never been married and that she therefore enjoy all the rights priviliges (sic) and claims of a single woman. And that this decree be placed upon the records of the said Court as evidence of the said divorce. By the Court."

◆ ◆ ◆

April Term 1842 #38 Feb. 8, 1842 -"To the Honorable the Judges of the Court of Common Pleas of Cumberland County -The petition of Jesse Powell Respectfully Represents That your petitioner in the month of August A.D. 1837 was contracted in matrimony and married to a certain Lydia Bitner, and although by the laws of God as well as by their mutual vows and faith plighted to each other they were reciprocally bound to that uniform kindness and regard which ought to be inseparable from the marriage state, yet so it is that the said Lydia from the month of August 1838, hath wilfully and maliciously absented herself from your petitioner -without just or reasonable cause and such desertion hath persisted in for the term of three years and upwards and yet doth continue to absent herself from your petitioner. Wherefore your petitioner further showing that he hath resided in this state for two years and upwards previous to the filing this petition prays your Honors that a subpoena may issue from said Court directed to the said Lydia commanding her to appear at the next term of the said Court to answer this petition and also that a decree of said Court may be made granting your petitioner a divorce from the society, fellowship and company of the said Lydia in all time to come, and from the marriage bond aforesaid as if he had never been married or as if the said Lydia were naturally dead And he will pray etc." (signed Jesse Powell.)

April Term 1842 #38 Feb. 8, 1842 -"Cumberland County S.S. -Before the subscriber a Justice of the Peace in and for said County personally came the within named Jesse Powell who being duly sworn according to law says that the facts set forth in the within petition are true, to the best of his knowledge and belief, and that the said complaint is not made out of levity or by collusion between him and his said wife and for the mere purpose of being freed and separated from each other, but in sincerity and truth for the causes mentioned in the within petition. Sworn and subscribed the eighth day of February A.D. 1843 Before me." (signed William Irvine and Jesse Powell.) -Notation on front of this document -"15th Feb. 1842. Subpoena awarded By the Court. Graham."

Feb. 17, 1842 -"Cumberland County S.S. -The Commonwealth of Pennsylvania to Lydia Powell Greeting -Whereas Jesse Powell on the fifteenth day of February A.D. 1842 preferred a petition to the Judges of the Court of Common Pleas of Cumberland County, praying that for the causes therein set forth he might be divorced from the bonds of matrimony entered into with you the said Lydia Powell, and the said Judges having awarded a subpoena -We command you the said Lydia Powell that setting aside all business and excuses whatsoever, you be and appear in your proper person before our Judges at Carlisle at our County Court of Common Pleas there to be held the Eleventh day of April next, to answer the petition or libel of the said Jesse Powell, and shew cause if any you have why he should not be divorced from the bonds of matrimony agreeably to the acts of Assembly in such case made and provided. Witness Samuel Hepburn Esquire, President of our said Court at Carlisle the seventeenth day of February A.D. 1842 For Geo. Sanderson Prothonotary." (signed John Main.) -Notation on front of this document -"Not to be found in my Bailiwick, So answers," (signed Paul Martin Shrff.) -"Shrff. Martin (fee) 18 3/4 cts. Graham."

April 15, 1842 -"Cumberland County S.S. -The Commonwealth of Pennsylvania to Lydia Powell Greeting -Whereas Jesse Powell on the 15th day of February A.D. 1842 preferred a petition to the Judges of the Court of Common Pleas of Cumberland County praying that for the causes therein set fourth (sic) he might be divorced from the bonds of matrimony entered into with you the said Lydia Powell, and the said Judges having awarded an alias subpoena -we command you as we heretofore command you that setting aside all other business and excuses whatsoever you be and appear in your proper person before our Judges at Carlisle at our County Court of Common Pleas there to be held the second Monday of August next to answer the petition or libel of the said Jesse Powell, and shew cause if any you have why he shall not be divorced from the bonds of matrimony agreeably to the acts of assembly in such case made and provided and hereof you are not to fail -Witness Samuel Hepburn Esquire at Carlisle the 15th day of April A.D. 1842." (signed Geo. Sanderson Prothonotary.) Notations on the front and back of this document -"Not to be found in my Bailiwick, so answers." (signed Paul Martin Shrff.) "Shrff. Martin's (fee) 18 3/4¢" "Sworn to and subscribed by Paul Martin Esq. Shff. the 18th November 1842 Before" (signed Geo. Sanderson, Prothy. Paul Martin, Shff.)

Nov. 21, 1842 -"Jesse Powell vs. Lydia Powell: No. 38 April Term 1842 Alias Subpoena Sur Divorce returnable to August T. 1842 -And now, to wit, 21st November 1842 proof being made that defendant could not be found in Cumberland County -The Sheriff of said County is directed to cause notice to be published in our newspaper printed in said county for four successive weeks prior to the 9th day of January A.D. 1843 -requiring the said Lydia Powell to appear on said day, to answer to the complaint of the said Jesse Powell." -"Filed 21 Nov. 1842."

Dec. 15, 1842 -"Jesse Powell vs. Lydia Powell: No. 38 April T. 1842 Subpoena Sur Divorce -Agreeably to an order of court made on the 21st day of November 1842 the said Lydia Powell is hereby notified to appear before the Judges of the Court of Common Pleas of Cumberland County at Carlisle on Monday the 9th day of January 1843 to answer to the complaint of the said Jesse Powell (signed Paul Martin Shff.) "Carlisle December 15th 1842." -"Cumberland County S.S. -George Sanderson Esq. being duly sworn says that he published the above in the *American Volunteer* for four successive weeks agreeably to order of the Court. Sworn and subscribed the 9th Jany. 1843 Before John Main for Thos. H. Criswell Prothy." (signed Geo. Sanderson.) -"Filed 9th Jany. 1843"

Jan. 9, 1843 -"Jesse Powell vs. Lydia Powell: In the Court of Common Pleas of Cumberland County Summons in Divorce -And now, to wit, 9th January A.D. 1843, on proof of the publications of notice in our newspaper printed in Cumberland County for four successive weeks prior to the present Term of said Court, requiring the said Lydia Powell to appear on this day to answer to the complaint of the aforesaid Jesse Powell -Whereupon the Court appoints (illegible first name) Redsacker Esq. of Elizabeth Town, Lancaster County, Pennsylvania, a commissioner to take depositions to be read in evidence and the hearing of the above stated case. By the Court."

Feb. 14, 1843 -"Jesse Powell vs. Lydia Powell: In the Court of

Common Pleas of Cumberland County No. 38 April Term 1843 Subpoena Sur Divorce. And now, to wit, 14th February 1843 on proof of the marriage of the aforesaid parties, and that the Defendant Lydia Powell had wilfully absented herself from the habitation of her husband the aforesaid, Jesse Powell, without a reasonable cause, for and during the term and space of two years and more -The Court do sentence and decree that the aforesaid Jesse Powell and Lydia Powell be divorced and separated from the nuptial ties or bonds of matrimony, and that all and every the duties, rights and claims accruing to either of the said parties at any time heretofore, in pursuance of said marriage shall cease and determine and the said parties shall severally be at liberty to marry again in like manner as if they never had been married. -By the Court." "State of Pennsylvania Cumberland County S.S. -I, Thomas H. Criswell Prothonotary of the Court of Common Pleas of Cumberland County do certify that the above is a true copy of the decree of the court made in the case of the application of Jesse Powell for a divorce from his wife Lydia Powell. In testimony whereof have set my hand and the seal of the said Court at Carlisle the sixteenth day of February in the year of our Lord one thousand eight hundred and forty three." (signed Thos. H. Criswell Prothonotory.)

♦ ♦ ♦

August Term 1842 #1 April 11, 1842 -"To the Hon. the Judges of the Court of Common Pleas of Cumberland County -The petition of George Swigert respectfully represents, that some time in the spring of the year eighteen hundred and thirty nine your petitioner was legally contracted in marriage with one Elizabeth Hostler, and as her husband was reputed by all his neighbors, and resided with the said Elizabeth as her husband for the space of about nine months, during all which time he behaved as an affectionate husband ought to do. And whereas the laws of God require that this solemn contract should continue during their joint lives and ought not to be annulled for light trifling causes, and that each should fulfill the duties of the solemn vows they took upon themselves; yet so it is that the said Elizabeth, your petitioner's wife, forgetting and disregarding the duties of the marriage contract with your petitioner did on or about the 25th day of February in the year 1842 wilfully and maliciously desert and absent herself from the habitation of your petitioner, without a reasonable cause and hath so wilfully and maliciously continued to absent herself for and during the term and space of two years and upwards, and still continues to absent herself. Your petitioner further represents that he is a citizen of this Commonwealth and has resided therein one year and upwards next preceding this his application. He therefore prays your Honours to grant him a divorce from the bonds of matrimony with the said Elizabeth and he will pray etc." (signed George Swigert.) -- "Cumberland County S.S.

-Personally before the subscriber one of the Justices of the Peace in and for said County came the within named George Swigert who being duly sworn according to law doth depose and say that the facts set forth in the foregoing petition are true to the best of his knowledge and belief, and that the said complaint is not made out of levity, or by collusion between the said husband and wife, for the mere purpose of being freed and separated from each other, but in sincerity and truth for the causes mentioned in the within petition. Sworn and subscribed this 11th April A.D. 1842 before me." (Signed David J. Smith, J.P. and George Swigert.) -"11th April 1842. Subpoena awarded By the Court."

April 15, 1842 -"Cumberland County S.S. -The Commonwealth of Pennsylvania to Elizabeth Swigert Greeting -Whereas George Swigert, on the eleventh day of April A.D. 1842 preferred a petition to the Judges of the Court of Common Pleas of Cumberland County praying that for the causes therein set forth he might be divorced from the bonds of matrimony entered into with you the said Elizabeth Swigert and the said Judges then awarded a subpoena, We command you the said Elizabeth Swigert, that setting aside all other business and excuses whatsoever you be and appear in your proper person before our Judges at Carlisle, at our County Court of Common Pleas there to be held the second Monday of August next, to answer the petition or libel of the said George Swigert, and shew cause if any you have why the said George Swigert your husband shall not be divorced from the bonds of matrimony agreeably to the acts of assembly in such case made and provided. And hereof you are not to fail -Witness Samuel Hepburn Esquire at Carlisle the 15th day of April A.D. 1842." (Signed Geo. Sanderson, Prothonotary.) Notation on the front of this document -"Served personally and by copy, 26th May, 1842. So answers, Paul Martin Shrff. Shff. Martin's fee $1.44 Brandeberry."

Aug. 9, 1842 -"George Swigert vs. Elizabeth Swigert: No. 1 Aug. 1842 In the Court of Common Pleas of Cumberland County No. 1 August Term 1842 Subpoena Sur divorce -And now, to wit, 9th August 1842 on motion of Mr. Reed Rule that William Irvine Esquire be appointed a commissioner to take testimony etc. and reduce the same to writing exparte on ten days notice to the Defendant and that the case be disposed of at the next term in the testimony so taken. By the Court." -"Cumberland County S.S. -I George Sanderson Prothonotary of the Court of Common Pleas of said County do certify that the above rule is entered of record in said Court. In testimony whereof I have hereunto set my hand and the seal of said Court at Carlisle this 12th day of October A.D. 1842 For Geo. Sanderson Prothy." (Signed John Main.)

Sept. 20, 1842 -"To the defendant. Please to take notice that the testimony of witnesses will be taken in pursuance of the above rule before William Irvine Esq. at his office in Carlisle on Wednesday the twelveth (sic) day of October next, between the hours of ten o'clock in the morning and four in the afternoon. 20 Sept. 1842." (Signed John Reed Atty. for Plff.)

Sept. 28, 1842 -"Cumberland County S.S. -Before me the subscriber a Justice of the Peace in and for said County personally came Robert McCanty who upon his solemn oath according to Law doth say that he served a copy of the within Rule and Notice upon Elizabeth Swigert by handing her a true copy of the same this Day the 28th Sept. 1842. Sworn and subscribed Sept. 28th 1842 before me." (Signed Wm. Irvine and R. McCantny, Cost.)

Oct. 12. 1842 -"In pursuance of the annexed rule and motion the following witnesses appeared at my office in Carlisle on the twelfth day of October 1842 between the hours of ten o'clock A.M. and four in the afternoon and being severally first and duly sworn according to law depose and say as follows viz: Felix Swigart being duly sworn says "that he is a son of George Swigart and know that the said George Swigart and Elizabeth lived together in North Middleton Township in Cumberland County as man and wife. On Sunday in February 1840 my father set off to go to Chambersburg. I lived in the house at the time. Elizabeth his wife appeared to be affectionate and kind to him at that time. He started off she gave him her hand to bid him good bye. She asked him when he would be back. He said he did not know just as he would get through with his business. On the Monday following Jas. Dunn and I commenced threshing there was no one at home but my sister. She started to school in the morning so there was no one left at the house but Mrs. Swigart. I saw her passing in and out of the house opening the potato hole and her daughter Elizabeth came up from Snyder's before that she had been sending things off to Snyder's and Father told her it would no do and not to do so. In the evening my sister came home from school. I went up to the house. Mrs. Swigart was there but had sent off the cupboard furniture and her daughter was gone. In the evening two travellers came there and staid (sic) all night. She went off about midnight in that night and took with her all the moveable property -three beds and bedding a bureau with the things in the drawers -chairs -table and a variety of other things. The house was stripped and in the morning she was gone. I saw the track where the wagon had come to take away the things. She did not let any one know she was going but carried off everything secretly. She never returned to live with George Swigart since that night. She has returned to the house secretly by night and carried off other property since and has lived separate and apart ever since from George Swigart. She was not driven off but went of her own accord in the absence of George Swigart as above stated. She lives now in North Middleton township and has a separate establishment of her own. Sworn and subscribed

Before me as above stated." (signed Wm. Irvine and Felix Swigart.)

Oct. 12, 1842 -"Catharine Swigart being duly sworn says she is a daughter of George Swigart and lived at home after her father was married to Mrs. Hostler. They lived something like a year together. The day before she went off from my father's house I was at school. When I returned in the evening dishes and other cupboard furniture had been sent off. My father was absent at the time at Chambersburg. She went off that night secretly she took with her the chief portion of the moveable property in the house such as beds bedding chairs bureaus -clothing. She took all her own and some of mine. She has never returned to live in the family since. She continues to live in a separate establishment of her own. She came back afterwards in the night and carried off some of my father's clothing and some of mine with silver spoons and other articles. My father was not cross but good to her while she lived with him. She had no reason for going away. She was very pleasant to my father the morning before he went to Chambersburg. She did not tell any of us she was going away. Sworn and subscribed Before me as above stated." (signed William Irvine and Catharine Swigert.)

Oct. 12, 1842 -"Elizabeth Sites being duly sworn. I know the parties. They lived together as my neighbors. After she left Swigert she came to live in sight of us. She bought a house and lot and lived in it. Swigart had sold a bedstead to one Bonheater after Mrs. Swigert left him and she found it out where it was and she went there in their absence in the night and took it off. She told me so herself. She showed me in her house where she lived after she left Swigart pitchers tumblers silver tea spoons cups and saucers and a heap of things she said she got these at Swigart's the time she made the last haul. One set of cups and saucers she said were at Swigart's when she went there first to live and "When I first saw them I was determined to slip them away and give them to my daughter Betsy when she got married" but she had left Swigart before Betsy was married and could not get her hands on them. She said there were either three cups or three saucers wanting of the set but says she "I intend to make another haul." I said to her ain't you afraid to go back at night and of getting hurt if they would hear you in the house. She said She was not a bit afraid to go there anytime and she was determined to make another haul and keep in at it as long as she could find anything to take. At another time she showed me a handbox in her house. It had two quilts and other articles in it which she said she had taken from Swigart and did not wish him to take from her. She asked me to let her bring them to my house and not to let my husband know for if ever she came to law with Swigart she wished to have the neighbours take her part. She said she wanted to keep them from Swigart so that he would not see them for if he did he would know them and take them. I lived near Swigart and wife before she went away and I saw or know nothing to give her any reason for going. He treated her well so far as I knew. I thought he treated her as nice as any woman should be treated. I heard her say several times that she never would go back to live with Swigart. Sworn and subscribed Before me Oct. 12th 1842 as above stated." (signed Wm. Irvine and by mark Elizabeth Sites.)

Oct. 12, 1842 -"John Kitch being duly sworn says that Swigart is a man of property and of sufficient means to support his family. I have been there often about the house and always saw plenty of everything. I came to Swigart's one day in March or April 1840 after Mrs. Swigart had gone off. Sheriff Myers was there. They were searching after some property she had taken away. The sheriff requested me to go with him down to Snyder's. He was a son of hers by a former husband. We went there as far as the barn. Swigert, his son and me stopped at the barn. The Sheriff went to the house. It was locked. He could not get in. It was in the forenoon of the day. We got the door of the granary open and went in and found some of the property there. At first when we went to the house the door was fastened. She talked to me through the glass above the door. After some time she retreated into the door of the back room. She had a gun in her hand cocked and swore if anybody would come into that room she would shoot them. A bureau case without the drawers was found in the house and some other articles. She came out and swore and blackguarded the party. There were some papers in a bundle that she had taken off. Sworn and subscribed Before me Oct. 12th 1842 as above stated." (signed Wm. Irvine and John Kitch.)

Oct. 12, 1842 -"The Reverend J. Ulrich being duly sworn deposeth and says as follows. I was present at my own house in the Borough of Carlisle of the 28th day of March 1839 when Geo. Swigert and Mrs. Eliz. Snyder (formerly Eliz. Hosler) came there and were joined in marriage at which time I performed the ordinary ceremony. Sworn and subscribed at the time and place above stated Before me." (signed Wm. Irvine and J. Ulrich Pastor of the Ev. Luth. Church of Carlisle.)

Oct. 12, 1842 -"John Myers Esq. being duly sworn says he was present and knows the facts as stated in the testimony of John Kitch and that they are there truly stated. He further says that he was there another time to look after the property which had been taken from Swigart's house by Mrs. Swigart. He was acting as Sheriff at the time. The doors were locked of Snyder's house where she was were locked. She and some other woman had scalding water and they threatened to scald him if he came in. He was kept out and did not get any of the property. Sworn and subscribed Before me Oct. 12th 1842 above stated." (signed Wm. Irvine and John Myers.)

Oct. 12, 1842 -"I certify that the above depositions were duly taken this day at the time and place appointed as by pursuance and under my direction and reduced to writing by my authority agreeably to rule of court and behold my hand and seal this 12th day of Octr. 1842." (signed William Irvine. Seal.)

Nov. 17, 1842 -"In the Court of Common Pleas of Cumberland County No. 1 August Term 1842 George Swigert vs. Elizabeth Swigert: Subpoena Sur Divorce Served. And now, to wit, 17th November 1842 Divorce decreed, By the Court and order that Elizabeth Swigert pay the following cost on the proceeding to wit:

Sheriff Martin		$1.44
Attorney		3.00
Clerk Sanderson		3.00
Justice Irvine		1.77
Witnesses		$9.21
Rev. John Ulrich	$0.25	
Felix Swigert	.43	
Catharine Swigert	.43	
John Myers Esq.	.55	
John Kitch	.49	
Elizabeth Sites	.49	$2.64
		$11.85

The Sheriff is authorized to collect the above cost from Elizabeth Swigert, agreeably to the order of the court by direction of George Swigert. Test. John Main for Geo. Sanderson Prothonotary."

Jan. 11, 1843 -"Cumberland County S.S. -Paul Martin Esq. being duly sworn according to law doth say that he demanded the amount of the within bill of costs in pursuance of the within order of court from Elizabeth Swigert on the 9th inst. and she refused to pay the same. Sworn and subscribed this 11th Jany. A.D. 1843 Before." (Signed Thos. H. Criswell Prothy. and Paul Martin, Shrff.)

Nov. 17, 1842 -"Now to wit Nov. 17th 1842 in the case of the application of George Swigert for a divorce from the bonds of matrimony with Elizabeth Swigert, upon due proof taken in accordance with the order of the Court, on due consideration the Court decree a divorce and separation from the nuptial ties or bonds of matrimony between the said George and Elizabeth and that the marriage is null and void, and that all and every the duties, rights and claims accruing to either of the said parties at any time theretofore in pursuance of the said marriage shall cease and determine and the said parties shall severally be at liberty to marry again in like manner as if they never had been married, and that the said Elizabeth pay all of the costs of this proceeding. By the Court." Filed 17 Nov. 1842.

Nov. 21, 1842 -"The Sheriff is authorized to collect the costs agreeably to the order of the court of Elizabeth Swigert. 21 Nov. 1842." (signed George Swigert.) "Geo. Sanderson Esq. Prothy. -please make out a bill of all the costs in this case with an order of Court for the payt. of it by Elizabeth Swigart at the order of George Swigert (illegible word) on the other side, authorizing the Shff. to collect it and hand it to the Sheriff for collection." (signed John Reed.)

♦ ♦ ♦

August Term 1842 #25 May 20, 1842 -"To the Judges of the Court of Common Pleas of Cumberland County -The petition of Nancy Carothers by her next friend David Parnell -Respectfully Represents that in the month of April 1839 she was lawfully married to Andw. Carothers then of Dickinson Township Cumberland County and continued to live and cohabit with him as his wife in the said Township of Dickinson and had by him issue one child. That about one year after her marriage the said Andw. Carothers her husband treated her and her child cruelly and barbarously and on or about the 3 Feb. 1841 the said Andrew Carothers did maliciously abandon his family and left his said wife and child without the means of support. She therefore prays your Honors to grant her a divorce from bed and board and also to allow her such alimony as her husband's circumstances will admit." (signed Nancy Carothers by her next friend David Pennell.) "Cumberland County sct. Personally appeared before me a Justice of the Peace in and for said County Nancy Carothers who being duly sworn doth depose and say that the facts set forth in the above petition are true to the best of her knowledge and belief and that the said complaint is not made out of levity or by collusion between her and her husband and for the mere purpose of being freed and separated from each other, but in sincerity and truth for the causes mentioned in the said petition. Sworn and Subscribed the 20 May 1842 Before me." (signed William Irvine and Nancy Carothers.)

June 11, 1842 -"Cumberland County s.s. -The Commonwealth of Pennsylvania to Andrew Carothers Greeting -Whereas Nancy Carothers by her next friend David Penwell (sic) on the 20th day of May 1842 preferred a petition to Samuel Hepburn Esq. President Judge of the Court of Common Pleas of Cumberland County praying that for the causes therein set fourth (sic) she might be divorced from the bonds of matrimony entered into with you the said Andrew Carothers and that she be allowed such alimony as your circumstances will admit. And the said Judge having awarded a Subpoena, We command you the said Andrew Carothers that setting aside all other business and excuses whatsoever you be and appear in your proper person before our Judges at Carlisle at our county Court of Common Pleas there to be held the second Monday of August next to answer the petition or libel of the said Nancy Carothers by etc. and shew cause if any you have why the said Nancy Carothers your wife shall not be divorced from the bonds of matrimony, and allowed such alimony as your circumstances will admit agreeably to the acts of assembly in such case made and provided -and hereof you are not to fail. Witness Samuel Hepburn

Esquire at Carlisle the Eleventh day of June A.D. 1842. For Geo. Sanderson, Prothonotary." (signed John Main.) Notation on the front of this document -"Not executed by order of Plaintiff's Attorney, so answers" (signed Paul Martin Shrff.) Shff. Martin's fee 77 cts.

◆ ◆ ◆

November Term 1842 #37 Sept. 6, 1842 -"To the Honorable the Judges of the Court of Common Pleas of Cumberland County -The Libel of Elizabeth Hall by her next friend Charles Bell, Esq. -Respectfully showeth -That your Libellant on the 24th day of May in the year of our Lord one thousand eight hundred and thirty seven was contracted in matrimony and married to a certain John L.N. Hall and from that time until the 24th day of September in the year aforesaid lived and cohabited with the said John L.N. Hall as his wife and as such was owned and acknowledged by him and so deemed and reputed by her neighbors and acquaintances and although by the laws of God, as well as by their mutual vows and faith plighted to each other they were bound to that uniform constancy and regard which ought to be inseparable from the marriage state; yet so it is that the said John L.N. Hall from the said 24th day of September in the year aforesaid hath wilfully and maliciously deserted and absented himself from the habitation of this Libellant without any just or reasonable cause and such desertion hath persisted in from that time until the present and yet doth continue to absent himself from the said Libellant and wherefore your libellant further showeth that she is a citizen of the state of Pennsylvania and has resided therein for upwards of one whole year previous to the filing of this her libel. She therefore prays your honors that a subpoena may issue forth to summon the said John L.N. Hall to appear at the next Court of Common Pleas to be held in and for the County aforesaid at Carlisle on the second Monday of November next to answer the complaint aforesaid. And also that a decree of the said Court may be made for the divorcing of him the said John L.N. Hall from the society, fellowship and company of this Libellant in all time to come, and her this Libellant from the marriage bond aforesaid as if she had never been married or as if the said John L.N. Hall were naturally dead. And this Libellant will pray etc." (Signed Elizabeth Hall By her next friend Chas. Bell.) "Cumberland County s.s. -Elizabeth Hall the within named Libellant being duly sworn according to law says the facts contained in the within and foregoing libel are true to the best of her knowledge and belief, and that the said complaint is not made out of levity, and collusion between her and the said John L.N. Hall, and for the mere purpose of being freed and separated from each other, but in sincerity and truth for the causes mentioned in the said Libel. Sworn before me this 6th day of September A.D. 1842." (signed William Irvine and Elizabeth Hall.)

Sept. 13, 1842 -"Cumberland County S.S. -The Commonwealth of

Pennsylvania to John L.N. Hall Greeting -Whereas Elizabeth Hall by her next friend Charles Bell Esquire, on the 13th day of September 1842 preferred a petition to Judge Stuart one of the Associate Judges of the Court of Common Pleas of said County in vacation, praying that for the causes therein set forth she might be divorced from the bonds of matrimony entered into with you the said John L.N. Hall, and the said Judge having awarded a subpoena -We command you the said John L.N. Hall, that setting aside all other business and excuses whatsoever, you be and appear in your proper person before our Judges at Carlisle at our county Court of Common Pleas there to be held the second Monday of November next to answer the petition or libel of the said Elizabeth Hall by etc. and shew cause if any you have why the said Elizabeth Hall your wife should not be divorced from the bonds of matrimony agreeably to the acts of Assembly in such case made and provided, and hereof you are not to fail. Witness Samuel Hepburn Esquire at Carlisle the thirteenth day of September A.D. 1842 for Geo. Sanderson, Prothy." (signed John Main.)

Nov. 21, 1842 -"Cumberland County S.S. -Paul Martin Sheriff being sworn in open court doth say that John L.N. Hall the Defendant is not to be found in the county aforesaid. Sworn and subscribed 21 Nov. 1842." (signed Geo. Sanderson, Prothy. and Paul Martin, Shrff.) Notation on the front of this document "Shff. Martin's fee 18 3/4 cts. Gaullagher."

Nov. 28, 1842 -"Cumberland County s.s. -The Commonwealth of Pennsylvania John L.N. Hall Greeting: Whereas Elizabeth Hall by her next friend Charles Bell Esquire on the 13th day of November 1842 preferred a petition to Judge Stuart one of the aforesaid Judges of the Court of Common Pleas of said county, in vacation praying that for the causes therein set forth she might be divorced from the bonds of matrimony entered into with you the said John L.N. Hall, and the said Judge having awarded a subpoena, we command you, as we have heretofore commanded you, that setting aside all other business and excuses, you be and appear in your proper person before our Judges at Carlisle at our County Court of Common Pleas there to be held the second Monday of January next to answer the petition or libel of the said Elizabeth Hall by etc. and shew cause if any you have why the said Elizabeth Hall your wife shall not be divorced from the bonds of matrimony agreeably to the acts of assembly in such case made and provided and hereof you are not to fail. Witness Samuel Hepburn Esquire at Carlisle the 28th day of November A.D. 1842 For Geo. Sanderson Prothy." (signed John Main.)

Feb. 14, 1843 -"Cumberland County, s.s. -Paul Martin Sheriff being sworn in open court doth say that John L.N. Hall the defendant is not to be found in the County aforesaid. Sworn and subscribed Before T.H. Criswell Prothy. Feby. 14, 1843." (signed Paul Martin.) "Now to wit 14th of Feby. 1843 the Court order and direct the Sheriff to render notice to be published in one newspaper printed in this county for four weeks successively prior to the first day of next term requiring the said John L.N. Hall to appear in Court on said day to answer the complaint of the said Elizabeth Hall By the Court." Notation on the front of this document -"Not to be found in my Bailiwick so answers, Paul Martin Shrff. Gaullagher."

April 15, 1843 -"Elizabeth Hall by her next friend Charles Bell Esq. vs John L.N. Hall: Subpoena in divorce No. 37 Nov. T. 1843 -Now to wit, 15th April 1843 it appearing to the Court that the sheriff made publication in this case agreeably to the order of Court and the said defendant not appearing in Court to answer the complaint of the said Elizabeth the Court order and direct that depositions be taken exparte by the said Elizabeth before David Smith Esqr. to be read in evidence on the hearing of her application as aforesaid at the next argument and Orphan's Court. By the Court. Apl. 15 1843." "Filed 15th April 1843."

April 22, 1843 -"Elizabeth Hall by her next friend Charles Bell vs. John L.N. Hall: Application for divorce in the Court of Common Pleas of Cumberland County -In pursuance of an order of court in the above case to take depositions to be read in evidence on the hearing and trial of said case personally appeared before the subscriber a Justice of the Peace in and for said County Mrs. Rachel Kline who being duly affirmed according to law doth say that the aforenamed Elizabeth Hall was intermarried with the aforesaid John L.N. Hall sometime in the month of May 1838 in Carlisle, that said affirmant was present at the marriage, that they were married by the Rev. Mr. Aurand -that the said John L.N. Hall resided and lived with his said wife a few months after said marriage -after which he wilfully and maliciously deserted and absented himself from the habitation of his said wife without any reasonable cause and has continued to absent himself from that time until the present for a period of four or five years and for more than two years previous to the filing of this petition of the said Elizabeth for a divorce. Said affirmant doth further say that the said Elizabeth is a citizen and resident of Cumberland County. Affirmed and subscribed this 22 day of April 1843." (signed David Smith and Rachel Kline.)

April 22, 1843 -"Also at same time appeared John Irwin who being duly sworn according to law doth say that he was acquainted with the said John L.N. Hall and Elizabeth Hall. That they lived together as man and wife for some months in the year 1838 in Carlisle -that the said John L.N. Hall some time in said year wilfully and maliciously deserted and absented himself from the habitation of his said wife without any reasonable cause and has continued to absent himself from that time until the present a period of more than two years previous to the filing of the petition of the same Elizabeth for a divorce. Sworn and subscribed this 22 day of April 1843." (signed David Smith and John Irwin.) Notation on the front of this document -"Filed 25th 1843."

April 25, 1843 -"Elizabeth Hall by her next friend Charles Bell vs. John L.N. Hall: Application for a divorce -Now to wit 25th of April 1843 the Court after hearing the depositions of witnesses taken in this case on the part of the aforesaid Libellant and after mature deliberation do order, adjudge and decree that the said Elizabeth Hall Libellant be divorced and separated from the said John L.N. Hall and that all and every the duty, rights, and claims accruing to either of the said parties by reason of the said marriage shall henceforth cease and determine and the said parties be severally at liberty to marry again in like manner as if they had never been married. By the court. Test. Thos. H. Criswell Prothy."

◆ ◆ ◆

August Term 1843 #148 Aug. 12, 1843 -"To the Honorable the Judges of the Court of Common Pleas of Cumberland County -The petition of Elizabeth Krider by her step -father and next friend George Carns Respectfully Represents That your Libellant on the 25th day of Feby. A.D. 1830 was contracted in matrimony and married to a certain David Krider and lived and cohabited with him as his wife and as such was owned and acknowledged by him and so deemed and reputed by all her neighbors and acquaintances. And although by the laws of God as well as by their mutual vows and faith plighted to each other, they were reciprocally bound to that uniform kindness and regard which ought to be inseparable from the marriage state -Yet so it is that the said David Krider, disregarding his duties as her husband, did at sundry times offer such indignities to her person as to render her condition intolerable and life burthensome and did by cruel and barbarous treatment endanger her life, and by means of the previous did force her to withdraw from his house and family. Wherefore your libellant further showing that she is a citizen of the Commonwealth of Pennsylvania and hath resided therein for more than two years previous the filing of this petition -prays your Honors that a subpoena may be issued by said Court directed to the said David Krider commanding him to appear at the next term of the said Court to answer this petition -And also that a decree of said Court may be made granting this Libellant a divorce from the society fellowship and company of the said David Kryder (sic) in all time to come and from the marriage bond aforesaid as if she had never been married or as if the said David Kryder (sic) were naturally dead. And she will pray etc." (signed Witness J.H. Graham, Elizabeth Krider by her mark, also By her step father and next friend George Karns.) "Cumberland County s.s. -Before the subscriber a Justice of the Peace in and for said County personally came the within named Elizabeth Krider who being duly sworn according to law says that the facts set forth in the within libel are true to the best of her knowledge and belief. And that the said complaint is not made out of levity or by collusion between her and her said husband and for the mere purpose of being freed and separated from each other, but in sincerity and truth for the causes mentioned in the within petition or libel. Sworn and subscribed the 12th August 1843 Before." (signed David Smith, J.P. also by her mark Elizabeth Krider.) Notation on the front of this document -"Subpoena awarded 14th August 1843 By the Court. Graham."

Aug. 17, 1843 -"Elizabeth Krider vs. David Krider: Application for a divorce to the Court of Common Pleas of Cumberland County -I David Krider offer to appeal in this case without either writ or service and I further hereby acknowledge the truth of the facts stated in the petition of libellant to have the same effect as if the same had been regularly proved to the satisfaction of the court in the mode prescribed by law -Witness my hand and seal the 17th day of August A.D. 1843 -Witness" (signed J. Holsaple and Isaac Hrighrey? and David Krider.) (Seal.) Notation on the front of this document,"Filed 19th Augt. 1843"

♦ ♦ ♦

November Term 1842 #5 Nov. 9, 1842 -"To the Honourable the Judges of the Court of Common Pleas of Cumberland County -The petition of John Casey Respectfully showeth that your petitioner on the third day of March in the year of our Lord One thousand Eight Hundred and forty two was lawfully joined in marriage with Martha Casey, his present wife, and from that time hath lived and in all respects demeaned himself as a kind and loving husband. And although by the laws of God as well as by the natural vows plighted to each other, they were bound to that chastity which ought to be inseparable from the marriage state, yet, the said Martha in violation of the marriage vow hath for a considerable time past, given herself up to adulterous practices, and been guilty of adultery with Abraham P. Erb. Wherefore your libellant further showing that he is a citizen of the State of Pennsylvania and has resided therein for upwards of one whole year previous to the filing of this his libel, prays your Honours that a subpoena may issue forth to summon the said Martha to appear at the January Term next of this Court, to answer the complaint aforesaid. And also that a decree of this Honourable Court may be made for the divorcing her the said Martha Casey from the society, fellowship and company of this libellant for all time to come: and him the libellant from the marriage bond aforesaid, as if he had never been married, or as if the said Martha were naturally dead -And this libellant will pray etc." (signed Jno. Casey.) "Cumberland County s.s. -The above named John Casey being duly sworn says, that the facts contained in the above libel are true to the best of his knowledge and belief, and that the said complaint is not made out of levity, and by collusion between him and his said wife, and for the mere purpose of being freed and separated from each other, but in sincerity and truth for the causes mentioned in said libel." (signed Jno. Casey.) "Sworn and subscribed before me this 9 day of November A.D. 1842." (signed Jas. Kennedy Justice of the Peace.) Notation on the front of this document, "16 November 1842 -Subpoena awarded. By the Court. Casey."

Nov. 17, 1842 -"John Casey vs. Martha Casey: In the Com. Pleas of Cumberland Co. Issue Subpoena in Divorce. To Geo. Sanderson Esq. Prothy." (signed Jos. Casey atty. for Plff. 17th Nov. 1842.") Notation on the fron of this document,"Filed 17th Nov. 1842."

Nov. 17, 1842 -"Cumberland County s.s. -The Commonwealth of Pennsylvania to Martha Casey Greeting: Whereas John Casey on the sixteenth day of November A.D. 1842 preferred a petition to the Judges of the Court of Common Pleas of Cumberland County praying that for the causes therein set forth he might be divorced from the bonds of matrimony entered into with you the said Martha Casey, and the said Judges have awarded a subpoena. We command you that setting aside all other business and excuses whatsoever, you be and appear in your proper person before our Judges at Carlisle at our County Court of Common Pleas there to be held the second Monday of January next being the ninth day of said month, to answer the petition or libel of the said John Casey, and shew cause if any you have why the said John Casey your husband shall not be divorced from the bonds of matrimony agreeably to the acts of Assembly in such case made and provided, and hereof you are not to fail. Witness Samuel Hepburn Esquire at Carlisle the seventeenth day of November A.D. 1842. For Geo. Sanderson Prothonotary." (signed John Main.) Notations on the front of this document -"Subpoena Sur Divorce Returnable 9th Jany. 1843. Served personally and by copy 10th December, 1842. So answers," (signed Paul Martin Shrff.) "Shff Martin's bill $1.97 1/2 Casey."

April 10, 1843 -"John Casey vs. Martha Casey: In the Court of Common Pleas of Cumberland County -No. 5 January Term 1843 Subpoena Sur Divorce -And now, to wit 10th April 1843 James R. Irvine Esq. appointed a Commissioner to take the depositions of witnesses in this case on part of the Plaintiff -By the Court." -"Cumberland County s.s. -I Thomas H. Criswell Prothonotary of the Court of Common Pleas of said county, do certify that the above is a true extract taken from the records of said Court. In testimony whereof I have hereunto set my hand and the seal of said Court at Carlisle the 16th day of June A.D. 1843 For Thos. H. Criswell Prothy." (signed John Main.)

July 31, 1843 -"To Martha Casey, Defendant -You are hereby notified that under a Rule of Court, of which the above is a copy, depositions will be taken in said cause, before me at my office in the Borough of Newville on Friday August 11th 1843 between the hours of 10 A.M. and 3 P.M. at which time and place you are requested to attend." (signed James R. Irvine Commissioner July 31, 1843.)

November Term 1842 #5 Aug. 11, 1843 -"Cumberland County s.s. -James Widner personally appeared before me one of the Justices of the Peace in and for said County, and being sworn says, that on the thirty first day of July 1843 he served the within notice by having a true copy of the same in the hands of the within -named defendant Martha Casey, and further says not. Sworn and subscribed Augt. 11, 1843 before" (signed James R. Irvine and James Widner.)

Aug. 11, 1843 -"Depositions of witness produced, sworn and examined before James R. Irvine, at his office in the Borough of Newville on Friday Augt. 11, 1843 between the hours of 10 A.M. and 3 P.M. of said day in obedience to the Rule of Court and notice hereto attached, to be read in a cause depending in said Court in which John Casey is Plaintiff and Martha Casey Defendant -Plaintiff present, Defendant not appearing. -James Kennedy Esq. being produced, sworn and examined doth depose and say, in the evening of the eighth day of Octr. last, I was called into Major Casey's house, and had some conversation with his wife Martha Casey, and during that conversation, she (Martha Casey) acknowledged that she had criminal intercourse with a certain Abraham P. Erb, on Sabbath night (if I am not mistaken) the 28th day of Augt. last past, and afterwards made oath of that fact before me as a Justice of the Peace and further saith not. Sworn and subscribed Augt. 11, 1843 before" (signed James R. Irvine and Jas. Kennedy.) Notation on the front of this document "25 cts. paid."

Aug. 15, 1843 -"John Casey vs. Martha Casey: In the Court of Common Pleas of Cumberland County No. 5 January Term 1843 Subpoena Sur Divorce -And now to wit, 15th August 1843, the Court do sentence, adjudge and decree that the marriage of said parties is and shall be henceforth null and void, and all and every the duties, rights and claims accruing to either of said parties at any time heretofore, in pursuance of said marriage, shall cease and determine, and be totally dissolved, and that the said John Casey be at full liberty to marry again. By the Court." -"State of Pennsylvania County of Cumberland s.s. -I Thomas H. Criswell Prothonotary of the Court of Common Pleas of said County, do certify, that the above is a true copy of the decree of the Court made in the case of the application of John Casey for a Divorce from his wife Martha Casey, taken from the records of said Court. In testimony whereof I have hereunto set my hand and the seal of said Court at Carlisle the 28th day of October A.D. 1843." (signed Thos. H. Criswell Prothonotary.)

♦ ♦ ♦

January Term 1845 #6 Oct. 14, 1844 -"To the Honorable the

Judges of the Court of Common Pleas of Cumberland County -The Libel of Margry Mahoney by her next friend John Walker -Respectfully showeth That your Libellant on the eleventh day of August in the year of our Lord one thousand eight hundred and thirty six was contracted in matrimony and married to a certain Dennis Mahoney and from that time until the first day of March one thousand eight hundred and thirty seven lived and cohabited with the said Dennis Mahoney as his wife and as such was owned and acknowledged by him and so deemed and reputed by her neighbours and acquaintances. And although by the laws of God as well as by their mutual vows and faith plighted to each other, they were bound to that uniform constancy and regard which ought to be inseparable from the marriage state: yet so it is that the said Dennis Mahoney from the said first day of March in the year 1837 last aforesaid hath wilfully and maliciously deserted and absented himself from the habitation of this Libellant without any just or reasonable cause. And such desertion hath persisted in for the term of two years and upwards, and yet doth continue to absent himself from the said Libellant. Wherefore your Libellant further shewing that she is a citizen of the state of Pennsylvania and has resided therein for upwards of one whole year previous to the filing of this her Libel prays your Honors that a subpoena may issue forth to summon the said Dennis Mahoney to appear in this Honorable Court at next January term, to answer the complaint aforesaid. And also that a decree of this Honorable Court may be made for the divorcing of him the said Dennis Mahoney from the society, fellowship and company of this Libellant in all time to come and her this Libellant from the marriage bond aforesaid as if she had never been married or as if the said Dennis Mahoney were naturally dead. And this Libellant will pray etc." (signed Test. H. Gaullagher and Margry Mahoney by her mark.) "By her next friend" (signed John Walker.) -"Cumberland County s.s. -Personally appeared before the subscriber a Justice of the Peace in and for said County Margry Mahoney the above named Libellant who being duly sworn says, the facts contained in the above libel are true to the best of her knowledge and belief, and that the said complaint is not made out of levity, and collusion between her and the said Dennis and for the mere purpose of being freed and separated from each other, but in sincerity and truth for the causes mentioned in said libel. Sworn and subscribed before me this 14th day of October 1844." (signed William Irvine and Margry Mahoney by her mark.) Notation on the front of this document -"Subpoena awarded By the Court 18th Nov. 1844. Gaullagher."

Nov. 22, 1844 -"Cumberland County S.S. -The Commonwealth of Pennsylvania to Dennis Mahony Greeting: Whereas Margery Mahony on the eighteenth day of November A.D. 1844 preferred a petition to the Judges of the Court of Common Pleas of Cumberland County, pray(ing) that for the causes therein set forth she might be divorced from the bonds of matrimony entered into with you the said Dennis Mahony, and the said Judges having awarded a subpoena -We command you the said Dennis Mahoney that setting aside all business and excuses whatsoever, you be and appear in your proper person before our Judges at Carlisle at our County Court of Common Pleas there to be held the thirteenth day of January next, to answer the petition or libel of the said Margry Mahony, and shew cause if any you have why she should not be divorced from the bonds of matrimony agreeably to the acts of Assembly in such case made and provided. Witness Samuel Hepburn Esquire, President of our said Court at Carlisle the twenty second day of November A.D. 1844." (signed Thos. H. Criswell Prothonotary.) Notation on the front of this document -"Defendant not to be found in my bailiwick -11 Decr. 1844. So answers" (signed A. Longsdorf Shrf.) Shff. fees 18 3/4 cts. Gaullagher.

Feb. 11, 1845 -"Adam Longsdorf being affirmed in open court doth say that the Defendant in this case is not to be found in his bailiwick. Affirmed and subscribed 11 Febry. 1845 in open court." (signed Test. Thos. H. Criswell Prothy. and Adam Longsdorf.)

◆ ◆ ◆

April Term 1845 #17 Feb. 10, 1845 -"To the Honorable the Judges of the Court of Common Pleas of Cumberland County -The libel of Rachel Ritner by her brother and next friend William Black -Respectfully Represents that your Libellant on the 8th day of December in the year of our Lord one thousand eight hundred and thirty six was contracted in marriage to a certain John Ritner, and from that time until the 26th day of July one thousand eight hundred and thirty nine lived and cohabited with the said John Ritner as his wife and as such was owned and acknowledged by him, and so deemed and reputed by her neighbours and acquaintances. And although by the laws of God, as well as by their mutual vows and faith plighted to each other, they were bound to that uniform constancy and regard which ought to be inseperable from the marriage state: Yet so it is that the said John Ritner from the said 26th day of July in the year 1839 last aforesaid hath wilfully and maliciously deserted and absented himself from the habitation of the Libellant, without any just or reasonable cause. And such desertion hath persisted in for the term of two years and upwards, and yet doth continue to absent himself from the said Libellant -Wherefore your Libellant further shewing that she is a citizen of the state of Pennsylvania, and has resided therein for upwards of one whole year previous to the filing of this her libel prays your Honours that a subpoena may issue to summon the said John Ritner to appear in this Honorable Court at next April term to answer the complaint aforesaid. And also that a decree of this Honorable Court, may be made for the divorcing of him the said John Ritner from the society, fellowship and company of this Libellant in all time to come, and her this Libellant from the marriage bond aforesaid as if she had never been married or as if the said John Ritner were naturally dead. And this Libellant will pray etc." (signed Rachel C. Ritner by her next friend William Black) -"Cumberland County s.s. -Personally appeared before the subscriber a Justice of the Peace in and for said county Rachel C. Ritner the Libellant aforesaid who being duly sworn says the facts contained in the foregoing libel are true to the best of her knowledge and belief, and that the said complaint is not made out of levity, and collusion, between her and the said John Ritner, and for the mere purpose of being freed and separated from each other, but in sincerity and truth for the causes mentioned in said libel. Sworn and subscribed Before me this 10th February 1845" (signed David Smith, J.P. and Rachel C. Ritner.) Notation on the front of this document -"Subpoena awarded By the Court 11th Febry. 1845." Adair."

Feb. 12, 1845 -"Cumberland County, S.S. -The Commonwealth of Pennsylvania to John Ritner Greeting: Whereas Rachel C. Ritner on the eleventh day of February A.D. 1845 preferred a petition to the Judges of the Court of Common Pleas of Cumberland County, praying that for the causes therein set forth she might be divorced from the bonds of matrimony entered into with you the said John Ritner, and the said Judges having awarded a Subpoena -We command you, the said John Ritner that setting aside all business and excuses whatsoever you be and appear in your proper person before our Judges at Carlisle at our County Court of Common Pleas there to be held the fourteenth day of April next to answer the petition or libel of the said Rachel C. Ritner, and shew cause if any you have why she should not be divorced from the bonds of matrimony agreeably to the act of assembly in such case made and provided. Witness Samuel Hepburn Esquire, President of our said Court at Carlisle the twelfth day of February A.D. 1845." (signed Thos. H. Criswell Prothonotary) Notation on the front of this document -"Defendant not to be found in my bailiwick March 19th 1845. So answers" (signed A. Longsdorf Shrff.) "Shff's fee 18 3/4 cts. Adair."

April 16, 1845 -"Cumberland County s.s. -Adam Longsdorff Esq. Shrff., being duly affirmed says the within named respondent John Ritner is not to be found in this County. Affirmed and subscribed in open Court this 16th April 1845 Before" (signed Thos. H. Criswell Prothy. and A. Longsdorff, Shrff.)

◆ ◆ ◆

April Term 1845 #28 Feb. 21, 1845 -"To the Honorable Samuel Hepburn President Judge of the Court of Common Pleas of Cumberland County -The petition of Maria Hetrick by her uncle and next friend Edward Prendergass Respectfully Represents -That your libellant on the nineth day of May A.D. 1816 was contracted in matrimony and married to a certain Abraham Hetrick and from that time until the month of April A.D. 1839 lived and cohabited with him as his wife and as such was owned and acknowledged by him and deemed and reputed by all her neighbors and acquaintances. And although by the laws of God as well as by their mutual vows and faith plighted to each other, they were reciprocally bound to their uniform kindness and regard which ought to be inseparable from the marriage state. But so it is that the said Abraham Hetrick hath by cruel and barbarous treatment endangered the life of your libellant and hath offered such indignities to her person as to render her condition intolerable and life burthensome and thereby forced her to withdraw from his house and family and for the last year hath refused to provide for your libellant a suitable maintenance. She therefore prays that a subpoena may be awarded to the said Abraham Hetrick returnable at the next Term of the Court to shew cause why the court should not grant your libellant a divorce from bed and board and also allow her such alimony as the circumstances of the said Abraham Hetrick will admit of. And she will pray etc." (signed Witness J.H. Graham, Maria Hetrick by her mark.) "by her next friend (signed Edward Pendergass) -"Cumberland County s.s. -Before the Hon. Samuel Hepburn President Judge of the Court of Common Pleas of Cumberland County personally came the within named Maria Hetrick who being duly sworn according to law says that the facts continued in the within and foregoing libel are true to the best of her knowledge and belief and that the said complaint is not made out of levity or by collusion with her said husband but in sincerity and truth for the causes mentioned in said petition or libel. Sworn and Subscribed 21 Feby. 1845 Before" (signed Saml. Hepburn and Maria Hetrick by her mark.) -Notation on the front of this document "No. 28 Apr. Term 1845 Maria Hetrick by her next friend Edward Pendergrass vs. Abraham Hetrick Petition for a divorce from bed and board and for alimony 21 February A.D. 1845 Subpoena awarded." (signed Saml. Hepburn.) "filed 21st Feby. 1845 Graham."

Feb. 22, 1845 -"Cumberland County S.S. -The Commonwealth of Pennsylvania to Abraham Hetrick Greeting: Maria Hetrick on the twenty first day of February A.D. one thousand Eight hundred and forty five preferred a petition to the Judges of the Court of Common Pleas of Cumberland County praying that for the causes therein set forth she might be divorced from the bonds of matrimony entered into with you the said Abraham Hetrick and the said Judges having awarded a subpoena, We command you the said Abraham Hetrick that setting aside all business and excuses, whatsoever, you be and appear in your proper person before our Judges at Carlisle at our County Court of Common Pleas there to be held the fourteenth day of April next to answer the petition or libel of the said Maria Hetrick, and shew cause if any you have why she should not be divorced from the bonds of matrimony agreeably to the acts of assembly in such case made and provided. Witness Samuel Hepburn Esquire, President of our said Court at Carlisle the twenty second day of February A.D. 1845." (signed Thos. H. Criswell Prothonotary) -Notation the front of this document -"Subpoena Sur Divorce Returnable 14th April 1845 28th Feby. 1845 Served by copy So answers" (signed A. Longsdorf Shrff.) "Shff. fee $1.27 1/2. Graham."

April 21, 1845 -"Hetrick vs. Hetrick: Subpoena Sur Divorce No. 28 April Term 1845 -In this case the subpoena having issued for a divorce from the bonds of matrimony and not for a divorce from bed and board and for alimony agreeably to the petition of the libellant -on motion of Mr. Graham the Court awards another subpoena returnable the first day of the next August Term for a divorce from bed and board and for alimony agreeably to the petition of the libellant." -Notation on the front of this document -"Filed 21st Apr. 1845."

Nov. 17, 1845 -"Cumberland County, S.S. -The Commonwealth of Pennsylvania to the Sheriff of Cumberland County, Greeting: We command you that you attach Joseph Barbour so that you have him forthwith before the Judges of the Court of Common Pleas now holding at Carlisle, for the County of Cumberland, to answer us of a contempt in not obeying our writ of subpoena, issued out of our said court, in a certain action wherein Maria Hetrick is plaintiff and Abraham Hetrick is defendant. Hereof fail not. Witness Samuel Hepburn Esqr., President of the said court at Carlisle, the 17th day of November in the year of our Lord, one thousand eight hundred and forty five." (signed Thos. H. Criswell, Prothonotary) -Notation on the front of this document: "Hetrick vs. Hetrick: Attacht. for Jos. Barbour Non est inventus So answers" (signed J.F. Lamberton Dp. Shff. and A. Longsdorf, Shrff.) "Prot. C. 37 1/2 cts."

undated -"Maria Hetrick vs. Abraham Hetrick: No. 28 Aprl. T. 1845 Petition for Divorce -The said Libellant comes and says that she ought not be barred from having a decree of divorce from bed and board and for such alimony as the circumstances of the said Abraham Hetrick will admit for because she says that the said Abraham hath by cruel and barbarous treatment endangered the life of the said libellant and did offer such indignities to her person as to render her condition intolerable and life burthensome and did force her to withdraw from her house and family and hath for the last year and more doth refuse to provide for the said libellant a suitable maintenance as set forth in the said libellant's petition to the Court and of this she puts herself upon the County -and she positively and wholly denies that the temper disposition and acts of the said libellant have been such during the time she lived and cohabited with him the said respondent as to render his life burthensome and conditions intolerable and she publishes and denies that she wholly refused and neglected to do and perform the ordinary duties of a wife or mother toward and for the said Abraham Hetrick and his children and the said libellant doth further protest and deny that at the special insistence and request of the said libellant the said Abraham Hettrick (sic) did make lawful and reasonable maintenance for her on the 14 Oct 1839 by an agreement in writing that could be enforced by her the said libellant -nor has the said Abraham nor any one for him, paid to the said libellant annually with interest $2083.33 as is alleged by the said Respondent -But that the said Respondent hath neglected and still doth refuse to provide for your said libellant a suitable maintenance as the said libellant hath alleged in his said petition. This she is ready to verifty. She therefore puts herself upon the county. ---To the rejoinder of the Respondent the libellant says -that the said A. Hetrick hath refused and still doth refuse to provide for the said libellant a suitable maintenance as she hath heretofore alleged and that he hath not tendered and offered to pay the said libellant such reasonable maintenance." Notation on the front of this document -"with No. 28 Apr. 1845."

◆ ◆ ◆

August Term 1845 #2 April 17, 1845 -"Cumberland County S.S. -The Commonwealth of Pennsylvania to John Ritner Greeting: Whereas Rachel Ritner on the eleventh day of February A.D. 1845 preferred a petition the Judges of the Court of Common Pleas of Cumberland County praying that for the causes therein set forth she might be divorced from the bonds of matrimony entered into with you the said John Ritner that setting aside all business and excuses whatsoever you be and appear in your proper person before our Judges at Carlisle at our County Court of Common Pleas there to be held the tenth day of August next to answer the petition or libel of the said Rachel C. Ritner, and shew cause if any you have why she should not be divorced from the bonds of matrimony agreeably to the acts of assembly in such case made and provided. Witness Samuel Hepburn Esquire, President of our said Court at Carlisle the seventeenth day of April A.D. 1845." (signed Thos. H. Criswell Prothonotary.) Notation on the front of this document -"No. 2 Augt. Term 1845 Rachel C. Ritner vs. John Ritner Subpoena Sur divorce Returnable 10th Augt. 1845 Defendant not to be found in my bailiwick So answers" (signed A. Longsdorf Shrff.) "Shff's fee 18 3/4 cts. Adair."

◆ ◆ ◆

August Term 1845 #10 undated -"Mariah (sic) Hettrick (sic) by her next friend Edward Pendegrass vs. Abraham Hettrick (sic): No. 28 April Term 1845 (Note -front of document says No. 10 August Term 1845) Petition for Divorce -Abraham Hettrick (sic) the respondent protesting that the petition or libel of the said Mariah (sic) Hettrick (sic) is not sufficient in form or substance to entitle the said libellant to such decree as she claims appears by his attorneys William M. Biddle and Frederick Watts Esquires and answer to the petition and libel of the said Mariah (sic) Hettrick (sic) by her next friend Edward Pendegrass: that true it is that the said Abraham and the said Mariah (sic) were duly united in the bond of matrimony and continued to live and cohabit together as man and wife as set forth in the said petition: But the said Abraham doth deny that he hath by cruel and barbarous treatment endangered the life of the said libellant and hath not offered such indignities to her person as to render her condition intolerable and life burthensome and did not force her to withdraw from his house and family and hath not for the last year refused to provide for the said libellant a suitable maintenance: but on the contrary the conduct temper disposition and acts of the said libellant have been such, during the time she lived and cohabited with the said respondent, as to render his life burthensome and condition intolerable that she wholly refused and neglected to do and perform the ordinary duties of a wife, or a mother towards and for the said Abraham Hettrick (sic) and her children: and the said Abraham Hettrick (sic) doth further answer and aver that at the insistence and request of the said libellant he did make a provision for her maintenance to wit on the 14 December A.D. 1839 an agreement in writing was entered into by the said libellant by which the said respondent was induced to sell and despose of a farm of which he was then seized and possessed to one Philip Zeigler for the purpose of creating an investment in the said farm to the amount of two thousand and Eighty three dollars thirty three cents the interest of which was to be paid by the said Philip Zeigler to the said libellant annually: and the said respondent doth aver that the said Philip Zeigler hath paid and hath always been ready and willing to pay to the said libellant the said interest annually: and therefore he prays that the petition of the said libellant may be dismissed. ----To the supplication of the Libellant the respondent by her said Attorney rejoins -That the said Abraham Hettrick (sic) hath refused and still doth refuse to provide for the said libellant a suitable maintenance as she alleged: but on the contrary the said sum of $2083.33 was put into the hands of the said Philip Zeigler at the insistence request knowledge and consent of the said libellant the interest of which sum the said Philip agreed and bound himself to pay to the said libellant annually and the said Philip hath paid and offered and tendered to pay to the said libellant the said interest annually to wit the sum of one hundred and twenty five dollars and the said principle sum of $2083.33 is still in the hands and possession and care of the said Philip Zeigler upon the trusts aforesaid and the interest of which he is willing to pay to the said libellant."

April 28,1845 -"Cumberland County S.S. -The Commonwealth of

Pennsylvania to Abraham Hetrick Greeting: Whereas Maria Hetrick on the 21st day of February one thousand Eight hundred and forty five preferred a petition to the Judges of the Court of Common Pleas of Cumberland County praying that for the causes therein set forth she might be divorced from bed and board and also that she might be allowed such alimony as the circumstances of the said Abraham Hetrick will admit of and the said Judges having awarded a Subpoena We command you the said Abraham Hetrick that setting aside all business and excuses, whatsoever you be and appear in your proper person before our Judges at Carlisle at our County Court of Common Pleas there to be held the eleventh day of August next to answer the petition or libel of the said Maria Hetrick and shew cause if any you have why you should not be divorced from bed and board and also be allowed such alimony as the circumstances of you the said Abraham Hetrick will admit of agreeably to the Acts of Assembly in such case made and provided. Witness Samuel Hepburn Esqr. President of our said Court at Carlisle the twenty Eighth day of April A.D. 1845." (signed Thos. H. Criswell Prothonotary) -Notation on the front this document -"No. 10 Augt.Term 1845 Maria Hetrick by her next friend Edward Pendegrass vs. Abraham Hetrick Subp. Sur Divorce Returnable eleventh Augt. 1845 9th May 1845 Served by copy So answers." (signed A. Longsdorf Shrff.) "Shff. fee $1.27 1/2 Graham."

Dec. 13, 1845 -"Maria Hettrick by her next friend Edward Pendegrass vs. Abrm. Hettrick: No. 10 Aug. Term 1845 In the Common Pleas of Cumberland County -Subpoena Sur Divorce -Now to wit 13 December 1845 The parties agree that all the allegations and facts stated in the petition and pleadings be withdrawn and that the decree for the payment of alimony be made with the same effect as if the cause had been tried and a verdict for the plaintiff. And the parties agree that the following be the decree of the Court that the said Abraham Hettrick do pay or cause to be paid to the said Mariah Hettrick the sum of One Hundred and fifty dollars in full compensation for the support of herself and payment of her own expenses up to the day of the date thereof and farther that he will pay or cause to be paid to her on the 1st day of January 1847 the sum of Two hundred dollars and on each first day of January thereafter the sum of two Hundred dollars, and this proceeding and agreement to have the same force and effect as if it had been attained by an adverse proceeding and decree of the Court. And the Prothonotary is hereby authorized to enter the same upon the records of the Court of Common Pleas. 13 December 1845." (signed illegible first name Watts, Atty. for Deft. and J.H. Graham, Atty. for Plaintiff) -Notation on the front of this document -"No. 10 Aug. T. 1845 Mariah Hettrick by her next friend Edward Pendegrass vs. Abrm. Hettrick agreement and settlement by the parties. Filed 13th Decr. 1845."

Nov. 18, 1845 -"M. Hetrick vs. A. Hetrick Plffs. witness at Nov. T. 1845

Paid -Thomas Bell 2 days	$1.25	
10 miles circular	.30	$1.55
Paid -John Wondertech	1.25	
7 miles circular	.21	$1.46
Paid -John Armstrong	1.25	
12 miles circular	.36	$1.61
-Francis Eckles Esq.	1.25	
14 miles circular	.42	$1.67
Paid -John Gross	1.25	
18 miles circular	.54	$1.79
Paid -Joseph Kenegy	1.25	
12 miles circular	.36	$1.61
Paid -Andrew Monnasmith	1.25	
8 miles circular	.24	$1.49
Paid -Frederick Illefritz	1.25	
5 miles circular	.15	$1.40
Paid -Mathew B. Rodgers	1.25	
6 miles circular	.18	$1.43

Taxed and sworn to by M. B. Rodgers the 18th Nov. 1845 Before John Main for Thos. H. Criswell Prothy.

Paid -William Baker 2 days	$1.00	$1.00
Paid -Edward Pendergrass for serving		
Subpoena on 14 witness	$1.40	
28 miles circular	.84	$2.24
		$17.25

Received from W.M. Beetem our costs in the above case in full." (signed William Baker, M. B. Rodgers, Edward Pendergrass, Andrew Monnasmith, John Gross by his mark, John Armstrong, Thos. Bell, Fredk. Illefritz by his mark, John Wondertech, Test. John Main.)

"Defts. wits. at Nov. T. 1845 M. Hetrick vs. A. Hetrick:

Stephen Piper	$1.25
8 miles circular	.24
	$1.49

Recd. 18th Dec. 1845 from W.M. Beetem one 49/100 Dollars in full of the above bill of costs." (signed Test. John Main and Stephen Piper by his mark.)

Jan. 14, 1847 -"1847 January 14th Sir pay to the Bearer James Williamson the moneys due me as a witness in the Abraham Hetrick case." (signed Joseph Kenege.) "Recd. 14 Jany. 1847 from W.M. Beetem, Prot. One dollar and Sixty one cents in full of the above order." (signed James Williamson.) Notation on the front of this document -"10 Nov. T. 1845 Hetrick vs. Hetrick Bill of costs."

◆ ◆ ◆

November Term 1845 #2 Aug. 12, 1845 -"To the Honorable the

Judges of the Court of Common Pleas of Cumberland County -The petition of David Irving respectfully represents -That he was legally united in marriage with Rosanna Van Kirk about sixteen years ago, then lived with her up until February 1842, since which time she has refused to live and cohabit with your petitioner, and has wilfully and maliciously deserted his habitation -Your petitioner further represents that his said wife since the said February 1842, and during the time of her desertion has been living in adultery with various persons, and conducting herself as a common prostitute. He therefore prays your honors to grant such relief as the Act of Assembly in such case made and provided and he will pray etc." (signed David Irvine) -"Cumberland County sct. -David Irvine the above named petitioner being duly sworn according to law says that the facts set forth in the above petition are true to the best of his knowledge and belief -that his complaint is not made out of levity, or by collusion between him and his said wife, and for the mere purpose of being freed and separated from each other, but in sincerity and truth and for the causes mentioned in his petition. Sworn and Subscribed before me this 12 Aug. 1845." (signed David Smith, J.P. and David Irvine) -Notation on the front of this document -"No. 2 Nov. T. 1845 Petition of David Irvine for a divorce. Subpoena awarded 12th Augt. 1845 By the Court. filed 12 Augt. 1845."

Aug. 18, 1845 -"Cumberland County S.S. -The Commonwealth of Pennsylvania to Rosanna Irvine Greeting: Whereas David Irvine on the twelfth day of August A.D. One thousand Eight Hundred and forty five preferred a petition to the Judges of the Court of Common Pleas of Cumberland County praying that for the causes therein set forth he might be divorced from the bonds of Matrimony entered into with you the said Rosanna Irvine, and the said Judges having awarded a subpoena, therefore, We command you the said Rosanna Irvine that setting aside all business and excuses whatsoever you be and appear in your proper person before our Judges at Carlisle at our County Court of Common Pleas there to be held the tenth day of November next to answer the petition or libel of the said David Irvine, and shew cause if any you have why he should not be divorced from the bonds of Matrimony agreeably to the acts of Assembly in such case made and provided. Witness Samuel Hepburn Esquire President of our said Court at Carlisle the eighteenth day of August in the year of our Lord one Thousand Eight Hundred and Forty five." (signed Thomas H. Criswell Prothonotary) -Notation on the front of this document -"No. 2 November T. 1845 David Irvine vs. Rosanna Irving Subpoena Sur Divorce October 28, 1845 Served personally and by copy, So answers." (signed Jas. F. Lamberton, D. Shrff. and A. Longsdorf, Sheriff) "Shff.'s bill $1.19 1/2 Todd."

Nov. 10, 1845 -"David Irvine vs. Susannah (*sic*) Irvine: Sub. Sur divorce. Now, to wit 10 Nov. 1845 -The writ in this case having been returned served -on motion of L. Todd, David Smith, Esq. is appointed a Commissioner to take depositions to be reqd in evidence in this case -to be taken exparte on ten days notice. By the Court." -Notation on the front of this document -"No. 2 Nov. T. 1845 filed 10 Nov. 1845."

◆ ◆ ◆

April Term 1846 #1 Jan. 16, 1846 -"To the Honorable the Judges of the Court of Common Pleas of Cumberland County -The petition of John Shank of the Borough of New Cumberland -Respectfully Represents -That on the 22 July 1841 he was lawfully married with Catherine Deyer and continued to live with her for more than three years and during that time conducted himself as a loving husband should do. Although by the Laws of God as well as by her plighted faith and Statute of Pennsylvania the said Catherine was bound to that chastity which ought to be inseparable from the marriage state yet the said Catherine in violation thereof has for considerable time past given herself up to adulterous practices and has been guilty of adultery with different persons. Your petitioner, being a citizen of Pennsylvania, therefore prays your Honors to award a subpoena directed to the said Catherine Shank to appear at the next Court to be held on the second Monday of April 1846 and shew cause why the said Court should not make a decree that the said John Shank should be divorced from the bonds of matrimony entered into with the said Catherine Deyer and he as in duty bound will pray etc." (signed John Shank) -"Cumberland County sct. -Personally appeared before me a Justice of the Peace in and for said County John Shank who being duly sworn doth depose and say that the facts set forth in the foregoing petition are true to the best of his knowledge and belief. Sworn and Subscribed the 16 Jan. 1846 Before me." (signed Peter A. Ege and John Shank) Notation on the front of this document -"No. 1 April T. 1846 John Shank vs. Catherine Shank: Subpoena Sur divorce -Subpoena awarded." (signed Saml. Hepburn Jany. 16, 1846) "Filed 16 Jany. 1846 Watts."

Jan. 16, 1846 -"Cumberland County s.s. -The Commonwealth of Pennsylvania to Catharine Shank Greeting: Whereas John Shank on the 16th day of January A.D. 1846 preferred a petition to the Hon. Samuel Hepburn President Judge of the Court of Common Pleas of Cumberland County (in vacation) praying that for the causes therein set forth he might be divorced from the bonds of matrimony entered into with the said Catharine Shank, late Catharine Deyer and the said Judge having awarded a subpoena. Therefore we command you the said Catharine Shank that setting aside all business and excuses whatsoever, you be and appear in your proper person before our Judges at Carlisle at our County Court of Common Pleas there to be held the 13th day of April next to answer the petition or libel of the said John Shank, and shew cause if any you have why he should not be divorced from the Bonds of matrimony agreeably to the acts of Assembly in such case made and provided -Witness Samuel Hepburn Esquire at Carlisle the 16th day of January A.D. 1846." (signed W.M. Beetem -Prothonotary.) --

Jan. 19, 1846 -"Lancaster County sct. -Personally appeared before me a Justice of the Peace in and for said County Joseph Donaly who being duly sworn doth depose and say that he served a true copy of the within Subpoena on Catherine Shank on the nineteenth day of January A.D. 1846. Sworn and Subscribed the 19th day of January A.D. 1846 Before me." (signed Jacob Foreman and Joseph Donely.)

April 16,1846 -"The Court having received due proof of the service of the subpoena according to law do hereby order and decree that J. T. Anderson Esq. of Marietta, Lancaster County be and is hereby appointed a commissioner to take testimony to be read in the final hearing of this cause. 16 April 1846. By the Court." -Notation on the front of this document -"No. 1 April T. 1846 John Shank vs. Catharine Shank Subpoena Sur Divorce Returnable 13th Apl. 1846 New Cumbl. J.T. Anderson Esq. of Marietta Lan. Co. to be appointed Commisioner to take testimony. Watts."

April 18, 1846 -"Cumberland County Sct. -The Commonwealth of Pennsylvania to J. T. Anderson, Esq. of Marietta, Lancaster County, Greeting. -Know ye that in confidence of your prudence and fidelity, we have appointed you and these presents do give unto you full power and authority in pursuance of an order made in our County Court of Common Pleas for the said County of Cumberland in a certain case of Subpoena sur Divorce, wherein John Shank is Plaintiff and Catharine Shank is Defendant, at a certain day and place by you for that purpose by you to be appointed, all and every person or persons who may be named to you. -And then and there to examine each of them the said witnesses touching the premises and reduce their testimony to writing, and when you have so done you are to send the same before us in our County Court of Common Pleas aforesaid, and this writ, under your hand and seal. Witness the Honorable Samuel Hepburn Esq. President of our said Court of Common Pleas, at Carlisle, the 18th day of April, A.D. 1846." (signed W.M. Beetem Prothy.) -"The execution of this rule appears in a certain schedule hereto annexed."

May 11, 1846 -"Charles Malhorn Sworn -I am acquainted with Catherine Shank. She lived next door to me in Marietta; the first that I took notice there was such late setting up in the house and cutting up. Halderman was to come up to employ John Shank to work on his farm and when John would be gone Haldeman would come and stay at the house. When he would go in the door was locked. I have several times tryed (*sic*) the door a few minutes after he would go in. One night when John was not at home Haldeman came to the house with his sleigh with the bell muffled between eight and ten o'clock at night the back way and took Catherine away in the sleigh and was away about an hour and a half and he brought her back in the back way. For a couple of weeks Haldeman was there nearly half of his time. I have often seen her call men in off the pavement. Sworn and Subscribed before me May 11th 1846." (signed J.T. Anderson and Charles Malhorn.)

May 11, 1846 -"Allen Ruby sworn -I am acquainted with Catherine Shank, I have often seen men in the house under suspicious circumstances. I have heard reported of her that she allowed familiar intercourse with other men while her husband lived with her. Sworn and Subscribed before me May 11th 1846." (signed Allen S. Ruby and J. T. Anderson.)

May 11, 1846 -"Adeline Shafer Sworn -I am acquainted with Catherine Shank. I lived in the house with her while she lived with her husband; her conduct with men was scandalous while I lived with her as she spent half a day several times with different men upstairs by themselves when her husband was absent and several times she got her husband to go off to Mount Pleasant about two miles from where they live; so as to get other men with her. When other men would come in she would take them around the neck and kiss them -I saw Lewis Worley in bed with her and I saw Henry Isanberger in bed with her. I threatened that I would tell her husband; she said that she did not care whether I did or not; if she expected anyone she would try to get me off. When I came to the house several times that she had got me off I found some man with her. I know that one Feltenberger was with her one night in the back room. She told me that her and one Haldeman was on the bed in the room together. I knew that he was in the room with her. Mr. Feltenberger told me that he had to send Shank and his wife away from the oar (sic) banks on account of her conduct with the men. John Shank her husband was well thought of himself as he was a good worker and was much pitied. Sworn and Subscribed before me May 11th 1846." (signed J. T. Anderson and Adeline Shafer by her mark.)

May 11, 1846 -"Depositions of Allen Ruby, Adeline Shafer and Charles Malhorn of the Borough of Marietta, Lancaster County Pennsylvania produced sworn and examined this eleventh day of May A.D. 1846 at the office of J.T. Anderson Esquire by virtue of a rule for the examination of witnesses in a certain cause now depending before the Court of Common Pleas at Carlisle Cumberland County wherein John Shank is plaintiff and Catherine Shank is defendant. Certified under my hand and seal at the Borough of Marietta Lancaster County the eleventh day of May A.D. 1846." (signed J. T. Anderson Justice of the Peace Lancaster County.) Notation on the front of this document; "No. 1 April Term 1846 Shank vs. Shank Commission Filed 10th Augt. 1846."

Aug. 10, 1846 -Notation on the front of this document -"No. 1 April Term 1846 John Shank vs. Catherine Shank Final decree of divorce Filed 10th August, 1846" -"In the matter of the Libel of John Shank for a divorce from his wife Catharine Shank -Now, to wit, 10 Aug. 1846 The Commissioner heretofore appointed to take testimony in the case have returned the depositions of the witnesses and the Court having duly considered the whole case do now order decree and sentence that the said John Shank is hereby divorced and separated from the nuptial ties or bonds of matrimony and that all any every the duties rights and claims accruing to either of the said parties at any time heretofore in pursuance of the said marriage shall cease and determine and the said parties shall severally be at liberty to marry again in like manner as if they never had been married. By the Court."

◆ ◆ ◆

November Term 1846 #6 Aug. 11, 1846 -"To the Honorable the Judges of the Court of Common Pleas for the County of Cumberland. -The Petition of Jane Cummins by David Chestnut her next friend, Repectfully Showeth -That your libellant on the 19th day of February in the year of our Lord one thousand Eight Hundred and Thirty Nine was contracted in matrimony and married to a certain James C. Cummins, and from that time until about the 15th day of August in the year of our Lord one thousand Eight Hundred and forty, lived and cohabited with him as his wife, and as such was owned and acknowledged by him, and so deemed and reputed by all her neighbors and acquaintances; and although by the laws of God, as well as by their mutual vows and faith plighted to each other, they were reciprocally bound to that kindness and uniform regard which ought to be inseparable from the marriage state; yet so it is that the said James C. Cummins from the said 15th day of August or therabout in the year of our Lord one thousand eight Hundred and Forty hath wilfully and maliciously absented himself from the habitation of this Libellant without just or reasonable cause. And such desertion has persisted in for the term of two years and upwards and yet doth continue to absent himself from the said Libellant. Wherefore your Libellant further showing that she is a citizen of this State, and hath resided therein for one whole year and more previous to the filing of this petition, prays your Honors that a Subpoena shall issue from the said Court directed to the said James C. Cummins commanding him to appear at the next Term of the said Court to answer the Petition; and also that a decree of the said Court may be made divorcing him the said James C. Cummins from the society, fellowship and company of this Libellant in all time to come, and Jane Cummins this Libellant from the marriage bond aforesaid, as if she had never been married, or as if the said James C. Cummins were naturally dead. And this Libellant will pray." (signed Jane Commons by her next friend David Chestnut) --"The above named Jane Cummins being duly sworn, says, the facts contained in the above Libel are true to the best of her knowledge and belief, and that the said complaint is not made out of levity, and collusion between her and the said James C. Cummins and for the mere purpose of being freed and separated from each other, but in sincerity and truth, for the causes mentioned in the said Libel. Sworn before me this Eleventh day of August 1846." (signed James Mackey and Jane Commons.) -Notation on the front of this document -"No. 6 November Term 1846 Jane Cummins by her next friend David Chestnut vs. James C. Cummins Petition for Divorce 18th Augt. 1846 Subpoena awarded By the Court. Watts."

Aug. 18, 1846 -"Cumberland County S.S. -The Commonwealth of Pennsylvania to James C. Cummins, Greeting: Whereas, Jane Cummins by her next friend David Chestnut, on the 18th day of August A.D. 1846, preferred a petition to the Court of Common Pleas of Cumberland County, praying that for the causes therein set forth, she might be divorced from the bonds of matrimony entered into with you the said James C. Cummins -and the Court awarded a Subpoena. We therefore command you the said James C. Cummins, that setting aside all business and excuses whatsoever you be and appear in your proper person before our Judges at Carlisle, at our County Court of Common Pleas, there to be held the 9th day of November, next, to answer the petition or libel of the said Jane Cummins your wife, and shew cause if any you have why she should not be divorced from the bond of matrimony entered into with you, agreeably to the act of Assembly in such case made and provided. Hereof fail not. Witness Samuel Hepburn, Esq. President of our said Court at Carlisle the 18th day of August, A.D. 1846." (signed W.M. Beetem, Prothy.)

Dec. 12, 1846 -"Cumberland County, Sct. -A. Longsdorf Esq. being duly affirmed according to law doth depose and say that the Deft. J.C. Cummins is not to be found in my bailiwick. Affirmed and Subscribed the 12th day of Decr. 1846 Before" (signed W.M. Beetem, Prot. and A. Longsdorf, Shrff.) -Notation on the front of this document -"No. 6 November T. 1846 Jane Cummins by her next friend David Chesnut vs. James C. Cummins Subpoena Sur Divorce 12 Octr 1846 Deft. not to be found in my bailiwick, So answers" (signed A. Longsdorf, Shrff.) "Shff. fee $0.18 3/4 Watts."

Dec. 17, 1846 -"Cumberland County, Sct. -The Commonwealth of Pennsylvania to James C. Cummins Greeting: Whereas, Jane Cummins by her next friend David Chesnut, on the 18th day of August, A.D. 1846 preferred a petition to the Court of Common Pleas of Cumberland County, praying that for the causes therein set forth, she might be divorced from the bonds of matrimony entered into with you the said James C. Cummins -and the Court awarded a Subpoena -We therefore command you, as we have heretofore commanded you the said James C. Cummins, that setting aside all business and excuses whatsoever you be and appear in your proper person before our Judges, at Carlisle, at our County Court of Common Pleas, there to be held the 11th day of January next, to answer the petition or libel of the said Jane Cummins your wife -and show cause if any you have why she should not be divorced from the bonds of matrimony entered into with you agreeably to the act of Assembly in such case made and provided. Hereof fail not. -Witness Samuel Hepburn, Esq. President of our said Court, at Carlisle the 17th day of December, A.D. 1846." (signed W.M. Beetem, Prot.)

November Term 1846 #6 Jan. 8, 1847 -"Cumberland County, S.S. -James Hoffer Esq. Sheriff being duly sworn according to law doth depose and say that the Defendant James C. Cummins in the within writ, is not to be found in my bailiwick on Dec. 30, 1846. Sworn and Subscribed before me 8 Jany. 1847." (signed W.M. Beetem, Prot. and James Hoffer, Shrff.)

April 19, 1847 -"Cumberland County, S.S. -James Hoffer Esq. Shrff. being duly sworn according to law doth depose and say that he caused notice to be published in one newspaper printed in said county for four successive weeks prior to the first day of the Apr. T. 1847, requiring the said James C. Cummins to appear on that day to answer the complaint of the said Jane Cummins. Sworn and Subscribed the 19th April 1847 Before me." (signed W.M. Beetem, Pro. and James Hoffer, Shrff.) -Notation on the front of this document -"No. 6 November T. 1846 Jane Cummins by her next friend David Chesnut vs. James C. Cummins Alias Subpoena sur Divorce Retble. 11th January, 1847. Decr. 30th 1846 Deft. not to be found in my bailiwick, so answers" (signed James Hoffer, Shff.) "Shff. Hoffer's fee $0.18 3/4 do on ado $1.50 Watts."

◆   ◆   ◆

November Term 1846 #22 Sept.5,1846 -"To the Honorable John Stuart one of the Judges of the Court of Common Pleas of Cumberland County -The petition of Susannah Harris by her next friend Peter Lindsey Respectfully Represents -That your libellant on the 4th day of September A.D. 1845 was contracted in matrimony and married to a certain Enoch Harris and from that time until the (left blank) day of April 1846 lived and cohabited with him as his wife and as such was owned and acknowledged by him and so deemed and reputed by all her neighbors and acquaintances, and although by the laws of God as well as by their mutual vows and faith plighted to each other they were reciprocally bound to that uniform kindness and regard which ought to be inseparable from the marriage state, yet so it is that the said Enoch Harris on the said (left blank) day of April 1846 and at various other days and times prior to that date, did by cruel and barbarous treatment endanger the life of your libellant and did offer such indignities to her person as to render her condition intolerable and life burthensome and thereby force her to withdraw from his house and society and companionship -Wherefore your libellant further showing that she hath resided in this state for more than two years previous to this date -Prays your Honor that a subpoena may issue from said court directed to the said Enoch Harris commanding him to appear at the next term of the said court to answer this petition and also that a decree of said Court may be made granting this libellant a divorce from the society fellowship and company of the said Enoch Harris in all time to come and from the bond of matrimony as if she had never been married or as if the said Enoch Harris were naturally dead. And she will pray etc." (signed Susannah Harris by her next friend Peter Lindsey) -"Cumberland County s.s. -Before the subscriber a Justice of the Peace in and for said county personally came the within named Susannah Harris who being duly sworn according to law says that the facts contained in the within libel are true to the best of her knowledge and belief -And that the said complaint is not made out of levity or by collusion between her and her said husband and for the mere purpose of being freed and separated from each other, but in sincerity and truth for the causes mentioned in the within petition or libel. Sworn and Subscribed the 5 September 1846 Before me" (signed J. Holsaple, J.P. and Susannah Harris) -Notation on the front of this document -"No. 22 November T. 1846 Petition of Susannah Harris by her next friend for a divorce 5 Septb. 1846 Subpoena awarded by" (signed John Stuart) "Filed 8th September 1846."

Sept. 8, 1846 -"Cumberland County S.S. -The Commonwealth of Pennsylvania to Enoch Harris, Greeting: Whereas Susannah Harris, by her next friend Peter Lindsey, on the 5th day of September, A.D. 1846, preferred a petition to the Honorable John Stuart, one of the Judges of the Court of Common Pleas of Cumberland County, praying that for the causes therein set forth, she might be divorced from the bonds of matrimony entered into with you the said Enoch Harris -and the said Judge Stuart awarded a Subpoena. We therefore command you the said Enoch Harris, that setting aside all business and excuses whatsoever you be and appear in your proper person before our Judges at Carlisle at our County Court of Common Pleas there to be held the 9th day of November, next, to answer the petition or libel of the said Susannah Harris, your wife, and shew cause if any you have why she should not be divorced from the bonds of matrimony entered into with you, agreeably to the acts of Assembly in such case made and provided. Hereof fail not. Witness, Samuel Hepburn, Esq. at Carlisle, the 8th day of September A.D. 1846." (signed W.M. Beetem, Prothy.)

Dec. 15, 1846 -"Cumberland County s.s. -A. Longsdorf, Esq.

being duly affirmed according to law doth depose and say that the Defendant is not to be found in my bailiwick. Affirmed and Subscribed before me Dec. 15, 1846. (signed W.M. Beetem, Prot. and A. Longsdorf, Shrff.) -Notation on the front this document -"No. 22 November T. 1846 Susannah Harris by her next friend Peter Lindsey vs. Enoch Harris Subpoena sur Divorce Octr. 17, 1846 Deft. not to be found in my bailiwick So answers" (signed A. Longsdorf, Shrff.) "Shff.'s fee $0.18 3/4 Graham."

Dec. 17, 1846 -"Cumberland County, S.S. -The Commonwealth of Pennsylvania to Enoch Harris Greeting: Whereas Susannah Harris by her next friend Peter Lindsey, on the 5th day of September A.D. 1846 preferred a petition to the Honorable John Stuart, one of the Judges of the Court of Common Pleas of Cumberland County, praying that for the causes therein set forth, she might be divorced from the bonds of matrimony entered into with you the said Enoch Harris -and the said Judge Stuart, awarded a Subpoena -We therefore command you the said Enoch Harris, as we have heretofore commanded you, that setting aside all business and excuses whatsoever you be and appear in your proper person before our Judges at Carlisle at our County Court of Common Pleas there to be held the 11th day of January next, to answer the petition or libel of the said Susannah Harris, your wife, and show cause if any you have why she should not be divorced from the bond of matrimony entered into with you agreeably to the act of Assembly in such case made and provided. Hereof fail not. -Witness Samuel Hepburn, Esq. at Carlisle the 17th day of December, A.D. 1846." (signed W.M. Beetem, Prot.) -Notation on the front of this document -"No. 22 Nov T. 1846 Susannah Harris by her next friend Peter Lindsey vs. Enoch Harris, Alias Subpoena Sur Divorce Retble. 11th Jany. 1847. Decr. 30th 1846 Deft. not to be found in my bailiwick so answers" (signed James Hoffer, Shff.) -"Shff. Hoffer's fee $0.18 3/4 do on ado $1.50 Graham."

April 19, 1847 -"In the Court of Common Pleas of Cumberland County -Susannah Harris by her next friend Peter Lindsey vs. Enoch Harris: No. 22 November T. 1846 Subpoena Sur Divorce -19th April, 1847, On motion of Mr. Graham, in open court, Dr. James R. Irvine appointed a Commissioner to take depositions in this case to be read upon the hearing of the same at the next court of Common Pleas, to be held in and for said county, on the fourth Monday of August, 1847. By the Court."

July 15, 1847 -"Cumberland County, s.s. -I do certify that the above is a true copy of the appointment of Dr. J. R. Irvine, a Commissioner, to take Depositions etc. in the above case. In testimony whereof I have hereunto set my hand, and affixed the seal of said Court, at Carlisle, the 15th day of July, A.D. 1847." (signed W.M. Beetem Prot.)

Sept. 4, 1847 -"Depositions of witnesses produced sworn and

examined before James R. Irvine, at his office in the Borough of Newville on Saturday the 4th day of Septr. 1847 in pursuance of the rule of Court, hereto attached. Eleanora Wilt having been first duly sworn, deposes as follows. I saw my sister Susannah Wilt married to Enoch Harris. The ceremony was performed at my house in Westpennsborough township on the 4th day of Sept. 1845 by the Rev. Robt. McCachrew -From the time of their marriage they occupied the same house with me until Sunday the 26th day of April 1846. For some days prior to the last mentioned date Enoch Harris was ill tempered and cross, and refused to speak to his wife, or to any other person about the house, and for sometime previous to that date also, he (Harris) acted in such a way that we all were afraid he would do us harm. On Sunday night April 26,1846 Harris retired early to bed without speaking to any person, his wife (my sister) and myself sat up late, being afraid to go to bed until John Ashburn a young man who lived in the family, and the only man (except Mr. Harris) in the family, should come in. It was about 11 o'clock when John Ashburn came in, and shortly after he came in we went to bed. As my sister and I were going to bed I said to her that if she was afraid to go to bed with Harris, she had better sleep in my room -she replied that she would try it awhile longer for he could not hurt her much as long as John Ashburn was so near her, sleeping in the next room to her. A short time after I went to bed I heard my sister Mrs. Harris calling to John Ashburn, that she wanted to get up -I at once rose and went into John Ashburn's room, and then went down stairs for light; whe I returned she was coming out, she appeared much alarmed, and ran across to my room, I went in also, and we shut the door and fastened it. About half an hour afterward, Harris came to the door, and threatened to break open the door, and did attempt to force open the door. I told him he should not come in and he said he would and that if I did not open it he would break it and this he repeated often. At this time John Ashburn came to the door and I called to him to prevent Harris from breaking the door and if necessary to knock him down. I heard John Ashburn threatening him that if he did not leave the door he would have to hurt him, and would knock him down. He then went to his own room, after scolding a good deal. On the next morning my sister left the house and did not return until Tuesday evening. On Monday Harris carried his bed from the room they had occupied to a room down stairs and procured a chain and padlock, and fastened the door of the room the shutters of the windows were also closed and fastened by him. He had also an axe in the room. He remained in the house on Monday night and left on Tuesday morning. On Wednesday I went before a Justice of the Peace in Springfield, and brought a suit against Harris of "Surety of the Peace". He was arrested upon the warrant issued by the Justice and committed to jail. A few days afterward he returned to the house, but did not come in. His trunk and clothes were taken out to him, and he left, and has not returned since. I understood that he had gone to the State of New Jersey. Sworn and Subscribed before" (signed James R. Irvine and Eleanora Wilt.)

Sept. 4, 1847 -"John Ashburn having been first duly sworn, doth depose as follows. I was living with the Misses Wilt for some time before and after the 26th April 1846. For some time before that date we were all afraid of Enoch Harris. I was afraid of my own life. He appeared angry and sullen and would not speak to any person. I had for some time been talking to him and trying to induce him to behave properly, and telling him that he had deceived his wife. The only reply made by him was that he had also been deceived. On Sunday night 26th April 1846 I was at preaching and came home at about Eleven o'clock, and found Mrs. Harris and her sister Miss Wilt setting up, and they said they were afraid to go to bed on account of the manner in which Harris acted. I went to bed a short time after. I was in bed about half an hour, when I heard Mrs. Harris calling me by name. She said she wanted out or up, which she said I am not certain. I slept in the room adjoining the one in which they were. I called to him to let her out, if she wanted out. He answered that I had no right to interfere. I replied that he should no abuse her, and I would interfere. I then opened the door of their room and Mrs. Harris ran out and went into her sister's room. About half an hour afterward he came out of his own room and went to the door of Eleanor Wilt's room, and endeavoured to break it open by pressing against it with his feet and knees and using all his force to effect his object. Eleanor told me to put him away, and if necessary to knock him down. I threatened to do it and told him I would be forced to hurt him, if he not go away, and after a long time he did go away. On the next day I asked him if he was going to cut up any more, but he gave me no answer. On that day also he removed his bed down stairs, and procured a chain padlock from a neighbour, and fastened the door on which he placed his bed. He also fastened the shutters of the room. He left on Monday and was back once or twice until Wednesday, when he was taken into custody by the Constable. After he was taken into custody I opened the room he had occupied, and found an axe, which had been missed, and suspected that he had it. Some days afterward he returned. I gave him his trunk and clothing, and I have not seen him since. Sworn and Subscribed Before" (signed James R. Irvine and John Ashburn.)

Sept. 4, 1847 -"Cumberland County, s.s. -I, James R. Irvine Commissioner, named in the order of Court hereto attached, do certify that the within and foregoing depositions of Eleanora Wilt and John Ashburn were duly taken and subscribed before me, at the time and place stated in the caption thereto (the said witnesses having been first duly sworn according to law) Witness my hand at

Newville 4 Sept. 1847" (signed James R. Irvine) -Notation on the front of this document -"No. 22 November Term 1846 Harris vs. Harris: Proceedings in Divorce Filed 8th Sept. 1847."
Sept. 8, 1847 -"Susan Harris by her next friend Peter Lindsey vs. Enoch Harris: In the Common Pleas of Cumberland County No. 22 November Term 1846 Subpoena Sur Divorce -And now, to wit, 7th September A.D. 1847 Doct. James R. Irvine Esq. the Commissioner having returned to the Court here the depositions of witnesses taken before him on the part of the libellant, and the same being read and heard by the court, and the court after mature deliberation being satisfied therewith and proclamation being made for the Respondent to come forth and he not appearing, the Court do order, adjudge and decree that the said Susan Harris be divorced and separated from the bond of matrimony contracted with the said Enoch Harris the Respondent -and that all and every the duties rights and claims accruing to either of the said parties by reason of the said marriage shall hence forth cease and determine and the said parties be severally at liberty to marry again in like manner as if they had never been married. By the Court Sept. 8th 1847" -Notation on the front of this document -"No. 22 November T. 1846 Susan Harris vs. Enoch Harris Decree in Divorce Filed 8th Sept. 1847."

◆ ◆ ◆

November Term 1846 #52 Oct. 12, 1846 -"To the Honorable the Judges of the Court of Common Pleas of Cumberland County - The Libel of Sarah Marlin by her Father and next friend Joseph T. Ward, M.D. -Respectfully Showeth, That your libellant on the 12th day of Septr. in the year of our Lord one thousand and eight hundred and forty two was contracted in matrimony, and married to a certain Henry Marlin and from that time until the 19th day of April in the year of our Lord one Thousand Eight Hundred and forty three lived and cohabited with the said Henry Marlin as his wife, and as such was owned and acknowledged by him, and so deemed and reputed by her nieghbors and acquaintances. And although by the laws of God as well as by their mutual vows and faith plighted to each other, they were bound to that uniform constancy and regard which ought to be inseparable from the marriage state; yet so it is, that the said Henry Marlin from the 19th day of April in the year of our Lord one thousand eight hundred and forty three hath wilfully and maliciously deserted and absented himself from the habitation of this Libellant without any just or reasonable cause. And such desertion hath persisted in for the term of two year, and upwards, and yet doth continue to absent himself from the said Libellant. Wherefore your Libellant further showing that she is a citizen of the state of Pennsylvania and hath resided therein for upwards of one whole year previous to the filing of this Libel, prays your Honors that a subpoena may issue forth to summon the said Henry Marlin to appear in this Honorable Court at November Term next, to answer the complaint aforesaid. -And also that a decree of this Honorable Court may by made for the divorcing of him the said Henry Marlin from the society, fellowship and company of this Libellant in all time to come, and Sarah Marlin this Libellant from the marriage bond aforesaid, as if she had never been married, or as if the said Henry Marlin were naturally dead. And this Libellant etc." (signed Sarah Marlin By her father and next friend Jos. T. Ward.) -"Cumberland County, s.s. -The above named Sarah Marlin being duly affirmed, says, the facts contained in the above Libel are true to the best of her knowledge and belief, and that the said complaint is not made out of levity, and collusion between her and the said Henry Marlin, and for the mere purpose of being freed and separated from each other, but in sincerity and truth, for the causes mentioned in the said Libel. Affirmed before me this (left blank) day of October 1846." (signed David Smith and Sarah Marlin.) -Notation on the front of this document -"No. 52 November Term 1846 Petition of Sarah Marlin for a Subpoena in divorce. Subpoena awarded returnable on the 1st day of the next term of Court." (signed Saml. Hepburn) "Oct. 12 1846 Filed 12th October 1846 Watts."

Oct. 12. 1846 "Cumberland County Sct. -The Commonwealth of Pennsylvania to Henry Marlin Greeting: Whereas, Sarah Marlin by her father and next friend Joseph T. Ward, M.D. on the 12th day of October A.D. 1846, preferred a petition to the Court of Common Pleas of Cumberland County, praying that for the causes therein set forth, she might be divorced from the bonds of matrimony entered into with you the said Henry Marlin, and the Judges of the same court awarded a Subpoena. -We therefore command you the said Henry Marlin that setting aside all business and excuses whatsoever you be and appear in your proper person before our Judges, at Carlisle at our County Court of Common Pleas, there to be held on the 9th day of November, next, to answer the petition or libel of the said Sarah Marlin, by her father and next friend Joseph T. Ward, M.D. and shew cause if any you have why she should not be divorced from the bonds of matrimony entered into with you, agreeably to the act of Assembly in such case made and provided. Hereof fail not. Witness Samuel Hepburn, Esq. at Carlisle, the 12th day of October, A.D. 1846." (signed W.M. Beetem, Prothy.)

Dec. 30, 1846 -"Cumberland County, s.s. -A. Longsdorf Esq. being duly affirmed according to law doth depose and say that the Defendant is not to be found in my bailiwick. Affirmed and Subscribed the 30 Decr. A.D. 1846 Before me." (signed W.M. Beetem, Prot. and A. Longsdorf, Shrff.) -Notation on the front of this document -"No. 52 November T. 1846 Sarah Marlin by her father and next friend Jos. T. Ward, M.D. vs. Henry Marlin Subpoena Sur Divorce Retble. 9th Nov. 1846 15th Octr. 1846 Deft. not to be found in my bailiwick. So. answers" (signed A. Longsdorf, Shrff.) "Shff.'s fee $0.18 3/4 Watts."

Dec. 30, 1846 -"Cumberland County, Sct. -The Commonwealth of Pennsylvania to Henry Marlin, Greeting: Whereas, Sarah Marlin by her father and next friend Joseph T. Ward, M.D. on the 12th day of October, A.D. 1846 preferred a petition to the Court of Common Pleas of Cumberland County, praying that for the causes therein set forth she might be divorced from the bonds of matrimony entered into with you the said Henry Marlin, and the Judges of the same, court awarded a Subpoena. We therefore command you, as we have heretofore commanded you, the said Henry Marlin, that setting aside all business and excuses whatsoever you be and appear in your proper person before our Judges, at Carlisle, at our county Court of Common Pleas, there to be held on the 11th day of January next, to answer the petition or libel of the said Sarah Marlin, by her father and next friend Joseph T. Ward, M.D. and shew cause if any you have why she should not be divorced from the bonds of matrimony entered into with you agreeably to the act of Assembly in such case made and provided. Hereof fail not. Witness, Samuel Hepburn, Esq. at Carlisle, the 30th day of December, A.D. 1846." (signed W.M. Beetem, Prot.)

Jan. 8, 1847 -"Cumberland County, S.S. -James Hoffer Esq. Sheriff being duly sworn according to Law, doth depose and say that the Defendant in the within writ, is not to be found in my bailiwick on Decr. 30, 1846. Sworn and Subscribed before me, 8 Jany. 1847." (signed W.M. Beetem, Prot. and James Hoffer, Shff.) -Notation on the front of this document -"No. 52 November T. 1846 Sarah Marlin, by her father and next friend Joseph T. Ward, M.D. vs. Henry Marlin Alias Subpoena for Divorce Retble. 11th January, 1847 Decr. 30th 1846 Deft. not to be found in my bailiwick, so answers." (signed James Hoffer, Shff.) "Shff. Hoffer fee $0.18 3/4 do on adv. $1.50 Watts."

April 19, 1847 -"In the Court of Common Pleas of Cumberland County -Sarah Marlin by her father and next friend Jos. T. Ward, M.D. vs. Henry Marlin: No. 52 November T. 1846 Subpoena Sur Divorce -19th Apl. 1847. On motion of Mr. Watts, in open court, David Smith, Esq. appointed a Commissioner to take depositions in this case, to be read upon the hearing of the same at the next Court of Common Pleas, to be held in and for said county, on the 27th day of April, 1847. By the Court."

April 26, 1847 -"Cumberland County, s.s. -I hereby certify that the above is a true copy of the appointment of D. Smith, Esq. Commissioner in the above case. In testimony whereof I have hereunto set my hand and affixed the seal of said court, at Carlisle, the 26th day of April, A.D. 1847." (signed W. M. Beetem, Prothy.)

April 26, 1847 -"Sarah Marlin by her father and next friend Dr.

Jos. T. Ward vs. Henry Marlin: Cumberland County S.S. -Personally appeared before me David Smith a Commissioner to take the testimony in this case, Fanny McManus who being duly sworn doth depose and say that in or about the month of September 1842 she was present at and witnessed the ceremony of marriage performed by the Revd. Henry Aurana between Henry Marlin and Miss Sarah Ward the Daughter of Dr. Jos. T. Ward, that she had understood and believes that the said Henry Marlin deserted his wife about three years ago, and although she has known the said Sarah Marlin since, she has not seen the said Henry Marlin and has no knowledge of where he is or has been for the last three years. Sworn to and Subscribed before me April 26th 1847." (signed David Smith and Fanny MacManus.)

April 26, 1847 -"Also, at the same time and place personally came Charles Reed who being duly sworn doth depose and say that he was personally acquainted with Henry Marlin and his wife Sarah Marlin. That they continued to live together as man and wife up to about the month of May 1844, that he the said Henry Marlin about that time went off from this part of the Country, and deserted his wife. That deponent has since that time been acquainted with the said Sarah Marlin and verily believes that her husband has not been with her or contributed in any manner to her support since he left her as before mentioned and deponent further saeth (*sic*) that he has no knowledge where the said Henry Marlin now is. Sworn to and Subscribed before me April 26th 1847." (signed C.W. Reed and David Smith.)

November Term 1846 #52 April 26, 1847 -"Also at the same time and place personally came Margaret McManus, who being duly sworn doth depose and say that in or about the month of September 1842 she was present at and witnessed the ceremony of marriage performed by the Revd. Henry Aurand between Henry Marlin and Miss Sarah Ward Daughter of Jos. T. Ward. That she has understood, and believes, that the said Henry Marlin deserted his wife about three years ago, and although she has known the said Sarah Marlin since, she has not seen the said Henry Marlin, and has no knowledge of where he is or has been for the last three years. Sworn to and Subscribed before me April 26th 1847." (signed David Smith and Margaret MacManus.)

April 27, 1847 -"Now, to wit, 27 April 1847 The Court upon due consideration of the premises do hereby order and decree that the said Sarah Marlin be and is truly divorced from the bond of matrimony or nuptial ties entered into by her the said Sarah Marlin and the said Henry Marlin and that all and every the duties, rights and claims accruing to either of the said Henry Marlin or the said Sarah Marlin at any time heretofore in pursuance of the said marriage shall cease and determine. And the said parties shall severally be at

Liberty to marry again in the like manner as if they never had been married. By the Court." Notation on the front of this document -"No. 52 Novr. T. 1846 Sarah Marlin by her father and next friend Dr. Jos. T. Ward vs. Henry Marlin. Depositions Filed 27th April, 1847."

◆ ◆ ◆

November Term 1846 #54 -Oct. 12, 1846 -"To the Honorable the Judges of the Court of Common Pleas of Cumberland Co. -The Libel of Ann Amelia Brisbane by her next friend Martin Cornman -Respectfully Sheweth That your Libellant in the month of April A.D. One thousand Eight hundred and forty was contracted in matrimony and married to a certain Edward Brisbane and from that time until April the 24th A.D. One thousand Eight hundred and forty four lived and cohabited with the said Edward as his wife and as such was owned and acknowledged by him and so deemed and reputed by her neighbors and acquaintances. And although by the laws of God as well as by their mutual vows and faith plighted to each other, they were bound to that uniform constancy and regard which ought to be inseparable from the marriage state; yet so it is that the said Edward from the twenty fourth of April A.D. One thousand Eight hundred and forty four hath wilfully and maliciously deserted and absented himself from the habitation of this Libellant without any just or reasonable cause. And such desertion hath persisted in for the term of two years and upwards, and yet doth continue to absent himself from the said Libellant. Wherefore your Libellant further showing that she is a citizen of the State of Pennsylvania, and has resided therein for upwards of one whole year previous to the filing of this her libel prays your Honors that a subpoena may issue forth to summon the said Edward Brisbane to appear in this Honorable Court at November term next to answer the complaint aforesaid. And also that a decree of said Honorable Court may be made divorcing of him the said Edward Brisbane from the society, fellowship and company of this Libellant in all time to come, and she this Libellant from the marriage bond aforesaid as if she had never been married, or as if the said Edward Brisbane were naturally dead. And this Libellant will pray etc." (signed Ann Amelia Brisbane.) "by her next friend" (signed Martin Cornman.) -"Cumberland County s.s. -The within named Ann Amelia Brisbane being duly sworn says the facts contained in the above libel are true to the best of her knowledge and belief, and that the said complaint is not made out of levity and collusion between her and her said husband and for the mere purpose of being freed and separate from each other, but in sincerity and truth for the causes mentioned in said Libel. Sworn and Subscribed before me this 12th October A.D. 1846." (signed Saml. Hepburn and Ann Amellia Brisbein [sic].) "Subpoena awarded returnable on the 1st day of next term etc. Oct. 14th 1846 (signed Saml. Hepburn.) -Notation on the front of this document -"No. 54

Nov. T. 1846 A.A. Brisbane vs. Edward Brisbane Petition and affidavit Filed 16th Oct. 1846 Riddle."

Oct. 16, 1846 -"Cumberland County, Sct. -The Commonwealth of Pennsylvania to Edward Brisbane Greeting: Whereas Ann Amelia Brisbane, late Ann Amelia Gould by her next friend Martin Cornman preferred a petition on the 14th day of October, A.D. 1846, to the Court of Common Pleas of Cumberland County praying that for the causes therein set forth, she might be divorced from the bonds of matrimony entered into with you the said Edward Brisbane -and the Judges of said court awarded a Subpoena -We therefore command you the said Edward Brisbane, that setting aside all business and excuses, whatsoever, you be and appear in your proper person before our Judges, at Carlisle, at our county Court of Common Pleas, there to be held the 9th day of November, next, to answer the petition or libel of the said Ann Amelia Brisbane, late Ann Amelia Gould, your wife -and shew cause if any you have why she should not be divorced from the bond of matrimony entered into with you agreeably to the act of Assembly in such case made and provided. Hereof fail not. Witness Samuel Hepburn, Esquire, at Carlisle, the 16th day of October, A.D., 1846. (signed W.M. Beetem, Prothy.)

Nov. 16, 1846 -"Cumberland County, s.s. -Adam Longsdorf Esq. Shff. being duly affirmed according to law doth depose and say that the Defendant Edward Brisbane is not to be found in my bailiwick. Affirmed and Subscribed in open Court, the 16 Nov. 1846." (signed W.M. Beetem, Prothy. and A. Longsdorf, Shrff.)

April 19, 1847 -"Cumberland County, s.s. -J. Hoffer, Esq. Shff. being duly sworn according to law, doth depose and say that he caused notice to be published in one newspaper printed in said county for four successive weeks prior to the first day of the Apr. T. 1847 requiring the said Ed. Brisbane to appear on that day to answer the complaint of the said Catharine (*sic*) Brisbane. Sworn and subscribed the 19th Apl. 1847 before me." (signed W.M. Beetem, Pro. and James Hoffer, Shff.) -Notation on the front of this document -"No. 54 November T. 1846 Ann Amelia Brisbane late Ann Amelia Gould by her next friend Martin Cornman vs. Edward Brisbane Supboena Sur Divorce Retble. 9th Nov. 1846 Octr. 17, 1846 Deft. not to be found in my bailiwick So Answers" (signed A. Longsdorf Shrff.) "Shff.'s fee $0.18 3/4. Riddle."

Nov. 16, 1846 -"Cumberland County, s.s. -The Commonwealth of Pennsylvania, to Edward Brisbane Greeting: Whereas Ann Amelia Brisbane, late Ann Amelia Gould, by her next friend Martin Cornman, preferred a petition, on the 14th day of October, A.D. 1846, to the Court of Common Pleas of Cumberland County praying that for the causes therein set forth, she might be divorced from the bond of matrimony entered into with you the said Edward Brisbane -and the Judges of said Court awarded a Subpoena. We therefore command you the said Edward Brisbane, as we have heretofore commanded you, that setting aside all business and excuses whatsoever, you be and appear in your proper person before our Judges of the Court of Common Pleas, at Carlisle, there to be held the 11th day of January next, to answer the petition or libel of the said Ann Amelia Brisbane, late Ann Amelia Gould your wife -and shew cause if any you have why she should not be divorced from the bond of matrimony entered into with you agreeably to the act of Assembly in such case made and provided. Hereof fail not. -Witness Samuel Hepburn, Esquire, at Carlisle, the 16th day of November, A.D. 1846." (signed W.M. Beetem, Prot.)

Jan. 8, 1847 -"Cumberland County, Sct. -I J. Hoffer, Esq. Shff. being duly sworn according to law doth depose and say that the Deft. in the within writ, is not to be found in my bailiwick. Sworn and Subscribed before me 8 Jany. 1847." (signed W.M. Beetem, Prot. and James Hoffer, Shff.) -On the front of this document is this notation -"No. 54 November T. 1846 Ann Amelia Brisbane, late Ann Amelia Gould, by her next friend Martin Cornman vs. Edward Brisbane Alias Subpoena sur Divorce Retble. 11th January 1847 Decr. 30, 1846 Deft. not to be found in my bailiwick, so answers" (signed James Hoffer, Shff.) "Shff. Hoffer's fee $0.18 3/4 do on adj. $1.50. Riddle."

April 19, 1847 -"In the Court of Common Pleas of Cumberland County -Ann Amelia Brisbane late Ann A. Gould by her next friend Martin Cornman vs. Edward Brisbane: No. 54 November Term 1846 19th April 1847 On motion of Mr. Riddle, in open court, David Smith, Esq. appointed a Commissioner to take depositions in this case, to be read upon the hearing of the same, at the next Court of Common Pleas to be held in and for said county, on the 23rd day of August, 1847. By the Court."

July 1, 1847 -"Cumberland County, s.s. -I do certify that the above is a true extract, taken from the records of the Court of Common Pleas of said county in the above stated case. In testimony whereof I have hereunto set my hand and affixed the seal of said Court at Carlisle the 1st July, A.D. 1847." (signed W.M. Beetem, Prot.) -Notation on the front of this document -"No. 54 August T. 1847 with No. 54 Nov. 1846 Brisbane vs. Brisbane Commission."

July 2, 1847 -"In pursuance of the annexed commission to take the depositions of witnesses in the case of Ann Amelia Brisbane late Ann A. Gould by her next friend Martin Cornman vs. Edward Brisbane, Personally appeared before me the said Commissioner Sarah Jane Kelly, a witness on the part of the said Ann Amelia Brisbane who being duly sworn deposeth and sayeth, I was a witness to the marriage of Ann A. Gould to Edward Brisbane aforesaid. The said parties were married by the Revd. John Ubrich in May one thousand Eight hundred and forty. The only other witness present was a young man by the name of Jacob Biel, who does not now reside in this part of the country. After the marriage of the said Ann to the said Edward they lived together about three weeks as man and wife. He then left her and returned some time after, when the parties again lived together. But this spring three years ago he left her and has never returned to her since, without any reasonable cause for so doing, and has done nothing toward her suport (sic) or maintenance nor that of the two children that he had by the said Ann. She the said Ann having since he left supported herself and children. I do not know where the said Edward went to. Sworn to and Subscribed before me July 2nd 1847." (signed David Smith and Sarah Jane Kelly.)

Aug. 21, 1847 -"Frederick Gould being also duly sworn deposes and says, that Edwsard Brisban (sic) the husband of the said Ann wilfuly (sic) and malitiousesly (sic) deserted hir (sic) and has been absent from the habitation of the said Ann without a reasonable cause and since April one thousand Eight hundred and forty four. That during all that time deponent has heard nothing of him, nor has the said Edward since he has deserted his wife as aforesaid done anything towards hir (sic) mentance (sic) or support. Sworn to and Subscribed before me August 21st 1847." (signed David Smith and by his mark Frederick Gould.)

Aug. 21, 1847 -"Mary Wetzel being also duly sworn deposes and says, in the spring of 1844, Deponent lived in the house with Ann Brisban (sic) and hir (sic) husband and it was in April in that year that the said Brisban (sic) deserted his wife. That since April one thousand Eight hundred and forty four deponent has heard nothing of the said Edward nor has she known where he went to or where he is. That he deserted his wife without any reasonable cause, and since he left hir (sic) has done nothing towards hir (sic) suppor (sic) or mentance (sic), that the said Edward has two children by the said Ann and that the said Ann has been obleged (sic) to support hirself (sic) and these children for the last three years and four months. Sworn to and Subscribed before me August 21st 1847." (signed David Smith and by her mark Mary Wetzel.)

November Term 1846 #54 Aug. 21, 1847 -"James Calleo also being duly sworn deposes and says, that he knows that the said Edward Brisban (sic) deserted his wife last April three years ago without any reasonable case (sic). That deponent went with him thirty miles from Carlisle but that the said Edward traveled in another direction. Deponent don't know where nor has he ever hered (sic) anything of him since, nor has the said Edward since done any thing (sic) towards the support of his wife and children, but they have ben (sic) supported by the said Ann. Sworn to and Subscribed before me August 21st 1847." (signed David Smith and James Calleo.)

Aug. 23, 1847 -"Ann Amelia Brisbane late Ann A. Gould by her next friend Martin Cornman vs. Edward Brisbane: In Common Pleas of Cumberland County No. 54 November Term 1846 -And now to wit the twenty third of August A.D. One thousand Eight hundred and forty seven David Smith Esquire the Commissioner, having returned to the Court here the depositions of witnesses taken before him on the part of the Libellant, and the same being read and heard by the Court, and the Court after mature deliberation being satisfied therewith and proclamation being duly made for the Respondent to come forth and he not appearing, the Court do order adjudge and decree that the said Ann Amelia Brisbane the Libellant be divorced and separated from the bond of matrimony contracted with the said Edward Brisbane the respondent, and that all and every the duties rights and claims accruing to either of the said parties by reason of the said marriage shall henceforth cease and determine, and the said parties, be severally at liberty to marry again in like manner as if they never had been married. By the Court."

◆ ◆ ◆

April Term 1847 #47 Nov. 13, 1846 -"To the Honorable Samuel Hepburn President Judge of the Court of Common Pleas of Cumberland County -The petition of Susan Carey by her next friend John Kreitzer Respectfully Represents That your libellant in the month of November A.D. 1842 was contracted in matrimony and married to a certain James Carey and from that time until May A.D. 1846 lived and cohabited with him as his wife and as such was owned and acknowledged by him and so deemed and reputed by all her neighbors and acquaintances and altho (sic) by the laws of God as well as by their mutual vows and faith plighted to each other, they were reciprocally bound to that uniform kindness and regard which ought to be inseperable from the marriage state yet so it is that the said James Carey hath offered such indignities to her person as to render her condition intolerable and life burthensmome and thereby forced her to withdraw from his house and family -Wherefore your libellant further showing that she hath resided in this state for two years and upwards previous to the filing of this petition -Prays your Honors that a subpoena may issue from said Court directed to the said James Carey commanding him to appear at the next term of said Court to answer this petition -And also that a decree of said Court may be made granting this Libellant a divorce from the society fellowship and company of the said James Carey in all time to come and from the marriage bond aforesaid as if she had never been married, or as if the said James Carey were naturally dead. And she will pray." (signed witness D.H. Graham Susan Carey by her mark.) "By her next friend" (signed John Kreitzer.) -"Cumberland County, s.s. -Before me a Justice of the Peace in and for said County personally came the within named Susan Carey who being duly sworn according to Law, says that the facts contained in the within libel are true to the best of her knowledge and belief -And that the said complaint is not made out of levity or collusion between her and her said husband and for the mere purpose of being freed and seperated from each other but in sincerity and truth for the causes mentioned in the within petition or libel. Sworn and Subscribed the 13 Novr. 1846 Before me" (signed David Smith and by her mark Susan Carey.) -Notation on the front of this document -"No. 47 April T. 1847 Petition of Susan Carey for a divorce from the bond of matrimony -Subpoena awarded by Saml. Hepburn March 25th 1847 Filed 25 March 1847 Graham."

March 25, 1847 -"Cumberland County, s.s. -The Commonwealth of Pennsylvania to James Carey Greeting, Whereas, Susan Carey by her next friend John Kreitzer, on the 25th day of March, A.D. 1847 preferred a petition to the Honorable Samuel Hepburn President Judge of the Court of Common Pleas of Cumberland county, praying that for the causes therein set forth, she might be divorced from the bonds of matrimony entered into with you the said James Carey and the President Judge of said court awarded a Subpoena. We therefore command you the said James Carey, that setting aside all business and excuses whatsoever you be and appear in your proper person, before our Judges, at Carlisle, at our county Court of Common Pleas, there to be held on the 12th day of April, next, to answer the petition or libel of the said Susan Carey, by her next friend John Kreitzer -and show cause if any you have why she should not be divorced from the bonds of matrimony entered into with you, agreeably to the act of Assembly in such case made and provided. Hereof fail not. Witness (signed Samuel Hepburn, Esquire, at Carlisle the 25th day of March, A.D. 1847 W.M. Beetem Prot.)

April 27, 1847 -"Cumberland County, s.s. -Robert McCartney, Esq. Deputy Sheriff being duly sworn according to Law doth depose and say that he served the within writ personally and by copy 29 March 1847 on James Carey -Sworn and Suscribed the 27th day of Apl. 1847 before me." (signed W.M. Beetem Pro. and R. McCartney.) -Notations on the front of this document -"No. 47 April Term 1847 Susan Carey, by her next friend John Kreitzer vs. James Carey Subpoena for Divorce Retble. 12th April, 1847 29 Mar. 1847 served personally and by copy so answers" (signed R. McCartney Dp. Shff. and James Hoffer Shff.) Shff. Hoffer fee $1.20 1/2 Graham."

April Term 1847 #47 Sept. 7, 1847 -"I hereby discontinue all proceedings in this case 7th Sept. 1847." (signed Susan Carey.)

♦

April Term 1848 #11 Feb. 4, 1848 -"To the Honr. Samuel Hepburn, President Judge of the Court of Common Pleas of Cumberland County -The libel of Mary Brumboch, formerly Mary Windemaker, by her brother and next friend William Windemaker -Respectfully Sheweth -That your libellant on the 8th day of November 1844, was contracted in matrimony and married to a certain Samuel Brumboch. And although by the laws of God, as well as by their mutual vows and faith plighted to each other, they were bound to that uniform constancy and regard which ought to be inseparable from marriage state; yet so it is that the said Samuel from the tenth of November A.D. One thousand Eight hundred and forty four hath wilfully and maliciously deserted and absented himself from the habitation of this Libellant without any just or reasonable cause. And such desertion hath persisted in for the term of two years and upwards, and yet doth continue to absent himself from the said Libellant. Wherefore your Libellant further showing that she is a citizen of the State of Pennsylvania, and has resided therein for upwards of two years previous to the filing of this her libel prays your Honors that a subpoena may issue forth to summon the said Samuel Brumboch to appear in this Honorable Court at April term next to answer the complaint aforesaid. And also that a decree of said Honorable Court may be made divorcing of him the said Samuel Brumboch from the society, fellowship and company of this Libellant in all time to come, and she this Libellant from the marriage bond aforesaid as if she had never been married, or as if the said Samuel Brumboch were naturally dead. And this Libellant will pray etc." (signed Mary Brumboch by her mark.) "by her next friend" (signed William Windemaker.) -"Cumberland County s.s. -The within named Mary Brumboch being duly sworn says the facts contained in the above libel are true to the best of her knowledge and belief, and that the said complaint is not made out of levity and collusion between her and her said husband and for the mere purpose of being freed and separate from each other, but in sincerity and truth for the causes mentioned in said libel. Sworn and Subscribed before me this 4th Feby. A.D. 1848" (signed Saml. Hepburn and Mary Brumboch by her mark.)

Feb. 7, 1848 -"Cumberland County, Sct. -The Commonwealth of Pennsylvania to Samuel Brumboch, Greeting: Whereas Mary Brumbach, formerly Mary Windemaker, by her brother and next friend, William Windemaker, on the 7th day of February A.D. 1848, preferred a petition to the Honr. Samuel Hepburn, President Judge of the Court of Common Pleas of Cumberland County, praying that for the causes therein set forth she might be divorced from the bonds of matrimony entered into with you the said Samuel Brumbach. -Whereupon: 7th Feby. 1848, the said Judge awarded a Subpoena. We, therefore command you, the said Saml. Brumbach, that setting aside all business and excuses whatsoever, you be and appear, in your proper person before our Judges of the Court of Common Pleas, to be held at Carlisle, in and for the County of Cumberland on the 10th day of April next to answer the petition or libel of the said Mary Brumbach, formerly Mary Windemaker, by her brother and next friend William Windemaker, and shew cause, if any you have why she should not be divorced from the bonds of matrimony entered into with you agreeably to the act Assembly in such case made and provided. Hereof fail not. Witness, Samuel Hepburn Esq. at Carlisle, the 7th day of February, A.D. 1848." (signed W.M. Beetem, Prot.)

April 13, 1848 -"Cumberland County, S.S. -Robt. McCartney (Dept. Sheriff) be duly sworn, deposeth that he served the within writ, by leaving a copy with an adult member of defendant's family. Sworn and Subscribed this 13th day of April 1848." (signed W.M. Beetem Prot. and R. McCartney Dp. Shff.) -Notation on the front of this document -"No. 11 April T. 1848 Mary Brumboch, formerly Mary Windemaker, by her brother and next friend William Windemaker vs. Samuel Brumboch Subpoena sur Divorce Retble: 10th April, 1848. Feby. 11, 1848. Served by leaving a copy with an adult member of his family. So answers" (signed R. McCartney Dp. Shff. and James Hoffer Shff.) "Shff. Hoffer's fee $1.35 1/2 Miller."

April 13, 1848 -"In the Court of Common Pleas of Cumberland County -Mary Brumboch, formerly Mary Windemaker, by her brother and next friend William Windemaker vs. Samuel Brumboch: No. 11 April Term, 1848 Subpoena sur Divorce 13th April, 1848, On motion of Mr. Miller, William B. Mullen, Esq. appointed a Commissioner to take the depositions of witnesses to be read on the hearing of this case (Exparte rule on ten days notice.) By the Court."

May 5, 1848 -"Cumberland County, Sct. -I Wm. M. Beetom, Prothonotary of the Court of Common Pleas of said county, do certify that the above is a true extract, taken from the records of the Court of Common Pleas of said county. In testimony whereof I have hereunto set my hand and affixed the seal of said Court, at Carlisle, the 5th day of May, A.D. 1848." (signed W.M. Beetem Prot.) -Notation on the front of this document -"No. 11 April T. 1848 Mary Brumboch, formerly Mary Windemaker, by her brother and next friend William Windemaker vs. Samuel Brumboch Rule to take Depositions Miller."

Aug. 29, 1848 -"Mary Brumboch formerly Mary Windemaker vs. Samuel Brumboch: No. 11 April T. 1848 To Samuel Brumboch Sir, you are hereby notified that the depositions of witnesses in the above case will be taken to be read in evidence on the hearing, before Wm. B. Mullen Esq. on Monday the 11 day of Sept. next, at 10 o'clock in the forenoon, When and where you may attend if you think proper." (signed Wm. H. Miller Atty. for Libellant 29th Augt. 1848.) Notation on the front of this document -"I hereby accept notice, waiving the ten day notice required. 5th Sept. 1848" (signed by his mark Samuel Broombaugh and witness Wm. B. Mullen.)

April Term 1848 #11 May 10, 1848 -"Mary Brumboch, formerly Mary Windemaker, by her brother and next friend William Windemaker vs. Samuel Brumboch: No. 11 April Term 1848 Subpoena Sur Divorce To Saml. Brumboch, Take notice that depositions to be read in evidence, on the hearing of the above case, will be taken before Wm. B. Mullen Esq., a Commissioner appointed by the court for that purpose, at his office in South Middleton Township, on Saturday, the twelfth day of August 1848 between 9 o'clock A.M. and 4 o'clock P.M. -when and where you may attend and cross examine if you think proper." (signed W.H. Miller Atty. for Libellant 10th May 1848.)

Aug. 7, 1848 -"Cumberland County, S.S. -Before me a Justice of the Peace in and for said county, personally appeared Charles Ringewalt, who being duly affirmed says that he served a true copy of the within writ on Samuel Brumboch, on Tuesday the first day of August 1848. Sworn and Subscribed before me the seventh day of August 1848." (signed Wm. B. Mullin and Charles Ringewalt.) -Notation on the front of this document -"Windemaker vs. Brumbach: Notice to take depositions on 10 days' notice C. Ringwalt's cost 16¢."

Aug. 12, 1848 -"No. 11 Apr. 1848 Windemaker vs. Broombaugh: Cumberland County, S.S. -Before me the subscriber one of the Justices of the Peace in and for said County, came William Windemaker, on the part of libelant (sic) who after being duely (sic) sworn according to law doath (sic) depose and say that I know the parties in this case. I think it is about five years since they were married, they were married by Mathew Moore Esqr. Broombaugh was with her two nights since they were married. They were married in my house. Broombaugh left libelant of his accord, two days after they were married he left her. I never heard Broombaugh say he would not live with libelant. Sworn and Subscribed before me this 12th day of August A.D. 1848." (signed Wm. B. Mullin and by his mark William Windemaker.)

Aug. 12, 1848 -"No. 11 Apr. 1848 Windemaker vs. Broombaugh: Cumberland County, S.S. -Before me the subscriber one of the Justices of the Peace, in and for said County, personally came Michael Yengst, on the part of libelant (sic), who afer being duly sworn according to law doth depose and say that I know the parties in this case. I was at the house but can't tell when they were married, don't know the year they were married by Mathew Moore, Esqr. Broombaugh has not lived with libelant (sic) since they were married, I know the fact that Broombaugh deserted her of his own accord, from the time they were first married. I have heard Broombaugh say he never would live with libellant, and further saith not. Sworn and Subscribed before me the 12th day of August A.D. 1848." (signed Wm. B. Mullin and Michael Yengst by his mark.)

Aug. 12, 1848 -"Windemaker vs. Broombaugh: No. 11 Apr. 1848 Cumberland County, S.S. -Before me the subscriber one of the Justices of the Peace in and for said County, came Richard Windemaker, on the part of libelant (sic), who after being duly sworn according to law, douth (sic) depose and say, I know the parties in this case. They were married on Sunday evening about five years ago. They were married by Mathew Moore, Esq. Broombaugh has not lived with libelant (sic) since they were married, I know that. Libelant (sic) would have lived with Broombaugh, if he had been satisfied to live with her. He left her the next day after they were married. He only stayed one night with her after they were married. I never heard Broombaugh saying he would not live with her, and further saith not. Sworn and Subscribed before me this 12th day of August A.D. 1848." (signed Wm. B. Mullen and by his mark Richard Windemaker.)

Sept. 9, 1848 -"Mary Broombaugh, formerly Mary Windemaker vs. Samuel Broombaugh: No. 11 Apr. 1848 Cumberland County, S.S. Before me the subscriber a commissioner appointed by the court to take depositions in this case, came Michael Yengst, on the part of (the) libelant (sic), who after being duly sworn according to law, doth depose and say, that I know the parties in this case. I know the fact that Samuel Broombaugh has deserted libelant (sic) for more than two years. I can further state that Broombaugh, has never contributed to her support, during that time, and further saith not. Sworn and Subscribed before me the 9th day of September A.D. 1848." (signed Wm. B. Mullin and by his mark Michael Yenst.)

Sept. 12, 1848 -"Mary Brumboch, formerly Mary Windermaker, by her brother and next friend William Windemaker vs. Samuel Brumboch: No. 11 April Term 1848 Subp. Sur Divorce -And now this 12th day of September 1848, the Examiner Wm. B. Mullen Esq. having returned to the Court here the depositions of witnesses taken before him on part of the libellant and the same being read and heard by the Court and the Court after mature and solemn deliberation being satisfied therewith and proclamation being duly made for the respondent to come forth, and he not appearing the Court do order and adjudge and decree that the said Mary Brumbach the libellant be divorced and seperated from the bond of matrimony contracted with the said Samuel Brumboch, and that all and every the duties, rights and claims accruing to either of the said parties by reason of the said marriage shall henceforth cease and determine; and the said parties be severally at liberty to marry again in like manner as if they had never been married. By the Court." -Notation on the front of this document -"No. 11 April Term 1848 Mary Brumboch formerly Mary Windemaker vs. Saml. Brumbach -Decree of Court in Divorce Filed 12th Septr. 1848."

◆　　　　　◆　　　　　◆

April Term 1848 #15 Feb. 15, 1848 -"To the Honourable the Judges of the Court of Common Pleas of Cumberland County -The Petition of Henry Peters respectfully represents: That your petitioner on the first day of January in the year of our Lord one thousand eight hundred and forty, was bound in matrimony, and married to a certain Susana Buzzard and from that time until the month of January in the year of our Lord one thousand eight hundred and forty three lived and cohabited with the said Susana as his wife, and as such was owned and acknowledged by her, and so deemed and reputed by their neighbours and acquaintances. And although by the laws of God, as well as by their mutual vows and faith plighted to each other, they were bound to that uniform constancy, and regard which ought to be inseparable from the marriage state. Yet so it is that the said Susana in violation of her marriage vow, hath for a considerable time past, being at such time domiciled within the Commonwealth of Pennsylvania, given herself up to adulterous practices, and been guilty of adultery with a certain William Holmes and with diverse other persons to your petitioner unknown. Wherefore your libellant further showing that he is a citizen of the State of Pennsylvania and has resided therein for upwards of one whole year previous to the filing of this his libel, prays your honours that a subpoena may issue forth to summon the said Susana to appear in this honourable court at the next term to answer his complaint aforesaid, as also that the Court may decree a divorce and separation from the nuptial ties or bonds of matrimony with the said Susana, and he will pray etc." (signed Henry H. Peters.) -"Cumberland County S.S. -Henry Peters the above named petitioner being duly sworn according to law doth say that the facts set forth in the foregoing petition are true to the best of his knowledge and belief, and that the said complaint is not made out of levity, or by collusion between them the said Henry and Susana his wife and for the mere purpose of being freed and separated from each other, but in sincerity and truth for the causes mentioned in said petition or libel. Sworn and Subscribed this 15th day of February A.D. 1848." (signed Geo. Fleming and Henry H. Peters.) -Notation on the front of this document -No. 15 April Term, 1848 Petition of Henry Peters for a divorce 15th Feby. 1848 Subpoena awarded By the Court. Brandeburry."

Feb. 15, 1848 -"Cumberland County, S.S. -The Commonwealth of Pennsylvania to the Sheriff of Cumberland County Greeting: Whereas, Henry H. Peters did on the 15th day of February, A.D. 1848 prefer his petition to our said Judges of our Court of Common Pleas for the county of Cumberland, praying that for the causes therein set forth, that he might be divorced from the bonds of matrimony entered into with you Susanna Peters formerly Susanna Buzzard. We do therefore command you, the said Susanna Peters formerly Susanna Buzzard, that setting aside all other business and excuses whatsoever, you be and appear in your proper person before our Judges at Carlisle, at a Court of Common Pleas, there to be held for the County of Cumberland, on the 10th day of April, next to answer the petition or libel of the said Henry H. Peters, and to show cause, if any you have, why the said Henry H. Peters, your husband, should not be divorced from the bonds of matrimony agreeably to the acts of General Assembly in such case made and provided. And hereof fail not. Witness the Honorable, Samuel Hepburn Esq. President of our said Court, at Carlisle, the 15th day of February, A.D. 1848." (signed W.M. Beetem Prot.)

April 13, 1848 -"Cumberland County, S.S. -Robert McCartney being duly sworn according to law doth say that he served a copy of the within Subpoena, on the said Susana Peters by delivering her a copy on the 19 Feb. 1848. Sworn and Subscribed this 13 April 1848." (signed W.M. Beetem Prot. and R. McCartney.) -Notation on the front of this document -"No. 15 April T. 1848 Henry H. Peters vs. Susanna Peters, formerly Susanna Buzzard Subpoena sur Divorce Feby. 19, 1848 Served personally and by copy, So answers" (signed R. McCartney, Dp. Shff. and James Hoffer Shff.) "Shff. Hoffer's fee $2.56 1/2. Brandeburry."

April 13, 1848 -"In the Court of Common Pleas of Cumberland County -Henry H. Peters vs. Susana Peters formerly Susanna Buzzard: No. 15 April Term 1848 13 April 1848 On motion of Mr. Brandeburry, David Smith Esq. appointed a Commissioner to take testimony in this case, at his office in the Borough of Carlisle on Monday the 24th day of April 1848 at 10 o'clock in the forenoon. By the Court.

April 14, 1848 -"Cumberland County, SS. -I do certify that the above is a true extract taken from the records of the Court of Common Pleas of said County. In testimony whereof I have hereunto set my hand, and affixed the seal of said Court at Carlisle the 14th day of April A.D. 1848." (signed W.M. Beetem Prot.)

April 15, 1848 -"To Mrs. Susana Peters Respondent: You will take notice that in pursuance of the foregoing Rule, depositions to be read on the hearing of the above case on Tuesday, the 25th instant at an adjourned Court to be held in Carlisle, will be taken before David Smith Esquire, at his office in the Borough of Carlisle on Monday the 24th instant between the hours of 10 o'clock A.M. and 4 o'clock P.M. of said day when and where you may attend, if you think proper." (signed S.G. Brandeburry, Atty. for Libellant April 15, 1848.)

April 17, 1848 -"Cumberland County, S.S. -Jas. M. Allen being duly sworn, doth say, that he served a copy of the within Rule of Court duly certified under the seal of said Court and a copy of the within notice to take depositions, on the within named Susanna Peters, on Monday the 17th day of April 1848 by delivering the same to her personally. Sworn and Subscribed this 17th day of April 1848 before me." (signed Geo. Fleming and Js. M. Allen.) -"I accept notice of the within Rule of Court and notice to take depositions, and waive all objections as to the time." (signed by her mark Susana Peters

Test. Js. M. Allen.) Notation on the front of this document -"No. 15 April T. 1848 Peters vs. Peters: In Divorce. Depositions. Filed 25 April, 1848."

April Term 1848 #15 April 24, 1848 -"In pursuance to the foregoing rule personally appeared before me the Subscriber a Justice of the Peace in and for the county of Cumberland Revd. Henry Aurand who being duly sworn, says I married a Mr. Peters to a Miss Busard on the first day of January 1838, 39 or 40 I can't recollect which. I kep (sic) no record of there (sic) marrige (sic). The man now attending as party in this suit is the same person which I marrid (sic) to Miss Bosard, at the above stated time. Sworn to and Subscribed before me April 24th 1848." (signed David Smith and Henry Aurand.)

April 24, 1848 -"J.E. Bonham being also sworn deposes and says at the January Sessions 1848 I assisted in the trial for fornication and Bastardy against Alfred Brannon in which Susan (sic) Peters was the prosecutrix. She swore that Alfred Brannon was the father of hir (sic) child, and he was convicted of Fornication and acquitted of Bastardy. was not prosecuting attorney at the time but took a part in the prosecution at the instance of William Holmes. Brannon the Defendant alleged at the trial that William Holmes was the real father of said child. Sworn before me April 24th 1848." (signed David Smith and J. Elliot Bonham.)

April 24, 1848 -"Cumberland County S.S. -Personally appeared before me the Subscriber a Justice of the Peace in and for said County Joseph Lobach who being duly sworn says I am acquainted with Henry Peters and Susan his wife. The said Henry Peters was sent to the Penitentiary in the whinter (sic) of 1843 and his wife Susan was brougt (sic) to the Poor house of Cumberland County, on the 12th day of November 1844 and was delivered of a child on the 13th day of November 1844 and remained in the poor house until the 24th day of March 1845. Said Peters has not been in the neighbourhood (sic) since in the whinter (sic) of 1843 until some time in the month of January 1848. Sworn to and Subscribed before me April 24th 1848." (signed Jos. Lobach.) "Justice fee 50 cts."

April 24, 1848 -"L.G. Brandeberry, Esq. also being duly sworn says Henry Peters was tried in January court in Carlisle in 1843 and was convicted of murder in the second degree or manslauter (sic) and sentenced to imprisonment to Estern (sic) Penitentiary for five years. I saw him in his cell in June 1843. I did not see him in this part of the country from that time until January 1848 and he has been here ever since. I have not seen his wife here since he returned. I believe she resides in Harrisburgh. I don't know that Peters has ever seen his wife or been with hir (sic) since he has returned. Sworn to and Subscribed before me April 24th 1848." (signed David Smith and L.G. Brandeberry.) -"I also certify that the foregoing depositions were taken before me at the time and place specified in the rule in pursuance of the libelant, no one appearing for the respondent." (signed David Smith Commissioner.)

April 25, 1848 -"And now to wit April 25th 1848 in the matter of the application of Henry Peters for a divorce from the bonds of matrimony with Susanna his wife, the Court upon due consideration of the premises, and after hearing the cause and the evidence offered on part of the Libellant, and upon due proof of notice having been served on the said Susanna Peters, the wife of said Henry Peters, do order and decree, that the said Henry Peters be divorced and separated from the bonds of matrimony with the said Susanna, and that all and every the duties, rights, and claims accruing to either of the said parties at any time heretofore in pursuance of the said marriage, shall cease and determine, and the said Henry shall be at liberty to marry again in the like manner as if they never had been married, By the Court." -Notation on the front of this document -"No. 15 April Term, 1848. Peters vs. Peters: Decree of Court. Filed 25th April, 1848."

◆ ◆ ◆

April Term 1848 #16 Feb. 15, 1848 -"To the Honorable the Judges of the Court of Common Pleas of Cumberland County -The Petition of Elisabeth Reinald by her next friend Tho. Craighead Jr. Respectfully Represents -That about the month of April 1842 she was lawfully joined in marriage with Henry Reinald. That in the month of May 1845 the said Henry Reinald maliciously deserted your petitioner his said wife without any reasonable cause and has been absent ever since from her habitation and has in no manner since contributed to her support. She therefore prays your Honors to award a Subpoena to the said Henry Reinald to appear at the next Court and shew cause why the said Court should not decree that the said Elizabeth should be divorced from the bonds of matrimony entered into as stated. And she will pray etc." (signed Elisabeth Reinald by her next friend Thos. Craighead Jr.) -"Cumberland County sct. -Personally appeared before me a Justice of the Peace in and for said said County, Elizabeth Reinald who being duly sworn doth depose and say that the facts set forth in the above petition are true to the best of her knowledge and belief and that the said complaint is not made out of levity or by collusion between her and her husband and for the mere purpose of being freed and separated from each other, but in sincerity and truth for the causes set forth in her said petition. Sworn and Subscribed the 15 Feb. 1848 Before me." (signed Thos. Craighead Jr. and Elisabeth Reinald.) -On the front of this document -"No. 16 April T. 1848 Petition of Elizabeth Reinald for a Divorce. 15th Feby. 1848 Subpoena awarded By the Court. Watts."

Feb. 15, 1848 -"Cumberland County, Sct. -The Commonwealth of Pennsylvania to Henry Reinald Greeting: Whereas, Elizabeth Reinald, by her next friend Thomas Craighead Jr. did on the 15th day of

February, A.D. 1848, prefer her petition to our Judges of our Court of Common Pleas for the County of Cumberland, praying for the causes therein set forth that she might be divorced from the bonds of matrimony entered into with Henry Reinald. We do therefore command you, the said Henry Reinald, that setting aside all other business and excuses whatsoever, you be and appear in your proper person before our Judges, at Carlisle, at a Court of Common Pleas, there to be held for Cumberland County on the 10th day of April next, to answer the petition or libel of the said Elizabeth Reinald, and to show cause if any you have, why the said Elizabeth Reinald your wife should not be divorced from the bond of matrimony, agreeably to the acts of General Assembly in such case made and provided. And hereof fail not. Witness, the Honorable, Saml. Hepburn, Esq. President, of our said Court, at Carlisle the 15th day of February A.D. 1848." (signed W.M. Beetem Prot.)

April 25, 1848 -"Cumberland County sct. -Personally appeared in open court James Hoffer Sheriff who being duly sworn doth depose and say that the defendant in this case was not to be found in his bailiwick and therefore he returned the writ Non est inventus. Sworn and Subscribed the 25 Apr. 1848." (signed W.M. Beetem Prot. and James Hoffer Shff.) -Notation on the front of this document -"No. 16 April Term, 1848 Elizabeth Reinald, by her next friend Thos. Craighead Jr. vs. Henry Reinald Subpoena Sur Divorce N.E.I. So answers" (signed James Hoffer Shff.) "Shff. Hoffer's fee $0.18 3/4 Watts."

May 4, 1848 -"Cumberland County, Sct. -The Commonwealth of Pennsylvania to Henry Reinald, Greeting: Whereas Elizabeth Reinald, by her next friend Thomas Craighead Jr. Esq. did on the 15th day of February, A.D. 1848, prefer her petition to our Judges of our Court of Common Pleas, for the county of Cumberland, praying for the causes therein set forth, that she might be divorced from the bonds of matrimony entered into with Henry Reinald. We do therefore command you, as we have heretofore commanded you, the said Henry Reinald, that setting aside all other business and excuses whatsoever, you be and appear, in your proper person before our Judges at Carlisle, at a Court of Common Pleas there to be held for Cumberland county, on the 28th day of Augt. next, to answer the petition or libel of the said Elizabeth Reinald and to show cause, if any you have why the said Elizabeth Reinald, your wife, should not be divorced from the bonds of matrimony, agreeably to the acts of Assembly in such case made and provided. And hereof fail not. Witness the Honorable, Samuel Hepburn Esq. President, of our said court, at Carlisle, the 4th day of May A.D. 1848." (signed W.M. Beetem Prot.)

Nov. 22, 1848 -"Cumberland County, Sct. -James Hoffer, Esq. Shff. being duly sworn according to law, doth depose and say that the Deft. within mentioned is not to be found in my bailiwick. Sworn and Subscribed the 22d Nov. 1848 Before me." (signed W.M. Beetem Prot. and James Hoffer Shff.) Notation on the front of this document -"No. 16 April Term, 1848 Elizabeth Reinold by her next friend Thos. Craighead Jr. vs. Henry Reinold Alias Subpoena sur Divorce Writ advertised four weeks prior to Court. N.E.I. So answers" (signed James Hoffer Shff.) "Shff. Hoffer's fee $0.18 3/4 Do on advers. $1.50 Watts."

Jan. 18, 1849 -"In the Court of Common Pleas of Cumberland County. Elizabeth Reinold by her next friend Thomas Craighead Junr. vs. Henry Reinold: No. 16 April Term 1848 Subpoena Sur Divorce. 18th Jany. 1849 On motion of Mr. Watts F.A. Mateer Esq. appointed a Commissioner to take the depositions of witnesses, at his office, in Hoguestown to be read in evidence on the hearing of this case, at the next argument Court, 13th Feby. 1849. To meet exparte. By the Court."

Jan. 22, 1849 -"Cumberland County SS -I, James F. Lamberton Prothonotary of the Court of Common Pleas of said county do certify that the foregoing is an extract taken from the records of the Court of Common Pleas of said County, in said case. In testimony whereof I have hereunto set my hand and the seal of said court, at Carlisle the 22nd day of January A.D. 1849." (signed Jas. F. Lamberton Prothy.)

Feb. 5, 1849 -"Febr. 5th A.D. 1849. The execution of the above Commission appears by the depositions hereto annexed -Witness my hand." (signed F.A. Mateer Comm.) "Agreeable to the annexed Commission the following witnesses came before me F.A. Mateer and by virtue of said Commission were duly qualified as follows (to wit):

Feb. 5, 1849 -"Cumberland County, S.S. -Jacob Bricker of the towns. of Silver Springs in said County, aged 67 years and upwards being produced sworn and examined deposeth and saith, I am acquainted with Henry Reinold and Elizabeth his wife. They were married at my house in said township, by the Revd. Mr. Stroh sometime in Apr. A.D. 1842. I was present at the marriage; and further saith not. Sworn and Subscribed February 5th A.D. 1849 before me." (signed Jacob Bricker and F.A. Mateer, Comm.)

"Cumberland Co., S.S. -Abr. Keembots (sic) of the towns. of Silver Spring in said County County (sic), aged 46 years and upwards, being produced, affirmed and examined doth depose and say that I am acquainted with Henry Reinold and Elizabeth his wife. I know they were married. Henry Reinold rented a room in my house and moved his furniture there and commenced housekeeping with his wife on the 7th day of April A.D. 1842. That he left his wife in haymaking of that year. I did not see him again till next haymaking when he came and took his mowing scythe away. His wife moved to Perry County sometime before he came back the last time. I know he cut timber on her land and pealed (sic) some bark and made use of the money that he made very little provision for her support while he did live with her, and further saith not. Sworn and Subscribed the 5th day of Febr. A.D. 1849 before me." (signed Abraham Keenbirtz and F.A. Mateer Coms.)

Feb. 5, 1849 -"Cumberland Co., S.S. -Leha Longsdorff, widow of the towns. of East Pennsboro, towns. in said County aged 27 years and upward being produced sworn and examined doth depose and say that I am a sister of Elizabeth Reinold. That she was married to Henry Reinold sometime in the year A.D. 1842. That he took a horse that belonged to Elizabeth and me and sold it without our consent. That all he bought for the use of his family out of the money was one bag full of grain, that we got the horse from our grandfather. That he left his wife in haymaking, after they were married, and did not leave her anything to live on. She came home to us sometime after harvest of the same year. That Henry Reinold came back sometime in April of the next year. Then when he was at home he sold her side saddle and twelve pounds of wool, without her consent and made use of the money. That he cut timber, and pealed (sic) bark on her land and made use of the money. That he left her again about the first of May of the same year. That he came again about six months afterwards. That he provided nothing for her support when at home, she lived in her own house and made use of her own furniture for housekeeping. That it will be four years next May since he left her altogether. That he was back once since to see her, but did not take up with her. I wanted him to buy dresses for his children but he would not do it. He did not do anything at all for them, or his wife. That the last time he was at home Elizabeth told him she was going to get a divorce; and further saith not. Sworn and Subscribed the 5th day of Febr. A.D. 1849 before me." (signed Leah Longddorf and F.A. Mateer Comms.) -Notation on the front of this document -"No. 16 April Term 1848 Depositions Elizabeth Reinold vs. Henry Reinold: Sur Divorce Thos. Craighead paid Justice Mateer $1.09 Filed 13th Feby. 1849. Witnesses paid by plff.

Jacob Bricker	$0.62 1/2
Leah Longsdorff	$1.10
Abrm. Keenbritz	$0.92 1/2
	$2.75 "

Feb. 13, 1849 -"Elizabeth Reinold vs. Henry Reinold: Divorce Now, to wit, 13 Feb. 1849 the Court having heard the testimony taken in this case upon due consideration of the premises do hereby order and decree that the said Elizabeth Reinold and Henry Reinold be and they are hereby divorced and separated from the nuptial ties and bonds of matrimony and their marriage is hereby nullified and dissolved and that all the duties rights and claims accruing to either of the said parties at any time heretofore in pursuance of the said marriage shall cease and determine and the said parties are severally at liberty to marry again in like manner as if they never had been married. By the Court." -Notation on the front of this document -"No. 16 April T. 1848 Reinold vs. Reinold: Divorce Decree Filed 13 Feby. 1849."

♦ ♦ ♦

August Term 1848 #1 March 22, 1848 "To the Honorable the Judges of the Court of Common Pleas of Cumberland County -The petition of Margaret Jones by her next friend Jacob Gross respectfully represents -That she was legally united in holy wedlock to Conrad Jones on the 10th Nov. 1840, by the Revd. Henry Aurand, and that he continued to live and cohabit with her up until September 1845, at which time, although bound by the laws of God sworn to maintain and provide for her and to treat her as a husband should treat his wife, yet disregarding his duties and obligations, and violating his faith, he at that time wilfully and maliciously deserted your petitioner, and absented himself from her habitation without any reasonable or just cause, and has for more than the period of two years, refused and neglected to cohabit and live with your petitioner and to provide for her wants and necessities. Your petitioner further represents that she is a citizen of the Commonwealth of Pennsylvania, and has resided in said state one year and upwards before the presenting of this petition. She therefore prays your Honors to award a Subpoena to the said Conrad Jones, as directed by the Act of Assembly in such cases made and provided, and she will ever pray etc." (signed by her mark Margaret Jones.) -"Cumberland County sct. -Margaret Jones, the above petitioner being duly sworn according to law says, that the facts set forth in the above petition are true to the best of her knowledge and belief, and that the aforesaid complaint is not made out of levity or by collusion between her and her said husband, and for the mere purpose of being freed and separated from each other, but in sincerity and truth for the causes mentioned in her said libel. Sworn and Subscribed before me this 22nd March 1848." (signed David Smith and by her mark Margaret Jones.) -Notation on the front of this document -"No. 1 August T. 1848 Petition of Margaret Jones by her next friend Jacob Gross for a Subpoena Sur Divorce, 11th April 1848, Subpoena awarded By the Court. Filed 10 April, 1848. Todd."

April 10, 1848 -"Cumberland County Sct. -The Commonwealth of Pennsylvania to the Sheriff of Cumberland County Greeting: Whereas, Margaret Jones by her next friend Jacob Gross, on the 10th day of April A.D. 1848, did prefer her petition to our said Judges of our Court of Common Pleas for the county of Cumberland, praying that for the causes therein set forth that she might be divorced from the bonds of matrimony entered into with you Conrod Jones. We, do therefore command you the said Conrod Jones, that setting aside all other business and excuses whatsoever you be and appear in your proper person before our Judges, at Carlisle, at a Court of Common Pleas, there to be held for the county of Cumberland, on the 28th day of August, next, to answer the petition or libel of the said Margaret Jones, and to show cause, if any you have, why the said Margaret Jones your wife, should not be divorced from the bonds of matrimony, agreeably to the acts of Assembly in such case made and provided. And hereof fail not. Witness the Honorable Samuel Hepburn, Esq. President of our said Court, at Carlisle the 10th day of April A.D. 1848." (signed W.M. Beetem, Prot.)

Aug. 28, 1848 -"Cumberland County sct. -Robert McCartney, Dept. Shff., being duly sworn according to law says he served the within writ on Conrod Jones, per serving the copy on the 1 Aug. 1848 -sworn and subscribed before me the 28 Aug. A.D. 1848." (signed R. McCartney Dp. Shff.) -Notation on the front of this document -"No. 1 August T. 1848 Margaret Jones by her next friend Jacob Gross vs. Conrod Jones Subpoena Sur Divorce July 1st 1848 Served personally and by copy, So Answers" (signed R. McCartney Dp. Shff. and James Hoffer Shff.) "Shff. Hoffer's fee $1.84 1/2. Todd."

Aug. 28, 1848 -"In the Court of Common Pleas of Cumberland County -Margaret Jones by her next friend Jacob Gross vs. Conrod Jones: No. 1 August Term 1848 28th August 1848, On motion of Mr. Todd, in open court, David Smith, Esq. appointed a Commissioner to take depositions in this case, at his office in Carlisle, on Monday the 11th Sept. 1848, at 10 o'clock, A.M. to be read upon the hearing of the same, at the next Argument Court, to be held at Carlisle, in and for the county aforesaid, on Tuesday the 12th day of September 1848. By the Court. --Cumberland County, Sct. -I do certify that the above is an extract taken from the records. In testimony whereof I have hereunto set my hand and affixed the seal of the Court of Common Pleas, the 2nd day of September A.D. 1848." (signed W.M. Beetem Prot.)

Aug. 30, 1848 -"Margaret Jones vs. Conrod Jones: In the Common Pleas of Cumberland County Subpoena Sur Divorce -Sir: Take notice that depositions on the part of the libellant in this case will be taken before the subscriber, a Commissioner appointed by the Court for that purpose, on Monday, the 11th day of September next, at 10 o'clock A.M., at my office in the Boro of Carlisle, when and where you may attend to cross examine, if you think proper." (signed David Smith Coms. 30 Aug. 1848.)

Sept. 5, 1848 -"The service of this writ sworn to before me by W.G. Hamilton on Const. of YY Towns. Sept. 5th A.D. 1848. Cost 64¢." (signed W.G. Hamilton and F.A. Mateer Justice of the Peace.) -Notation on the front of this document -"No. 1 August T. 1848 Jones vs. Jones: Rule to take Depositions Retble. 12th Sept. 1848."

Sept. 11, 1848 -"In pursuance to the annexed rule of Court personally appeared before me David Smith a commissioner there named at his office in the Borough of Carlisle on Monday the 11th day of September 1848, at two o'clock in the forenoon (sic) of said day the following witness prodused (sic) on the part of the libellant and due process having been made of notice to Conrod Jones the defendant of the trial and place of taking depositions in the case Rev. Henry Aurand being duly sworn deposes and says I was the pastor of the German Reformed Church in the Borough of Carlisle in 1840. I married Conrad Jones to Miss Margaret Snyder the 10th day of November 1840 according to law and the custom of the church. The certificate attached to my deposition marked D.Y. was given by me at the time to Margaret Snyder now Mrs. Jones." (signed Henry Aurand.) -Certificate attached initialed D.Y. "What God hath joined together, let no man put asunder. I certifify that on the 10th day of Novr. 1840 I have solemnized the Rites of Matrimony between Mr. Conrad Jones and Miss Margaret Snyder according to Law. Witness my hand." (signed Henry Aurand Minister of the Gospel.)

Sept. 11, 1848 -"Also Jacob Pence being duly affirmed deposes and says. I have been acquainted with Margaret Jones and Conrad Jones parties in this suit for five years. They resided in Hoguestown. I lived in the same house with them for three years. Mr. Jones deserted his wife three years ago this faul (sic). Mr. Jones had no cause for deserting his wife to the best of my knowledge. Mr. Jones has done nothing towards the support of Mrs. Jones and child since he has deserted them that I know of. Mr. Jones now boards at the Tavern in Hoguestown and has no residence and no intercourse with Mrs. Jones. Mrs. Jones has to hire out in order to mentain (sic) herself." (signed Jacob Pence.)

Sept. 11, 1848 -"Also at the same time and place Frederick Brakenmaker being duly affirmed deposes and says. I have known the parties in this suit for five years and better. They resided in Houguestown. I worked with Mr. Jones before he deserted his wife. It is about three years ago since Mr. Jones deserted his wife. I worked with Mr. Jones up until the time he deserted his wife. Mr. Jones had no just or reasonable cause for leaving his wife that I know of. Shortly after Mr. Jones deserted his wife he broke up his shop and has since been working through the country. Mr. Jones has not contributed any thing towards the support and mentance (sic) of his wife and child since the time he deserted her and I have hered (sic) him say that he would not. Mrs. Jones has been obliged to hire out since that time to mentain (sic) herself and child. She is now hired hired out. Mr. Jones now boarded at Mr. Grier's Tavern, and has no house home or residence. He only works now and then." (signed Frederick Brakenmaker.)

Sept. 11, 1848 -"I do certify that the above and foregoing depositions of the Revd. Henry Aurand, Jacob Pence and Frederick Brakenmaker were taken before me David Smith at my office in the Borough of Carlisle between the hours of ten and twelve o'clock of

Monday the 11th day of September 1848 according to notice duly served, they having been severally sworn and affirmed before the taking of there (sic) depositions. Witness my hand and seal at Carlisle the 11th day of September A.D. 1848." (signed David Smith.)

Jacob Pence one day and 18 miles circular .79
Frederick Brakenmaker one day and 18 miles circular .79
Revd. H. Aurand .25
Taking Depositions 1.00
$2.83

Notation on the front of this document -"No. 1 August T. 1848 -Jones vs. Jones: Depositions -Filed 12th Sept. 1848."

August Term 1848 #1 Sept. 12, 1848 -"Margaret Jones by her next friend Jacob Gross vs. Conrod Jones: No. 1 Aug. T. 1848 Sub. Sur Divorce -And now, to wit, 12th September 1848, David Smith, Esq., the Commissioner appointed by the Court in this case, having returned to the Court here the depositions of witnesses taken before him, on the part of the libellant, the same being read and heard by the Court. The Court after mature deliberation being satisfied there with (sic), and the respondent not appearing, the Court do order, adjudge and decree that the said Margaret Jones, the libellant be divorced and separated from the bond of matrimony contracted with the said Conrod Jones, the respondent, and that all and every the duties, rights, and claims accruing to either of the said parties by reason of the said marriage shall henceforth cease and determine, and the said parties be severally at liberty to marry again, in like manner as if they never had been married and that Deft. pays the costs of this proceeding. By the Court Sept. 12, 1848." -Notation on the front of this document -"No. 1 August T. 1848. Jones vs. Jones: Decree of the Court. Filed 12th Sept. 1848. Todd."

◆ ◆ ◆

August Term 1848 #2 April 11, 1848 -"To the Honorable the Judges of the Court of Common Pleas of Cumberland County -The petition of Sarah Ann McCabe by her next friend John Gilmore -Respectfully showeth, That your Libellant on the 11th day of July in the year of our Lord one thousand eight hundred and forty five was contracted in matrimony and married to a certain William McCabe and from that time until the 20th day of November in the year of our Lord one thousand eight hundred and forty five -lived and cohabited with him as his wife, and as such was owned and acknowledged by him, and so deemed and reputed by all her neighbors and acquaintances; and although by the laws of God, as well as by their mutual vows and faith plighted to each other, they were reciprocally bound to that kindness and uniform regard which ought to be inseparable from the marriage state; yet so it is, that the said William McCabe from the 20th day of November in the year of our Lord one thousand eight hundred and forty five hath wilfully and maliciously deserted and absented himself from the habitation of this libellant without any just or reasonable cause -and such desertion hath persisted in for the term of two years and upwards, and yet doth continue to absent himself from the said libellant. Wherefore your libellant further showing that she is a citizen of the state of Pennsylvania, and has resided therein for upwards of one whole year previous to the filing of this her libel, prays your Honors that a subpoena may issue forth to summon the said William McCabe to appear in this Honorable Court on the first day of August term next to answer the complaint aforesaid. And also that a decree of this Honorable Court may be made for the divorcing of him the said William McCabe from the society, fellowship and company of this libellant in all time to come, and her this libellant from the marriage bond aforesaid as if she had never been married or as if the said William were naturally dead. And this libellant will pray." (signed Sarah Ann McCabe by her next friend John Gilmore.) --"The above named Sarah Ann McCabe being duly sworn says that the facts contained in the above libel are true to the best of her knowledge and belief, and that the said complaint is not made out of levity and collusion between her and the said William McCabe and for the mere purpose of being freed and separated from each other but in sincerity and truth for the causes mentioned in the said libel. Sworn and subscribed before me this 11th day of April 1848." (signed David Smith J.P. and Sarah Ann McCabe.) -Notation on the front of this document -"No. 2 Augt. T. 1848. The petition of Sarah Ann McCabe for a divorce. 12th April 1848 Subpoena awarded by the court Filed 12th April, 1848. Gaullagher."

August Term 1848 #2 April 12, 1848 -"Cumberland County, Sct. -The Commonwealth of Pennsylvania to the Sheriff of Cumberland County, Greeting -Whereas Sarah Ann McCabe by her next friend John Gilmore, did on the 12th day of April, A.D. 1848, prefer a petition, to our said Judges of our Court of Common Pleas, for the County of Cumberland, praying for the causes therein set forth, that she might be divorced from the bonds of matrimony entered into with you Wm. McCabe. We, do therefore command you, the said William McCabe, that setting aside all other business and excuses whatsoever you be and appear in your proper person before our Judges, at Carlisle, at a Court of Common Pleas, there to be held for the County of Cumberland, on the 28th day of August next, to answer the petition or libel of the said Sarah Ann McCabe, your wife, to show cause if any you have, why the said Sarah Ann McCabe, your wife, should not be divorced from the bond of matrimony, agreeably to the act of Assembly, in such case made and provided. And hereof fail not. Witness the Honorable Samuel Hepburn, Esq. President of our said Court, at Carlisle, the 12th day of April, A.D.

1848." (signed W.M. Beetem, Prot.)

Aug. 29, 1848 -"Cumberland County S.S. -James Hoffer Sheriff of said County being duly sworn according to law in open court doth say that the within named William McCabe was not and could not be found in said County. Sworn and subscribed before me this 29th Augt. 1848." (signed W.M. Beetem -Prot. and James Hoffer Shff.) -Notation on the front of this document -"No. 2 August T. 1848 Sarah Ann McCabe by her next friend John Gilmore vs. William McCabe Subpoena sur Divorce N.I.H.J.L. So answers James Hoffer Shff. Shff. Hoffer's fee $0.18 3/4 Gaullagher."

Aug. 29, 1848 -"Cumberland County, Sct. -The Commonwealth of Pennsylvania to the Sheriff of Cumberland county Greeting: Whereas, Sarah Ann McCabe, by her next friend John Gilmore, did on the 12th day of April, A.D. 1848, prefer a petition to our said Judges of our Court of Common Pleas, for the county of Cumberland, praying for the causes therein set forth, that she might be divorced from the bonds of matrimony entered into with you William McCabe. We do therefore command you the said William McCabe, as we have heretofore commanded you that setting aside all other business and excuses whatsoever, you be and appear in your proper person, before our Judges, at Carlisle, at a Court of Common Pleas, there to be held for the county of Cumberland on the 13th day of November next, to answer the petition or libel of the said Sarah Ann McCabe, and to show cause, if any you have, why the said Sarah Ann McCabe, your wife, should not be divorced from the bonds of matrimony agreeably to the act of Assembly in such case made and provided. And hereof fail not. Witness the Honorable Saml. Hepburn, Esq. President of our said Court, at Carlisle, the 29th day of August, A.D. 1848." (signed W.M. Beetem, Prot.)

Nov. 22, 1848 -"Cumberland County, Sct. -James Hoffer, Esq. Sheriff of Cumberland County being duly sworn according to law doth depose and say that Defendant is not to be found within my bailiwick. Sworn and Subscribed, the 22d Nov. 1848, before me." (signed W.M. Beetem Prot. and James Hoffer Shrff.) -Notation on the front of this document -"No. 2 August T. 1848. Sarah Ann McCabe by her next friend Jno. Gilmore vs. William McCabe Alias Subpoena sur Divorce. N.E.I. Writ advertised four weeks prior to Court, So answers" (signed James Hoffer Shff.) "Shff. H.'s fee $0.18 3/4 advertising $1.50 Gaullagher."

Jan. 18, 1849 -"In the Court of Common Pleas of Cumberland County -Sarah Ann McCabe by her next friend Jno. Gilmore vs. William McCabe: Subpoena Sur Divorce No. 2 August Term 1848 18th Jany. 1849 On motion of Mr. Gaullagher, Geo. Fleming "Esqr." appointed a Commissioner to take the depositions of witnesses at his office in Carlisle to be read in evidence on the hearing of this case, at the next argument Court. 13th Feby. 1849. To meet exparte.

-Cumberland County -I James F. Lamberton Prothonotary of the Court of Common Pleas of said county do certify that the above is an extract taken from the records of the Court of Common Pleas of said County in said case. In testimony whereof I have hereunto set my hand and the seal of said court at Carlisle, the 23rd day of January A.D. 1849." (signed Jas. F. Lamberton Proth.)

Feb. 8, 1849 -"Cumberland County S.S. -In pursuance of the above rule of Court personally appeared before me a Justice of the Peace in and for said County John Underwood who being duly affirmed according to law doth say that he is acquainted with Sarah Ann McCabe and William McCabe named in the above rule -that he was present at their marriage -that they were united in marriage by the Rev. Henry Aurand sometime in the month of August 1845. That the said William wilfully and maliciously deserted and absented himself from the habitation of his said wife Sarah Ann in the month of November 1845 without any reasonable cause, and that he has continued in such wilfull and malicious desertion and absence from that time until the present and still continues in the same without any reasonable cause. Sworn and affirmed 8 Febry. 1849." (signed John Underwood and George Fleming.)

Feb. 8, 1849 -"Also at same time appeared Elizabeth Egolf who being duly sworn according to law doth say that she is acquainted with Sarah Ann McCabe and William McCabe named in the above rule. That she was present at their marriage. That they were united in marriage by the Rev. Henry Aurand in the month of August 1845. That the said William wilfully and maliciously deserted and absented himself from the habitation of his said wife Sarah Ann in the month of November 1845 without any reasonable cause, and that he has continued in such wilful and malicious desertion from that time until the present and still continues in the same without any reasonable cause. Sworn and subscribed 8 Febry. 1849." (signed by her mark Elizabeth Egolf and by George Fleming.) -Notation on the front of this document -"No. 2 August Term 1848 Sarah Ann McCabe by her next friend vs. William McCabe: Rule to take Depositions Filed 13th Feby. 1849. Gaullagher."

Feb. 13. 1849 -"Sarah Ann McCabe by her next friend John Gilmore vs. William McCabe: Subpoena sur Divorce No. 2 Augt. T. 1848 -Now to wit 13th Febry. 1849 the court after hearing the depositions of John Underwood and Elizabeth Egolf taken before Geo. Fleming Esqr. read, and after mature deliberation being satisfied therewith and proclamation being made for the said William McCabe the Respondent to come forth, and he not appearing the Court do order, adjudge, and decree that the said Sarah Ann McCabe the Libellant be divorced and separated from the bond of matrimony contracted with the said William McCabe the Respondent, and that all and every the duties, rights, and claims accruing to either of the said parties by reason of the said marriage shall henceforth cease and determine, and the said parties be severally at liberty to marry again in like manner as if they never had been married. By the Court." -Notation on the front of this document -"No. 2 August T. 1848 Sarah Ann McCabe by her next friend vs. William McCabe Decree of Divorce Filed 13th Feby. 1849."

◆ ◆ ◆

November Term 1848 # 9 Sept. 7, 1848 -"The libel of Elizabeth Donnelly her father and next friend Benjamin Ebersole Respectfully Showeth -That your libellant on the twentieth day of September One thousand eight hundred and forty four was contracted in matrimony and married to a certain James Donnely and from that time until the first day of October One thousand Eight hundred and forty four lived and cohabited with the said James Donnelly and as her husband he was acknowledged by all her neighbors and so deemed by himself. And although by God's laws as well as by their mutual vows plighted to each other, they were bound to that uniform constancy and regard which is inseparable from the marriage state; yet so it is that the said James Donnelly from the first day of October One thousand Eight hundred and forty four hath wilfully absented himself from, and maliciously deserted the hatitation and abode of your Libellant without any reasonable cause. The said desertion and absence have continued for two years and upwards and yet does continue. Your libellant represents further that she has resided in the state of Pennsylvania as a citizen thereof for one whole year and upwards before the filing of this petition. She therefore prays your Honor to grant a subpoena to summon the said James Donnelly to appear in this Honorable Court at the next term (to wit at November next) to answer her complaint. She further prays that a decree may be made divorcing the said James Donnelly from the society and company of your libellant (a vinculo matrimonii) as though they the said James and your libellant had never been married, or as if the said James was naturally dead. And she will pray." (signed Elizabeth Donly by her next friend Benjamin Ebersole.) -"Cumberland County, S.S. -The above named Elizabeth Donnelly being duly sworn says that the facts contained in the above libel are true and that the complaint is not made out of levity or collusion between the libellant and respondent, but for the mere purpose of being freed from each other, and in sincerity and truth for the causes contained in the above libel. Sworn and Subscribed before me this (blank) day of Sept. 1848." (signed Elizabeth Doly (sic) and Saml. Hepburn.) "To the Hon. Samuel Hepburn President Judge of the Court Common Pleas of Cumberland County" -Notation on the front of this document -"No. 9 November T. 1848. Elizabeth Donnelly by her next friend etc. vs. Jas. Donnelly Divorce Subpeona awarded returnable 1st day of next term. (signed Saml. Hepburn Prest. Judge Sept. 7, 1848.) "Filed 7th

Septr. 1848. Adair."

Sept. 7, 1848 -"Cumberland County, Sct. -The Commonwealth of Pennsylvania to the Sheriff of Cumberland County Greeting: Whereas, Elizabeth Donnelly, by her father and next friend Benjamin Ebersole, on the 7th day of September A.D. 1848, did prefer a petition to our said Judges of our Court of Common Pleas for the county of Cumberland, praying for the causes therein set forth, that she might be divorced from the bond of matrimony entered into with you James Donnelly. We do therefore command you the said James Donnelly, that setting aside all other business and excuses whatsoever you be and appear in your proper person, before our Judges, at Carlisle, at a Court of Common Pleas, there to be held for the county of Cumberland, on the 13th day of November next, to answer the petition or libel of the said Elizabeth Donnelly, and to show cause, if any you have why the said Elizabeth Donnelly your wife, should not be divorced from the bond of matrimony, agreeably to the acts of Assembly in such case made and provided. And hereof fail not. Witness the Honorable Saml. Hepburn, Esq. President of our said Court, at Carlisle, the 7th day of September, A.D. 1848." (signed W.M. Beetem Prot.)

April 10, 1849 -"Cumb. Co., s.s. -Jas. Hoffer Sheriff being duly sworn says that the respondent Jas. Donnelly is not to be found in his bailiwick. Sworn and Subscribed 10th Apl. 1849 before me." (signed Jas. F. Lamberton, Prot. and James Hoffer Shff.) -Notation on the front of this document -"#9 November T. 1848. Elizabeth Donnelly by her father and next friend Benjamin Ebersole vs. James Donnelly Subpoena sur Divorce N.E.I. So answers." (signed James Hoffer Shff.) "Shrff. H.'s fee $0.18. 3/4 Adair."

Aug. 28, 1849 -"And now, to wit Aug. 28th 1849 proof and return being duly made as to the alias subpoena being returned in open Court and publication thereof having been made according to law Geo. Ege Esquire is appointed a Commissioner to take depositions to be read on the hearing. The Commission returnable on Tuesday the 11th Sept. 1849. By the Court. 28 Aug. 1849."

November Term 1848 #9 April 10, 1849 -"Cumberland County Sct. -The Commonwealth of Pennsylvania to the Sheriff of Cumberland County Greeting: Whereas Elizabeth Donnelly, by her next friend Benjamin Ebersole, on the 7th day of September A.D. 1848 did prefer a petition to our said Judges of our Court of Common Pleas for the County of Cumberland, praying for the causes therein set forth, that she might be divorced from the bonds of matrimony entered into with you James Donnelly. We do, therefore command you the said James Donnelly as we have heretofore commanded you that setting aside all other business and excuses whatsoever you be and appear in your proper person, before our Judges at Carlisle at a Court of Common Pleas, there to be held for the County of Cumberland on the 27th day of August next, to answer the petition or libel of the said Elizabeth Donnelly, and to shew cause if any you have why the said Elizabeth Donnelly your wife, should not be divorced from the bonds of matrimony agreeably to the acts of Assembly in such case made and provided. And hereof fail not. Witness the Honorable Frederick Watts President of our said Court at Carlisle the 10th day of April A.D. 1849." (signed Jas. F. Lamberton Prothy.) -Notation on the front of this document -"No. 9 November T. 1848 Elizabeth Donnelly by her father and next friend Benjamin Ebersole vs. James Donnelly Alias Subpoena Sur Divorce N.E.I.V. Writ advertised four weeks prior to return day 12 Nov. 1849 -So Answers" (signed James Hoffer Shff.) "Shff. Hoffer's fee $0.18 3/4. Advertising $2.50. total $2.68 3/4. Adair."

Aug. 28, 1849 -"Cumberland Co., S.S. -Jas. Hoffer Sheriff says that respondent is not to be found in his bailiwick and he published the legal notice in three papers printed in this County. Sworn and Subscribed before me 28 Aug. 1849." (signed Jas. F. Lamberton Prot. and James Hoffer Shff. and R. McCartney Dp. Shff.)

Nov. 12, 1849 -"Cumberland Co. -R. McCartney Dep. Sheriff being by me duly sworn says notice was published of the within application according to law and the order of the Court of 11th Sept. 1849, the former publication having been by the Court deemed insufficient. Sworn and Subscribed before me 12 Novr. 1849." (signed James F. Lamberton Prothy. and R. McCartney Dp. Shff.)

Aug. 28, 1849 -"In the Court of Common Pleas of Cumberland County -Elizabeth Donnelly by her father and next friend Benjamin Ebersole vs. James Donnelly: No. 9 November Term 1848 Subpoena Sur Divorce -And now, to wit Aug. 28, 1849 proof and return being duly made as to the alias Subpoena being returned in open Court and publication thereof having been made according to law, Geo. Ege Esquire is appointed a Commissioner to take depositions to be read on the hearing. The commission returnable on Tuesday the 11th Sept. 1849 By the Court." -"Cumberland County S.S. -I James F. Lamberton Prothonotary of the Court of Common Pleas of said County, do certify that the above is true extract, taken from the records of the Court of Common Pleas of said County. In testimony whereof I have hereunto set my hand and affixed the seal of said Court at Carlisle the 29th day of August A.D. 1849." (signed Jas. F. Lamberton Prothy.) -Notation on the front of this document -"No. 9 November T. 1848 Geo. Ege. Esqr. Commission Donnelly vs. Donnelly Adair."

Sept. 7, 1849 -"No. 9 of November Term 1848 Elizabeth Donnelly by her father and next friend Benjamin Ebersole vs. James Donnelly: Subpoena Sur Divorce By virtue of a Commission issued to me from the Court of Common Pleas of Cumberland County, the following depositions were taken to wit. -Cumberland County, s.s. -The Revd.

J.N. Hoffman being by me duly sworn says that on the twentieth of September A.D. 1844, he joined in marriage Elizabeth Ebersole this libellant with James Donnelly according to the rites and ceremonies of the Lutheran Church. Sworn and subscribed before me the 7th September 1849." (signed Geo. Ege and John N. Hoffman.)

"Rev. J.N. Hoffman   31
Justice Ege   22 1/2"

November Term 1848 #9 Sept. 7, 1849 -"Cumberland County s.s. -Personally appeared before me a Justice of the Peace in and for said County, Benjamin Ebersole Jr. who being duly sworn says that his sister Elizabeth was born in the State of Pennsylvania and resided therein more than one whole year previous to the filing of her petition for a divorce from James Donnelly. That she was married, to the said James Donnelly sometime in the fall of 1844, that after their marriage she resided with her father and that said Donnelly refused and neglected to live with her, and in the same fall, he did wilfully and maliciously desert the said Elizabeth from her habitation and from the County of Cumberland without a reasonable cause for and during the time and space of two years and upward, to wit, from the fall of 1844 to the present time. That he has not since been heard of by me or to my knowledge by my sister Elizabeth or any of the family, except that I heard that he was in Lebanon County in the fall of 1844 after his desertion of my sister Elizabeth. Sworn and subscribed before me 7th September 1849." (signed Benjamin Ebersole and Geo. Ege.) "Justice Ege costs 36" -Notation on the front of this document -"No. 9 Nov. T. 1848 Donnelly by her next friend vs. James Donnelly Subpoena Sur Divorce Return of Commission issued to me by the Court of Common Pleas of Cumberland County." (signed Geo. Ege Justice of the Peace.)

"Costs Rev. Hoffman   31
Justice Ege   59

Filed 11 Sept. 1849 Adair."

Nov. 12, 1849 -"Elizabeth Donnelly by her father and next friend Benjamin Ebersole vs. James Donnelly: Subpoena sur Divorce In the Court of Common Pleas of Cumberland County -Now, to wit Novr. 12, 1849 the Examiner George Ege Esq. having returned to Court here the depositions of witnesses taken before him on the part of the libellant and the same after proof being made of publication according to law being read and heard by the Court, and the Court after mature deliberation being satisfied therewith and proclamation being duly made for the respondent to come forth and he not appearing the Court, Do order and decree, That the said Elizabeth Donnelly the libellant be divorced and separated from the bond of matrimony contracted with the said James Donnelly the respondent and that all and every the duties rights and claims accruing to either of said parties by reason of said marriage shall henceforth cease and determine and the said parties be severally at liberty to marry again in like manner as though they had never been married. The Court do further award costs to the said Elizabeth Donnelly in whose behalf this decree is passed; according to the Acts of Assembly in such case made and provided. By the Court." (signed Fredr. Watts Proth.) -Notation on the front of this document -"No. 9 Nov. T. 1848 Donnelly vs. Donnelly Divorce Decree of Court a vinculo matrimonii Filed 12 Nov. 1849 Adair."

♦ ♦ ♦

January Term 1849 #3 Oct. 30, 1848 -"To the Honourable, the Judges of the Court of Common Pleas for the County of Cumberland -The petition of Elizabeth Whisler by her brother and next friend Jacob Low, respectfully represents, that your libellant on the fourteenth day of June in the year of our Lord one thousand eight hundred and forty six was bound in matrimony and married to a certain Abraham Whisler of said county, and from that time until sometime in the first part of September, in the year of our Lord one thousand eight hundred and forty six lived and cohabited with the said Abraham Whisler as his wife, and as such was owned and acknowledged by him and so deemed and reputed by their neighbours and acquaintances. Yet so it is that the said Abraham Whisler disregarding his duties as a husband did on the fourteenth day of August in the year our Lord one thousand eight hundred and forty six by cruel and barbarous treatment endanger her life, and at sundry other times offered such indignities to her person as to render her condition intolerable and life burdensome, and thereby force her to withdraw from his house and family, since which time he has made no provision for her maintenance or support, and she has no separarate estate in her own right for such purpose. She has been absent from her said husband and without any aid or support from him ever since the said first part of September one thousand eight hundred and forty six. Wherefore your libellant further showing that she is a citizen of this state, and hath resided therein for upwards of one whole year previous to the filing of this petition, prays your honors that a subpoena may issue from the said court directed to the said Abraham Whisler, commanding him to appear at the next term of the said court, to answer this petition; and also that a decree of the said court may be given granting this libellant a divorce from bed and board, and also allowing her such allimony as the said Abraham Whisler's circumstances will admit of agreeably to the acts of Assembly in such case made and provided, and that such other proceedings be had as this case requires so as to accomplish the object of her said petition. And the said libellant as in duty bound will pray etc." (signed by her mark Elizabeth Whisler.) "by her brother and next friend" (signed Jacob Low and Test. J. Ellis Bonham.) -"Cumberland County s.s. -The above named Elizabeth Whisler maketh oath and saith, that the facts set forth in the foregoing petition are true to the best of her knowledge and belief, and that said complaint is not made out of levity and collusion between the said petitioner and the said Abraham Whisler her husband, and for the mere purpose of being freed and separated from each other, but in sincerity and truth and for the causes mentioned in the above petition. Sworn and subscribed before me this 30th day of October A.D. 1848." (signed Geo. Fleming J.P. and by her mark Elizabeth Whisler.) -Notation on the front of this document -"No. 3 January T. 1849 Petition of Elizabeth Whisler by her brother and next friend Jacob Low for a divorce from bed and board and alimony. 13th Nov. 1848. Subpoena awarded By the Court."

Nov. 13, 1848 -"Cumberland County, Sct. -The Commonwealth of Pennsylvania to the Sheriff of Cumberland County, Greeting: Whereas, Elizabeth Whisler by her brother and next friend Jacob Low, did on the 13th day of November, A.D. 1848, prefer her petition to our Judges of our Court of Common Pleas for the county of Cumberland, praying, for the causes therein set forth, that she, the said Elizabeth Whisler, might be divorced from the bonds of matrimony entered into with you Abraham Whisler, and be allowed such alimony as your circumstances will admit. We do therefore command you, the said Abraham Whisler that setting aside all other business whatsoever, you be and appear in your proper person before our Judges, at Carlisle, at a Court of Common Pleas, there to be held for the said county of Cumberland on the 8th day of January next, to answer the petition or libel of the said Elizabeth Whisler, and to show cause, if any you have, why a divorce should not be granted to the said Elizabeth Whisler, your wife, and a decree for alimony be made agreeably to the act of General Assembly in such case made and provided. And hereof fail not. Witness the Honorable Samuel Hepburn, Esq. President of our said Court, at Carlisle, the 13th day of November, A.D. 1848." (signed W.M. Beetem -Prot.) -Notation on the front of this document -"No. 3 January T. 1849 Elizabeth Whisler by her Brother and next friend Jacob Low vs. Abraham Whisler Subpeona sur Divorce and for alimony Nov. 27th 1848 Served personally and by copy. So answers" (signed R. McCartney Dp. Shff. and James Hoffer Shff.) -"Shff. Hoffer's fee $2.40 1/2. Bonham."

Dec. 11, 1848 -"To the Honorable the Judges of the Court of Common Pleas of Cumberland County -To the petition or libel of Elizabeth Whisler filed in the said Court the said Abrm. Whisler answers: That true it is he was married to the said libellant on or about the 14 June 1846 but it is not true that he disregarded his duties as a husband or treated the said libellant cruelly and barbarously or that he did endanger her life: nor did he offer such indignities to her person as to force her to withdraw from his house and family. But on the contrary the said Abrm. Whisler the respondent avers and reserves to himself the right to prove if it becomes necessary that the said libellant after her marriage with the respondent refused to perform any of the duties of a wife and in her conduct and demeaner was outrageous and violent and in her associations exceptionable and that she voluntarily left the house and home of the respondent and refused to return and has ever since remained absent. It is true that the said respondent has not contributed in any way to the support of the said libellant since her desertion nor is he in law bound to make any such provision for her." (signed Abraham Whisler.) -Notation on the front of this document -"No. 3 Jany. T. 1849 Eliz. Whisler by her next friend Jacob Low vs. Abm. Whisler Filed 19 Jany. 1849."

Dec. 11, 1848 -"Cumberland County sct. -Abrm. Whisler personally appeared before me and being duly affirmed doth say that the facts set forth in the within answer are true to the best of his knowledge and belief. Affirmed and subscribed the 11 December 1848 Before me." (signed Geo. Fleming and Abraham Whisler.)

Jan. 19, 1849 -"To the Honourable the Judges of the Court of Common Pleas of Cumberland County -To the answer of Abraham Whisler filed in the said court the said libellant by her attorney, comes and says, that protestesting (sic), all and singular the matters and things in the said respondent's plea, alleged in bar of her libels and prayer, are not true, she is ready to verify the said matters and things by her in her said libel and prayer set forth, and prays that a jury may be called to inquire thereof, according to the form of the several Acts of Assembly in this behalf made and provided." (signed J. Ellis Bonham, Attorney for Libellant.) -Notation on the front of this document -"No. 3 January T. 1849 Elizabeth Whisler by her next friend Jacob Low vs. Abrm. Whisler Filed 19 Jan. 1849."

◆ ◆ ◆

January Term 1849 #15 Dec. 18, 1848 -"To the Hon. Samuel Hepburn Esq. President Judge of the Court of Common Pleas of Cumberland County -The Petition of David Shoffner Respectfully Represents -That on the 7 December 1843 he was lawfully joined in marriage with Elizabeth Duey and continued to reside with her and she with me until about the 14 August 1844 when she the said Elizabeth refused to perform any of the duties of a wife for and towards your petitioner. And at that time she the said Elizabeth did wilfully and maliciously desert and absented herself from the habitation of her husband your petitioner without any reasonable cause and hath continued to absent herself ever since. He therefore prays your Honor to award a subpoena to the said Elizabeth Shoffner to appear at the next Court and answer the petition or libel and shew cause why the said Court should not make a decree divorcing the said David Shoffner from the bonds of matrimony entered into by him with the said Elizabeth, and he as in duty bound will pray etc."

(signed David Shoffner.) -"Cumberland County, sct. -Personally appeared before me a Justice of the Peace in and for said County David Shoffner who being duly sworn doth depose and say that the facts set forth in the above petition or libel are true to the best of his knowledge and belief and that the said complaint is not made out of levity or by collusion between him and his said wife and for the mere purpose of being freed and separated from each other, but in sincerity and truth for the causes mentioned in the said petition or libel. Sworn and Subscribed the 18 December 1848 Before me." (signed David Smith and David Shoffner.) -Notation on the front of this document -"No. 15 Jany. T. 1849 Petition of David Shoffner for a Divorce Subpoena awarded returnable 19 Jany. 1849" (signed Saml. Hepburn Decr. 18, 1848.) "Filed 18th Decr. 1848."

Dec. 18, 1848 -"Cumberland County S.S. -The Commonwealth of Pennsylvania to the Sheriff of Cumberland County Greeting: Whereas David Shoffner, did on the 18th day of December 1848, prefer his petition to the Honorable Samuel Hepburn, President Judge of our Court of Common Pleas for the County of Cumberland, praying for the causes therein set forth, that he might be divorced from the bonds of matrimony entered into with you Elizabeth Duey. We do therefore command you, the said Elizabeth Duey, that setting aside all other business and excuses whatsoever you be and appear in your proper person before our Judges at Carlisle, at a Court of Common Pleas, there to be held for the county of Cumberland, on the 19th day of January next, to answer the petition or libel of the said David Shoffner, and to show cause, if any you have, why the said David Shoffner, your husband, should not be divorced from the bonds of matrimony, agreeably to the Acts of General Assembly in such case made and provided. Hereof fail not. Witness the Honorable Samuel Hepburn President of our said Court, at Carlisle, the 18th day of Decr. A.D. 1848 for J.F. Lamberton, Prot." (signed W.M. Beetem.) -Notation on the front of this document -"No. 15 January T. 1849 David Shoffner vs. Elizabeth Shoffner formerly Elizabeth Duey Subpoena Sur Divorce. Watts."

Dec. 29, 1848 -"Cumberland County, sct. -Personally appeared before me a Justice of the Peace in and for said County Abraham Coble who being duly affirmed doth depose and say that he served the within subpoena on Elizabeth Shoffner on the 29th day of December 1848 by giving her a true copy thereof after reading it to her. Affirmed and Subscribed the 29th day of December 1848 Before me." (signed Thos. Craighead Jr. and Abram Coble.)

Jan. 19, 1849 -"In the Court of Common Pleas of Cumberland County David Shoffner vs. Elizabeth Shoffner: No. 15 January Term 1849 Subpoena Sur Divorce -19th Jany. 1849 on motion of Mr. Watts Thos. Craighead, Esqr. appointed a Commissioner to take the depositions of witnesses at his office to be read in evidence on the trial of this case at the next arguments Court, 13 Feby. 1849. To meet exparte. By the Court." -Notation on the front of this document -"No.15 January T.1849 David Shoffner vs. Elizabeth Shoffner Rule to take depositions. Watts."

Jan. 22, 1849 -"Cumberland County S.S. -I James F. Lamberton Prothonotary of the Court of Common Pleas of Cumberland County do certify that the foregoing is an extract taken from the records of the Court of Common Pleas of said County, in said case. In testimony whereof I have hereunto set my hand and the seal of said court, at Carlisle the 22nd day of January A.D. 1849."

Feb. 3, 1849 -"February 3d 1849 The execution of the above Commission appears by the depositions hereto annexed. Witness my hand." (signed Thos. Craighead Jr. Commissioner.)

Feb. 3, 1849 -"Agreeable to the annexed Commission the following witnesses came before me Thomas Craighead Jr. and by virtue of said Commission were duly qualified as follows viz. -Cumberland County s.s. -The Rev. David Bossler of the Borough of Harrisburg aged forty eight years and upwards being produced sworn and examined doth depose and say that. I am a minister of the Gospel. I was called upon to marry David Shoffner to Elizabeth Duey and that I did marry said David Shoffner to said Elizabeth Duey on the 7th day of December A.D. 1843. Further saith not. Sworn and Subscribed before me the 3d day of Feb. 1849." (signed D. Bossler and Thos. Craighead Jr. Com.)

January Term 1849 #15 Feb. 3, 1849 -"Cumberland County S.S. -Samuel Page of the County of Dauphin aged 26 years and upwards, being produced, sworn and examined, doth depose and say -That I am acquainted with David Shoffner and slightly acquainted with his wife Elizabeth Shoffner. I know that they were married. I was asked to haul a load of goods by David Shoffner, from where he then lived in a house of Joshua Elders, with Frederick Duey his fatherinlaw (sic). It was about the last of August or first of September 1844. I sent the wagon up with my hired boy. I followed the wagon. Soon after they had began to load the wagon when I got there. I helped to load the wagon and made all ready to start. Shoffner was moving to his brotherinlaws (sic) Jacob Sheetz. The goods was taken to Sheetz's and unloaded. Elizabeth Shoffner the wife swore she would not go along with her husband. I tried to persuade her to go along but she utterly refused. I then went upstairs to a room where she was to try to persuade her to go with her husband. She still refused. Her husband requested me to try to persuade her to go along with him, but she still refused. I then tried to persuade her to come to my house on Sunday, and I and my wife would take her to her husband in the carriage. My house is about halfway to where her husband moved to. She still refused. I then came out and told her husband to ask her once more to go along. She then replied that he might kiss her damned arse she would not go along. Said I wish he would have no luck no where. I then started off with the wagon and said no more to her. Sworn and Subscribed before me Feb. 3d 1849." (signed Thos. Craighead Jr. Commissioner and Samuel Page.)

Feb. 3, 1849 -"Cumberland County s.s. -George Holtzberger of the County of Dauphin aged forty five years and upwards being produced sworn and examined doth depose as follows -viz: Saith that I am acquainted with David Shoffner and his wife Elizabeth Shoffner. I knew them both before they were married and afterwards. They were married I think seventh of December 1843. They lived together as man and wife until August or September 1844. I was not present when David Shoffner moved his household stuff away. They have not lived together since David moved his goods away from Joshua Elder. The wife's father Frederick Duey and David Shoffner lived together in one house. They had it rented from Joshua Elder. Elizabeth Shoffner remained with her father until the next April. David Shoffner often complained to me he could not live comfortably with his wife. I rather advised him to move away from her father's, and may be (sic) it would do better with them further saith not. Sworn and subscribed before me the 3d day of February 1849." (signed Thos. Craighead Jr. Commissioner and George Holtzberger by his mark.) -"Cumberland County S.S. -I do certify that the foregoing and annexed depositions were duly sworn to taken and subscribed before me at my office in Whitehill by virtue and authority of the rule hereto annexed. Witness my hand and seal at Whitehill aforesaid the 3d day of February A.D. 1849." (signed Thos. Craighead Jr. Commissioner.) -Notation on the front of this document -"No. 15 January T. 1849 Depositions David Shoffner vs. Elizabeth Shoffner: Divorce Filed 13th Feby. 1849 Witnesses Samuel Page, George Holtzberger, Rev. D. Bossler: Paid by Plff."

Feb. 13, 1849 -"David Shoffner vs. Elizabeth Shoffner: Divorce Now to wit 13 Feb. 1849 the subpoena in the case having been duly and legally served a commissioner appointed to take testimony and the same having been taken and submitted to the Court: it is thereupon ordered and decreed that the said David Shoffner and Elizabeth Shoffner be and they are hereby divorced and separated from the nuptial ties and bonds of matrimony and their marriage is hereby nullified and dissolved and that all and any the duties rights and claims accruing to either of the said parties at any time heretofore in pursuance of the said marriage shall cease and determine and the said parties are severally at liberty to marry again in like manner as if they never had been married. By the Court." -Notation on the front of this document -"No. 15 January T. 1849 Shoffner vs. Shoffner: Divorce Decree Filed 13 Feby. 1849."

◆   ◆   ◆

April Term 1849 #27 Feb. 15, 1849 -"To the Honble. The Judges of the Court of Common Pleas of Cumberland County -The libel of Ann Smith late Ann McKinney by her next friend Philip Messersmith Respectfully Sheweth -That your libellant on the 8th May A.D. One thousand Eight hundred and twenty Eight was contracted in matrimony and married to a certain Thomas Smith and from that time until the 3d of July A.D. One thousand Eight hundred and forty two lived and cohabited with the said Thomas as his wife and as such was owned and acknowledged by him and so deemed and reputed by her acquaintances and neighbours. And although by the laws of God as well as by their mutual vows and faith plighted to each other they were bound to that uniform constancy and regard which ought to be inseparable from the marriage state; yet so it is that the said Thomas from the said 3d of July A.D. One thousand Eight hundred and forty two hath wilfully and maliciously deserted and absented himself from the habitation of this libellant without any just or reasonable cause, and such desertion hath persisted in for the term of two years and upwards, to wit from the said 3d July A.D. 1842 up to this day, and still doth continue to absent himself from this libellant. Wherefore your libellant further showing that she is a citizen of the State of Pennsylvania and has resided therein for upwards of one whole year previous to the filing of this her libel prays your Honors that a subpoena may issue forth to summon the said Thomas Smith to appear in this Honorable Court at April term next to answer the complaint aforesaid. And also that a decree of said Honorable Court may be made divoricing of him the said Thomas Smith from the society fellowship and company of this libellant in all time to come and she this libellant from the marriage bond aforesaid as if she had never been married or as if the said Thomas Smith were naturally dead. And this libellant will pray etc." (signed Ann Smith by her next friend P. Messersmith.) -"Cumberland County SS -The within named Ann Smith being duly sworn deposeth that the facts contained in the above and foregoing libel are true to the best of her knowledge and belief, and that the said complaint is not made out of levity and collusion between her and her said husband and for the mere purpose of being freed and separated from each other, but in sincerity and truth for the causes mentioned said libel. Sworn and Subscribed before me this 15th day of February A.D. 1849." (signed Ann Smith and David Smith.) -"Subpoena awarded 19th Feby. 1849" (signed John Stuart.) -Notation on the front of this document -"No. 27 April T. 1849 Ann Smith by her next friend Philip Messersmith vs. Thomas Smith Filed 19th Feby. 1849. Biddle."

Feb. 19, 1849 -"Cumberland County, SS -The Commonwealth of Pennsylvania, to the Sheriff of Cumberland County, Greeting: Whereas, Ann Smith late Ann McKinney by her next friend Philip Messersmith, did on the 19th day of February, A.D. 1849, prefer a petition to our said Judges of our court of Common Pleas, for the county of Cumberland, praying for the causes therein set forth, that she might be divorced from the bonds of matrimony entered into with you the said Thomas Smith. We do therefore command you the said Wm. McCabe, that setting aside all other business and excuses, whatsoever, you be and appear in your proper person, before our Judges, at Carlisle, at a Court of Common Pleas, there to be held for the County of Cumberland on the 9th day of April, next, to answer the petition or libel of the said Ann Smith, and to show cause, if an you have, why the said Ann Smith, your wife, should not be divorced from the bonds of matrimony agreeably to the acts of Assembly in such cases made and provided. And hereof fail not. Witness the Honorable Samuel Hepburn, Esq. President of our Court, at Carlisle, the 19th day of February A.D. 1849 for J.F. Lamberton -Prot." (signed W.M. Beetem.)

Sept. 10, 1849 -"Cumb. Co. s.s. -Robert McCarny being duly sworn says that the defendant Thomas Smith is not in his bailiwick. Sworn and Subscribed before me 10th Sept. 1849." (signed Jas. F. Lamberton Prot. and R. McCartny.) -Notation on the front of this document -"No. 27 April Term 1849 Ann Smith, late Ann McKinney, by her next friend Philip Messersmith vs. Thomas Smith Subpoena sur Divorce N.E.I. So answers" (signed James Hoffer Shff.) "Shff. Hoffer's fee $0.18 3/4. Biddle."

April 10, 1849 -"Cumberland County Sct. -The Commonwealth of Pennsylvania to the Sheriff of Cumberland County -Greeting: Whereas Ann Smith late Ann McKinney by her next friend Philip Messersmith did on the 19th day of February A.D. 1849 prefer a petition to our said Judges of our Court of Common Pleas, for the County of Cumberland, praying for the causes therein set forth, that she might be divorced from the bonds of matrimony entered into with you the said Thomas Smith. We do therefore command you, that setting aside all other business and excuses whatsoever, you be and appear in your proper person before our Judges, at Carlisle at a Court of Common Pleas, there to be held for the County of Cumberland on the 27th day of August next, to answer the petition or libel of the said Ann Smith, and to shew cause, if any you have, why the said Ann Smith, your wife, should not be divorced from the bonds of matrimony agreeably to the acts of Assembly in such case made and provided. And hereof fail not. Witness the Honorable Frederick Watts Esqr. President of our said Court at Carlisle the 10th day of April 1849." (signed Jas. F. Lamberton, Prothy.) -Notation on the front of this document -"No. 27 April Term 1849 Ann Smith late Ann McKinney, by her next friend Philip Messersmith vs. Thomas Smith Alias Subpoena Sur Divorce N.E.I. and writ advertised four weeks prior to return day 12th Nov. 1849. So answers." (signed James Hoffer Shff.)

-Shff. Hoffer fee $0.18 3/4

Advertising $2.50
$2. 68 3/4 Biddle."
Sept. 11, 1849 -"Cumberland County S.S. -James Hoffer Esqr. Sheriff of said County being duly sworn according to law, says that he advertised the within writ for four weeks prior to the return day as directed by the Court and that the said Defendant could not be found in this County." (signed James Hoffer Shff.) "Sworn and Subscribed before me 11th Sept. 1849" (signed Jas. F. Lamberton Prothy.)

Nov. 12, 1849 -"Cumberland County s.s. -Robert McCartney deputy Sheriff being duly sworn deposeth that he caused notice to be published in one newspaper in this County for four weeks sucessively prior to the first day of this term requiring the said Thomas Smith to appear on said day to answer the complaint of the said Ann Smith. Sworn and Subscribed before Jas. F. Lamberton Prothy. Nov. 12, 1849." (signed R. McCartney Dp. Shff.)

Nov. 12, 1849 -"Ann Smith late Ann McKinney by her next friend vs. Thomas Smith: Divorce In this case a subpoena and alias subpoena having been returned that deft. could not be found, and notice having been regular published for four weeks since the return of the alias subpoena. The said Ann Smith by her next friend Philip Messersmith now respectfully requests the Court to appoint a Commissioner to take testimony in the case. 12 Nov. 1849." (signed W.M. Bidell Atty. for Libellant.) -Notice on the front of the document -"No. 27 April Term 1849 Filed 12 Nov. 1849 George Ege Esq. appointed Commissioner to take the testimony and Friday the 18th Dec. 1849 appointed for formal hearing. By the Ct. 12 Nov. 1849."

April Term 1849 #27 Dec. 18, 1849 -"In the Court of Common Pleas of Cumberland County No. 27 April Term 1849 -Ann Smith late Ann McKinney, by her next friend Philip Messersmith vs. Thomas Smith: Subpoena Sur Divorce 12th Nov. 1849 a Subpoena and alias Subpoena having been returned that the defendant could not be found and notice having been regularly published for four weeks since the return of the alias Subpoena. The said Ann Smith by her next friend etc. respectfully request the Court to appoint a Commissioner to take testimony in this case. George Ege Esq. appointed commissioner to take the testimony and Tuesday the 18th Decr. 1849 appointed for final hearing. By the Court. -Cumberland County SS -I do certify that the above is a true extract taken from the records of the Court of Common Pleas of said county. In testimony whereof I have hereunto set my hand and the seal of said Court at Carlisle this 24th day of November A.D. 1849." (signed Jas. F. Lamberton Prothy.) -Notation on the front of this document -"No. 27 April T. 1849 Smith etc. vs. Smith: Geo. Ege Esqr. appointed Comm. to take testimony etc."

Nov. 24, 1849 -"Ann Smith late Ann McKinney by her next friend

Philip Messersmith vs. Thomas Smith: Libel for Divorce -Before me George Ege Esq. commissioner appointed by the Court, to take testimony in this case, as appears by the commission hereunto annexed, Personally appeared James Davis, who being first duly sworn, deposeth and saith as follows. I knew Thomas Smith and Ann Smith his wife, the parties in this proceeding. I have first known them about thirteen years ago -when I first knew Smith and wife they lived in M. Curtis' house in Louther Street. After that they lived in the house of Simon Smith, and after that in the house of Geo. McCoy, and during all that time, the said Thomas lived and cohabited with the said Ann as his wife, and as such owned and acknowledged her, and they were deemed and reputed as man and wife by their acquaintances and neighbors they the said Smith and wife had children. Smith left his wife about eight years ago, since which time he has not returned, and for the last seven or eight years since the desertion of his wife by said Smith, she has had a family of small children to support. I know of no just or reasonable cause for said Smith leaving his wife. Sworn and Subscribed before me 24th November 1849." (signed Geo. Ege Commissioner and James Davis.)

Nov. 24, 1849 -"At the same time and place personally came Charles G. Murray who being duly sworn deposeth and saith that he has known Thomas Smith and Ann his wife for upwards of twelve years. That they lived and cohabited together as man and wife. That the said Ann was owned and acknowledged by the said Thomas as his wife and they were always deemed and reputed as man and wife by their acquaintances and neighbors. They have five small children when I knew them. I knew them when they lived in M. Curtis' house, Simon Smith's house and the house of Geo. McCoy. About seven or eight years ago, the said Smith deserted his said wife, without any just or reasonable cause known to the deponent and has continued such desertion ever since, never having returned since he left his wife and family, but leaving her all that time to support herself and little children. Sworn and subscribed before me 24th November 1849." (signed Geo. Ege and Charles G. Murray.) -Notation on the front of this document -"No. 27 April T. 1849 Ann Smith by her next friend etc. vs. Thomas Smith Filed 18 Decr. 1849."

Dec. 18, 1849 -"Ann Smith late Ann McKinney, by her next friend Philip Messersmith vs. Thomas Smith: In the Court of Common Pleas of Cumberland County No. 27 April Term 1849 -And now to wit the 18th December A.D. 1849 the Commissioner George Ege Esq. having returned to the Court here the depositions of witnesses taken before him on the part of the libellant, and the Court after mature deliberation, being satisfied therewith, and proclamation being duly made for the Respondant to come forth, and he not appearing the Court do order adjudge and decree that the said Ann Smith the Libellant, be divorced and separated from the bond of matrimony contracted with the said Thomas Smith the Respondant and that all and every the duties, rights and claims accruing to either of the said parties, by reason of the said marriage, shall henceforth cease and determine, and the said parties be severally at liberty to marry again in like manner as if they never had been married. By the Court." (signed Fred. Watts President Judge 18 Dec. 1849.) -Notation on the front of this document -"No. 27 April T. 1849 Smith etc. vs. Smith: Decree of Court."

◆ ◆ ◆

April Term 1849 #38 March 7, 1849 -"To the Honble. the Judges of the Court of Common Pleas of Cumberland County -The petition of Elinora Barron by her father and next friend George Wahl Respectfully Showeth -That your Libellant on the sixth day of November A.D. One thousand Eight hundred and forty seven was contracted in matrimony and married to a certain Joseph F. Barron and from that time until the sixth of March A.D. One thousand Eight hundred and forty nine, lived and cohabited with him as his wife, and as such was owned and acknowledged by him and so deemed and reputed by all her neighbours and acquaintances and although by the laws of God as well as by their mutual vows and faith plighted to each other they were reciprocally bound to that kindness and uniform regard which ought to be inseparable from the marriage state; yet so it is, that the said Joseph F. Barron did prior to the said sixth day of March A.D. 1849 offer such indignities to her person as to render her condition intolerable and life burdensome and thereby force her to withdraw from his house and family. Wherefore your libellant further showing that she is a citizen of this state and hath resided therein for one whole year and more previous to the filing of this petition prays your Honors that a subpoena shall issue from said Court directed to the said Joseph F. Barron, commanding him to appear at the next April term of the said Court to answer this petition, and also that a decree of the said Court may be made for the divorcing of him the said Joseph F. Barron from the society fellowship and company of this Libellant in all time to come, and she the Libellant from the marriage bond aforesaid, as if she had never been married or as if the said Joseph F. Barron were naturally dead. And she will pray etc." (signed Elinora Barron by her next friend George Wahl.) Cumberland County S.S. -The above named Elinora Barron being duly sworn, says that the facts contained in the above libel are true to the best of her knowledge and belief, and that the said complaint is not made out of levity and collusion between her, and the said Joseph F. Barron, and for the mere purpose of being freed and separated from each other, but in sincerity and truth for the causes mentioned in the said libel. Sworn and Subscribed before me this seventh day of March A.D. 1849." (signed Eleanora Barron and James J. Smith, J.P.) -"Subpoena awarded 9th March 1849." (signed

John Stuart.) -Notation on the front of this document -"No. 38 April T. 1849 E. Barron vs. J.F. Barron: Filed 9 March 1849."

March 9, 1849 -"Cumberland County SS -The Commonwealth of Pennsylvania the Sheriff of Cumberland County Greeting, Whereas, Elinora Barron by her father and next friend George Wahl did on the 9th day of March 1849 prefer her petition to the Honorable John Stuart Associate Judge of our Court of Common Pleas for the County of Cumberland, praying for the causes therein set forth, that she might be divorced from the bonds of matrimony entered into with you Joseph F. Barron. We do therefore command you, the said Joseph F. Barron, that setting aside all other business and excuses whatsoever, you be and appear in your proper person before our Judges at Carlisle at a Court of Common Pleas, there to be held for the County of Cumberland, on the 9th day of April next, to answer the petition or libel of the said Elinora Barron, your wife, should not be divorced from the bonds of matrimony agreeably to the Acts of General Assembly in such case made and provided. Hereof fail not. Witness the Honorable John Stuart and John Clendenin Associate Judges of our said Court at Carlisle the 9th day of March A.D. 1849." (signed Jas. F. Lamberton, Prothy.) -Notation on the front of this document -"No. 38 April Term 1849 Elinora Barron by her father and next friend George Wahl vs. Joseph F. Barron Subpoena Sur Divorce Feby. 9, 1849 Served personally and by copy So answers" (signed R. McCartny Dp. Shff. and James Hoffer Shff.) "Shff. Hoffer's fee $1.20 1/2. Biddle."

April 24, 1849 -"To the Honourable the Judges of the Court of Common Pleas of Cumberland County -The answer of Joseph F. Barron to the libel of Eleonora Barron by her father and next friend George Wahl praying for a divorce. The respondent saving and reserving to himself all manner of benefit and advantage of exception to the manifold untruths, incertainties and imperfections, in the said libel contained, for answer thereto or as much thereof as he is advised it is necessary to answer, admits, that the said Eleonora Barron was joined with this respondent in the holy bonds of matrimony on the ninth day of November A.D. one thousand eight hundred and forty seven, and not on the sixth day of November A.D. one thousand eight hundred and forty seven as the said Eleonora Barron has set forth in her libel. And this respondent protests that she the said libellant has not demeaned herself as a dutiful and loving wife, but by the indulgences of a violent temper has embittered his life. And the said respondent avers that he has always since the said marriage, conducted himself as a husband ought to do towards the said Eleonora Barron, and he wholly denies that he ever beat or abused the said Eleonora Barron, or by barbarous or cruel treatment, rendered her condition intolerable or life burdensome, or that he ever gave her cause, or obliged her to depart from his house, but he says, that the said Eleonora Barron left his house without any just cause. All of which matters and things this respondent is ready to verify, to maintain and prove, and humbly pleadeth the same in bar to the libel of the said Eleonora Barron, and prays that a jury may be called to enquire thereof, according to the forms of the several acts of Assembly in this behalf made and provided. April 24th 1849." (signed Joseph F. Barron.) -"Cumberland County, ss -Personally came before me a Justice of the Peace in and for the County of Cumberland and state of Pennsylvania, the above named Joseph F. Barron, who being duly sworn according to law, declared upon his solemn oath, that the statements in the foregoing answers made are true, to the best of his knowledge and belief. Sworn and subscribed before me this 24th day of April A.D. 1849." (signed Joseph F. Barron and Geo. Ege, Justice of the Peace.) -Notation on the front of this document -"No. 38 April T. 1849 Answer of Joseph F. Barron to the libel of Elonora Barron, in divorce Filed 25 April 1849."

Aug. 14, 1849 -"Cumberland County, SS. -The Commonwealth of Pennsylvania, to George L. Reighter, A.T. Green, Snyder Rupley, Charles Reighter, John Reighter, Catharine Beltzoover, Eliza Bell (colored), Thomas Humes, Ephraim Black Greeting: We command you, and each of you, that laying aside all business and excuses, you be and appear in your proper person before the Judges of the Court of Common Pleas, at Carlisle, at a Court of Common Pleas, there to be held for the county of Cumberland, the 27th day of August 1849 at 10 o'clock in the forenoon of that day, to testify all and singular, those things you shall know in a certain action of Divorce pending and undetermined between Elinora Barron by her father and next friend Geo. Wahl Plaintiff, and Joseph F. Barron Defendant (on the part of the Defendant). And this, you are not to omit under the penalty of One Hundred Pounds. Witness the Honorable Frederick Watts, at Carlisle, the 14th day August in the year of our Lord, one thousand eight hundred and forty-nine. (signed Jas. F. Lamberton, Prothonotary.) -Notation on the front of this document -"No. 38 April Term 1849 Barron vs. Barron: Subps. Aug. 24, 1849 Served on all the within named witnesses So answers" (signed R. McCartny.) "Shff. Hoffer's fee $2.08 1/2 25cts."

Jan. 19, 1850 -"Elinora Barron etc. vs. Jos. F. Barron: No. 38 April T. 1849 Plff. Witnesses at Jany. T. 1850 Paid Prothy L. -Majr. Sanno 2 days and 1 mile $1.31" -Notation on the front of this document -"No. 30 Apl. T. 1849 Barron etc. vs. Barron: M. Sanno wit. Filed 19 Jany 1850."

Jan. 15, 1850 -"Eleanora Barron vs. Jos. F. Barron: 38 April T. 1849 -Now to wit 15 Jan. 1850 the Jury having found for the plaintiff the Court do hereby order and decree that the said Eleanora Barron and the said Jos. F. Barron be divorced and separated from the nuptial ties or bonds of matrimony and all and every the duties rights and claims accruing to either of the said parties at any time heretofore in pursuance of the said marriage shall cease and determine and the said parties shall severally be at liberty to marry again as if they never had been married. And that judgement be entered in this issue for the costs of the same against the defendant. By the Court." (signed Fred. Watts.) -Notation on the front of this document -"No. 38 April T. 1849 Barron etc. vs. Barron: Decree of Court Filed 15 Jany 1850."

♦ ♦ ♦

August Term 1849 #84 June 5, 1849 -"To the Honorable the Judges of the Court of Common Pleas of Cumberland County. -The petition of Catharine Myers late Catharine Heavinger, by her father and next friend John Heavinger, respectfully showeth, That his daughter Catharine Heavinger was lawfully joined in wedlock, on the 19 day of March 1847, to George W. Myers, by the Rev. Mr. Kempfer; the said George W. Myers was thus both by the laws of God and man bound to cherish, protect and maintain the said Catharine, but on the contrary neglectful of his duty, he wilfully and maliciously and without any just cause, within one week after the solemnization of his nuptials, abandoned and deserted his wife, the said Catharine, and now since has wholly failed and refused to provide for and maintain her, the said Catharine, and thrown her upon her own resources. Your petitioner further represents that the said Catharine is a citizen of the State of Pennsylvania, and has been such for more than one year last past, and before the preparing of this petition. He therefore prays your Honor to award a subpoena sur Divorce against the said George W. Myers, commanding him to appear at the next August Term, to shew cause why the bonds of matrimony entered into with him by the said Catharine, should not be dissolved etc. and to extend to her all other the remedies provided in such case by the act of Assembly, and he will pray etc." (signed John Heavner.) -"Cumberland County sct. -Personally appeared before me the subscriber a Justice of the Peace in and for the said County, Catharine Myers, who being duly sworn according to law, says that the facts set forth in the above petition are true to the best of her knowledge and belief, and that her said complaint is not made out of levity or by collusion between her and her said husband, George W. Myers, and for the mere purpose of being freed and separated from each other, but in sincerity and truth for the causes mentioned in her said petition. Sworn and subscribed before me 5th June 1849." (signed Catharine Myers and M. Holcomb.) -Notation on the front of this document -"No. 84 August Term 1849 Petition of Catharine Myers by her father and next friend John Heavinger, for a divorce -Subpoena Awarded 6 Jan. 1849." (signed Fred. Watts -"Filed 6th June 1849."

August Term 1849 #84 June 7, 1849 -"Cumberland County SS

-The Commonwealth of Pennsylvania to the Sheriff of Cumberland County Greeting: Whereas Catharine Myers late Catharine Heavinger by her father and next friend John Heavinger did on the 6th day of June A.D. 1849 prefer a petition to our said Judges of our Court of Common Pleas for the County of Cumberland, praying for the causes therein set forth, that she might be divorced from the bonds of matrimony entered into with you the said Geo. W. Myers. We do therefore command you the said George W. Myers that setting aside all other business and excuses whatsoever, you be and appear in your proper person before our Judges at Carlisle, at a Court of Common Pleas there to be held for the County of Cumberland on the 27th day of August next, to answer the petition or libel of the said Catharine Myers and shew cause if any you have why the said Catharine Myers your wife, should not be divorced from the bonds of matrimony agreeably to the Acts of Assembly in such case made and provided. And hereof fail not. Witness the Honorable Frederk. Watts, President of our said Court at Carlisle the 7th day of June 1849." (signed Jas. F. Lamberton Prothy.)

Aug. 27, 1849 -"Cumberland County sct. -James Hoffer Esq. Sheriff of our said County being duly sworn according to law says that the defendant in this writ, is not to be found in his bailiwick. Sworn and Subscribed before me 27 Aug. 1849." (signed James Hoffer Shrff. and Jas. F. Lamberton Prothy.) -Notation on the front of this document -"No. 84 August Term 1849 Catharine Myers late Catharine Heavinger by her father and next friend John Heavinger vs. George W. Myers Subpoena Sur Divorce N.E.I. So answers" (signed James Hoffer Shff.) -"Shff. Hoffer's fee $0.18 3/4. Todd."

Sept. 18, 1849 -"Cumberland County SS -The Commonwealth of Pennsylvania to the Sheriff of Cumberland County Greeting: Whereas Catharine Myers late Catharine Heavinger by her father and next friend John Heavinger did on the 6th day of June A.D. 1849 prefer a petition to our said Judges of our Court of Common Pleas for the County of Cumberland praying for the causes therein set forth, that she might be divorced from the bonds of matrimony entered into with you the said Geo. W. Myers. We do therefore command you as we have heretofore commanded you the said George W. Myers that setting aside all other business and excuses whatsoever, you be and appear in your proper person before our Judges at Carlisle, at a Court of Common Pleas there to be held for the County of Cumberland, on the 12th day of November next, to answer the petition or libel of the said Catharine Myers and to shew cause if any you have why the said Catharine Myers your wife should not be divorced from the bonds of matrimony agreeably to the Acts of Assembly in such case made and provided -and hereof fail not. Witness the Honorable Frederick Watts President of our said Court at Carlisle the 18th day of September 1849." (signed Jas. F. Lamberton Prothy.)

Nov. 12, 1849 -"Cumberland County sct. -Robert McCartney Depy. Shff. being duly sworn according to law says that the respondent Geo. Myers is not to be found in Cumberland County. Sworn and subscribed before me 12 Nov 1849." (signed Jas. F. Lamberton Pro. and R. McCartny Dp. Shff.)

Jan. 14, 1850 -"Cumberland County sct. -David Smith Esq. Shff. being duly sworn according to law says that he caused notice of the within application to be published in one newspaper in Carlisle for four weeks successively, prior to this date, as directed by the order of Court. Sworn and subscribed before me 14 Jany. 1850" (signed Jas. F. Lamberton, Pro. and David Smith Shrff.) -Notation on the front of this document -"No. 84 August Term 1849 Catharine Myers late Catharine Heavinger by her father and next friend John Heavinger vs. George W. Myers 14 Jan. 1850 Michael Holcomb Esq. appointed Commissioner to take testimony and the 12 Feb. fixed for final hearing. By the Ct. Alias Subpoena Sur Divorce Non est inventus So answers" (signed James Hoffer Shff.) -"Writ advertised four weeks prior to 14 Jany. 1850. So answers" (signed David Smith Shrff.) -"Shff. Hoffer's fee $0.18 3/4 do S. $1.50 advertising. Todd."

Jan. 14, 1850 -"In the Court of Common Pleas of Cumberland County Catharine Myers late Catharine Heavinger by her father and next friend John Heavinger vs. George W. Myers: No. 84 August Term 1849 Subpoena Sur Divorce 14 Jany. 1850 Michael Holcomb Esq. appointed Commissioner to take testimony and the 12th Feby. fixed for final hearing. By the Court. -Cumberland County Sct. -I do certify that the above is a true extract taken from the records of said Court. In testimony whereof I have hereunto set my hand and seal of office at Carlisle the 7th day of January A.D. 1850." (signed Jas. F. Lamberton Prothy.) -Notation on the front of this document -"No. 84 August T. 1849 Myers etc. vs. Myers: M. Holcomb Esq. apptd. Com. Filed 12 Feby. 1850 Cumberland County ss. -I do certify that the depositions attached to this order of Court was taken before me this 12th February A.D. 1850. Costs 50cts. paid by L. Todd, Esq." (signed M. Holcomb Justice of the Peace.)

Jan. 28, 1850 -"In pursuance of the annexed commission to me directed, the following witnesses were examined to wit -William Wert being duly sworn according to law, says I am well acquainted with the Revd. J. Kempfer who now resides in the State of Maryland, I am also acquainted with his hand writing, having seen him write and having also corresponded with him. The Certificate of Marriage between George W. Myers and Catharine Heavener attached hereto and marked M.H. is to the best of my knowledge and belief in his hand writing. Sworn and subscribed before me 28th Jan. 1850." (signed M. Holcomb and William Wert.)

Jan. 28, 1850 -"Also at the same time and place, Michael Sanno, being duly sworn according to law, says, I am acquainted with the parties to this suit, immediately after the marriage of the parties, George W. Myers, maliciously and without any just cause deserted his wife and has not contributed anything towards her support ever since and that she has been dependent on her own exertions for support. Sworn and subscribed before me this 28th Jan. 1850." (signed M. Holcomb and Michael Sanno.)

Jan. 28, 1850 -"Also at the same time and place, Mrs. Margaret Miller, being duly sworn according to law says, I am acquainted with George W. Myers and Catharine his wife, shortly after their marriage he the said George maliciously abandoned her without any reasonable cause, and has never contributed anything towards her support, nor had any communication with her ever since, and the said Catharine has maintained herself during this time. Sworn and subscribed before me 28th Jan. 1850." (signe M. Holcomb J.P. and Mrs. Marget [sic] Miller.)

Jan. 28, 1850 -"Marriage Certificate -This is to certify that Mr. George W. Myer of Carlisle Cumberland County State of Pennsylvania and Miss Catharine Hevener of the same place, were lawfully jointed together in holy wedlock, on the nineteenth day of March, in the year of our Lord one thousand eight hundred and forty seven. May the God of all grace enable you faithfully to fulfil the solemn covenant made in his presence, and after having lived together in a state of holy joy and pious friendship, may you meet in heaven in perfect happiness never to be terminated." (signed J. Kaempffer Minister of the Ev. Luth. Church, Carlisle.) -" (M.H.) -"Notation on the front of this document -"Mrs. Catharine Myer, Carlisle with No. 84 Aug. 1849"

Feb. 12, 1850 -"Catharine Myers by her father and next friend Jno. Heavner vs. George W. Myers: No. 84 Aug. T. 1849 -Subpoena sur divorce -And now to with 12th February 1850, Michael Holcomb the Commissioner in this case, having returned to the Court here the depositions of witnesses taken before him on the part of the libellant, and the same being read and heard by the Court, and the Court after mature deliberation being satisfied therewith, and proclamation being duly made for the respondent to come forth, and he not appearing, the Court do order, adjudge and decree that the said Catharine Myers, the libellant, be divorced and separated from the bond of matrimony contracted with the said George W. Myers, the respondent, and that all and every the duties, rights and claims accruing to either of the said parties by reason of the said marriage, shall henceforth cease and determine, and the said parties be severally at liberty to marry again, in like manner as if they never had been married: and further that the respondent pay the costs of these proceedings. By the Court." (signed Fred. Watts President.) -Notation on the front of this document -"No. 84 August T. 1849 Myers vs. Myers: Decree of the Court Filed 12 Feby 1850. Todd.)

♦ ♦ ♦

August Term 1849 #118 -July 5, 1849 -"To the Honourable Fredk. Watts President Judge of the Court of Common Pleas for the County of Cumberland -The libel of Edatha Woodley by her next friend David Webster Respectfully showeth, That your libellant on the thirty first day of January, in the year of our Lord one thousand eight hundred and forty was bound in matrimony, and married to a certain Edmond Woodley, and from that time until the twenty fourth day of June in the year of our Lord one thousand eight hundred and forty six lived and cohabited with the said Edmond Woodley as her husband, and as such was owned and acknowledged by their neighbours and acquaintances. And although by the laws of God, as well as by their mutual vows and faith plighted to each other, they were bound to that uniform constancy and regard which ought to be inseparable from the marriage state, yet so it is, that the said Edmond Woodley, the said parties being domiciled within the Commonwealth of Pennsylvania from the (left blank) day of November in the year of our Lord one thousand eight hundred and forty two, hath wilfully and maliciously deserted and absented himself from the habitation, society and fellowship of this libellant without any just or reasonable cause, and still hath persisted in such desertion for the term of two years and upwards, and still doth continue to absent himself from the said libellant. Wherefore your libellant further showing that she is a citizen of the state of Pennsylvania and has resided therein for upwards of one whole year previous to the filing of this her libel, prays your Honor that a subpoena may issue forth to summon the said Edmond Woodley to appear at the said Court of Common Pleas at the August Term next, to answer her complaint aforesaid. And also, that this honorable Court may decree a decree of divorce and a separation from the said nuptial ties or bonds of matrimony, hereunto uniting, as above mentioned, this libellant to and with the said Edmond Woodley and she will pray etc." (signed Edatha Woodley by her next friend David Webster.) -"Cumberland County ss -Edatha Woodley within named personally appeared before me the subscriber a Justice of the Peace in and for the county aforesaid, and being by me first duly sworn saith that the facts set forth in the foregoing petition are true to the best of her knowledge and belief, and that the said complaint is not made out of levity and collusion between the petitioner and the said Edmond Woodley, and for the mere purpose of being freed and separated from each other, but in sincerity and truth, and for the causes mentioned in the above petition. Sworn and subscribed before me this 5th day of July A.D. 1849." (signed Geo. Ege and Edille (sic) Woodley -Notation on the front of this document -"No. 118 August T. 1849 Filed 11 July 1849 Subpoena Awarded." (signed Fred. Watts 10 July 1849.)

August Term 1849 #118 July 11, 1849 -"Cumberland County SS -The Commonwealth of Pennsylvania to the Sheriff of Cumberland County Greeting: Whereas Edatha Woodley by her next friend David Webster did on the 10th day of July A.D. 1849 prefer a petition to our said Judges of the Court of Common Pleas, for the County of Cumberland, praying for the causes therein set forth, that she might be divorced from the bonds of matrimony entered into with you the said Edmond Woodley. We do therefore command you the said Edmond Woodley, that setting aside all other business and excuses whatsoever, you be and appear in your proper person before our Judges, at Carlisle, at a Court of Common Pleas, there to be held for the County of Cumberland on the 27th day of August next to answer the petition or libel of the said Edatha Woodley and to shew cause if any you have, why the said Edatha Woodley, your wife should not be divorced from the bonds of matrimony agreeably to the Acts of Assembly in such case made and provided. And hereof fail not. Witness the Honorable Frederick Watt, President of our said Court, at Carlisle the 11th day of July A.D. 1849." (signed Jas. F. Lamberton Prothy.)

Aug. 28, 1849 -"Cumberland County ss -Robert McCartny Deputy Sheriff of said county being duly sworn deposes and says that the foregoing return that the defendant was now not residing in town to the best of his knowledge and belief. Sworn and subscribed before me 28 Aug. 1849." (signed Jas. F. Lamberton Prothy. and R. McCartny.) -Notation on the front of this document -"No. 118 August T. 1849 Edatha Woodley by her next friend David Webster vs. Edmond Woodley Subpoena Sur Divorce N.E.I. So answers" (signed James Hoffer Shff.) "Shrff. Hoffer's fee $0.18 3/4. Bonham."

July 11, 1849 -"Cumberland County SS -The Commonwealth of Pennsylvania to the Sheriff of Cumberland County Greeting: Whereas Edatha Woodley by her next friend David Webster did on the 10th day of July A.D. 1849 prefer a petition to our said Judges of our Court of Common Pleas, for the County of Cumberland, praying for the causes therein set forth, that she might be divorced from the bonds of matrimony entered into with you the said Edmond Woodley. We do therefore command you the said Edmond Woodley, that setting aside all other business and excuses whatsoever, you be and appear in your proper person before our Judges at Carlisle, at a Court of Common Pleas, there to be held for the County of Cumberland on the 27th day of August next to answer the petition or libel of the said Edatha Woodley and to shew cause if any you have, why the said Edatha Woodley, your wife should not be divorced from the bonds of matrimony agreeably to the Acts of Assembly in such case made and provided. And hereof fail not. Witness the Honorable Frederick Watts, President of our said Court, at Carlisle the 11th day of July A.D. 1849." (signed Jas. F. Lamberton Prothy.)

Aug. 28, 1849 -"Cumberland County ss -Robert McCartney Deputy Sheriff of said county being duly sworn deposes and says that the foregoing return that the defendant was non est inventus is true to the best of his knowledge and belief. Sworn and subscribed before me 28 Aug. 1849." (signed Jas. F. Lamberton Prothy. and R. McCartny.) -Notation on the front of this document -"No. 118 August T. 1849 Edatha Woodley by her next friend David Webster vs. Edmond Woodley Subpoena Sur Divorce N.E.I. So answers" (signed James Hoffer Shff.) -"Shff. Hoffer's fee $0.18 3/4. Bonham."

Sept. 3, 1849 -"Cumberland County SS -The Commonwealth of Pennsylvania to the Sheriff of Cumberland County Greeting: Whereas Edatha Woodley by her next friend David Webster did on the 10th day of July A.D. 1849 prefer a petition to our said Judges of our Court of Common Pleas for the County of Cumberland praying for the causes therein set forth that she might be divorced from the bonds of matrimony entered into with you the said Edmond Woodley. We do therefore command you the said Edmond Woodley as we have heretofore commanded you, that setting aside all business and excuses whatsoever you be and appear in your proper person before our Judges at a Court of Common Pleas there to be held for the County of Cumberland on the 12th day of November next, to answer the petition or libel of the said Edatha Woodley, your wife and to shew cause if any you have why the said Edatha Woodley your wife should not be divorced from the bonds of matrimony agreeably to the acts of Assembly in such case made and provided. And hereof fail not. Witness the Honorable Frederick Watts President, of our said Court at Carlisle the 3d September A.D. 1849." (signed Jas. F. Lamberton Prothy.)

Nov. 5, 1850 -"Cumberland County ss -Personally appeared before me the subscriber a Justice of the Peace in and for said County Robert McCartny, late deputy Sheriff, who being duly sworn according to law deposes and says that the foregoing return that the defendant was non est inventus is true to the best of his knowledge and belief. Sworn and subscribed before me this 5th day of Nov. 1850." (signed R. McCartny and Stephen Keepers.) -Notation on the front of this document -"No. 118 August T. 1849 Edatha Woodley by her next friend David Webster vs. Edmond Woodley Alias Subpoena Sur Divorce Non est inventus So answers" (signed James Hoffer Shff.) "Shff. Hoffer's fee $0.43 3/4. Bonham."

Nov. 11, 1850 -"Edatha Woodley by her next friend David Webster vs. Edmond Woodley: No. 118 Aug. T. 1849. Subpoena sur Divorce On motion of Mr. Bonham, proof having been made on the return of the subpoena and alias subpoena, that the said Edmond Woodley could not be found. It is hereby ordered that notice be given by the sheriff by publication in one newspaper in the borough of Carlisle, for four weeks sucessively, to the said Edmond Woodley, agreeably to the act of Assembly, to appear on the 17th day of December 1850, to answer the complaint of the said Edatha Woodley. Nov. 11th 1850. By the Court." -Notation on the front of this document -"No. 118 August T. 1849 Filed 11 Nov. 1850."

Dec. 17, 1850 -"Edatha Woodley by her next friend vs. Edmond Woodley: No. 118 Aug. T. 1849 On proof of publication of motion by Sheriff in accordance with the order of Court, on motion of Mr. Bonham A.L. Sponsler Esq. appointed Commissioner to take depositions on the part of the Complainant, exparte. Dec. 17th 1850. By the Court." -Notation on the front of this document -"No. 118 Aug. T. 1849 Filed 17 Decr. 1850"

Dec. 28, 1850 -"Cumberland County SS -I James F. Lamberton Prothonotary of the Court of Common Pleas of said County do certify that the above is true extract taken from the records of said Court. In testimony whereof I have hereunto set my hand and affixed the seal of said Court at Carlisle this 28th day of December A.D. 1850." (signed Jas. F. Lamberton Prothy.) -Notation on the front of this document -"No. 118 August T. 1849 Woodley vs. Woodley."

Jan. 2, 1851 -"In persuance of the foregoing order of Court in the matter of an application of Edatha Woodley against Edmund Woodley for a divorce the following witnesses were produced sworn and examined on the part of the Complaintant. Cumberland County SS -Margery Holly being duly sworn according to law deposes and says I have known Edmund Woodley and Edatha Woodley some six or seven years. They lived together as man and wife up until the time Mr. Woodley left Carlisle about four years ago. They were living at the Carlisle Barracks. Edmund Woodley told me before he left that he did not intend to do anything more for his wife Edatha Woodley. That he had another wife in Canada to whom he was going and that he would not live with his present wife any longer. Edmund Woodley went away a few days after this conversation occurred and has not lived with her since. I do not know where Edmund Woodley now resides. I have frequently heard both Edmund Woodley and Edatha Woodley say that they were man and wife. Editha (sic) Woodley has lived in Carlisle ever since Edmond Woodley left her, further deponent saith not. Sworn and subscribed before me this 2d day of January 1851." (signed Margery Holly and A. L. Sponsler J.P.)

August Term 1849 #118 Jan. 2, 1851 -"The following Marriage Certificate was produced before me by the complainant which is hereto attached marked (A). State of Michigan Wayne County: To whom it may concern -I hereby certify that on the 31st day of January 1840 at Dearborn in said County Edmund Woodley of the Army of the United States aged 24 years and Editha Leger of said County aged 18 years united by me in the bonds of matrimony. Given under my hand at Dearborn this 31st day of January 1840." (signed Thomas M. Sweeny Justice of Peace.)

Jan. 2, 1851 -"David Webster being duly sworn deposes and says I have known Editha Woodley for 3 years past during which time Edmund Woodley has not been living with her. During said time she has been living in Carlisle and at the Carlisle Barracks and is at present residing in the Borough of Carlisle. Sworn and subscribed before me the 2d day of January 1851." (signed David Webster and A.L. Sponsler J.P.)

Jan. 2, 1851 -"Cumberland County ss -I do certify that the foregoing depositions were duly taken before me a Commissioner appointed by the Court to take depositions on the part of the Complaintant in an application on part of complainant for a divorce suit No. 118 Aug. Term 1849 in the Court of Common Pleas of Cumberland County as appears by the order of the court hereto prefixed all of which is respectfully submitted as witness my hand and seal at my office in Carlisle the 2d day of Jan. 1851." (signed A.L. Sponsler J.P.) -Notation on the front of this document -"No. 118 August T. 1849 Filed 13 Jany. 1851 Commissioner's costs for taking Depositions -50 cts. paid by Complainent."

Jan. 13, 1851 -"And now to wit, January 1851, The Examiner Alfred L. Sponsler Esqr. having returned to Court hire (sic) the depositions of Depositions (sic -apparently error for "witnesses") taken before him on the part of the libellant and the same being read and heard by the Court, after mature deliberation, the Court being satisfied therewith do order and decree that the said Edatha Woodley, the libellant be divorced and separated from the bonds of matrimony contracted with Edmond Woodley the respondent and that all and every the duties rights and claims accruing to either of the parties be severally at liberty to marry again in like manner as though they had never been married. The Court do further award costs to the said Editha Woodley according to the acts of assembly in such case made and provided. By the Court." (signed Fred. Watts Prot. 13 Jan. 1851.) -Notation on the front of this document -"No. 118 August T. 1849 Woodley vs. Woodley: Decree Filed 13 Jany. 1851."

◆   ◆   ◆

November Term 1849 #1 Aug. 30, 1849 -"To the Hon. the Judges of the Court of Common Pleas of Cumberland County -The petition of Elizabeth O'Sullivan by her next friend John Brannon Respectfully represents That your petitioner on the 9th day Jany. Eighteen hundred and forty four was lawfully joined in marriage with Timothy O'Sullivan and from that time till the 14th day of July 1849 lived and cohabited with the said O'Sullivan as his wife and was owned and acknowledged by him and so reputed by all her acquaintances and although by the laws of God and their mutual vows they were bound to each other to that regard which ought to be inseparable from the married state, yet the said Timothy O'Sullivan has offered such indignities to the person of your petitioner as to render her condition intolerable and life burdensome; and therefore was she compelled to abandon him. Your Libellant showing moreover that she is a citizen of the State of Pennsylvania and has resided in said state more than one year before the filing of this her libel prays your Honors that a subpoena issue to summon the said Timothy O'Sullivan to appear in this Honorable Court at November Term next to answer this complaint and that a decree may be made to divorce the said Timothy from the society and company of this Libellant forever, and her the said Libellant, from the marriage bond aforesaid as though they had never been married or as if he were naturally dead. And this Libellant will pray etc." (signed Elizabeth O'Sullivan by her next friend John Brannon.) -"Cumberland County SS -The above named Elizabeth O'Sullivan being duly sworn says that the facts contained in the above libel are true to the best of her knowledge and belief and that this complaint is not made out of levity and collusion between her and the said Timothy O'Sullivan and for the mere purpose of being separated from each other, but in sincerity and truth for the causes mentioned in the said Libel. Sworn and subscribed before me this 30th day of August 1849." (signed Elizabeth O'Sullivan and Geo. Ege. Justice of the Peace.) -Notation on the front of this document -"No. 1 November Term 1849 Elizabeth O'Sullivan by her next friend John Brannon vs. Timothy O'Sullivan Libel in Divorce Subpoena awarded By the Court 30 Aug. 1849 Filed 30th Aug. 1849. Adair."

Aug. 30, 1849 -"Cumberland County SS -The Commonwealth of Pennsylvania to the Sheriff of Cumberland County Greeting: Whereas Elizabeth O'Sullivan by her next friend John Brannon on the 30th day of August A.D. 1849 did prefer a petition to our said Judges of our Court of Common Pleas for the County of Cumberland, praying for the causes therein set forth that she might be divorced from the bonds of matrimony entered into with you Timothy O'Sullivan. We do therefore command you the said Timothy O'Sullivan that setting aside all other business and excuses whatsoever you be and appear in your proper person, before our Judges, at Carlisle at a Court of Common Pleas, there to be held for the County of Cumberland on the 12th day of November next, to answer the petition or libel of the said Elizabeth O'Sullivan and to show cause if any you have why the said Elizabeth O'Sullivan your wife, should not be divorced from bonds of matrimony, agreeably to the acts of Assembly in such case made and provided. And hereof fail not. Witness the Honorable Frederick Watts President of our said Court, at Carlisle the 30th day of August A.D. 1849." (signed Jas. F. Lamberton, Prothy.)

Nov. 12, 1849 -"Cumberland Co. S.S. -Robert McCartney Deputy Shff. being duly sworn says that the within subpoena was served personally and by copy on Timothy O'Sullivan on the 6th Sept. 1849.

Sworn and subscribed before me 12th Novr. 1849" (signed R. McCartney Dp. Shff.) -Notation on the front of this document -"No. 1 November Term 1849 Elizabeth O'Sullivan by her next friend John Brannon vs. Timothy O'Sullivan Subpoena Sur Divorce Sept. 6, 1849 Served personally and by copy So answers" (signed R. McCartney Dp. Shff. and James Hoffer Shff.) "Shff. Hoffer's fee $1.20 1/2 Adair."

Nov. 12, 1849 -"In the Court of Common Pleas for Cumberland County Elizabeth O'Sullivan by her next friend etc. vs. Timothy O'Sullivan: Subpoena sur Divorce The said Elizabeth O'Sullivan the libellant, now to the Court respectfully represents that a subpoena sur divorce was awarded to her against Timothy O'Sullivan by this Honble. Court to wit No. 1 Nov. T. 1849 which said subpoena was by the Sheriff of Cumberland County returned on oath to the said Court, on Monday the 12th day of November 1849 that the same "was served personally and by copy on Timothy O'Sullivan on the 6th Sept. 1849" as by the record of said Court appears. She therefore prays your Honors to appoint an examiner to take the depositions of witnesses to be read on the hearing of the said subpoena Novr. 12 1849." (signed Elizabeth O'Sullivan.)

Nov. 13, 1849 -"Now to wit, 13th Novr. 1849 the Court appoints Geo. Ege Esq. an examiner to take depositions as prayed for, he to make return of the same to this court on Tuesday the 18 Dec. 1849. Due notice of the time and place of taking the same to be given to the respondent." -Notation on the front of this document -"No. 1 Novr. T. 49 Elizabeth O'Sullivan by her next friend etc. vs. Timothy O'Sullivan Petition of Libellant for Commissioner to take depositions Filed 13 Nov. 1849. Adair."

November Term 1849 #1 Nov. 13, 1849 -"In the Court of Common Pleas of Cumberland County Elizabeth O'Sullivan by her next friend John Brannon vs. Timothy O'Sullivan: No. 1 Nov. Term 1849 Subpoena Sur Divorce 13 Nov. 1849 Petition of Libellant for Commissioner filed Nov. 13, 1849 on motion of Mr. Adair and proof of the service of the writ on Deft. Geo. Ege Esq. appointed an examiner to take the depositions as prayed for, to make return of the same to this court on Tuesday the 18th Decr. 1849 Due notice of the time and place of taking the same to be given to the respondent, By the Court." -"Cumberland County SS -I do certify that the above is a true extract taken from the records of the Court of Common Pleas of said County. In testimony whereof I have hereunto set my hand and the seal of office at Carlisle the 19 day of November A.D. 1849." (signed Jas. F. Lamberton Prothy.)

Nov. 23, 1849 -"To Timothy O'Sullivan You are hereby notified that depositions to be read on the above case will be taken by virtue of the above decree of the Court before Geo. Ege Esq. The Examiner appointed by said Court on Friday the 14th day of December next, between the hours of two and five o'clock P.M., in the jail of Cumberland County November 23rd 1849." (signed S.D. Adair Atty. for libellant.)

Dec. 15, 1849 -"Cumberland Co. SS -David Smith Shff. of Cumberland Co. being duly sworn says he served a copy of the within decree of the Court together with a copy of the certificate of the prothy and a copy of the notice to take depositions on Timothy O'Sullivan on Friday the 23d day Novr. 1849 Sworn and subscribed before me this 15 Decr. 1849." (signed Geo. Ege J.P. and David Smith Shff.) -Notation on the front of this document -"No. 1 November T. 1849 Geo. Ege Esq. appointed examiner etc. O'Sullivan vs. O'Sullivan: Commr. to take depositions Subp. in divorce Nov. 23d 1849 Served personally and by copy So answers" (signed David Smith Shrff.) Shff. Smith's fee $0.83."

Dec. 6, 1849 -"Cumberland County, SS. -The Commonwealth of Pennsylvania to Leah Wise, John Gillen, T.P. Dwen, Joseph Shrom, Elizabeth Lisbon Greeting: We command you, and each of you, that laying aside all business and excuse, you be and appear in your proper persons before George Ege Esq. a Commissioner appointed by the Court of Common Pleas of said county, on Friday, the 14th day of December at the Carlisle jail between the hours of 2 and 5 o'clock in the afternoon of that day, to testify and give evidence on behalf of the libellant in a certain action of divorce, pending in the Court of Common Pleas of Cumberland County in which E. O'Sullivan is the libellant and T. O'Sullivan respondent. Herein fail not, on pain of One Hundred Dollars each. Witness the said George Ege, Esquire, at Carlisle, the 6th day of Dec. A.D. 1849." (signed Geo. Ege.)

Dec. 14, 1849 -"By virtue of the foregoing dunn of the Court of Common Pleas of Cumberland County, in the matter of the application for a Divorce from the bonds of matrimony by Elizabeth O'Sullivan against Timothy O'Sullivan I George Ege Esq. appointed examiner to take depositions on the part of the libellant, do make the following return, that on Friday the fourteenth day of December A.D. 1849, appeared before me, the following witnesses, between the hours of two and five P.M. in the jail of Cumberland County to testify on the part of the libellant -John Gillen being sworn, says, I have known Elizabeth O'Sullivan for twenty years and upwards, she was the widow of John Dwen, when she married Timothy O'Sullivan, according to the best of my knowledge. They have been married four or five years, the Revd. McMahn told me he had married them. McMahn is a priest of the Catholic Church, and was then. I don't know what the conduct of T. O'Sullivan was to his wife and all I know is from hearsay. From hearsay the conduct of O'Sullivan to his wife, was very bad, indeed, that he abused her very much and called her very bad names, if what I heard be true, it would render her life intolerable. I know that Timothy O'Sullivan and Elizabeth his wife, near lived together, as man and wife, from the time of their marriage, untill O'Sullivan was sent to prison, by the Court of Quarter Sessions of Cumberland County. I heard different persons say that O'Sullivan treated his wife badly, I heard your own wife say. Mr. O'Sullivan asked John Gillen, whether he had not been responsible for bringing suit against his wife for slander on these same grounds. The question was ruled as not being pertinent. I have known Mrs. O'Sullivan from the time I was trustee for her, to have a propensity to run in debts beyond her means. Question by O'Sullivan -Do you know whether my wife, was One hundred dollars in debts, at the time I married her. I don't know whether or not. The libellant will, for sake of stopping an investigation which is improper, admit that Mrs. Dwen, at the time of her marriage to O'Sullivan, was indebted to the amount of one hundred dollars, but adds at the same time, that O'Sullivan had nothing, neither not was personal, out of which, to pay the same, that the libellant is seized and possessed of real estate, from the proceeds of which, the respondent has lived and dispersed of the proceeds thereof, from the time of the marriage, untill the institution of these proceedings. The libellant objects, to any examination, of the amounts between the parties, as they are now in court." (signed John Gillen.)

Dec. 14, 1849 -"T. P. Dwen, sworn, says, O'Sullivan objects to the testimony of Dwen, because he is interested. T. O'Sullivan and Mrs. Dwen the libellant, were married in Harrisburg in January A.D. 1844, to the best of my knowledge, by the Revd. McMahn. I was in Harrisburg at the time, but was not present at the marriage. I went down with them from Carlisle, they came back to O'Donnely, when they staid (sic), and there they said they were married. O'Sullivan since their marriage was in the habit of coming home drunk, and whipped his wife, blackened her eyes, and punished her, untill she was black and blue. I saw him whip her, with his fists, and was still beating her, when I interfered. Such conduct has been carried on towards her since about ten months after they were married. I was absent seven or eight months, and during that time, I know nothing about it. O'Sullivan's conduct to his wife, has been such as to render her life burthensome and her condition intolerable. He not only saw her beaten black and blue several times, but O'Sullivan did not even bring enough to support her." (signed Thomas P. Dwen.)

Dec. 14, 1849 -"Leah Wise, sworn, say I lived with Mrs. O'Sullivan more than one year. When O'Sullivan came home, he would run through the house and throw himself on the floor. He sometimes bullied his wife, hit her with his fists and pulled her by the nose, he blackened her face and eyes, more than once, he called her hard names, his wife had to run out of the house. When he beat her, she ran out into the entry, when Mrs. O'Sullivan was in bed, he brought a pistol up and said he was going to get it fixed, he was drunk then, then he ran down, it was after Mrs. O'Sullivan was in bed, I was in the same room with Mrs. O'Sullivan one night he came home. Mrs. O'Sullivan lighted the candle for him, and he threw himself on the bed. Mrs. O'Sullivan said she was going to leave him. O'Sullivan then said, he would put an end to her before that. Mrs. O'Sullivan went that night to Mrs. Carney, she took the youngest child with her, the other child was in bed with him. I went with Mrs. O'Sullivan and staid (sic) with her. I went after Thomas, Mrs. O'Sullivan sent me for him. He went with us to Mr. Carney, it was eleven or twelve o'clock at night. Mrs. O'Sullivan was afraid that O'Sullivan was following me, and I am about ten years old. I took the pistol to the room where Mrs. O'Sullivan sleeps, that was our sleeping room. I was sleeping when he came into the room. I saw you strike Mrs. O'Sullivan in the face. We had enough of bread but not enough of meat, sometimes enough and sometimes not, he brought meat home when he went to market." (not signed by Leah Wise.)

November Term 1849 #1 Dec. 14, 1849 -Joseph Shrom, sworn, deposeth and saith, that on the ninth day of January 1844, Timothy O'Sullivan and his wife were married. For sometime after they were married, he treated her as well as a woman should be treated by a man, but directly after he got matters into his own hands, I saw a good shot of a change. He seemed very surly, kept on in that way for some time. Thomas Dwen came into house one evening after dark, and told me to come in quick, that O'Sullivan was killing his mother. I got up from my supper, I went in, Mrs. O'Sullivan was crying, O'Sullivan was in a great possession. I asked them what was the matter, O'Sullivan said, he had ordered Tom out of the room, he struck down with his right hand, and said, that (illegible word) of mine said, he should not go. Mrs. O'Sullivan told him that Thomas had as good a right in the room as he had. O'Sullivan said he had no right there at all, O'Sullivan then said that he wanted to put him out the room, and said that heroine of mine, pointing to his wife, said he should not put him out. His wife then said that O'Sullivan had struck her. O'Sullivan said he did not strike her, that he only pushed her from him. She then said that he did strike her, and he said he did not. O'Sullivan said he would show how he had done it, he said he had took her by the arms, behind her back, and pushed her with his right hand, up against the wall. They still went on sparring for some time, there was then another rumpus in the house. I saw her, I think, the very next day after, one of her eyes was very black. I asked her if she had been at an Irish wedding. She said it was O'Sullivan had struck her and blackened her eyes. Sometime after that they had another tarrup, when both her eyes were as black as they would be. I live adjoining, nothing but a fine (illegible word). Mrs. O'Sullivan would not make her appearance as on the street, for two weeks, they went on pretty much in the same rough way, untill the 28th of October 1847. He then beat her unmercifully that night. Next morning, she went up to Esquire Smith's to bind him over. She stopped as she came back at my door. She was crying, she said the Squire would not give her law. Her right eye was very black, the left eye was black on the under side just above the right eye, on the forehead, there was a visible stroke. On the right cheek there was another visible stroke. On the left jaw there was another visible stroke. She told me to only feel her head, she said just feel my head. I drew my right hand down over the left side of her head. I would compare it to nothing else, than drawing my hand over a bag of apples, or a bag of potatoes, from the lumps that was on it. I told her to come along with me. We went to Squire Smith's and had him bound over and sentenced into recognizance, she went to the country, I think the same day. She said she could live with him no longer. She staid (sic) in the country three or four days. A short time after, she came home she took him back. She was confined to her bed, somewhere in the neighbourhood of three months. Since that I don't know that he struck her at all, but they lived a very rough life for man and wife. About a month or six weeks, after she was able to go about, the child was born. From after the child was born his conduct was very bad. His wife dare not speak to my wife across the fence for want he would bullyrag her, saying they were talking about him. The conduct of O'Sullivan to his wife, without entering into particulars, was such as to render her life uncomfortable and unhappy in the extreme. I have heard her say frequently that she had a notion to put an end to herself to put herself out of his mark. From the time he got matters into his own hands his bad conduct towards her commenced and continued untill he was commited to prison or untill she left him. From what I know of him, she could not live with him with happiness or safety to herself. Cross examined by O'Sullivan. I was not present at their marriage. I was twice in their house. I never saw O'Sullivan strike his wife. It was from her situation and what she told me that I knew O'Sullivan had abused her these different times her eyes were blackened. The room that the fighting was in had a bed in it and there was fire in the stove. Tom went into the fire and O'Sullivan ordered or put him out. I don't know whether there was a fire in the other room or not, I was not in it. I don't know what was the matter with Mrs. O'Sullivan when she was sick, but it was immediately after she got the beating. Mrs. O'Sullivan's face is very much marked with the small pox, it is raised around the lower part of her face or around her jaws. O'Sullivan and myself are not on friendly terms but the families are as intimate as they were ever." (signed Joseph Shrom.)

Dec. 14, 1849 -"Elizabeth Leyman, sworn, deposeth and saith, that my parents lived five years in the house where O'Sullivan lived, and I lived one year. It is six years since we first moved into the house. It is the same house that O'Sullivan lived in during the time, during all that time he would come in drunk. I heard him several times scolding his wife. One evening I was upstairs I heard a great noise. That same night I saw that Mrs. O'Sullivan had a black eye, bruised in the face. O'Sullivan's conduct to his wife, from what I saw and heard, was very bad." Cross examined by O'Sullivan "We overheard the two back rooms up stairs. I did not see O'Sullivan come in after bed time, but I heard him come in. I don't know whether there was sufficient in the house for food or not. I once or twice eat (sic) at their lath, there was enough. Mrs. O'Sullivan's temper is good enough, but she is passionate when people want to tramp upon her." (signed by her mark Elizabeth Leyman.)

Dec. 14, 1849 -"Cumberland County ss, I do certify, that the foregoing depositions were taken before me, at the Carlisle jail on Friday the fourteenth day of December 1849. The witnesses all having been sworn and examined in presence of Timothy O'Sullivan the respondent and L.D. Adair attorney for the libellant." (signed Geo. Ege Examiner.) "Examiner's costs $3.34."

Dec. 18, 1849 -"E. O'Sullivan by her next friend etc. vs. Timothy O'Sullivan: Sub. sur divorce Now, to wit Decr. 18th 1849, the examiner Geo. Ege having returned to Court here the depositions of witnesses taken before him on the part of the libellant and the same being read and heard by the Court, after mature deliberation the Court being satisfied therewith Do order and decree that the said Elizabeth O'Sullivan the libellant be divorced and separated from the bond of matrimony contracted with Timothy O'Sullivan the respondent and that all and every the duties rights and claims accruing to either of the parties by reason of said marriage shall henceforth cease and determine and the said parties be severally at liberty to marry again in like manner as though they had never been married. The Court do further award costs to the said Elizabeth according to the Acts of Assembly in such case made and provided. By the Court." (signed Fred. Watts 18 Decr. 1849) -Notation on the front of this document -"No. 1 November Term 1849 E. O'Sullivan by her next friend etc. vs. T. O'Sullivan Report of Examiner Filed 18 Decr. 1849."

◆ ◆ ◆

April Term 1850 #2 Jan. 10, 1850 -"To the Honorable the Judges of the Court of Common Pleas of Cumberland County. The petition of Caroline Eichelberger by her next friend Peter Sipe Respectfully represents that your petitioner was on the (left blank) day of September 1843 lawfully joined in marriage with Levi Eichelberger. He from that time, for a period of a few weeks lived and cohabited with her, and demeaned himself in all respects as a kind and affectionate husband, and although by the laws of God, as well as by the mutual vows plighted to each other to that constancy and uniform regard, which ought to be inseparable from the marriage state, yet the said

Levi in violation of his marriage vow, hath wilfully and maliciously deserted and absented himself from your petitioner without reasonable cause, and has contributed nothing towards her maintenance and support from that time until the present; being a period of more than six years. Wherefore your petitioner being a resident of the said County of Cumberland for the last six years and upwards, prays your Honors that a subpoena may issue in due form of law, directed to the said Levi Eichelberger commanding him to appear at the next Court of Common Pleas, for said County to answer your petioner's libel, and shew cause if any he has why, your said petitioner shall not be divorced from the bond of matrimony etc. And she will pray etc." (signed by her mark Caroline Eichelberger.) -"Cumberland County ss -The above named Caroline Eichelberger being duly sworn, doth depose and say, that the facts contained in the above petition are true to the best of her knowledge and belief and that said complaint is not made out of any levity, or collusion between her and the said Levi Eichelberger for the purpose of being freed and separated from each other, but in sincerity and truth for the causes mentioned in said petition or libel. Sworn and subscribed before me this 10th day of January 1850." (signed Thos. Craighead Jr. Justice of the Peace and Caroline Eichelberger by her mark.) -Notation on the front of this document -"No. 2 April T. 1850 Subpoena awarded by the Court returnable first day of next term 14 Jan. 1850 Filed 14 Jany. 1850 Hepburn."

Jan. 14, 1850 -"Cumberland County SS -The Commonwealth of Pennsylvania to the Sheriff of Cumberland County Greeting -Whereas Caroline Eichelberger by her next friend Peter Sipe did on the 14th day of January 1850 prefer a petition to our said Judges of our Court of Common Pleas for the county of Cumberland praying for the causes therein set forth, that she might be divorced from the bonds of matrimony entered into with you Levi Eichelberger. We do therefore command you, the said Levi Eichelberger that, setting aside all other business and excuses whatsoever, you be and appear in your proper person before our Judges at Carlisle, at a Court of Common Pleas there to be held for the County of Cumberland, on the 8th day of April next, to answer the petition or libel of the said Caroline Eichelberger and to shew cause if any you have why the said Caroline Eichelberger your wife, should not be divorced from the bonds of matrimony agreeably to the Acts of Assembly in such case made and provided. And hereof fail not. Witness the Honorable Frederick Watts President of our said Court at Carlisle the 14th day of January 1850." (signed Jas. F. Lamberton Prothy.) -Notation on the front of this document -"No. 2 April Term 1850 Caroline Eichelberger by her next friend Peter Sipe vs. Levi Eichelberger 26 Aug. 1850 Alias Subpoena awarded By the Ct. Subpoena Sur Divorce N.E.I. So answers" (signed David Smith Sheriff.) Shff. Smith's fee

$0.18 3/4. Hepburn."

Oct. 1, 1850 -"Cumberland County SS -The Commonwealth of Pennsylvania to the Sheriff of Cumberland County Greeting -Whereas Caroline Eichelberger by her next friend Peter Sipe did on the 14th day of January 1850 prefer a petition to our said Judges of our Court of Common Pleas for the County of Cumberland praying for the causes therein set forth, that she might be divorced from the bonds of matrimony entered into with you Levi Eichelberger. We do therefore command you, as we have heretofore commanded you, the said Levi Eichelberger that, setting aside all other business and excuses whatsoever, you be and appear in your proper person before our Judges at Carlisle at a Court of Common Pleas there to be held for the county of Cumberland, on the 11th day of November next, to answer the petition or libel of the said Caroline Eichelberger, and to shew cause if any you have why the said Caroline Eichelberger your wife, should not be divorced from the bonds of matrimony agreeably to the acts of Assembly in such case made and provided. And hereof fail not. Witness the Honorable Frederick Watts President of our said Court at Carlisle the 1st day of October, 1850." (signed Jas. F. Lamberton Prothy.) -Notation on the front of this document -"No. 2 April T. 1850 Caroline Eichelberger by next friend Peter Sipe vs. Levi Eichelberger Alias Subpoena Sur Divorce N.E.I. So answers" (signed David Smith Shrff.)

-"Shff. Smith's fee $0.18 3/4
Prothy.   .12 1/2
                          .31 1/2   Hepburn."

Nov. 11, 1850 -"Cumberland County SS -Personally appeared before me the subscriber a Justice of the Peace in and for the said County David Smith Shrff. who being duly sworn according to law deposes and says that the foregoing return that the Defendant was non est inventus is true to the best of his knowledge and belief. Sworn and Subscribed before me November 11th 1850." (signed M. Holcomb J.P. and David Smith Shrff.)

Jan. 21, 1851 -"To the Hon. the Judges of the Court of Comm. Pleas of Cumb. Coy. -The petition of Caroline Eichelberger by her next friend Peter Sipe Respectfully represents that a subpoena for a divorce was awarded by sd. Court in favor of your petitioner to Levi Eichelberger to N 2 Apr T. 1850 and alias which was regularly published by the Sheriff of sd. County agreeably to the order of said Court commanding the said Levi to appear at the days and times there mentioned. That there has been no appearance she therefore prays the Court to appoint a Commissioner to take the testimony in the Case and report the same to the sd. Court on the 25 day of March next." (signed Caroline Eichelberger by her next friend Peter Sipe per Saml. Hepburn their atty. Jay. 21st 1851." -Notation on the front of this document -"No. 2 April Term 1850 Thos. Craighead Jr.

Appointed Commissioner to take the testimony By the Ct. 21 Jan. 1851."

Nov. 11, 1850 -"In the Court of Common Pleas of Cumberland County Caroline Eichelberger by her next friend Peter Sipe vs. Levi Eichelberger: No. 2 April T. 1850 Subpoena Sur Divorce 11 Nov. 1850 On motion of Mr. Hepburn, proof having been made by the Sheriff that the said Levi Eichelberger could not be found etc. 21 Jany. 1851 Thos. Craighead Jr. appointed Commissioner to take the testimony -By the Court." -"Cumberland County Sct. I do certify that the above is a true extract taken from the records of the Court of Common Pleas of said County. Witness my hand the seal of said Court at Carlisle this 21 Jany. 1851." (signed Jas. F. Lamberton Prothy.)

Feb. 17, 1851 -"To the Honorable the Judges of the Court of Common Pleas of Cumberland County -Having recd. this Commission, I in due time called before me the testimony found pertinent to the case, per the depositions hereto annexed all which are respectfully submitted. Witness my hand Feby. 17th 1851." (signed Thos. Craighead Jr.) -Notation on the front of this document -"No. 2 April T. 1850 Eichelberger etc. vs. Eichelberger: Com. to Thos. Craighead Jr."

Feb. 14, 1851 -"Catharine (sic) Eichelberger by her next friend Peter Sipe vs. Levi Eichelberger: In the Court of Common Pleas of Cumberland County Agreeably to the Commission annexed hereto I Thomas Craighead Jr. of said County, did call before me the following persons, and after having examined them on their oath or affirmation touching the matter in controversy reduced their testimony to writing, witness my hand and seal." (signed Thos. Craighead Jr.)

Feb. 14, 1851 -"Cumberland County ss -Personally appeared before me Elizabeth G. Morrison of Hampden Township Cumberland County widow aged fifty years who being duly sworn doth depose and say, that I am acquainted with Caroline Eichelberger and has known her about eight years. I also knew Levi Eichelberger her husband. They were reputed to be married in November 1843, or thereabouts. The evening they were married they came to my house together, as man and wife. I saw their marriage certificate. The next day he went away and returned. Several times afterwards he went away and returned, for about a week or so. He then went away, and I have not seen him since. I don't know that he ever provided for her. He never paid me for their boarding, either himself or wife, but went off and left her destitute and unprovided for. Sworn and Subscribed befor me Feby. 14th 1851." (signed Thos. Craighead Jr. Commissioner and Elizabeth G. Morrison.)

Feb. 14, 1851 -"Cumberland County ss -Personally appeared before me, Margaret M. Oyster, widow, aged thirty years a resident of Hampden Township, Cumberland County, who being duly affirmed doth affirm and say -That I am well acquainted with the above named Caroline Eichelberger. I also knew her husband Levi Eichelberger, in November 1843 or thereabouts. They came to my mother's house (Elizabeth G. Morrison) together as man and wife. They had their marriage certificate with them. I saw it and read it. They were married by Lewis Zearing Esquire late of Mechanicksburg (sic) deceased. They staid (sic) one night at my mother's. The next day he went away. She staid (sic) and he returned in a day or so and done so for several days, say eight or ten days. He then went away and has not returned to her since. He never has provided for her, but abandoned her to the cold charities of the world, with an infant to support by her own industry. Eichelberger and his wife boarded at my mother's during time he staid (sic) with her, and I am of opinion he never has paid her. It is now over seven years since the said Levi Eichelberger left, or abandoned his said wife Caroline. Further saith not. Affirmed and Subscribed before me Feby. 14th 1851." (signed Thos. Craighead Jr. Commissioner and Mrs. Margaret M. Oyster.)

Feb. 17, 1851 -"Cumberland County ss -Personally appeared before me this 17th day of February A.D. 1851 William R. Gorgas Esquire a resident of Lower Allen Township said County aged forty four 44 years who after being duly affirmed according to law, doth affirm and say that he was acquainted with Levi Eichelberger and Caroline his wife. And that the said Caroline lived with my mother (Catharine Gorgas) in the year 1843, and that the said Caroline left my mother's family about in September of that year, and that she was reported to be married to the said Levi Eichelberger soon after she left my mother's, or some time same fall. Said Eichelberger a short time after their marriage left his said wife and staid (sic) away until the summer of 1844. He then returned and staid (sic) a short time. My impression is he did not go to see his wife at all. He then started off, and has not been back since. He never to my knowledge provided or done anything for her. I think it was in October 1845 she returned and lived again with my mother, brought her child with her, and provided altogether for herself and child by her own industry and remained there two years and a half. She was a working industrious good housekeeper and we found no fault to her that we know of. My mother lives in part of the same house I live in. Further saith not. Affirmed and Subscribed before me Feby. 17th 1851." (signed Thos. Craighead Jr. Com. and Wm. R. Gorgas.)

March 25, 1851 -"And now to wit 25th March 1851. The testimony in the case of the libel of Caroline Eichelberger for a divorce from the bonds of matrimony with Levi Eichelberger, being presented to the said Court. Upon due consideration it is ordered decreed and adjudged that the bonds of matrimony or nuptial ties contracted between the said Caroline and Levi Eichelberger be and the same are hereby dissolved and annulled and all and every the duties rights and claims accruing to the said parties at any time theretofore in pursuance of the said marriage shall cease and determine, and the said Caroline shall be at liberty to marry again in the like manner as if she had never been married. And that the said Levi Eichelberger shall pay the costs of this proceeding. -By the Court." (signed Fred. Watts President.) -Notation on front -"No. 2 April T. 1850 Filed March 25 1851."

◆ ◆ ◆

April Term 1850 #14 Jan. 28, 1850 -"To the Honble. the Judges of the Court of Common Pleas of Cumberland County -The petition of Catherine Wharfe late Catherine Black by her next friend Jacob Duey Respectfully Sheweth -That your petitioner on the twenty seventh of March A.D. (1849) One thousand Eight hundred and forty nine was lawfully joined in marriage with James Wharfe, and from that time until the nineteenth day of December last past lived and cohabited with him the said James Wharfe as his wife and as such was owned and acknowledged by him and so deemed and reputed by all her neighbours and acquaintances; and altho by the laws of God as well as by their mutual vows, they were reciprocally bound to that uniform regard which ought to be inseparable from the marriage state, yet so it is that the said James Wharfe has offered such indignities to the person of your petitioner as to render her condition intolerable and her life burthensome and thereby forced her to withdraw from his house and company. Wherefore your Libellant further showing that she is a citizen of the State of Pennsylvania and has resided therein for upwards of one whole year previous to the filing of this her libel prays your Honors that a subpoena may issue forth to summon the said James Wharfe to appear in this Honorable Court at April term next to answer the complaint aforesaid. And also that a decree of this Court may be made for the divorcing of him the said James Wharfe from the society fellowship and company of this libellant in all time to come and this libellant from the marriage bond aforesaid as if she had never been married, or as if the said James Wharfe were naturally dead. And this libellant will pray etc." (signed Catherine Wharfe by her next friend Jacob Duey.) -"Cumberla County ss -The above named Catherine Wharfe being duly sworn deposeth, that the facts contained in the above libel are true to the best of her knowledge and belief, and that the said complaint is not made out of levity and collusion between her and him the said James Wharfe, and for the mere purpose of being freed and separated from each other, but in sincerity and truth for the causes mentioned in said libel. Sworn and Subscribed before me this 28th January A.D. 1850." (signed Catharine Wharfe and Jas. F. Lamberton Prothy.) -Notation on the front of this document -"No. 14 April Term 1850 Catherine Wharfe by her next friend Jacob Duey vs. James Wharfe Filed 28 Jany. 1850 Libel for divorce Subpoena awarded." (signed Fred. Watts Prest. Judge.) "28 Jan. 1850 75 prd. Biddle."

Jan. 21, 1850 -"Cumberland County SS -The Commonwealth of Pennsylvania to the Sheriff of Cumberland County Greeting: Whereas Catharine Wharfe late Catharine Black by her next friend Jacob Duey on the 28th day of January A.D. 1850, did prefer a petition to our said Judges of our Court of Common Pleas for the County of Cumberland, praying for the causes therein set forth, that she might be divorced from the bonds of matrimony entered into with you James Wharfe. We do therefore command you the said James Wharfe that setting aside all other business and excuses whatsoever you be and appear in your proper person, before our Judges, at Carlisle at a Court of Common Pleas, there to be held for the County of Cumberland on the 8th day of April next, to answer the petition or libel of the said Catharine Wharfe and to show cause if any you have why the said Catharine Wharfe your wife, should not be divorced from the bonds of matrimony agreeably to the Acts of Assembly in such case made and provided. And hereof fail not. Witness the Honorable Frederick Watts President of our said Court, at Carlisle the 28th day of January A.D. 1850." (signed Jas. F. Lamberton Prothty.) -Notation on the front of this document -"No. 14 April Term 1850 Catharine Wharfe by her next friend Jacob Duey vs. James Wharfe Subpoena Sur Divorce Feby. 1, 1850 Served personally and by copy So answers." (signed David Smith Shrff.) -"Shff. Smith's fee $1.20 1/2. Biddle."

April 20, 1850 -"Cumberland County SS -David Smith Esq. Sheriff being sworn deposeth and saith that he served the within writ personally and by copy on James Wharfe on the 1st February A.D. 1850. Sworn and subscribed before me this 20th April 1850." (signed Jas. F. Lamberton Prot. and David Smith Shrff.)

April 20, 1850 -"Wharfe by her next friend vs. Wharfe: April Term 1850 Subpoena in Divorce -The subpoena in this case having been returned, and due proof that the same was served on the said defendant personally and by copy on the first of Feby. last and said J. Wharfe not appearing nor no person for him, the Court appoint Michael Holcomb Esq. a Commissioner to take testimony on the part of the Libellant. By the Court." (signed Fred. Watts Prot. 20 April 1850.) -Notation on the front of this document -"No. 14 April T. 1850 Wharfe vs. Wharfe: Commr. Filed 20 April 1850."

April 26, 1850 -"Cumberland County Sct -I do certify that the above is copy of the entry made by the Court in said case. In testimony whereof I have hereunto set my hand and affixed the seal of said Court at Carlisle this 26th day of April A.D. 1850." (signed Jas. F. Lamberton Proth.)

April 26, 1850 -"Catherine Wharfe by her next friend Jacob Duey vs. James Wharfe: In the Common Pleas of Cumberland County

Libel for Divorce No. 14 of April term 1850 -Sir Take notice that the depositions of witnesses to be read in evidence on the hearing of this case will be taken before Michael Holcomb Esqr. the Commissioner appointed by the Court to take the testimony, at his office in Carlisle on Monday the 29th instant between the hours of nine o'clock and eleven o'clock in the morning of that day, when and where you can attend to cross examine. To Mr. James Wharfe 26th April 1850" (signed W.M. Biddle Atty. for Libellant.)

April 29, 1850 -"Cumberland County SS -Thomas M. Biddle being duly sworn deposeth that he served the within notice on James Wharfe by giving him a copy of the same on Friday the 26th of April instant. Sworn and subscribed this 29th April 1850." (signed Thos. M. Biddle.)

April 29th, 1850 -"In pursuance of the annexed commission to me to take testimony on the part of the Libellant in the Subpoena for Divorce in the case of Catharine Wharfe by her next friend Jacob Duey against James Wharfe. Proof of service of the annexed notice to take depositions on James Wharfe having been made, the following testimony was taken in pursuance thereof, the same having commenced in the hours stated in said rule and continued until completed, James Wharf not attending or any person on his behalf. Sarah Brinn, being duly sworn according to law, sayeth that she had a conversation with James Wharf of the borough of Carlisle, the defendant, and that he admitted to her that he had compelled his wife to put her legs up over his shoulders, that he had forced her so to do and in that way had connection with her, that he had also had connection with her, by laying her on a trunk, and in any and every way that he pleased. The deponent further states that the said Wharf acknowledged and told to her that he had treated his wife badly by having connection with her as he had done, and that he knew he had injured her, and that she would frequently complain and hallow out when he had to do with her, as he did. Sworn and subscribed before me 29th April 1850." (signed M. Holcomb and Sarah Brinn.)

April 29, 1850 -"Sarah Black, being duly sworn according to law, saith, I am the mother of Catharine Wharf, she was married to James Wharf in March 1849 in Carlisle, by Rev. Mr. Hoffman, and lived with said Wharf about nine months. Towards the end of that time my daughter complained of the way in which her husband treated her and said that he had injured her by said treatment, and that he would continue and persist in so using her notwithstanding all her entreaties to him not to do so. That a month or two before she left her said husband the said Catharine was confined to her bed, for more than three weeks, which was occasioned by the falling of her womb, which projected from her person. That the said Catharine was in such a state that deponent did think that she could not recover. That her the said Catharine at the time was but little over fifteen years of age. The deponent has no doubt that the condition of her daughter as described was owing to the cruel and barbarous treatment of her husband James Wharf. That after the said Catharine was able to get about, she left her husband and came to live with deponent (her mother) refusing any longer to live with him. Sworn and subscribed before me 29th April 1850." (signed M. Holcomb and Sarah Black.)

April 29, 1850 -"Dr. Hargrove Hinkley, being duly sworn according to law, saith, that he attended Mrs. Catharine Wharfe, some three or four month ago. She was suffering at the time from Prolepsus (sic) of the womb of a very severe character. At one time the womb protruded from the vulvae or external labia and accompanied by a profuse leucorreal (sic) discharge with the usual attendant symptoms of such a disease. Her situation I attributed to the too frequent and unnatural connection of her husband with her, causing as it necessary would a relaxation of the vaginal canal and a falling of the womb. She was somewhat relieved by the medical treatment but not effectually cured, and probably never will be. Sworn and subscribed before me 29th April 1850." (signed M. Holcomb and Hargrove Hinkley.)

April 30, 1850 -"Catharine Wharfe by her next friend Jacob Duey vs. James Wharfe: In the Common Pleas of Cumberland County No. 14 April Term 1850 -And now the 30th April A.D. One thousand Eight hundred and fifty the Commissioner Michael Holcomb Esq. having returned to the Court here the depositions of witnesses taken before him on the part of the Libellant and the same being read and heard by the Court, the Court after mature and solemn deliberation being satisfied therewith, and proclamation being duly made for the Respondent to come forth and he not appearing, the Court do order adjudge and decree that the said Catherine Wharfe the Libellant be divorced and separated from the bond of matrimony contracted with the said James Wharfe the Respondent, and that all and every the duties rights and claims accruing to either of the said parties by reason of the said marriage shall henceforth cease and determine and the said parties be severally at liberty to marry again in like manner as if they had never been married. By the Court." (signed Fred. Watts Pres. Judge.) -Notation on the front of this document -"No. 14 April Term 1850 Filed 30 April 1850."

◆ ◆ ◆

January Term 1851 #24 Nov. 25, 1850 -"To the Honorable the Judges of the Court of Common Pleas of Cumberland County -The libel of Mary Fellers, by her next friend Wm. Corbett Respectfully Sheweth -That your libellant on the 11th of August A.D. 1836, was bound in matrimony, and married to a certain Henry Fellers, and from that time until the 10th day of September, A.D. 1850 lived and cohabited with the said Henry Fellers, as his wife, and as such was owned and acknowledged by him, and so deemed and reputed by their neighbours and acquaintances. And although by the laws of God, as well as by their mutual vows and faith plighted to each other, they were bound to that uniform constancy and regard which ought to be inseparable from the marriage state, yet so it is, that the said Henry Fellers did on the 10th day of September 1850, the said parties being at that time domiciled within the Commonwealth of Pennsylvania, and at various other days and times turn this libellant (his wife) out of doors, and did beat, abuse, and threaten to kill her, and did offer such other indignities to her person as to render her condition intolerable, and life burdensome, and by cruel and barbarous treatment, to endanger her life. Wherefore your libellant further showing that she is a citizen of this state, and hath resided therein for upwards of one whole year previous to the filing of this petition, prays your honors, that a subpoena may issue from the said Court directed to the said Henry Fellers, commanding him to appear at the next term of the said Court, to answer this petition: and also that this honorable court may decree a divorce and separation from the said nuptial ties or bonds of matrimony, heretofore uniting, as before mentioned, this libellant to and with the said Henry Fellers. And the said libellant will pray etc." (signed Test. Wm. H. Miller and Mary Fellers and Wm. Corbett by his mark.) -"Cumberland County SS -Personally appeared before me, one of the Justices of the Peace in and for said County, Mary Fellers, who being duly sworn deposeth, that the facts contained in the foregoing petition or libel are true, and that the said complaint is not made out of levity or collusion between this libellant, and her said husband, and for the mere purpose of being freed and separated from each other, but in sincerity and truth for the causes mentioned in said petition or libel. Sworn and subscribed before me this 25th day of November 1850." (signed Geo. Ege and Mary Fellers by her mark.) -Notation on the front of this document -"No. 24 January T. 1851 Petition of Mary Fellers by her next friend Wm. Corbett for divorce Subpeona awarded By the Court 17th Decr. 1850 Mary Fellers by her next friend Wm. Corbett vs. Henry Fellers: Sur Issue Subp. for divorce To Proth. Lamberton Wm. H. Miller Atty. for Libl. 30th Decr. 1850 Filed 30th Decr. 1850 Miller."

Dec. 30, 1850 -"Cumberland County ss -The Commonwealth of Pennsylvania to the Sherriff of Cumberland County Greeting Whereas Mary Fellers by her next friend William Corbett did on the 17th day of December A.D. 1850 prefer a petition to our said Judges of our Court of Common Pleas, for the County of Cumberland, praying for the causes therein set forth, that she might be divorced from the bonds of matrimony entered into with you the said Henry Fellers. We do therefore command you the said Henry Fellers that setting aside all other business and excuses whatsoever you be and appear in your proper person before our Judges at Carlisle, at a Court of Common Pleas there to be held for the County of Cumberland on the 13th day of January next to answer the petition or libel of the said Mary Fellers and to shew cause if any you have, why the said Mary Fellers your wife should not be divorced from the bonds of matrimony agreeably to the acts of assembly in such case made and provided. And hereof fail not. Witness the Honorable Frederick Watts President of our said Court at Carlisle this 30th day of December A.D. 1850." (signed Jas. F. Lamberton Prothy.) -Notation on the front of this document -"No. 24 Jany. T. 1851 Mary Fellers by her next friend William Corbett vs. Henry Fellers Subpoena Sur. Divorce Decr. 30, 1850 Served personally and by copy So answers (signed E. Cornman Dep. Shff. and David Smith Shff.) -"Shff. Smith's fee $1.20 Miller."

Jan. 14, 1851 -"To the Hon. the Judges of the Court of Common Pleas of Cumberland County the petition of Mary Fellers by her next friend Wm. Corbett by their atty. Wm. H. Miller Respectfully Represents -That a petition of said libellant, a subpoena sur divorce was awarded by your Hon. consent and against Henry Fellers, the (illegible word) of the sd. (illegible) which subpoena was issued, to No. 24 January Term 1851 -returnable to this Court. Your petitioner therefore prays your Hon. Court, to appoint a Commissioner, to take depositions, in said case, to be read before your Honorable Court, on the hearing, to meet exparte on ten days notice to said Henry Fellers." (signed Mary Fellers by her next friend Wm. Corbett by Wm. H. Miller their atty. 14th Jany. 1851) -Notation the front of this document -"No. 24 Jany. T. 1851 Petition of Mary Fellers etc. for a Commissioner to take depositions in the Int. Sur divorce vs. Henry Fellers Geo. Ege Esq. appointed Commissioner to take testimony By the Court 15 Jan. 1851 Filed 15 Jany. 1851."

January Term 1851 #24 March 25, 1851 -"To the Honorable the Judges of the Court of Common Pleas of Cumberland County -Henry Fellers in answer to the subpoena awarded against him by your honorable Court commanding him to appear and shew cause why a bill of Divorce should not be granted to his wife Mary Fellers. Respectfully Represents: That it is not true as is alleged in the petition of his wife Mary Fellers that he offered to her indignities nor has he so comported himself towards her as to render her life intolerable. Nor are the statements set forth in her petition true as a whole nor in part. Your respondent hath good reason to believe and doth believe that evil and designing persons are now instigating his wife to seek for the divorce prayed for out of ill feeling they bear towards him. And your Respondent would further represent that he is now confined in the jail of this county and is therefore at present unable to produce evidence which he otherwise could and which when produced he does not doubt will show to the entire satisfaction of your honors that no such divorce should or ought to be granted. He therefore prays your honorable Court either to dismiss the libel presented to you by his said wife or order a trial of the case by a jury of his countrymen before whom he can appear and vindicate himself from the charges made against him by your libellant. And he will ever pray etc." (signed Henry Fellers by his mark and Jas. R. Smith.) -On other side of paper (this side extremely hard to read. -E.T.) -"Jacob Westfall: Henry Brown: Called her every thing bad. Do nothing but curse and swear. Not fit to have a family or be herd (sic). Alexr. Ligget: Clock broken. Riots (an illegible word.) -so frequent I did not go down. Isaac Vanandoll: For 15 or 20 minutes blackguarding her all time. Could hardly speak when he was in home. Sarah Springs: Said he would kill her if it were not for the law. Adam Spring: Thompson Ligget: Saw her put out and heard she kept in cornfield." -Notation on the front of this document -"No. 24 January T. 1851 Answer of Henry Fellers Sub. Div. Filed 25 March 1851."

April 28, 1851 -"Mary Fellers by her next friend Wm. Corbett vs. Henry Fellers No. 24 Jan. Term 1851: And now to wit -28th April 1851. The following issue is formed, in the above case, to be tried by jury. The fact of the marriage of the said Mary Fellers, and Henry Fellers is admitted. And the libellant, now avers, that the said Henry Fellers, from the year 1840 up to the bringing of this suit, has offered such indignities to the person of the said Mary Fellers, as to render her condition intolerable, and life burdensome, and that for these reasons, she is entitled to a divorce from the society, fellowship and company of the said Henry Fellers for all time to come, and from the marriage bond aforesaid, as if the said parties had never been married. And the said Henry Fellers denies these facts, and the said libellant's right to be so divorced. Judgement to be in accordance, with the facts found by the jury -and if the libellant's allegations are sustained, by the verdict -then the Court to decree, a divorce from the bonds of matrimony, according to the prayer of libellant." (signed Wm. H. Miller Atty. for Libellant and Jas. R. Smith Atty. for Deft. 1st May 1851.) -Notation on the front of this document -"No. 24 Jany. T. 1851 Mary Fellers by her next friend Wm. Corbett vs. Henry Fellers Issue to try the facts Filed May 6th 1851."

Aug. 18, 1851 -"Cumberland County, SS -The Commonwealth of Pennsylvania, To Andrew Rickwine, Henry Leib, Jacob Westfall, Henry Brown, Alexander Liggett, Philip Lutz, Isaac Vanasdall, Sarah Springs, Adam Springs, Thompson Liggett, Robert Gill Greeting: We command you, and each of you, that laying aside all business and excuses, you be and appear in your proper person before the Judges of the Court of Common Pleas, at Carlisle, at a Court of Common Pleas, there to be held for the County of Cumberland, the 25th day of August 1851 at 10 o'clock in the forenoon of that day, to testify all and singular, those things you shall know in a certain action of

Divorce pending and undetermined between Mary Fellers etc. Plaintiff, and Henry Fellers Defendant (on the part of the Plaintiff). And this you are not to omit under the penalty of One Hundred Pounds. Witness the Honorable Frederick Watts, at Carlisle, the 18th day of August in the year of our Lord, one thousand eight hundred and fifty one." (signed Jas. F. Lamberton Prothonotary.) -On other side of paper -"August 19th 1851 Served personal on Leib, Westfall and Rickwine and Philip Lutz. Brown personal and on Springs and wife
copy serving .60 cts.
.20 cts.
Mileage .80 cts.
$1.40
So answers J. Young Const. August 21st 1851 served on Vanasdall and T. Liget (sic) and Elexander (sic) Liggett personal
serving .30
Mileage .30
$2.00
So answers J. Young Const. Jonathan Young is constable of (Monroe?)." -Notation on the front of this document -"No. 24 Jany. T. 1851 Fellers vs. Fellers: Subp."
Aug. 25, 1851 -"Mary Fellers etc. vs. Henry Fellers: No. 24 Jany. T. 1851 Plffs. wits. at August T. 1851.

Andrew Rickwine	1 day and 6 miles	$0.98 1/2
Henry Leib	1 day and 5 miles	.92 1/2
Jacob Westfall	1 day and 5 miles	.92 1/2
Henry Brown	1 day and 6 miles	.98 1/2
Alex Liggett	1 day and 6 miles	.98 1/2
Philip Lutz	1 day and 6 miles	.98 1/2
Isaac Vanasdal	1 day and 6 miles	.98 1/2
Sarah Springs	1 day and 6 miles	.98 1/2
Adam Springs	1 day and 6 miles	.98 1/2
Thompson Liggett	1 day and 6 miles	.98 1/2
Robert Gill	1 day and 8 miles	1.10 1/2

The above bill taxed and sworn to by Mary Fellers, 25 Aug. 1851." (signed Jas. F. Lamberton Proth.)
1 Subp. .43
Const. Young Ser Sub. 3.40
Taxing bill .18 3/4
$4.01 3/4
$14.85 1/4"
Notation on the front of this document -"No. 24 Jany. T. 1851 Fellers etc. vs. Fellers: Plff's bill and Wits. Filed 25th Augt. 1851."
Aug. 28, 1851 -"Mary Fellers by her next friend Wm. Corbett vs. Henry Fellers: No. 24 January T. 1851 in the Court of Common Pleas of Cumberland County -Petition for divorce from the bonds of matrimony, on the grounds of intolerable treatment -Replication

denying the facts, and asking an issue -Issue directed by the Court to try the facts. -Verdict for Plaintiff. And now to wit the 26th day of August in the year of our Lord One thousand Eight Hundred and fifty one -a jury of the county having been called, and sworn to try the above issue -returned to the Court a verdict for plaintiff, to wit on the 28th day of August A.D. 1851. Whereupon the Court do order, adjudge and decree that the said Mary Fellers the libellant and Plaintiff be divorced and separated from the bond of matrimony contracted with the said Henry Fellers, and that all and every the duties, rights, claims accruing to either of the said parties by reason of the said marriage shall henceforth cease and determine, and the said parties be severally at liberty to marry again in like manner as if they never had been married. By the Court." (signed Fred. Watts Prest.) -Notation on the front of this document -"No. 24 Jany. T. 1851 Mary Fellers by her next friend Wm. Corbett vs. Henry Fellers: Decree of Court."

◆　　　　◆

August Term 1851 #3 April 18, 1851 -"To the Honorable the Judges of the Court of Common Pleas of Cumberland County -The petition of Mary Ramp respectfully represents that your libellant about (left blank) years since was contracted in matrimony and married to a certain William Ramp and since that time until about the 15 March 1849 and cohabited with him as his wife and as such was owned and acknowledged by him and so deemed and reputed by all her neighbors and acquaintances. And although by the laws of God as well as by their mutual vows and faith plighted to each other, they were reciprocally bound to that uniform kindness and regard which ought to be inseparable from the marriage state, yet so it is that the said Wm. Ramp hath offered such indignities to her person as to render her condition intolerable and life burdensome and hath thereby forced her to withdraw from his house and family. Wherefore your libellant further showing that she hath resided in this state for two years and upwards immediately preceding this application prays your Honors that a subpoena may issue from said Court directed to the said William Ramp, commanding him to appear at the next term of said Court to answer this petition, and also that a decree of said Court may be made granting this libellant a divorce from bed and board and also to allow her such alimony as the circumstances of the said William Ramp will admit of. And she will pray etc." (signed Mary Ramp by her next friend Samuel Heberlig.) -"Cumberland County SS -Mary Ramp being duly affirmed according to law, says that the facts set forth in the above libel are true to the best of her knowledge and belief, and that the said complaint is not made out of levity or collusion between her and her husband, but in sincerity and truth for the causes mentioned in the foregoing petition. Affirmed and subscribed the (left blank) April 1851 Before me." (signed

Henry D. Daelhousen and Mary Ramp by her mark.) -Notation on the front of this document -"No. 3 August T. 1851 Petition of Mary Ramp wife of Wm. Ramp for a divorce a mensa et thoro and alimony -Subpoena Awarded By the Court 18 Apl. 1851. Filed 18 April 1851. Graham."

April 18, 1851 -"Cumberland County SS -The Commonwealth of Pennsylvania to William Ramp, Greeting: Whereas Mary Ramp on the 18th day of April One thousand, eight hundred and fifty one, preferred a petition to the Judges of the Court of Common Pleas of Cumberland County praying that for causes therein set forth, she might be divorced from bed and board and that she might be allowed such alimony as the circumstances of the said William Ramp will admit of, and the said Judges having awarded a subpoena. We command you the said William Ramp that setting aside all business and excuses, whatsoever, you be and appear in your proper person before our Judges at Carlisle, at our County Court of Common Pleas there to be held the 25th day of August next, to answer the petition or libel of the said Mary Ramp and shew cause if any you have why she should not be divorced from bed and board and why she should not be allowed such alimony as the circumstances of you the said William Ramp will admit of, agreeably to the Acts of Assembly in such case made and provided. Witness Frederick Watts Esqr. President of our said Court at Carlisle the eighteenth day April A.D. 1851." (signed Jas. F. Lamberton Prothy.) -"I hereby authorize and depute J.P. Rhoads to execute the above writ agreeably to law. Witness my hand and seal this 29th day of July A.D. 1851." (signed David Smith Shrff.)

July 31, 1851 -"Cumberland County ss -J.P. Rhoads having been sworn says that he served the within Subpoena Sur Divorce on William Ramp personally and by copy on the 31st day of July A.D. 1851. Sworn and Subscribed before me the 31st July 1851." (signed David Wherry, J.P. and John P. Rhoads.) -Notation on the front of this document -"No. 3 August Term 1851 Mary Ramp by her next friend Samuel Heberlig vs. William Ramp Subp. Sur Divorce etc. July 31, 1851 Served formally and by copy So answers" (signed David Smith Shff.) -"Shff. Smith's fee $2.72. Graham."

August Term 1851 #3 Aug. 25, 1851 -"To the Honourable the Judges of the Court of Common Pleas for Cumberland County Penna. -The answer of William Ramp to the Libel of Mary Ramp by her next friend Samuel Heberlig, praying for a divorce a mensa et thoro and alimony. This respondent saving and reserving to himself the manifold errors, inconsistencies and imperfections in the said Libel set forth, for answer thereto, or as much thereof as he is advised it is necessary to answer, admits that on the (left blank) day the Libellant has set forth in her libel she was joined with this respondent in the holy bonds of matrimony, and protests that the said Respondent hath not offered such indignities to her person as to render her condition intolerable and life burdensome and hath not thereby forced her to withdraw from his house and family. And the said respondent avers that he has always since the said marriage conducted himself as a husband ought to do towards the said Mary Ramp and wholly denies that he ever abused the said Mary Ramp, or offered any indignities to her person as to render her condition intolerable or life burdensome or that he ever gave her cause or obliged her to depart from his house, but says that the said Mary Ramp left his house without any just cause. This respondent further avers, that he always has been willing and now offers to receive the said Mary Ramp and cohabit with her again, and to use her as a good husband husband ought to do. Wherefore he prays that the said libel may be dismissed with costs etc." (signed William Ramp.) -"Cumberland County ss -William Ramp being sworn according to law saith that the facts set forth in the foregoing answer are true. Sworn and Subscribed before me. Aug. 25, 1851." (signed Jas. F. Lamberton Prothy. and William Ramp.)

Aug. 29, 1851 -"Now, to wit, 29 Aug. 1851 the Petitioner having presented an application for an issue as provided by the Act of Asembly the respondent declines to acquiesce in such direction by the Court but says that the Court will make such order as they deem best. The Court therefore order the petitioner asserting to at that depositions be taken by either party on ten days notice to the other party to be read on the final hearing upon which the Court will make a decree. By the Court." -Notation on the front of this document -"No. 3 August Term 1851 Answer of William Ramp to the Libel of Mary Ramp by her next friend. Filed Aug. 26, 1851"

Aug. 26, 1851 -"Mary Ramp by her next friend Samuel Heberlig vs. William Ramp: In the Court of Common Pleas of Cumberland County No. 3 August Term 1851 -Petition for divorce "a mensa et thoro" and alimony. And now to wit 26 August 1851 The Respondent having filed his answer in the above stated case -The following issue is directed by the court to be tried by a jury. The fact of the marriage of the said Mary Ramp and William Ramp being admitted by Respondent in his answer. The said libellant now avers that the said William Ramp has offered such indignities to her person as to render her condition intolerable and life burdensome and thereby forced her to withdraw from his house and family and that she is entitled to a divorce "a mensa et thoro" and to alimony. And the said William Ramp denies the above comments and the said libellant's right to be so divorced. Judgement to be entered in accordance with the facts found by the Jury and if libellant's allegations are sustained by the verdict, the court to decree a divorce "a mensa et thors" and also such alimony to libellant as the circumstances of the said William Ramp will admit of." -Notation on the front of this document -"No. 3

T. 1851 Mary Ramp by her next friend etc. vs. William Ramp Issue directed by the court. Filed Aug. 26, 1851"
July 30, 1851 -"Mary Ramp by her next friend Samuel Heberlig vs. William Ramp: No. 3 August Term 1851 Application for a divorce from bed and board and for alimony in the Court of Common Pleas of Cumberland County -To William Ramp -You are hereby notified that depositions to be read in evidence in the above stated case, in pursuance of a rule of Court, will be taken at the office of Robt. Middleton Esq. in Mifflin township on the fourth day of September 1851 between the hours of ten and four o'clock of that day." (signed J.H. Graham Atty. for Mary Ramp.) -"Served by giving Wm. Ramp a copy of the within notice on 30th July 1851 at 11 a.m. o'clock of said day. Served on oath." (signed Samuel Heberlig.) -Notation on the front of this document -"Depositions of Wm. Ramp Jury with No. 3 Aug. 1851 Justice's costs-

taking depositions	.73 cts.
Subpoena	.09 cts.
Serving Witnesses	.03 cts.
	.85 cts."

Sept. 1, 1851 -"Caption of a deposition of a witness sworn and examined on the 1st day of September A.D. 1851 at the office of Robt. Middleton Esq. in Mifflin Township County of Cumberland between the hours of 12 o'clock and 9 p.m. of said day to be read in evidence before the honourable Frederick Watts President and Judge of the several courts of Cumberland Perry and Juniata Countys in Pennsylvania and the honourable John Stuart and John Clendennin his associates in Cumberland County in the case of the application of Mary Ramp by her next friend Saml. Heberlig for a divorce from bed and board and for a living versis William Ramp Senr. in the Court of Common Pleas of Cumberland County No. 3 August term 1851. By virtue of the annexed Rule of Court. William Ramp Junr. of Mifflin Township aged about 28 yrs. being produced and sworn and examined by me on the 1st day of Sept. 1851 between the hours of 2 o'clock and 8 o'clock in the evening of said day -is as follows -Interrogatory first what passed between your father and mother when she left him. (Answer) He drank very hard and attempted to hang himself and chased us all out of the house at night and we were afraid of him. On Friday he shot in the house and John and the women all run (sic) to the cornfield and I went to Frazer's and brought him down and I thought the old man had shot himself and we found him lying on the floor and I told Frazer to turn him over and see whether he was shot or not. On Friday before Mother left Father was going to hang himself with a hankerchief (sic). Mother begged on him not to hang himself and I went in and took the hankerchief (sic) from him of his neck and I was afraid of father and thought father would take his own life or mother's life was in danger. When he was drunk more than once he threatened to hang himself. My mother was afraid to stay at night and after mother and sister Katty left on Friday night father went to the barn. I thought to hurt them and to the spring house to hurt them and said 'I'll find you yet you Bitches you'" ----(Question.) Did your father ever take your mother by the hair. --At one time my father came out of the house into the field and caught my mother by the hair and father throwed the stove down the night of Sam Maxwell's sale and was drunk when he thrown (sic) it down and it was full of fire. Last spring two years ago I was afraid of my life that father would hurt me somehow because he tried to hurt me in Newberg and I carried a pistol to protect myself. Mother told father if he would not do better she would leave him and he said she might go as fast as she liked and I told him so too and he told me she might go as quick as she liked." (signed William Ramp.) -"I certify that the above witness was duly qualified and examined before me at my office as stated in the Caption and subscribed his deposition in my presence. William Ramp Senr. being present also Samuel Heberlig next friend to Mary Ramp the parties and witness having been duly notified to appear at my office on the 4th Sept. inst. voluntarily came this day September 1st to have the above deposition taken so that William Ramp Junr. could start to the west on tomorrow morning the 2nd Sept. In testimony whereof I have hereunto subscribed my name and seal at Mifflin Township the first day of September A.D. 1851." (signed Robert Middleton Justice of Peace.)

August Term 1851 #3 Oct. 20, 1851 -"Mary Ramp by her next friend Samuel Hiberlig vs. William Ramp: In the Court of Common Pleas of Cumberland County -Proceedings for a divorce from bed and board and for alimony -Sir To William Ramp Defendant -You will please take notice that in pursuance of a rule of Court entered in the above case depositions to be read in evidence on the hearing of the same before the Court, will be taken at the office of Robert Middleton Esq. in Mifflin Township Cumberland County on Thursday the 6th November 1851 between the hours of ten o'clock A.M. and five o'clock P.M. of that day and if necessary the taking of said depositions will be continued on Friday the 7th November between the said hours until the depositions of all the witnesses produced on part of libellant are taken." (signed D.H. Graham Atty. for Mary Ramp 20 October 1851.)

Oct. 31, 1851 -"Cumberland County SS -Andrew Hailor constable being duly sworn according to law deposeth and says that he served the within notice on William Ramp the within named defendant by personally giving him a true copy thereof on the twenty-eighth day of October 1851. Sworn and subscribed the 31st day of October 1851 before me." (signed A. Hailor and Robt. Middleton.) -Notation on the front of this document -"No. 3 Aug. T. 185 Ramp vs. Ramp: depositions."

Nov. 6, 1851 -"Caption of depositions of witnesses produced and sworn and examined at the office of Robt. Middleton Esq. one of the Justices of the Peace in and for the County of Cumberland and township of Mifflin on Thursday the sixth day of November 1851 between the hours of ten o'clock A.M. and five o'clock P.M. of said day in obedience to a rule of Court and notice hereto attached to be read in a cause depending in said Court in which Mary Ramp by her next friend Samuel Heberly is plaintiff and William Ramp is defendant. George Lay of the township of Mifflin in the County of Cumberland aged about twenty six and upwards being produced sworn and examined on behalf of the plaintiff in the title of this deposition named doth depose as follows viz: I am acquainted with William Ramp. I have known him between five and six years. I never knew him to abuse his wife while I was there. I was called on to watch him at one time about three or four years ago by one of his daughters to stay with him as he was going to hang himself. I did stay with him. I cannot say whether his family was afraid or not. They never said they were afraid. Wm. Ramp was going to hang himself. He had fastened himself to a little apple tree. I saw that this was at the time I was called to stay with him. He was spreeing it at that time as far as I know he spreed it but one time when I lived on the place. I don't know of his getting drunk often but I have often heard say so. When I was attending him I was there three nights. I was never called on but three nights. There never was a butcher knife taken from him when I was by." Cross examination of George Lay -"Upon counting up tis five years since I was called on to watch Wm. Ramp and since I lived on his place I have lived within one mile to four of Wm. Ramp ever since when he was tied to a tree that I spoke of. He was tied with a pair of suspenders. He was standing on the ground when I saw him. His suspenders were tied to the tree. I never saw Wm. Ramp abuse his wife while I was there. When I was there he did not abuse or treat his wife unkindly. Sworn and subscribed this 6th day of November before me and in my presence as stated in the caption." (signed Robt. Middleton and George Lay by his mark.)

Nov. 6, 1851 -"Ezra Williams of the township of Hopewell being produced and sworn and examined aged about forty nine -on behalf of the plaintiff -Five years ago I undertook to do a job of shoemaking for Wm. Ramp. I went to Mr. Ramp. I heard quarrelling when I came back and found William Ramp was on a spree and Mrs. Ramp came out crying and said Billy was or a spree and asked me to stay. Billy lay down by the stove and was very drunk and did not know what he was doing. He had liquor in a corner cupboard and went upstairs frequently. He was on a spree when ever he could get liquor. I have been at his family twice when he was on a spree and he was quarreling with his family both times. Since his wife left him he has been spreeing it occasionally whenever he could get liquors without paying for it altogether himself. I have lived with him since the old lady left and he was a real fine fellow when he was sober. He was not under the influence of liquor more than four times during the time I lived there something like four months. He came home for a few times nice and straight and then he came home a couple of times not very ordinary neither for man nor beast woman or child. When we first moved into Ramp's house there was a cot of bed clothing and human clothing. They were indecently tainted with the contents of the human stomach. They were thrown out in both ways. When or how it was done I don't know or can't tell. Billy Ramp slept in that bed before we came there. The washing that was to be done there was no woman in the county could do it and I done the half of the washing myself." Cross examination of Ezra Williams -"I do not know whether Mr. Ramp abused his wife or who caused the quarrell. It was his general practice to get drunk when he can get liquor. I never was on a spree but once with Billy Ramp on a bear hunt. At this time Billy Ramp lay in Montgomery's barnyard and the (beast?) had to do as it could. I saw him fall off his horse and lay there. I kept to get him on once an he fell off again and we left him. I did not say that William slept in that room that was described before I came there but afterward there was there was no other person slept there but him and no persons but himself. Direct examination resumed. William Ramp said that if his wife did not go away he would give her a damned kicking. He told us this after we came to live there. William Ramp said I will be damned if ever I threaten to shoot my woman or myself but By God I promised to give her good kicking. He said he was going to give her a kicking because she said he was going to shoot himself. Sworn and subscribed before me this 6th day of November 1851." (signed Robt. Middleton and Ezra Williams.)

Nov. 6, 1851 -"John Haller sworn deposes as follows. This fall two years ago I was at Mr. Ramp's husking before the election and he was in a spree. We were in the field husking and Mr. Ramp started of home and we heard a gun fired of and William Ramp said he had shot himself. We then started to the house and his daughter came. She thought Dady had shot himself. When we went into the house Billy Ramp was lying in the room and the gun was shot of and standing up in the corner of the room. I was there several nights and I saw no bad conduct when I was there between him and his wife. Before I was married I was there three or four days during the time of this husking and saw no bad treatment of his wife. I got up out of bed me and John Cook and William Ramp and his mother and sister and went up to Mr. Frazier's and stayed there all night. The reason we went up to Frazier's we were all afraid of him. William Ramp and me came back next morning and got the old woman into the house and Katty and got breakfast and went to the field to husk corn and nothing said either way. The next day the old woman and daughter came down to where we were husking corn and complained that he had kicked at her and she was afraid of him and she left William Ramp that evening that we were husking corn. I am married to their daughter." Cross examination of John Haller -"I cannot tell who shot of the gun. I was in the cornfield. I do not know whether it was that gun that was shot of. Myself and Cook got out of bed Mrs. Ramp was in the kitchen. She was not in bed that night. Mrs. Ramp staid (sic) that night we went up to Frazier's that Ramp would kill her. I did not hear Mr. Ramp abuse or threaten her. I never at any time saw Mr. Ramp abuse or threaten Mrs. Ramp. Sworn and subscribed before me the 6th day of November 1851." (signed Robt. Middleton and John Haller.)

August Term 1851 #3 Nov. 6, 1851 -"Ezra Williams recalled. After I moved to Ramp's place it frequently occurred that he dirtied the beds and clothes in the manner I stated before. He went to bed with his boots and clothes on. As he got of his beast when he was in liquor he was in the habit of making threats. He threatened in this way that if Samuel Heberlig would take any hand in this thing between him and his woman he would shoot him. He was abusive. Mr. Ramp said that if my wife or any of the Heberligs would come into my house to take anything away I would be God damned if he would not shoot them and he had three guns in the house. Billy Ramp came into our house and laid behind the stove and threw up the contents of his stomach like any dog would do that over loaded his stomach. Mr. Ramp complained because my wife would not take it away and I told her never mind Susan there is another house. Mr. Ramp dirtied the bed when he was under the influence of liquor. I cannot say once that he did not do it when under the influence of liquor. He did it every time that I carried him of the horse or that I recollect of his being in liquor. Sworn and subscribed before me this 6th day of Novmb. 1851." (signed Robt. Middleton and Ezra Williams.)

Nov. 6, 1851 -"Catharine Haller deposes after being sworn as follows. The following deposition is reduced to writing by Wm. H. Miller, by consent of parties. I am a daughter of Wm. Ramp. I was married last April two years. The first time my mother left father was three years this fall. In the next spring she was back again awhile, but left him in March finally -that is last March two years ago. She then came to where I was living with my sister. This was about six miles from where he lived. When I lived at home, Father did not use mother well. Once when we we husking corn, he kicked her, or kicked towards her. He was in the kitchen, and she came in and he caught her by the arm, and I got up and pushed him away. Then me and mother ran out, and went to the cornfield. He kicked at mother in the kitchen. I don't know whether he hit her or not. He kicked towards her I know. I was scared at the time. Once before when he came home from the election he threatened to kill both mother and me. He was drunk. He came towards us and we ran away. We went out of the house, and when he went back, we went into the house, but we did not go to bed that night. We were afrald he would kill us. He did not go to bed himself, till near daylight. He had scolded mother that evening, and called her every thing that he knew. Before we brought him in every time he came home drunk, he would abuse and scold mother. He came home drunk frequently and he would frequently say to mother, when he was drunk, that some of her children were not his. These things have been going on, abusing her in this way, since ever I can recollect anything and continued it as long as I was at home. After she went back the second time, he continued it again just as bad, and sometimes worse. I was there sometimes and at the time of corn husking, in the evening, he get us to go to bed, and all evening he carried an iron corn husker in his hand, walking about through the room, but would not go to bed himself. We often got out of bed at night for fear he would kill us. He would lie behind the stove. At the time of corn husking, he came into the room. I don't know what time he went to the dresser and got a knife. There had been no threats before he came into the room, where we were. When he came to the door he blew out the candle, then we got up. He laid the knife on the window. We found it there the next morning. Me and mother went up to Frazer's. Cross Ex. by Dr. Hepburn -The night of the election, when we all came back into the house, he sat down by the fire. He asked us why we would not go to bed. We did not tell him why. After this, that night, he did not threaten us, or use any ugly language. I never heard mother scold father, she didn't dare do so, he was always too cross to her. He didn't have liquor very often at home. He would get drunk most every time he would go away. He was sometimes a week away drinking -I mean that he would be away a week sometimes, and came home drunk. I did not see him drink when he was away. There were months sometimes when he did not get drunk. The night he had the corn husker and walked the floor, he did not say what he was going to do with it. He made no threats. The night he took the knife he did not threaten to do us any injury. The reason we were afraid was because he walked the floor all night. He had threatened before to kill us but not that night. Sworn and Subscribed before me this 6th day of Nov. 1851." (signed Robt. Middleton and Catharine Haller by her mark.)

Nov. 6, 1851 -"Richard Druet (sic) being produced and sworn did depose and say as follows: I was working at Ramp's. I was in the meadow when some of the children came to me to come and settle their father. I went to the house and saw him walking in the room and I asked what was wrong and he raised up a chair in his hand and came towards me. Cross examination of Richard Druet -It may be ten or fifteen years ago for what I know. I was at Mrs. Ramp's house frequently until she went away. I have seen people (fight?) a great deal more frequently than they did and others worse. I have seen him the worse of liquor many a time. Sworn and Subscribed before me the 6th November A.D. 1851." (signed Robt. Middleton and Richard Drewet [sic].)

Nov. 6, 1851 -"Mary Myers being produced and sworn did depose as follows I am a daughter of Mrs. Ramp's. My father's conduct up to the time she left him was not very good. He did not use her as he ought to. He always scolded her every time he came home and called her everything he knowed. He said some of the children was not his and called her every thing he knew and sometimes it was after midnight before he would quit scolding. He would swear and make threats. He came home too drunk and I helped to loosen the horse. I put away the horse and coaxed him into the house. There was no person there but me and my mother. I coaxed him to ly (sic) down beside the stove. Till about midnight he would not go to bed. He always lay beside the stove when he was drunk. Me and mother had gone to bed. After midnight he got up and crawled about the floor and hunted in the bed and drawers and desk where there was (sic) knives and corn huskers and I told mother to jump up that he know he was hunting something. He said to mother in English it was well for you you got up or you would have been badly scared but not as badly scared as hurt. Mother don't understand English but I do. Father knew mother don't understand English. Father asked me what was the reason I was there. I told him I was sleeping with mother. The time Peter Carman lived there he came home drunk more than once but a certain Monday he came home and began cursing and swearing and pounded on the table when we were at dinner. Peter jumped up scared and father was scolding and swearing all after noon (sic). Father has made us all run out of the house more than once because he was scolding and threatening and kicked at me. I never saw father strike or kick at mother. I never saw him to do it. I have heard him threaten her. More than once he kept liquor in the house he hid it once and I found it. Cross examination of Mary Myers as follows. The night when my father was hunting in the desk and drawer he did not say what he was hunting or what he wanted. When he was sober he did not use mother as well as he ought. Sworn and Subscribed before me the 6th day of November 1851." (signed Robt. Middleton and Mary M. Myers.)

Nov. 6, 1851 -"John Ramp being produced and sworn did depose as follows: This fall three years I was at father's at a corn husking frolic. The old man husked corn until night along with the rest of us that day. He felt the liquor a good deal at supper. On the following Friday I went to the field to him where he was drinking cider. I said to him you ought not to drink that sour cider. He said would not like to have my property and I said No I can live if it must be without it and then he said he would go right home and he would shoot himself and I told my brother William he said so to me and he said you had better follow him and I followed him to the house but he went faster than I did. When I got to the gate the women came running out of the house and I ran around the house towards the bridge but the gun cracked before I got to the bridge. The gun must have been fired in the room as the door was shut. The window of the room father was in faced towards the bridge. One or more of the panes of glass was broken but I cannot say what broke the glass. After Frazer came down brother William and Frazier went into the room. I looked into the room and father lay on his back. He then got up and went to the spring house for more cider. Father called her a whore and bad names. I heard this myself. He was very frequently intoxicated and he was then abusive to his family. Cross examination of John Ramp. I am certain father shot of (sic) the gun althoug (sic) I did not see it. I did not see any mark of shot or any thing else in the room." (signed John Ramp.) "I certify that the foregoing witnesses were duly qualified and examined at the time and place stated in the caption and subscribed their depositions in my presence at Mifflin Township before Robert Middleton on 6th November 1851."

```
"Justice taking depositions              $4.04
swearing and witnesses                    .24
2 subpoenas for 11 witnesses              .36
swearing constable to serve               .06
of subpoena and notice                    .00
                                        $4.70

Samuel Heberlig Serving Subpoenas
on seven witnesses                        .70
Mileage                                   .72
                                        $1.42
Constable Farter's costs
Serving notice on Wm. Ramp and
serving subpoenas                       $1.66
                                        $7.78"
```

"Examined on 6th Novr. 1851 Plaintiff's bill of costs of witnesses before Esq. Middleton

```
John Ramp        1 day    .25
                 4 miles  .24
                          .49                    .49
George Lay       1 day    .25
                 5 miles  .30
                          .55                    .55
```

Mary Myers	1 day	.25	
	6 miles	.36	
		.61	.61
John Haller	1 day	.25	
	8 miles	.48	
		.73	.73
Catharine Haller	1 day	.25	
	8 miles	.48	
		.73	.73
Rich. Druett	1 day	.25	
9 miles		.54	
		.79	.79
David Hann	1 day	.25	
8 miles		.48	
		.73	.73
"Ezra Williams	1 day	.25	
10 miles		.66	
		.91	.91
			$5.05

The within bill taxed before me the sixth day of November 1851." (signed Robt. Middleton Justice of the Peace.)

Feb. 23, 1852 -"Mary Ramp by her next friend Saml. Heberlig vs. William Ramp: No. 3 Augt. Term 1851 in the Court of Common Pleas of Cumb. Co. Proceedings in divorce from bed and board, and for alimony. Mr. Wm. Ramp Defendant: You will hereby take notice that in pursuance of a rule of Court entered in the above case depositions to be read in evidence part of libellant, on the hearing of the same before the Court, will be taken at the office of James R. Irvine Esq. in the Borough of Newville on Thursday the 18th day of March next, between the hours of 10 o'clock A.M., and five o'clock P.M. of that day, when and where you are invited to attend, and cross examine." (signed Fred. Watts and Wm. H. Miller Atty. for Libellant 23d Feb. 1852.)

Feb. 27, 1852 -"Cumberland County, ss -John Stevick personally appears before me a Justice of the Peace for said County, and being duly affirmed, saith that he served the within notice upon William Ramp, by leaving a true copy thereof in his hands on the 27th day of February #1852 Affirmed and Subscribed 1852 before" (signed David Wherry J.P. and Palm Stevick.) -Notation on the front of this document -"Mary Ramp etc. Wm. Ramp Notice to take depositions

Costs Serving notice by c.	.10
Mileage 16 miles	.42
	.52"

(signed John Stevick.)

March 18, 1852 -"Depositions of witnesses produced, sworn, or affirmed and examined at the office of James R. Irvine in the Borough of Newville, on the 18th day of March 1852, between the hours of 10 o'clock A.M. and 5 o'clock P.M. in pursuance of the notice hereto attached: The Plaintiff Saml. Heberlig, and Deft. Wm. Ramp being both present. Thomas Hefflefinger having been first duly sworn says. I know Wm. Ramp. I know him to own real estate. He owns two farms, one of them situate in Hopewell Township Cumbd. County and containing about 200 acres; the other, situate in Mifflin Township in the same county containing about 200 acres. The first farm named I should suppose would sell for eight or nine dollars per acre cash, the land is part slate, part free stone: the house on it is bad. The barn is a tolerably good bank barn. The second farm named above has on it a tolerably good house and barn, land, slate and free stone mixed. I should not think it would be worth more than six or seven dollars per acre cash. I think both farms have gone down with a year or two, and are not as good as they were at that time. I know Mr. Ramp to have some personal property consisting in part of four head of horses, a waggon, tillery and usual farming implements. He lived upon and farmed the place in Hopewell township for one year, at least, ending about a year ago. He lived for part of last year and now lived near his Mifflin farm. I know Wm. Ramp worked hard. I never saw him abusing his family anytime that I have been in his house. I have noticed that his family was well fed and well clothed. For some years past I have not visited his house often. Sworn and Subscribed before" (signed James R. Irvine and Thomas Hefflefinger.)

March 18, 1852 -"John M. Miller having been first duly sworn says. I am acquainted with Wm. Ramp's two farms. I consider the farm in Hopewell Township worth eight dollars per acre cash. The farm in Mifflin township is, I think, worth six dollars per acre cash. I do not know what personal property he has except four head of horses, a wagon, tillery and farming implements. About eighteen months ago I was riding in company with Wm. Ramp and while talking of the difficulty between his wife and himself, he said that he would spend all his property, before he would knock under and allow his wife to get any of it. I know that at the time he said this the lawsuit between them had commenced. I never knew Ramp to destroy anything or to lay about not working. I never saw him disturbing any of his family, but I have been but little about his house. I know that Ramp's personal property was sold about a year since by David Wherry acting as his agent. The personal property he now owns he has bought since, with the exception of the wagon and one horse. Sworn and Subscribed before" (signed James R. Irvine and John M. Miller.)

March 18, 1852 -"James McDonnel having been first sworn says. Ramp once told me that his wife had applied for a divorce and the third of his property, and said that she might have the divorce, but not the thirds of his property. He also told me he could not have a wife and pay a housekeeper. He also told that he intended to have a new house and new wife, whether joking or not I cannot tell. It is hard to tell when he is joking. He was at the time in liquor. I saw him last year working on his Hopewell farm, making rails and harvesting and other work. Sworn and Subscribed before" (signed James R. Irvine and James McDonnel.)

March 18, 1852 -"Adam Failor having been first sworn says, In 1846 or 1847 I was hunting with Wm. Ramp. He was sober during part of the hunt and not sober during the other part. Ezra Williams was with us. During that hunt I held his horse while Williams assisted him to get into the saddle, and he was so intoxicated that he nearly fell over on the other side. I prevented him from falling and he was at last mounted and rode off and a short time after we found him on the ground, his horse standing beside him. We wanted to help him on his horse again. He would not get on, and we left him there. He told us to go on and he would follow. We waited for him frequently on the road, but did not see him afterwards. Sworn and Subscribed Before" (signed James R. Irvine and Adam Failor.)

March 18, 1852 -"John Holler having been first duly affirmed says, Ramp has told me that he would spend all his property before his wife should have a cent of it. This was about three years ago since the first difficulty with his wife. He further said that he would go to Carlisle and get money and give a Judgment on his property, so that those that were trying to get something for his wife could not get any of it. He told me at another time that he was to blame in part for his wife leaving him, but he could not bear all the blame, she was in fault also. I was living in Ramp's house when Miss Miller left him. Miss Miller left his house at night. Before she left she came running into the part of the house where I resided crying, and she asked me to back to Ramp's part, while she got her clothes, for she said she would stay with him no longer. I told my wife to go with her and as soon as she got her clothes she left the house and the next day came back and took what things she had left. Ramp was in the kitchen when she ran out of it to us. Ramp boarded with me three or four months. At one time when at the table told me the fish was lousey and the butter stunk, and I was glad when he quitted (sic) boarding with me. My wife washed for him, when he began to board with me. After a while she refused to wash for him any longer, saying that his clothes were so filthy that the thoughts of washing them was enough to make her vomit. I have known him to come home with a loaded pistol. If he has a grudge against any person he is disposed to be quarrelsome, and will revenge himself if he gets the chance. This all occurred within three years back since he and his wife separated. I have known to quarrel with John Heberlig. I have no hard feelings against Wm. Ramp. Affirmed and Subscribed Before" (signed James R. Irvine and John Holler.)

August Term 1851 #3 March 18, 1852 -"Susan Williams having been first sworn says, I lived with Wm. Ramp. I came to live with him about two years since. Shortly after I was there I found his clothes and they were very dirty. His bed and clothes were covered with human dirt. He said to me that his wife did not love him, and he did not care anything about her. That when she went to bed she was like an old sow and would lay grunt till morning. Once when he was drunk he said that she need not make such a fuss that he could have poison in her coffee and she would not have known it. He said if he had done right the second time she went away, he would have given her a d___d good kicking and then let her go. He said that he would get a step-mother for his children. He said that Peggy Miller wanted him to go to bed with her, but he would not do it, when he could get the old woman (her mother) behind the door for a quarter. He was in the habit of laying about the stove and vomiting when drunk. I have heard him say that two guns and a pistol loaded and would shoot Wm. Knettle or any of the Heberligs that would come on his premises to interrupt anything belonging to him. He also said at the same time that he would shoot his wife if she came upon his premises to disturb any of his property, for she had already taken more than he allowed her to have, that she could not have taken herself away all that she had, that some of the Heberligs must have taken away some of the things for her. While I lived with him he was quarreling all the time --disputing, complaining about the baking and cooking, and housekeepings -and could not be satisfied with anything. He also said that he never could get any bread fit to eat baked by his wife -sometimes it was dough; she could bake good bread if she pleased, he said but would not do it for him, she was too spiteful. Sworn and Subscribed Before" (signed James R. Irvine and Susan Williams by her mark.)

March 18, 1852 -"Mary Ann Myers having been first sworn says, during the month of Feby. last, Wm. Ramp came to my house, and told my mother, Mary Ramp, his wife, (who lives with me) in my presence, that he wished her to go home with him. She answered -I don't think you want me and he replied -No, I don't want you for I had two women last night, one in bed and one out of bed. I never knew of any person trying to persuade Mrs. Ramp to leave her husband. At the time the above conversation occurred, my father Wm. Ramp was somewhat in liquor, and talked a great. Ramp's words were -to my mother -I had two women last night, one in bed with me, and one out of bed. When my father and mother and myself lived together, he was very quarrelsome, scolding and storming about the house. Once when he was quarrelling and fighting with my mother, I interfered and he kicked at me. My youngest sister lived in the house at the same time. This last occurrence took place 5 or 6 years ago. At the time we had to get a man to watch father all the time. We were all afraid that he would do mischief to himself or to others. He threatened to hang himself at the same time. I was at my father's house at the time my mother returned after leaving him the first time. I cleaned up the house, and made the beds; there were five beds, and all of them were so filthy that they were not fit for any person to sleep in. He had been sleeping in the beds; they were covered with human dirt. He had not been sick at the time. Just before my mother left father the second time, he told her she might go, that no person could keep her anyhow. That the article of agreement made between him and his wife, was worth nothing, not even so much waste paper. Before my mother left the second time -I heard father call my mother all kinds of hard names, such as whore, bitch -told her some of her children were not his. I would not live with my father, if he would give me $100 a day -I could not do so, he behaves too badly, too hogishly. I have heard one of his house keepers say they could not live with him. Sworn and Subscribed Before" (signed James R. Irvine and Mary Ann Myers.)

August Term 1851 #3 March 18, 1852 -"Thomas Hefflefinger recalled. I was at Wm. Ramp's at one time when he was drunk in bed. He got up, while I was there and waiked out. Sarah Neidigh was in the room at the time. When he left the room she went up to the bed, and taking up the bedclothes, turned her head away and covered the bed with them sayinq she had never seen such a bed. There was a loud smell at the same time. It was the smell of human filth. She said she could not tell how she would wash them and would charge two dollars for doing so. Sworn and Subscribed before" (signed James R. Irvine and Thomas Heffelfinger.) -"Cumberland County ss -I do certify that the above witnesses were duly qualified and examined, at the time and place stated in the caption Before" (signed James R. Irvine March 18, 1852.)

Items of Costs

Justice J.R. Irvine (Paid by Saml. Heberlig.)	$2.12 1/2
John Stevich serving notice and Subpoena	3.12
Adam Heberlig serving subpoena	1.44
Witness Thos. Hefflefinger one day and 16 m. (cir.)	1.10 1/2
Witness Jno. M. Miller one day and 20 miles (cir.)	1.22 1/2
Witness James McDonnel one day and 18 miles (cir.)	1.16 1/2
Witness Adam Failor one day and 14 miles (cir.)	1.04 1/2
Witness John Holler one day and 18 miles (cir.)	1.16 1/2
Witness Mary Ann Myers one day and 16 m. (cir.)	1.10 1/2
Witness Susan Williams one day and 22 m. (cir.)	<u>1.28 1/2</u>
	$15.78"

Feb. 18, 1853 -"Mary Ramp by her next friend Samuel Heberlig vs. William Ramp: No. 3 August T. 1851 in the Common Pleas of Cumberland County -Divorce etc. -And now to wit -the 18 day of February A.D. 1853 -the examiners Robert Middleton Esq. and

James R. Irvine Esq. having returned to the Court here the depositions of witnesses taken before them on the part the libellant, and the same being read and heard by the court, and after mature and solemn deliberation, being satisfied therewith, and the respondent William Ramp, having also been heard by his counsel, and depositions read on his part, and he having shown no sufficent cause why the prayer of the libellant should not be granted, the Court do order, adjudge and decree that the said Mary Ramp the libellant be divorced and separated from the bed and board, society and fellowship of the said William Ramp the respondent for all time to come; and that the sum of one hundred and twenty dollars, be allowed and the same is hereby charged upon and directed to be paid by the said William Ramp the respondent to her the said Mary Ramp the libellant, from the filing of her libel to the time of this decree, for the expenses of her maintenance and support during that time, and that the further sum of sixty dollars per year payable quarterly be allowed, and the same is hereby charged upon and directed to be paid by the said William Ramp the respondent, to her the said Mary Ramp the libellant, annually, for the comfort, maintenance, and support of herself and family, from the date of this decree, to the time of her death or untill this be revoked or annulled by due course of law. By the Court" -Notation on the front of this document -"No. 3 Augt. 1851 Ramp vs. Ramp: Decree of Court filed 19 February 1853."

♦ ♦ ♦

April Term 1852 #25 Jan. 10, 1852 -"To the Honourable the Judges of the Court of Common Pleas for the county of Cumberland -The libel of Magdalena Whitman by her father and next friend Michael Albright respectfully showeth: That your libellant petitioner, on the 11th day of June 1840 was contracted in matrimony and married to a certain Jacob Whitman and from that time until the tenth day of April 1848 lived and cohabited with the said Jacob Whitman as wife, and as such was owned and acknowledged by him, and so deemed and reputed by her neighbours and acquaintances; and although by the laws of God, as well as by their mutual vows and faith plighted to each other, they were bound to that uniform constancy and regard which ought to be inseparable from the marriage state, yet, so it is, that the said Jacob Whitman from the 10th day of April 1848 hath wilfully and maliciously deserted and absented himself from the habitation of this libellant petitioner, without any just or reasonable cause, and such desertion hath persisted in for the term of two years and upwards, and yet doth continue to absent himself from the said libellant. Wherefore your libellant further showeth that she is a citizen of the State of Pennsylvania, and has resided therein for upwards of one whole year previous to the filing of this libel, prays your honours that a subpoena may issue forth, to summon the said Jacob Whitman, to appear in this honorable court at April term next, to answer the complaint aforesaid, and also, that a decree of this honourable court may be made for the divorcing of her, the said Magdalena Whitman from the society, fellowship, and company of the sd. Jacob Whitman in all time to come, and release this libellant from the marriage bond aforesaid as if she had never been married, or as if the said Jacob Whitman were naturally dead. And etc. (signed by her mark Magdelane Whitman.) -"Cumberland county ss -The above named Magdalena Whitman being duly sworn says the facts contained in the above libel are true to the best of her knowledge and belief; and that the said complaint is not made out of levity and collusion between her and the said Jacob Whitman and for the mere purpose of being freed and separated from each other, but in sincerity and truth for the causes mentioned in the said libel. Sworn before me this 10th day of January A.D. 1852." (signed J. Longenecker Justice of the Peace and Magdalena Whitman by her mark.) -Notation on the front of this document -"No. 25 April Term 1852 Filed Feby. 21 1852 20 February 1852 Subpoena awarded J.H. Graham Prest. Judge Issue Subpoena for divorce in this case." (signed S.W. Hyser.) Feb. 21, 1852 To Prothy. Cumb. Coy."

Feb. 21, 1852 -"Cumberland County Sct. -The Commonwealth of Pennsylvania to the Sheriff of Cumberland County Greeting: Whereas Magdalena Whitman by her father and next friend Michael Albright on the 20th day of February A.D. 1852 did prefer a petition to our said Judges of our Court of Common Pleas for the County of Cumberland, praying for the causes therein set forth, that she might be divorced from the bonds of matrimony entered into with you Jacob Whitman. We do therefore command you the said Jacob Whitman that setting aside all other business and excuses whatsoever you be and appear in your proper person before our Judges at Carlisle at a Court of Common Pleas, there to be held for the County of Cumberland on the 12th day of April next, to answer the petition or libel of the said Magdalena Whitman and to shew cause if any you have why the said Magdalena Whitman your wife, should not be divorced from the bonds of matrimony, agreeably to the Acts of Assembly in such case made and provided. And hereof fail not. Witness the Honorable James H. Graham President of our said Court, at Carlisle this 21 day February A.D. 1852 for Geo. Zinn Prothy." (signed Jas. F. Lamberton Esq.)

April 19, 1852 -"Cumberland County SS -David Smith, Sheriff of Cumberland County being sworn says that the within named Jacob Whitman cannot be found in his bailiwick, to the best of his knowledge and belief. Sworn and Subscribed before me 19 April 1852." (signed George Zinn Prothy. and David Smith Shff.) -Notation on the front of this document -"No. 25 April T. 1852 Magdalena Whitman by her father and next friend Michael Albright vs. Jacob Whitman Subpoena Sur Divorce 19th April 1852 Als Subp. Sur Divorce awarded By the Court N.E.I. So answers" (signed David Smith Shrff.) "Shff. Smith's fee $0.18 3/4. N.W. Hepburn."

April 19, 1852 -"Cumberland County Sct. -The Commonwealth of Pennsylvania to the Sheriff of Cumberland County Greeting: Whereas Magdalena Whitman by her father and next friend Michael Albright on the 20th day of February A.D. 1852 did prefer a petition to our said Judge of our Court of Common Pleas for the County of Cumberland, praying for the causes therein set forth, that she might be divorced from the bonds of matrimony entered into with you Jacob Whitman. We do therefore command you, as you heretofore have been commanded the said Jacob Whitman that, setting aside all other business and excuses whatsoever, you be and appear in your proper person before our Judges at Carlisle at a Court of Common Pleas, there to be held for the County of Cumberland, on the 23d day of of August next, to answer the petition or libel of the said Magdalena Whitman your wife, should not 1 divorced from the bonds of matrimony, agreeably to the acts of Assembly in such case made and provided. And hereof fail not. Witness the Honorable James H. Graham President of our said Court, at Carlisle this 19 April A.D. 1852." (signed George Zinn Prothy.)

August 23, 1852 -"Cumberland County Sct. -David Smith Sheriff of Cumberland County being sworn says that the within named defendant cannot be found in his bailiwick to the best of his knowledge and belief. Sworn and Subscribed before me 23 August 1852." (signed George Zinn Prothy. and David Smith Shrff.) -Notation on the front of this document -"No. 25 April T. 1852 Magdalena Whitman by her father and next friend Michael Albright vs. Jacob Whitman Als. Subpoena Sur Divorce Shff. Smith's fee $0.18 3/4. N.W. Hepburn."

♦ ♦ ♦

August Term 1852 #48 July 9, 1852 -"To the Honorable James H. Graham, President Judge of the Court of Common Pleas of the County of Cumberland -The petition of Nathan Deh, of the township of North Middleton -Respectfully Represents -That your petitioner on the 17th day of June 1852, was lawfully joined in marriage with Catharine Ellwinger, and from that time hath lived and in all respects demeaned himself as a kind and loving husband. And although by the laws of God, as well as by the natural vows plighted to each other they were bound to that chastity which ought to inseparable from the marriage state, yet the said Catharine, since her marriage to the said Nathan, has been delivered of a still born child, to wit, on the 4th day of July last, which child was begotten by a certain (first name left blank) Bennet, about Christmas last, by the confession of the said Catharine and further that said child was not begotten by said libellant. Wherefore your libellant further shewing that he is a citizen of the state of Pennsylvania and has resided therein for upwards of one whole year previous to the filing of this his libel, prays your honor that a subpoena may issue forth to summon the said Catharine to appear at the next term of the said court, to answer the complaint aforesaid. And also that a decree of this honorable court may be made for the divorcing of her, the said Catharine from the society, fellowship and company of this libellant in all time to come and him, this libellant from the marriage bond aforesaid as if he had never been married or as if the said Catharine were naturally dead. And he will pray etc." (signed Nathan Deh.) -"Cumberland County SS. -The above named Nathan Deh being duly sworn says that the facts contained in the foregoing libel are true to the best of his knowledge and belief; and that the said complaint is not made out of levity and by collusion between him the said Nathan and her the said Catharine, and for the mere purpose of being freed from each other, but in sincerity and truth for the causes mentioned in said libel. Sworn and Subscribed before me this 9th day of July 1852." (signed Nathan Deh and M. Holcomb Justice of the Peace.) -"Nathan Deh vs. Catharine Deh: Sur Issue Sub. Sur divorce To Geo. Zinn Jr. Esq. Prothy." (signed Wm. H. Miller 9th July 52.) -Notation on the front of this document -"No. 48 August Term 1852 Nathan Deh vs. Catharine Deh: Summons Sur divorce 9 July 1852 Subpoena Awarded." (sign J.H. Graham Prest. Judge.) "filed 9 July 1852 Plff. for tax and writ -Miller."

July 9, 1852 -"Cumberland County S.S. -The Commonwealth of Pennsylvania to the Sheriff of Cumberland County Greeting: Whereas Nathan Deh on the 9th day of July A.D. 1852 did prefer a petition to our said Judge of our Court of Common Pleas for the County of Cumberland praying for the causes therein set forth, that he might be divorced from the bonds of matrimony entered into with you Catharine Deh. We do therefore command you the said Catharine Deh, that, setting aside all other business and excuses whatsoever you be and appear in your proper person before our Judges at Carlisle at a Court of Common Pleas, there to be held for the County of Cumberland on the 23d day of August next to answer the petition or libel of the said Nathan Deh and to shew cause if any you have why the said Nathan Deh your husband, should not be divorced from the bonds of matrimony agreeably to the Act of Assembly in such case made and provided. And hereof fail not. Witness the Honorable James H. Graham President of our said Court at Carlisle this 9th day of July A.D. 1852." (signed George Zinn Prothy.)

July 12, 1852 -"Cumberland County ss -E. Cornman Deputy Sheriff being sworn says that he served the within writ personally and by copy on Catharine Deh on the 12th day of July 1852. Sworn and Subscribed before" (signed Geo. Zinn Prothy. 23d August 1852 and E. Cornman.) -Notation on the front of this document -"No. 48

August Term 1852 Nathan Deh vs. Catharine Deh Subpoena Sur Divorce Shff. Smith's fee $1.35 1/2. Miller."

♦ ♦ ♦

November Term 1852 #3 August 23, 1852 -"To the Honourable the Judges of the Court of Common Pleas of Cumberland County The petition of Levi Lyon Respectfully Sheweth -That your petitioner on or about the 15 day of September A.D. 1851 was bound in matrimony and married to a certain Julia Woodly and from that time until the last day of September 1852 lived and cohabited with the said petitioner as her husband and as such was owned and acknowledged by her and so deemed and reputed by their neighbours and acquaintances. And although by the laws of God as well as by their mutual vows and faith plighted to each other they were bound to that uniform constancy and regard which ought to be inseparable from the marriage state, yet so it is that the said Julia in violation of her marriage vow hath for a considerable time past being at such time domiciled within the Commonwealth of Pennsylvania given herself up to adulterous practices, and been guilty of adultery with diverse persons. Wherefore your libellant further shewing that he is a citizen of the State of Pennsylvania and has resided therein for upwards of one whole year previous to filing of this his libel prays your honors that a subpoena may issue forth to summon the said Julia to appear in this honorable court at the November term next to answer his complaint aforesaid. And also that this honorable court may decree a divorce and separation from the said nuptial ties or bonds of matrimony heretofore uniting as above mentioned this libellant to and with the said Julia. Cumberland County ss Levi Lyon the above libellant being duly sworn deposes and says that the facts contained in said petition or libel are true to the best of his knowledge and belief and that the said complaint is not made out of levity or by collusion between the said husband and wife and for the mere purpose of being freed and separated from each other but in sincerity and truth for the causes mentioned in the said petition or libel. Sworn and Subscribed before 23rd August 1852." (signed Geo. Ege and Levi Lyon by his mark.) -Notation on the front of this document -"No. 3 November Term 1852 Petition of Levi Lyon for Subpoena Sur divorce 23rd August 1852 Subpoena awarded By the Court filed 23d August 1852."

Aug. 23, 1852 -"Cumberland County SS -The Commonwealth of Pennsylvania to the Sheriff of Cumberland County Greeting: Whereas Levi Lyon on the 23d day of August A.D. 1852 did prefer a petition to our said Judge of our Court of Common Pleas for the county of Cumberland, praying for the causes therein set forth that he might be divorced from the bonds of matrimony entered into with you Julia Woodly. We do therefore command you the said Julia Lyon that setting aside all other business and excuses whatsoever you be and appear in your proper person before our Judges at Carlisle at a Court of Common Pleas, there be held for the County of Cumberland on the 8 day of November next to answer the petition or libel of the said Levi Lyon and to shew cause if any you have why the said Levi Lyon your husband, should not be divorced from the bonds of matrimony, agreeably to the Acts of Assembly in such case made and provided. And hereof fail not. Witness the Honorable James H. Graham President of our said Court at Carlisle this 23d day of August A.D. 1852." (signed George Zinn Prothy.) -Notation on the front of this document -"No. 3 November Term 1852 Levi Lyon vs. Julia Lyone Subpoena Sur Divorce 30 Oct. 1852 Served personally and by copy So answers" (signed E. Cornman Dep. Shff. and David Smith Shff.) "Shff. Smith's fee $0.95 1/2. Penrose."

♦ ♦ ♦

January Term 1853 #3 Oct. 25, 1852 -"To the Honble. The Judges of the Court of Common Pleas of Cumberland County -The petition of Catharine Eichelberger by her next friend Levi Eberly Respectfully Showeth -That your petitioner was on the fourth of August A.D. One thousand Eight hundred and thirty three lawfully joined in marriage with Jacob Eichelberger her present husband and from that time until the month of August A.D. One thousand Eight hundred and fifty one when the said Jacob Eichelberger deserted her; lived and cohabited with him and hath in all respects demeaned herself as a kind and affectionate wife, and although by the laws of God as well as by the mutual vows plighted to each other they were bound to that uniform constancy and regard which ought to be inseparable from the marriage state yet so it is that the said Jacob in violation of his marriage vow hath for a considerable time past given himself up to adulterous practices and been guilty of adultery with a certain Mary Huber (with whom since the 27th June last past he has been living as her husband) and with diverse other persons to your petitioner unknown. Wherefore your libellant further shewing that she is a citizen of the Commonwealth of Pennsylvania, and hath resided therein for more than one whole year previous to the filing of this her petition, prays your Honors that a subpoena may issue in due form of law directed to the said Jacob Eichelberger commanding him to appear in this Honorable Court to answer the complaint aforesaid: And also that a decree of this Honorable Court may be made for the divorcing of her the said Catharine from the bond of matrimony as if she had never been married. And she will pray etc." (signed Catharine Eichelberger by her next friend Levi Eberly.) -"Cumberland County SS -The above named Catharine Eichelberger being duly affirmed according to law doth depose and say that the facts contained in the foregoing petition or libel are true to the best of her knowledge and belief; and that the said complaint is not made out of levity, or by collusion between her the said Catharine Eichelberger and the said Jacob Eichelberger her husband, and for the mere purpose of being separated from each other, but in sincerity and truth for the causes mentioned in the said petition or libel. Affirmed and Subscribed this 25th October 1852 before me" (signed Geo. Ege and Catharine Eichelberger.) -Notation on the front of this document -"No. 3 January Term 1853 Catharine Eichelberger by her next friend Levi Eberly vs. Jacob Eichelberger filed 8 Nov. 1852 Subpoena in divorce. 8 Novr. 1852 Subpoena awarded returnable to the Jany. T. 1853 By the Court."

Nov. 8, 1852 -"Cumberland County Sct -The Commonwealth of Pennsylvania to the Sheriff of Cumberland County Greeting -Whereas Catharine Eichelberger by her next friend Levi Eberly did on the 8th day of November A.D. 1852 prefer a petition to our said Judges of our Court of Common Pleas for the County of Cumberland praying for the causes therein set forth, that she might be divorced from the bonds of matrimony entered into with you the said Jacob Eichelberger. We do therefore command you the said Jacob Eichelberger that setting aside all other business and excuses whatsoever you be and appear in your proper person before our Judges at Carlisle, at a court of Common Pleas there to be held for the County of Cumberland on the 10th day of January next to answer the petition or libel of the said Catharine Eichelberger and to show cause if any you have why the said Catharine Eichelberger your wife should not be divorced from the bonds of matrimony agreeably to the acts of Assembly in such case made and provided -and hereof fail not. Witness the Honorable James H. Graham President of our said court at Carlisle the 8th day of November 1852." (signed George Zinn Prothy.) -"Cumberland County Sct -Jos. McDarmond, Sheriff, being sworn says that the within named Jacob Eichelberger cannot be found in his bailiwick to the best of his knowledge and belief. Sworn and subscribed before me 7 January 1853." (signed George Zinn Prothy. and Jos. McDarmond Shff.) -Notation on the front of this document -"No. 3 January Term 1853 Catharine Eichelberger by her next friend Levi Eberly vs. Jacob Eichelberger Subpoena in Divorce Shff. McDarmond's fee $0.18 1/4. Biddle."

Jan. 13, 1853 -"Cumberland County Sct. -The Commonwealth of Pennsylvania to the Sheriff of Cumberland County, Greeting Whereas Catharine Eichelberger by her next friend Levi Eberly did on the 8th day of November A.D. 1852 prefer a petition to our said Judges of our Court of Common Pleas for the County of Cumberland, praying for the causes therein set forth, that she might be divorced from the bonds of matrimony entered into with you the said Jacob Eichelberger. We do therefore command you the said Jacob Eichelberger, that setting aside all other business and excuses whatsoever, you be and appear in your proper person before our Judges at Carlisle, at a Court of Common Pleas there to be held the County of Cumberland on the 11th day of April next to answer the petition or libel of the said Catharine Eichelberger, and to show cause if any you have why the said Catharine Eichelberger, your wife should not be divorced from the bonds of matrimony agreeably to the acts of Assembly in such case made and provided -and hereof fail not. Witness the Honorable James H. Graham President of our said Court at Carlisle the 13 day of January 1853." (signed George Zinn Prothy.)

April 9, 1853 -"Cumberland County Sct -Joseph McDarmond Sheriff being sworn says that the within named Jacob Eichelberger cannot be found in his bailiwick to the best of his knowledge and belief. Sworn and Subscribed before" (signed George Zinn Prothy and J.L. McDarmond Shff 9th April 1853.) "Joseph McDarmond Sheriff being duly sworn says that notice was published in two newspapers printed in the Borough of Carlisle." -Notation on the front of this document -"No. 3 April Term 1853 Catharine Eichelberger by her next friend Levi Eberly vs. Jacob Eichelberger Alias Subpoena Sur Divorce April 9th 1853 writ returned Non est inventus So answers" (signed Jos. McDarmond Shff.) -"Shrff. McDarmond's fee $0.18 1/4. Henderson."

Aug. 22, 1853 -"Catharine Eichelberger by her next friend Levi Eberly vs. Jacob Eichelberger: No. 3 Apl. T. 1853 Joseph McDarmond Sheriff being duly sworn says that notice was published in two newspapers in the Borough of Carlisle for four weeks successively prior to the 22nd day of August A.D. 1853 -the first day of the present term, requiring the said defendant Jacob Eichelberger to answer the complaint of the said Catharine Eichelberger and to show cause if any why she should not be divorced from the bonds of matrimony, agreeably to the acts of Assembly in such case made and provided. Sworn and subscribed before me 22 Aug. 1853." (signed Geo. Zinn Prothy. and J.L. McDarmond Shff.) -Notation on the front of this document -"With No. 3 April 1853 filed 22 Aug. 1853 22d Aug. 1853 Wm. D. Shupp Esq. apptd. Commissioner to take testimony By the Court."

Aug. 22, 1853 -"Catharine Eichelberger by her next friend Levi Eberly vs. Jacob Eichelberger: No. 3 April Term 1853 Alias Subpoena Sur Divorce 22 Aug. 1853 Wm. D. Shupp Esq. appointed Commissioner to take testimony etc. By the Court." -"Cumberland County SS: I Geo. Zinn Prothy. of the Court of Common Pleas of said county do certify that the above is a true extract taken from the records of said court. Given under my hand the seal of said Court at Carlisle the 26th day of A.D. 1853." (signed Geo. Zinn Prothy.)

Sept. 21, 1853 -"Catharine Eichelberger by her next friend Levi Eberly vs. Jacob Eichelberger: No. 3 April Term 1853 Alias Subpoena Sur Divorce etc. -Depositions of Lewis Bricker, Rev. Samuel Eberly, Matthias Bitner Esq. and James M. Flender, witnesses produced, sworn and examined by me the twenty-first day of September

A.D. 1853, at my office in Shiremanstown Lower Allen township by virtue of the annexed rule of Court of Common Pleas. And taken at the instance (sic) of the Plntff. The said Lewis Bricker personally appeared and being duly sworn doth depose and say: I am well acquainted with the parties in this suit Catharine Eichelberger and Jacob Eichelberger, I knew Mr. Eichelberger before his marriage. I was in their house and know that the parties lived and cohabited together as man and wife. It is about fourteen years since I was in the habit of occasionally calling at their house. I was well acquainted with the Rev. Emanuel Keller and with his wife. The Rev. Emanuel Keller died the 11th of April A.D. 1837 and his wife died about two years after that. I was acquainted with Mr. Keller's hand writing. I believe the certificate marked A and dated the 4th day of Augt. 1833 and purporting to be the certificate of Mr. Jacob Eichelberger's marriage to Catharine Eberly (the present parties in this suit) to be the hand writing of Emanuel Keller, and that the same is a genuine certificate of the said Rev. Emanuel Keller. And further deponent saith not. Examination taken and reduced to writing and by the witness subscribed and sworn to, this 21st day of September A.D. 1853." (signed W.D. Shoop Commissioner and Lewis Bricker.)

Sept. 21, 1853 -"At the same time and place appeared the Rev. Samuel Eberly who being duly affirmed doth depose and say: I am acquainted with the parties in this suit the libellant and respondent. I have been acquainted with them from their childhood up; I recollect the time when they got married; it is about twenty years since their marriage. I was not present at the marriage. They lived and cohabited together as man and wife. They lived together till within between two and three years; at which time the respondent left his wife and absented himself from the habitation of the said libellant Catharine Eichelberger. I know of no cause that he had for thus leaving her. His desertion was willful and I believe malicious. He still persists in absenting himself. It is more than two years since Mr. Jacob Eichelberger told me he would no longer provide for his family. He assigned no reason to me why he left his wife, and I think he had none. And further deponent saith not. Examination taken and reduced to writing and by the witness subscribed and affirmed to this 21st day of September A.D. 1853." (signed W.D. Shoop Commissioner and Samuel Eberly Sr.)

Sept. 21, 1853 -"At the same time and place appeared Matthias Bitner Esq. who being duly affirmed doth depose and say: I am acquainted with the parties in this suit the libellant and respondent. I was acquainted with Jacob Eichelberger from his boyhood up. It is about eight or ten years since I became acquainted with Catharine Eichelberger. At that time they lived together and cohabited as man and wife. I know that he left and deserted his wife the said Catharine Eichelberger. In the spring of 1851 he refused to pay the store bill which his wife had purchased at my store. The goods had been for the use of the family and were partly groceries and partly dry goods. He rufused to pay all goods that had been purchased after June or July 1850. It is now more than three years since he has wilfully and maliciously deserted his family. It was about June or July A.D. 1850 when he notified me that he would no longer pay for any articles whatever his wife might buy. I know that he is married again because he told me so. He Jacob Eichelberger the repallant (sic) told me that he was married to a lady (whose name I have forgotten) of Lancaster County. I know of no reasons that he had for deserting his family. The parties to this suit have five children living and they have some that are dead. And further deponent saith not. Examination taken and reduced to writing and by the witness subscribed and affirmed to this 21st day of September A.D. 1853." (signed W.D. Shoop Commissioner and M. Ritner.)

Sept. 21, 1853 -"At the same time and place appeared James M. Flender who being duly affirmed doth depose and say: I am acquainted with the parties (Catharine Eichelberger and Jacob Eichelberger) in this suit. I know that they lived and cohabited together as man and wife. I know that the said Jacob Eichelberger has wilfully and maliciously deserted and absented himself from the habitation of the said libellant Catharine Eichelberger without any reasonable cause. I have lived with the parties, and all appeared to be right between them. It is about three years since he left her, and about that long since he told me he would no more provide for the said libellant. He told me he was married. He is at this time married to a lady at Dillersville Lancaster County. I have forgotten her name. I have seen the woman to whom he is married since his marriage to her. I knew her before her married. They have two children; I mean in this last marriage. The parties in this suit have five children living and some that are dead. And further deponent saith not. Examination taken and reduced to writing and by the witness subscribed and affirmed to this 21st day of Sept. A.D. 1853." (signed W.D. Shoop Commissioner and James M. Flender.)

Sept. 21, 1853 (Marriage certificate marked "A" pasted on document) "What God hath joined together, let no man put asunder. I certify that on the 4th day of Augt. 1833 I have solemnized the rite of matrimony between Mr. Jacob Eichelberger and Miss Catharine Eberly according to law. Witness my hand Emanuel Keller Minister of the Gospel." -"At the execution of the commission "to take testimony etc." in the case of "Catharine Eichelberger by her next friend Levi Eberly vs. Jacob Eichelberger" the above "certificate" of "Emanuel Keller" was produced and shown to Lewis Bricker and by him deposed unto at the time of his examination, and is the certificate refered to by him as the paper marked A." (signed W.D. Shoop Commissioner.) -Notation on the front of this document -"No. 3 April

Term 1853 Eichelberger vs. Eichelberger Divorce filed 8 November 1853. Biddle."

Nov. 8, 1853 -"Catharine Eichelberger by her next friend Levi Eberly vs. Jacob Eichelberger: No. 3 April Term 1853 Alias Subpoena Sur Divorce -And now to wit the 8th November A.D. 1853 the Commissioner William D. Shoop Esq., having returned to the Court here the depositions of witnesses taken before him on the part of the libellant and the same being read and heard by the Court, and the Court after mature and solemn deliberation being satisfied therewith, and proclamation being duly made for the Respondent to come forth and he not appearing, the Court do order adjudge and decree that the said Catharine Eichelberger the Libellant be divorced and separated from the bond of matrimony contracted with the said Jacob Eichelberger the Respondent and that all and every the duties rights and claims, accruing to either of said parties by reason of the said marriage shall henceforth cease and determine, and the said parties be severally at liberty to marry again in like manner as if they never had been married. Respondent to pay all costs of the proceedings. By the Court." -Notation on the front of the document -"No. 3 April Term 1853 Eichelberger vs. Eichelberger Decree of Court filed 8 November 1853. Biddle."

◆   ◆   ◆

January Term 1853 #4 Nov. 8, 1852 -"To the Honorable the Judges of the Court of Common Pleas of Cumberland County -The libel of Suzan (sic) Peters by her next friend Jacob Sadler Respectfully Sheweth That your libellant was on the 21st day of January 1851 lawfully joined in marriage with Samuel Peters and lived and cohabited with the said Samuel Peters, as his wife and as such was owned and acknowledged by him and so deemed and reputed by their neighbors and acquaintances. And although by the laws of God, as well as by their mutual vows and faith plighted to each other, they were bound to that uniform constancy and regard which ought to be inseparable from the marriage state, yet so it is that the said Samuel Peters in violation of his marriage vow hath for a considerable time past being at such time domiciled within the Commonwealth of Pennsylvania, given himself up to adulterous practices and been guilty of adultery with a certain Polly Shamberger and diverse other persons to your petitioner unknown. And further that the said Samuel Peters hath wilfully and maliciously deserted your petitioner. Wherefore libellant further showing that she is a citizen of this State, and has resided therein for upwards of one whole year previous to the filing of this petition, prays your honors, that a subpoena may issue from the said Court directed to the next term of the said Court, to answer this petition, and also that the honorable Court may decree a divorce and separation from the said nuptial ties or bonds of matrimony, heretofore uniting, as before mentioned this libellant with the said Samuel Peters. And the said libellant will pray etc." (signed Susan Peters by her next friend Jacob Sadler.) -"Cumberland County SS. Personally appeared before me one of the Justices of the Peace in and for said County, Suzan (sic) Peters, who being duly sworn deposeth that the facts set forth in the foregoing petition or libel are true, and that the said complaint is not made out of levity or collusion between this libellant and her said husband, and for the mere purpose of being freed and separated from each other, but in sincerity and truth for the causes mentioned in said petition or libel. Sworn and Subscribed before me this 8th day of November 1852." (signed Geo. Ege J.P. and Susan Peters by her mark.) -Notation on the front of this document -"No. 4 January Term 1853 Petition of Suzan Peters by her next friend Jacob Sadler for a divorce filed 8 Nov. 1852 8th Novr. 1852 Subpoena awarded returnable at next term By the Court Suzan Peters by her next friend Jacob Sadler vs. Samuel Peters: To George Zinn Esq. Prothy. Sir Issue Subpoena sur divorce." (signed R.M. Henderson Atty. for Plff. 8 Nov. 1852.)

Nov. 8, 1852 -"Cumberland County Sct. -The Commonwealth of Pennsylvania to the Sheriff of Cumberland County Greeting: Whereas Susan Peters by her next friend Jacob Sadler did on the 8th day of November A.D. 1852 prefer a petition to our said Judges of our Court of Common Pleas for the County of Cumberland praying for the causes therein set forth, that she might divorced from the bonds of matrimony entered into with the said Samuel Peters. We do therefore command you the said Samuel Peters, that setting aside all other business and excuses whatsoever you be and appear in your proper person before our Judges at Carlisle at a Court of Common Pleas there to be held for the County of Cumberland on the 10th day of January next to answer the petition or libel of the said Susan Peters and to show cause if any you have why the said Susan Peters your wife should not be divorced from the bonds of matrimony agreeably to the Acts of Assembly in such case made and provided -And hereof fail not. Witness the Honorable James H. Graham President of our said Court at Carlisle the 8th day of November 1852." (signed George Zinn Prothy.)

Jan. 7, 1853 -"Cumberland County Sct. Jos. McDarmond, Sheriff, being sworn says that the within named Samuel Peters, cannot be found in his bailiwick to the best of his knowledge and belief. Sworn and subscribed before me 7 January 1853." (signed George Zinn Prothy. and Jos. McDarmond Shff.) -Notation on the front of this document -"No. 4 January Term 1853 Susan Peters by her next friend Jacob Sadler vs. Samuel Peters Subpoena Sur Divorce Shff. McDarmond's fee $0.18 1/4. Henderson."

Jan. 13, 1853 -"Cumberland County Sct. -The Commonwealth of Pennsylvania to the Sheriff of Cumberland County Greeting Whereas Susan Peters by her next friend Jacob Sadler did on the 8 day of

November A.D. 1852 prefer a petition to our said Judges of our Court of Common Pleas for the County of Cumberland praying for the causes therein set forth, that she might be divorced from the bonds of matrimony entered into with the said Samuel Peters. We do therefore command you the said Samuel Peters, that setting aside all other business and excuses whatsoever you be and appear in yor proper person before our Judges at a Court of Common Pleas there to be held for the County of Cumberland on the 11th day of April next to answer the petition or libel of the said Susan Peters, and to show cause if any you have why the said Susan Peters your wife, should not be divorced from the bonds of matrimony agreeably to the Acts of Assembly in such case made and provided -and hereof fail not. Witness the Honorable James H. Graham President of our said Court at Carlisle the 13th day of January 1853." (signed George Zinn Prothy.)

April 9, 1853 -"Cumberland County Sct -Joseph McDarmond Sheriff being sworn says that the within named Samuel Peters cannot be found in his bailiwick to the best of his knowledge and belief. April 9th 1853 Sworn and Subscribed before me" (signed George Zinn Prothy and Jos. McDarmond Shff.) -Notation on the front of this document -"No. 4 April Term 1853 Susan Peters by her next friend Jacob Sadler vs. Samuel Peters Alias Subpoena Sur Divorce April 9th 1853 writ returned Non est inventus So answers" (signed J.L. McDarmond Shff.) -"Shff. McDarmond's fee $0.18 1/2. Henderson."

Aug. 22, 1853 -"Susan Peters by her next friend Jacob Sadler vs. Samuel Peters: No. 4 April Term 1853 Joseph McDarmond Sheriff being duly sworn says that notice was published in two newspapers in the Borough of Carlisle for four weeks successively prior to the 22d day of August A.D. 1853 the first day of the present term requiring the said defendant Samuel Peters to answer the complaint of the said Susan Peters and to show cause if any why she should not be divorced from the bonds of matrimony agreeably to the Acts of Assembly in such case made and provided. Sworn and Subscribed before me 22 Aug. 1853." (signed Geo. Zinn Prothy and Jos. McDarmond Shff.) -Notation on the front of this document "With No. 4 April 1853 filed 22 Aug. 1853 22 Aug. 1853 Wm. D. Shupp (sic) Esq. appointed commissioner to take testimony etc. By the Court."

Aug. 22, 1853 -"Susan Peters by her next friend Jacob Sadler vs. Samuel Peters: No. 4 April Term 1853 Alias Subpoena Sur Divorce 22 Aug. 1853 Wm. D. Shupp (sic) appointed Commissioner to take testimony etc. By the Court. Cumberland County S.S. -I Geo. Zinn Prothy., of the Court of Common Pleas of said County do certify that the above is a true extract taken from the records of said Court. Given under my hand and the seal of said Court at Carlisle the 26th Augst. A.D. 1853." (signed Geo. Zinn Prothy.)

Sept. 17, 1853 -"Susan Peters by her next friend Jacob Sadler vs. Samuel Peters: No. 4 April Term 1853 Alias Subpoena Sur Divorce etc. Depositions of Elizabeth Simmons and Jacob McCartney witnesses produced sworn and examined by me at my office in Shiremanstown by virtue of the annexed rule of court. Taken at the instance (sic) of the Plaintiff on the seventeenth day of September A.D. 1853 at the office of W.D. Shoop Esq. in Shiremanstown in the county of Cumberland and state of Pennsylvania. The said Elizabeth Simmons personally appeared and being duly sworn doth depose and say: I am well acquainted with Samuel Peters. I had some acquaintance with him before his marriage to Susan Simmons, which was sometime in the month of January A.D. 1851. They had one child born in the month of July following. He left her in about seven weeks after the child was born. About eight days before he left his wife he said in my presence that he was better acquainted with a certain female (whom he named) than he was with his wife. I do not think that he had any knowledge of her prior to his marriage. I saw him in company with this same female in the green lane which leads from Hoguestown late one evening either in the last week of June or the first week in July. They were both laying on the ground and they were close together. I was going home from the store; I had been there for sugar. It was twilight; this was in the same year of his marriage and prior to the birth of the child. I frequently heard him say that he would not live without having connections with other women. And further deponent saith not. Sworn and subscribed by making her mark before me this 17 Sept. 1853." (signed W.D. Shoop Commissioner and Elizabeth Simmons by her mark.)

Sept. 17, 1853 -"At the same time and place appeared Jacob McCartney who being duly sworn doth depose and say, I was acquainted with Samuel Peters. I became acquainted with him after his marriage. I saw him at the camp meeting in Mr. Bricker's woods, in the month of September 1851. I heard him ask a female (name omitted) on Sunday evening at the campmeeting to go with him out into the woods. She replied the leaves are too wet to night (sic), but to morrow (sic) night I will go with you. It had rained that day. I was standing close by at the time and heard distinctly what was said. We went home together that night and on the road home I upbraided him for his conduct with this female. He then told me that he had been with her the night before at a certain house and that he (Samuel Peters) had had connections with her. He told me the same evening that he intended to leave his wife; but before he left her he intended to make another one (child) for her. I told him if he done that he ought to be tarred and feathered. This was also said in reply to my upbraiding him for his conduct and not staying at home with his wife as a man should do. This same female has had an illegitamate (sic) child since that time, at nine months after the campmeeting. And further deponent saith not. Sworn and subscribed before me this 17th Sept. A.D. 1853." (signed W.D. Shoop Commissioner and Jacob McCartney.) -Notation on the front of this document -"No. 4 April Term 1853 filed 8 November 1853."

Nov. 8, 1853 -"Suzan Peters by her next friend Jacob Sadler vs. Samuel Peters: And now the eighth day of November A.D. 1853 the Commissioner W.D. Shoop Esq. appointed to take testimony, having returned to the Court the depositions of witnesses taken before him on the part of the libellant and the same being read and heard by the Court and proclamation being duly made for the defendant to come forth and not appearing, the Court do order adjudge and decree that the said Susan Peters, be divorced and separated from the bond of matrimony contracted with the said Samuel Peters, the defendant, and that all and every the duties, rights and claims accruing to either of the said parties by reason of the said marriage shall henceforth cease and determine, and the said parties be severally at liberty to marry again in like manner as if they never had been married. And that the respondent pay the costs of the proceedings. By the Court. -"Notation on the front of this document -"No. 4 April Term 1853 filed 8 November 1853."

♦   ♦   ♦

April Term 1853 #29 Feb. 1853 -"To the Hon. The Judges of the Court of Common Pleas of Cumberland County -The petition of Lydia Brownawell by her father and next friend Samuel Senseman Respectfully Represents -That in the month of August 1851 she the said Lydia was lawfully joined in wedlock with Henry Brownawell and continued to live and cohabit with him after that time for and during the period of about one year during which she demeaned and behaved herself as a dutiful wife should do but the said Henry Brownawell unmindful of his marriage vow and disregarding the duty and protection which he owed to his said wife did by cruel and barbarous treatment endanger his wife's life and did offer such indignities to her person as to render her condition intolerable and life burthensome and has thereby forced her to withdraw from his house and family. She therefore prays your Honors to subpoena the said Henry Brownawell to appear before your Honorable Court to answer the complaint of the said Lydia Brownawell and shew cause why she should not be divorced from the bonds of matrimony for which she prays." (signed Lydia Brownewell By her next friend Saml. Senserman.) -"Cumberland County sct. Personally appeared before me a Justice of the Peace in and for said County Lydia Brownawell who being duly sworn doth depose and say that the facts contained in the above petition are true to the best of her knowledge and belief and that the said complaint is not made out of levity or by collusion between her and her said husband and for the mere purpose of being freed and separated from each other but in sincerity and truth for the causes mentioned in the said petition. Sworn and Subscribed the (left blank) day of Feb. 1853 Before me." (signed John Palmer and Lydia Brownawell.) -Notation on the front of this document -"No. 29 April Term 1853 Lydia Brownawell vs. Henry Brownawell Petition for a Subpoena 18 February 1853 Subpoena is awarded by the Court. By the Court. Filed 18 February 1853. Watts and Parker."

Feb. 18, 1853 -"Cumberland County Sct. -The Commonwealth of Pennsylvania to the Sheriff of Cumberland County Greeting Whereas Lydia Brownawell by her father and next friend Samuel Senseman on the 18th day of February A.D. 1853, did prefer a petition to our said Judges of our Court of Common Pleas for the County of Cumberland praying for the causes therein set forth, that she might be divorced from the bond of matrimony entered into with you Henry Brownawell. We therefore do command you the said Henry Brownawell that setting aside all other business and excuses whatsoever, you be and appear in your proper person, before our Judges at Carlisle at a Court of Common Pleas, there to be held for the County of Cumberland on the 11th day of April next to answer the petition or libel of the said Lydia Brownawell and to show cause if any you have why the said Lydia Brownawell your wife, should not be divorced from the bonds of matrimony, agreeably to the Acts of Assembly in such case made and provided. And hereof fail not. Witness the Honorable James H. Graham President of our said Court at Carlisle this 18th day of February A.D. 1853." (signed George Zinn Prothy.)

Aug. 22, 1853 -"Now to wit 22 Aug. 1853 on return of Watts and Parker the Court appoints F.A. Mateer Esq. as a Commissioner to take the testimony of witnesses to be read in evidence in the Hearing of this case. By the Court." -Notation on the front of this document -"No. 29 April Term 1853 Lydia Brownawell by her father and next friend Samuel Senseman vs. Henry Brownawell Subpoena Sur Divorce 12th March 1853 Served personally and by Copy So answers" (signed James Widner Dept. Sheriff for Jos. McDarmond Shff.) "Sheriff McDarmond's fee $1.92 1/2. Watts and Parker."

Aug. 22, 1853 -"In the Court of Common Pleas of Cumberland County Lydia Brownawell by her father and next friend Saml. Senseman vs. Henry Brownawell: No. 29 April Term 1853 Subpoena Sur Divorce Now to wit 22 Aug. 1853 on motion of Watts and Parker the Court appoint F.A. Mateer Esq. as Commissioner to take the testimony of witnesses to be read in evidence in the hearing of this case." -"Cumberland County S.S. -I George Zinn Prothy. of the Court of Common Pleas of said County do certify that the above is a true extract taken from the records of said Court. Given under my hand and the seal of said Court at Carlisle the 22d day of August A.D. 1853. (signed George Zinn Prothy.)

Aug. 25, 1853 -"Cumberland Co. S.S. -I certify that in conformity with the foregoing Commission the depositions hereto annexed were duly taken and subscribed before me as aforesaid. In testimony whereof I have hereunto set my hand at Hogestown County of Cumberland the 25th day of August A.D. 1853." (signed F.A. Mateer Justice of the Peace.) "Prothy. fee pd. $0.25."

Aug. 22, 1853 -"Cumberland Co. S.S. Before me one of the Justices of the Peace in and for the County of Cumberland personally appeared Catharine Gross late Catharine Litzenger being of the age of twenty five years who upon her solemn affirmation doth depose and say I am well acquainted with Lydia Brownewell, wife of Henry Brownewell the defendant in this case. I lived with them in July 1852. I nursed her during her confinement, while she was sick and in bed heard Brownewell swear that she must leave his house, and if she did not go he would put her out and her things with her. She was not able to be up at that time. This took place about the 20th or 25th of the month, seen him afterwards take her clothes and other articles out of the bureau, was at a neighbours house on the 31st and when I returned home I found Mrs. Brownell's furniture out of the house. Brownewell asked me to go to her father's and persuade her to come back again. Told me next morning that he did not think she would stay away when he turned her out. On the 6th of August following Mrs. Brownewell and me were at Mr. Orris's and when returning Brownewell met us in the vicinity of Mr. Senseman's (Mrs. Brownewell's father) and caught hold of his wife and dragged her past her fathers to his own house in a violent manner and took her in and locked the door. She resisted but she could not get loose from him. Seen Mr. Senseman run out and take the child out of her arms. Heard Brownwell tell Mr. Senseman to come and her from him if he could. Felt very much afraid that night that he would kill her before morning, seemed to be in a great passion. Further saith not. Affirmed and subscribed the 22nd day of August 1853 before me" (signed F.A. Mateer Justice of the Peace and Catharine Gross.)

Aug. 25, 1853 -"Cumberland Co. S.S. -Before me one of the Justices of the Peace in and for the county of Cumberland, personally came David Orris who being duly sworn doth depose and say I am fifty years of age. Am well acquainted with Lydia Brownewell wife of the defendant in these proceedings. My farm joins the one on which Brownewell lived in 1852. About the 30th of July of the same year I was sent for by Mr. Senseman family. Went over and heard from them that Brownewell had been abusing his wife. Was requested by them to go into Brownewell's and try to peacefy (sic) him. Went in and found him and his wife in one of (the) back rooms. He was holding her round the body. She was making some effort to get loose from him; asked him what was wrong? He told me he had done something he ought not to have done. Asked him why he done so. Told me when he got angry he did not care what he done. Heard his wife ask him if she had ever gave him any reason to abuse her as he had been doing. Said she did not. Seen her furniture on the porch and in the yard. Heard him say that he had put it out. Heard him say that he had put her out of the house at the same time. Believe Brownwell has left the neighbourhood with another woman. The current report of the neighbourhood justifys (sic) me in saying so. Further saith not. Sworn and subscribed the 25th day of August 1853 before me" (signed F.A. Mateer J.P. and David Orris.)

Aug. 25, 1853 -"Cumberland Co. S.S. -Before me a Justice of the Peace in and for the county of Cumberland personally came George Houk Jr. who being duly sworn doth depose and say I am thirty years of age, am well acquainted with the parties named in these proceedings. Went to Brownewell's house about the 6th of Aug. 1852 by the request of Mrs. Senseman to try and get him to let his wife have her clothing etc., found the house locked up. Brownewell and his wife were in the house. I was in company with some other men. Spoke to him through the door and asked him to let us in. After some time he did open the door and came out. I asked him if he had put his wife out of the house as was reported. Said he did. Asked him why he done so. Told me it began about some trifling affair, and when he got into a passion he did not care what he done. Said if his wife would give him a divorce he would give her all that belonged to her and a hundred dollars besides. Said if he had a divorce he would not care about her. That he could do then as he pleased. Ask him what he meant by doing as he pleased. Said he could then get married again whenever he wished to do so. Have heard it said that Brownewell went away with another woman, believe it to be a current report of the neighbourhood. Sworn and subscribed the 25th day of August 1853." (signed George Hauck and F.A. Mateer J.P.)

Aug. 25, 1853 -"Cumberland Co. S.S. -Before me one of the Justices of the Peace in and for the county of Cumberland personally appeared William Brunner, who being of the age of sixteen years was duly sworn, doth depose and say I know Henry Brownwell and Lyda his wife. I was in the orchard on the farm he lived on in 1852 and heard some person screaming as if in distress. I ran towards the house, seen him have his wife in the road and was dragging her towards the house. She seemed to be very much frightened, and was trying to get away from him. Seen him take her into the yard. Have heard it said that he is gone to the west with another woman, it is generally believed to be true. Sworn and subscribed the 25th day of August 1853 before me." (signed F.A. Mateer J.P. and William H. Brunner.)

Aug. 25, 1853 -"Cumberland Co. S.S. -Before me one of the Justices of the Peace in and for the county of Cumberland personally came Joseph Millizen who being duly sworn doth depose and say I am past thirty five years of age. Was in company with George Houk Jr. at Henry Brownewell's the defendant in this case about the 6th of

Aug. 1852, heard Brownewell say he had turned his wife out of the house. I spoke to him, by himself, to give his wife what belonged to her. Said he would do so cheerfully if they would clear him of her so that he could go and get married again. For said he to live with her I cannot, and never will. Heard it said this week that Brownewell had went to the west with another woman. Believe it to be a current report of the neighbourhood, further saith not. Sworn and subscribed the 25th day of August 1853 before me" (signed F.A. Mateer J.P. and Joseph Millizen.)

Aug. 25, 1853 -"Cumberland Co. S.S. -Before me one of the Justices of the Peace in and for the county of Cumberland personally came George Buttorff who being duly sworn doth depose and say I am sixty six years of age. Am well acquainted with the parties to these proceedings. About the 6th of August 1852 I heard some person screaming, believed it to be Mrs. Brownewell. Went down to Mrs. Senseman's as soon as I could get there to see what was the matter. Learned from them that Brownewell had dragged his wife into the house. I live about eight rods from where Brownewell lived at that time. I was in my own house at the time. I have heard that Brownewell went away with another woman. Further saith not. Sworn and subscribed the 25th day of August 1853 before me. (signed F.A. Mateer J.P. and George Buttorff.)

Aug. 25, 1853 -"Cumberland Co. S.S. -Before me one of the Justices of the Peace in and for the county of Cumberland personally came David Emminger who being duly sworn doth depose and say I am sixty four years of age. I had some conversation with Henry Brownewell the defendant in this case. He requested me to go to Mr. Senseman's and try to get his wife to come back and live with him. Asked him what was wrong that he had turned her out of the house. Told me that they differed about some trifling thing and when he got into a passion he did not care what he done. Said, he took her by the arm and put her out. This conversation took place about the 8th of Aug. 1852. Believe from the common talk of the neighbourhood that he went away with another woman. Sworn and subscribed the 25th day of August 1853 before me" (signed F.A. Mateer J.P. and David Emminger.) -Notation on the front of this document -"No. 29 April Term 1853 Brownawell vs. Brownawell: Divorce case Depositions filed 30 August 1853."

Aug. 30, 1853 -"Lydia Brownawell by her father and next friend vs. Henry Brownawell: Divorce Now, to wit, 30 Aug. 1853 the Court having heard and duly considered this case do hereby order and decree that the said Lydia Brownawell and Henry Brownawell be and they are hereby divorced from the bonds of matrimony and their nuptial ties and all and every the duties rights and claims which have accrued to either of the said parties at any time heretofore in pursuance of their marriage shall now cease and determine and they shall severally be at liberty to marry again in like manner as if they never had been married. By the Court." (signed J.H. Graham Prest. Judge etc.) -Notation on the front of this document -"No. 29 April Term 1853 filed 30 August 1853."

◆ ◆ ◆

April Term 1853 #39 March 9, 1853 -"To the Honorable James H. Graham, President Judge of the Court of Common Pleas of the County of Cumberland -The petition of Hannah Weaver, by her mother and next friend Rebecca Weaver (signed by her mark.) Respectfully sheweth. That your petitioner was on the 24th of October A.D. 1847, lawfully joined in marriage with Joseph Weaver, her present husband, and from that time until the 25th of October 1847, lived and cohabited with him, and hath in all respects demeaned herself as a kind and affectionate wife; and although by the laws of God, as well as by the mutual vows plighted to each other, they were bound to that uniform constancy and regard which ought to be inseparable from the marriage state, yet so it is, that the said Joseph in violation of his marriage vow, from the said 25th day of October 1847 up to the present time, hath wilfully and maliciously deserted and absented himself from the habitation of this petitioner without any just or reasonable cause. Wherefore your petitioner further showing that she is a citizen of the Commonwealth of Pennsylvania, and hath resided therein for more than one whole year previous to the filing of this her petition, prays your Honor that a subpoena may issue in due form of law directed to the said Joseph Weaver, commanding him to appear at the next Court of Common Pleas of said County, and to answer the complaint aforesaid; and also that a decree of the Court of Common Pleas aforesaid may be made for the denouncing of her the said Hannah Weaver from the bond of matrimony, as if she had never been married. And she will pray etc. Witness -" (signed William Fagan and Hannah Weaver by her mother and next friend Rebecca Weaver who signed by her mark) -"Cumberland County S.S. -The above named Hannah Weaver, being duly sworn according to law, doth depose and say, that the facts contained in the foregoing petition or libel are true and to the best of her knowledge and belief; and that the said complaint is not made out of levity, or by collusion between her the said Hannah, and the said Joseph, and for the mere purpose of being freed and separated from each other, but in sincerity and truth, for the causes mentioned in said petition or libel. Sworn and subscribed before me this 9th day of March A.D. 1853." (signed J.H. Graham and Hannah Weaver by her mark.) -"Hannah Weaver by her mother and next friend Rebecca Weaver vs. Joseph Weaver: To Geo. Zinn Esq. Prothy. Sir Issue Subpoena for divorce a vinculo matrimonii (signed W.H. Miller Atty. for Pet. 9th March 1853.) -Notation on the front of this document -"No. 39 April Term 1853 Hannah Weaver by her mother and next friend Rebecca Weaver vs. Joseph Weaver filed 16 March 1853 Subp. sur divorce 9th March 1853 Subpoena awarded." (signed J.H. Graham.) -"Miller."

March 16, 1853 -"Cumberland County S.S. -The Commonwealth of Pennsylvania to the Sheriff of Cumberland County Greeting: Whereas Hannah Weaver by her mother and next friend Rebecca Weaver did on the 9th day of March 1853 prefer a petition to our said Judges of our Court of Common Pleas for the County of Cumberland praying for the causes therein set forth, that she might be divorced from the bonds of matrimony entered into with you Joseph Weaver. We do therefore command you the said Joseph Weaver that setting aside all other business and excuses whatsoever, you be and appear in your proper person before our Judges at Carlisle at a Court of Common Pleas there to be held for the County of Cumberland on the 11th day of April next to answer the petition or libel of the said Hannah Weaver, and to show cause if any you have why the said Hannah Weaver your wife, should not be divorced from the bonds of matrimony agreeably to the Acts of Assembly in such case made and provided -and hereof fail not. Witness the Honorable James H. Graham President of our said Court at Carlisle the 16th day of March A.D. 1853." (signed George Zinn Prothy.) -Notation on the front of this document -"No. 39 April Term 1853 Hannah Weaver by her mother and next friend Rebecca Weaver vs. Joseph Weaver Subpoena Sur divorce March 1853 I acknowledge the service of the within Subpoena Sur divorce April 9th 1853 writ returned Non est inventus So answers" (signed Jos. McDarmond Shff.) -"Shff. McDarmond's fee $0.18 1/4. Miller."

◆ ◆ ◆

August Term 1853 #32 May 20, 1853 -"To the Honorable the Judges of the Court of Common Pleas of the County of Cumberland. The petition of Elizabeth Traub by her friend George Spongenberg, respectfully showeth That your petitioner was on the 1st day of February 1849 lawfully joined in marriage with John Traub her present husband and from that time until the 11th day of October A.D. 1850 lived and cohabited with him and hath in all respects demeaned herself as a kind and affectionate wife; and although by the laws of God as well as by the mutual vows plighted to each other they were bound to that uniform constancy and regard which ought to be inseparable from the marriage state yet so it is that the said John Traub in violation of his marriage vow, from the 11th day of October A.D. 1850 hath wilfully and maliciously deserted and absented himself from the habitation of this petitioner without any just cause and such desertion hath persisted in for the term of two years and upwards and yet doth continue to absent himself from the said petitoner. Wherefore your petioner further showing that she is a citizen of the Commonwealth of Pennsylvania and hath resided therein for more than one year previous to the filing of this her petition prays your Honors that a subpoena may issue in due form of law directed to the said John Traub commanding him to appear in this Honorable Court, at August term next to answer the complaint aforesaid. And also that a decree of this Honorable Court may be made for the divorcing of her the said Elizabeth Traub from the bond of matrimony as if she had never been married. And she will pray etc." (signed in German script by George Spongenberg.) -"Cumberland County S.S. The above named Elizabeth Traub being duly sworn according to law doth depose and say that the facts contained in the above petition or libel are true to the best of her knowledge and belief; and that the said complaint is not made out of levity or by collusion between her the said Elizabeth Traub and her husband the said John Traub, and for the mere purpose of being freed and separated from each other, but in sincerity and truth, for the causes mentioned in the said petition or libel. Sworn and subscribed before me a Justice of the Peace of Cumberland County this 20th day of May A.D. 1853." (signed M. Holcomb, J.P. and Elizabeth Traub.) Notation on the front of this document -"No. 32 August Term 1853 7th June 1853 Subpoena awarded." (signed J.H. Graham Judge etc.) -"filed 7 June 1853 22 Aug. 1853 Alias subpoena awarded By the Court. Wolf."

June 7, 1853 -"The Commonwealth of Pennsylvania to the Sheriff of Cumberland County Greeting Whereas Elizabeth Traub by her next friend George Spongenberg did on the 7th day of June 1853 prefer her petition to our said President Judge of our Court of Common Pleas for the State of Pennsylvania and County of Cumberland praying for the causes therein set forth, that she might be divorced from the bonds of matrimony entered into with you John Traub. We do therefore command you the said John Traub, that setting aside all other business and excuses whatsoever, you be and appear in your proper person before our Judges at Carlisle at a Court of Common Pleas, there to be held for the County of Cumberland, on the twenty second day of August next to answer the said petition or libel of the said Elizabeth Traub etc. and to show cause, if any you have, why the said Elizabeth Traub your wife, should not be divorced from the bonds of matrimony, agreeably to the Acts of General Assembly in such case made and provided. And hereof fail not. Witness the Honorable James H. Graham Esq. President of our said Court at Carlisle the 7th day of June A.D. 1853." (signed George Zinn Prothy.)

Aug. 19, 1853 -"Cumberland County S.S. -Joseph McDarmond being sworn says that the defendent John Traub cannot be found within his bailiwick. Sworn and Subscribed before me 19 Aug. 1853." (signed Geo. Zinn Prothy. and Jos. McDarmond Shff.) -Notation on the front of this document -"No. 32 August Term 1853 Elizabeth Traub by her next friend George Spongenberg vs. John Traub Subpoena Sur Divorce N.E.I. Shff. McDarmond's fee $0.18 3/4. Wolf."

♦ ♦ ♦

August Term 1853 #33 June 13, 1853 -"To the Honorable James H. Graham President Judge of the Court of Common Pleas of Cumberland County -The petition of George W. Smith of North Middleton Township, Cumberland County respectfully showeth -That your petitioner was on or about the fifteenth day of January A.D. 1846 lawfully joined in marriage with Rebecca Jacobs his present wife and from that time lived and cohabited with her and hath in all respects demeaned himself as a kind and loving husband; and although by the laws of God, as well as by their mutual vows plighted to each other, they were bound to that constancy and uniform regard and chastity which ought to be inseparable from the marriage state yet so it is that the said Rebecca in violation of her marriage vow hath for a considerable time past, being at such time domiciled within the Commonwealth of Pennsylvania, given herself up to adulterous practices, and been guilty of adultery with diverse persons. Wherefore, your libellant further shewing that he is a citizen of this State and hath resided therein for upwards of one whole year previous to the filing of this his petition, prays your honors that a subpoena may issue in due form of law, directed to the said Rebecca, commanding her to appear at the next Court of Common Pleas to be held at Carlisle, to answer the petitioner's libel and to show cause if any she hath, why the petitioner should not be divorced from the bond of matrimony. And he will pray etc." (signed George W. Smith) -"Cumberland County SS. -The within named George W. Smith being duly sworn according to law doth depose and say that the facts contained in the above petition or libel are true to the best of his knowledge and belief. And that the said complaint is not made out of levity or by collusion between him and the said Rebecca his wife and for the mere purpose of being freed and separated from each other -but in sincerity and truth for the causes mentioned in the said petition or libel. Sworn and subscribed before me this 13th day of June A.D. 1853." (signed Geo. Ege and George W. Smith.) -Notation on the front of this document -"No. 33 August Term 1853 The petition of George W. Smith for a Divorce. Filed 14 June 1853 14th June 1853 Subpoena awarded." (signed J. Graham Judge etc.) -"George W. Smith vs. Rebecca Smith: To Geo. Zinn Prothy. Issue subpoena sur divorce." (signed R.M. Henderson Atty. for Pltff.)

June 14, 1853 -"The Commonwealth of Pennsylvania to the Sheriff of Cumberland County Greeting, Whereas George W. Smith did on the 13th day of June 1853, prefer his petition to James H. Graham President Judge of our Court of Common Pleas for the State of Pennsylvania and County of Cumberland, praying for the causes therein set forth, that he might be divorced from the bonds of matrimony entered into with you Rebecca Smith. We therefore command you, the said Rebecca Smith, that setting aside all other business and excuses whatsoever, you be and appear in your proper person before our Judges at Carlisle at a Court of Common Pleas, there be held for the County of Cumberland on the 22d day of August next, to answer the petition or libel of the said George W. Smith and to show cause, if any you have, why the said George W. Smith your husband should not be divorced from the bonds of matrimony, agreeably to the Acts of General Assembly in such case made and provided -And hereof fail not. Witness the Honorable James H. Graham Esq. President of our said Court at Carlisle the 14th day of June A.D. 1853." (signed George Zinn Prothy. -"25 August 1853 Micl. Holcomb Esq. appointed Commissioner to take testimony etc. By the Court." -Notation on the front of this document -"No. 33 August Term 1853 George W. Smith vs. Rebecca Smith Subpoena Sur Divorce June 20th 1853 Served personally and by copy So answers" (signed James Widner Dept. Shff.) -"Shff. McDarmond's fee $1.08. Henderson."

Aug. 25, 1853 -"With No. 33 Aug. 1853 Among the Records of the Court of Common Pleas of Cumberland County the following proceedings were had, to wit: George W. Smith vs. Rebecca Smith: No. 33 August Term 1853 Subpoena Sur divorce 25 August 1853 Michl. Holcomb Esq. appointed Commissioner to take testimony etc. -Cumberland County S.S. -I Geo. Zinn Prothy. of the Court of Common Pleas of said county do certify that the above is a true extract taken from the records of said court. Given under my hand and the seal of the said court at Carlisle the 12 Sept. 1853." (signed Geo. Zinn Prothy.)

Sept. 24, 1853 -"Geoge W. Smith vs. Rebecca Smith: No. 33 August Term 1853 Subpoena sur Divorce, etc. Depositions of George P. Myers, Alfred Brannon and Henry Glass, produced sworn and examined by me at my office in the borough of Carlisle, by virtue of the annexed Rule of Court. Taken at the instance of the plaintiff on the 24th day of September, in the borough of Carlisle County of Cumberland, at my office. -George P. Myers, sworn, I do know Rebecca Smith, that she is a woman of notorious bad character for chastity, that she has left her husband and is in the habit of going with other men, and is reputed a general whore, and has been living at houses known to be houses of ill-fame and separate and apart from her husband. Sworn and subscribed before me 24th Sept. 1853." (signed M. Holcomb Commissioner and George P. Myers.)

Sept. 24, 1853 -"Alfred Brannon, sworn, I have been acquainted with Rebecca Smith, wife of George W. Smith, over one year, she is notorious for bad habits, is considered a whore, has left her husband, and is in the habit of resorting to houses of ill-fame, and did keep a house of ill-fame herself, and was in the habit of keeping soldiers in her house, and other persons, married men and others. Sworn and subscribed before me the 24th Sept. 1853." (signed M. Holcomb Commissioner and Alfred Brannon.)

Sept. 24, 1853 -"Henry Glass, sworn, I have known Rebecca Smith wife of George W. Smith for several years that she is a woman of bad character from general report, for drinking and whoring and kept an idle and disorderly house in the borough of Carlisle and was in the habit of absenting herself from husband. Sworn and subscribed before me the 24th Sept. 1853" (signed M. Holcomb Commissioner and Henry Glass.)

"Costs
Witnesses

G.P. Myers	.50
A. Brannon	.50
H. Glass	.50
M. Holcomb Commissioner	2.00

$3.50" -Notation on the front of this document -"No. 33 August Term 1853 George W. Smith vs. Rebecca Smith: 23 Aug. T. 1853 Depositions filed 16 November 1853."

Nov. 14, 1853 -"George W. Smith vs. Rebecca Smith: In the Court of Common Pleas of Cumberland County -No. 33 August T. 1853 -And now the 14th day of November 1853 -The Commissioner Michael Holcomb Esq., having returned to the Court the depositions of witnesses taken before him on the part of the libellant, and the same being read and heard by the Court, and the Court after mature and solemn deliberation being satisfied therewith and proclamation being duly made for the respondent to come forth and she not appearing, the Court do order, adjudge and decree that the said George W. Smith the libellant be divorced and separated from the bond of matrimony contracted with the said Rebecca Smith the respondent, and that all and every the duties, rights and claims accruing to either of the said parties by reason of the said marriage shall henceforth cease and determine and the said parties be severally at liberty to marry again in like manner as if they never had been married. By the Court." -Notation on the front of this document -"No. 33 August T. 1853 George W. Smith vs. Rebecca Smith: decree filed 16 Nov. 1853."

◆ ◆ ◆

November Term 1853 #2, Aug. 22, 1853 -"The Commonwealth of Pennsylvania to the Sheriff of Cumberland County Greeting: Whereas Elizabeth Traub by her next friend George Spongenberg did on the 7th day of June 1853 prefer her petition to our said President Judge of our Court of Common Pleas for the State of Pennsylvania and County of Cumberland praying for the causes therein set forth, that she might be divorced from the bonds of matrimony entered into with you John Traub. We do therefore command you the said John Traub, that, setting aside all other business and excuses whatsoever, you be and appear in your proper person before our Judges at Carlisle at a Court of Common Pleas, there to be held for the County of Cumberland on the fourteenth day of November next to answer the said petition or libel of the Elizabeth Traub etc. and to show cause, if any you have, why the said Elizabeth Traub your wife should not be divorced from the bonds of matrimony agreeably to the Acts of General Assembly in such case made and provided. And hereof fail not. Witness the Hon. James H. Graham Esq. President of our said Court at Carlisle the 22d day of August A.D. 1853." (signed George Zinn Prothy.)

Feb. 25, 1854 -"Cumberland County S.S. -Joseph McDarmond being sworn says that the defendant John Traub cannot be found within his bailiwick 11th Nov. 1853. Sworn and Subscribed before me 25th Feby. 1854." (signed Geo. Zinn Prothy. and Jos. McDarmond Shff.) -Notation on the front of this document -"No. 2 November Term 1853 Elizabeth Traub by her next friend Geo. Spongenburg vs. John Traub Alias Subpoena Sur Divorce N.E.I. So answers" (signed Jos. McDarmond Shff.) -"Shff. McDarmond's fee $0.18 3/4. Wolf."

April 8, 1854 -"Elizabeth Traub by her next friend George Spongenberg vs. John Traub: No. 2 November Term 1853 -Joseph McDarmond being duly sworn deposes and says that notice was published in one newspaper in the Borough of Carlisle for four weeks successively prior to the 10th day April A.D. 1854 the first day of the present term requiring the said John Traub the defendant to answer the said complaint of the said Elizabeth Traub and to show cause if any why she should not be divorced from the bonds of matrimony agreeably to the act of assembly in such case made and provided. Sworn and Subscribed before me this 8 April 1854." (signed Geo. Zinn Prothy. and Jos. McDarmond Shff.) -Notation on the front of this document -"No. 2 November T. 1853 Traub vs. Traub Subpoena Sur divorce Affidavit of Shff. Shff. McDarmond for advt. $1.50 filed 8 April 1854."

April 13, 1854 -"Elizabeth Traub by her next friend George Spongenberg vs. John Traub: No. 2 November T. 1854 Alias Subpoena Sur Divorce 13 April 1854 Stephen Keepers Esq. is appointed Commissioner in this case to take depositions. -Cumberland County S.S. -I Geo. Zinn Prothy. of the Court of Common Pleas of said county do certify that the above is a true extract taken from the records of said court. Given under my hand and the seal of said Court at Carlisle this 14th day of April A.D. 1854." (signed Geo. Zinn Prothy.)

April 15, 1854 -"Elizabeth Traub by her next friend George Spongenberg vs. John Traub: In pursuance of the annexed rule personally appeared before me the subscriber a Commissioner appointed for the purpose, Michael Holcomb Esq. who after being sworn according to law deposes and says, that Elizabeth Traub was married to John Traub, some where (sic) about five years ago and he continued about in this country untill about four years ago, when he left this Country, he has not been here or contributing in any way for the support of his wife, ever since he went away, she has had to make her own living by hiring out. Sworn and subscribed before me this 15th April 1854." (signed Stephen Keepers and M. Holcomb.)

April 15, 1854 -"Personally appeared before me the subscriber a Commissioner appointed for the purpose, William Barnitz who after being duly affirmed according to law, deposes and says, that Elizabeth Traub was married to John Traub, some where (sic) about five years ago, and he continued about in this country untill about four years ago, when he left this Country, he has not been here or contributed in any way for the support of his wife ever since he went away, she has had to make her own living by hiring out. Affirmed to and subscribed before me this 15th April 1854." (signed Stephen Keepers and Wm. Barnitz.)

April 15, 1854 -"Elizabeth Traub by her next friend George Spongenberg vs. John Traub: In pursuance of the annexed rule personally appeared before me the subscriber a Commissioner appointed for the purpose, James H. Waggoner who after being duly affirmed according to law deposes and says that Elizabeth Traub was married to John Traub some where (sic) about five years ago, and he continued about in this County untill about four years ago, when he left this Country, he has not contributed in any way for the support of his wife ever since he went away, she has had to make her own living ever since by hiring out. Affirmed to and subscribed before me this 15th April 1854 (signed Stephen Keepers and James H. Waggoner) -Notation on the front of this document -"No. 2 November T. 1853 Elizabeth Traub vs. John Traub Depositions filed 21 April 1854."

April 21, 1854 -"Elizabeth Traub vs. John Traub: Now to wit 21 April 1854 the Court having heard the testimony taken by the Commissioner upon due consideration of the premises do order and decree that the said Elizabeth Traub be and she is hereby divorced from the bond of matrimony entered into with the said John Traub and that she be at full liberty to marry again as if she never had been married -By the Court" -Notation on the front of this document -"No. 2 November T. 1853 filed 21 April 1854."

◆ ◆ ◆

November Term 1853 #6 Aug. 25, 1853 -"To the Honorable the Judges of the Court of Common Pleas of Cumberland County -The petition of John J. Boyer of Carlisle in the County aforesaid Respectfully Showeth That your petitioner was on the 30th day of June A.D. 1852 lawfully joined in marriage with Sarah A. Boyer his present wife and from that time until in or about the 1st day of July 1853 lived and cohabited with her and hath in all respects demeaned himself as a kind and affectionate husband and although by the laws of God as well as by the mutual vows plighted to each other they were bound to that uniform constancy and regard which ought to be inseparable from the marriage state yet so it is that the said Sarah in violation of her marriage vow hath for a considerable time past given herself up to adulterous practices and been guilty of adultery with a certain Henry Peters and diverse other persons to your petitioner unknown. Wherefore your petitioner further showing that he is a citizen of the Commonwealth of Pennsylvania and hath resided therein for more than one whole year previous to the filing of this his petition prays your Honors that a subpoena may issue in due form of law directed to the said Sarah Boyer commanding her to appear in this Honorable Court at November Term next to answer the complaint aforesaid: And also that a decree of this honorable Court may be made for the divorcing of him the said John J. Boyer from the bond of matrimony as if he had never been married and he will ever pray." (signed John J. Boyer) -"Cumberland County S.S. -The above named John J. Boyer being duly sworn according to law deposes and says that the facts contained in the above petition or libel are true to the best of his knowledge and belief and that the said complaint is not made out of levity or by collusion between him the said John J. Boyer and the said Sarah his wife and for the mere purpose of being freed and separated from each other but in sincerity and truth for the causes mentioned in the said petition or libel. Sworn and subscribed this 25th day of August 1853." (signed Stephen Keepers J.P. and John J. Boyer.) -Notation on the front of this document -"No. 6 November Term 1853 Petition of John J. Boyer for Divorce 26 August 1853 Subpoena awarded By the Court filed 26 Aug. 1853. Penrose."

Aug. 26, 1853 -"To the Commonwealth of Pennsylvania to the Sheriff of Cumberland County Greeting: Whereas John J. Boyer on the 26th day of August 1853 preferred his petition to our said Judges of our Court of Common Pleas for the State of Penna. and County of Cumberland, praying for the causes therein set forth that he might be divorced from the bonds of matrimony entered into with you Sarah A. Boyer. We therefore command you the said Sarah A. Boyer, that setting aside all other business and excuses whatsoever, you be and appear in your proper person before our Judges at Carlisle at a Court of Common Pleas, there to be held for Cumberland County on the 14th day of November next to answer the petition or libel of said John J. Boyer and to show cause, if any you have, why the said John J. Boyer your husband, should not be divorced from the bonds of matrimony agreeably to the acts of General Assembly in such case made and provided. And hereof fail not. Witness the Hon. James H. Graham President of our said court at Carlisle the 26th day of August A.D. 1853." (signed George Zinn Prothy.) -Notation on the front of this document -"No. 6 November Term 1853 John Boyer vs. Sarah A. Boyer Subpoena Sur Divorce August 29th 1853 Served by Copy So answers" (signed James Weaver Dept. Shff.) -"Shff. McDarmond's fee $0.95 1/4. Penrose."

◆   ◆   ◆

November Term 1853 #32 Oct. 15, 1853 -"To the Honorable the Judges of the Court of Common Pleas of Cumberland County -The petition of Sarah Leiby whose maiden name was Sarah Bare by her brother and next friend Henry Bare ----Respectfully Represents That in the year One thousand Eight Hundred and thirty three she was lawfully married to James Leiby in Adams County Pennsylvania and continued to reside and live with him as his wife until about the year 1844 when she separated from him for the cause that the said James Leiby had before that been guilty of adultery by having had carnal knowledge of the body of one Mary Pie in the town of Newburg Cumberland County Pennsylvania of which your petitioner alleges the said James Leiby was guilty and that he has often since been guilty of adultery by having had carnal knowledge of the bodies of other women whose names are not known to your petitioner. He therefore as the Brother and next friend of the said Sarah prays your Honors to award a Subpoena directed to the said James Leiby commanding him to appear at the next term of your court to answer this complaint and shew cause why the said Sarah should not be divorced from the bonds of matrimony entered into by her with the said James Leiby and he as in duty bound will pray etc." (signed Henry Bare.) -"Cumberland County sct. -Henry Bare the petitioner and Sarah Leiby personally appeared before me a Justice of the Peace and being duly sworn according to law do depose and say that the facts contained in the foregoing petition or libel are true to the best of their knowledge and belief and that the said complaint is not made out of levity or by collusion between the said husband and wife and for the mere purpose of being freed and separated from each other, but in sincerity and truth for the causes mentioned in the said petition or libel. Sworn and subscribed the 15th of October 1853 Before me" (signed F. Eckels and Henry Bare and Sarah Leiby by her mark.) -Notation on the front of this document -"No. 32 November Term 1853 Sarah Leiby by her brother and next friend Henry Bare vs. James Leiby filed 15th October 1853 15 Oct. 1853 Subpoena awarded." (signed J.H. Graham Prest. Judge etc.)

Oct. 15, 1853 -"The Commonwealth of Pennsylvania to the Sheriff of Cumberland County: Greeting, Whereas Sarah Leiby by her Brother and next friend Henry Bare did on the 15th day of October

A.D. 1853 prefer her petition to our said President Judge of our Court of Common Pleas for the State of Pennsylvania and County of Cumberland praying for the causes therein set forth, that she might be divorced from the bonds of matrimony entered into with you James Leiby. We do therefore command you the said James Leiby, that setting aside all other business and excuses whatsoever you be and appear in your proper person before our Judges at Carlisle at a Court of Common Pleas, there to be held for the County of Cumberland on the 14th day of November next, to answer the petition or libel of the said Sarah Leiby, and to show cause, if any you have, why the said Sarah Leiby your wife should not be divorced from the bonds of matrimony, agreeably to the Act of Assembly in such case made and provided -And hereof fail not. Witness the Honorable James H. Graham, President of our said Court at Carlisle the 15th day of October A.D. 1853." (signed Geo. Zinn Prothy.) -Notation on the front of this document -"No. 32 November T. 1853 Sarah Leiby by her Brother and next friend Henry Bare vs. James Leiby Subpoena Sur Divorce Oct. 31st 1853 Served personally So answers" (left unsigned.) -"Shff. McDarmond's fee $0.96." (signed Jos. McDarmond Shff.) "Watts and Parker."

Sept. 12, 1854 -"Sarah Leiby by her brother and next friend Henry Bare vs. James Leiby: Subpoena Sur Divorce Now, to wit, 12 September A.D. 1854 upon due consideration of the premises and after having the proof taken in pursuance of the Commission heretofore appointed by the Court for that purpose, the Court do hereby order and decree that the said Sarah Leiby be and is hereby divorced and separated from the nuptial ties or bonds of matrimony existing or which have ever heretofore existed between her and the said James Leiby and that all and every the duties rights and claims accruing to either of the said parties at any time heretofore shall cease and determine and the said Sarah Leiby shall be at liberty to marry again in the like manner as if they never had been married. By the Court." (signed J.H. Graham, Prest. Judge.) -Notation on the front of this document -"No. 32 November Term 1853 filed 12 Sept. 1854."

◆   ◆   ◆

Jan. Term 1854 #2 Aug. 19, 1853 -"The Commonwealth of Pennsylvania to the Sheriff of Cumberland County Greeting Whereas Sophia Rice of the Borough of Carlisle and County aforesaid by her next friend George Folland did on the 22d day of August 1853 prefer her petition to our said President Judge of our Court of Common Pleas for the State of Pennsylvania and County of Cumberland praying for the causes therein set forth, that she might be divorced from the bonds of matrimony entered into with you Peter Rice. We therefore command you the said Peter Rice, that setting aside all business and excuses whatsoever, you be and appear in your proper person before our Judges at Carlisle at a Court of Common Pleas there to be held for the County of Cumberland on the ninth day of January next to answer the said petition or libel of Sophia Rice etc. and to show cause, if any you have, why the said Sophia Rice your wife should not be divorced from the bonds of matrimony agreeably to the Acts of General Assembly in such case made and provided. And hereof fail not. Witness the Hon. James H. Graham President of our said Court at Carlisle the 19th day of August A.D. 1853." (signed George Zinn Prothy.)

Jan. 9, 1854 -"Cumberland County S.S. -Joseph McDarmond being sworn says that Peter Rice the defendant can not be found within the County. Sworn and Subscribed before me the 9 Jany. 1854." (signed Geo. Zinn Prothy. and Jos. McDarmond Shff.) -"Geo. Ege Esq. appointed Commissioner to take depositions. By the Court." -Notation on the front of this document -"No. 3 January Term 1854 Sophia Rice of the Borough of Carlisle by her next friend George Folland vs. Peter Rice Alias Subpoena Sur divorce N.E.I. Shff. McDarmond's fee $0.18. Penrose."

April 8, 1854 -"Sophia Rice of the Borough of Carlisle by her next friend George Foland vs. Peter Rice: No. 2 Jan. T. 1854 -Joseph McDarmond Sheriff being duly sworn deposes and says that notice was published in one newspaper in the Borough of Carlisle for four weeks successively prior to the 10th day of April A.D. 1854 the first day of the present term requiring the said Peter Rice the defendant to answer the said complaint of the said Sophia Rice and to show cause if any why she should not be divorced from the bonds of matrimony agreeably to the acts of Assembly such case made and provided. Sworn and Subscribed before me this 8th April 1854." (signed Geo. Zinn Prothy. and Jos. McDarmond Shff.) -Notation on the front of this document -"No. 2 Jany. T. 1854 Rice vs. Rice filed 8 Apl. 1854 Subpoena sur Divorce Affidavit of Sheriff. Shff. McDarmond's fee for advt. $1.50."

Jan. Term 1854 #2 Aug. 28, 1854 -"Sophia Rice of the Borough of Carlisle by her next friend George Foland vs. Peter Rice: No. 2 January Term 1854 Alias Subpoena Sur Divorce And now to wit the 28th day of August A.D. 1854 the Commissioner George Ege having returned to the Court here the depositions of witnesses taken before him on the part of the libellant and the same being read and heard by the Court -and the Court after mature and solemn deliberation being satisfied therewith and proclamation being duly made for the Respondent to come forth and he not appearing the Court do order adjudge and decree that the said Sophia Rice the Libellant be divorced and separated from the bond of matrimony contracted with the said Peter Rice the Respondent -and that all and every the duties rights and claims accruing to either of said parties by reason of said marriage shall henceforth cease and determine and the said parties be severally at liberty to marry again in like manner as if they never had been married. By the Court." -Notation on the front of this document -"No. 2 Jan. Term 1854 Rice vs. Rice Decree of Court filed 28 Aug. 1854. Penrose."

◆ ◆ ◆

April Term 1854 #3 April 13, 1854 -"Shearer Ellen Ginn Colored Woman by her next friend and father vs. Edward Ginn: No. 3 April Term 1854 Subpoena Sur Divorce 13 April 1854 A.B. Sharp Esq. appointed Commissioner to take depositions on 5 days notice. By the Court. -Cumberland County S.S. -I Geo. Zinn Prothy. of the Court of Common Pleas of said County do certify that the above is a true extract taken from the records of said Court. Given under my hand and the seal of said Court at Carlisle the 12th May 1854." (signed Geo. Zinn Prothy.) -Notation on the front of this document -"No. 3 April Term 1854 Commission to A.B. Sharp Esq. to take testimony."

July 24, 1854 -"Ellen Ginn by her next friend and father Cato Natts vs. Edward Ginn: In the Court of Common Pleas for Cumberland County No. 3 April T. 1854 July 24, 1854 Mr. Edward Ginn Sir: You will take notice that the undersigned having been appointed by said County to take testimony Commissioner in the above case of Divorce between your said wife and yourself. Will meet at his office in the Borough of Carlisle for that purpose on Saturday the 29th inst. at ten o'clock in the forenoon, when and where you may attend if you think fit." (signed A.B. Sharp Commissioner.) -Notation on the front of this document -"I hereby accept service of the within. July 24, 1854." (signed Edward Ginn.)

July 29, 1854 -"No. 3 Apr. 1854 Ellen Ginn (colored woman) by her father and next friend Cato Natts vs. Edward Ginn (colored man): No. 3 April Term 1854 in the Common Pleas of Cumberland County -Depositions of Elizabeth Lee, and Lena Green produced sworn and examined by me at the office of W.J. Shearer in the Borough of Carlisle, by virtue of the annexed Rule of Court; this 29th day of July 1854."

July 29, 1854 -"Elizabeth Lee being duly sworn doth depose and say -I have known Ellen Ginn all her life and have known her and her husband to live disagreeably for the last seven years. I have seen him beat her in an insufferable manner once. That was a year last May. She went to sue him and went by my house. He followed her there and attempted to search my house for her. He said if he got his hands on her he would kill her and he had understood she intended sueing him for abusing her. She did sue the next morning and after that they separated and have not lived together since. I have not spoken to Edward Ginn for the last six months, but before that I have heard him say repeatedly that she should never have a peaceful life. I am confident she has never had a peaceable life for the last seven years. He always abused her when she came home to see her mother or talked of doing so. I considered her life in danger all the time she was with him. It was on account of her children that she lived with him and bore his abuse as long as she did. For the last seven years she supported herself, him, and their children by her own labor, until they parted. I now recollect of him knocking her down and kicking her in the presence of a number of persons some three years since in my mother's yard. Edward Ginn is a drunkard and has been for the last seven years and is never sober when he can get liquor. In the last two years he has been in Gaol (sic) about half the time. Previous to that he has been in Gaol (sic) at different times for various offences." Cross Examined by Edward Ginn -"She never left the house o'clock at night when you were not there. She moved her things to her mother's when you were in Gaol (sic), at the suggestion of Esq. Ege, and that she might not have rent to pay." In asking again -"Mrs. Ginn has always bore an excellent character for industry, chastity and other good qualities of character. I have known her from the cradle. She is working in Harrisburg now because she is afraid to remain hear (sic). Sworn and subscribed before me 24 July 1854." (signed A.B. Sharp and Elizabeth Lee by her mark.)

July 24, 1854 -"Lena Green being duly sworn doth depose and say -I have known these parties for four or five years. Both at the Forge and at Carlisle. I saw him knock her down and her incensable (sic) for five or ten minutes. I did not know of any cause of anger he had. She had just got over a spell of the fever. She was very weak at the time. He struck her on the side of the head. I lived with them about a year at the Forge, and during that time I saw him frequently striking and abusing her. During that time I considered her life in danger. He frequently came home drunk and often threatened to shoot and kill her. I knew them when they lived in Ningard's house; they lived down stairs (sic) and my mother up stairs (sic). I could hear him strike her with the handle of an umbrella when I was up stairs (sic) with my mother. I did not see him strike her then, but I did afterwards. I saw him strike her once with his cane once with an umbrella cane and once with his hand, and have seen him strike her with other things at other times. He knocked her down sometimes when he struck her. I have heard him threaten to poison her in my own house. It was on account of her children that she remained with him as long as she did. She is afraid of her life, and interferring with her mother, is the reason of her residing at Harrisburg. Edward Ginn is a drunken character and is never sober when he can get liquor. I have heard him threaten since she left him, that he would murder her whenever he got hand on her. Mrs. Ginn is a virtuous and inourtinous (sic, industrious?) woman and I have never heard anything against her from any one. Sworn and subscribed before me this 29th of July 1854." (signed A.B. Sharp and Lena Green by her mark.)

Sept. 12, 1854 -"Ellen Ginn by her father and next friend Cato Natts vs. Edward Ginn: No. 3 April Term 1854 And now to wit: the 12th day of September A.D. 1854 the Commissioner, A.B. Sharp Esq. having returned to the Court here the depositions of witnesses taken before him on the part of the petitioner, and the same being read and heard by the Court, and the Court after mature deliberation being satisfied therewith, and proclamation being duly made for the respondent to come forth, and he not appearing the Court do order adjudge and decree that the said Ellen Ginn, the petitioner be divorced and separated from the bond of matrimony contracted with the said Edward Ginn the respondent and that all and every the duties, rights, and claims accruing to either the said parties by reason of said marriage shall thenceforth cease and determine and the said parties be severally at liberty to marry again in like manner as they had never been married. By the Court." -Notation on the front of this document -"No. 3 April Term 1854 filed 12 Sept. 1854."

◆ ◆ ◆

Aug. 1854 Term #38 July 11, 1854 -"The petition of Leah Eberly by her brother and next friend Samuel Albright Respectfully Showeth -That your petitioner on the 29th day of November A.D. 1849 was lawfully joined in marriage with Samuel Eberly Jr. and from that time until the 16th day of May 1854 lived and cohabited with the said Samuel Eberly Jr. as his wife and was owned and acknowledged by him and so deemed and reputed by all her neighbors and acquaintances, and although by the laws of God, as well as by their mutual vows, they were reciprocally bound to that uniform regard which ought to be inseparable from the marriage state, yet so it is, that the said Samuel Eberly Jr. has offered such indignities to the person of your petitioner as to render her condition intolerable and her life burthensome and hereby forced her to withdraw from his house and company. Wherefore your Libellant further showing that she is a citizen of Pennsylvania and has resided therein for upwards of one whole year previous to the filing of this her Libel prays your Honors that a subpoena may issue forth to summon the said Samuel Eberly Jr. to appear in this Honorable Court at the next term to answer the complaint aforesaid. And also that a decree of this Honble. Court may be made for the divorcing of him the said Samuel Eberly Jr. from the society fellowship and company of this Libellant in all time to come from the marriage bond aforesaid, as if they had never been married or as if the said Samuel Eberly Jr. were dead and this Libellant will pray etc." (signed Leah Eberly by her next friend Samuel Albright.) -"Cumberland County S.S. -The above named Leah Eberly being duly affirmed says that the facts contained in the foregoing libel are true to the best of her knowledge and belief, and that the said complaint is not made out of levity and collusion, between her and her said husband and for the mere purpose of being freed and separated from each other, but in sincerity and truth, for the causes mentioned in said libel. Affirmed and Subscribed before me this 11th day of July A.D. 1854." (signed G.W. Criswell, J.P. and Leah Eberly.) -Notation on the front of this document -"No. 38 August Term 1854 Leah Eberly by her next friend Saml. Albright vs. Samuel Eberly Jr. Sub. Sur Divorce 15 July 1854 Subpoena awarded." (signed J.H. Graham Prest. Judge etc.) -"filed 15 July 1854. Biddle."

July 15, 1854 -"The Commonwealth of Pennsylvania to the Sheriff of Cumberland County Greeting Whereas Leah Eberle by her next friend Saml. Albright did on the 15th day of July 1854 prefer her petition to the President Judges of our Court of Common Pleas for the state of Pennsylvania and County of Cumberland praying for the causes therein set forth that she might be divorced from the bonds of matrimony entered into with you Samuel Eberle Jr. We do therefore command you, the said Samuel Eberle Jr. that setting aside all other business and excuses whatsoever you be and appear in your proper person before our Judges at Carlisle at a Court of Common Pleas there to be held for the County of Cumberland on the 28th day of August next to answer the petition or libel of the said Leah Eberle and to show cause if any you have why the said Leah Eberle your wife should not be divorced from the bonds of matrimony, agreeably to the acts of General Assembly in such case made and provided -And hereof fail not. Witness the Honorable James H. Graham Esq. President of our said Court at Carlisle this 15th day of July A.D. 1854." (signed Geo. Zinn Prothy.)

Aug. 28, 1854 -"Cumberland County S.S. -Joseph McDarmond Sheriff being duly sworn says that he served the within subpoena by certified copy left at the dweling (sic) house of defendant in presence of an adult member of his family on the 26th day of July 1854. Sworn and subscribed before me this 28th day of August 1854." (signed George Zinn Prothy. and Jos. McDarmond Shff.) -"Shff. McDarmond's fee $2.12." -Notation on the front of this document -"No. 38 August Term 1854 Leah Eberle by her next friend Saml. Albright vs. Samuel Eberle Jr. Subpoena Sur Divorce. Biddle."

◆ ◆ ◆

Aug. 1854 Term #60 July 1854 -"To the Honble. the Judges of the Court of Common Pleas of Cumberland County -The petition of Rebecca Hughes by her step father and next friend John Ritner -Respectfully Represents That your petitioner on the 21st June A.D. 1849 was lawfully joined in marriage with John Hughes and from that time until January A.D. 1852 lived and cohabited with him the said John Hughes as his wife and as such was owned and acknowledged by him and so deemed and reputed by all her neighbours and acquaintances and altho. by the laws of God as well as by their mutual vows, they were reciprocally bound to that uniform regard which ought to be inseparable from the marriage state yet so it is that the said John Hughes has offered such indignities to the person of your petitioner as to render her condition intolerable and her life burthensome, and thereby forced her to withdraw from his house and company. Wherefore your Libellant further shewing that she is a citizen of the State of Pennsylvania, and has resided therein for upwards of one whole year previous to the filing of this her libel, prays your Honors that a subpoena may issue forth to summon the said John Hughes to appear in this Honorable Court at the next August term of said Court, to answer the complaint aforesaid: And also that a decree of this Honble. Court may be made for the divorcing of him the said John Hughes from the society fellowship and company of this Libellant in all time to come, and she the Libellant from the marriage bond aforesaid, as if she had never been married or as if the said John Hughes were naturally dead. And she will pray etc." (signed Rebecca Hughes by her next friend John Ritner.) -"Cumberland County ss -The above named Rebecca Hughes being duly affirmed says that the facts contained in the within Libel are true to the best of her knowledge and belief, and that the said complaint is not made out of levity and collusion between her and her said husband, and for the mere purpose of being freed and separated from each other, but in sincerity and truth, for the causes mentioned in the said Libel. Affirmed before me this (left blank) day of July A.D. 1854." (signed M. Holcomb and Ann Rebecca Hughes.) -Notation on the front of this document -"No. 60 August Term 1854 15 Aug. 1854 Subpoena awarded By the Court. T.M. Biddle."

Aug. 15, 1854 -"Cumberland County S.S. -The Commonwealth of Pennsylvania to the Sheriff of Cumberland County -Greeting Whereas Rebecca Hughes by her step father and next friend John Ritner did on the 15th day of August 1854 prefer her petition to our said Judges of our Court of Common Pleas for the State of Pennsylvania, and County of Cumberland praying for the causes therein set forth, that she might be divorced from the bonds of matrimony entered into with you John Hughes. We do therefore command you the said John Hughes, that setting aside all other business and excuses whatsoever, you be and appear in your proper person before our Judges at Carlisle at a Court of Common Pleas, there to be held for the County of Cumberland on the 28th day of August next, to answer the petition or libel of the said Rebecca Hughes, and to show cause, if any you have, why the said Rebecca Hughes your wife, should not be divorced from the bonds of matrimony, agreeable to the acts of general assembly in such case made and provided -And hereof fail not. Witness the honorable James H. Graham Esquire President of our said Court at Carlisle the 15th day of August A.D. 1854." (signed George Zinn Prothy.)

Aug. 28, 1854 -"Cumberland County S.S. -Joseph McDarmond being sworn says the defendant John Hughes can not be found within the County of Cumberland. Sworn and Subscribed before me the 28th day of August 1854." (signed George Zinn Prothy. and Jos. McDarmond Shff.) -"Shff. McDarmond's fee $0.18 3/4." -Notation on the front of this document -"No. 60 August Term 1854 Rebecca Hughes by her step father and next friend John Ritner vs. John Hughes Subpoena Sur Divorce Now to wit 28 Aug. 1854 Proof having been made that the Deft. cannot be found in the County alias Subpoena awarded returnable at the next term. By the Court. T.M. Biddle."

◆ ◆ ◆

November Term 1854 #1 Aug. 23, 1855 -"Rebecca Hughes by her step father and next friend John Ritner vs. John Hughes: No. 1 Nov. Term 1854 -Joseph McDarmond Sheriff being duly sworn deposes and says that notice was published in one newspaper in the Borough of Carlisle for four weeks successively prior to the 27th day of August A.D. 1855 the first day of the present term requiring the said John Hughes the defendant to answer the said complaint of the said Rebecca Hughes and to show cause if any why she should not be divorced from the bonds of matrimony agreeably to the acts of Assembly in such case made and provided. Sworn and Subscribed before me 23 Augt. 1855." (signed P. Quigley Dep. Prothy. and Jos. McDarmond Shff.)

Aug. 27, 1855 -"27 Aug. 1855 James F. Lamberton Esq. appt. Comm. to take depositions etc. By the Court." -Notation on the front of this document -"No. 1 November Term 1854 Rebecca Hughes by her next friend vs. John Hughes Alias Subpoena Sur Divorce Affidavit of Sheriff Filed 23d Augt. 1855 Shff. McDarmond Cost on publishing $2.00."

Aug. 27, 1855 -"In the Court of Common Pleas of Cumberland County -Rebecca Hughes by her Step Father and next friend John Ritner vs. John Hughes Entered 29 August 1854: No. 1 November Term 1854 Alias Subpoena Sur Divorce N.E.I. Notice published in one newspaper for 4 weeks successively prior to 27th Aug. 1855 Now to wit 27th August A.D. 1855 James F. Lamberton Esq. Appointed Commissioner to take depositions, to be read in the hearing of this case, as evidence etc. By the Court. Given under my hand the seal of said Court at Carlisle the 13th day of September A.D. 1855." (signed D.K. Noell Prothonotory per P. Quigley Dep. Prothy.) -Notation on the front of this document -"No. 1 November Term 1854 Rebecca Hughes by her Step Father and next friend John Ritner vs. John Hughes: Alias Subpoena Sur Divorce Commission to take Depositions 12th Nov. 1855 held under advisement -By the Court. Biddle & Penrose."

Aug. 29, 1854 -"Cumberland County Sct. -The Commonwealth of Pennsylvania to the Sheriff of Cumberland County Greeting Whereas

Rebecca Hughes by her Step Father and next friend John Ritner did on the 15th day of August 1854 prefer her petition to our said Judges of our Court of Common Pleas for the State of Pennsylvania and County of Cumberland praying for the causes therein set forth that she might be divorced from the bonds of matrimony entered into with you John Hughes. We do therefore command you the said John Hughes that setting aside all other business and excuses whatsoever, you be and appear in your proper person before our Judges at Carlisle at a Court of Common Pleas, there to be held for the County of Cumberland on the 13th day of November next to answer the petition or libel of the said Rebecca Hughes, and to show cause, if any you have, why the said Rebecca Hughes your wife should not be divorced from the bonds of matrimony, agreeably to the act of general assembly in such case made and provided -And hereof fail not. Witness the Hon. James H. Graham Esq. President of our said Court at Carlisle the 29th day of August A.D. 1854." (signed Geo. Zinn Prothy.)

Nov. 7, 1854 -"Cumberland County S.S. -Joseph McDarmond Sheriff being duly sworn says the defendant John Hughes can not be found within the County of Cumberland. Sworn and Subscribed before me 7 Nov. 1854." (signed Geo. Zinn Prothy. and Jos. McDarmond Shff.) -"Shff. McDarmond's fee $0.18 3/4. -Notation on the front of this document -"No. 1 November T. 1854 Rebecca Hughes by her Step Father and next friend John Ritner vs. John Hughes Alias Subpoena Sur Divorce T.M. Biddle."

Oct. 23, 1855 -"With No. 1 Nov. 1854 In the Court of Common Pleas of Cumberland County -Rebecca Hughes by her father and next friend John Ritner vs. John Hughes: No. 1 November T. 1854 Als. Subp. Sur Divorce N.E.I. -In pursuance of the annexed Commission to me, to take testimony on the part of the Libellant in the above stated case -I attended at the public house of Raymond and Kendig in Portsmouth, Dauphin County on the twenty third day of October A.D. 1855, when the following testimony was taken." (signed Jas. F. Lamberton Comm.)

Oct. 23, 1855 -"Mrs. Ann Etter being duly affirmed according to law, sayeth that she has known John Hughes of Portsmouth, Dauphin County and Rebecca his wife for a number of years, they lived in Portsmouth, she the said Rebecca came to my house, after some time the Defendant came, and plead (sic) very much for her the said Rebecca to return with him to his house and said that he the Defendant knew that, he had treated her the said Rebecca very badly, but would do so no more. The said John Hughes was and is now, a very intemperate, worthless man, has done nothing to support his wife for at least three years. Affirmed and subscribed before me this 23rd October 1855." (signed Jas. F. Lamberton and Ann Etter.)

Oct. 23, 1855 -"Elizabeth Strine being duly affirmed according to law sayeth, that she has known John Hughes and Rebecca his wife for five or six years that, he was and is a very intemperate man, the deponent further states, that she lived with a Mrs. Murry on the first floor, whilst Mrs. Hughes lived with the Defendant in the second story of the same house, that she saw the Defendant knock down the stove pipe, overthrow the table and break the dishes one evening, she the said Rebecca ran down stairs and wanted to remain in Mrs. Murry's room, appearing very much frightened and afraid of her husband. Affirmed and subscribed before me this 23rd October 1855." (signed Jas. F. Lamberton and Elizabeth Strine.)

Oct. 23, 1855 -"Geo. Washington Hughes being duly affirmed according to law, sayeth, that he knows John Hughes and Rebecca his wife, they lived in Portsmouth, have known them for many years, the Defendant would at times go to his house under the effects of liquor and knock things around -am a brother to the Defendant, he the Defendant has no means of support, has furnished his wife with nothing for several years, is doing no good for himself or any body (sic) else, is rather intemperate. Affirmed and Subscribed before me this 23 October 1855." (signed G. Washington Hughes and Jas. F. Lamberton.)

Nov. 12, 1855 -"Rebecca Hughes by her Step Father and next friend John Ritner vs. John Hughes: No. 1 November Term 1854 Alias Subpoena sur Divorce N.E.I. And now to wit the 12th day of November A.D. 1855, the Commissioner James F. Lamberton Esq. having returned to the Court here the depositions of witnesses taken before him on the part of the libellant and the same being read and heard by the Court, and the Court after mature and solemn deliberation being satisfied therewith, and proclamation being duly made for the Respondent to come forth and he not appearing the Court do order and decree that the said Rebecca Hughes, the libellant be divorced and separated from the bond of matrimony contracted with the said John Hughes the Respondent and that all and every the duties, rights, and claims accruing to either of said parties by reason of said marriage shall henceforth cease and determine, and the said parties be severally at liberty to marry again in like manner as though they never had been married." -Notation on the front of this document -"with No. 1 Nov. 1854."

◆ ◆ ◆

Nov. Term 1854 #9 Sept. 12, 1854 -"To the Honorable the Judges of the Court of Common Pleas of Cumberland County: The petition of Jane Cuff by her next friend Samuel Ashford respectfully showeth: That your petitioner was on the twenty-third day of March A.D. 1848, lawfully joined in marriage with John Cuff her present husband, and from that time until the first day of August A.D. 1853, lived and cohabited with him and hath in all respects demeaned herself as a kind and affectionate wife, and although by the laws of God as well as by the mutual vows plighted to each other they were bound to that uniform constancy and regard which ought to be inseparable from the marriage state, yet so it is that the said John Cuff in violation of his marriage vow, hath for a considerable time past given himself up to adulterous practices; and been guilty of adultery with a certain Rosanna Johnston and diverse other persons to your petitioner unknown. Wherefore your petitioner further showing that she is a citizen of the Commonwealth of Pennsylvania and hath resided therein more than one whole year previous to the filing of this her petition prays your Honors that a subpoena may issue in due form of law, directed to the said John Cuff, commanding him to appear in this Honorable Court at November Term next to answer the complaint aforesaid. And also that a decree of this honorable Court may be made for the divorcing of her her the said Jane Cuff from the bond of matrimony as if she had never been married. And she will pray etc." (signed Jane Cuff by her next friend Samuel Ashford who signed by his mark.) -"Cumberland County SS. -The above named Jane Cuff being duly Sworn according to law doth depose and say that the facts contained in the above petition are true to the best of her knowledge and belief; and that the said complaint is not made out of levity or by collusion between her the said Jane Cuff and the said John Cuff her husband and for the mere purpose of being freed and separated from each other, but in sincerity and truth for the causes mentioned in the said petition. Sworn and Subscribed before me this 12th September 1854." (signed Geo. Zinn Prothy. and Jane Cuff.) -Notation on the front of this document -"No. 9 November T. 1854 with No. 11 Aug. 1855 12 Sept. 1854 Subpoena awarded By the Court filed 12 Sept. 1854."

Sept. 12, 1854 -"The Commonwealth of Pennsylvania to the Sheriff of Cumberland County Greeting Whereas Jane Cuff by her next friend Samuel Ashford did on the 12th day of September 1854 prefer her petition to our said Judges of our Court of Common Pleas for the State of Pennsylvania and County of Cumberland praying for the causes therein set forth that she might be divorced from the bonds of matrimony entered into with you John Cuff. We do therefore command you the said John Cuff that setting aside all other business and excuses whatsoever, you be and appear in your proper person before our Judges at Carlisle at a Court of Common Pleas there to be held for the County of Cumberland on the 13th day of November next to answer the petition or libel of the said Jane Cuff. And to show cause, if any you have, why the said Jane Cuff your wife should not be divorced from the bonds of matrimony agreeably to the acts of General Assembly in such case made and provided -And hereof fail not. Witness the Honorable J.H. Graham Esq. President of our said Court at Carlisle the 12th day of Sept. A.D. 1854."

(signed Geo. Zinn Prothy.)

Nov. 7, 1854 -"Cumberland County SS -Joseph McDarmond Sheriff being duly sworn says the defendant can not (sic) be found within the County of Cumberland. Sworn and Subscribed before me 7th Nov. 1854." (signed George Zinn Prothy. and Jos. McDarmond Shff.) -"Shff. McDarmond's fee $0.18 3/4." -Notation on the front of this document -"No. 9 November Term 1854 with No. 11 Aug. 1855 Jane Cuff by her next friend Samuel Ashford vs. John Cuff Subpoena Sur Divorce 25 Nov. 1854 alias Subpoena awarded By the Court Shearer."

Nov. 25, 1854 -"Cumberland County S.S. -The Commonwealth of Pennsylvania to the Sheriff of Cumberland County Greeting Whereas Jane Cuff by her next friend Samuel Ashford did on the 12th day of September 1854 prefer her petition to our said Judges of our Court of Common Pleas for the State of Pennsylvania and County of Cumberland praying for the causes therein set forth that she might be divorced from the bonds of matrimony entered into with you John Cuff. We do therefore command you the said John Cuff that setting aside all other business and excuses whatsoever, you be and appear in your proper person before our Judges at Carlisle at a Court of Common Pleas there to be held for the County of Cumberland on the 8th day of January next to answer the petition or libel of the said Jane Cuff. And to shew cause, if any you have, why the said Jane Cuff your wife should not be divorced from the bonds of matrimony agreeably to the acts of General Assembly in such case made and provided -And hereof fail not. Witness the Honorable James H. Graham Esqr. President of our said Court at Carlisle the 25th day of November A.D. 1854." (signed George Zinn Prothy. -Notation on the front of this document -"No. 9 January Term 1855 with No. 11 Aug. Term 1855 Jane Cuff by her next friend Samuel Ashford vs. John Cuff Alias Subpoena Sur divorce Shearer."

◆ ◆ ◆

Aug. Term 1855 #1 April 6, 1855 -"To the Honorable the Judges of the Court of Common Pleas of Cumberland County. The petition of Jacob Lesher of Hopewell Township in said county Respectfully Represents. That your petitioner was on the 30th day of March 1843, lawfully joined in marriage with Elizabeth Nickey, his present wife and from that time till the 15th day of December 1845 lived and cohabited with her and in all respects conducted himself as a kind and affectionate husband yet the said Elizabeth in violation of her marriage vows, and without any just and reasonable cause hath willfully and maliciously deserted and absented herself from the habitation of this petitioner and such desertion hath persisted for the term of nine years and upwards and yet doth continue to absent herself from the said petitioner: Wherefore your petitioner further representing that he is a citizen of the Commonwealth of Pennsylvania, and hath resided therein for more than one whole year previous to the filing of this his petition, prays your Honors, that a subpoena may issue in due form of law, directed to the said Elizabeth commanding her to appear in this Honorable Court at the August Term next and answer the complaint aforesaid: And also that a decree of this Honorable Court may be made for the divorcing of him the said Jacob Lesher from the bond of matrimony, as if he had never been married. And he will pray etc." (signed Jacob Lesher.)

April 6, 1855 -"Cumberland County SS -The said Jacob Lesher being duly sworn according to law says that the facts set forth in the foregoing petition are true to the best of his knowledge and belief; and that the said complaint is not made out of levity or collusion between him the said Jacob Lesher and the said Elizabeth his wife and for the mere purpose of being freed and separated from each other but in sincerity and truth, for the causes mentioned in said petition. Sworn and subscribed before me this 6th day of April 1855." (signed Abraham Hostetter and Jacob Lesher.) -Notation on the front of this document -"No. 1 August T. 1855 Petition of Jacob Lesher for a Divorce etc. 11 April 1855 Subpoena awarded By the Court Filed 11 Apl. 1855. Colwell & McClure."

April 11, 1855 -"Cumberland County S.S. -The Commonwealth of Pennsylvania to the Sheriff of Cumberland County Greeting Whereas Jacob Lesher did on the 11th day of April 1855, prefer his petition to our said Judges of our Court of Common Pleas for the State of Pennsylvania and County of Cumberland, praying for the causes therein set forth, that he might be divorced from the bonds of matrimony entered into with you Elizabeth Lesher. We do therefore command you, the said Elizabeth Lesher, that setting aside all other business and excuses whatsoever, you be and appear in your proper person before our Judges at Carlisle at a Court of Common Pleas, there to be held for the County of Cumberland on the 27th day of August next to answer the petition or libel of the said Jacob Lesher, your husband, and to shew (sic) cause if any you have why the said Jacob Lesher your husband should not be divorced from the bonds of matrimony, agreeably to the Acts of Assembly, in such case made and provided. And hereof fail not. Witness the Honorable James H. Graham, Esq. President of our said Court at Carlisle this 11th day of April 1855." (signed P. Quigley Dep. for D.K. Noell Prothy.)

May 17, 1855 -"Cumberland County SS -Joseph McDarmond Sheriff having been duly sworn says that he served the within subpoena on Elizabeth Lesher personally and by certified copy on the 15th day of May 1855. Sworn and Subscribed before me 17th May 1855." (signed P. Quigley Dep. Prothy. and Jos. McDarmond Shff.) -"Shff. McDarmond's fee $3.40." -Notation on the front of this document -"No. 1 August Term 1855 Jacob Lesher vs. Elizabeth Lesher Subpoena Sur Divorce 27 Aug. 1855 Benj. Duke Esq. apptd.

Commissioner to take depositions etc. By the Court Filed 27 Augt. 1855. Colwell & McClure."

Aug. 27, 1855 -"In the Court of Common Pleas of Cumberland County No. 1 August Term 1855 Jacob Lesher vs. Elizabeth Lesher Entered 11 April 1855 Colwell & McClure: Subpoena Sur Divorce 15 May 1855 Served personally and by certified copy on Elizabeth Lesher. Now to wit 27th August 1855 Benjamin Duke Esq. appointed Commissioner to take depositions etc. in the above case. By the Court. Given under my hand and the seal of said Court this 12th day of September A.D. 1855." (signed D.K. Noell Prothonotary per P. Quigley Dep. Prothy.) -Notation on the front of this document -"No. 1 August Term 1855 Jacob Lesher vs. Elizabeth Lesher: Sub. Sur Divorce Commission to take Depositions etc. Colwell & McClure."

Sept. 29, 1855 -"To Mrs. Elizabeth Lesher, Whereas the undersigned has received a commission issuing out of the Court of Common Pleas of the County of Cumberland, State of Pennsylvania, to me directed for the examination of witnesses in a certain suit or action now depending in said Court for a divorce in which Jacob Lesher is the libellant or petitioner and you, the said Elizabeth Lesher, are the respondent: Now you are hereby notified that I will execute the said commission on behalf of the said libellant or petitioner at the office of Robert P. McClure in the Borough of Shippensburg County of Cumberland aforesaid on Saturday the 20th day of October next at 10 o'clock in the forenoon of the said day when and where you may attend with your witnesses if you think proper. Witness my hand and seal this 29th day of September A.D. 1855." (signed Benjamin Duke Commissioner.) -Notation on the front of this document -"Notice to Mrs. Elizabeth Lesher."

Oct. 20, 1855 -"Cumberland County SS. Before me Benjamin Duke Commissioner appointed to take testimony etc. personally came Hugh Smith Constable of Southampton Township Franklin County Pennsylvania who being duly sworn says that he served this notice personally and by copy on Mrs. Elizabeth Lesher on the Fourth day of October 1855 before me." (signed Benjamin Duke and Hugh Smith.)

Oct. 20, 1855 -"No. 1 Aug. 1855 Jacob Lesher vs. Elizabeth Lesher: In the Court of Common Pleas Cumberland County -No. 1 August Term 1855 Subpoena Sur Divorce Depositions of witnesses produced sworn and affirmed and examined on the 20th day of October A.D. 1855 at the office of R.P. McClure in the Borough of Shippensburg by virtue of a commission hereto annexed to Benjamin Duke directed for the examination of witnesses in a certain cause depending in said Court, wherein Jacob Lesher is Plaintiff and Elizabeth Lesher defendant. The Plaintiff appeared, but no person appeared on behalf of the defendant, due proof having been made of the service of the notice hereto annexed upon her on the 4th day of

October 1855 at the time and place of taking the depositions. Revd. James Mackey of Shippensburg produced and affirmed on behalf of the Libellant (Jacob Lesher) deposeth as follows: I am acquainted with Jacob Lesher and Elizabeth his wife. I knew her before her marriage, her maiden name was Elizabeth Nickey. They were married by me on 31th March 1843 as my record shoes (sic) to which I now refer to ascertain the date, it is the records kept by me in my own hand writing. Affirmed and Subscribed October 20th 1855 before me" (signed Benjamin Duke Commissioner and James Mackey.)

Oct. 20, 1855 -"Peter Stouffer of Hopewell Township Cumberland Co. produced and affirmed on behalf of the Libellant Jacob Lesher, deposes as follows: I am acquainted with Jacob Lesher and Elizabeth his wife. I live about an eighth of a mile from Jacob Lesher's place of residence, Jacob Lesher was married to Elizabeth Nickey, some ten or twelve years ago, I think. They lived together a few years, how many I can not state exactly. She left him before my wife died, my wife died in Nov. 1848. Elizabeth Lesher has not lived with her husband Jacob Lesher since that time; at the time she went away I saw her father's waggon at Jacob Lesher's house loding (sic) her furniture. They had two children, I do not know whether they had more or not. She appeared to care very little for the children, one of the children is dead, the other Jacob Lesher has in his care. I do not know that Elizabeth Lesher had any cause for leaving her husband Jacob Lesher. He appeared to provide well for his family. I do not know where she is now living, but it is the common rumer (sic) that she is married again and lives in Franklin County. Affirmed and Subscribed October 1855 before." (signed Benjamin Duke Commissioner and Peter Stouffer.)

Oct. 20, 1855 -"David Lesher Jr. of Hopewell Township Cumberland County produced and sworn on behalf of the libellant Jacob Lesher deposes as follows: I am a brother of Jacob Lesher. He and I live on the same farm, some forty rods apart, and have lived there ever since we were married except for about eight months, which time he lived in another house, though in the same neighbourhood (sic). My brother Jacob was married, I think it was March 30th 1843, to Elizabeth Nicky, I was married the 28th March 1843 and Jacob was married married two days afterwards. My brother Jacob and his wife Elizabeth lived together two years and a half. She then left his house and went home to her father's. He lived in Hopewell Township. Her father came to Jacob's house with his waggon to take her and her furniture away, she went with her father. My brother Jacob gave them up her furniture. She has never lived with Jacob since. I would have known it, if they would have lived together since that time. She had no cause for leaving Jacob that I know of. He treated her well and provided well for his family.

They had two children. When she went away she took the youngest with her and left the other with brother Jacob, and it is still living with him. The child she took was about two or three years old, when it was brought back to my brother Jacob's. That child died when it was about six years old. She attended the funeral but she did not go back to Jacob's house from the funeral. She went from the grave yard with her brother in law Mr. Strowman. She seemed to care nothing about the children. I do not know where Mrs. Lesher is living now. It is said she is living with John Hartzog in Franklin County. Sworn and Subscribed October 20th 1855 before" (signed B. Duke Commissioner and David Lesher Jr.)

Oct. 20, 1855 -"Hugh Smith of Orrs Town produced and sworn on behalf of the Libellant Jacob Lesher, deposeth as follows: I am acquainted with Jacob Lesher and Elizabeth his wife. I think it is about ten years since they were married. They were at my house the same day they were married I think her name before her marriage was Elizabeth Nicky. I knew that Elizabeth Lesher left her husband Jacob Lesher some six or eight years ago. They have not lived together since. I lived about six or seven miles from them, I frequently visited them when in the neighbourhood they lived in. They had two children that I know of, one of the children is dead. I was at the funeral, Mrs. Lesher attended the funeral, but did not return to the house of J. Lesher, the death of the child was within the last six years. On the fourth day of October 1855 I served a notice on Mrs. E. Lesher to attend if she saw proper at the time and place appointed to take depositions in this case. I found her at the house of John Hertzog in Green Township Franklin County Penna. She was in bed at the time I went there. She had a child apparently about four or five days old. She acknowledged that the child was hers. She was suckling it at the time. I asked her if she was married. She said she was married to John Hartzog that it was no use to deny it any longer, said he was a very good man, and treated her very well. I asked her if she did not think it was a violation of the law for her to mary (sic) again. She replied that she considered it a violation of the law of God according to scripture, but did not know that it was a violation of the laws of man. She excused herself by saying she had to make her living by going from place to place, and had to work harder than she was able to bear. She said she would not attend at the time and place appointed for taking depositions in the case, that she had no objection to Jacob Lesher obtaining a divorse (sic) from her, that she wished he might get it without any trouble, and that she wished him well. I do not know that Elizabeth Lesher had any cause for leaving Jacob Lesher. He treated her well and provided well for his family as far as I know. I was frequently back and forward, and had a good opertunity (sic) of knowing. Sworn and Subscribed before me Oct. 20, 1855." (signed Benjamin Duke Commissioner and Hugh Smith.)

-"I hereby certify that the above witnesses were duly qualified and examined at the time and place stated in the above caption, and subscribed their depositions in my presence." (signed Benjamin Duke Commissioner.) -"Commissioner's fee for taking depositions $2.50." -Notation on the front of this document -"No. 1 Aug. Term 1855 Jacob Lesher vs. Elizabeth Lesher: Subp. Sur Divorce Depositions Filed 12th Nov. 1855. Colwell and McClure."

Nov. 12, 1855 -"Jacob Lesher vs. Elizabeth Lesher: In the Court of Common Pleas of Cumberland County No. 1 Aug. Term 1855 In the matter of the petition of Jacob Lesher for a divorce from his wife Elizabeth Now to wit: 12th November 1855 The commissioner Benjamin Duke Esq. having returned the depositions taken by him in the said matter after three weeks notice duly served on the respondent of the time and place of taking them, and the same being read and heard by the Court, and due proclamation having been made for the respondent to come forth, and she not appearing. The Court after due consideration of the premises do order sentence and decree that the said Jacob Lesher be divorced and separated from the nuptial ties or bonds of matrimony contracted with the said Elizabeth Lesher the respondent. By the Court." -Notation on the front of this document -"No. 1 Aug. T. 1855 Jacob Lesher vs. Elizabeth Lesher Decree of Court Filed 12th Nov. 1855 Colwell and McClure."

Nov. 21, 1855 -"D.K. Noell Esq. Sir, Please pay to R.P. McClure my fees as a Commissioner in the case of Jacob Lesher against Elizabeth Lesher, and this shall be your receipt for the same. Rec. payment of the above $2.50 Nov. 21, 1855." (signed R.P. McClure and Benjamin Duke.) -Notation on the front of this document -"No. 1 Aug. T. 1855 Recd."

◆ ◆ ◆

Aug. Term 1855 #11 April 26, 1855 -"Cumberland County SS -The Commonwealth of Pennsylvania to the Sheriff of Cumberland County Greeting Whereas Jane Cuff by her next friend Samuel Ashford did on the 12th day of September 1854, prefer her petition to our said Judges of our Court of Common Pleas for the State of Pennsylvania and County of Cumberland and praying for the causes therein set forth that she might be divorced from the bonds of matrimony entered into with you John Cuff. We do therefore command you the said John Cuff that setting aside all other business and excuses whatsoever you be and appear in your proper person before our Judges at Carlisle at a Court of Common Pleas there to be held for the County of Cumberland on the 27th day of August next to answer the petition or libel of the said Jane Cuff and to shew (sic) cause, if any you have, why the said Jane Cuff your wife should not be divorced from the bonds of matrimony agreeably to the Acts of General Assembly in such case made and provided -And hereof fail not. Witness the Honorable J.H. Graham President of our said Court at Carlisle the 26th day of April 1855." (signed P. Quigley, Dep. for D.K. Noell, Prothy.)

Aug. 27, 1855 -"Cumberland County SS -Joseph McDarmond Shff. being duly sworn says that the defendant John Cuff can not be found within the County of Cumberland. Sworn and Subscribed before me 27 Augt. 1855." (signed P. Quigley Dep. Prothy. and Jos. McDarmond Shff.) -"Shff. McDarmond's fee $0.18 3/4." -Notation on the front of this document -"No. 11 August Term 1855 Jane Cuff by her next friend Samuel Ashford vs. John Cuff Alias Subpoena Sur Divorce. Shearer."

Jan. 28, 1856 -"Cumberland County, S.S. -The Commonwealth of Pennsylvania the Sheriff of Cumberland County Greeting Whereas Jane Cuff by her next friend Samuel Ashford did on the 12th day of September 1854 prefer her petition to our said Judges of our Court of Common Pleas for the State of Pennsylvania and County of Cumberland, and praying for the causes therein set forth that she might be divorced from the bonds of matrimony entered into with you John Cuff. We, do therefore command you as we have heretofore commanded you the said John Cuff that setting aside all other business and excuses whatsoever you be and appear in your proper person before our Judges at Carlisle at a Court of Common Pleas there to be held for the County of Cumberland, on the 14th day of April next to answer the petition or libel of the said Jane Cuff, and to shew (sic) cause, if any you have, why the said Jane Cuff your wife should not be divorced from the bonds of matrimony agreeably to the Acts of General Assembly in such case made and provided; And hereof fail not. Witness the Honorable James H. Graham President of our said Court at Carlisle the 28th day of January A.D. 1856." (signed D.K. Noell Prothonotary per P. Quigley Dep. Prothy.)

May 13, 1856 -"13 May 1856 Leitzbron and Squire, M. Holcomb appointed commissioner to take testimony etc. on ten days notice By the Court -Notation on the front of this document -"No. 11 August Term 1855 Jane Cuff by her next friend Samuel Ashford vs. John Cuff Alias Subpoena Sur divorce 21th February 1856 Served personally and by certified copy on Defendant So answers" (signed Jacob Bowman Sheriff.) -"Sheriff Bowman's fee $1.20. Shearer."

May 14, 1856 -"In the Court of Common Pleas of Cumberland County -Jane Cuff by her next friend Samuel Ashford vs. John Cuff: No. 11 August T. 1855 Subpoena Sur Divorce 21 Feby. 1856 Served personally and by certified copy on Defendant. Now to wit 13th May 1856 -M. Holcomb Esq. appointed Commissioner to take testimony on ten days notice. By the Court. Given under my hand and the seal of said Court at Carlisle the 14th day of May A.D. 1856." (signed D.K. Noell Prothonotary per P. Quigley Dep. Prothy.) -Notation on the front of this document -"No. 11 Augt. T. 1855 Cuff vs. Cuff Commr.

to take testimony. Shearer."

May 24, 1856 -"In pursuance of the foregoing Commission to me directed, and notice given to the defendant, and parties having met at my office in the borough of Carlisle, on Saturday the 24th May 1856, the following depositions were taken: Susan Ashford, sworn, John Cuff left my sister Jane, this last April three years ago, and that his wife Jane Cuff has had to maintain herself ever since, and the said John Cuff has not contributed any thing (sic) for her support ever since, and she principally made her living by hiring out, they were married about eight years ago. Sworn and subscribed before me the 24th day of May 1856." (signed M. Holcomb, J.P. and Susan Ashford by her mark.)

May 24, 1856 -"Jane Golden, sworn, I do know John Cuff the husband of Jane Cuff, she is still living. I seen John Cuff at Misses Buchanan's in the City of Philadelphia in the fall of 1853, and he was living with a colored woman of the name of Rosanna Johnston as her husband, and he was at service up in the City, and he rented a room from Mrs. Buchanan for himself and Rosanna. They held themselves out in the boarding house as man and wife. They lived and roomed together as man and wife. They had but one room and was but one bed in the room. Myself and sister called on them while they were boarding at Buchanans. We found them setting together on the sofa. My sister asked him if he was not Jane Cuff's husband. He said no; his brother was Jane Cuff's husband. Rosanna said he was her husband, she called him husband. He never denied being her husband, but represented himself as being her husband. They were living at Mrs. Young's before that as husband and wife. Sworn and subscribed before me the 24th day of May 1856." (signed M. Holcomb J.P. and Jane Golden by her mark.) -Notation on the front of this document -"Jane Cuff by her next friend Saml. Ashford vs. John Cuff Testimony taken in the above case by Mr. Holcomb Esq. Commr. appointed by the Court With No. 11 Aug. 1855."

Aug. 28, 1856 -"Jane Cuff by her next friend Saml. Ashford vs. John Cuff: No. 11 Aug. Term 1855 in the Common Pleas of Cumberland County And now, to wit the 28th day of August A.D. 1856 the Commissioner, M. Holcomb Esq., having returned to Court the depositions of witnesses taken before him on the part of the libellant and the same being made and heard by the Court, and the Court after mature and solemn deliberation being satisfied therewith and proclamation being duly made for the respondent to come forth, and he not appearing, the Court do order and adjudge and decree that the said Jane Cuff the libellant be divorced and separated from the bond of matrimony contracted with the said John Cuff, the respondent, and that all and every the duties, rights, and claims accruing to either of said parties by reason of said marriage shall henceforth cease, and determine, and the said parties be severally at liberty to marry again, in the like manner as if they had never been married. By the Court." Notation on the front of this document -"No. 11 Augt. T. 1855 Cuff vs. Cuff Decree of Court Filed 28th Augt. 1856. Shearer."

◆ ◆ ◆

Jan. Term 1856 #2 Sept. 10, 1855 -"To the Honourable the Judges of the Court of Common Please (sic) of Cumberland County, The petition of Rosanna Reckstraw by her next friend Jacob Landis respectfully represents; That your libellant on the seventeenth day of March A.D. One thousand eight hundred and fifty one was contracted in matrimony and married to a certain William Reckstraw, and from that time until the fourteenth day of March A.D. One thousband eight hundred and fifty three lived and cohabited with him as his wife, and as such was owned and acknowledged by him, and so deemed and reputed by all her neighbors and acquaintances and although by the laws of God as well as by their mutual vows and faith plighted to each other they were reciprocally bound to that kindness and uniform regard which ought to be inseparable from the marriage state yet so it is that the said William Reckstraw from the said fourteenth day of March A.D. One thousand eight hundred and fifty three hath willfully and maliciously absented himself from the habitation of this libellant without just or reasonable cause, and such desertion has persisted in for the term of two years and upwards, and yet doth continue to absent himself from the said libellant. Wherefore your libellant further showing, that she is a citizen of the State of Pennsylvania and has resided therein for upwards of one whole year previous to the filing of this her libel, and now resides in the said County, prays your Honour that a Subpoena may issue to summon the said William Reckstraw to appear in this Honourable Court at the next term, to answer the complaint aforesaid, and also that a decree of this Honourable Court may be made for divorcing of him the said William Reckstraw from the society, fellowship, and company of this libellant in all time to come and this libellant from the marriage bond aforesaid as if she had never been married or as if the said William Reckstraw were naturally dead and this libellant will pray etc." (signed Rosannah Rakestraw by her next friend Jacob G. Landes.) -"Cumberland County SS. Personally appeared before the Subscriber one of the Justices of the Peace in and for said County the above named Rosanna Reckstraw, who on her oath lawfully administered doth say, that the facts contained in the above libel, are true to the best of her knowledge and belief, and that the said complaint is not made out of levity or by collusion between her and the said William Reckstraw and for the mere purpose of being freed from each other but in sincerity and truth for the causes mentioned in the said libel. Sworn and Subscribed this tenth day of Sept. A.D. 1855 before me." (signed Charles Wilber and Rosannah

Rakestraw.) -Notation on the front of this document -"No. 2 Jany. T. 1856 The petition of Rosanna Reckstraw for Divorce 14th Nov. 1855 Subp. awarded By the Court Filed 14th Nov. 1855 Alias Sub. allowed 25 Jan. 1856 By the Court. Williamson and Hepburn."

Nov. 14, 1855 -"Cumberland County SS. The Commonwealth of Pennsylvania to the Sheriff of Cumberland County GREETING. Whereas Rosanna Reckstraw, by her next friend Jacob G. Landis did on the 14th day of November 1855, prefer her petition to our said Judges of our Court of Common Pleas for the State of Pennsylvania and County of Cumberland, praying for the causes therein set forth that she might be divorced from the bonds of matrimony entered into with you William Reckstraw. We do therefore command you the said William Reckstraw, that setting aside all other business and excuses whatsoever, you be and appear in your proper person before our Judges at Carlisle at a Court of Common Pleas there to be held for the County of Cumberland on the 14th day of January next, to answer the petition, or libel of the said Rosanna Rakestraw, and to shew (sic) cause if any you have, why the said Rosanna Reckstraw (sic), should not be divorced from the bonds of matrimony agreeably to the Acts of General Assembly in such case made and provided: -And hereof fail not. Witness the Honorable James H. Graham Esq. President of our said Court at Carlisle the 14th Novr. A.D. 1855." (signed D.K. Noell Prothonotary per P. Quigley Dep. Prothy.)

Jan. 14, 1856 -"Cumberland County SS -Jacob Bowman Sheriff being sworn says that William Rockstraw (sic) the deft. cannot be found within the County Jany. 14th 1856 Sworn and Subscribed before me." (signed D.K. Noell Prothy. and Jacob Bowman Sheriff.) -"Shff. Bowman's fee $0.18 3/4" -Notation on the front of this document -"No. 2 January T. 1856 Rosanna Reckstraw by her next friend Jacob G. Landis vs. William Reckstraw Subp. Sur Divorce Filed 14 Jany. 1856 Williamson and Hepburn."

Jan. 25, 1856 -"Cumberland County,s.s. -The Commonwealth of Pennsylvania to the Sheriff of Cumberland County GREETING. Whereas Rosanna Reckstraw by her next friend Jacob G. Landis, did on the 14th day of November 1855 prefer her petition to our Judges of our Court of Common Pleas for the State of Pennsylvania and County of Cumberland, praying for the causes therein set forth that she might be divorced from the bonds of matrimony entered into with you William Reckstraw. We do therefore command you as we have heretofore commanded you the said William Reckstraw, that setting aside all other business and excuses whatsoever, you be and appear in your proper person before our Judges at Carlisle at a Court of Common Pleas there to be held for the County of Cumberland on the 14th day of April next to answer the petition or libel of the said Rosanna Rakestraw, and to shew (sic) cause if any you have, why the said Rosanna Reckstraw should not be divorced from the bonds of matrimony agreeably to the Acts of General Assembly, in such case made and provided: -And hereof fail not. Witness the Honorable James H. Graham President of our said Court at Carlisle the 25th day of January A.D. 1856." (signed D.K. Noell Prothy. per P. Quigley Dep. Prothy.)

April 10, 1856 -"Cumberland County SS -Jacob Bowman Sheriff being duly sworn says that the deft. William Reckstraw can not be found within the County. Sworn and Subscribed before me." (signed P. Quigley Dep. Prothy. and Jacob Bowman Shrff.) -Notation on the front of this document -"No. 2 January T. 1856 Rosanna Reckstraw by her next friend Jacob G. Landis vs. William Reckstraw: Alias Subpoena Sur divorce Shff. Bowman's fee $0.18 3/4. Hepburn."

April 15, 1856 -"In the Court of Common Pleas of Cumberland County Rosanna Reckstraw by her next friend Jacob G. Landis vs. William Reckstraw: No. 2 January Term 1856 Alias Subpoena Sur divorce And now to wit; 15th April 1856 the Alias Subpoena in this case having been returned by the Sheriff of the said County, and proof having been made that the said William Reckstraw, could not be found within the said County of Cumberland. The Court order that the Sheriff of the said County, cause notice to be published in one of the newspapers in the said County for four weeks successively prior to the first day of the next term, of the said Court, requiring the said William Reckstraw to appear on the said day to answer the complaint of the said Rosanna Reckstraw. By the Court. Cumberland County, SS." (signed D.K. Noell Prothy. per P. Quigley Dep. Prothy.) -Notation on the front of this document -"No. 2 Jany. T. 1856 R. Reckstraw vs. Wm. Reckstraw Published in one newspaper for four weeks successively as by direction of the decree of the Court So answers" (signed Jacob Bowman Shff.) -"Shff.Bowman's fee $0.18 3/4 advt. $2.00 total $2.18 3/4. Geo. W. Criswell Esq. appointed Commissioner to take depositions on the hearing of this case By the Court Filed 25th Augt. 1856 Williamson & Hepburn for publication."

Aug. 29, 1856 -"In the Court of Common Pleas of Cumberland County No. 2 January Term 1856 Rosanna Reckstraw by her next friend Jacob G. Landis vs. William Reckstraw: Subpoena Sur Divorce Now to wit, 25th August 1856 George W. Criswell appointed Commissioner to take depositions on the hearing of this case By the Court. Given under my hand and the seal of said Court at Carlisle the 29th day of August A.D. 1856." (signed D.K. Noell Prothy. per P. Quigley Dep. Prothy.) -Notation on the front of this document -"No. 2 Jany. T. 1856 R. Reckstraw vs. Wm. Reckstraw: Geo. W. Criswell Commr. to take depositions Williams & Hepburn."

Nov. 7, 1856 -"Cumberland County SS -Personally appeared before me one of the Justices of the Peace in and for the said County Christian Eberly of East Pennsboro township County aforesaid (yeoman) who upon his solemn affirmation according to law doth say

I was well acquainted with William Rackstraw. I know he deserted his wife Rosanna and one child sometime in the spring of 1853. He left his wife in a destitute condition and I have not heard from him since he left. Further saith not. Affirmed and Subscribed before me this 7th day of Novem. 1856." (signed G.W. Criswell and C. Eberly.)

Oct. 23, 1856 -"Cumberland County SS. -Personally appeared before me one of the Justices of the Peace in and for the said County Jacob G. Landes of York County yeoman who upon his solemn affirmation according to law saith I knew William Rackstraw and he deserted his wife Rosanna some time (sic) in March A.D. 1853. He had not provided any thing (sic) for his wife to keep house or live upon for six months before he left her, and I have not heard any thing (sic) from since the time that he left and deserted his wife as before mentioned. Further saith not. Affirmed and Subscribed before me this 23 day of October 1856." (signed G.W. Criswell and Jacob G. Landes.) -Notation on th front of this document -"No. 2 Jany. T. 1856 Reckstraw vs. Reckstraw Filed 11th Nov. 1856."

Nov. 11, 1856 -"Rosanna Rackstraw by her next friend Jacob G. Landis vs. William Reckstraw: No. 2 Jany. T. 1856 In Common Pleas of Cumb. Cty. -And now the 11th day of Novr. A.D. 1856 the Examiner George W. Criswell Esq. having returned to the Court here the depositions of witnesses taken before him on the part of the Libellant, and the same being read and heard by the Court, and the Court after mature and solemn deliberation, being satisfied therewith, and proclamation being duly made for the Respondent to come forth, and he not appearing, the Court do order, adjudge and decree, that the said Rosanna Reckstraw the Libellant be divorced and separated from the bond of matrimony contracted with the said William Reckstraw the Respondent, and that all and every the duties, rights and claims, accruing to either of the said parties by reason of the said marriage, shall henceforth cease and determine, and the said parties be severally at liberty to marry again in like manner as if they never had been married and that the Defendant pay the costs. By the Court." -Notation on the front of this document -"No. 2 Jany. T. 1856 Reckstraw vs. Reckstraw Decree of Court Filed 11th Nov. 1856."

◆ ◆ ◆

Aug. Term 1856 #3 April 12, 1856 -"To the Honorable the Judges of the Court of Common Pleas of Cumberland County -The petition of John Arnold of the township of Frankford township (sic) County aforesaid -Respectfully Represents -That your libellant was on the 22nd day of October A.D. 1842 lawfully joined in marriage with Margaret Stoner his present wife and from that time until, the 10th day of April A.D. 1854 lived and cohabited with her and hath in all respects demeaned himself as a kind and affectionate husband and although by the laws of God as well as by the mutual vows plighted to each other they were bound to that uniform constancy and regard which ought to be inseparable from the marriage state yet so it is that the said Margaret in violation of her marriage vow from the said 10th day of April A.D. 1854 hath wilfully and maliciously deserted and absented herself from the habitation of the libellant without any just or reasonable cause and such desertion hath persisted in for the term of two years and upwards and yet doth continue to absent herself from the said libellant. Wherefore your libellant further shewing (sic) that he is a citizen of this Commonwealth and hath resided therein for more than one whole year previous to the filing of this his libel prays your Honors that a subpoena may issue in due form directed to the said Margaret commanding her to appear in this Honorable Court at the next term to answer the complaint aforesaid. And also that a decree of this Honorable Court may be made for the divorcing of him the said John Arnold from the bond of matrimony as if he had never been married. And he will ever pray etc." (signed John Arnold.) -"Cumberland County SS -The above named John Arnold being duly affirmed according to law doth affirm and say that the facts contained in the above libel or petition are true to the best of his knowledge and belief and that the said complaint is not made out of levity or by collusion between him the said John Arnold and the said Margaret his wife and for the mere purpose of being freed and separated from each other but in sincerity and truth for the causes mentioned in said petition or libel. Affirmed and Subscribed before me this 12th day of April 1856." (signed Stephen Keepers and John Arnold.) -Notation on the front of this document -"No. 3 August T. 1856 Libel of John Arnold for Subpoena sur Divorce 14th April 1856 Subpoena Awarded By the Court Filed 14th April 1856 Penrose & Biddle."

 Aug. Term 1856 #3 April 14, 1856 -"Cumberland County, SS. -The Commonwealth of Pennsylvania to the Sheriff of Cumberland County GREETING Whereas John Arnold did on the 14th day of April 1856 prefer his petition to our said Judges of our Court of Common Pleas for the State of Pennsylvania and County of Cumberland praying for the causes therein set forth that he might be divorced from the bonds of matrimony entered into with you Margaret Arnold. We do therefore command you the said Margaret Arnold that setting aside all other business and excuses whatsoever, you be and appear in your proper person before our Judges at Carlisle at a Court of Common Pleas, there to be held for the County of Cumberland on the 25th day of August next to answer the petition or libel of the said John Arnold your Husband, and to shew (sic) cause if any you have why the said John Arnold your Husband should not be divorced from the bonds of matrimony, agreeably to the Acts of Assembly in such case made and provided. And hereof fail not. Witness the Honorable James H. Graham Esquire, President of our said Court at Carlisle this 14th day of April A.D. 1856." (signed D.K. Noell Prothonotary per P. Quigley, Dep. Prothy.) -Notation on the front of this document -"No. 3 August T. 1856 John Arnold vs. Margaret Arnold Subpoena Sur Divorce August 18th 1856 N.E.I. So answers" (signed Jacob Bowman Shff.) -"Sheriff Bowman's fee $0.18 3/4 25th August 1856 Alias Subpoena awarded By the Court. Biddle & Penrose."

Aug. 29, 1856 -"Cumberland County, SS. The Commonwealth of Pennsylvania to the Sheriff of Cumberland county GREETING: WHEREAS, John Arnold did on the 14th day of April 1856, prefer his petition to our said Judges of our Court of Common Pleas for the State of Pennsylvania, and County of Cumberland, praying for the causes therein set forth, that he might be divorced from the bonds of matrimony entered into with you Margaret Arnold. We do therefore command you the said Margaret Arnold, as we have heretofore commanded you that setting aside all other business and excuses whatsoever, you be and appear in your proper person before our Judges at Carlisle, at a Court of Common Pleas there to be held for the County of Cumberland, on the tenth day of November next, to answer the petition or libel of the said John Arnold and to shew (sic) cause, if any you have, why the said John Arnold should not be divorced from the bonds of matrimony agreeably to the Acts of General Assembly in such case made and provided. And hereof fail not. Witness the Honorable James H. Graham, Esq., President of our said Court, at Carlisle, the 29th day of August A.D. 1856." (signed D.K. Noell Prothonotary per P. Quigley Dep. Prothy.) -Notation on the front of this document -"No. 3 August T. 1856 John Arnold vs. Margaret Arnold: Alias Subpoena Sur Divorce Retble. 10th Nov. 1856. N.E.I. So answers" (signed Jacob Bowman Sheriff.) "Filed 18th Sept. 1856 Shff. Bowman's fee $0.18 3/4. Biddle & Penrose."

Jan. 10, 1857 -"John Arnold vs. Margaret Arnold: Court of Common Pleas of Cumberland County Subpoena Sur Divorce No. 3 August Term 1856 Alias Subpoena to November Term 1856 Jacob Bowman Esq. High Sheriff of Cumberland County being duly sworn according to law deposes and says that notice was published in one newspaper in the Borough of Carlisle for four weeks successively prior to the 12th day of January A.D. 1857 the first day of the present term requiring the said Margaret Arnold the defendant to answer the said complaint of the said John Arnold and to shew (sic) cause if any she have why the said John Arnold should not be divorced from the bonds of matrimony agreeably to the acts of Assembly in such case made and provided. Sworn and Subscribed this 10th day of Jan. T. 1857." (signed P. Quigley Dep. Prothy. and Jacob Bowman Shff.) -Notation on the front of this document -"No. 3 August T. 1856 Arnold vs. Arnold Subpoena sur Divorce and Alias Subpoena Affidavit of the Publication 12 Jany. 1857 Michl. Holcomb

Esq. apptd. Commissioner to take testimony etc. By the Court Filed 12 Jany. 1857."

Jan. 12, 1857 -"In the Common Pleas of Cumberland County No. 3 August Term 1856 John Arnold vs. Margaret Arnold; Subpoena Sur Divorce 18th Augt. 1856 N.E.I. 25th Augt. 1856 Alias Sub. awarded N.E.I. 12th Jany. 1857 Affidavit of notice of publication N.E.I. Now to wit 12th January 1857 Michael Holcomb Esq. appointed Commissioner to take testimony etc. By the Court given under my hand and the seal of said Court at Carlisle the 22d day of January A.D. 1857." (signed D.K. Noell Prothonotary per P. Quigley Dep. Prothy.) -Notation on the front of this document -"No. 3 August Term 1856 John Arnold vs. Margaret Arnold: Subp. Sur Divorce Michael Holcomb Commr. to take testimony Filed 23d Feby. 1857. Penrose & Biddle."

Jan. 14, 1857 -"John Arnold vs. Margaret Arnold: M. Holcomb Comr. $2.50: Subpoena sur Divorce In the Court of Common Pleas of Cumberland County the following witnesses being produced and sworn. Henry Strine, sworn, I live in Frankford township, Cumberland county, and State of Pennsylvania, that I am well acquainted with John Arnold and Margaret Arnold, and that they were man and wife, and lived together as such. That the said Margaret Arnold has left the said John Arnold, and has been absent from him between two and three years. That the said John Arnold did always provide well for her in every respect, and that the said Margaret Arnold, was in the habit of treating him very badly, and is now absent in the West and has been there for upwards of two years. Sworn and subscribed before me the 14th January 1857." (signed M. Holcomb J.P. and Henry Strine by his mark.)

Jan. 14, 1857 -"William Y. Kennedy, sworn, I live in Frankford township, Cumberland County, Pennsylvania. I have known John Arnold and Margaret his wife for ten years and upwards. They lived near me and were tenants of mine in the year 1852. In the year of 1854, he lived in a house of Daniel Myers in the said township. His wife resided with him in this house of Myers until the 10th day of April 1854. This house of Myers is about one mile from where I now reside and did reside at that time. On the said 10th day of April 1854, Margaret Arnold left her said husband John Arnold. On that day I hauled part of her things from the house, and Henry Smith at the same time hauled the balance. We hauled them to her son David, in said township. She at this time told me that she never would live with Arnold again and since that time she has not lived with him, and she has lived out of the State nearly two years. She left the State, the April after she left her husband. I know of no reason why she thus deserted him. I always thought that he treated her as well as I treated my wife, or as a wife ought to be treated. She was a very singular tempered woman and was in the habit of scolding Arnold very violently. Arnold always took it very peaceably. I never seen him do any thing (sic) but get up and walk away from her, when she would abuse him. I think Arnold and his wife were married in the year 1841, and once before this last time she left him for nearly two years. When I hauled her things away in April 1854 she assigned for a reason that he would not pay her for keeping house for him. Arnold always provided well for his family. Sworn and subscribed before me." (signed M. Holcomb and Wm. Y. Kennedy.)

Jan. 14, 1857 -"Michael Minich, sworn, I know John Arnold and Margaret his wife. I knew them from the time they were married. We lived neighbors in Frankford township, in this county. Margaret Arnold left her husband three years ago this spring. I know of no cause of her leaving him. I had frequent opportunities of seeing how he treated her. He always treated her very well, and provided well for her. She behaved very badly towards him. She would abuse him shamefully, and he would quietly walk away from her. Arnold is a man of good character, excellent character. Sworn and subscribed before me." (signed M. Holcomb and Michael Minich.)

Jan. 14, 1857 -"Daniel Myers, affirmed, I live in Frankford township, in said county. John Arnold and wife were tenants of mine in 1853 and 1854. They were tenants of mine when she left him. She left him about the commencement of April 1854. William Y. Kenneday (sic) and Henry Smith hauled her goods away from the house, and she has not lived with Arnold since. I know of no reason for her leaving her husband. Arnold always treated her well, and provided well for her. She was in the habit of using rough language to him, and as I saw myself, when she would do this, he would get his hat and walk away without saying any thing (sic) to her. As far as I know Arnold bears a first rate character. Affirmed and subscribed before me." (signed M. Holcomb and Daniel Myers.)

Jan. 26, 1857 -"Cumberland County SS. -James McDowel, Esq. sworn, I know John Arnold and Margaret his wife. I have knowed (sic) them both for ten years. They resided in my neighborhood, some time (sic) prior to January 1st 1855, the said Margaret left the residence of her husband and has not resided with him since. How many months before the said first day of January 1855, she left her said husband I cannot say. I do know that she went West to the State of Iowa, some time (sic) in the month of April 1855, and has not been in this State to my knowledge since. I know of no reason why the said Margaret should have deserted the said John as above mentioned. As far as I know he treated her well. I have been in their house several times and seen them together there, and I always thought he treated her with kindness and respect, just as a husband should treat a wife. She was a high tempered woman and I have heard her scolding him and he kept quit (sic) and made no reply. The residence of these parties was in Frankford township in this County, and John Arnold is still a resident of this county and always has been so, since I knew him. Sworn and subscribed before me the 26th day of January, 1857." (signed James L. McDowell.)

Feb. 23, 1857 -"John Arnold vs. Margaret Arnold: Subpoena sur Divorce And now to wit the 23d day of February A.D. 1857 the Commissioner Michael Holcomb Esq. having returned to the Court here the depositions of witnesses taken before him on the part of the libellant and the same being read and heard by the Court and the Court after mature and solemn deliberation being satisfied therewith and proclamation being duly made for the Respondent to come forth and she not appearing. The Court do order and decree that the said John Arnold the libellant be divorced and separated from the bond of matrimony contracted with the said Margaret Arnold the respondent and that all and every the duties, rights and claims accruing to either of said parties by reason of said marriage shall thenceforth cease and determine and the said parties severally be at liberty to marry again in the like manner as if they never had been married. By the Court." -Notation on the front of this document -"No. 3 August T. 1856 Arnold vs. Arnold Subpoena Sur Divorce Decree Filed 23d Feby. 1857"

◆ ◆ ◆

Aug. Term 1856 #20 May 28, 1856 -"To the Hon. the Judges of the Court of Common Pleas of Cumberland County, the petition of John R. Leidig a citizen of Cumberland County respectfully showeth That your petitioner was on the 30th day of July 1851 lawfully joined in marriage with Sarah Jane Miller his present wife and that he lived and cohabited with her for a period of over two years and did in all respects demean himself as a kind and loving husband, and although by the laws of God as well as by the mutual vows plighted to each other they were bound to that constancy and uniform regard and chastity which ought to be inseparable from the marriage state, yet so it is that the said Sarah Jane in violation of her marriage vow hath for a considerable time past, being at such time domiciled within the Commonwealth of Pennsylvania, given herself up to adulterous practices and been guilty of adultery with a certain (John Bilsmoyer, and diverse other persons -these words all crossed out) person whose name is unknown to your petitioner. Wherefore your petitioner further showing that he is a citizen of this state, and has resided therein for upwards of one whole year previous to the filing of this his petition, prays that a subpoena may issue in due form of law, directed to the said Sarah Jane commanding her to appear at the next Court of Common Pleas to be held at Carlisle to answer the petitioner's libel, and to show cause if any she hath why the petitioner should not be divorced from the bonds of matrimony. And he will ever pray etc." (signed John R. Leidig.) -"Cumberland County SS. -Personally appeared before me a Justice of the Peace in and for said County, the within named libellant John R. Leidig, who being duly sworn according to law says that the facts set forth in the within petition are true to the best of his knowledge and belief, and that the said complaint is not made out of levity and collusion between him and the said within named Sarah Jane Leidig, and for the mere purpose of being freed and separated from each other, but in sincerity and truth, and for the causes mentioned in his within petition. Sworn and subscribed before me the 28th May 1856." (signed Stephen Keepers and John R. Leidig.) -Notation on the front of this document -"No. 20 Augt. T. 1856 Petition of John R. Leidig for a Divorce 31st May 1856 Subpoena awarded By Court Filed 2d June 1856. Smith."

May 31. 1856 -"Cumberland County, ss -The Commonwealth of Pennsylvania to the Sheriff of Cumberland County, Greeting Whereas John R. Leidig, did on the 31 May 1856, prefer his petition to our said Judges of our Court of Common Pleas, for the State of Pennsylvania and County of Cumberland, praying for the causes therein set forth that he might be divorced from the bonds of matrimony entered into with you Sarah Jane Leidig. We do therefore command you the said Sarah Jane Leidig, that setting aside all other business and excuses whatsoever, you be and appear in your proper person before our Judges at Carlisle, at a Court of Common Pleas there to be held for the County of Cumberland on the 25th day of August next to answer the petition or libel of the said John R. Leidig and to shew (sic) cause if any you have, why the said John R. Leidig should not be divorced from the bonds of matrimony, agreeably to the Acts of General Assembly in such case made and provided. Witness the Honorable James H. Graham President of our said Court at Carlisle the 31st day of May A.D. 1856." (signed D.K. Noell, Prothonotary per P. Quigley, Dep. Prothy.) -Notation on the front of this document -"No. 20 August T. 1856 John R. Leidig vs. Sarah Jane Leidig: Subpoena Sur divorce June 25th 1856 Served personally and by certified copy on Sarah Jane Leidigh (sic) So answers" (signed Jacob Bowman Shff.) -"Shff. Bowman's fee $2.76 Smith."

Aug. 25, 1856 -"John R. Leidig vs. Sarah Jane Leidig, No. 20 August T. 1856 Subpoena Sur Divorce To the Honorable the Judges of the Court of Common Pleas of Cumberland County. The petition of John R. Leidig by his attorney Jas. R. Smith respectfully represents that the subpoena awarded in the above case has been returned by the sheriff "Served personally and by certified copy on Sarah Jane Leidig," and that there is no appearance for her. He therefore prays your honorable Court to appoint a Commissioner to take testimony to be read in evidence on the hearing of the above case -said testimony to be taken at any time on ten days notice to either party. And he will pray etc." (signed John R. Leidig by his attorney Jas. R. Smith) -Notation on the front of this document -"No. 20 Augt. T.

1856 John R. Leidig vs. Sarah J. Leidig Petition for a Commissioner etc. Filed Aug. 25th 1856 25th August 1856 Charles Wilber appointed a Commissioner to take testimony on ten days notice. By the Court. Smith."

"John R. Leidig vs. Sarah Jane Leidig: In the Court of Common Pleas of Cumberland County No. 20 August T. 1856 Subpoena Sur Divorce 25th June 1856 Served personally and by certified copy on Sarah Jane Leidig. Now to wit 25th August 1856 Charles Wilbur appointed a Commissioner to take testimony on ten days notice. By the Court. Given under my hand and the seal of said Court at Carlisle the 29th day of August A.D. 1856." (signed D.K. Noell Prothy. per P. Quigley Dep. Prothy.) -Notation on the front of this document -"No. 20 Augt. T. 1856 John R. Ledig vs. Sarah Jane Leidig: Charles Wilbur Commr. to take depositions on ten days notice. Smith."

undated -"John R. Ledig vs. Sarah Jane Ledig: In the Court of Common Pleas of Cumberland County No. 20 Aug. T. 1856 Subpoena Sur divorce To Sarah Jane Ledig: You are hereby notified that a Commission has been issued to me to take testimony to be had on the hearing of the above case in pursuance of my duties I will take testimony at my office in West Fairview on Saturday the first day of November next between the hours of 9 & 12 o'clock A.M. when and where you may attend to examine witnesses if you see proper to." (signed Charles Wilber J. of the Peace.)

Oct. 16, 1856 -"Cumberland County SS -Personally appeared before me A. Coble who being duly sworn says he served the within notice on Sarah Jane Leidig by leaving a copy with her on the 16th October 1856 Sworn and subscribed before me this 16th Oct. 1856." (signed Charles Wilbur J.P. and Abram Coble.) -Notation on the front of this document -"Notice Sarah Jane Leidig October 16th 1856 Served by Copy." (signed A. Coble.)

Nov. 1, 1856 -"In pursuance of the foregoing rule and notice the following witnesses were produced and sworn and examined before me at my office in West Fairview Cumberland County and State of Pennsylvania on the first day of November 1856 between the hours of nine and twelve o'clock A.M. of said day on the part of the plaintiff. John Bilmyer sworn says I know John and Sarah Jane Leidig as husband and wife. Esq. Agnany married them. My wife told me she was present at the marriage. My wife is dead. Was sister to Serry Jane Leidig. Some time after the said Leidig and Sarah Jane were married she the said Sarah Jane came to my house with a strange man whose name I do not know and remained there for one or two days and nights and while there they sleped (sic) in the same bed together. This was in the year of 1853 or 4. They started from my house together towards Humels Town. They returned in two or three weeks to my house and wanted to stay there again. I told Sarah Jane she might stay there as long as she wanted to but I would not keep the man who was with her that man was was not John R. Leidig her husband. They went away together after I refused to keep the man. Sworn and subscribed before me the first day of November 1856." (signed Charles Wilbur J.P. and John Billmir.)

Nov. 1, 1856 -"David Agnany Esq. sworn says, I am a Justice of the Peace in Perry County. I married John R. Leidig to Sarah Jane Miller in my office in Perry County on the 30th day of July 1851. These are the parties to this suit that I married. Sworn and subscribed before me on the first day of November 1856." (signed Charles Wilbur J.P. and David Angney.)

Nov. 1, 1856 -"William Brooks sworn says I was married to Sarah Jane Leidig by Gacob (sic) Bruner Esq. on the 28th day of last August and we have lived and cohabited together since that time as man and wife. Sworn and subscribed before me the first day of Nov. 1856." (signed Charles Wilbur J.P. and William Brooks.) -Notation on the front of this document -"No. 20 August Term 1856 John R. Leidig vs. Sarah J. Leidig Filed 10th Nov. 1856 Smith."

Nov. 10, 1856 -"John R. Leidig vs. Sarah Jane Leidig: No. 20 Aug. T. 1856 Sub. Sur divorce And now to wit 10th Novr. 1856 Charles Wilber the Commissioner having returned to the Court here the deposition of witnesses taken before him on the part of the libellant and the same being read and heard by the Court the Court after mature deliberation being satisfied therewith and proclamation being duly made for the respondent to come forth and she not appearing, the Court do order, adjudge and decree that the said John R. Leidig the libellant be divorced and separated from the bonds of matrimony contracted with the said Sarah Jane Leidig the respondent, and that all and every the duties, rights and claims accruing to either of the said parties by reason of the said marriage shall henceforth cease and determine, and the said parties be severally at liberty to marry again in like manner as if they never had been married. By the Court." -"Notation on the front of this document -"No. 20 August Term 1856 Leidig vs. Leidig Sub. Sur divorce Decree of Ct. Filed 10th Nov. 1856. Smith."

◆ ◆ ◆

Nov. Term 1856 #5 Aug. 27, 1856 -"To the Honorable the Judges of the Court of Common Pleas of Cumberland County the petition of Ann King of the Borough of Carlisle, and County aforesaid by her next friend John Mell Respectfully Represents That your petititioner was on the 24th day of November A.D. one thousand eight hundred and fifty-three joined in marriage with William R. King her present husband. That within a few days after the said marriage and before the said parties had cohabited and lived together and although by the laws of God, as well as by the mutual vows plighted to each other they were bound to that uniform constancy and regard which ought to be inseparable from the marriage state yet so it is that the said William R. King in violation of his marriage vow from the (left blank) day of January A.D. one thousand eight hundred and fifty-four or thereabouts hath wilfully and maliciously deserted and absented himself from the habitation of this petitioner without any just or reasonable cause and such desertion hath persisted in for the term of two years and upwards and yet doth continue to absent himself from your said petitioner. Wherefore your petitioner further showeth that she is a citizen of the Commonwealth of Pennsylvania and hath resided therein for more than one whole year previous to the filing of this her petition. She therefore prays your Honor that a subpoena may issue in due form of law directed to the said William R. King commanding him to appear in the said Court of Common Pleas at the November Term next to answer the complaint aforesaid And also that a decree of the Court may be made for the divorcing of the said Ann King from the bond of matrimony as if she had never been married. And she is in duty bound will ever pray etc." (signed Annie King.) -"Cumberland County ss -The above named Ann King being duly sworn according to law doth depose and say that the facts set forth in the above petition or libel are true to the best of her knowledge and belief and that the said complaint is not made out of levity or by collusion between her the said Ann King and her husband the said William R. King and for the mere purpose of being freed and separated from each other but in sincerity and truth for the causes mentioned in the said petition or libel. Sworn and subscribed before me the 27th August 1856." (signed M. Holcomb J.P. and Annie King.) -Notation on the front of this document -"No. 5 November T. 1856 Petition of Ann Mell by her father and next friend John Mell for Divorce Aug. 27 1856 Subpoena Sur divorce awarded by the Court Filed Aug. 27 1856. Penrose & Biddle."

Aug. 29, 1856 -"Cumberland County,SS. -The Commonwealth of Pennsylvania to the Sheriff of Cumberland County, GREETING: WHEREAS, Annie King, by her father, and next friend did on the 27th day of August A.D. 1856 prefer her petition to our said Judges of our Court of Common Pleas for the State of Pennsylvania, and County of Cumberland, praying for the causes therein set forth, that she might be divorced from the bonds of matrimony entered into with you William R. King. We do therefore command you the said William R. King that setting aside all other business and excuses whatsoever, you be and appear in your proper person before our Judges, at Carlisle, at a Court of Common Pleas there to be held for the County of Cumberland, on the 10th day of November next, to answer the petition or libel of the said Annie King and to shew (sic) cause, if any you have, why the said Annie King should not be divorced from the bonds of matrimony agreeably to the Acts of General Assembly in such case made and provided. And hereof fail not. Witness the Honorable JAMES H. GRAHAM, Esq., President of our said Court, at Carlisle the 29th day of August A.D. 1856." (signed J.H. Graham.) -Notation on the front of this document -"No. 5 November T. 1856 Annie King by her father and next friend John Mell vs. William R. King Subpoena sur divorce N.E.I. So answers" (signed Jacob Bowman Sheriff.) "Sworn and Subscribed 10th Nov. 1856 before me" (signed P. Quigley Dep. Prothy.) "17th Nov. 1856 alias Subpoena awarded By the Court Shff. Bowman's fee $0.18 3/4. Penrose & Biddle."

Nov. 17, 1856 -"CUMBERLAND COUNTY, SS. -The Commonwealth of Pennsylvania to the Sheriff of Cumberland County, GREETING: WHEREAS, Annie King by her father and next friend John Mell did on the 27th day of August A.D. 1856, prefer her petition to our said Judges of our Court of Common Pleas for the State of Pennsylvania, and County of Cumberland, praying for the causes therein set forth, that she might be divorced from the bonds of matrimony entered into with you William R. King. We do therefore command you the said William R. King that setting aside all other business and excuses whatsoever, you be and appear in your proper person before our Judges, at Carlisle, at a Court of Common Pleas there to be held for the County of Cumberland, on the twelfth day of January next, to answer the petition or libel of the said Annie King and to shew (sic) cause, if any you have, why the said Annie King should not be divorced from the bonds of matrimony agreeably to the Acts of General Assembly in such case made and provided. And hereof fail not. Witness the Honorable JAMES H. GRAHAM, Esq., President of our said Court, at Carlisle, the 17th day of November A.D. 1856." (signed D.K. Noell Prothonotary per P. Quigley Dep. Prothy.) -Notation on the front of this document -"No. 5 November T. 1856 Annie King by her Father and next friend John Mell vs. William R. King: Alias Subpoena Sur divorce Retble. 12th Jany. 1857 December 5th 1856 N.E.I. So answers" (signed Jacob Bowman Sheriff.) -"Sworn and subscribed 9th Decr. 1856 before me" (signed P. Quigley Dep. Prothy.) -"Shff. Bowman's fee $0.18 3/4. Penrose & Biddle."

April 18, 1857 -"Annie King by her Father and next friend John Mell vs. William R. King: Court of Common Pleas of Cumberland County No. 5 Nov. Term 1856 Cumberland County ss -Jacob Bowman High Sheriff of the said County being duly sworn according to law deposes and says that notice was published in one newspaper in the Borough of Carlisle for four weeks successively prior to the 13th day of April A.D. 1857 the first day of the present term requiring the said William R. King the defendant to answer the said complaint of the said Annie King and to shew (sic) cause if any he have (sic) why the said Annie King should not be divorced from the bonds of matrimony agreeably to the Acts of Assembly in such case made and provided. Sworn and Subscribed this 18th day of April 1857."

(signed P. Quigley Dep. Prothy. and Jacob Bowman, Shrff.) -Notation on the front of this document -"No. 5 November T. 1856 Ann King by her next friend John Mell vs. W.R. King Alias Subpoena sur divorce Affidavit of the publication of notice etc. Filed 23d April 1857 23d April 1857 Stephen Keepers Esq. apptd. Commissioner to take depositions etc. By the Court."

April 28, 1857 -"In the Court of Common Pleas of Cumberland County Penrose & Biddle: Annie King by her Father and next friend John Mell vs. William R. King: No. 5 November Term 1856 Subpoena Sur Divorce N.E.I. So answers Jacob Bowman Shrff. 17th Nov. 1856 Alias Subp. awarded By the Court. 5th Decr. A. Subp. returned N.E.I. so answers Jacob Bowman Shrff. 25th April 1857 Affidavit of publication of notice filed Now to wit 23d April 1857 Stephen Keepers Esq. appointed Commissioner to take depositions etc. By the Court Given under my hand and the seal of said Court at Carlisle the 28th day of April A.D. 1857." (signed D.K. Noell Prothonotary Per P. Quigley Dep. Prothy.) -Notation on the front of this document -"No. 5 November T. 1856 Annie King by her Father and next friend John Mell vs. Wm. R. King: Stephen Keepers appointed Commissioner to take testimony Filed 24th Augt. 1857 By order of the Court. Penrose & Biddle."

Aug. 19, 1857 -"In pursuance of the annexed Commission to me directed, the following depositions were taken on the part of the libellant, Annie King, on (left blank) day of August A.D. 1857. Robert McCartney being duly sworn deposes and says I know Anna King, have known her since her childhood. I knew William R. King her husband. They were married in the fall or winter of 1853. She was verry (sic) young at the time only about fifteen years of age. King went away from Carlisle within two or three months after their marriage leaving his wife and has not to my knowledge been back since. He seemed to be roving worthless sort of person not fit to take care of a family. He has done nothing towards providing for his wife. I know of no reason for his leaving Carlisle. Sworn to and subscribed before me this 19th August 1857." (signed Stephen Keepers and R. McCartney.)

Aug. 19, 1857 -"William Bentz, being duly sworn, deposes and says, I am a brotherinlaw (sic) of Anna King, am married to her sister. She was married to William R. King in the fall or winter of 1853. She was very young at the time of her marriage I think not quite fifteen years old. King left Carlisle some two months after there (sic) marriage, and has not been back since to my knowledge. He made no provision for the support of his wife whatever. I considered him a worthless man, not fit to support or take care of a family. I know of no reason for his leaving. Sworn to and subscribed before me this 19th August 1857." (signed Stephen Keepers and Wm. Bentz.)

Aug. 20, 1857 -"Michael Holcomb, Esq. being duly sworn

according to law deposes and says, That he was well acquainted with Annie King, the daughter of Mr. John Mell of the Borough of Carlisle. That the said Annie King was married several years ago to a man named King. She was verry (sic) young at the time of her marriage. King was a stranger in the place and had only been here a short time when the marriage occurred. King left shortly after the marriage a verry (sic) short time after and has not been here since so far as I know. I know of no reason for King's leaving and his wife has ever since her marriage been suported (sic) by Mr. John Mell, her father. I don't suppose Annie was more than fifteen when she was married and I have known her from the time she was a child. King was to all appearance a man of but little character and not able to support a family. He was by no means industrious. Sworn to and subscribed before me this 20 August 1857." (signed Stephen Keepers and M. Holcomb.)

Aug. 24, 1857 -"Annie King by her father and next friend John Mell vs. William R. King: Court of Common Pleas of Cumberland County No. 5 Nov. Term 1856 And now to wit the 24th day of August A.D. 1857 the Commissioner Stephen Keepers Esq. having returned to the Court here the depositions of witnesses taken before him on the part of the libellant and the same being read and heard by the Court and the Court after mature and solemn deliberation being satisfied therewith and proclamation being duly made for the respondent to come forth and he not appearing. The Court order and decree that the said Annie King the libellant be divorced and separated from the bond of matrimony contracted with the said William R. King the respondent and that all and every the duties, rights, and claims accruing to either of said parties by reason of the said marriage shall thenceforth cease and determine and the said parties severally be at liberty to marry again in the like manner as if they had never been married. By the Court." -Notation on the front of this document -"No. 5 Nov. T. 1856 King vs. King Decree Filed 24th August 1857. Penrose."

◆ ◆ ◆

Nov. Term 1856 #23 Oct. 7, 1856 -"To the Hon. Jas. H. Graham Prest. Judge of the Court of Common Pleas of Cumberland County -The petition of Nicolas Nearon respectfully showeth -That your petitioner on the twelveth (sic) day of December A.D. 1853 was lawfully joined in marriage with Rebecca Bowermaster now Nearon and from that time hath lived and cohabited with her until the fourth day of July A.D. 1854. And although by the laws of God, as well as by the natural vows plighted to each other, they were bound to that chastity which ought to be inseparable from the marriage state, yet the said Rebecca Nearon in violation of the marriage vow, hath for a considerable time past given herself up to adulterous practices and been guilty of adultery with a certain William White and with diverse other persons to your petitioner unknown. Wherefore your petitioner further shewing that he is a citizen of Pennsylvania and has resided therein for the whole period of his life, prays your Honor that a subpoena may issue to summon the said Rebecca Nearon to appear at the next term of the said Court to answer the complaint aforesaid. And also that a decree of the said Court may be made for the divorcing of the said Rebecca from the society, fellowship and company of this petitioner in all time to come and this petitioner from the marriage bond aforesaid as if they had never been married or as if the said Rebecca Nearon were naturally dead. And your petitioner will pray etc." (signed Nicolas Nearon.) -"Cumberland County SS. -The above named Nicolas Nearon being duly sworn says that the facts contained in the within libel are true to the best of his knowledge and belief. And that the said complaint is not made out of levity and by collusion between him and the said Rebecca and for the mere purpose of being freed and separated from each other -but in sincerity and truth for the causes mentioned in the said libel. Sworn and Subscribed before me this seventh day of October A.D. 1856." (signed Stephen Keepers and Nicolas Nearon.) -Notation on the front of this document -"No. 23 Novr. T. 1856 Nicolas Nearon vs. Rebecca Nearon: petition for subpoena in Divorce 8th Octr. 1856 Subpoena awarded." (signed J.H. Graham.) "Filed 8th Octr. 1856. Henderson."

Oct. 8, 1856 -"CUMBERLAND COUNTY SS. The Commonwealth of Pennsylvania, to the Sheriff of Cumberland county, GREETING: WHEREAS, Nicholas Nearon did on the Eighth day of October A.D. 1856, prefer his petition to our said Judges of our Court of Common Pleas for the State of Pennsylvania, and County of Cumberland, praying for the causes therein set forth, that he might be divorced from the bonds of matrimony entered into with you Rebecca Nearen. We do therefore command you the said Rebecca Nearen that setting aside all other business and excuses whatsoever, you be and appear in your proper person before our Judges, at Carlisle, at a Court of Common Pleas there to be held for the County of Cumberland, on the tenth day of November next, to answer the petition or libel of the said Nicholas Nearen and to shew (sic) cause, if any you have, why the said Nicholas Nearen should not be divorced from the bonds of matrimony agreeably to the Acts of General Assembly in such case made and provided. And hereof fail not. Witness the Honorable JAMES H. GRAHAM, Esq., President of our said Court, at Carlisle, the Eighth day of October A.D. 1856." (signed D.K. Noell, Protonotary, per P. Quigley Dep. Prothy.) "10 Novr. 1856 Genl. Thomas C. Miller appointed Commr. to take testimony on ten days notice to Deft. By the Court." -Notation on the front of this document -"No. 23 November T. 1856 Nicholas Nearen vs. Rebecca Nearen: Subpoena Sur divorce October 8th 1856 Served personal (sic) and by certified copy on Rebecca Nearen. So answers (signed Jacob Bowman Sheriff.)

-"Shff. Bowman's fee $3.04 Henderson."

Nov. 10, 1856 -"Nicholas Nearen vs. Rebecca Nearen: In the Court of Common Pleas of Cumberland County No. 23 November Term 1856 Subpoena Sur divorce 8th October 1856 Served personally and by certified copy on Rebecca Nearen. Now to wit 10th November 1856 Genl. Thomas C. Miller appointed Commissioner to take testimony to be read in evidence on the hearing of said case, the testimony to be taken at any time on ten days notice to Defendant. By the Court. Given under my hand and the seal of said Court at Carlisle the 10th day of November A.D. 1856." (signed D.K. Noell Prothonotary per P. Quigley Dep. Prothy.)

Dec. 5, 1856 -"To Rebecca Nearen the Defendant -You are hereby notified that depositions of witnesses to be read in evidence on the hearing of the above case, on part of Libellant will be taken before Genl. T.C. Miller at his office in Dickinson township, on Saturday the 20th day of December instant, between the hours of 9 o'clock A.M. and 5 o'clock P.M. of said day, when and where you may attend and cross examine if you see proper. 5 Decr. 1856." (signed Nicholas Nearon.)

Dec. 13, 1856 -"Cumbl. County SS. Personally appeared before me the subscriber one of the Justices of the Peace in and for said county Samuel Coover who upon his solemn oath doth depose and say that he served this subpoenia (sic) on deft. Rebecca Nearon, on the 9th day of December 1856 and further this deponent sayeth not. Sworn and Subscribed the 13th Dec. 1856." (signed T.C. Miller, J.P. and Samuel Coover.) -Notation on the front of this document -"No. 23 November 1856 Nicholas Nearen vs. Rebecca Nearen: Subp. Sur Divorce Commission to take depositions Genl. Thos. C. Miller Commissioner S. Coover serving this Subp. 10 Miles Filed 20th Jany. 1857. Henderson."

Dec. 20, 1856 -"David Witherow being first duly affirmed deposeth as follows viz, That on the night of either the 28th or 29th of June 1853 I saw Rebecca Nearen the defendant in this suit, committing the act of adultery in as much as I saw her prostrate on the table in the kitchen of Pltf., and a certain William White on top of her. I know they did commit the act for I saw her bare legs and him said White between them and from what I saw and heard I know the act of copulation was performed, for I was not more than 12 feet off at the time and looking through a crack in the door but so wide that I could se (sic) distinctly what was done as I have stated, and that at the time he Nicholas Nearon the Pltff. was confined to his bed in a perfectly disabled condition so much so that he could not turn himself in bed without assistance. I spent much time in attending to his wants. He lay 5 months, this was occassioned by a severe cut in his knee with an axe. I also say that from my observation while waiting on him that the said defendant behaved in a recklas (sic) and wanton manner by neglecting to attend to the wants of Pltff., by running about the neighbourhood, thereby neglecting him and her household duties, and further this deponent sayeth not." (signed David Witherow.) -"Affirmed and Subscribed before me this 20 day of December A.D. 1856." (signed T.C. Miller.)

Nov. Term 1856 #23 Dec. 20, 1856 -"Also personally appeared same day viz. 20th Dec. 1856 Jno. S. Dunlap who being duly affirmed doth depose and say that Nicholas Nearon the Pltff. and his wife Rebecca lived in a tenant House of Myers at the time he cut his knee that he lay several months unable to work. That his wife Rebecca neglected to attend to him as she ought and she finally left him and that she never returned to him that I know of. He was then taken to his mother's carried on a litter and further this deponent sayeth not." (signed John S. Dunlap.) "Affirmed and Subscribed before me this 20th day of Dec. 1856." (signed T.C. Miller.)

Dec. 20, 1856 -"Also personally came before me same day viz. 20th Decr. 56 James Dunlap who upon his solemn affirmation doth depose and say that the facts just stated and above related in the deposition of his brother Jon. S. Dunlap are about all I know in the matter. That I was one of the men that helped to carry him on the litter to his mother's. There were 4 or 5 of us Danl. Mash, David Witherow, Layfiette (sic) Brown and perhaps others. I think those were the men." (signed James Dunlap.) "Affirmed and Subscribed before me this 20th Dec. 1856" (signed T.C. Miller.)

Dec. 20, 1856 -"Also personally appeared before me same day viz. 20th Decr. 1856 Peter Vantz who upon his solemn affirmation doth depose and say that whilst Pltff. N. Nearon lay disabled with his sore leg, he frequently seen Rebecca Nearon deft. running about with other men to public gatherings at night. That her conduct was rather suspicious, and she neglected to attend to her sick husband as she ought, and that she finally left him before he got well, and that she never has returned to him since. She told me she never would return to him that she did not care a dam (sic) about him and further this deponent sayeth not. (signed Peter Vantz.) "Afd. and Subscribed this 20th Decr. 1856 before me the Subscriber." (signed T.C. Miller.) "I certify that the foregoing depositions were taken before me on Saturday the 20th day of Decr. 1856, between the hours of 9 A.M. and 5 P.M. Each of said witnesses being first duly sworn or affirmed, and that they were reduced to writing by me. The said Plaintiff being present -but the defendant not being present, nor any one for her. Witness my hand the day and year above written." (signed T.C. Miller.)

Jan.20, 1857 -"Nicholas Nearen vs. Rebecca Nearen: In the Court of Common Pleas No. 23 Nov. T. 56 -And now the 20 day of January A.D. 1857 -The Commissioner Thomas C. Miller Esq. having returned to Court the depositions of witnesses taken before him on the part of the Libellant and the same being read and heard by the Court. And the Court after mature and solemn deliberation, being satisfied therewith and proclamation being duly made for the Respondent to come forth and she not appearing the Court do order adjudge and decree that the said Nicholas Nearen the Libellent be divorced and separated from the bond of matrimony contracted with the said Rebecca Nearen the respondent and that all and every the duties rights and claims accruing to either of the said parties by reason of the marriage shall henceforth cease and determine and the said parties be severally at liberty to marry again in like manner as if they had never been married. By the Court." -Notation on the front of this document -"No. 23 Nov. T. 1856 Nicholas Nearen vs. Rebecca Nearen: No. 23 Nov. T. 56 Decree Filed 20th Jany. 1857."

◆ ◆ ◆

Aug. Term 1857 #2 April 4, 1857 -"To the Honorable the Judges of the Court of Common Pleas of Cumberland County The petition of David Hoover of Dickenson township Respectfully Represents -That your petititioner was married to Barbara Timmons in July 1835, and from that time until the latter part of March 1843, lived and cohabited with her, and hath in all respects demeaned himself as a kind and affectionate husband; and although by the laws of God, as well as by the mutual vows plighted to each other, they were bound to that uniform constancy and regard which ought to be inseparable from the marriage state yet so it is that the said Barbara, in violation of her marriage vow, hath for a considerable time past given herself up to adulterous practices, and been guilty of adultery with a certain John Roor, and diverse other persons, to your petitioner unknown. Wherefore your libellant further showing that he is a citizen of the Commonwealth of Pennsylvania, and hath resided therein for more than one whole year previous to the filing of this his petition, prays your Honors that a Subpoena may issue in due form of law, directed to the said Barbara, commanding her to appear at the next term of the Court of Common Pleas of said County, to answer the complaint aforesaid: And also that a decree of said Court may be made for the divorcing of him the said David Hoover from the bond of matrimony, as if he had never been married. And he will pray etc." (signed David Hoover.) -"Cumberland County SS. -The above named David Hoover being duly sworn according to law doth depose and say, that the facts contained in the foregoing petition or libel are true, to the best of his knowledge and belief; and that the said complaint is not made out of levity, or by collusion between him the said David Hoover and the said Barbara his wife, and for the mere purpose of being freed and separated from each other, but in sincerity and truth, for the causes mentioned in said petition or libel. Sworn and Subscribed before me, this 4th April 1857." (signed M. Holcomb J.P. and David Hoover.) -Notation on the front of this document -"No. 2 August T.

1857 Petition of David Hoover for divorce 17 April 1857 Subpoena awarded By the Court. Filed 17th April 1857. Miller."

April 17, 1857 -"CUMBERLAND COUNTY, SS. -The Commonwealth of Pennsylvania, to the Sheriff of Cumberland county, GREETING: WHEREAS, David Hoover of Dickinson Township did on the seventeenth day of April A.D. 1857, prefer his petition to our said Judges of our Court of Common Pleas for the State of Pennsylvania, and County of Cumberland, praying for the causes therein set forth, that he might be divorced from the bonds of matrimony entered into with you Barbara Timmons. We do therefore command you the said Barbara Hoover that setting aside all other business and excuses whatsoever, you be and appear in your proper person before our Judges, at Carlisle, at a Court of Common Pleas there to be held for the County of Cumberland, on the twenty fourth day of August next, to answer the petition or libel of the said David Hoover, and to shew (sic) cause, if any you have, why the said David Hoover, should not be divorced from the bonds of matrimony agreeably to the Acts of General Assembly in such case made and provided. And hereof fail not. Witness the Honorable JAMES H. GRAHAM, Esq., President of our said Court, at Carlisle, the Seventeenth day of April A.D. 1857." (signed D.K. Noell, Prothonotary, Per P. Quigley Dep. Prothy.) -Notation on the front of this document -"No. 2 August Term 1857 David Hoover vs. Barbara Hoover: Subpoena Sur divorce 21st May 1857 Served personally and by certified copy on Barbara Hoover So answers" (signed Jacob Bowman Sheriff.) -"Sheriff Bowman's fee $2.33 1/2. Miller."

Aug. 26, 1857 -"David Hoover vs. Barbara Hoover: No. 2 Aug. T. 1857 Subpoena Sur Divorce To the Hon. the Judges of the Court of Common Pleas of Cumberland County The petition of David Hoover, the above libellant, by W.H. Miller his atty. -Respectfully Represents That the Subpoena in the above case has been returned by the Sheriff, as follows "21st May 1857 -Served personally and by certified copy on Barbara Hoover," He therefore prays that a Commissioner may be appointed to take depositions of witnesses to be read in the above case, and prove the points set forth in the petition of libellant. And he will pray etc." (signed David Hoover by his Atty. W.H. Miller 26th Augt. 1857."

Aug. 28, 1857 -"28 August 1857 Thos. C. Miller Esq. appointed Commissioner to take depositions on ten days notice to Barbara Hoover By the Court." Notation on the front of this document -"No. 2 Aug. T. 1857 -David Hoover vs. Barbara Hoover: Petition for Commissioner to take depositions Filed 28th August 1857."

Sept. 19, 1857 -"David Hoover vs. Barbara Hoover: In the Common Pleas of Cumberland County No. 2 Augst. Term 1857 To Mrs. Barbara Hoover -You will hereby take notice that I have been appointed by the Court of Common Pleas as Commissioner to take testimony in the above case, on the application of David Hoover: And that I will attend to taking depositions in the above case, on part of the said David Hoover, (to be read in evidence on the hearing of the case) at my office near Cumberland Furnace, in Dickenson township, Cumberland County, on Saturday the 3d day of October 1857, between the hours of 9 o'clock A.M. and 4 o'clock P.M. of said day, when and where you may attend and cross examine if you see proper." (signed T.C. Miller Commissioner Sept. 19, 1857.) -Notation on the front of this document -"No. 2 Augt. T. 1857 David Hoover vs. Barbara Hoover Subpoena Sur Divorce Com. to take depositions David Hoover paid costs $5.80 Sent by T.C. Miller In care of James Davis."

Sept. 25, 1857 -"Cumberland county SS. -Personally came before me T.C. Miller one of the Justices of the Peace in and for said county J.L. Henry who upon his solemn oath doth say that he served this notice on Deft. the 23d day Sept. 1857." (signed J.L. Henry.) -"Sworn and Subscribed before me the 25 Sept. 1857." (signed T.C. Miller.) "With No. 2 Aug. 1857."

Sept. 21, 1857 -"Cumberland County, SS. -The Commonwealth of Pennsylvania to Elizabeth Beetem, Catherine Pechert (of Jno.), Elizabeth Deckert, Jno. Crismore, Mary Ann Kechler, Jno. Auld Esq., E. Coover. We command you and each of you, that laying aside all business and excuses whatsoever, you and each of you be and appear in your proper persons, before T.C. Miller on Saturday the third day of October at 10 o'clock in the fournoon (sic) of the said day; then and there TO TESTIFY THE TRUTH, according to your knowledge, on behalf of the David Hoover in a certain action between David Hoover Plaintiff, and Barbara Hoover Defendant. And hereof fail not, under the penalty of the Court. Witness T.C. Miller Esquire, one of our Justices of the Peace in and for said County, the 21st day of Sept. A.D. 1857." (signed T.C. Miller) -On the Front of this document -"Sept. 24st 1857

Milage (sic)	$0.60	
Service	$0.50	
	$1.10	
Constable J.L. Henry 3		
After Costs for second service		
Milage (sic)	$0.24	
Service	$0.20	
	$0.44	
	$1.54	
Witnesses	Elizabeth Beetem	.31
pd.	Catherine Pechert	.56
	Elizabeth Deckert	.31
	Jos. Crisman	.37
	Mrs. Kechler	.44

Jno. Auld	.41
Eph. Coover	.31
	$2.71
	$1.54
	$4.25
Miller	$2.11
	$6.36
off from Mrs. Peckert	.56
	$5.80 "

Aug. 28, 1857 -Miller -David Hoover vs. Watts & Parker -Barbara Hoover: In the Common Pleas of Cumberland County No. 2 August Term 1857 Subpoena Sur Divorce 21 May 1857 served personally and by certified copy on Barbara Hoover. Now to wit 28 August 1857 Thomas C. Miller Esquire appointed Commissioner to take depositions on ten days notice to Barbara Hoover. By the Court. In testimony whereof I have hereunto set my hand and affixed the seal of said Court at Carlisle the 28th day of August A.D. 1857." (signed D.K. Noell, Prothonotary Per P. Quigley Dep. Prothy.) -Notation on the front of this document -"No. 2 August Term 1857 David Hoover vs. Barbara Hoover: Subp. Sur Divorce Thos. C. Miller Esq. appointed Commissioner to take depositions on ten days notice to Barbara Hoover. September 23d 1857 Served personally on defendant.

Milage (sic)	$0.12
Service	$0.20
	$0.32

James L. Henry Constable Cumberland Co. SS. Personally came before T.C. Miller a Justice of the Peace in and for said Co. J.L. Henry who upon his solemn oath doath (sic) say that he served this writ on Deft. the 23d Sept. 57." (signed J.L. Henry.) -"J.L. Henry Sworn and Subscribed before me the 25 Sept. 1857." (signed T.C. Miller.)

Oct. 3, 1857 -"3rd Oct. 1857 by virtue and in accordance to the command of the above writ the following depositions were taken (viz) -Jno. Auld Esqr. being duly affirmed doth depose and say. I think it was sometime in 1843 or 1844 that David Hoover and his wife Barbara met before me and entered into a written agreement, to separate as man and wife. I drew up the agreement of Release. The condition of which was that he David Hoover was to pay her the interest of Three hundred Dollars annually during her natural life. This was duly executed before me, and I was desired to keep it by both parties, and do so for some 3 or 4 years, then the said Barbara called on me and requested that I would give it up to him said David. I did so. About this time she fel (sic) in with a man named Jno. Kuhn and after some time she came and swore a child to said Kuhn. The matter was settled before the prosecuting Attorney. I was present at the time and Kuhn paid her $100. and further this deponent sayeth not." (signed John Auld.)

Oct. 3, 1857 -"Mrs. Elizabeth Beetem being duly affirmed doth depose and say, Barbara Hoover at one time told me that she had commited adultery. I think it was 14 or 15 years ago but I considered her crazy at the time and further this deponant sayeth not." (signed by her mark Elizabeth Beetem Witness T.C. Miller.)

Oct. 3, 1857 -"Mrs. Elizabeth Deckert being duly sworn doth depose and say that the said Barbara, swore that she would put fire to and burn up the damd. old House. She also sworn before me that she would destroy every thing (sic) she could and further this deponent sayeth not." (signed Elizabeth Decker.)

Oct. 3, 1857 -"Mary Ann Keckler being duly affirmed doth depose and say, The said Barbara said she would destroy every thing (sic) she could and would do worse than even she did and further sayeth not." (signed by her mark Mary Ann Kechler and Witness T.C. Miller.)

Oct. 3, 1857 -"Joseph Mahan being duly affirmed doth depose and say, some 15 years ago I was at Hoover's house. Hoover and his wife were quarreling. She flew at him and a scuffle issued. She behaved in an outrageous manner. Hoover and I of late years have had frequent conversations. He always said he never would take up or live with her, and to the best of my knowledge he never has. I was living at Johnston's at the time she was pregnant to Jno. Kuhn. She told me she was, and going up to Shippinsburg (sic) to get married to him. Well, they did get a Gig and went up to Sheppensburg (sic) and when they came back they repoarted (sic) that they were married. They passed for man and wife. They went up to Squire Auld to throw up the (illegible word), and that she was a free woman and Hoover was a free man and further sayeth not." (signed Joseph Machon.)

Oct. 3, 1857 -"Jno. Christmore, being duly sworn doth depose and say, I heard Barbara Hoover say that she would burn the damd (sic) old house but she was crazy at the time. She was chained to the floor at the time. It was 15 years ago and further sayeth not." (signed by his mark Jno. Chrismore Witness T.C. Miller.)

Oct. 3, 1857 -"Witness in behalf of defendant Jno. Kelly afd. David Hoover told me that he would kill his wife Barbara and put her into the fire if she did not give up the (illegible word). He told me that she was going up to Shippensburg to get married to Jno. Kuhn. I believe they did go up and (illegible word) said they were married. Afterward she had a child to Jno. Kuhn and sworn it before Squire Auld. The child is yet living and about 9 years old, and further sayeth not." (signed Jno. Kelly by his mark.)

Oct. 3, 1857 -"Saml. Coover, sworn, says, I seen her when she was crazy. She appeared to be uneasy about her soul's salvation. I seen her pray in (Tommy?) Sheps kitchen." (signed Samuel Coover.)

Oct. 3, 1857 -"Mary Ann Johnston aft. says, Barbara Hoover lived with me. She was saving and industrious and cleanly and decent. I could find no fault with her. She lived with me four years. I never had any one about me that was more kind to me and my family. She would rise at the hour of midnight to oblige me." (signed Mary Ann Johnson.)

Oct. 3, 1857 -"Ephraham Coover afd., says, Barbara Hoover lived with me. She did well and was respectable. I never heard any thing (sic) against her until that affair hapened (sic) with Kuhn and her I never say any thing (sic) wary. Koon (sic) told me that they were not married." (signed E.L. Coover.)

Oct. 11, 1857 -"David Hoover vs. Barbara Hoover: Subpoena Sur Divorce No. (left blank) Nov. Term 1857 Cumberland County SS. Personally came before me T.C. Miller one of the Justices of the Peace in and for said County David Galloway, Jno. Henninger, Aquilla Robison who upon their solemn affirmation doth declare and say that Pltff. and defendant for a number of years lived together as man and wife and it was believed and we believe that they were such, and no one doubt it, it is said and no one doubts it that we know of." (signed David Galloway John Henninger and Aquilla Robison.) -"Affirmed and Subscribed before me this Eleventh day of October 1857 and I do this by virtue of a commission isd. out of Court directing me to take depositions in this case." (signed T.C. Miller.) -Notation on the front of this document -"With No. 2 Aug. 1857."

Oct. 20, 1857 -"David Hoover vs. Barbara Hoover: In the Common Pleas of Cumberland County No. 2 Aug. T. 1857 Subp. Sur Divorce And now to wit, 20th Oct. 1857 the Commissioner Thomas C. Miller having returned to the Court here the depositions of witnesses taken before him on the part of the petitioner and the same having been read and heard by the Court, and the Court after mature deliberation having been satisfied therewith and proclamation being duly made for the defendant to come forth, and she not appearing, the Court do order, adjudge and decree that the said David Hoover the petitioner be divorced and separated from the bonds of matrimony contracted with the said Barbara Hoover the defendant, and that all and every the duties, rights, and claims accruing to either the said parties by reason of said marriage shall thenceforth cease and determine, and that said parties be severally at liberty to marry again in like manner as if they had never been married. By the Court." -Notation on the front of this document -"No. 2 August T. 1857 David Hoover vs. Barbara Hoover Decree of Divorce Filed 20th October 1857. Miller."

♦   ♦   ♦

Jan. Term 1858 #5 Nov. 7, 1857 -"To the Honorable the Judges of the Court of Common Pleas of Cumberland County. The petition of Mary Jane Haines of the Borough of Shippensburg, County aforesaid by her next friend Benjamin Snodgrass of the said Borough respectfully represents: That your petitioner the said Mary Jane Haines was on the Ninth day of October A.D. 1851 lawfully joined in marriage with Lewis Haines her present husband and from that time until the fifteenth day of February A.D. 1855, or thereabout, lived and cohabited with him and hath in all respects demeaned herself as a kind and affectionate wife; and although by the laws of God as well as by the mutual vows plighted to each other they were bound to that uniform constancy and regard which ought to be inseparable from the marriage state yet so it is that the said Lewis Haines in violation of his marriage vow, from the said fifteenth day of February A.D. 1855 hath wilfully and maliciously deserted and absented himself from the habitation of the petitioner without any just or reasonable cause and such desertion hath persisted in for the term of two years and upwards and yet doth continue to absent himself from the said petitioner. Wherefore your petitioner further showing that she is a citizen of Pennsylvania and hath resided therein for more than one whole year previous to the filing of this her petition prays your Honors that a subpoena may issue in due form of law directed to the said Lewis Haines commanding him to appear in the Honorable Court at the January Term next to answer the complaint aforesaid: And also that a decree of this Honorable Court may be made for the divorcing of her the said Mary Jane Haines from the bond of matrimony as if she had never been married. And she will pray etc." (signed Mary Jane Haines by her next friend Benjamin Snodgrass.) -Cumberland County SS. The above named Mary Jane Haines being duly affirmed according to law deposes and says that the facts contained in the above and foregoing petition or libel are true to the best of her knowledge and belief: and that the said complaint is not made out of levity, or by collusion between her, the said Mary Jane Haines and the said Lewis her husband and for the mere purpose of being freed and separated from each other, but in sincerity and truth for the causes mentioned in said petition or libel. Affirmed and subscribed before me the 7th day of November 1857." (signed James Mackey and Mary Jane Haines by her mark.) -Notation on the front of this document -"No. 5 January T. 1858 Petition of Mary Jane Haines by her next friend Benjamin Snodgrass for a divorce from her husband Lewis Haines. 12th November 1857 Subpoena awarded By the Court. Colwell & McClure."

Nov. 12, 1857 -"CUMBERLAND COUNTY, SS. -The Commonwealth of Pennsylvania, to the Sheriff of Cumberland county, GREETING: WHEREAS, Mary Jane Haines by her next friend Benjamin Snodgrass did on the twelfth day of November 1857, prefer a petition to our said Judges of our Court of Common Pleas for the State of Pennsylvania, and County of Cumberland, praying for the causes therein set forth, that she might be divorced from the bonds of matrimony agreeably to the Acts of General Assembly in such case made and provided. And hereof fail not. Witness the Honorable JAMES H. GRAHAM, Esq., President of our said Court, at Carlisle the twelfth day of November A.D. 1857." (signed D.K. Noell, Prothonotary, per P. Quigley Dep. Prothy.) -Notation on the front of this document -"No. 5 January Term 1858 Mary Jane Haines by her next friend Benjamin Snodgrass vs. Lewis Haines: Subpoena Sur Divorce N.E.I. So answer" (signed Jacob Bowman Shff.) -"18th Jany. 1858 Alias Subpoena awarded By the Court. Sheriff Bowman's fee $0.18 3/4. Colwell & McClure."

Jan. 18, 1858 -"CUMBERLAND COUNTY, SS. -The Commonwealth of Pennsylvania, to the Sheriff of Cumberland County, GREETING: WHEREAS, Mary Jane Haines by her next friend Benjamin Snodgrass, did on the twelfth day of November 1857, prefer a petition to our said Judges of our Court of Common Pleas for the State of Pennsylvania, and County of Cumberland, praying for the causes therein set forth, that she might be divorced from the bonds of matrimony entered into with you Lewis Haines. We do therefore command you the said Lewis Haines, as we have heretofore commanded you that setting aside all other business and excuses whatsoever, you be and appear in your proper person before our Judges, at Carlisle, at a Court of Common Pleas there to be held for the County of Cumberland, on the twelfth day of April next, to answer the petition or libel of the said Mary Jane Haines and to shew (sic) cause, if any you have, why the said Mary Jane Haines should not be divorced from the bonds of matrimony agreeably to the Acts of General Assembly in such case made and provided. And hereof fail not. Witness the Honorable JAMES H. GRAHAM, Esq., President of our said Court, at Carlisle, the Eighteenth day of January A.D. 1858." (signed P. Quigley, Prothonotary.)

April 16, 1858 -"Now to wit: 16 April 1858. In the matter of the Alias subpoena sur divorce, Mary Jane Haines by her next friend Benjamin Snodgrass vs. Lewis Haines, the Sheriff having made a return of the same that the said defendant cannot be found in the said County of Cumberland the Court do order and direct the Sheriff to cause notice to be published in one newspaper printed in the Borough of Carlisle for four weeks successively prior to the first day of the August Term of the Court of Common Pleas of said County next (illegible word) requiring the said defendant Lewis Haines to appear on the said day to answer to the said complaint. By the Court." -Notation on the front of this document -"No. 5 January T. 1858 Mary Jane Haines by her next friend Benjamin Snodgrass vs. Lewis Haines: Alias Subpoena Sur Divorce N.E.I. So answers" (signed Jacob Bowman Shff.) -"Shff. Bowman's fee $0.18 3/4. Filed 16th Apl. 1858 as to order. Colwell & McClure."

April 16, 1858 -"In the Common Pleas of Cumberland County No.

5 January T. 1858 Mary Jane Haines by her next friend Benjamin Snodgrass vs. Lewis Haines: Alias Subp. Sur Divorce Now to wit 16 April 1858. The Court do order and direct the Sheriff to cause notice to be published in one newspaper, printed in the Borough of Carlisle for four weeks successively prior to the first day of the August Term of the Court of Common Pleas of said County, requiring the said Defendant Lewis Haines to appear on the said day to answer to the said complaint. By the Court. Given under my hand and the seal of said Court at Carlisle the 16th April 1858." -(signed P. Quigley Prothy.) -Notation on the front of this document -"No. 5 Jany. Term 1858 M.J. Haines vs. Lewis Haines: 23d August 1858 Published in one newspaper as within I am commanded So answers" (signed Jacob Bowman, Sheriff.)-

"Sheriff Bowman $1.50
advert. $1.50
                   $3.00

Now to wit Aug. 23, 1858 Dr. John W. Lewis appointed Commissioner to take testimony in this case at Fayetteville, Franklin County, Pa. Filed 23d Augt. 1858. Colwell & McClure."

Aug. 23, 1858 -"Mary Jane Haines by her next friend Benjamin Snodgrass vs. Lewis Haines: In the Court of Common Pleas Of Cumberland County No. 5 January Term 1858 Subpoena Sur Divorce Now to wit 23d August 1858, Dr. John McClean appointed Commissioner to take testimony in the case at Fayetteville Franklin County Pa. By the Court. In testimony whereof I have hereunto set my hand and the seal of said Court at Carlisle the 23d day of August A.D. 1858." (signed P. Quigley Prothy.) -Notation on the front of this document -"No. 5 Jany. Term 1858 Mary Jane Haines by her next friend Benj. Snodgrass vs. Lewis Haines. Colwell & McClure."

Jan. Term 1858 #5 Sept. 17, 1858 -"Depositions of Witnesses produced sworn and affirmed, and examined by me, the 17th day of September A.D. 1858, between the hours of 10 o'clock A.M. and 3 o'clock P.M. at the Public House of Anthony Rupert, in Fayetteville Franklin County, Pa. by virtue of the annexed rule of the Court of Common Pleas of Cumberland County, for taking testimony in a certain cause, depending in said Court: Subpoena Sur Divorce, Wherein Mary Jane Haines, by her next friend Benjamin Snodgrass, is Plaintiff and Lewis Haines Defendant, said witnesses being produced and examined on the part of the petitioner, or plaintiff in said cause, the Defendant not being present, and no person appearing for him -the Plaintiff being present personally and by counsel."

Sept. 17, 1858 -"Franklin County Pa. SS. -This is to certify that on the 9th day of October A.D. 1851 before me James L. Horner a Justice of the Peace in and for said county Lewis Hains of Westminster Carrol (*sic*) Co., Md. and Mary Jane Wilson of Fayetteville Franklin County, Pa. were legally joined together in mariage (*sic*). Each of them being of full age and declaring themselves free from prior engagements or other lawful impediments in witness thereof they the said Lewis Haines and Mary Jane Wilson she assuming the name of her husband as I the said Justis (sic) and other the witnesses have hereunto set our hands and seals." (signed James L. Horner, Lewis F. Haines, Mary Jane Haines, Henry Mellinger, Sarah Mellinger, Mary J. Prinzer, Jacob Hollinger.) -Notation on the front of this document -"Certificate of Marriage."

Sept. 17, 1858 -"James L. Horner being sworn says: I am a Justice of the Peace residing in Green Township Franklin County. I was a Justice of the Peace in 1851. I am acquainted with Mary Jane Haines and Lewis Haines the parties to this case. They were married by me on the 9th day of October A.D. 1851, in Fayetteville, Franklin County. The name of the Plaintiff before her marriage was Mary Jane Wilson. I gave the parties a marriage certificate, which is the same hereunto annexed, and marked A. I knew the parties to this case to have lived separate and apart more than two years ago. Mrs. Haines living with her mother and Lewis Haines elsewhere; and it was well known here that the said Lewis Haines had separated from his wife the said Mary Jane Haines. Sworn and Subscribed before me the 17th of September 1858." (signed J.L. Horner and John McLean.)

Sept. 17, 1858 -"Catharine Shearman being sworn says I live in Fayetteville Franklin County. I am acquainted with Mary Jane Haines and Lewis Haines, the parties to this case. I knew the parties to have lived in this place as man and wife about five years ago, and afterward to wit between three and four years ago I knew the parties to live apart, the said Mary Jane Haines living in this place and Lewis Haines, at the same time living in the borough of Chambersburgh. During the time the parties were living separate and apart. At the request of the said Mary Jane Haines I spoke to the said Lewis Haines with regard to his taking up with his wife again. He told me at that time, that he would never take up with her again as long as the Sun was in the Firmament. I told him that was wrong, and that it was his duty to take up with his wife again. He then said he would never do so, seeming at the same time to be displeased that I mentioned the subject to him. I then told him that he ought to do something for his wife and child, and he replied that he could not, or would not, I do not recollect which, but that if his child died, if they would let him know, he would see that it was burried (sic) decently -the child being sick at that time. So far as I know, the parties have not lived together since. The said Lewis Haines, left this place for the West in the Spring of 1856, and I have not seen him or known him to have been in this place or neighborhood since. In the conversation above referred to the said Lewis Haines told me that the reason he left his wife was that she was so cross that he could not live with her, and besides, he had her mother's whole family to keep, and this was the only reason he gave for leaving her. Sworn and subscribed before me the 17th day of Sep. A.D. 1858." (signed by her mark Catharine Shearman and John McLean.)

Sept. 17, 1858 -"William Piper being sworn says I live in Fayetteville Franklin County. I am acquainted with Mary Jane Haines and Lewis Haines, the parties to this case. I knew them to live in this place (Fayetteville) as man and wife, about five years ago and in conversation with the said Lewis Haines before the separation of the parties he frequently told me that he would leave his wife the said Mary Jane, and that he would have left her long ago if it were not on account of his children. I knew Mrs. Haines to live in this place in the summer of 1855, and the said Lewis to live in the borough of Chambersburg, in the fall of the same year (1855), and I understood the parties to have separated at that time, and the said Lewis Haines left the following spring for the West, and that I have not seen the said Lewis Haines, nor heard of him having been in this place or neighborhood since. In a conversation with the said Lewis Haines after the parties had separated, he told me that they had separated, and that he would never take up with her again, stating as a reason for leaving her, that she was so cross that he could not live with her, and beside he had her mother's family to keep; and so far as I have known or seen the parties have not lived together since. I have known the said Lewis Haines at times to be intoxicated. Sworn and subscribed before me the 17th day of Sept. A.D. 1858." (signed William Piper and John McLean.)

Sept. 17, 1858 -"Elen Wilson being sworn says I live in Shippensburgh Cumberland County and have lived there for two years in June last. I previously lived in Fayetteville Franklin County. Mary Jane Haines is my daughter. She was married to Lewis Haines on the 9th day of October 1851. They lived in Fayetteville after their marriage. They were married in Fayetteville. Afterwards they removed to Adams County and after residing there ten months returned to Fayetteville and lived there till the fall of 1854, when they removed to Chambersburgh. He left my daughter Mary Jane Haines about the middle of February 1855. He the said Lewis Haines has not lived with my daughter since that time, and it is more than three years since I saw him last. He is said to be in the West at this time. My daughter lives in Shippensburgh, Cumberland County, at this time in my family. Part of the time the parties lived together as man and wife they lived in the house with me. At times he treated my daughter kindly, at other times he treated her harshly and roughly. At times he would get drunk. They have had two children, one of whom (the only one living) lives with me at Shippensburgh. He has contributed nothing towards the support of the child since he left my daughter. As far as I saw or knew my daughter always treated him with kindness, as I had an opportunity of knowing having been frequently at their house, and as they lived in the same house with me for a considerable length of time. My daughter went with me to Shippensburgh, when I moved there, and has lived there ever since. I have never seen Lewis Haines at Shippensburgh since he left my daughter. Sworn and Subscribed before me the 17th day of Sept. 1858." (signed Ellen Wilson and John McLean.)

Sept. 17, 1858 -"William M. Rupert sworn, says I live in Fayetteville Franklin County. I have known Lewis Haines about six years. He told me that he was married to the Plaintiff in this case, Mary Jane Haines. They lived together as man and wife in this place for some years after their marriage. I know that he the said Lewis Haines left his wife, and he told me afterwards, that he would never take up or live with her again. As near as I can recollect it is about three years or little more since they separated. Lewis Haines went to the West two years ago last spring, and I have not seen him here since. The said Lewis Haines would at times become intoxicated. He never gave me any reason for leaving his wife. After their separation he lived for some time in Chambersburgh while Mrs. Haines lived in Fayetteville; afterwards the parties lived in Fayetteville; but not together. Sworn and Subscribed before me the 17th day of Sept. 1858." (signed William M. Rupurt and John McLean.) "I do hereby certify, that the above witnesses were duly qualified and examined, at the time and place stated in the above caption and subscribed their depositions in my presence." (signed John McLean Commissioner.) "Costs

James L. Horner witness	.50 cts.	paid by Plaintiff
Room 1 day	$1.00	paid by Plaintiff
Commissioner fee	$2.00	paid by Plaintiff
	$3.50"	

Nov. 12, 1858 -"Mary Jane Haines by her next friend Benjamin Snodgrass vs. Lewis Haines: No. 5 January Term 1858 Subpoena Sur Divorce Now to wit 12th November 1858 The Court having heard all the proofs and allegations of the parties do hereby order, sentence and decree that the said Mary Jane Haines and the said Lewis Haines be and they are hereby divorced from the bonds of matrimony or nuptial ties and all and every the duties, rights and claims arising or accruing to either of the said parties at any time heretofore in pursuance of the said marriage shall cease and determine and the said parties shall severally be at liberty to marry again as if they had never been married. By the Court." -Notation on the front of this document -"No. 5 Jany. T. 1858 Mary Jane Haines by her next friend Benjamin Snodgrass vs. Lewis Haines Decree Filed 12th November 1858. Colwell & McClure."

◆ ◆ ◆

Jan. Term 1859 #1 Nov. 1, 1858 -"To the Honorable the Judges of the Court of Common Pleas of Cumberland County -The petition of Ann Nisley by her father and next friend John Warner Respectfully

Represents -That your petitioner on the seventeenth day of June A.D. one thousand eight hundred and fifty eight was bound in matrimony and married to John K. Nisley of the said County and from that time until about four weeks since (left blank) lived and cohabited with the said J.K. Nisley as his wife and as such was owned and acknowledged by him and so deemed and reputed by their neighbours and acquaintances. And although by the laws of God as well as by their mutual vows and faith plighted to each other, they were bound to that uniform constancy and regard which ought to be inseparable from the marriage state yet so it is that the said J.K. Nisley from the 7th the said day of October A.D. 1858 to the present time the said parties being at that time and still domiciled in the State of Pennsylvania wilfully and maliciously absented himself from the habitation of your petitioner and abandoned and deserted her without just or reasonable cause and has persisted in such desertion. Wherefore your petitioner further shewing (sic) that she is a citizen of this state and hath resided therein for upwards of one whole year previous to the filing of this petition prays your Honors that a subpoena may issue from the said Court directed to the said John K. Nisley commanding him to appear at the next term of the Court to answer this petition and also that a decree of the said court may be given granting to your petitioner a divorce from bed and board and allowing her such alimony as the said John K. Nisley's circumstances will admit of so as the same do not exceed the third part of the annual profit or income of his estate or of his occupation and labor. And your petitioners as in duty bound will ever pray etc." (signed Ann Knisely.) "Cumberland County SS. The above named Ann Nisley being duly affirmed according to law doth say that the facts set forth in the above petition are true to the best of her knowledge and belief and that the said complaint is not made out of levity or by collusion between her the said Ann Nisley and the said J.K. Nisley her husband and for the mere purpose of being freed and separated from each other but in sincerity and truth for the causes mentioned in the said petition. Affirmed and Subscribed this 1st day of November 1858." (signed Stephen Keepers and Ann Kniseley.) -Notation on the front of this document -"No. 1 January Term 1859 Libel of Ann Nisley for a divorce a mensa et thoro and alimony 8th November 1858 Subpoena Awarded By the Court. Penrose."

Nov. 8, 1858 -"CUMBERLAND COUNTY, SS. The Commonwealth of Pennsylvania, to the Sheriff of Cumberland county, GREETING: WHEREAS, Ann Nisley, by her father and next friend John Warner, did on the eight day of November 1858, prefer a petition to our said Judges of our Court of Common Pleas for the State of Pennsylvania, and County of Cumberland, praying for the causes therein set forth, that she might be divorced from the bonds of matrimony entered into with you John K. Nisley (with claim of Alimony). We do therefore command you the said John K. Nisley that setting aside all other business and excuses whatsoever, you be and appear in your proper person before our Judges, at Carlisle, at a Court of Common Pleas there to be held for the County of Cumberland, on the tenth day of January next, to answer the petition or libel of the said Ann Nisley by her father and next friend John Warner and to shew (sic) cause, if any you have, why the said Ann Nisley should not be divorced from the bonds of matrimony agreeably to the Acts of General Assembly in such case made and provided. And hereof fail not. Witness the Honorable JAMES H. GRAHAM, Esq., President of our said Court, at Carlisle. the Eighth day of November A.D. 1858." (signed P. Quigley, Prothonotary.) -Notation on the front of this document -"No. 1 January Term 1859 Ann Nisley by her Father and next friend John Warner vs. John K. Nisley: Subpoena Sur Divorce Nov. 12th 1858 Served personally and by copy, So Answers" (signed S. Keepers Dept. Sheriff per R. McCartney Shrff.) -"Sheriff's Costs $2.52 16th April 1859 Issues Awarded By the Court. Penrose."

Nov. 25, 1858 -"To the Honorable the Judges of the Court of Common Pleas of Cumberland County, The Answer of John K. Nisley, to the libel of Ann Nisley by her father and next friend John Warner, against him filed on the 8th day of November 1858. This respondent, saving to himself all manner of benefit, and advantage of exception to the manifold untruths, uncertainties, and imperfections in the said libel contained, for answer thereto, or and so much thereof as this respondent is advised it is in any way material for him to make answer, answers and says, that true it is that the said Ann Nisely, on the 17th day of June A.D. 1858, was lawfully joined in marriage with this respondent. Yet this respondent doth expressly deny the charge of having maliciously and wilfully deserted and absented himself from her, the said Ann Nisely, as is stated in the libel of the said Ann Nisely. But this respondent doth aver that the said Ann Nisely has maliciously deserted this respondent. All which matters and things the respondent is ready to verify and maintain and prove: and humbly pleadeth the same in bar to the libel of the said Ann Nisely, which he prays may be dismissed, and this respondent allowed his reasonable costs in this behalf." (signed J.K. Kniseley.) -"Cumberland County SS. Personally appeared before me a Justice of the Peace in and for said County, John K. Nisely, the above named respondent, who being duly affirmed according to law deposeth that the facts set forth in the foregoing answer are true to the best of his knowledge and belief. Sworn and Subscribed before me this 25th November 1858." (signed David Smith J.P., and J.K. Knisley.) -Notation on the front of this document -"No. 1 January T. 1859 Ann Nisely by her next friend vs. John K. Niseley Answer of defendant Filed 25 Nov. 1858. Miller."

Jan. Term 1859 #1 Aug. 8, 1859 -"CUMBERLAND COUNTY, S.S.

The Commonwealth of Pennsylvania to Edward Fissel, Sarah Coover, Michael Smyser, John Eichelberger, John Nelson, Deihart Stoner Junr., Abraham Smyser, Detric Stoner Senr. GREETING: We command you, and each of you, that laying aside all business and excuses, you be and appear in your proper person before the Judges of the Court of Common Pleas, at Carlisle, at a Court of Common Pleas, there to be held for the County of Cumberland, the twenty second day of August 1859 at 10 o'clock in the forenoon of that day, to testify all and singular, those things you shall know in a certain action of Subpoenia Sur Divorce pending and undetermined between Ann Nisley, by her father and next friend John Warner, Plaintiff, and John K. Nisley, Defendant, (on the part of the Plaintiff). And this you are not to omit under penalty of One Hundred pounds. Witness the Honorable James H. Graham, at Carlisle, the Eight day of August in the year of our Lord, one thousand eight hundred and fifty-nine." (signed P. Quigley Prothonotary.) -Notation on the front of this document -"No. 1 Jany. T. 1859 Ann Nisley by her father and next friend John Warner vs. John K. Nisley: Sub. Plff. (said) .25 Penrose Sarah Fisle, Rebeckca Fisle, Manuel Bowman, Margaret Bowman, A. Candella Bowman, Sarah Fisle, Jacob Zowke, Elizabeth Cochlin."

Aug. 8, 1859 -"CUMBERLAND COUNTY S.S. The Commonwealth of Pennsylvania, To David Kniseley, Elizabeth Kniseley, Abraham Shaffer, Edmond Fishel, Isaac Fishel, Rebaca (sic) Fishel, Catharine Renicker GREETING: WE command you, and each of you, that laying aside all business and excuses, you be and appear in your proper person before the Judges of the Court of Common Pleas, at Carlisle, at a Court of Common Pleas, there to be held for the County of Cumberland, the twenty second day of August 1859 at 10 o'clock in the forenoon of that day, to testify all and singular, those things you shall know in a certain action of Subpoena Sur Divorce pending and undetermined between Ann Nisley by her Father and next friend John Warner Plaintiff, and John K. Nisley Defendant, (on the part of the Defendant.) And this you are not to omit under penalty of One Hundred pounds. Witness the Honorable James H. Graham, at Carlisle, the Eighth day of August in the year of our Lord, one thousand eight hundred and fifty-nine." (signed P. Quigley Prothonotary.) -Notation on the front of this document. -"No. 1 Jany. T. 1859 Ann Nisley by her Father and next friend John Warner vs. John K. Nisley Subp. Deft. paid .25 Miller."

Aug. 7, 1860 -"CUMBERLAND COUNTY, S.S. The Commonwealth of Pennsylvania, To Abraham Smyser, John Nelson, Detrich Stoner Sen., Jacob Coover, Edward Fishel, Isaac Fishel, William Himes, Jacob Zook, William Smyser, Hecter McCay, Emanuel Bowman, Rebecca Fishel, Leah Fishel, Margaret Bowman, Mary Stevens, Elizabeth Cocklin, Mandela Bowman, Lavina Zook, Lydia Duey, Jane Bricker, Ann Rennaker, John Eichelberger GREETING: We command you, and each of you, that laying aside all business and excuses, you be and appear in your proper person before the Judges of the Court of Common Pleas, at Carlisle, at a Court of Common Pleas, there to be held for the County of Cumberland, the Twenty seventh day of August 1860 at 10 o'clock in the forenoon of that day, to testify all and singular, those things you shall know in a certain action of Subp. Sur Divorce, with claim of Alimony pending and undetermined between Ann Nisley by her Father and next friend John Warner Plaintiff, and John K. Nisley Defendant, (on the part of the Plaintiff). And this you are not to omit under penalty of One Hundred pounds. Witness the Honorable James H. Graham, at Carlisle, the seventh day of August in the year of our Lord, one thousand eight hundred and sixty." (signed P. Quigley Prothonotary.) -Notation on the front of this document -"No. 1 January T. 1859 Ann Nisley by her Father and next friend John Warner vs. John K. Nisley Subp. Plff. paid .25 Penrose."

Aug. 22, 1859 -"Ann Nisley by her father and next friend John Warner vs. John K. Nisley: No. 1 Jany. T. 1859 Plff. Bill and Act. at Aug. T. 1859.

Edward Fissel	1 day	15 miles	$1.52 1/2
Jacob Coover	1 day	14 miles	$1.46 1/2
John Eichelberger	1 day	16 miles	$4.78 1/2
Service on Sub.	14 miles $1.40		
	30 miles $1.80		
John Nelson	1 day	15 miles	$1.52 1/2
Deitrick Stoner Jnr.	1 day	14 miles	$1.46 1/2
Deitrick Stoner Sr.	1 day	14 miles	$1.46 1/2
Isaac Fisher	1 day	14 miles	$1.46 1/2
Emanuel Bowman	1 day	12 miles	$1.34 1/2
Elizabeth Cocklin	1 day	12 miles	$1.34 1/2
Prothy. Q. Taxing Bill			.18 3/4
			$16.57 1/4

Taxed and Affirmed to 22d August 1859 (by J. Eichelberg) P. Quigley: Defts. Bill and costs at Augt. T. 1859

Abraham Sheaffer	1 day	14 miles	$1.46 1/2
Elizabeth Kneisley	1 day	14 miles	$1.46 1/2
Deft. Subp.		.25	
	7	.70	
Mileage	.20	1.60	$2.55
	Prothy. Q. Taxing Bill		
(paid by Deft.)	.18 3/4		
			$5.66 3/4

-Notation on the front of this document -"No. 1 Jany. T. 1859 Ann Nisley vs. J.K. Nisley: Plff. Bill and costs at Augt. T. 1859."

Aug. 27, 1860 -"Ann Nisley vs. John K. Nisley: No. 1 Jany. T. 1859

McCartney	2.52	2.52
Plff. Bill and Writ at former term	16.57	.18 3/4
Atty.	1.25	1.25
Plff. Bill and W. at Augt. T. 1860	16.57	.18 3/4
Prothy. Q.	3.50	3.50
27 August 1860 paid Prothy. Q.		7.64 1/2
by Atty. Miller	$40.41	
Deduct Docket costs		
		7.64 1/2
		$32.77"

Aug. 27, 1860 -"Ann Nisley vs. John K. Nisley: No. 1 August T. 1860 Plff. Bill at Augt. 1860

Abrm. Smyser	1 day	12 miles		$1.34 1/2
John Nelson	1 day	15 miles		1.52 1/2
Detrick Stoner	1 day	12 miles		1.34 1/2
Jacob Coover	1 day	12 miles		1.34 1/2
Edward Fissle	1 day	15 miles		1.52
Isaac Fisle	1 day	12 miles		1.34 1/2
Wm. Himes	1 day	6 miles		.98 1/2
Wm. Smyser	1 day	12 miles		1.34 1/2
Hector McKay	1 day	15 miles		1.52
Emanuel Bowman	1 day	12 miles		1.34 1/2
Margaret Bowman	1 day	12 miles		1.34 1/2
Elizabeth Cocklin	1 day	12 miles		1.34 1/2
Mandela Bowman	1 day	12 miles		1.34 1/2
John Eichelberger	1 day	16 miles	1.52	
Serving Subp.	21 miles	2.62	2.62	
	46 miles	1.38	1.38	5.52
Subp. plff.				.25
Prothy. Q. taxing Bill				.18 3/4
				$23.60 3/4"

Jan. Term 1859 #1 Aug. 27, 1860-
"Recd. of Prothy. Q. my costs in this case:

Hector B. McKay	1.52	
John M. Nelson	3.04	
William Himes	.98	
D.R. Sterner Jr.	1.46	
E. Cocklin	2.69	
E. Bowman	2.69	
M. Bowman	1.34 1/2	
Mandela Bowman	1.34 1/2	
John Eichelberger	10.30	25.37

Edmund Fishel	3.04	28.41
Isaac Fishel	2.81	31.22
Abraham Smyser	1.34	32.56

March 17, 1859 -"Nisely vs. Nisely: In the Court of Common Pleas of Cumberland County -No. 1 Jan. Term 1859 Cumberland County ss And now to wit 17th March 1859 the libellant Ann Nisely by W.M. Penrose attorney avers and says that protesting all and singular the matters and things in the respondent's answer alledged in bar of her libel and prayer are not true she is ready to verify the said matters and things by her in her said libel and prayer set forth and prays that a jury may be called to inquire thereof according to the form of the several Acts of Assembly in this behalf made and provided." (signed W.M. Penrose Atty. per Libellant.) -Notation on the front of this document -"No. 1 Jan. Term 1859 Nisely vs. Nisely Replication Filed 17th March 1859."

♦ ♦ ♦

April Term 1859 #22 Feb.8, 1859 -"To the Hon. the Judges of the Common Pleas of Cumberland County -The petition of Caroline Nickle by her next friend Conrad Herde respectfully sheweth that your petitioner was on the 11th day of November 1856 lawfully joined in marriage with John Nickle her present husband by Stephen Keepers, a Justice of the Peace in and for said County and from that time lived and cohabited with him and hath in all things demeaned herself as a kind and loving wife; and although by the laws of God as well as by the mutual vows plighted to each other they were bound to that constancy and uniform regard and chastity which ought to be inseparable from the marriage state. Yet so it is, that the said John Nickel from the 12 day of November 1856 hath, the said parties being at that time domiciled within the Commonwealth of Pennsylvania wilfully and maliciously absented himself from the habitation of this libellant and abandoned his family without just or reasonable cause and has from the said date persisted in such desertion. Wherefore your petitioner further shewing (sic), that she is a citizen of this State and hath resided therein for upwards of one whole year previous to the filing of this petition, prays Your Honors that a Subpoena may be issued in due form of law directed to the said John Nickel commanding him to appear at the next Court of Common Pleas to be held at Carlisle in the County of Cumberland to answer the petitioner's libel, and to shew (sic) cause if any he hath why the petitioner should not be divorced from the bonds of matrimony. And she will pray etc." (signed Caroline Nickel by her mark by her next friend Conrad Herde who signed in German and witnessed by Jas. R. Smith.) -"State of Pennsylvania Cumberland County SS -The above named Caroline Nickel being duly sworn according to law, doth depose and say that the facts contained in the above petition or libel, are true to the best of her knowledge and belief, and that the said complaint is not made out of levity, or by collusion between her and the said John Nickel her husband and for the mere purpose of being freed separated from each other, but in sincerity and truth for the causes mentioned in said petition or libel. Sworn and Subscribed before me this 8th Feby. A.D. 1859." (signed Caroline Nickel by her mark and David Smith J.P.) -Notation on the front of this document -"No.22 April Term 1859 Caroline Nickle by her next friend Conrad Herd vs. John Nickle 11th Feby. 1859 Subpoena awarded." (signed J.H. Graham Prest. Judge.) -"Filed 11th Feby. 1859 Smith."

Feb. 11, 1859 -"CUMBERLAND COUNTY, S.S. The Commonwealth of Pennsylvania, to the Sheriff of Cumberland county, GREETING: WHEREAS, Caroline Nickle, by her next friend Conrad Hurd did on the Eleventh day of February 1859, prefer a petition to our said Judges of our Court of Common Pleas for the State of Pennsylvania, and County of Cumberland, praying for the causes therein set forth, that she might be divorced from the bonds of matrimony entered into with you John Nickel. We do therefore command you the said John Nickle that setting aside all other business and excuses whatsoever, you be and appear in your proper person before our Judges, at Carlisle, at a Court of Common Pleas there to be held for the County of Cumberland, on the Eleventh day of April next, to answer the petition or libel of the said Caroline Nickle and to shew (sic) cause, if any you have, why the said Caroline Nickel should not be divorced from the bonds of matrimony agreeably to the Acts of General Assembly in such case made and provided. And hereof fail not. Witness the Honorable JAMES H. GRAHAM, Esq., President of our said Court, at Carlisle, the Eleventh day of February A.D. 1859." (signed P. Quigley Prothonotary.) -Notation on the front of this document -"No. 22 April Term 1859 Caroline Nickel by her next friend Conrad Hurd vs. John Nickel: Subpoena Sur Divorce April 9th 1859 Defendant not to be found in my bailiwick so answers" (signed R. McCartney Shff.) -"On motion in open Court Alias Subp. awarded 12th Apl. 1859 By the Court." Shff. McCartney fee $0.83. Smith."

April 12, 1859 -"CUMBERLAND COUNTY. S.S. The Commonwealth of Pennsylvania, to the Sheriff of Cumberland county, GREETING: WHEREAS, Caroline Nickle by her next friend Conrad Hurd did on the Eleventh day of February 1859, prefer a petition to our said Judges of our Court of Common Pleas for the State of Pennsylvania, and County of Cumberland, praying for the causes therein set forth, that she might be divorced from the bonds of matrimony agreeably to the Acts of General Assembly in such case made and provided. And hereof fail not. Witness the Honorable JAMES H. GRAHAM, Esq., President of our said Court, at Carlisle, the Twelfth day of April A.D. 1859." (signed P. Quigley Prothontary.) -Notation on the front of this document -"No. 22 April Term 1859

Caroline Nickel by her next friend Conrad Hurd vs. John Nickel: Alias Subp. Sur Divorce Retble. 22d August 1859 June 6th 1859 writ returned Non Est Investus So answers" (signed R. McCartney Shff.) -"Shff. McCartney fee $0.26 3/4. Smith."

Aug. 27, 1859 -"Elizabeth Nickel by her next friend Conrad Hurd vs. John Nickel: In the Court of Common Pleas of Cumberland County No. 22 April Term 1859 Alias Subpoena Sur Divorce Now to wit 27th August 1859. The Court do order and direct the Sheriff, to cause notice to be published in one newspaper printed in the Borough of Carlisle for four weeks successively, prior to the first day of the November Term of the Court of Common Pleas of said County, requiring the said Defendant John Nickel to appear on the said day to answer to the said complaint etc. By the Court. Given under my hand and the seal of said Court at Carlisle the 26th day of September A.D. 1859." (signed P. Quigley Prothonotary.) -Notation on the front of this document -"No. 22 April T. 1859 Caroline Nickel by her next friend Conrad Hurd vs. John Nickel: Notice to Defendant to be published by Shff. for 4 weeks etc. Nov. 7th 1859 The within notice to the Defendant published in one newspaper as within I am directed. So answers" (signed R. McCartney Shff.) -"Shff. McCartney's fee $2.50. Smith."

Nov. 14, 1859 -"Caroline Nickel by her next friend Conrad Hurd vs. John Nickel: No. 22 April T. 1859 In the Common Pleas of Cumberland County Subpoena Sur Divorce Now to wit 14th November 1859, David Smith Esquire appointed Commissioner to take testimony to be read in the hearing of this case. By the Court. Attest" (signed P. Quigley Prothy.) -Notation on the front of this document "No. 22 Apl. T. 1859 Caroline Nickel vs. John Nickel. Smith."

Dec. 19, 1859 -"Deposition of witnesses produced sworn and examined by me the 19th day of December 1859 at my office in Carlisle by virtue of the annexed Commission issued out of the Court of Common Pleas for the examination of witnesses in a certain proceeding for devorce (sic) then pending between Caroline Nickle by her next friend C. Hurd vs. John Nickle. Nancy Moudy being duly sworn sayeth I am the wife of William Moudy formerly the Tavernkeeper in the Borough of Carlisle. I knew Caroline Swanger. She lived with me in 1856. She was hired by me to do housework. At the time Caroline Swanger lived at our house, John Nickle boarded at our house. John Nickle and Caroline Swanger were married at our house by Stephen Keepers Esq. John Nickle left after the night of there (sic) marriage and never staid (sic) with her a night after that. He left this county and went to Chambersburg and left there and went west. Caroline had a child. She mentained (sic) her child and self by her own labours. Sworn and Subscribed before me." (signed Nancy Moudy and David Smith.)

Dec. 19, 1859 -"Stephen Keeper sworn on the 11th day of November 1856 I was a Justice of the Peace in and for the Borough of Carlisle duly qualified on the said day, I married at the house of William Moudy John Nickle and Caroline Swanger. Immediately after the marriage John Nickle abandoned his wife and has not since returned to her. Since that time she has mentained (sic) herself by her own labours and industery (sic) as a servant in Langeleys. Sworn and Subscribed before me." (signed Stephen Keepers and David Smith.)

Dec. 19, 1859 -"Saha (sic) Humes sworn I have known Caroline Nickle. She was working as a servant at Dr. Lumases. She had a child called Laura Nickle. I became acquainted with hir (sic) by her calling on me to board her child. I offered to board the child at one dollar per week. She said she was not able to pay that, that hir (sic) wages was not sufficient to pay one dollar pr. week but would give seventy five cents and I agreed to take and board the child fer (sic) seventy five cents pr. week. Afterward I told hir (sic) I could not aford (sic) to board the child fer (sic) seventy five cents a week. She said she would give all her wages one dollar and that was all she had to depend upon. I boarded the child about three months prior to April 1859 and its mother paid me its board. I have no acquaintance with John Nickle. I never knew his wife to have any means of support only what she earned. Sworn to and Subscribed before me." (signed David Smith and Sarar (sic) Humes by hir (sic) mark.)

Dec. 19, 1859 -"Martha Beatman (sic) sworn I have known John Nickle and Caroline his wife. I knew them before they were married. Shortly after there (sic) marriage Nickle abandoned his wife. He left Carlisle and has not been back here since. Shortly after the abandonment and desertion of his wife by Nickle she went to her Grandmother Mrs. Swanger and was there confined. Sometime after her child was born she came to Carlisle and lived in the family with her child of Christian Long at fifty cents pr. veek. Four or five days befor (sic) the death of Mrs. Long, she brought her child to me to board and I boarded hir (sic) child, at seventy five cents pr. week and she went to Mrs. Irish at one dollar and twenty five cents per week. After she left Mrs. Irish she went to Dr. Loomases to live. From the time of her marriage up to the filing of this suit I know she received no support from hir (sic) husband, but hir (sic) means of living had for hirself (sic) and child were earned by her. The child I boarded was called Laura Nickle. It must now be about three years old. Sworn and Subscribed before me." (signed David Smith and Martha Bateman.)

April Term 1859 #22 Dec. 19, 1859 -"Barbara Leidigh sworn I have known Caroline Swonger while living at Col. Moudys. She was hired there. I also knew John Nickle. I understood that John Nickle and Caroline Swonger were married. John Nickle has not lived with his wife since I herd (sic) of there (sic) marriage. After they were married John Nickle went away and I have not seen him since. After hir (sic) confinement she hired out as a servant in differant (sic) familys (sic), at Christian Long's, M. Irishe's and Dr. Loomas. While she was living at Mr. Irishe's and Mr. Loomase's she had hir (sic) child bording (sic) at Martha Bateman's and Mrs. Hume's. The child's name was Laura. She had no means of support for hirself (sic) and child on what she earned by her labour to my knowledge. Sworn to and Subscribed before me." (signed David Smith and Barbara Leidigh who signed in German script.) -Notation on the front of this document -"No. 22 Apl. T. 1859 Nickel vs. Nickel Smith."

Dec. 20, 1859 -"Caroline Nickel by her next friend C. Herd vs. John Nickel: No. 22 April T. 1859 Subpoena in Divorce Now to wit 20th Decr. 1859, after hearing the evidence in this case and upon due consideration of the premises the Court doth hereby order and decree that the said Caroline Nickel be and she is hereof divourviced (sic) from the bonds of matrimony entered into with the said John Nickel, and all and every the duties, rights and claims accruing to either of the said parties at any time heretofore in pursuance of their marriage shall cease and determine, and the said parties shall severally be at liberty to marry again in the like manner as if they never had been married. By the Court." -Notation on the front of this document -"No. 22 April T. 1859 Caroline Nickel vs. John Nickel Filed 20th Decr. 1859. Smith."

◆ ◆ ◆

Aug. Term 1859 #7 April 19, 1859 -"To the Honorable the Judges of the Court of Common Pleas of Cumberland County: The petition of Mary Jane Ruggles of the borough of Carlisle by her next friend John McClintock respectfully showeth that your petitioner was on or about the 25th day of December 1839, lawfully joined in marriage with Alexander Ruggles her present husband and from that time until about the fifteenth day of June A.D. 1857, lived and cohabited with him and hath in all respects demeaned herself as a kind and affectionate wife. And although by the laws of God as well as by the mutual vows plighted to each other they were bound to that uniform constancy and regard which ought to be inseparable from the marriage state, yet so it is that the parties being at the time domiciled within the Commonwealth of Pennsylvania the said Alexander Ruggles has offered such indignities to the person of your petitioner as to render her condition intolerable, and her life burdensome, and thereby forced her to withdraw from his house and family. Wherefore your petitioner further showing that she is a citizen of the State of Pennsylvania and has resided therein for upwards of one whole year previous to filing this her petition, prays your Honors that a subpoena may issue in due form of law directed to the said Alexander Ruggles commanding him to appear in this Honorable Court at August term next to answer the complaints aforesaid. And also that a decree of this Honorable Court may be made for divorcing of her the said Mary Jane Ruggles from the bond of matrimony, as if she had never been married. And she will ever pray." (signed Mary Jane Ruggles by her mark and Att. M. Holcomb.) -"Cumberland County SS. The above named Mary Jane Ruggles being duly sworn according to law doth depose and say that the facts set forth in the above petition are true to the best of her knowledge and belief. And that the said complaint is not made out of levity or by collusion between her the said Mary Jane Ruggles and her husband the said Alexander Ruggles, and for the mere purpose of being freed and separated from each other but in sincerity and truth for the causes mentioned in the said petition." (signed Mary Jane Ruggles by her mark and Attest. M. Holcomb.) -"Sworn and Subscribed before me, this 19th day of April A.D. 1859." (signed M. Holcomb, J.P.) -Notation on the front of this document -"No. 7 August Term 1859 Petition of Mary J. Ruggles by her next friend Jno. McClintock for Sub. Sur Divorce vs. Alexander Ruggles 22d April 1859 Subp. Awarded By the Court Filed 22d April 1859. Shearer."

April 22, 1859 -"CUMBERLAND COUNTY, S.S. The Commonwealth of Pennsylvania to the Sheriff of Cumberland county, GREETING: WHEREAS, Mary Jane Ruggles by her next friend John McClintock did on the 22nd day of April A.D. 1859, prefer her petition to our said Judges of our Court of Common Pleas for the State of Pennsylvania, and County of Cumberland, praying for the causes therein set forth, that she might be divorced from the bonds of matrimony entered into with you Alexander Ruggles. We do therefore command you the said Alexander Ruggles that setting aside all other business and excuses whatsoever, you be and appear in your proper person before our Judges, at Carlisle, at a Court of Common Pleas there to be held for the County of Cumberland, on the Twenty second day of August next, to answer the petition or libel of the said Mary Jane Ruggles and to shew (sic) cause, if any you have, why the said Mary Jane Ruggles should not be divorced from the bonds of matrimony agreeably to the Acts of General Assembly in such case made and provided. And hereof fail not. Witness the Honorable JAMES H. GRAHAM, Esq., President of our said Court, at Carlisle, the twenty second day of April A.D. 1859." (signed P. Quigley Prothonotary.) -Notation on the front of this document -"No. 7 August Term 1859 Mary Jane Ruggles by her next friend John McClintock vs. Alexander Ruggles: Subpoena Sur Divorce May 9th 1859 Served personally and by certified copy on the Defendant So answers" (signed R. McCartney Shff. and Stephen Keepers Dep. Shrff.) -"Shf. McCartney's fee $2.72. Shearer."

◆ ◆ ◆

Aug. Term 1859 #35 May 11, 1859 -"To the Honorable the Judges of the Court of Common Pleas for the County of Cumberland. The petition of Caroline Gibson by her next friend Rufus E. Shapely Sr. Respectfully Showeth: That your petitioner was on the eleventh day of June A.D. 1833 lawfully joined in marriage with John Gibson her present husband and from that time until the Nineteenth day of January A.D. 1849, lived and cohabited with her (sic, him) and hath in all respects demeaned hirself (sic) as a kind and affectionate wife and although by the laws of God as well as by the mutual vows plighted to each other they were bound to that uniform constancy and regard which ought to be inseparable from the marriage state yet so it is that the said John Gibson in violation of his marriage vow from the 19th day of January A.D. 1849 hath wilfully and maliciously deserted and absented himself from the habitation of this petitioner without any just or reasonable cause and such desertion hath persisted in for the term of ten years and upwards and yet doth continue to absent himself from the said petitioner. Wherefore your petitioner further showing that she is a citizen of the Commonwealth of Pennsylvania and hath resided therein for more than one whole year previous to the filing of this her petition prays your Honors that a Subpoena may issue in due form of law directed to the said John Gibson commanding him to appear in this honorable Court at (left blank) Term next to answer the complaint aforesaid. And also that a decree of this honorable Court may be made for the divorcing of her the said Caroline Gibson from the bond of matrimony as if she had never been married. And she will pray etc." (signed Caroline Gibson.) -"Cumberland County S.S. The above named Caroline Gibson being duly sworn according to law doth depose and say that the facts contained in the above petition or libel are true to the best of her knowledge and belief; and that the said complaint is not made out of levity or by collusion between her the said Caroline Gibson and her husband the said John Gibson and for the mere purpose of being freed and separated from each other, but in sincerity and truth for the causes mentioned in the said petition or libel." (signed Carolin Gibson.) -"Sworn and subscribed before me this 11th day of May A.D. 1859." (signed M.Holcomb.) -Notation on the front of this document -"No. 35 August Term 1859 Caroline Gibson by her next friend Rufus E. Shapley Sr. vs. John Gibson Petition for Divorce 28 May 1859 Subpoena Awarded" (signed J.H. Graham Judge.) -"Filed 3rd June 1859. Henderson."

June 3, 1859 -"CUMBERLAND COUNTY, S.S. The Commonwealth of Pennsylvania, to the Sheriff of Cumberland county, GREETING: WHEREAS, Caroline Gibson by her next friend Rufus E. Shapley Sr. did on the third day of June A.D. 1859, prefer her petition to our said Judges of our Court of Common Pleas for the State of Pennsylvania, and County of Cumberland, praying for the causes therein set forth, that she might be divorced from the bonds of matrimony entered into with you John Gibson. We do therefore command you the said John Gibson that setting aside all other business and excuses whatsoever, you be and appear in your proper person before our Judges, at Carlisle, at a Court of Common Pleas there to be held for the County of Cumberland, on the Twenty second day of August next, to answer the petition or libel of the said Caroline Gibson and to shew (sic) cause, if any you have, why the said Caroline Gibson should not be divorced from the bonds of matrimony agreeably to the Acts of General Assembly in such case made and provided. And hereof fail not. Witness the Honorable JAMES H. GRAHAM, Esq., President of our said Court, at Carlisle, the Third day of June A.D. 1859." (signed P. Quigley Prothonotary.) -Notation on the front of this document -"No. 35 August Term 1859 Caroline Gibson, by her next friend, Rufus E. Shapley Sr. vs. John Gibson: Subpoena Sur Divorce June 6th 1859 Writ returned Non est inventus so answers" (signed R. McCartney Shff.) -"Shff. McCartney's fee $0.26 3/4. Henderson."

Aug. 27, 1859 -"CUMBERLAND COUNTY, S.S. The Commonwealth of Pennsylvania, to the Sheriff of Cumberland county, GREETING: WHEREAS, Caroline Gibson by her next friend Rufus E. Shapley Senr. did on the third day of June A.D. 1859, prefer her petition to our said Judges of our Court of Common Pleas for the State of Pennsylvania, and County of Cumberland, praying for the causes therein set forth, that she might be divorced from the bonds of matrimony entered into with you John Gibson. We do therefore command as we have hertofore commanded you the said John Gibson that setting aside all other business and excuses whatsoever, you be and appear in your proper person before our Judges, at Carlisle, at a Court of Common Pleas there to be held for the County of Cumberland, on the Fourteenth day of November, next, to answer the petition or libel of the said Caroline Gibson and to shew (sic) cause, if any you have, why the said Caroline Gibson should not be divorced from the bonds of matrimony agreeably to the Acts of General Assembly in such case made and provided. And hereof fail not. Witness the Honorable JAMES H. GRAHAM, Esq., President of our said Court, at Carlisle, the 27th day of August A.D. 1859." (signed P. Quigley Prothonotary.)

Nov. 14, 1859 -"Now to wit 14 Nov. '59 The Court do order and direct the Sheriff to cause notice to be published in one newspaper, printed in the Borough of Carlisle for four weeks sucessively prior to the first day of the Jany. Term of the Court of Common Pleas of said County requiring the said defendant John Gibson to appear on the said day to answer the said complaint etc. By the Court." -Notation on the front of this document -"No. 35 August T. 1859 Caroline Gibson by her next friend Rufus E. Shapley Sr. vs. John Gibson Alias Subpoena Sur Divorce Oct. 14th 1859 Defendant not to be found in my Bailiwick. So answers" (signed R. McCartney Shff.)

-Shff. McCartney's fee $0.18 3/4. Henderson."

Aug. Term 1859 #35 Jan. 9, 1860 -"Caroline Gibson by her next friend Rufus E. Shapley Sr. vs. John Gibson: No. 35 August T. 1859 In the Court of Common Pleas of Cumberland County Subpoena Sur Divorce Now to wit 9th January 1860, M. Holcomb Esq. appointed Commissioner to take depositions to be read in evidence on the hearing of this case. By The Court Attest." (signed P. Quigley Prothy.) -Notation on the front of this document -"No. 35 Augt. T. 1859 Caroline Gibson vs. John Gibson: Commission to take testimony Filed 16th Jany. 1860 Justice fees $1.00. Henderson."

Jan. 14, 1860 -"Caroline Gibson by her next friend Rufus E. Shepley Sr. vs. John Gibson: No. 35 August T. 1859 Comm. Plea Cumd. County Subpoena Sur Divorce Depositions of witnesses produced, sworn and examined by me at my office in the borough of Carlisle, on the 14th January 1860, by virtue of the annexed commission. Rufus E. Shepley, Jr. sworn, deposeth and saith, I now (sic) Caroline Gibson and John Gibson. Caroline Gibson is the daughter of Rufus E. Shapley, Sr. She was married to John Gibson in the year 1833, at her father's house in Carlisle. I was present at the time they were married. They lived together until 1849 or 1850. They had four children, two now living. John Gibson left his wife in 1849 or 1850, to go to Californey (sic), and has not been back since. I do not know where he went and do not now (sic) where he is now, he has never been in this county since. He has made no provision for his wife or family, and believe he has entirely deserted them. He never visited to her to my knowledge, and if he did I would no (sic) it. She Caroline Gibson is dependent on her father for her support and maintenance. Sworn and subscribed before me 14th Jan. 1860." (signed M. Holcomb J.P. and Rufus E. Shapley Jr.)

Jan. 14, 1860 -"Charles Shepley, sworn, deposeth and saith, I was present at the marriage of John Gibson and Caroline Gibson the parties in this suit. I do not recollect the year when they were married. John Gibson left his wife in January 1849, and has not been at home since, and I know that he has not made any provision for wife or family, but has entirely deserted them. I was informed by my brother-in-law that he had been living with another women (sic) in the State of Illinois, and was engaged to be married and denied that he had a wife. My brother-in-law lives in the State of Illinois. She lives with her father, and has been ever since he left. Sworn and subscribed before me the 14th Jan. 1860." (signed Charles Shapley and M. Holcomb, J.P.)

Jan. 14, 1860 -"Joseph Sturner (sic), sworn, I know the parties to this suit. It is about 11 years since John Gibson left his wife, and has entirely abandoned her, and has made no provision for her whatever. She is now dependent on her father for her support. I do not know where he is now, except from hearsay. I know he has not been in Carlisle, since he left. I do not think he writes to his wife. Sworn and subscribed before me the 14th January 1860." (signed Joseph L. Sterner and M. Holcomb, J.P.)

Jan. 16, 1860 -"Caroline Gibson by her next friend Rufus E. Shapley Sr. vs. John Gibson: Subpoena Sur Divorce Cumberland County S.S. And now to wit January 16th A.D. 1860 -The Commissioner Michael Holcomb Esq. having returned to the Court the depositions taken in this case, The Court do after mature and solemn deliberation being duly satisfied therewith and proclamation being made for the respondent to come forth and he not appearing, The Court do order and decree that the said Caroline Gibson be divorced and separated from the bond of matrimony contracted with said John Gibson and that all and every the duties, rights and claims by reason of said marriage shall herewith cease and determine and the said parties be severally divorced and at liberty to marry again in like manner as if they had never been married. By the Court." -Notation on the front of this document -"No. 35 Augt. T. 1859 Gibson vs. Gibson: Decree Sur Divorce Filed 16 Jany. 1860. Henderson."

◆ ◆ ◆

Jan. Term 1860 #7 Nov. 28, 1859 -"To the Honorable the Judges of the Court of Common Pleas of Cumberland County -The petition of Mrs. Catherine Eppley by her brother and next friend John Kutz -Respectfully showeth that your petitioner on or about the 12th day of April A.D. 1854 was married to Dr. George M. Eppley and from that time until the 7th day of October A.D. 1854 lived and cohabited with him and hath in all respects demeaned herself as a kind and affectionate wife and although by the laws of God and by the mutual vows plighted to each other they were bound to that uniform constancy and regard which ought to be inseparable from the marriage state yet so it is that the said Dr. George M. Eppley in violation of his marriage vow from the 7th day of October A.D. 1854 (the parties being domiciled at the time within the Commonwealth of Pennsylvania) hath wilfully and maliciously absented himself from the habitation of this libellant and abandoned his family without just or reasonable cause and hath persisted in such desertion from the date last mentioned. Wherefore your petitioner further showing that she is a citizen of this state and hath resided therein for upwards of one whole year previous to the filing of this petition prays your Honors that a subpoena may issue from the said Court directed to the said Dr. George M. Eppley commanding him to appear at the next term of the Court to answer the petition and also that a decree of this Court may be given granting this libellant a divorce from bed and board and also allowing her such alimony as the said Dr. George M. Eppley's circumstances will admit of so that the same do not exceed the third part of the annual profit or income of his estate or of his

occupation and labor. And as in duty bound she will ever pray etc."
(signed C.C. Eppley.) -"Cumberland County S.S. The above named
Mrs. Catherine Eppley being duly affirmed according to law doth
depose and say that the facts contained in the above petition or libel
are true to the best of her knowledge and belief and that the said
complaint is not made out of levity or by collusion between her the
said Catherine Eppley and the said Dr. George M. Eppley her
husband and for the mere purpose of being freed and separated from
each other but in sincerity and truth for the causes mentioned in the
said petition or libel. Affirmed and Subscribed this 28th day of
November A.D. 1859 before me." (signed C.C. Eppley and J.B.
Drawbaugh, J.P.) -Notation on the front of this document -"No. 7
January T. 1860 Libel of Mrs. C. Eppley for a divorce a mensa et
thoro and alimony 29 Novr. 1859 Subpoena awarded." (signed J.H.
Graham Judge.) -"Filed 29th Nov. 1859 $1.25 paid by John Kutz
Penrose."

Nov. 29, 1859 -"CUMBERLAND COUNTY, SS. The Commonwealth
of Pennsylvania, to the Sheriff of Cumberland county, GREETING:
WHEREAS, Mrs. Catharine Eppley did on the 29th day of November
A.D. 1859, prefer a petition to our said Judges of our Court of
Common Pleas for the State of Pennsylvania, and County of Cumberland,
praying for the causes therein set forth, that she might be
divorced from the bonds of matrimony entered into with you George
M. Eppley (a mensa et thoro & alimony. We do therefore command
you the said George M. Eppley that setting aside all other business
and excuses whatsoever, you be and appear in your proper person
before our Judges, at Carlisle, at a Court of Common Pleas there to
be held for the County of Cumberland, on the ninth day of January
next, to answer the petition or libel of the said Catharine Eppley and
to shew (sic) cause, if any you have, why the said Catharine Eppley
should not be divorced from the bonds of matrimony agreeably to
the Acts of General Assembly in such case made and provided. And
hereof fail not. Witness the Honorable JAMES H. GRAHAM, Esq.,
President of our said Court, at Carlisle, the 29th day of November
A.D. 1859." (signed P. Quigley Prothonotary.) -Notation on the front
of this document -"No. 7 January Term 1860 Mrs. Catharine Eppley,
by her Brother and next Friend John Kutz vs. Dr. George M. Eppley:
Subpoena Sur Divorce, a mensa et thoro, & alimony Dec. 1st 1859
Served personally and by certified copy on the Defendant so answers"
(signed R. McCartney Shff.) -"Shff. McCartney's fee $2.96
Penrose."

◆ ◆ ◆

April Term 1860 #41 March 7, 1860 -"To the Honorable the
Judges of the Court of Common Pleas of Cumberland County The
petition of Nancy Perry by her next friend Andrew Gould Respectfully
showeth that your petitioner was on the fifth day of December A.D.

1856 lawfully joined in marriage with James S. Perry her present husband and from that time until the second day of June A.D. 1858 lived and cohabited with him and hath in all respects demeaned herself as a kind and affectionate wife and although by the laws of God as well as by the mutual vows plighted to each other they were bound to that uniform constancy and regard which ought to be inseparable from the marriage state. Yet so it is that the said James S. Perry in violation of his marriage vow from the second day of June A.D. 1858 hath wilfully and maliciously deserted and absented himself from the habitation of this petitioner without any just or reasonable cause and such desertion hath persisted in for the term of twenty months and upwards and yet doth continue to absent himself from the said petitioner, wherefore your petitioner further showeth that she is a citizen of the commonwealth of Pennsylvania and hath resided therein more than one whole year previous to the filing of this her petition, prays your Honors that a subpoena may issue in due form of law directed to the said James S. Perry commanding him to appear in this Honorable Court at the April Term next to answer the complaint aforesaid and also that a decree of this Honorable Court may be made for the securing of her the said Nancy Perry from the bond of matrimony as if she had never been married. And she will pray etc." (signed Nancy Perry by her next friend Andrew Gould.) -"Cumberland County SS. Personally appeared before me the subscriber a Justice of the Peace in and for said County the above named Nancy Perry who being duly sworn according to law doth depose and say that the facts as set forth in the above petition are true to the best of her knowledge and belief and that the said complaint is not made out of levity or by collusion between her the said Nancy Perry and her husband the said James S. Perry and for the mere purpose of being freed and separated from each other but in sincerity and truth for the causes mentioned in the said petition. Sworn and subscribed before me this (left blank) day of (left blank) A.D. 1860." (signed Nancy Perry and David Smith Justice of the Peace.) -Notation on the front of this document -"No. 41 April T. 1860 Nancy Perry by her next friend Andrew Gould vs. James S. Perry Petition for a Divorce 7 March 1860 Subpoena awarded." (signed J.H. Graham Judge.) -"Lee."

March 7, 1860 -"CUMBERLAND COUNTY, SS. The Commonwealth of Pennsylvania, to the Sheriff of Cumberland county, GREETING: WHEREAS, Nancy Perry, by her next friend Andrew Gould did on the seventh day of March A.D. 1860, prefer a petition to our said Judges of our Court of Common Pleas for the State of Pennsylvania, and County of Cumberland, praying for the causes therein set forth, that she might be divorced from the bonds of matrimony entered into with you James S. Perry. We do therefore command you the said James S. Perry that setting aside all other business and excuses whatsoever, you be and appear in your proper person before our Judges, at Carlisle, at a Court of Common Pleas there to be held for the County of Cumberland, on the ninth day of April next, to answer the petition or libel of the said Nancy Perry and to shew (sic) cause, if any you have, why the said Nancy Perry should not be divorced from the bonds of matrimony agreeably to the Acts of General Assembly in such case made and provided. And hereof fail not. Witness the Honorable JAMES H. GRAHAM, Esq., President of our said Court, at Carlisle, the seventh day of March A.D. 1860." (signed P. Quigley Prothonotary.) -Notation on the front of this document -"No. 41 April Term 1860." Nancy Perry by her next friend Andrew Gould vs. James S. Perry: Subpoena Sur Divorce March 26th 1860 Defendant not to be found in my Bailiwick so answers" (signed R. McCartney Shff.) -"Shff. McCartney's fee $0.18 3/4. Lee."

♦ ♦ ♦

INDEX

ADAIR, 166 167 191 194 238-241 263-265 269
AGNANY, 356 357
AGNEW, 2
ALBRIGHT, 13-15 298-300 331 332
ALEXANDER, 4 5 161
ALLEN, 8 67 151 224 225
ANDERSON, 34 200 201
ANGNEY, 357
ARMOR, 24
ARMSTRONG, 16 20 197
ARNOLD, 349-354
ASH, 1 3
ASHBURN, 207 208
ASHFORD, 336-338 343-345
ATLEE, 1 2
AUGHINBAUGH, 20 21
AUGNEY, 67
AULD, 367-369
AURANA, 212
AURAND, 184 212 225 230 232 233 236
BADEN, 9 69
BAKER, 2 46 197
BARBOUR, 193
BARE, 71-73 75 76 78 326 327
BARNET, 57-60
BARNITZ, 324
BARR, 75 153
BARRON, 251-254
BATEMAN, 386
BATESSER, 74
BAXTER, 71 72
BAXTESSER, 73 74
BAXTSER, 73
BEADER, 141
BEAR, 25 72
BEARE, 24
BEATMAN (sic), 385
BEETEM, 57-59 62 68 69 71 133 135 140 151 197 200 203-206 210 211 214 215 218 220 224 227 228 231 235 238 242 244 248 367 369
BEETOM, 57 220
BEIRBREWER, 13 15
BEIRBROWER, 14
BELL, 97 182-185 197 253
BELSHOOVER, 91
BELTZHOOVER, 91 131 132 144
BELTZOOVER, 253
BENDER, 28
BENNET, 300
BENTZ, 360
BERCH, 98-101 103
BERE, 24 25 77
BEYERS, 6
BIDDLE, 99 129 155 156 195 247-249 252 275 276 304 308 332-335 350-352 358-360
BIDELL, 249
BIEL, 216
BIERBREWER, 13
BIERBROWER, 13
BIGHAM, 160
BILLMIR, 357
BILMYER, 356
BILSMOYER, 354
BISBAN, 32

BITNER, 172 305
BLACK, 7 8 18 24 71 78-81 132 133 190 191 253 275-277
BLAINE, 10 11
BODEN, 9
BOGGS, 75-77
BOLLINGER, 165
BONHAM, 225 241 243 259-261
BOOR, 2
BOSARD, 225
BOSLER, 97
BOSSLER, 1 2 245 246
BOWER, 116-120
BOWERMASTER, 19 31-34 36 37 40 361
BOWERS, 116
BOWMAN, 16 344 347 348 351 355 359 360 362 363 366 372 373 379-381
BOYCE, 3
BOYER, 101 102 324-326
BRACKENRIDGE, 10
BRADEBERRY, 99
BRADY, 11 12
BRAKENMAKER, 232 233
BRANDEBERRY, 161 176 225
BRANDEBURRY, 223 224
BRANDEBURY, 100 105 163
BRANDT, 162-165
BRANNON, 225 262-264 321 322
BRANT, 51
BRETS, 147 148
BREWSTER, 32
BRICKER, 31-33 228 229 305 306 379
BRIGGS, 108 112
BRINDLE, 129
BRINN, 276
BRISBAN (sic), 216
BRISBANE, 213-215 217
BRISBEIN, 213
BROOKS, 357
BROOMBAUGH, 220-222
BROWN, 15 280 281 364
BROWNAWELL, 312 313 316
BROWNELL, 314
BROWNEWELL, 312 314-316
BROWNWELL, 315
BRUMBACH, 219-222
BRUMBOCH, 218-222
BRUNDEBURY, 162
BRUNER, 357
BRUNNER, 315
BUCHANAN, 1 3 345
BUCK, 32
BUSARD, 225
BUTTORFF, 316
BUYERS, 6 7
BUZZARD, 223
BYERS, 164
CAIRNS, 136 137 150 151
CALL, 33
CALLEO, 216
CAPP, 97
CAREY, 217 218
CARLSON, 13
CARMAN, 291
CARNEY, 267
CARNS, 185
CAROTHERS, 7 8 76 81 83 94 181
CARVER, 58
CASEY, 186-188
CAUFFMAN, 23 24
CHESNUT, 204
CHESTNUT, 202 203
CHRISMORE, 369
CHRIST, 71 75
CHRISTLEIB, 84
CHRISTLIEB, 44 46 48 83 85-88
CHRISTMORE, 369
CHURCH, 71 72 75
CLARK, 11 12 41 142
CLAYPOOLE, 3
CLENDENIN, 89-94 96 97 252
CLENDENNIN, 285
CLEPPINGER, 26 103
CLIPINGER, 110 113
CLIPPINGER, 30 31 103 105-107 111-113
COBLE, 244 356
COCHLIN, 379

COCKLEY, 123 124
COCKLIN, 379-381
COCKLY, 122
COLWELL, 339 340 343 371-373 376
COMMONS, 203
COOK, 160 288 289
COOVER, 363 367 368 370 379-381
CORBETT, 277-282
CORNMAN, 213-215 217 279 301 303
COUFFER, 25
COUSER, 18
COWAN, 29
COX, 37
CRAIGHEAD, 41 226-229 244-246 270-273
CRALL, 33
CREIGH, 7 82 124 136
CREVER, 6 7
CRISMORE, 367
CRIST, 72 75 76 78
CRISWELL, 161 171 174 175 180 183 185 187 188 190 191 193 194 196-198 332 348 349
CROCKETT, 41
CROLL, 30
CROWLEY, 78 79
CROWNELL, 9
CUFF, 336-338 343-346
CUMMINS, 202-204
CURTIS, 250
DAELHOUSEN, 160 161 283
DALHOUSER, 48
DAVENPORT, 62 63
DAVIS, 17 18 104 107 111 113 136 150 169-172 250 367
DECKER, 369
DECKERT, 367 369
DEH, 300-302
DENTLER, 6
DEWN, 266 267
DEYER, 199
DILL, 157
DILLER, 90 91 133-135
DININGER, 15
DISBROW, 76
DIVIRE?, 3 4
DOLY, 237
DONALY, 200
DONLY, 237
DONNELLY, 63 237-241
DONNELY, 237
DOUGLAS, 44
DOWN, 6
DOYLE, 16 17 19 22-24 40
DRAWBAUGH, 392
DREWET, 291
DRISBAUCH, 100
DRUET, 290
DRUETT, 293
DRUIRE?, 4
DUEY, 243-246 274-276 379
DUKE, 339-343
DUMB, 6
DUNCAN, 5
DUNFEE, 151 152 154
DUNLAP, 3 42 44 51 52 56 364
DUNN, 177
DURRE, 3
DWEN, 265 266
EATON, 108 109
EBERLE, 332
EBERLY, 160 303-305 307 308 331 332 348 349
EBERSOLE, 237-240
EBY, 30
ECKELS, 326
ECKLES, 197
EGE, 199 238-240 249 250 253 258 263-265 269 278 279 302 304 309 328 330
EGOLF, 236
EGULF, 64
EICHELBERG, 380
EICHELBERGER, 16 17 269-274 303-308 379-381
ELDER, 246
ELDERS, 245
ELLIOTT, 85 86
ELLWINGER, 300

ELY, 25
EMMERICK, 96 97
EMMINGER, 316
EPPLEY, 391 392
ERB, 40 71-74 78 186 188
ETTER, 18 335
EWIG, 25
EWING, 51-53
FAGAN, 317
FAHNESTOCK, 69-78
FAILOR, 295 297
FARTER, 292
FAUST, 115 116
FELLERS, 277-282
FERGERSON, 8
FISHEL, 379 382
FISHER, 15 16 77 90 380
FISLE, 379 381
FISSEL, 379 380
FISSLE, 381
FLEEGER, 41
FLEMING, 83-86 89 90 95-97 99 104-106 113 115 117 118 121-126 129 130 133-136 223 224 235 236 242 243
FLENDER, 305 307
FOLAND, 328
FOLK, 21
FOLLAND, 327 328
FOREMAN, 200
FOULK, 17 21 51 64 65
FOX, 28
FRALEY, 132 133
FRAZER, 285 292
FRAZIER, 288
FREIS, 69
FRIES, 69
FRIESE, 68 69
GAENSLEN, 127 128
GALBRAETH, 64
GALBRAITH, 61 62 65
GALBRATH, 62
GALBREATH, 62-64
GALLAGHER, 139 140 142 144 147
GALLOWAY, 370

GANNAN, 112
GARBER, 1 2
GAULLAGHER, 39 121 145 147 158 159 183 184 189 190 234-236
GAUMAN, 108
GEESE, 13
GELTENBERGER, 201
GENNSLER, 67
GENSLER, 65 66
GIBSON, 140 141 388-391
GILBERT, 28-30
GILL, 280 281
GILLEN, 265 266
GILLMORE, 29
GILMORE, 233-236
GINN, 329-331
GINNEY, 68
GIVLER, 36 38 39
GLASS, 321 322
GLENN, 10-13
GOLDEN, 345
GOOD, 120
GOODYEAR, 41 91
GORGAS, 273
GOULD, 67 214-217 392-394
GRAHAM, 86 87 124-126 134 135 137 148-151 173 185 186 192 193 196 206 217 218 283 285 286 299-301 303-305 309 310 313 317-321 323 326-328 332 335 337-339 344 347 348 350 351 355 358 359 361 362 366 372 378-380 383 387-389 392-394
GRAYSON, 7 8
GREEGER, 41
GREEN, 253 329-331
GRIER, 232
GROMAN, 51
GROSS, 95 129-131 197 230 233 314
GRUBB, 16
HAAK, 19-21
HAILOR, 286
HAINES, 370-376

HAINS, 373
HALDEMAN, 201
HALL, 3 182-185
HALLER, 288-290 293
HAMILTON, 141 231
HAMMERSLEY, 72 74
HANN, 293
HANNK, 20
HARBAUGH, 111
HARMAN, 90-93
HARMAND, 91
HARPER, 41 46 59 62 66 68-71 78 80
HARRIS, 5 204-209
HARRISON, 56 57
HARTZEL, 67 68
HARTZOG, 342
HAUCK, 315
HAUK, 160
HAUSE?, 63 64
HAVENSTICK, 31
HAVERSTOCK, 44
HEAP, 10 11
HEAVINGER, 254-256
HEAVNER, 254 257
HEBERLIG, 282-286 289 292-295 297
HEBERLIGS (THE), 296
HEBERLY, 287
HEFFLEFINGER, 46 47 294 297
HEISER, 31
HELFENSTEIN, 16
HELFENSTINE(?), 42
HELLER, 27
HELPENSTEIN, 32
HENDERSON, 305 309 320 321 362 363 388 390 391
HENNINGER, 370
HENRY, 367 368
HENWOOD, 22
HEPBUN, 135
HEPBURN, 85 137 139 143 146 147 149-152 155 156 158 159 162 163 165-167 170 171 173 174 176 181 183 190-194 196

HEPBURN (Continued)
198-200 203-206 210 211 213 215 217-220 224 227 231 234 235 237 238 242-244 248 270-272 290 300 347 348
HERD, 383 386
HERDE, 382
HERMAN, 88-90 93 94
HERSHEY, 41
HERTZOG, 342
HESSINGER, 36
HETRICK, 191-194 196 197
HETTRICK, 194-196
HEVENER, 257
HIBERLIG, 286
HICK, 20
HICKERNELL, 19
HILING, 38
HIMES, 379 381
HINKLEY, 277
HIPPEL, 120 121
HIPPLE, 122 123
HOCH, 43
HOFFER, 204 206 211 214 215 218 220 224 227 228 231 235 238 239 242 248 249 252 253 255 256 259 260 264
HOFFMAN, 240 276
HOKE, 164
HOLCOMB, 66 83 85 95 104 105 115 117 118 121 122 125 126 129 130 166 167 254 256 257 271 275-277 301 319 321 322 324 333 344 345 351-354 360 361 365 387 388 390 391
HOLLER, 295 297
HOLLINGER, 374
HOLLY, 261
HOLMES, 223 225
HOLSAPLE, 186 205
HOLSAPPLE, 51 52
HOLSHAPPLE, 52
HOLSHOPLE, 52 53
HOLSHOPPLE, 52 53
HOLSOPPLE, 53

HOLTSAPLE, 8
HOLTZBERGER, 246
HOOBER, 3 369
HOON, 85
HOOPER, 51
HOOVER, 110 111 130 134 365-370
HOPPLE, 144
HORNER, 373 374 376
HOSLER, 179
HOSTETTER, 339
HOSTLER, 114-116 175 178
HOUGH, 42
HOUK, 315
HOUSE, 38 39
HRIGHREY?, 186
HUBER, 303
HUGHES, 332-336
HULL, 32 33
HUME, 156 386
HUMES, 157 253 385
HUMES?, 63 64
HURD, 384
HYSER, 22 299
ILLEFRITZ, 197
INGERSOLL, 6
IRISH, 385
IRISHE, 386
IRVIN, 44 50 71-78 172
IRVINE, 35 42-44 49 51-53 89 95 117 140 141 171-173 176-182 187-189 198 206-209 293-298
IRVING, 198
IRWIN, 34 42 71 72 158 169 185
ISANBERGER, 201
ISRAEL, 8
JACOBS, 320
JAMES, 4 24
JOHNSON, 370
JOHNSTON, 337 345 370
JONES, 67 73-76 230-233
JORDAN, 2
KARNS, 185
KAUFMAN, 23
KEAMPFFER, 257

KECHLER, 367 369
KECKLER, 369
KEEMBOTS (sic), 228
KEENBIRTZ, 229
KEENBRITZ, 229
KEENEY, 171 172
KEEPER, 384
KEEPERS, 260 323-325 350 355 360-362 377 378 382 384 385 387
KELLER, 41 59 92 306 307
KELLY, 215 216 369
KELSO, 160
KEMPFER, 254 256
KENEGE, 197
KENEGY, 197
KENNEDAY, 353
KENNEDY, 153 154 187 188 352 353
KENTZ, 35-37
KEPLER, 169-171
KEPPLER, 171 172
KERNAN, 41
KETH, 30
KETRING, 37-39
KIMMEL, 168
KINDIG, 82
KING, 357-361
KIRK, 72
KITCH, 179 180
KLINE, 184
KNEISLEY, 380
KNETTLE, 60 159 296
KNISELEY, 378 379
KNISELY, 377
KNISLEY, 378
KOCK, 24
KOHLSTOCK, 17
KOON, 370
KREITZER, 217 218
KRIDER, 185 186
KRONE, 142-145
KRYDER, 185
KRYSHER, 144 163-165
KUHN, 368-370
KUNKLE, 55 56

KUNTZ, 15
KUTZ, 131 132 391 392
LAMB, 165 166 168
LAMBERTON, 122-124 193 198
  228 236 238 239 244 245 248
  249 252 253 255 256 259-261
  263 264 270-272 274 275 278
  279 281 283 284 299 334 336
LANDES, 346 349
LANDIS, 346-348
LANE, 15
LAUGHLIN, 153 154
LAY, 287 292
LEACH, 18
LEAS, 167 168
LECHLER, 7
LEDIG, 356
LEE, 329 330 393 394
LEEPER, 1 3
LEFEVER, 99
LEGER, 261
LEGGET, 280
LEGGETT, 280
LEIB, 280 281
LEIBY, 326 327
LEIDIG, 354-357
LEIDIGH, 355 385 386
LEITZBRON, 344
LEMER, 71 75 78
LEMOR, 74
LEONARD, 33
LESHER, 338-343
LEWIS, 6 70 72 73 76 100 373
LEYMAN, 268 269
LIGET, 281
LIGGETT, 281
LINDSAY, 50
LINDSEY, 49 204-206 209
LINE, 26 27 29 30
LINESWEAVER, 76
LISBON, 265
LITZENGER, 314
LIVINGSTON, 164 165
LOBACH, 89 96 130 135 225
LOBAUGH, 96
LOCHMAN, 147

LOGUE, 5-7 94 95
LONG, 7 385 386
LONGDDORF, 229
LONGENECKER, 299
LONGNECKER, 40 41 145 147
  148 160
LONGSDORF, 90 190 191 193
  194 196 198 203 205 206 210
  211 214
LONGSDORFF, 191 229
LOOMAS, 386
LOOMASES, 385
LOUGHRIDGE, 7
LOW, 164 241-243
LOWREY, 4
LOWRY, 4 5
LUMASES, 385
LUSK, 45 48 49 84-88
LUTZ, 280 281
LYNN?, 57
LYON, 2 302 303
LYONE, 303
MACHON, 369
MACKEY, 203 341 371
MACKLEY, 160
MACMANUS, 212
MAHAN, 369
MAHONEY, 189
MAHONY, 189 190
MAIN, 41 56 59 62 66 68 69 71
  80 159 166 167 171 173 174
  176 180 182 183 187 197
MALHORN, 200 201
MARKLE, 31
MARLIN, 209-213
MARQUART, 41
MARTIN, 9 11 12 156 158-161
  166 167 170 171 173 174 176
  180 182-184 187
MASH, 364
MATEER, 56 228 229 231 313-
  316
MATIER, 31
MATTER, 23 24
MAXWELL, 83-88 286
MAYHR, 158

MCALISTER, 1
MCCABE, 233-237 247 248
MCCACHREW, 207
MCCANTNY, 177
MCCANTY, 177
MCCARNY, 248
MCCARTNEY, 218 220 224 231
   239 242 249 256 260 263 264
   311 312 360 378 381 384 387
   389 390 392 394
MCCARTNY, 248 252 253 256
   259 260
MCCASKRY, 6
MCCAY, 82 83 379
MCCLEAN, 373
MCCLELLAND, 160
MCCLINTOCK, 386 387
MCCLURE, 81 339 340 343 371-
   373 376
MCCORKSAY, 50
MCCORMACK, 77
MCCORMICK, 7 73-75
MCCOY, 40 42 83 250
MCCURDY, 67 68
MCDARMOND, 304 305 309 310
   313 318-321 323 326-328 332
   334 335 338 339 344
MCDONNEL, 294 295 297
MCDOWEL, 353
MCDOWELL, 353 354
MCELWAIN, 53
MCELWINE, 54 55
MCKANDEL, 2
MCKAY, 381
MCKEAN, 3
MCKINNEY, 41 247-250
MCLAUGHLIN, 41
MCLEAN, 374-376
MCMAHN, 265 266
MCMANUS, 212
MEGARY, 100 101
MEGERY, 100
MELL, 357 359-361
MELLINGER, 374
MESSERSMITH, 247-250
METZ, 6

MEYERS, 31
MIDDLETON, 285-293 297
MILIZEN, 33-35
MILLER, 35 37 39 65 67-69 71
   75-77 86 87 105 106 111 113
   147 148 220 221 257 278-280
   289 293 294 296 297 301 302
   317 318 354 357 362-364
   366-370 378 379 381
MILLIZEN, 34 315 316
MINICH, 353
MITCHELL, 11 13 51
MOLTZ, 154 155 157
MONNASMITH, 197
MONTGOMERY, 6
MOODRY, 62
MOORE, 114 116 221 222
MORRISON, 272 273
MOUDY, 384 385
MULL, 13
MULLEN, 220-222
MULLIN, 221 222
MUMMA, 147 160
MURRAY, 250
MURRY, 336
MUSSELLMAN, 24
MUSSELMAN, 24 25
MYER, 257
MYERS, 7 33 35 133 135 137-
   140 143 144 146 147 149-152
   155 179 180 254-257 291 293
   296 297 321 352 353 364
NASH, 106-108 110 111 113
NATTS, 329 331
NAY, 93
NEAL, 17 21-24 52
NEAREN, 362-365
NEARON, 361-364
NEIDIGH, 297
NELSON, 6 379-381
NICKEL, 383-386
NICKEY, 338 341
NICKLE, 382-386
NICKY, 341
NINGARD, 330
NISELY, 378 382

NISLEY, 376-381
NOBLE, 8
NOELL, 339 340 343 344 347
 348 351 352 355 356 359 360
 362 363 366 368 372
O'BRIEN, 9 10
O'DONNELY, 266
O'SULLIVAN, 262-269
OLIVER, 17
ORRIS, 91 92 314 315
OVERHALTZER, 26
OVERHOLZER, 27
OWENS, 11 12
OYSTER, 272 273
PAGE, 245 246
PAGUE, 160
PALMER, 313
PARKER, 313 327 368
PARNELL, 181
PATTERSON, 5 13
PECHERT, 367
PECK, 141 142
PECKERT, 368
PENCE, 232 233
PENDEGRASS, 194-196
PENDERGASS, 192
PENDERGRASS, 192 197
PENNELL, 181
PENROSE, 7 303 325 326 328
 329 334 350 351 358-361
 377-379 382 392
PENWELL, 181
PERRY, 392-394
PETERS, 102 222-226 308-312
 325
PIPER, 7 197 375
PLICHT, 50
POWELL, 172-175
PRENDERGASS, 191
PRINZER, 374
QUIGLEY, 334 339 340 344 347
 348 351 352 355 359 360 362
 363 366 368 372 373 378-380
 384 387 389 390 392 394
RACKSTRAW, 349
RAKESTRAW, 346 347

RAMP, 282-289 291-298
RAMSAY, 65 66
RAMSEY, 31 33 37 41 42 54 55
 59 60 62-66 83 138
RAYER, 27
RAYNARD, 51
RAYNER, 51
RAYNOR, 51
RECHSTRAW, 346
RECKSTRAW, 347 348 349
REDSACKER, 174
REED, 20 21 33 39 55 56 61 62
 65 66 68 70 80 83 85 88 89
 93-96 99 104-106 113 115-
 118 121 125 127 129 130 132
 133 153 176 177 181 212
REIFSNYDER, 32
REIGHTER, 253
REINALD, 226 227
REINOLD, 228-230
RENICKER, 379
RENNAKER, 379
RHOADS, 283
RICE, 327-329
RICHARDSON, 27-30
RICHEY, 32 33 36 37
RICKWINE, 280 281
RIDDLE, 214 215
RINARD, 44-51
RINGEWALT, 221
RINGWALT, 221
RINNARD, 47-51
RITCHEY, 37
RITCHY, 36
RITNER, 15 17-20 190 191 194
 307 332-335
ROBERTSON, 103-113
ROBISON, 370
ROCKSTRAW, 347
RODEBAUGH, 31
RODGERS, 11 12 197
RODIBAUGH, 22
RODROCK, 13
ROLAND, 137-141
ROSE, 18 19
ROTHROCK, 13-15

ROUDEBAUGH, 31
RUBY, 201
RUDY, 27-30
RUGGLES, 386 387
RUPERT, 376
RUPLEY, 135 253
RUPP, 116-119
RUPURT, 376
RUTCHERS, 36 39
RUTH, 160
RYNARD, 44
SADLER, 308-310 312
SAILOR, 56
SANDERS, 139
SANDERSON, 135 137 139 140 143 144 146 147 149-153 155 156 158 159 163 164 166 167 170 171 173 174 176 180 182 183 187
SANNO, 21 22 44 253 256 257
SAUNDERS, 47
SAXTON, 23 42-44
SAYLER, 55 56
SAYLOR, 3 56
SCOTT, 17
SELLERS, 3
SEMM?, 13
SENSEBAUGH, 47
SENSEMAN, 312-316
SENSERMAN, 312
SERRERT, 14
SHAFER, 201
SHAFFER, 379
SHAMBERGER, 308
SHANER, 168 169
SHANK, 199-202
SHAPELY, 388
SHAPLEY, 388-391
SHARDY, 102
SHARP, 10 329-331
SHARRETTS, 64
SHEAFFER, 380
SHEANER, 165-168
SHEARER, 329 338 344-346 387
SHEARMAN, 374 375
SHEETZ, 245

SHELDEN, 17
SHELL, 9 12 13
SHELLY, 33 96 97
SHEPLEY, 13 390
SHEPS, 369
SHERBAHN, 156
SHERBAN, 118 119
SHERBURN, 156
SHIELDS, 19 22-24 26
SHOFFNER, 243-246
SHOOP, 306-308 311 312
SHROM, 265 267 268
SHUPP, 305 310
SIDLE, 159
SIMMONS, 29 30 311
SIMON, 120-124
SIPE, 269-272
SITES, 178-180
SIVERR?, 13
SLONAKER, 92
SMALL, 98 101
SMITH, 22 32 40-43 54 82 83 166 176 184-186 190 191 198 199 210-212 216-218 224- 226 230-234 244 247-251 256 265 268 270 271 275 279 280 283 299 300 302 303 320-322 340 342 353 355-357 378 382-386 393
SMYSER, 379 381 382
SNAVELY, 101 154-157
SNODGRASS, 79 81 84 98 116 122 123 126-129 136 138 142 143 146 371-373 376
SNYDER, 1 179 232
SPENCE, 62
SPONGENBERG, 318-320 322-324
SPONSLER, 23 261 262
SPRING, 280
SPRINGS, 280 281
STEEL, 2
STEEN, 157 158
STERNER, 381 391
STEVENS, 379
STEVICH, 297

STEVICK, 293
STEWART, 159 161
STINE, 163
STONER, 349 379-381
STOUFFER, 341
STRAYER, 19
STRINE, 336 352
STROH, 228
STROWMAN, 342
STUART, 99 142 145 159-161
  183 204-206 247 252 285
STURGEON, 41
STURNER, 390
SWAGER, 15
SWANGER, 13 384 385
SWEENY, 261
SWEIGART, 15 16
SWENGER, 14 15
SWENZE, 13
SWIGART, 177-180
SWIGER, 15
SWIGERT, 175-180
SWISHER, 11 12
SWONGER, 385
TAYLOR, 17
THOMAS, 120 124 125 127
THOMPSON, 56 57
THRUSH, 160
TIMMONS, 365 366
TODD, 13 14 16 133 149 198
  199 231 233 255-257
TORBET, 45
TORBETT, 46
TRANGER, 51
TRAUB, 318-320 322 324
TRAUGH, 14 21 22
TRIMBLE, 94
UBRICH, 215
ULRICH, 179 180
UNDERWOOD, 236
VANANDOLL, 280
VANASDAL, 281
VANASDALL, 280 281
VANFORIN, 11
VANKIRK, 198
VANTZ, 364

WAGGONER, 44 47 50 51 324
WAGNER, 145-148
WAHL, 251-253
WALKER, 189
WALLACE, 5 25-30
WALT, 22 23
WALTER, 97
WALTERS, 10 11 96 97
WARD, 209-213
WARNER, 119 376-380
WATT, 259
WATTS, 69 129 142 152 170 171
  195 196 199 200 203 204 210
  211 226-228 239 241 244 245
  248 251 253-255 257-260 262
  263 269-271 274 275 277 279
  281-283 285 293 313 327 368
WEAKLEY, 160
WEAVER, 7 9 12 13 43 60 317
  318 326
WEAVER?, 23
WEBSTER, 258-260 262
WEIDKNECHT, 26 28-30
WEIGANDT, 127-129
WEISE, 46
WEIST, 57-61
WEITZEL, 16
WERT, 256
WESTFALL, 280 281
WETZEL, 116 216
WHARF, 277
WHARFE, 274-277
WHERRY, 283 293 294
WHISLER, 102 241-243
WHITE, 140 141 361 363
WHITEMAN, 151 152
WHITMAN, 298-300
WIDNER, 188 313 321
WIEMER, 164 165
WIGHTMAN, 151-154
WILBER, 346 356 357
WILBUR, 356 357
WILLIAMS, 10 49 124-127 287-
  289 293 295-297
WILLIAMSON, 45 197 347 348
WILLS, 18

WILSON, 17 53-55 157-159 168
    373-376
WILT, 3 4 207 208
WINDEMAKER, 218-220 221 222
WINDERMAKER, 222
WINGLER, 2
WISE, 265-267
WITHEROW, 363 364
WOLF, 16 17 93 319
WOLFORD, 164
WONDERLICH, 16
WONDERTECH, 197
WOODBURN, 9
WOODLEY, 258-262
WOODLY, 302
WOODS, 148-150

WORKMAN, 8
WYMER, 162
YENGST, 221 222
YENST, 222
YOHE, 95-97
YOUNG, 71 72 78 88-93 99 281
ZACHARIAS, 71-73 78
ZEARING, 18 99-103 118 119
    155 167 168 273
ZEIGLER, 195
ZINN, 299-301 303-305 309 310
    313 317-319 321 323 326 328
    329 333-335 337 338
ZOOK, 379
ZOOKER, 107
ZOWKE, 379

www.ingramcontent.com/pod-product-compliance
Lightning Source LLC
Chambersburg PA
CBHW050832230426
43667CB00012B/1970